DARKNESS
FALLS ON
THE LAND
OF LIGHT

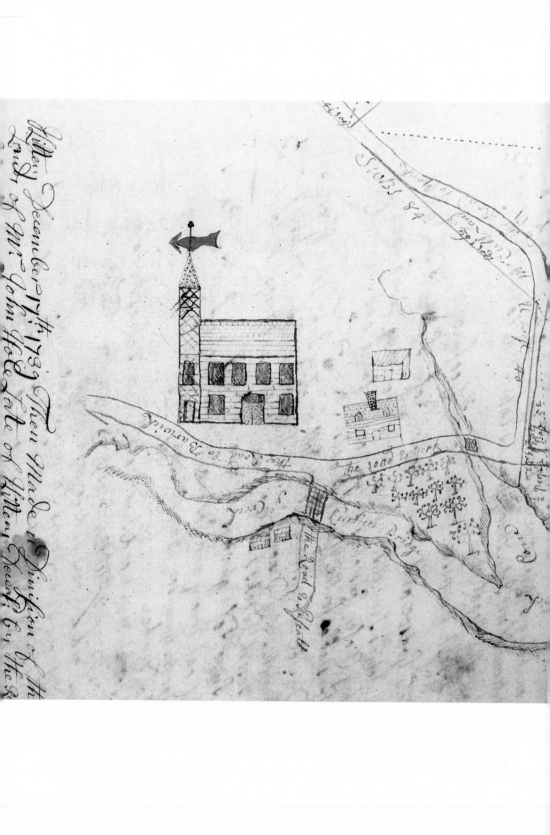

DARKNESS
FALLS ON
THE LAND
OF LIGHT

Experiencing Religious
Awakenings in Eighteenth-
Century New England

DOUGLAS L. WINIARSKI

Published for the Omohundro Institute of
Early American History and Culture, Williamsburg, Virginia,
by the University of North Carolina Press, Chapel Hill

The Omohundro Institute of Early American History and Culture is sponsored by the College of William and Mary. On November 15, 1996, the Institute adopted the present name in honor of a bequest from Malvern H. Omohundro, Jr.

Cover image: Relief cut of an earthquake, from *Earthquakes, Tokens of God's Power and Wrath* (n.p., 1744), concerning the earthquake felt in New England in June 1744. Rare Book Division, The New York Public Library. The New York Public Library Digital Collections. 1744. http://digitalcollections .nypl.org/items/94dcc09d-5c9a-b24d-e040-e00a180620e0

Library of Congress Cataloging-in-Publication Data
Names: Winiarski, Douglas Leo, author. | Omohundro
    Institute of Early American History & Culture.
Title: Darkness falls on the land of light : experiencing
    religious awakenings in eighteenth-century New
    England / Douglas L. Winiarski.
Description: Chapel Hill : Published for the Omohundro
    Institute of Early American History and Culture,
    Williamsburg, Virginia, by the University of North
    Carolina Press, [2017] | Includes bibliographical
    references and index.
Identifiers: LCCN 2016033871| ISBN 9781469628264
    (cloth : alk. paper) | ISBN 9781469628271 (ebook)
Subjects: LCSH: New England—Church history—18th
    century. | Great Awakening. | New England—Religious
    life and customs.
Classification: LCC BR520 .W56 2017 | DDC 277.4/07—dc23
    LC record available at https://lccn.loc.gov/2016033871

FRONTISPIECE John Godsoe, *Division of the Lands of Mr. John Hole.* 1739. Courtesy, Richard M. Candee

FOR MY PARENTS,
who have always
walked answerable
to their professions

ACKNOWLEDGMENTS

As I bring two decades of research on the religious history of eighteenth-century New England to a close, it is my great pleasure to recognize the people and institutions that made this book possible. *Darkness Falls on the Land of Light* draws on more than two hundred manuscript collections from more than sixty research archives, special collections libraries, historical societies, churches, and town offices scattered across sixteen states, three countries, and two continents. I wish to thank the archivists, librarians, curators, clerks, and other administrators who assisted me during my visits and who allowed me to quote and cite their incomparable manuscripts. I am especially grateful to Peggy Bendroth and Jeff Cooper at the Congregational Library and Archives in Boston for inviting me to serve on the steering committee for the New England Hidden Histories Project (NEHH). In the coming years, this digital history initiative will revolutionize public access to many of the relations and church records employed in this study.

Funding for *Darkness Falls on the Land of Light* was provided through generous grants from the American Council of Learned Societies, the Omohundro Institute of Early American History and Culture, and the University of Richmond. At the Institute, Fredrika Teute was an early champion of this project. I appreciated Fredrika's insights, patience, and guidance as I hammered this book into its present form. I hope it measures up to the ambitious work she encouraged me to write more than a decade ago. Following her retirement, Kaylan Stevenson, Nadine Zimmerli, and Paul Mapp expertly steered the manuscript through production. Along the way, Charles Cohen, Christine Heyrman, and an anonymous reviewer produced detailed readers' reports that challenged me to rethink, refine, and restructure every paragraph. Mark Cook designed the maps; Rebecca Wren prepared the chart; and Robbie St. John helped with research at a crucial moment as the project drew to a close.

Interested readers might wish to consult my earlier published essays, which contain more detailed discussions of some of the issues, individuals, and stories that appear in this book: "Popular Belief and Expression," in Mary Kupiec Cayton and Peter W. Williams, eds., *Encyclopedia of American Cultural and Intellectual History* (New York, 2001), III, 97–106; "The Education of Joseph Prince: Reading Adolescent Culture in Early Eighteenth-Century New England," in Peter Benes, ed., *The Worlds of Children, 1620–1920,* Dublin Seminar for New England Folklife, Annual Proceedings 2002 (Boston, 2004), 42–64; "'A Jornal of a Fue Days at York': The Great Awakening on the Northern New England Frontier," *Maine History,* XLII (2004), 46–85; "Souls Filled with Ravishing Transport: Heavenly Visions and the Radical Awakening in New England," *William and Mary Quarterly,* 3d Ser., LXI (2004), 3–46; "Jonathan Edwards, Enthusiast? Radical Revivalism and the Great Awakening in the Connecticut Valley," *Church History,* LXXIV (2005), 683–739; "Gendered 'Relations' in Haverhill, Massachusetts, 1719–1742," in Peter Benes, ed., *In Our Own Words: New England Diaries, 1600 to the Present,* I, *Diary Diversity, Coming of Age,* Dublin Seminar for New England Folklife, Annual Proceedings 2006/2007 (Boston, 2009), 58–78; "The Newbury Prayer Bill Hoax: Devotion and Deception in New England's Era of Great Awakenings," *Massachusetts Historical Review,* XIV (2012), 52–86; "New Perspectives on the Northampton Communion Controversy I: David Hall's Diary and Letter to Edward Billing," *Jonathan Edwards Studies,* III (2013), 268–280; "New Perspectives on the Northampton Communion Controversy II: Relations, Professions, and Experiences, 1748–1760," *Jonathan Edwards Studies,* IV (2014), 110–145; "New Perspectives on the Northampton Communion Controversy III: Count Vavasor's Tirade ...," *Jonathan Edwards Studies,* IV (2014), 353–382; and "Lydia Prout's Dreadfullest Thought," *New England Quarterly,* LXXXVIII (2015), 356–421.

Early in writing *Darkness Falls on the Land of Light,* I benefitted from my involvement with the Young Scholars in American Religion, an exceptional mentoring program sponsored by the Center for the Study of Religion and American Culture at Indiana University-Purdue University at Indianapolis. Stephen Prothero and Ann Taves offered sagely professional advice, and I enjoyed the comradery of Robert Brown, Julie Byrne, Martha Finch, Kathleen Flake, Clarence Hardy, Khyati Joshi, Kristin Schwain, Danielle Sigler, Rachel Wheeler, and David Yamane. Thanks to the center's director, Philip Goff, I recently partnered with Laurie Maffly-Kipp and a dynamic new cohort of young scholars, including Kate Bowler, Heath Carter, Kathryn Gin Lum, Joshua Guthman, Brett Hendrickson, Lerone Martin, Kate Moran, Angela Tarango, Stephen Taysom, T. J. Tomlin, David Walker, and Grace Yukich. Their scholarship and good cheer have inspired me to envision exciting new directions for my research.

In addition to the YSARs, friends and colleagues read preliminary drafts, answered questions, shared their research, and offered words of encouragement. Stephanie Cobb, Scott Davis, Frank Eakin, Jane Geaney, Mimi Hanaoka, Peter Kaufman, and Miranda Shaw have made the University of Richmond a remarkably collegial place to work. I also wish to thank Fred Anderson, Shelby Balik, Ross Beales, Jr., Peter Benes, Patricia Bonomi, Catherine Brekus, Richard Bushman, Jon Butler, Phyllis Cole, John Corrigan, Nina Dayton, Linford Fisher, Richard Godbeer, Christopher Grasso, Philip Gura, Susan Juster, Thomas Kidd, Ned Landsman, Tracy Levealle, Martha McNamara, Daniel Mandell, Stephen Marini, Joel Martin, Mary Beth Norton, Amanda Porterfield, Lynn Rhoads, Brett Rushforth, Erik Seeman, David Silverman, Alan Taylor, Michael Winship, Conrad Edick Wright, and the late Al Young. Ken Minkema lent his peerless knowledge of Jonathan Edwards to this project. Douglas Ambrose, Marie Griffith, Robert Gross, Evan Haefeli, Thomas Wilson, and Karin Wulf invited me to present my research at Harvard Divinity School, Hamilton College, the Early American History and Culture Seminar at Columbia University, the University of Connecticut Humanities Institute, and the Institute for Historical Studies at the University of Texas.

The members of the Fall Line Early Americanists (FLEA) reading group plowed through various drafts of this project for more than a decade, providing candid feedback and, more important, a vibrant intellectual community in central Virginia. Many, many thanks to FLEAs past and present, including Mathias Bergmann, Carolyn Eastman, Joshua Eckhardt, Rebecca Goetz, Terri Halperin, Jon Kukla, Robin Lind, Marion Nelson, John Pagan, Isabelle Richman, Philip Schwarz, and Ryan Smith. I owe a special debt of gratitude to Brent Tarter, who reviewed the entire manuscript at an early stage.

For more than two decades, Peter and Mary Ellen Falvey graciously opened their home whenever I was passing through the Boston area. I tested and refined the ideas presented in this book during countless coffeehouse chats with Mark Valeri at our old haunt, Stir Crazy, in Richmond. And to Roark Atkinson, Woody Holton, Edward Larkin, Mark McGarvie, Michael Moore, and Rachel Wheeler—stalwart colleagues and even better friends who kept me on task for many years—thank you!

Darkness Falls on the Land of Light operates in the spaces between and within the scholarship of three extraordinary mentors. I stumbled on the Haverhill relations during the 1990s while working on an independent study under the direction of David Hall, and his landmark *Worlds of Wonder, Days of Judgment* has never been far from my reach. I am thankful for David's continued support and friendship through the years. During my graduate school days at Indiana University, I learned to draw the study of New England Congregationalism through Jonathan Edwards and into the fractious culture inherited by the earliest Shaker converts—the twin poles of Stephen Stein's matchless scholarship. Robert Orsi's theoretical contributions to the study of popular and lived religion have illuminated my intellectual path at every turn.

I am grateful for the love and support of my siblings, Brian and Kerry Winiarski and Stephen Winiarski and Kira Przybylko. Thanks to my godson, Kevin, for always asking how the book was going, and to Chris, Brynn, Sam, and Grace for all the little things that come with being part of a wonderful family.

This book is dedicated to my parents, who nurtured the interests of a young boy growing up during the American Bicentennial and have inspired me ever since.

And much love to Nathan for everything else.

CONTENTS

MAPS

AAS American Antiquarian Society, Worcester, Mass.

AHI Carl Bridenbaugh, ed., *Gentleman's Progress: The Itinerarium of Dr. Alexander Hamilton, 1744* (Chapel Hill, N.C., 1948)

AHR *American Historical Review*

CH Thomas Prince, Jr., ed. *The Christian History* (Boston, 1743–1745)

CHS Connecticut Historical Society, Hartford, Conn.

CL Congregational Library and Archives, Boston

CSL Connecticut State Library, Hartford

CSM Colonial Society of Massachusetts, Boston

DDR Daniel Rogers, diary, 1740–175[3], Rogers Family Papers, 1614–1950, Ser. II, box 5B, New-York Historical Society

EAL *Early American Literature*

EAS *Early American Studies: An Interdisciplinary Journal*

EIHC *Historical Collections of the Essex Institute*

ESP Harold E. Selesky, ed., *Ezra Stiles Papers at Yale University,* microfilm (New Haven, Conn., 1976)

EWD E. H. Gillett, ed., "Diary of the Rev. Eleazar Wheelock, D.D., during His Visit to Boston, October 19, until November 16, 1741," *Historical Magazine and Notes and Queries, concerning the Antiquities, History, and Biography of America,* 2d Ser., V (1869), 237–240

NGD	William Kidder, [ed.], "The Diary of Nicholas Gilman" (master's thesis, University of New Hampshire, 1972)
PEM	Phillips Library, Peabody Essex Museum, Salem, Mass.
PHM	Pilgrim Society, Pilgrim Hall Museum, Plymouth, Mass.
SA	Sudbury Archives: A Collection of Historical Records Relating to Sudbury, Middlesex Co., Massachusetts, 1639–1850, Goodnow Library, Sudbury, Mass. (available online at *http://sudbury.ma.us /archives/*)
SGC I	Simon Gratz Autograph Collection, 1343–1928, Collection 250A, 633 boxes, Historical Society of Pennsylvania, Philadelphia
SGC II	Simon Gratz Autograph Collection, Collection 250B, 326 boxes, Historical Society of Pennsylvania, Philadelphia
SHG	John Langdon Sibley et al., *Sibley's Harvard Graduates: Biographical Sketches of Those Who Attended Harvard College, with Bibliographical and Other Notes*, 18 vols. (Cambridge, Mass., 1873–1999)
SSP I	Samuel P. Savage Papers, 1703–1848, MHS
SSP II	Samuel P. Savage Papers, II, 1710–1810, box 1, MHS
WCL	William L. Clements Library, University of Michigan, Ann Arbor
WJE	*The Works of Jonathan Edwards*, 26 vols. (New Haven, Conn., 1957–2008)
WJEO	*Works of Jonathan Edwards Online*, Jonathan Edwards Center, Yale University, New Haven, Conn. (available online at *http:// edwards.yale.edu*)
WMQ	*William and Mary Quarterly*, 3d Ser.
YUA	Manuscripts and Archives, Sterling Memorial Library, Yale University, New Haven, Conn.
YUB	Beinecke Rare Book and Manuscript Library, Yale University, New Haven, Conn.

The more than two hundred discrete manuscript collections cited in the pages that follow include diaries, journals, letters, commonplace books, sermon notes, devotional writings, church records, tax lists, court files, and other texts composed by men and women possessing a wide range of writing skills and literary acumen. In general, I have elected to present quotations from these texts using the expanded method described in Mary-Jo Kline, *A Guide to Documentary Editing*, 2d ed. (Baltimore, 1998), 157–158, 161–164, and Samuel Eliot Morison, "Care and Editing of Manuscripts," in Frank Freidel, ed., *The Harvard Guide to American History*, rev. ed. (Cambridge, Mass., 1974), I, 28–31. Occasional conjectural readings and grossly missing words appear in square brackets.

To assist readers and to facilitate future research, I have cited the more easily accessible published editions of these manuscripts whenever possible. The editors of these texts occasionally employ different transcription methods, most notably in the case of the modernized letterpress edition of *The Works of Jonathan Edwards*. I have attempted to check transcriptions appearing in nineteenth-century antiquarian histories and genealogies against the original manuscripts whenever possible, and I have silently corrected the handful of errors that I have encountered in these sources. Appendix B provides a roster of the major collections of church admission relations that I discuss throughout this study.

Biblical quotations are drawn from the King James translation commonly used in New England during the eighteenth century. I have not attempted to reconcile "Old Style" dates with the Roman Julian calendar adopted throughout the British Empire in 1752, nor have I retained the system of double dating used by provincial New Englanders who assumed that the year began on March 25 (e.g., Mar. 1, 1741/42). Adopting modern dates rarely poses significant historiographical challenges, except in one notable case that I discuss in Part 2, note 120.

The spelling of personal names and surnames varied considerably in eighteenth-century manuscript sources—even in texts authored by the same individual. I have adopted the most common modern spellings appearing in published vital records and genealogies. Likewise, town, county, and provincial boundaries changed frequently throughout the eighteenth century. I have elected to use place names that would have been familiar to eighteenth-century New Englanders, while including parenthetical references to modern locations. Thus, readers will occasionally encounter references to such places as the "waterside parish in Newbury (now Newburyport), Massachusetts," the "Lebanon Crank Society (now Columbia) Connecticut," or "Suffield, Massachusetts (now Connecticut)." To identify county and provincial borders, I have relied on Bruce C. Daniels, *The Connecticut Town: Growth and Development, 1635–1790* (Middletown, Conn., 1979); Richard W. Wilkie and Jack Tager, eds., *Historical Atlas of Massachusetts* (Amherst, Mass., 1991); Gordon DenBoer and John H. Long, comp., *Connecticut, Maine, Massachusetts, Rhode Island: Atlas of Historical County Boundaries*, ed. Long (New York, 1994), and Den-Boer, with George E. Goodridge, Jr., comp., *New Hampshire, Vermont: Atlas of Historical County Boundaries*, ed. Long (New York, 1993).

Essential research tools for identifying ministers, church officers, parish boundaries, and ecclesiastical events include *SHG;* Franklin Bowditch Dexter, *Biographical Sketches of the Graduates of Yale College: With Annals of the College History*, 6 vols. (New York, 1885–1912); Samuel L. Gerould, *The Congregational and Presbyterian Churches and Ministers of New Hampshire Connected with the General Association* (Lebanon, N.H., 1900); Albert Carlos Bates, ed., *List of Congregational Ecclesiastical Societies Established in Connecticut before October 1818* (Hartford, Conn., 1913); and Harold Field Worthley, *An Inventory of the Records of the Particular (Congregational) Churches of Massachusetts Gathered 1620–1805*, Harvard Theological Studies, XXV (Cambridge, Mass., 1970).

DARKNESS

FALLS ON

THE LAND

OF LIGHT

For my Part I can't but think ... That it is highly Incumbent on all who are not Seized with a Vertigo, to Stand upon their Guard, and in the most ardent Strains to lift up their Voice to the Most High, when the Religion of the Bible is like to be laid aside, for Some present immediate Inspirations—And not only so, but that Men should be often, and earnestly call'd upon and caution'd to Avoid that New Light which will lead Us into Darkness.—JOSIAH COTTON TO SAMUEL MATHER, 1742

Introduction

Deep in thought, Hannah Corey stood alone among the gravestones of the Sturbridge, Massachusetts, burial ground, gazing across the common at the Congregational meetinghouse. She and her husband, John, had affiliated with the church in the west parish of Roxbury by owning the covenant shortly after their marriage in 1741. Two years later, they moved to the recently settled frontier of central New England and proceeded to join the Sturbridge church in full communion. They had presented each of their four children for baptism shortly after their births. Now, during the fall of 1748, Corey faced serious—even supernatural—misgivings about her place within the sole, tax-supported religious institution in town.[1]

Corey had arrived early that afternoon for Caleb Rice's weekday lecture. As she sat in the empty pews awaiting the Sturbridge minister and her neighbors, the words of Jesus's stern rebuke to the moneychangers in Luke 19:46 suddenly darted into her mind: "My house is the house of prayer but ye have made it a den of thieves." Corey had a strong intimation that this was no ordinary meditation, daydream, or idle musing. Instead, she interpreted the scrip-

---

1. Testimony of Hannah Corey, Apr. 5, 1749, Sturbridge, Mass., Separatist Congregational Church Records, 1745–1762, CL (available online at NEHH); Robert J. Dunkle and Ann S. Lainhart, transcr., *The Records of the Churches of Boston and the First Church, Second Parish, and Third Parish of Roxbury, Including Baptisms, Marriages, Deaths, Admissions, and Dismissals* (Boston, 2001), CD-ROM, s.v. "John Corey"; *Vital Records of Roxbury, Massachusetts, to the End of the Year 1849*, 2 vols. (Salem, Mass., 1925), I, 76, II, 88; *Vital Records of Sturbridge, Massachusetts, to the Year 1850* (Boston, 1906), 39–40; Sturbridge, Mass., Congregational Church Records, 1736–1895, 37, 39, 61, MS copy, microfilm no. 863530, GSU. Previous studies of the Sturbridge schism include C. C. Goen, *Revivalism and Separatism in New England, 1740–1800: Strict Congregationalists and Separate Baptists in the Great Awakening* (Middletown, Conn., 1987), 101–103; William G. McLoughlin, *New England Dissent, 1630–1833: The Baptists and the Separation of Church and State*, 2 vols. (Cambridge, Mass., 1971), I, 457–460; Ola Elizabeth Winslow, *Meetinghouse Hill, 1630–1783* (New York, 1972), 231–236; and John L. Brooke, *The Heart of the Commonwealth: Society and Political Culture in Worcester County, Massachusetts, 1713–1861* (Amherst, Mass., 1989), 76–78.

tural words as an oracular communication from the Holy Spirit. It was the third revelation she had received that day. Two other biblical passages had impressed themselves on her mind as she walked along the road to the meetinghouse. Amos 3:3 and 2 Corinthians 6:17 spoke directly to her reservations regarding the fitness of the Sturbridge church. "Can two walk together, Except they be agreed"? "Come out from amongst them." The words thundered in her ears. Could she continue to walk with her neighbors in Christian fellowship? Was God commanding her to leave the church? With mounting concern, Corey confronted the troubling possibility that she had been worshipping for years in a den of thieves. "I thought," she later recalled, "I had rather ly down among the Graves then go into the meeting house." So she fled to the adjacent burial ground to collect herself and contemplate the meaning of God's powerfully intrusive messages.[2]

Corey eventually quelled her fears and returned to her pew, but, as she listened to Rice's sermon, she was overcome by a queer feeling. The entire meetinghouse "Seemed to be a dark place," she remembered. The minister, deacons, and congregation "lookt Strangely as if they ware all going Blindfold to destruction." Shaken by the peculiar turn of events, Corey and her husband abandoned their pew and retreated to the home of a neighbor named Isaac Newell. There, they gathered in prayer with a small group of disillusioned men and women who had just renounced their membership in the Sturbridge church. The dissenting faction included the town's first deacon, Daniel Fisk, his outspoken brother Henry, and perhaps a dozen former church members and discontented parishioners from several neighboring towns.[3]

One year earlier, the separatists had unilaterally dissolved all ties with Rice's church and, unsanctioned by any ecclesiastical or political authorities, embodied themselves into what would come to be called a Separate or "Strict" Congregational church. Henry Fisk defended their audacious action in a short narrative entitled "The Testimony of a People Inhabitting the Wilderness." During the fall of 1740, he explained, the famed touring evangelist George Whitefield passed through central Massachusetts and sparked an "extreordinary outpowering of the Spirit of God." Eleven people joined the Sturbridge church the following year, a figure twice the annual average. In a long passage laced with biblical allusions, Fisk described the awakened Sturbridge congregants as newborn babes who yearned for the "Sincere milk" of the preached

2. Testimony of Hannah Corey, Apr. 5, 1749, Sturbridge Separatist Congregational Church Records.

3. Ibid.; Henry Fisk, "The Testimony of a People Inhabitting the Wilderness," n.d. [January–February 1753], no. 397, *IBP*.

word. But when Rice closed his pulpit to the lively itinerant preachers who crisscrossed the region in emulation of Whitefield, his parishioners rebelled. Too many townspeople "ware for more order," Fisk complained, and thus had "lost there Spiritual life." Conflict smoldered during the next several years, as Sturbridge became "like a velley of dry Bones." The dissenters were forced to "forsake all" by withdrawing from communion. On September 5, 1748, they called John Blunt, a Connecticut layman with no formal education and no license from any association of Congregational ministers, to serve as the pastor of their illegal church.[4]

"Come and witness for the Holy Ghost," Fisk boldly proclaimed in a letter inviting leaders of the Separate Congregational movement from across New England to attend Blunt's ordination. "Our Lord and yours is doing a marvelus work" in Sturbridge. The wonders to which he alluded included a battery of charismatic practices modeled on the earliest Christian churches and the extraordinary gifts of the Holy Spirit that were poured out on the day of Pentecost. The Separates welcomed "unlarned" itinerants and urged them to share their preaching gifts with the assembly. Worship exercises featured a cacophony of noise, as members of the upstart congregation fell to the ground in distress, cried out in joy, sang hymns at the top of their voices, or prayed aloud for the conversion of their neighbors. Women spoke freely during their meetings, and they traveled abroad encouraging people in other towns to embrace the separatist cause. Some members believed that Blunt possessed miraculous healing powers. And, no sooner had they organized themselves into a dissenting church then Ebenezer Moulton arrived from the neighboring town of Brimfield with a new gift: adult, or believers', baptism. The logic of the Separates' zealous quest to purify the corrupt churches of New England's Congregational establishment had propelled them beyond the boundaries of the puritan tradition altogether.[5]

Hannah Corey initially hesitated to join the Separates, yet she had always been uncomfortable worshipping in the Sturbridge meetinghouse. At the time she was promoted to full membership in 1745, she knew her "Soul was one with Christ" but not in union with Rice and his parishioners. Still, she

4. Fisk, "Testimony of a People Inhabitting the Wilderness," n.d. [January–February 1753], no. 397, *IBP; GWJ*, 475; Sturbridge Congregational Church Records, 60.

5. Henry Fisk to the Canterbury, Conn., Separate Church, Sept. 5, 1748, no. 50, JTC; Testimonies of Sarah Blanchard and Sarah Martin, Apr. 5, 1749, Sturbridge Separatist Congregational Church Records; Solomon Paine, council minutes, Aug. 26, 1752, no. 94, JTC; Fisk, "Testimony of a People Inhabitting the Wilderness," n.d. [January–February 1753], no. 397, *IBP*; William G. McLoughlin, ed., *The Diary of Isaac Backus*, 3 vols. (Providence, R.I., 1979), I, 90–91.

worried about the propriety of withdrawing from communion, given the dissenters' reputation for making noisy disturbances in town. The prayer meeting at Newell's house erased all her doubts. Corey's reservations vanished, and she felt a "Sweet oneness of Soul" with the Separates. Comforting biblical verses poured into her head. "I knew what them words ment" in Hebrews 4:12, she wrote, "the voyce of the Lord is quick and powerfull, Sharper then a two edged Sword devilding the Soul and Spirit the joynts and marrow." Through personal revelations like these, she had learned to discern God's voice speaking directly to her and had "Evidenc Sealed to my Soul" that the dissenters' cause was a righteous one. Corey understood with perfect certainty that she had "pased from death to life" because, in the words of 1 John 3:14, she loved the Separate brethren. "I Se myself One in the Lord and one with them," Corey concluded, "and I cannot go without them." Less than three months later, the Coreys renounced the baptismal rites they had received as infants and were immersed by Moulton in the Quinebaug River alongside thirteen other Separates.[6]

Submitted at a disciplinary hearing during the spring of 1749, Hannah Corey's written account of her decision to abandon the Sturbridge Congregational church resonated with other testimonies presented by the dissenting faction. Their statements deployed biblical metaphors of light and darkness to differentiate their breakaway congregation from Rice's established church. On a previous Sabbath, Newell's sister Sarah Martin "went home as darck as eygept" after taking part in the Lord's Supper in the Sturbridge meetinghouse. The powerful emotions that Stephen Blanchard experienced during the meetings in Newell's home pierced his heart like a "light Shining in a dark plase." Corey's husband elected to worship among the dissenters "according to what Light god had given me." The Sturbridge Separates castigated their former brethren and sisters for perishing in "ignorance and Darkness" or "Labouring under Darkness."[7]

Even as the separatist controversy raged in Sturbridge during the fall of 1748, two other town residents, Moses and Ruth Holbrook, presented Rice with a pair of very different written statements. These brief autobiographical relations, as they were called, demonstrated the qualifications of potential candidates for full church membership. Whereas John and Hannah Corey

6. Testimony of Hannah Corey, Apr. 5, 1749, Sturbridge Separatist Congregational Church Records; Henry Fisk, "Testimony from the Brethren in Sturbridge," 1753, no. 396, *IBP*; McLoughlin, ed., *Diary of Isaac Backus*, I, 58–59.

7. Testimonies of Stephen Blanchard, John Corey, Sarah Martin, David Morse, and Jerusha Morse, Apr. 5, 1749, Sturbridge Separatist Congregational Church Records; Fisk, "Testimony of a People Inhabitting the Wilderness," n.d. [January–February 1753], no. 397, *IBP*.

criticized Rice's parishioners for languishing in spiritual darkness, the Holbrooks proudly proclaimed that they had been "born in the land of lite" and "livead under the preaching of the gospel." The Coreys embraced the warm fellowship of the Sturbridge Separates; the Holbrooks accentuated their pious upbringing within the Congregational establishment by parents who had devoted them to God's service in baptism as infants. Both couples scanned the natural world for wondrous manifestations of God's will, but they interpreted the same providential events in diametrically opposite ways. John Corey imagined that a powerful thunderstorm during the summer of 1748 was the voice of God commanding him to join the dissenters. This same meteorological event had awakened Ruth Holbrook's desire to close with Rice's established church.[8]

The two sets of testimonies diverged in other respects. The Coreys confidently declared that they worshipped among the small remnant of God's elect saints. The Holbrooks, by contrast, adopted a more cautious tone in their church admission relations. Both spouses lamented their inherent sinfulness and cited specific sins, including youthful disobedience, Sabbath breaking, and vain company keeping. Alluding to the terrifying words of 1 Corinthians 11:29, the Holbrooks even feared that they might eat and drink their own damnation by participating in the Lord's Supper unworthily. They begged for the prayers of the Sturbridge church and pledged to "walk acording to the profession" they had made. Except for a few minor details, the Holbrooks' relations were nearly identical in their content, style, and even physical appearance. Both documents were written by the same individual—probably Moses. Mirroring relations from dozens of churches in eastern and central Massachusetts, the Holbrooks' patterned discourse reinforced their willingness to submit to ecclesiastical institutions and communal expectations. The Coreys wrote as inspired individuals whose revelatory experiences impelled them to reject the authority of their minister and neighbors.[9]

Hannah and John Corey had not always condemned New England's Congregational establishment. They would have submitted relations nearly identical to those of the Holbrooks when they joined the Sturbridge church three years earlier. There was little to distinguish them from Moses and Ruth Holbrook in terms of wealth, social status, or family background. Both couples hailed from aspiring yeoman clans and had migrated to the new settlements of Worcester County in search of inexpensive land. Like most of their Stur-

---

8. Appendix B, Sturbridge, Mass., First Church, 12–13. For the full texts of Moses and Ruth Holbrook's relations, see George H. Haynes, *Historical Sketch of the First Congregational Church, Sturbridge, Massachusetts* (Worcester, Mass., 1910), 38–39; and Appendix C.

9. Appendix B, Sturbridge, Mass., First Church, 12–13.

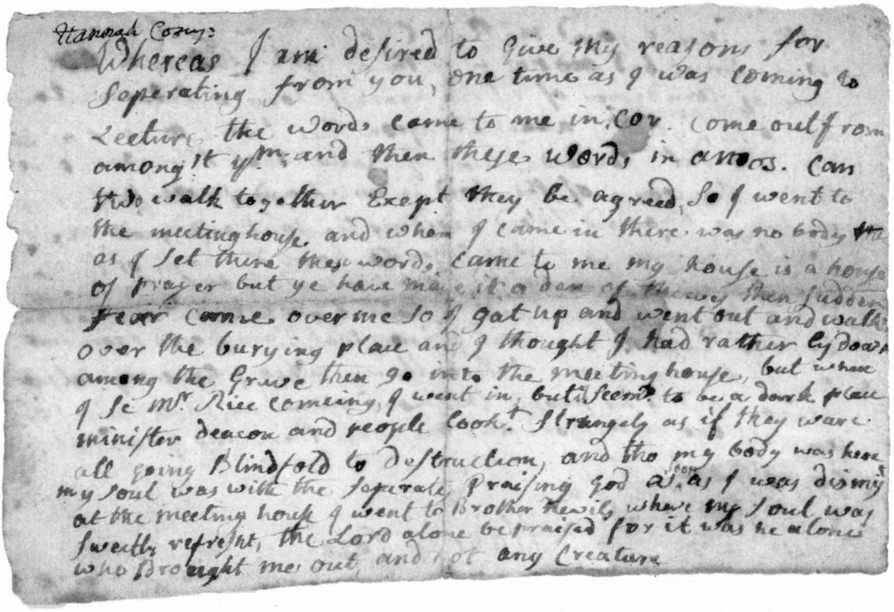

FIGURE 1 Testimony of Hannah Corey (front and back). April 5, 1749.
Courtesy, Congregational Library and Archives, Boston

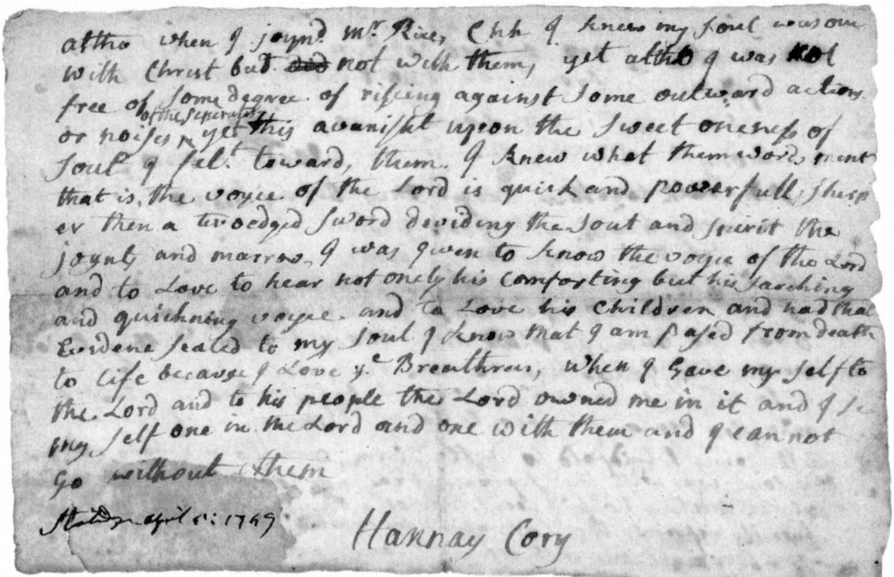

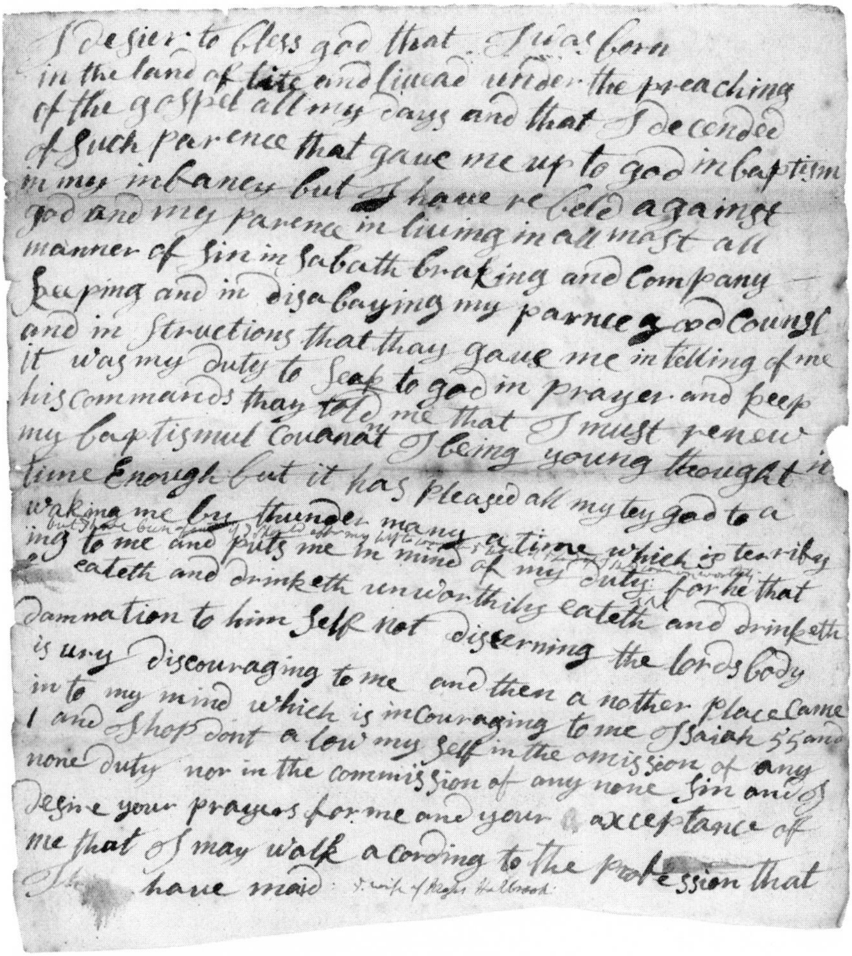
I desier to bless god that I was born
in the land of lite and liued under the preaching
of the gospel all my days and that I decended
of such parence that gave me up to god in baptism
in my infancy but I have rebeled against
god and my parence in living in all most all
manner of sin in Sabath braking and Company
keeping and in disobaying my parnce good counsel
and instructions that thay gave me in telling of me
it was my duty to seak to god in prayer and keep
his commands thay tole me that I must renew
my baptismul covanant I being young thought it
time enough but it has pleased all my tey god to a
waking me by thunder many a time which is tearibly
ing to me and puts me in mind of my duty for he that
eateth and drinketh unworthily eateth and drinketh
damnation to him self not discerning the lords body
is very discouraging to me and then a nother place came
in to my mind which is incouraging to me Isaiah 55 and
I and shop dont a low my self in the omission of any
none duty nor in the commission of any none sin and I
desire your prayers for me and your acceptance of
me that I may walk a cording to the profession that
I have maid

FIGURE 2 Relation of Ruth Holbrook. November 20, 1748.
Courtesy, Congregational Library and Archives, Boston

bridge neighbors, they lived in modest one-room houses furnished with a limited range of material goods. Diaries compiled by another Sturbridge resident who affiliated with Rice's church a decade later reveal an insular mental world shaped by the seasonal rhythms of the environment, the annual round of agricultural labor, the family life-course, and, only occasionally, local or regional politics. Born during the second decade of the eighteenth century, the Coreys and Holbrooks came of age, married, and started families during an intensive period of religious renewal and conflict, and both appear to have embraced the "pourful preaching" innovations that marked an era that later historians have called the Great Awakening in New England or, on a wider scale, the Protestant Evangelical Awakening.[10]

How did it come to pass that two families of roughly equal social status, who settled in the same town and once worshipped side by side in the same meetinghouse, came to view New England's dominant, established religious institution as a place of both gospel light and Egyptian darkness? Although they shared a worldview derived from their Reformed theological heritage, the Holbrooks and Coreys by 1750 were unwilling to sit together in the same building. They no longer spoke in a common religious idiom. The narratives they composed to support their respective decisions to affiliate and separate from the Sturbridge church disclosed a startling breach in what had once been an orderly, broadly inclusive religious culture.

■ *Darkness Falls on the Land of Light* examines the breakdown of New England Congregationalism and the rise of American evangelicalism during the eighteenth century. It is not a story of resurgent puritan piety but a tale of insurgent religious radicalism. The "New England Way"—the distinctive ecclesiastical system that shaped the Congregational tradition during the century following the puritan Great Migration of the 1630s—did not collapse under the weight of secularizing impulses, as Perry Miller and an earlier generation of social historians assumed. Nor was it plagued by the moribund formalism often denigrated by scholars of early evangelicalism.[11] Instead, a vibrant Con-

10. Ibid., 13; Sturbridge Congregational Church Records, 61; Holly V. Izard, "Another Place in Time: The Material and Social Worlds of Sturbridge, Massachusetts, from Settlement to 1850" (Ph.D. diss., Boston University, 1996), 82–119; Moses Weld, diaries, 1759–1773, Mss 663, NEHGS.

11. Key formulations of Perry Miller's declension thesis may be found in his *The New England Mind: From Colony to Province* (Cambridge, Mass., 1953), bks. III–IV (quote, 3); "Errand into the Wilderness," in Miller, *Errand into the Wilderness* (Cambridge, Mass., 1956), 1–15; and "Declension in a Bible Commonwealth," in Miller, *Nature's Nation* (Cambridge, Mass., 1967), 14–49. Christine Leigh Heyrman provides a summary and critique of the "communal breakdown" model of early New England social history in her *Commerce and Culture: The Maritime Communities of Colonial Massachusetts, 1690–1750* (New York, 1984), 13–20 (quote, 16). Although most scholars of New England puritanism have modified or abandoned Miller's thesis, negative judgments regarding the "laxity" and "formality" of "nominal" Congregationalists continue to anchor the introductory chapters of most general works on the Great Awakening, including Edwin Scott Gaustad, *The Great Awakening in New England* (New York, 1957), 13–15 ("laxity," 14); Goen, *Revivalism and Separatism in New England*, 3–4; J. M. Bumsted and John E. van de Wetering, *What Must I Do to Be Saved? The Great Awakening in Colonial America* (Hinsdale, Ill., 1976), 54–70; W. R. Ward, *The Protestant Evangelical Awakening* (Cambridge, 1992), 273–286; Mark A. Noll, *The Rise of Evangelicalism: The Age of Edwards, Whitefield, and the Wesleys*, A History of Evangelicalism: People, Movements, and Ideas in the English-Speaking World, I (Downers Grove, Ill., 2003), 27–49; and John Howard Smith, *The First Great Awakening: Redefining Reli-*

gregational establishment was buried under an avalanche of innovative and incendiary religious beliefs and practices during the middle decades of the eighteenth century. Acrimonious theological debate and sectarian schism had roiled the New England colonies a century earlier; and the region had witnessed previous "stirs," "harvests," and "awakenings."[12] But the surging religious fervor that engulfed New England in the wake of George Whitefield's 1740 preaching tour was unlike anything anyone had ever seen. It marked a dramatic break with the past. The primary agents inciting change were, not prominent ministers and theologians such as Jonathan Edwards, but unassuming men and women like Hannah and John Corey, whose burgeoning fascination with the drama of conversion and the charismatic gifts of the Holy Spirit drove them out of the churches of the Congregational standing order.

The pages that follow build on pioneering works of popular religion in early America and a wide range of studies that examine the complex relationship between religion and society in provincial New England. Whereas earlier scholars have treated the Whitefieldian revivals of the 1740s as a coda to the history of seventeenth-century puritanism, I characterize New England's era of great awakenings as the historical fulcrum on which the "shared culture" of David Hall's "world of wonders" tilted decisively toward Jon Butler's robust antebellum "spiritual hothouse."[13]

gion in British America, 1725–1775 (Madison, N.J., 2015), 39–63 ("formality," "nominal," 53). For the pejorative language of "nominal" Christians, see Thomas S. Kidd, *George Whitefield: America's Spiritual Founding Father* (New Haven, Conn., 2014), 119, 123, 130.

12. Douglas Winiarski, "Colonial Awakenings Prior to 1730," in Michael McClymond, ed., *Encyclopedia of Religious Revivals in America*, I, *A–Z* (Westport, Conn., 2007), 121–126. On sectarian dissent in seventeenth-century New England, see Philip F. Gura, *A Glimpse of Sion's Glory: Puritan Radicalism in New England, 1620–1660* (Middletown, Conn., 1984); David S. Lovejoy, *Religious Enthusiasm in the New World: Heresy to the Revolution* (Cambridge, Mass., 1985); Carla Gardina Pestana, *Quakers and Baptists in Colonial Massachusetts* (Cambridge, 1991); and Michael P. Winship, *Making Heretics: Militant Protestantism and Free Grace in Massachusetts, 1636–1641* (Princeton, N.J., 2002).

13. David D. Hall, *Worlds of Wonder, Days of Judgment: Popular Religious Belief in Early New England* (New York, 1989), 71; Jon Butler, *Awash in a Sea of Faith: Christianizing the American People* (Cambridge, Mass., 1990), 2. Earlier studies that have played a formative role in the development of this project include Robert G. Pope, *The Half-Way Covenant: Church Membership in Puritan New England* (Princeton, N.J., 1969); Charles E. Hambrick-Stowe, *The Practice of Piety: Puritan Devotional Disciplines in Seventeenth-Century New England* (Chapel Hill, N.C., 1982); John Corrigan, *The Prism of Piety: Catholick Congregational Clergy at the Beginning of the Enlightenment*, Religion in America (New York, 1991); Gerald F. Moran and Maris A. Vinovskis, eds., *Religion, Family, and the Life Course: Explorations in the Social History of Early America* (Ann Arbor, Mich., 1992); Richard P. Gildrie, *The Profane, the Civil, and the Godly: The Reformation of Manners in Orthodox New England, 1679–1749* (University Park, Pa., 1994); Susan Juster, *Disorderly Women: Sexual Politics and Evangelicalism in Revolutionary New England* (Ithaca, N.Y., 1994); James F. Cooper, Jr., *Tenacious of Their Liberties: The Congregationalists in Colonial Massachusetts,*

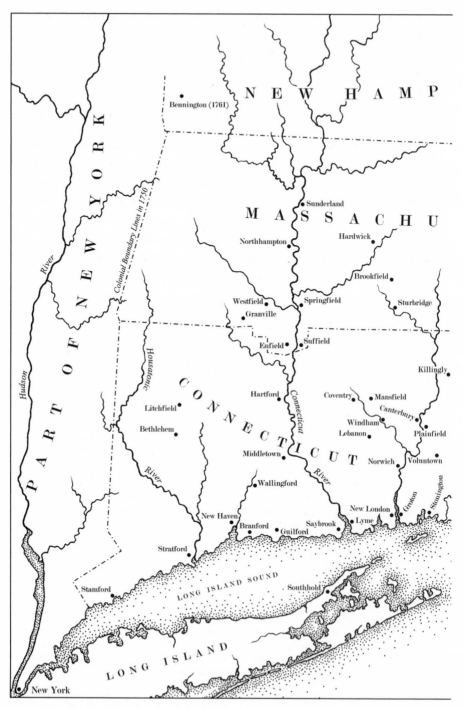

MAP 1 New England in 1750. Drawn by Mark Cook
Kittery and York are located in the Colony of Massachusetts, now part of Maine.

Like many colleagues who have turned to the study of lived religion, I seek to connect religious belief to practice, while situating both in a thick cultural context. Although historians of religion in provincial New England have long been accustomed to sorting ministers and their congregants into theological parties, temperaments, or ideal types, I place greater emphasis on the development of these categories over the course of the eighteenth century. Microhistorical case studies and aggregate data on church affiliation practices for thousands of individuals and families reveal ordinary people living through one of the most tumultuous periods in American religious history and emerging on the other side transformed.[14]

Much of the argument turns on the shifting religious experiences of lay men and women. Religious studies theorists frequently maintain that all experiences are mediated by or, to be more precise, constructed through language. Examining the religious lives of provincial New Englanders demands paying close attention to the changing vocabularies, grammars, tropes, idioms, and story frameworks they inscribed in their diaries, letters, devotional writings, and other personal papers as well as the practices that invested these

---

Religion in America (New York, 1999); Erik R. Seeman, *Pious Persuasions: Laity and Clergy in Eighteenth-Century New England,* Early America: History, Context, Culture (Baltimore, 1999); and Mark Valeri, *Heavenly Merchandize: How Religion Shaped Commerce in Puritan America* (Princeton, N.J., 2010). David D. Hall traces important historiographical trends in "On Common Ground: The Coherence of American Puritan Studies," *WMQ,* XLIV (1987), 193–229; "Narrating Puritanism," in Harry S. Stout and D. G. Hart, eds., *New Directions in American Religious History* (New York, 1997), 51–83; and "'Between the Times': Popular Religion in Eighteenth-Century British North America," in Michael V. Kennedy and William G. Shade, eds., *The World Turned Upside-Down: The State of Eighteenth-Century American Studies at the Beginning of the Twenty-First Century* (Bethlehem, Pa., 2001), 142–163.

14. Theoretical contributions to the study of "lived religion" include Robert A. Orsi, "Everyday Miracles: The Study of Lived Religion," in David D. Hall, ed., *Lived Religion in America: Toward a History of Practice* (Princeton, N.J., 1997), 3–21; and Orsi, *The Madonna of 115th Street: Faith and Community in Italian Harlem, 1880–1950,* 3d ed. (New Haven, Conn., 2010), xxxvii–xliii. On the turn to religious practices, see Laurie F. Maffly-Kipp, Leigh E. Schmidt, and Mark Valeri, eds., *Practicing Protestants: Histories of Christian Life in America, 1630–1965* (Baltimore, 2006). My allusion to "thick description" derives from Clifford Geertz's classic "Thick Description: Toward an Interpretive Theory of Culture," in Geertz, *The Interpretation of Cultures: Selected Essays* (New York, 1973), 3–30. I have also been influenced by older methodological debates involving the social history of ideas, especially the essays by Quentin Skinner collected in James Tully, ed., *Meaning and Context: Quentin Skinner and His Critics* (Princeton, N.J., 1988). Previous studies that sort provincial New Englanders into ideal types include Alan Heimert, *Religion and the American Mind: From the Great Awakening to the Revolution* (Cambridge, Mass., 1966), 3; Philip Greven, *The Protestant Temperament: Patterns of Child-Rearing, Religious Experience, and the Self in Early America* (Chicago, 1977), 12–14; and Richard Rabinowitz, *The Spiritual Self in Everyday Life: The Transformation of Personal Religious Experience in Nineteenth-Century New England* (Boston, 1989), xxviii–xxx.

discursive conventions with power and meaning. Throughout the colonial era, language drawn from the Reformed tradition provided the dominant idiom through which most people narrated both ordinary and extraordinary events in their lives. But the decade that culminated in the Sturbridge church schism witnessed a dramatic rupture in the ways that people such as the Holbrooks and the Coreys created meaningful worlds. New Englanders turned to vivid metaphors of darkness and light to describe the volatile situation. The title of this book seeks to capture the turmoil and creativity that prevailed in "post-Puritan" New England.[15]

I devote considerable attention to recovering the distinctive vocabularies that New Englanders themselves developed to articulate their rapidly changing religious culture. Many terms familiar to students of this period are anachronistic, pejorative, or misleading. As contemporary observers were quick to acknowledge, for example, provincial lay men and women did experience a "great awakening" during the 1740s; yet the meaning of events they alternately called a "great Reviveal of Religon" or "great Religious Commotions" remained bitterly contested.[16] The very concept of "a Revival of Religion"—a singular

15. I borrow the phrase "post-puritan" from Charles L. Cohen, "The Post-Puritan Paradigm of Early American Religious History," *WMQ*, LIV (1997), 696. For theoretical discussions of language and religious experience, see Wayne Proudfoot, *Religious Experience* (Berkeley, Calif., 1985), 216–227; Talal Asad, "The Construction of Religion as an Anthropological Category," in Asad, *Genealogies of Religion: Discipline and Reasons of Power in Christianity and Islam* (Baltimore, 1993), 27–54; Robert H. Sharf, "Experience," in Mark C. Taylor, ed., *Critical Terms for Religious Studies* (Chicago, 1998), 94–116; and Thomas A. Tweed, *Crossing and Dwelling: A Theory of Religion* (Cambridge, Mass., 2006), 54–79. Previous studies of religion in early America that adopt similar interpretive approaches include John Owen King III, *The Iron of Melancholy: Structures of Spiritual Conversion in America from the Puritan Conscience to Victorian Neurosis* (Middletown, Conn., 1983), 7–8; Michael J. Crawford, *Seasons of Grace: Colonial New England's Revival Tradition in Its British Context*, Religion in America (New York, 1991), 4–6; and Rodger M. Payne, *The Self and the Sacred: Conversion and Autobiography in Early American Protestantism* (Knoxville, Tenn., 1998), 1–12.

16. George Leon Walker, [ed.], *Diary of Rev. Daniel Wadsworth ..., 1737–1747* (Hartford, Conn., 1894), 71; Ivory Hovey, Sr., and Anne Hovey, to Ivory Hovey, Jr., Mar. 29, 1742, Hovey Family Papers, 1734–1901, PHM; Charles Lane Hanson, ed., *A Journal for the Years 1739–1803 by Samuel Lane of Stratham, New Hampshire* (Concord, N.H., 1937), 30. This study does not engage the historiographical debates that have developed in response to Jon Butler's landmark essay "Enthusiasm Described and Decried: The Great Awakening as Interpretative Fiction," *JAH*, LXIX (1982), 305–325, as well as his elaborations in "Whitefield in America: A Two Hundred Fiftieth Commemoration," *Pennsylvania Magazine of History and Biography*, CXIII (1989), 515–526; *Awash in a Sea of Faith*, 164–193; and *Becoming America: The Revolution Before 1776* (Cambridge, Mass., 2000), 196–204. Subsequent studies that have challenged or modified Butler's thesis include Crawford, *Seasons of Grace;* Harry S. Stout, *The Divine Dramatist: George Whitefield and the Rise of Modern Evangelicalism*, Library of Religious Biography (Grand Rapids, Mich., 1991); Timothy D. Hall, *Contested Boundaries: Itinerancy and the Reshaping of the Colonial American Religious World* (Durham, N.C., 1994); Juster, *Disorderly Women;* Frank Lambert, *"Pedlar in Divinity": George Whitefield and the*

and dramatic outpouring of the *"Work of the Spirit of GOD"* that was propagated from place to place seemingly under its own miraculous power—was less than a decade old at the time of Whitefield's first New England tour. Although seventeenth-century puritan divines had developed a coherent morphology of conversion, their provincial descendants struggled to categorize the rapid and often dramatically embodied experiences that Whitefield called the "new birth." As a result, many ministers and lay people began referring to the subjects of such experiences as "sudden," "new," or "young Converts." Later in the decade, Separate Congregationalists invented the expressions *"Half-membership"* and the "half way Covenant" to condemn innovations in baptismal practices that dated back nearly a century. Charles Chauncy and other clergymen resurrected the phrase "NEW-LIGHT" from the Antinomian controversy and the Quaker insurgencies of the seventeenth century to condemn what they considered to be religious disorders and excesses. Yale College president Ezra Stiles began referring to "Old Light" churches long after the revivals had subsided.[17]

Diaries, letters, and other eighteenth-century texts provide occasional glimpses of a new language of religious experience at the moment of creation. People learned to speak of "converting, as they call it" and how they *"got thro',* as they phrase it." They were "Mightily Comforted (and as the Term now is) have Received Light," or they "fell into what is called a Trance." Even

Transatlantic Revivals, 1737-1770 (Princeton, N.J., 1994); Lambert, *Inventing the "Great Awakening"* (Princeton, N.J., 1999); and Thomas S. Kidd, *The Great Awakening: The Roots of Evangelical Christianity in Colonial America* (New Haven, Conn., 2007). For broader historiographical trends, see Allen C. Guelzo, "God's Designs: The Literature of the Colonial Revivals of Religion, 1735-1760," in Stout and Hart, eds., *New Directions in American Religious History*, 141-172; Philip Goff, "Revivals and Revolution: Historiographic Turns since Alan Heimert's *Religion and the American Mind,*" *Church History*, LXVII (1998), 695-721; Christopher Grasso, *A Speaking Aristocracy: Transforming Public Discourse in Eighteenth-Century Connecticut* (Chapel Hill, N.C., 1999), 495-498; and Grasso, "A 'Great Awakening'?" *Reviews in American History*, XXXVII (2009), 13-21.

17. Ross W. Beales, Jr., "'Our Hearts Are Traitors to Themselves': Jonathan Mayhew and the Great Awakening," *Bulletin of the CL*, XXVII, no. 3 (1976), 8; Timothy Pickering, *The Rev. Mr. Pickering's Letters to the Rev. N. Rogers and Mr. D. Rogers of Ipswich ...* (Boston, 1742), 3; *GWJ*, 455; William Stevens Perry, ed., *Historical Collections Relating to the American Colonial Church* (Hartford, Conn., 1873), III, 368; EWD, 237; Winiarski, "'A Jornal of a Fue Days at York': The Great Awakening on the Northern New England Frontier," *Maine History*, XLII (2004), 70; Ebenezer Devotion, *An Answer of the Pastor and Brethren of the Third Church in Windham, to Twelve Articles, Exhibited by Several of Its Separating Members, as Reasons of Their Separation ...* (N[ew] London, Conn., 1747), 1; North Stonington, Conn., Congregational Church Records, 1727-1887, 116, microfilm no. 317, CSL; Charles Chauncy, *Seasonable Thoughts on the State of Religion in New-England ...* (Boston, 1743), vi; Franklin Bowditch Dexter, ed., *Extracts from the Itineraries and Other Miscellanies of Ezra Stiles, D.D., LL.D., 1755-1794 ...* (New Haven, Conn., 1916), 251.

Jonathan Edwards coined phrases for the "visible conversions (if I may so call them)" that he witnessed during the 1740s. Throughout this work, I employ words, phrases, and metaphors familiar to eighteenth-century clergymen and laypeople, such as a "holy walk, and conversation," "professors," "opposers," "Whitfeldarians," and the like.[18]

The last term, "Whitfeldarians," comes closest to naming those eighteenth-century Protestants whom contemporary historians have identified as evangelicals. Although this study is a regional contribution to the popular history of early evangelicalism, I seek to defamiliarize the category both to avoid the persistent "dissenter bias" that has dominated previous scholarship on religion in early America and to restore a greater sense of historical contingency to a movement that was still in its infancy in eighteenth-century New England.[19] With perhaps the notable exception of Cotton Mather, Congregational ministers rarely included the adjective "Evangelical" in their weekly sermons or theological works before 1740. Provincial lay men and women never used it at all. And neither group used the term in its nominal form to identify a distinctive group of people or a specific religious subculture. By the time that Hannah Adams of Medfield, Massachusetts, published the definitive edition of her *Dictionary of All Religions and Religious Denominations* in 1817, New Englanders had become accustomed to talking about the "diversity of sentiment among Christians" in terms of specific denominations, theological schools—including "Whitefieldites"—and even homegrown sectarian movements; but no entry in her celebrated early reference work yet bore the heading "Evangelical."[20]

For these reasons, I have bracketed *evangelicalism* for most of the pages

18. Francis L. Hawks and William Stevens Perry, eds., *Documentary History of the Protestant Episcopal Church, in the United States of America*, 2 vols. (New York, 1863–1864), I, 174; *South Carolina Gazette* (Charleston), Feb. 27–Mar. 6, 1742; Benjamin Throop, "Secret Interviews," 1741–1784, [4], CHS; DDR, Feb. 1, 1742; Jonathan Edwards to Thomas Prince, Dec. 12, 1743, in *WJE*, XVI, *Letters and Personal Writings*, ed. George S. Claghorn (New Haven, Conn., 1998), 120; Joseph Baxter, sermon fragment, n.d. [circa 1722–1743], Baxter-Adams Family Papers, 1669–1889, box 2, folder 19, MHS; Jonathan Edwards, "The Subjects of a First Work of Grace May Need a New Conversion," in *WJE*, XXII, *Sermons and Discourses, 1739–1742*, ed. Harry S. Stout and Nathan O. Hatch, with Kyle P. Farley (New Haven, Conn., 2003), 202; Andrew Croswell to Nathaniel and Daniel Rogers, Sept. 23, 1742, case 8, box 22, SGC I; Nathan Cole, "An Appeal to the Bible," Nathan Cole Papers, 1722–1780, I, 6, CHS.

19. John K. Nelson, *A Blessed Company: Parishes, Parsons, and Parishioners in Anglican Virginia, 1690–1776* (Chapel Hill, N.C., 2001), 9.

20. Hannah Adams, *A Dictionary of All Religions and Religious Denominations: Jewish, Heathen, Mahometan, Christian, Ancient and Modern*, intro. Thomas A. Tweed, Classics in Religious Studies, no. 8 (Atlanta, Ga., 1992), 320, 371. The *Oxford English Dictionary Online*, s.v. "evangelical," suggests that the nominal form of the term emerged among English Methodists during the 1790s.

that follow. Defining this word for a period in which it remained largely inoperative would run many of the same risks of "misplaced essentializing" that have often hindered seventeenth-century puritan studies.[21] David Bebbington's frequently cited quadrilateral definition—conversionism, biblicism, activism, and crucicentrism—masks far more than it illuminates the popular religious cultures of the eighteenth-century British Atlantic. In New England, Whitefield's fascination with conversion as an instantaneous event was quite unlike the more traditional seventeenth-century puritan morphology of conversion, which ministers and lay people often conceptualized as a lifelong pilgrimage through the wilderness of this world. Although provincial Congregationalists were steeped in the scriptures, during the Whitefieldian revivals and the decades that followed new converts such as Hannah Corey learned to think of the Bible as a detextualized voice that pierced their minds with supernatural force. W. R. Ward's hexagonal model of "top-drawer evangelicalism" bears little resemblance to the religious experiences described by lay men and women in eighteenth-century New England. Emphasizing lay experience and ecclesiastical innovations, Susan Juster's fourfold definition is much closer to the argument advanced in this study, but it nonetheless tends to reify a nascent religious temperament that came out of the religious revivals of the 1740s and remained constantly in motion throughout the eighteenth century.[22]

The "people called *New Lights*" diverged from their puritan ancestors in two specific ways: their preoccupation with Whitefield's definition of the new birth and their fascination with biblical impulses. These critical factors set many Whitefieldarians on a course to embrace increasingly radical beliefs and practices, including the bodily presence of the indwelling Holy Spirit,

21. Michael P. Winship, "Were There Any Puritans in New England?" *NEQ*, LXXIV (2001), 132.

22. D. W. Bebbington, *Evangelicalism in Modern Britain: A History from the 1730s to the 1980s* (London, 1989), 1–17; W. R. Ward, *Early Evangelicalism: A Global Intellectual History, 1670–1789* (Cambridge, 2006), 2–4; Juster, *Disorderly Women*, viii. Bebbington's definition has been cited in a wide range of studies, from general surveys and essay collections to specialized monographs. See, for example, Mark A. Noll, Bebbington, and George A. Rawlyk, eds., *Evangelicalism: Comparative Studies of Popular Protestantism in North America, the British Isles, and Beyond, 1700–1990*, Religion in America (New York, 1994), 6; Noll, *Rise of Evangelicalism*, 15–21; and Jonathan D. Sassi, *A Republic of Righteousness: The Public Christianity of the Post-Revolutionary New England Clergy*, Religion in America (New York, 2001), 146. A notable exception to this trend is Kidd's *Great Awakening*, which provides an important corrective to Bebbington's definition (xiv) and anticipates some of the issues that I address in this book. Catherine A. Brekus also adopts Bebbington's scheme, but her argument in *Sarah Osborn's World: The Rise of Evangelical Christianity in Early America* (New Haven, Conn., 2013) forthrightly acknowledges that the "new kind of faith that we now call evangelicalism" was a "loose coalition of leaders, ideas, and practices" that developed during the mid-eighteenth century and "took decades to come together" (5, 11).

continued revelation, dramatic visionary phenomena, and a strident desire to break fellowship with their kin and neighbors and worship with like-minded men and women who claimed similar experiences. Only the radicalism of the Whitefieldian revivals accounts for the unexpected splintering of the Congregational standing order that occurred during the middle decades of the eighteenth century, as religious institutions that once commanded the allegiance of more than 80 percent of the population in many New England towns devolved into a fractious spiritual marketplace of competing denominations and sects.[23] Since the last quarter of the twentieth century, scholars have been working to recover these so-called radical evangelicals from the periphery.[24] I place them in the eye of the tempests that engulfed and eventually tore apart New England's Congregational culture. In 1750, to be a Whitefieldarian was to be a religious radical.

Darkness Falls on the Land of Light is organized chronologically into five parts. Drawing on an exceptional collection of church admission relations from the town of Haverhill, Massachusetts, Part 1 examines the widely shared religious vocabulary through which church membership candidates during the period between 1680 and 1740 pledged to "walk answerably" to their doctrinal professions in the hope that a vengeful deity would not pour out affliction on their bodies, families, and communities. Provincial New Englanders inhabited a world punctuated by sudden deaths, infant mortality, natural disasters, epidemic diseases, and imperial warfare. Their devotional writings and practices directly addressed these temporal woes. Lay men and women might have worried about the salvation of their sinful souls—especially during the latter stages of life or in times of mortal danger—but they prayed just as fervently for good health, productive crops, pious children, safe journeys, and material blessings. The multiple demands of a "Godly Walk" entailed spiri-

23. Dean Dudley, *History and Genealogy of the Bangs Family in America* (Montrose, Mass., 1896), 8. I share Roger Finke and Roger Stark's interest in employing "economic concepts ... to analyze the success and failure of religious bodies," although I find their measurement techniques for the colonial era—and New England in particular—to be significantly flawed. For a more detailed critique and statement of the quantitative methodologies employed in this study, see Appendix A. Finke and Stark outline their "market-oriented" approach in *The Churching of America, 1776–2005: Winners and Losers in Our Religious Economy,* 2d ed. (New Brunswick, N.J., 2005), 8–12 (quotations, 9).

24. G. A. Rawlyk, *The Canada Fire: Radical Evangelicalism in British North America, 1775–1812* (Kingston, Ont., 1994), xvii. See also Stephen A. Marini, *Radical Sects of Revolutionary New England* (Cambridge, Mass., 1982); Clarke Garrett, *Origins of the Shakers: From the Old World to the New World* (Baltimore, 1988); Leigh Eric Schmidt, *Hearing Things: Religion, Illusion, and the American Enlightenment* (Cambridge, Mass., 2000); and Aaron Spencer Fogleman, *Jesus Is Female: Moravians and the Challenge of Radical Religion in Early America,* Early American Studies (Philadelphia, 2007).

tualizing everyday occurrences, meditating in secret, baptizing children in a timely fashion, and raising them in church fellowship. As with Anglican congregations elsewhere in England and British North America, the "practical Protestantism" that pervaded New England during a period once dismissed as its "Glacial Age" was tolerant, inclusive, steady, and comforting.[25]

The next three parts of the book explore the breakdown of New England's pervasive Congregational culture during a "Time of Great Awakenings." Framed by Nathan Cole's famous account of George Whitefield's 1740 visit to Middletown, Connecticut, Part 2 reconstructs the theological and rhetorical strategies through which the popular Anglican evangelist labored to persuade his audiences to repudiate the ideal of the godly walk. In its place, many New Englanders championed Whitefield's "doctrine of the new birth," the instantaneous descent and implantation of God's Holy Spirit. Circulating initially within epistolary networks and later through newspapers and magazines, heady reports of dramatic preaching performances, protracted religious meetings, and other innovative "Measures to Promote religion" convinced many "New Converts" that they were witnessing an unprecedented outpouring of the Holy Spirit, or what people began to call a singular *"Revival of Religion."*[26] Diaries, letters, sermon notes, church membership demographics, prayer bills, and even gravestone iconography registered an abrupt shift in lay piety, as New England lurched unexpectedly into what many believed was a new religious world.

Renewed emphasis on the theological doctrine of the Holy Spirit as an indwelling vital principle proved to be a perplexing issue for many Congregationalists. Part 3 tells the story of one man's struggle to discern its presence in the body of a young Boston revival convert named Martha Robinson. Neigh-

25. Appendix B, Boston, First Church, 10; John Barnard, *The Peaceful End of the Perfect and Upright Man: A Sermon, Occasioned by the Death of Mr. John Atwood ...* (Boston, 1714), 28; Clifford Kenyon Shipton, "The New England Clergy of the 'Glacial Age,'" CSM, *Publications, Transactions, 1933-1937*, XXXII (Boston, 1937), 53. I borrow the helpful phrase "practical Protestantism" from T. J. Tomlin, *A Divinity for All Persuasions: Almanacs and Early American Religious Life*, Religion in America (New York, 2014), 158. For comparisons with Anglicanism, see John Spurr, *The Restoration Church of England, 1646-1689* (New Haven, Conn., 1991), 279-330; W. M. Jacob, *Lay People and Religion in the Early Eighteenth Century* (New York, 1996), 1-19; Nelson, *Blessed Company*, 1-10; Louis P. Nelson, *The Beauty of Holiness: Anglicanism and Architecture in Colonial South Carolina* (Chapel Hill, N.C., 2008), 142, 222-224; and Lauren F. Winner, *A Cheerful and Comfortable Faith: Anglican Religious Practice in the Elite Households of Eighteenth-Century Virginia* (New Haven, Conn., 2010), 1-5, 19-26.

26. Benjamin Bradstreet, *Godly Sorrow Described, and the Blessing Annexed Consider'd* (Boston, 1742), title page; *GWJ*, 478; NGD, 194; Thomas Foxcroft to Jonathan Dickinson, Dec. 16, 1741, Charles Roberts Autograph Letter Collection, Haverford College Library, Haverford, Pa.; Thomas Prince, *It Being Earnestly Desired ...* (Boston, [1743]).

bors feared that Robinson was possessed by the Devil, but Hartford magistrate Joseph Pitkin found through a close inspection of physical signs and verbal utterances that her body had been alternately conscripted by Satan and the Holy Spirit. His surprising discovery positions the phenomenon of ecstatic spirit possession at the heart of the Whitefieldian new birth experience. During the revivals of the 1740s, New Englanders learned to associate the descent of the Holy Spirit with exercised bodies, impulsive biblical texts, and unusual visionary phenomena. The charismatic elements of this emerging conversion paradigm impelled many revival participants to engage in dramatic acts of ecclesiastical disobedience. The most notable of these events, the infamous New London bonfires of 1743, anchors the discussion in Part 4. Inspired by powerful native-born itinerants such as the incendiary James Davenport, Spirit-possessed radicals railed against the opponents of the revivals, branded their ministers and neighbors unconverted hypocrites, and embraced new gifts of preaching and worship. In time, the voices of scripture that dropped into their heads and sounded in their ears compelled them to break communion with the churches of the Congregational establishment altogether.

During the next several decades, ministers across New England struggled and frequently failed to corral the unruly religious experiences of their inspired parishioners. Part 5 recounts the strife that plagued not only well-established churches, such as Edwards's Northampton, Massachusetts, congregation, but also upstart separatist groups led by ardent revival proponents like the Separate Baptist minister Isaac Backus. Thrust into a dizzying and unstable religious marketplace, godly walkers and perfectionist seekers, Anglican conformists and "Nothingarians" trafficked in and out of the churches of the standing order at a startling rate. By 1780, religious insurgents had fomented what C. C. Goen once called a "permanent shattering" of the Congregational establishment. Not until the Second Great Awakening of the early nineteenth century would New Englanders finally come to terms with the pluralistic religious culture that arose during the decades following the revivals of the 1740s. The Epilogue sketches in broad strokes this final transformation of the New England way, as it unfolded during the lives of four generations of the Lane family of Hampton and Stratham, New Hampshire.[27]

The middle decades of the eighteenth century were the dark night of the collective New England soul, as ordinary people groped toward a radically restructured religious order. The outcome of that struggle—the travail of New

---

27. Dexter, ed., *Extracts from the Itineraries and Other Miscellanies of Ezra Stiles*, 105; Goen, *Revivalism and Separatism in New England*, xxvii.

England Congregationalism—transformed the once-puritan churches from inclusive communities of interlocking parishes and families into exclusive networks of gifted spiritual seekers. Then, as now, religion empowered men and women to question structures of authority. It also tore at the fabric of society.

■ In 1839, the amateur artist and popular historian John Warner Barber published a capsule history of Sturbridge in his celebratory *Historical Collections of Massachusetts*. The accompanying woodcut illustration depicting neatly walled fields and orderly buildings heralded the demographic permanence, economic prosperity, and political stability of the new nation. Atop a small rise at the center of the village, the twin spires of the Congregational and Baptist churches testified to the hegemony of the multidenominational Protestant order that had originated from the legal disestablishment of religion in Massachusetts a few years earlier. Barber's profile of Sturbridge highlighted the contributions of hardy pioneers like Daniel and Henry Fisk, who hewed a peaceable kingdom from the trackless wilderness. Although Barber acknowledged that some of the townspeople had "received *new light*" during the 1740s and separated to form the Sturbridge Baptist church, his laudatory account of the first century of the town's history subsumed religious conflict within a gazetteer of facts and figures on topography, population, farm acreage, and industrial production. One among dozens of local histories written during the decades before the Civil War, Barber's *Historical Collections* presented a vision of colonial history that merged seamlessly with evolving American values of civic engagement, religious pluralism, and participatory democracy.[28]

The troubled middle decades of the eighteenth century reveal a very different etiology of New England's iconic white villages, for the religious crisis that began with George Whitefield's 1740 preaching tour only intensified and deepened during the years that followed. On May 26, 1748, one month after Hannah and John Corey withdrew from communion in the Sturbridge church, angry townspeople descended on the Separates' meeting, laid hold of two dissenters from neighboring villages, and in a "hostile manner drew them out of

28. John Warner Barber, *Historical Collections, Being a General Collection of Interesting Facts, Traditions, Biographical Sketches, Anecdotes, etc., Relating to the History and Antiquities of Every Town in Massachusetts, with Geographical Descriptions* (Worcester, Mass., 1839), 607–608. On the construction of New England regional identity, see David D. Hall and Alan Taylor, "Reassessing the Local History of New England," in Roger Parks, ed., *New England: A Bibliography of Its History*, Bibliographies of New England History, VII (Hanover, N.H., 1989), xix–xxxi; William H. Truettner and Roger B. Stein, eds., *Picturing Old New England: Image and Memory* (New Haven, Conn., 1999); and Joseph A. Conforti, *Imagining New England: Explorations of Regional Identity from the Pilgrims to the Mid-Twentieth Century* (Chapel Hill, N.C., 2001).

View of the central village in Sturbridge.

FIGURE 3 "View of the Central Village in Sturbridge." From John Warner Barber, *Massachusetts Historical Collections, Being a General Collection of Interesting Facts, Traditions, Biographical Sketches, Anecdotes, Etc., Relating to the History and Antiquities of Every Town in Massachusetts, with Geographical Descriptions* (Worcester, Mass., 1839), 608. Courtesy, Colonial Williamsburg Foundation, Williamsburg, Virginia

town." The next year, a mob attacked another member of the separatist faction when he attempted to preach in a nearby town. In 1750, magistrates incarcerated John Corey and four other members of the reorganized Separate Baptist church after they refused to pay their ministerial taxes. Constables confiscated personal possessions from nearly every Baptist householder in Sturbridge to pay the salary of Congregational minister Caleb Rice. The destrained goods ranged from swine, heifers, steers, and oxen to saddles, kettles, pewter, warming pans, spinning wheels, and looking glasses. During a period of relative isolation in which most Sturbridge families owned little more than their land and buildings, the seizure of livestock, draft animals, tools, and material amenities had a devastating impact on the dissenters' struggle to wrest a meager competency from the stony uplands of central Massachusetts.[29]

29. Fisk, "Testimony of a People Inhabitting the Wilderness," n.d. [January–February 1753] no. 397, *IBP*, Fisk, "Testimony from the Brethren in Sturbridge," 1753, no. 396, Fisk et al. to the Sturbridge selectmen, May 5, 1749, no. 314, Anonymous, "Sturbridge Sufferings," Feb.

Sturbridge was wracked by a flood of recriminations, acrimonious town meetings, and protracted lawsuits during the 1750s. The rancor left scars that lingered well into the nineteenth century. "We verbally in a publick manner testifyed we profest a free Gosple," Henry Fisk bitterly recalled in words drawn from Psalm 120:7, "But we may only Say as David when I Speak for peace Lo they are for war." Only a handful of the Baptist dissenters ever reconciled with Rice's church. The rest remained socially and economically out of step with their Congregational neighbors for decades. Perhaps the best index of their persistent outsider status might be found among the gravestones of the Sturbridge burial ground. In 1749, Hannah Corey longed to lie down with the dead in a small clearing adjacent to the Congregational meetinghouse. A century later, however, this same site stood at the civic, economic, and religious heart of a quintessential New England village. Of the fifty-nine men and women who initially affiliated with the Separate Baptists, only three were buried in the Sturbridge town cemetery. Hannah and John Corey were not among them. They were likely interred in family plots or atop Fisk Hill, near the original site of the Baptist meetinghouse. Other alienated dissenters, embittered by years of maltreatment, departed for new settlements on the northern frontier.[30]

Late in the eighteenth century, Isaac Backus paused in his *Church History of New-England* to consider the state of religious affairs during the decades leading up to the Whitefieldian revivals of the 1740s. He entitled his chapter "A Review of Past Darkness." Backus's historical narrative would have found a sympathetic audience among the Coreys and other dissenters. But the Holbrooks and their neighbors who retained their membership in the Sturbridge Congregational church would not have agreed. For them, indeed, for a majority of the families that migrated to New England's near frontier during the 1730s, the towns of eastern Massachusetts constituted a thriving religious culture. They called it the "Gospel Land of Light."[31]

12, 1750, no. 326, Jonathan Perry, "Perry's Sufferings," Feb. 26, 1750, no. 326.5; Isaac Backus, *A Church History of New-England, Extending from 1690 to 1784 ...*, 2 vols. (Providence, R.I., 1784), II, 192.

30. Fisk, "Testimony of a People Inhabitting the Wilderness," n.d. [January–February 1753], no. 397, *IBP;* John L. Brooke, "'For Honour and Civil Worship to Any Worthy Person': Burial, Baptism, and Community on the Massachusetts Near Frontier, 1730–1790," in Robert Blair St. George, ed., *Material Life in America, 1600–1860* (Boston, 1988), 472–475.

31. Backus, *Church History of New-England,* II, 127; Appendix B, Sturbridge, Mass., First Church, 24. I borrow the phrase "near frontier" from Brooke, "'For Honour and Civil Worship," in St. George, ed., *Material Life in America,* 463.

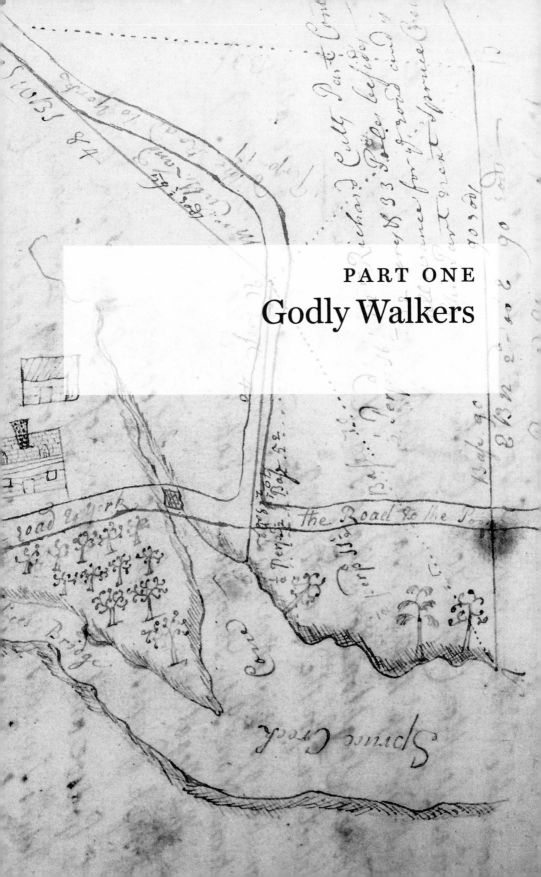

PART ONE
Godly Walkers

He called it "A Catalogue of Kindnesses." John Brown began recording the gifts contributed by his parishioners in a narrow account book on October 28, 1719, the day that he was ordained minister of the Congregational church in Haverhill, Massachusetts. The young Harvard College graduate maintained his catalog for close to a decade, making monthly notations alongside receipts for his salary and business transactions with his neighbors. Over time, the list swelled to just under twelve hundred separate contributions from more than 250 parishioners.[1]

The size and variety of the charitable items donated by the Haverhill congregation was impressive. The "free-gifts" of Brown's parishioners, which followed the annual subsistence cycle, ranged from spareribs to whole hogs, honeycombs to beehives, garden seeds to bushels of Indian corn. He received bass and salmon during the spring spawning runs, summer garden vegetables, turkeys from the fall slaughter, and sleigh loads of wood in winter. Most people gave foodstuffs, but there were other kinds of gifts as well. Young men volunteered physical labor in the form of fencing, carting, tilling, plowing, mowing, and haying at Brown's parsonage. Women shared biscuits, cakes, and minced pies from their kitchens. Wealthier parishioners offered luxuries such as wine, chocolate, spices, or, on a few rare occasions, hard currency. Even Haverhill's poorest residents endorsed Brown's ministry with a handful of beans, a few cabbages, or a cartload of dung for his fields along the Merrimack River.[2]

Like the turkeys and the tallows, the pigeons and the parsnips that Brown received each month from his congregants, his parish was unremarkable in almost every respect. The history of Haverhill mirrored that of many hinter-

1. John Brown, account book, 1718–1742, 65, MHS.
2. Ibid., 65.

land settlements that dotted the landscape of eastern Massachusetts. Founded in 1640 on the exposed frontier of Essex County, the small river town grew slowly during the second half of the seventeenth century. Devastated by native Americans and their French allies in 1697 and 1708, Haverhill eventually rebounded to roughly fifty families by the time of Brown's ordination before expanding rapidly during the next two decades. Its residents were principally the families of yeoman farmers and small craftsmen who pursued a seasonal round of work routines. As elsewhere in New England, the material standard of living in Haverhill grew slowly throughout the provincial period, as incorporation into a burgeoning Atlantic economy brought status commodities such as chairs, books, and tablewares. A handful of residents owned enslaved African Americans. Small cliques of elected leaders controlled town politics, which revolved around the usual business and controversies: laying out roads, dividing land, appointing officers, regulating livestock, resolving disputes, and collecting taxes for the maintenance of town buildings, the minister, and the schoolmaster.[3]

Brown published little during his life, and he rarely appeared in the diary ruminations of his contemporaries. But the Haverhill church nonetheless thrived under his quiet leadership. The town's original land grant extended more than ten miles into what is now New Hampshire, and irregular patterns of settlement resulted in the establishment of three new parishes in Haverhill as well as the creation of the town of Methuen during his ministry. Although these divisions siphoned off scores of taxpaying parishioners, Brown's church records indicate no eruptions of village factionalism. Boundary disputes with New Hampshire during the 1730s might have precipitated bitter political squabbles at the provincial level, but not in Brown's ecclesiastical world, where only a few sporadic cases of intemperance and fornication rippled across the surface of his quiescent country church. Between his ordination in 1719 and his death in 1742, Brown promoted 420 parishioners to full church membership; baptized 1,088 infants, children, and adults; and placed 325 congregants under the watch of the church through a ritual known as owning the covenant. With its tax-supported monopoly, the Haverhill church enjoyed unquestioned authority among the families in town.[4]

3. George Wingate Chase, *The History of Haverhill, Massachusetts, from Its First Settlement, in 1640, to the Year 1860* (1861; rpt. Somersworth, N.H., 1983), remains the standard history of Haverhill during the colonial period. For population figures, see Evarts B. Greene and Virginia D. Harrington, *American Population Before the Federal Census of 1790* (1932; rpt. Gloucester, Mass., 1966), 20, 24; and Josiah H. Benton, Jr., *Early Census Making in Massachusetts, 1643–1765 ...* (Boston, 1905).

4. Mary F. M. Raymond, comp., "Records of First Parish, Haverhill," 2 vols., I, 54–83, II,

The documentary record of Brown's ministry remains unsurpassed. In addition to a complete book of church records dating back to his ordination, hundreds of miscellaneous documents chronicle routine business ranging from weekly prayer requests to parish finances and cases of church discipline. Brown's published sermons reveal something of his theological orientation and homiletic style. He also served as clerk of the Bradford ministerial association. The most valuable surviving texts are the 235 church admission testimonies that the Haverhill minister carefully docketed and preserved for posterity. These brief autobiographical relations were read on the occasion when a parishioner advanced to full church membership. Among the 80 men and 155 women represented in the Haverhill collection were several notable town residents—including the famed Indian captive Hannah Duston—although most of the narratives were composed by or on behalf of ordinary townspeople who rarely left footprints in the historical record. The Haverhill relations are the second largest known group of Congregational church admission statements. They form what is arguably the richest archive of manuscripts pertaining to the religious experiences of lay men and women anywhere in the British Atlantic before 1740.[5]

Brown's "Catalogue of Kindnesses" and the extraordinary cache of manuscripts that document his pastorate stand as powerful reminders of the regular but often hidden workings of the Congregational establishment during the period between the revocation of the Massachusetts Bay charter in 1684 and the arrival of the eminent touring Anglican evangelist George Whitefield more than half a century later. When combined with demographic data on church affiliation and evidence from private devotional writings composed elsewhere in New England, they point toward a flourishing and pervasive religious culture. The men and women who brought their relations to Brown's parsonage came of age at the end of a century that had witnessed a series of adjustments that both strengthened the Congregational establishment and expanded its reach. An emerging cohort of sacerdotal clergymen—"catholick," or broadminded, in their theological sensibilities and organized into ministerial associations—emphasized the importance of religious practices in their weekly sermons. Expanding access to the sacraments of baptism and the Lord's Sup-

---

53–64, 73–81, 99–129, unpublished MS, 1895, Haverhill Public Library, Haverhill, Mass. For biographical information on Brown, see *SHG*, VI, 38–41.

5. A complete list of the Haverhill relations appears in Appendix B. For a wide range of miscellaneous papers from John Brown's pastorate, see Haverhill, Mass., First Congregational Church Records, 1719–2012, CL (available online at NEHH). See also Bradford, Mass., Ministers' Association, Records, 1719–1773, Franklin Trask Library, Andover Newton Theological School, Newton Centre, Mass.

per through revised church affiliation requirements might have tempered the reforming zeal of the puritan founders, but these ecclesiastical innovations also ensured nearly universal participation in the life of the church. Public rituals of fasting and thanksgiving harnessed private piety to the health, safety, wealth, and peace of the community and the colony. During the early decades of the eighteenth century, the rhythms of church affiliation in towns like Haverhill were closely attuned to the imperatives of family formation and social maturation, and women emerged as the primary source of religious authority in New England's little commonwealths.[6]

Provincial New Englanders associated church membership with a wide range of earthly needs, from coping with illness and raising children to alleviating epidemics and ensuring victory in military expeditions. Their relations marked a crucial milestone in a life dominated by devotional practices designed to garner protection from an increasingly disease-ridden, economically volatile, and war-weary society. The "bisness" of religion suffused every aspect of life. The same genealogical and commercial tropes that structured church admission testimonies also arose as the dominant idiom through which New Englanders explained the providential workings of their world. The God of early New Englanders was a "Debtor to none" who liberally dispensed credit in the form of temporal mercies in advance of the great day of reckoning. He was the "Great Benefactor" of their enterprises, the "Great Physician" to whom they turned in moments of affliction, and a "Heavenly father" who one day would provide his faithful children with a "portion" of his eternal estate.[7]

John Brown and his ministerial colleagues inveighed against the "Emtiness of all Earthly Enjoyments," and they enjoined their parishioners to imagine themselves as "Strangers and Pilgrims here upon the earth." Well-versed in Reformed theology, their parishioners understood that the diligent performance of religious duties would never merit salvation for them. They nonetheless persisted in the belief that their failure to observe solemn religious obligations would call down the wrath of God on their bodies, their families, and their towns. In their relations and devotional writings alike, lay men and

6. For an overview of these developments, see Michael P. Winship, "Congregational Hegemony in New England, from the 1680s to the 1730s," in Stephen J. Stein, ed., *The Cambridge History of Religions in America*, I, *Pre-Columbian Times to 1790* (New York, 2012), 282–302. On the "catholick spirit" in provincial Congregationalism, see John Corrigan, *The Prism of Piety: Catholick Congregational Clergy at the Beginning of the Enlightenment*, Religion in America (New York, 1991), 5.

7. John Gardner, journal, 1717–1718, 2 vols., I, 9, II, 15, Thomas Wren Ward Papers, 1717–1943, box 7, MHS; Benjamin Woods, journal, 1726–1730, [12, 18, 155], Diaries (Miscellaneous) Collection, 1681–1945, MS 181, YUA; *Letter-Book of Samuel Sewall*, MHS, *Collections*, 6th Ser., I, II (Boston, 1888), II, 12.

women paid close attention to the ways religion spoke to and offered solace for everyday privations. As one forthright diarist framed the issue, "Godliness was profitable for this life as well as to that which is to Come." The traditional puritan quest for assurance of salvation surfaced primarily in moments of acute crisis or in old age.[8]

Brown's parishioners in Haverhill accented this practical orientation toward the Christian life in the closing lines of their relations. "I Desire the Church to recieve me into their †tian [Christian] fellowship and Watch, and pray for me," explained one candidate, "that I may have Grace to walk inoffensively and Exemplarily, and profitably to my own Soul and the Good of my Neighbours." A godly "walk" or "well ordered Conversation," as it was more commonly called, was the key to safety and prosperity in this world, if not salvation in the next. Provincial New Englanders might have grown worldly during the early eighteenth century, but they were not secular by any modern definition of the term.[9]

I SIN IN COMING UNWORTHILY AND I SIN
IN STAYING AWAY UNWORTHILY

Among the most reliable and generous contributors to John Brown's "Catalogue of Kindnesses" were Ebenezer and Sarah Eastman. They also ranked among Haverhill's most prominent residents. Born in 1681, Ebenezer was a prosperous innkeeper and militia officer. His service in numerous military campaigns against the French, beginning with the 1711 assault on Port Royal and culminating in the siege of Louisbourg three decades later, generated a colorful body of family folklore during the nineteenth century. An enterprising entrepreneur, Eastman petitioned the town in 1721 to construct a wharf on the Merrimack River to facilitate "Trading by sea," which he described as "one way whereby I expect to gett my living and furnish out my good neighbors with many such nessisarys of life as are most conveniant." Within the decade, however, Eastman had reversed course, heading inland with a group of Haverhill proprietors to a new settlement at Pennacook (now Concord), New Hampshire. At the time of his death in 1748, his estate included exten-

8. Woods, journal, [107, 142]; Joseph Baxter, sermon on Gen. 47:9, Feb. 7, 1725, Dedham Historical Society, Dedham, Mass.

9. Appendix B, Haverhill, Mass., First Church, 17, 70, 140. Part 1 builds on the revisionist arguments advanced by Mark Valeri in *Heavenly Merchandize: How Religion Shaped Commerce in Puritan America* (Princeton, N.J., 2010), esp. 5–10. For a contrasting perspective, see Michael P. Winship, *Seers of God: Puritan Providentialism in the Restoration and Early Enlightenment*, Early America: History, Context, Culture (Baltimore, 1996), 148–149.

sive landholdings and livestock; mill complexes; farming, weaving, and black-
smithing tools; and an enslaved African American named Cesar.[10]

Sometime around 1714, Eastman married Sarah Peaslee, the daughter of a
Quaker yeoman and miller who was active in Haverhill town politics. During
the next two decades before moving to the New Hampshire frontier, the East-
mans had eight children. Sarah drifted away from her Quaker roots, and she,
along with her brother Nathaniel, emerged as a stalwart supporter of Brown's
ministry. One day during the winter of 1724, she appeared at Brown's parsonage bearing a small sheet of paper on which she had written a short autobiographical testimony:

> I deiser to blass god that I was born in a land of light and brought up
> under the light of the gospell. I have thought itt my duty to cum to the
> ordenances of baptism and the lords supper for sum Considrabell time
> but thinking mysalf unworthy of partacking of such holy ordenences has
> kapt me from Cuming sum Considrabell time. But of lat god has been
> sorly aflicting me by the dath of my mother and that in a vary offull man-
> ner which has ben a grat quickening to me in my duty. Thar has ben many
> plases of criptuer [scripture] has ben vary incoriging and quicking to
> me to Cum to thos ordinances as in Matthew 11 Chapter 28 vars [verse]
> Come unto me all ye that labour and are heavy laden and I will give you
> rest. And in vars 29 and 30 tack my yoke upone you and larn of me for I
> am meek and lowly in hart and ye shall find rest unto your souls for my
> yoak is easy and my burthen is light. And in Luke 9 Chapter and 26 vers
> for whosoever shall be ashamed of me and of my words of him Shall the
> son of man be ashamed when he shall Come in his own glory and in his
> fathers and of the holy angels. And in Isaiah 55 Chapter and 1 Vars ho
> every one that thirsteth Come ye to the waters. And in vars third encline
> your ears and Come unto me har [hear] and your Soul Shall live. And in
> many other plases has ben incorriging to me to Cum to the ordinances of
> baptisim and the Lords Super. I daiser [desire] to Cum dapending apon
> Christ for davin [divine] asistence and bagging your prayers for me that I
> May not Cum unworthily.

After discussing the contents of the relation and inquiring further into Eastman's theological knowledge, Brown "Propounded," or nominated, her to full

10. Chase, *History of Haverhill,* 254–256, 274, 276, 278, 283. For genealogical information, see Guy S. Rix, comp., *History and Genealogy of the Eastman Family of America . . .*
(Concord, N.H., 1901), 20–26; and *Vital Records of Haverhill, Massachusetts, to the End of
the Year 1849,* 2 vols. (Topsfield, Mass., 1910–1911), I, 102–103.

communion in the Haverhill church. For the next two weeks, she remained in this probationary state, as existing church members scrutinized her testimony. Then, on March 8, 1724, the Haverhill minister read her relation aloud, called for a vote, and admitted Eastman to full communion. Since she had been raised in a Quaker family, she presented herself and her five children for baptism on the same day. A little more than a month later, Eastman brought Brown a basket of parsnips.[11]

Despite its rough handwriting and idiosyncratic spelling, Eastman's relation was entirely conventional by the standards of the day. Early-eighteenth-century church admission narratives composed in parishes from the northern frontier to coastal Connecticut adhered to a common structure derived from six interchangeable components. Candidates typically began their narratives with several interlocking statements that established their family's religious pedigree. After acknowledging that they had failed to improve the means of grace offered to them as children, applicants chronicled various awakening events—illnesses, Indian raids, natural disasters, or, as in Eastman's case, family deaths—that they interpreted as the providential voice of God calling loudly for them to perform their sacramental duty by affiliating with the church and participating in the Lord's Supper. Most expressed concern and even terror at the prospect of consuming Christ's body and blood unworthily, but they also quoted or alluded to one or more encouraging scripture verses that buttressed their decision to join the church. Beginning in the 1720s, a growing number of candidates infused their relations with statements of Reformed theological doctrines on subjects ranging from the nature of the Trinity to the significance of the sacraments, while a minority of lay men and women were required to incorporate a confession of sin as a prerequisite for admission. Most people concluded their testimonies with a request for prayers on their behalf.

Eastman's 1724 relation was part of a unique genre of devotional literature with deep roots in the history of New England Congregationalism. Yet the formulaic nature of her carefully worded testimony reflected an important shift in the meaning of church membership, as New England towns evolved from zealous gathered communities of visible saints into the comprehensive, territorial parishes of the provincial era. Church admission relations were the lingua franca of religious experience in New England; the stock phrases that governed the genre provided a storehouse of tropes and ideas that oriented lay men and women in a rapidly changing colonial world.[12]

11. Appendix B, Haverhill, Mass., First Church, 58; Raymond, comp., "Records of First Parish, Haverhill," II, 55, 106; John Brown, account book, 82.

12. On the differences between seventeenth- and eighteenth-century church admission

■ Seventeenth-century puritan divines maintained a clear distinction between congregation and church. The former referred to the body of townspeople who were required by law to attend Sabbath meetings. The more restrictive conception of a church denoted an inner circle of visible saints who voted on ecclesiastical issues, subjected themselves to church discipline, and enjoyed privileged access to the sacraments of baptism and the Lord's Supper. According to the 1648 Cambridge *Platform of Church Discipline*, the first systematic exposition of New England ecclesiology, those seeking access to the *"doors* of the Churches of Christ upon earth" were expected to recite a "personall and publick *confession"* in which they stood before the church assembly and declared "Gods manner of working upon the soul."[13]

The daunting public spectacle capped a lengthy time of preparation. Prospective church members first appeared before the ruling elders in a private meeting several weeks in advance, when they articulated their desire to join the church and responded to a series of questions regarding their knowledge of Reformed theological doctrines. Successful applicants were then propounded for a period that usually lasted a fortnight but occasionally stretched over several months. During their probation, candidates labored to resolve disputes with other members of the community or acknowledged their moral transgressions in a formal confession of sin. On the appointed Sabbath, men and women stood before the congregation, spoke aloud their religious "experiences of a worke of grace upon their soules," and answered additional questions. In some churches, friends, neighbors, and family members offered supporting testimonies. Finally, the elder called for a vote, asked the applicant to assent to the church covenant, and extended the "right hand of Fellowship" to the newly admitted member.[14]

Seventeenth-century relations, such as those recorded by Cambridge, Massachusetts, minister Thomas Shepard during the 1640s, generally conformed

---

testimonies, see Susan Juster, *Disorderly Women: Sexual Politics and Evangelicalism in Revolutionary New England* (Ithaca, N.Y., 1994), 53–54. I sketch the evolution of the relation of faith genre over two centuries in "Religious Experiences in New England," in Amanda Porterfield, ed., *Modern Christianity to 1900*, A People's History of Christianity, VI (Minneapolis, Minn., 2007), 209–232.

13. Williston Walker, comp., *The Creeds and Platforms of Congregationalism* (1893; rpt. New York, 1991), 221, 223. On the development of the test of a relation, see Edmund S. Morgan, *Visible Saints: The History of a Puritan Idea* (New York, 1963), 64–112; and Patricia Caldwell, *The Puritan Conversion Narrative: The Beginnings of American Expression* (Cambridge, 1983), 45–116.

14. *Plymouth Church Records, 1620–1859*, CSM, *Publications*, XXII (Boston, 1920), 181, 183. For seventeenth-century church admission practices, see George Selement and Bruce C. Woolley, eds., *Thomas Shepard's Confessions*, CSM, *Pubs., Collections*, LVIII (Boston, 1981), 18–21.

to a narrative pattern that reflected the works of English divines who maintained that the experience of regeneration unfolded through a series of stages. The morphology of conversion often began with an incident that wrenched secure sinners out of their spiritual complacency and initiated a period of intensive introspection. Languishing under fears of impending divine wrath, the penitent faithful consulted with friends and family members and sought the advice of local pastors. Devotional routines such as Bible study, meditation, secret prayer, journal writing, and private rituals of covenant renewal afforded brief sanctuary from pervasive fears of living in bondage to sin. Broken sinners learned to rely on Christ alone for divine grace and occasionally experienced a fleeting sense that their salvation might be assured. They thereafter labored to recreate and routinize these refreshing moments. Despite periods of backsliding and persistent anxieties, earnest saints grew in grace over time and exhibited their transformed souls through sanctified behavior.[15]

From the outset, critics on both sides of the Atlantic balked at New England's anxiety-inducing standards for church membership. The practice of reciting relations as a term of communion elicited opposition from English Presbyterians, who questioned the scriptural foundation of the test and accused their colonial brethren of excessively narrowing the gates of the church. Similar complaints circulated among ministers in the Connecticut Valley during the 1640s. The intense public scrutiny engendered by the test of a relation sparked acrimony at Dedham, Massachusetts, and stalled the founding of churches at Dorchester and at John Eliot's model Indian mission village at Natick. In response to mounting criticism, the clergymen who gathered to draft the Cambridge *Platform* cautioned church members to exercise "tenderness" during the examination of prospective candidates and accept new communicants on the basis of the "weakest *measure* of faith." Tempering the reforming zeal of the puritan founders, this "judgment of charity," as it came to be known, marked an important first step toward making church membership more widely accessible.[16]

15. I borrow the phrase "morphology of conversion" from Morgan's classic *Visible Saints*, 66. David D. Hall surveys the extensive literature on seventeenth-century puritan spirituality in "On Common Ground: The Coherence of American Puritan Studies," *WMQ*, XLIV (1987), 213–222; and "Narrating Puritanism," in Harry S. Stout and D. G. Hart, eds., *New Directions in American Religious History* (New York, 1997), 67–68. See also Sarah Rivett, *The Science of the Soul in Colonial New England* (Chapel Hill, N.C., 2011), 70–124.

16. Walker, comp., *Creeds and Platforms of Congregationalism*, 222; Baird Tipson, "Invisible Saints: The 'Judgment of Charity' in the Early New England Churches," *Church History*, XLIV (1975), 460. For controversies over the test of a relation, see David D. Hall, *The Faithful Shepherd: A History of the New England Ministry in the Seventeenth Century* (Chapel Hill, N.C., 1972), 115–120; Tipson, "Samuel Stone's 'Discourse' against Requiring

During the next century, churches throughout New England steadily adjusted their admission standards. In 1697, the Cambridge church refused to impose the test of a relation on any future candidate of blameless conversation who responded adequately to the inquiries of church officers during a private conference. Two years later, the members of Benjamin Colman's upstart church at Boston's Brattle Square audaciously proclaimed that they would "lay aside the Relation of Experiences which were imposed in the other Churches in the Town." Among the most controversial leaders of this revisionist faction was Solomon Stoddard. According to one critic, the Northampton minister "cast off Relations" and allowed "all above 14 years of age, that live morally, and having Catechisticall knowledge of the Principalls of Religion, to the Lords Supper." Between 1700 and 1740, many long-standing and recently gathered churches in Massachusetts and eastern Connecticut eliminated the practice outright. Even as John Brown was writing scores of relations on behalf of his parishioners during the 1730s, members of the new church in Haverhill's west parish voted not to "Impose on any a Publick Relation of their Experiences as a Term or Indispensable Condition of Communion."[17]

Other Massachusetts churches modified the test by replacing oral testimonies with written statements. The Cambridge *Platform* originally included a provision for unduly fearful or infirm candidates to present their testimonies in private, and the church in Chelmsford extended this practice to all prospec-

Church Relations," *WMQ*, XLVI (1989), 786–799; Stephen Foster, *The Long Argument: English Puritanism and the Shaping of New England Culture, 1570–1700* (Chapel Hill, N.C., 1991), 161–163; and Charles L. Cohen, "Conversion among Puritans and Amerindians: A Theological and Cultural Perspective," in Francis J. Bremer, ed., *Puritanism: Transatlantic Perspectives on a Seventeenth-Century Anglo-American Faith* (Boston, 1993), 233–256.

17. Stephen Paschall Sharples, ed., *Records of the Church of Christ at Cambridge in New England, 1632–1830 …* (Boston, 1906), 121–122; *The Manifesto Church: Records of the Church in Brattle Square, Boston, with Lists of Communicants, Baptisms, Marriages, and Funerals: 1699–1872* (Boston, 1902), 3; Norman S. Grabo, "The Poet to the Pope: Edward Taylor to Solomon Stoddard," *American Literature*, XXXII (1960), 198–199; Haverhill, Mass., West Parish Congregational Church Records, 1735–1761, 87, CL (available online at NEHH). On Stoddard's church admission practices, see David D. Hall, "Editor's Introduction," in *WJE*, XII, *Ecclesiastical Writings* (New Haven, Conn., 1994), 38–43. For a sample of churches that eliminated the test of a relation before 1740, see William P. Upham, ed., *Records of the First Church in Beverly, Massachusetts, 1667–1772* (Salem, Mass., 1905), 60; George Ernest Bowman, ed., "Records of the First Parish in Brewster, Formerly the First Parish in Harwich, Mass.," *Mayflower Descendant*, VII (1905), 96; Walter Eliot Thwing, *History of the First Church in Roxbury, Massachusetts, 1630–1904* (Boston, 1908), 76–77; Franklin Bowditch Dexter, ed., *Extracts from the Itineraries and Other Miscellanies of Ezra Stiles, D.D., LL.D., 1755–1794 …* (New Haven, Conn., 1916), 259–260, 271, 280, 284; James Patrick Walsh, "The Pure Church: In Eighteenth-Century Connecticut" (Ph.D. diss., Columbia University, 1967), 243–247, 256; and James F. Cooper, Jr., *Tenacious of Their Liberties: The Congregationalists in Colonial Massachusetts*, Religion in America (New York, 1999), 270n.

tive church members in 1660. Citing the "odium put by some upon relations," John Fiske's parishioners submitted their relations in writing during a pastoral conference with the church elders. The Dorchester church voted several years later to allow women and young men to have their relations written down and read to the church. Within a few years, Boston's Old South Church had made accommodations for any candidate who "through scruple of Conscience" was unwilling to speak in public. Thomas Shepard might have been the principal architect of the test during the 1630s, but half a century later his son and namesake noted in the Charlestown record book that *"mens relations"* by "their own pronouncing" were "inconvenient" and would for the future be read in public. Dedham, Plymouth, and several churches in the Old Colony followed suit two decades later. By 1720, the practice was universal among churches that continued to require a relation as a term of communion.[18]

Written church admission testimonies composed during the provincial period differed markedly from their seventeenth-century oral predecessors. Surviving first-generation relations were rough transcriptions made by clergymen as they listened to the spoken testimonies of each candidate. Most eighteenth-century relations, by contrast, were composed in the minister's study during pastoral conferences with prospective communicants. The clergy's role in regulating admission expanded in direct proportion to the extent that oral testimonies receded from public view. According to the diary of Westborough, Massachusetts, minister Ebenezer Parkman, the practice of drafting a relation involved a series of reciprocal exchanges. In most cases, he merely served as a scribe, taking down the candidates' testimonies as they spoke or gathering "Minutes" that he later redacted into a completed text. Parkman encouraged his congregants to review and emend the final copy before signing it. Other parishioners brought their own written testimonies, which the Westborough minister sometimes felt obliged to "alter," "methodize," or, on rare occasions, rewrite altogether.[19]

18. Walker, comp., *Creeds and Platforms of Congregationalism*, 223; Robert G. Pope, ed., *The Notebook of the Reverend John Fiske, 1644–1675*, CSM, *Pubs., Colls.*, XLVII (Boston, 1974), 143; *Records of the First Church at Dorchester in New England, 1636–1734* (Boston, 1891), 46, 67; Hamilton Andrews Hill, *History of the Old South Church (Third Church) Boston, 1669–1884*, 2 vols. (Boston, 1890), I, 229; James F. Hunnewell, ed. "The First Record-Book of the First Church in Charlestown, Massachusetts," *NEHGR*, XXV (1871), 62; *Plymouth Church Records*, CSM, *Pubs.*, XXII (1920), 201–202; Dexter, ed., *Extracts from the Itineraries and Other Miscellanies of Ezra Stiles*, 330.

19. Ross W. Beales, Jr., "Literacy and Reading in Eighteenth-Century Westborough, Massachusetts," in Peter Benes, ed., *Early American Probate Inventories*, Dublin Seminar for New England Folklife, Annual Proceedings 1987 (Boston, 1989), 47–49n. On the process of

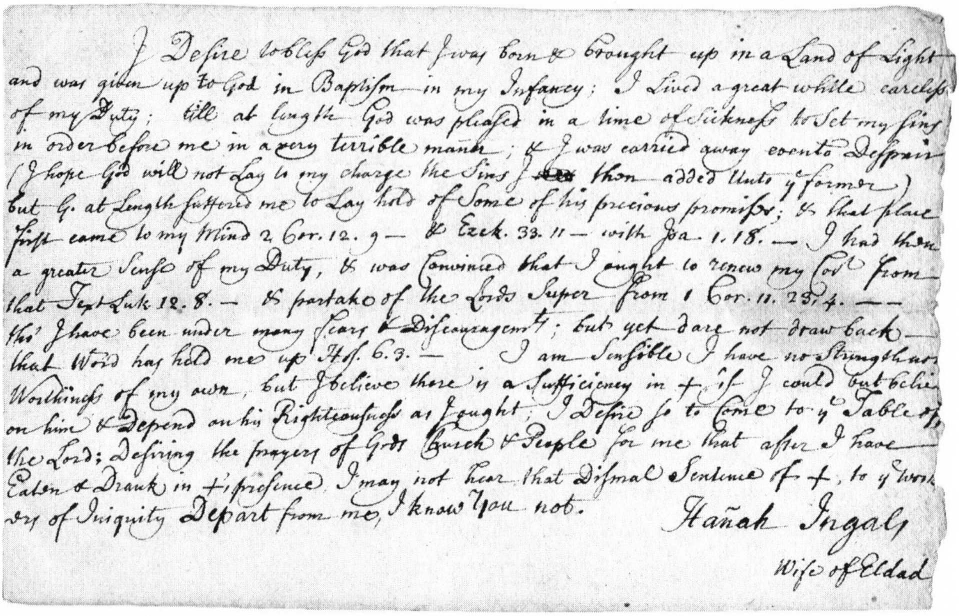
I Desire to bless God that I was born & brought up in a Land of Light and was given up to God in Baptism in my Infancy; I Lived a great while careless of my Duty; till at length God was pleased in a time of Sickness to Set my Sins in order before me in a very terrible manner; & I was carried away even to Despair (I hope God will not Lay to my charge the Sins I then added Unto ye former) but G. at Length suffered me to Lay hold of Some of his precious promises; & that place first came to my Mind 2 Cor. 12. 9 — & Ezek. 33. 11 — with Isa. 1. 18. — I had then a greater Sense of my Duty, & was Convinced that I ought to renew my Covt from that Text Luk. 12. 8. — & partake of the Lords Super from 1 Cor. 11. 23/4. —— tho' I have been under many fears & Discouragemts; but yet dare not draw back— that Word has held me up Hos. 6. 3. — I am Sensible I have no Strength nor Worthiness of my own, but I believe there is a Sufficiency in + if I could but believe on him & depend on his Righteousness as I ought; I Desire so to Come to ye Table of the Lord; desiring the prayers of Gods Church & People for me that after I have Eaten & Drank in +'s presence I may not hear that Dismal Sentence of +, to ye workers of Iniquity Depart from me, I know You not.

Hañah Ingals
Wife of Eldad

FIGURE 4 Relation of Hannah Ingals. March 31, 1723.
Courtesy, Congregational Library and Archives, Boston

The 235 Haverhill relations were the products of these evolving church admission practices. Almost two-thirds were composed in John Brown's elegant script. The young clergyman recorded each relation separately on small, uniform pieces of paper measuring approximately four by six inches, which he filled with terse biblical citations, frequent abbreviations, and shorthand symbols. On the reverse side, Brown identified each candidate, numbered the relation, and inscribed the dates on which the applicant had been propounded and admitted to the church. Only rarely did Brown alter the content of relations he received directly from his parishioners. The completed texts constituted a new genre of devotional literature that emphasized uniformity of rhetorical style, narrative content, and even physical appearance.[20]

---

recording seventeenth-century relations, see Charles Lloyd Cohen, *God's Caress: The Psychology of Puritan Religious Experience* (New York, 1986), 138–140.

20. Of the eighty-three Haverhill relations written in a hand other than Brown's, only three (3.6 percent) showed signs of significant editorial intervention, and fifty-four (65.1 percent) were read to the congregation as originally composed. Brown made minor or modest revisions—mostly spelling and grammatical changes—to the remaining twenty-six (31.3 percent). For a different perspective, see Erik R. Seeman, "Lay Conversion Narratives: Investigating Ministerial Intervention," *NEQ*, LXXI (1998), 629–634.

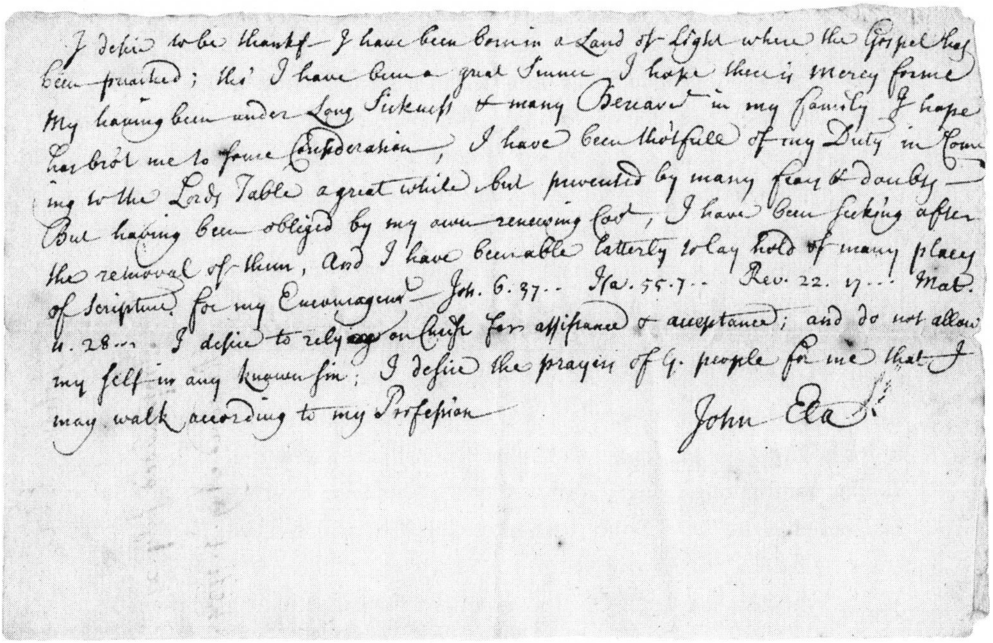
I desire to be thankf— I have been born in a Land of Light where the Gospel has
been preached; tho' I have been a great Sinner I hope there is mercy for me
My having been under Long Sickness & many Bereavemts in my family I hope
has brot me to serious Consideration; I have been thotfull of my Duty in Com
ing to the Lords Table a great while but prevented by many fears & doubts
But having been obliged by my own renewing Covt, I have been seeking after
the removal of them, and I have been able latterly to lay hold of many places
of Scripture for my Encouragemt— Joh. 6. 37.. Isa. 55. 7.. Rev. 22. 17.. Mat.
11. 28.. I desire to rely on Christ for assistance & acceptance; and do not allow
my self in any known sin; I desire the prayers of G. people for me that I
may walk according to my Profession
John Ela Sr

FIGURE 5 Relation of John Ela. August 4, 1734.
Courtesy, Congregational Library and Archives, Boston

As the eighteenth century progressed, these paper instruments increasingly assumed a contractual form that overshadowed the narrative structures of earlier oral church admission testimonies. Few church membership candidates claimed to have progressed any further than what seventeenth-century divines would have called the legal humiliation stage of conversion. New Englanders who reflected on their decisions to join the church in diaries and letters written between 1680 and 1740 understood affiliation as a measured choice and a solemn event but seldom the outcome of a protracted crisis. Boston magistrate Samuel Sewall was unusual in venting his angst-ridden meditations regarding his "Spiritual Estate" in his diary before joining Boston's Old South Church in 1677. Later writers simply recalled the date on which they were "Admitted regularly" or "Joyned in ful Communion with the church of Christ." Other diarists, including Sewall's son, Joshua Blanchard, the chief architect of the Old South meetinghouse in Boston, and Mehetabel Coit of New London, Connecticut, omitted mentioning their ascent to full communion altogether. Even Harvard College students John Barnard, Richard Brown, Samuel Brown, and Edward Holyoke, the future president of the college, eschewed or minimized this seemingly milestone event in their religious lives.[21]

By the time John Brown was ordained in 1719, the practice of composing written relations had decisively transformed the meaning of church affiliation. Established during the years surrounding the Antinomian controversy of the 1630s, the test of a relation initially served to inoculate New England's gathered churches against the revelatory claims of radicals such as Anne Hutchinson. With careful guidance from ministers such as Brown, prospective communicants in the early eighteenth century learned to anchor their religious experiences to communal expectations and established literary tropes. Candidates who had "come to years of Discretion" were expected to submit themselves to the discipline of the church, exhibit their knowledge of Reformed theology, and, above all, participate in the sacrament of the Lord's Supper. Joining the church in full membership, as one Haverhill woman summarized, was the "way of duty" required of all "Christs Disciples."[22]

■ The 1736 relation that John Brown penned for Lydia Page was among the shortest of his two-decade pastorate. "I believe the Bible to be the Word of God," the terse, 160-word statement began, "and I take the Assembly's Catechism to be agreable thereto." After commenting briefly on her catechetical

21. M. Halsey Thomas, ed., *The Diary of Samuel Sewall, 1674–1729*, 2 vols. (New York, 1973), I, 41; William Tudor, ed., *Deacon Tudor's Diary: Or "Memorandoms from 1709, etc. . . ."* (Boston, 1896), 2; "Extracts from the Diary of Rev. Jonathan Pierpont," *NEHGR*, XIII (1859), 256; Samuel Sewall, Jr., "Arithmetick and Copy-book," 1698–1772, 1, Samuel Sewall Papers, 1672–1815, MHS (available online at *www.masshist.org*); Abram English Brown, "The Builder of the Old South Meeting-House," *New England Magazine: An Illustrated Monthly*, New Ser., XIII (September 1895–February 1896), 396; Michelle Marchetti Coughlin, *One Colonial Woman's World: The Life and Writings of Mehetabel Chandler Coit* (Amherst, Mass., 2012), 34–36; "Autobiography of the Rev. John Barnard," MHS, *Colls.*, 3d Ser., V (Boston, 1836), 185; Lilley Eaton, comp., *Genealogical History of the Town of Reading, Mass. . . .* (Boston, 1874), 53–55; Cyrus Orcutt, ed., "Rev. Samuel Brown, of Abington," *NEHGR*, III (1849), 374; George Francis Dow, ed., *The Holyoke Diaries, 1709–1856* (Salem, Mass., 1911), 1. Evidence that Sewall, Jr., Blanchard, Richard Brown, and Holyoke were admitted to full communion may be found in Thwing, *History of the First Church in Roxbury*, 128; Richard D. Pierce, ed., *The Records of the First Church in Boston, 1630–1868*, CSM, *Pubs.*, XXXIX (Boston, 1961), 110; Joshua Coffin, transcr., "Facts and Developments concerning Formation, 1634–74, and Copy of Church Record, 1674–1745," June 23, 1700, PEM; and Sharples, ed., *Records of the Church of Christ at Cambridge*, 10.

22. Appendix B, Haverhill, Mass., First Church, 113. Studies that emphasize the conservative nature of the test of a relation during the seventeenth century include Janice Knight, *Orthodoxies in Massachusetts: Rereading American Puritanism* (Cambridge, Mass., 1994), 176–178; Michael G. Ditmore, "Preparation and Confession: Reconsidering Edmund S. Morgan's *Visible Saints*," *NEQ*, LXVII (1994), 298–319; Michael P. Winship, *Making Heretics: Militant Protestantism and Free Grace in Massachusetts, 1636–1641* (Princeton, N.J., 2002), 80–81; and Rivett, *Science of the Soul*, 96.

knowledge of Reformed theology, Page launched into a series of biblical quotations supporting her decision to apply for the privileges of full membership in the Haverhill church. She expressed initial trepidation at the prospect of participating in the public ordinance of the Lord's Supper, and she cited the "discouraging" words of 1 Corinthians 11:29 as the cause of her delay. But other "encouraging" scriptures allayed her fears. To be a "worthy receiver" of the Lord's Supper, as Page's relation indicated, meant mastering the right doctrinal beliefs and demonstrating a familiarity with specific biblical texts. This was no conversion narrative.[23]

Church membership professions—theological propositions strung together in series of "I believe" statements—gradually supplanted experiential relations in many Massachusetts parishes. Congregants in Braintree started supplementing their relations with a written declaration of their beliefs as early as 1676. When Joseph Green joined the Roxbury church two decades later, he met with minister Nehemiah Walter before composing an elaborate theological profession, which the deacon read aloud on the day he was admitted to full communion. The "Account of her knowledge and Experience" that thirteen-year-old Deborah Garret recited to the admiration of church members in Scituate in 1713 consisted entirely of formulaic responses to eight catechism questions posed by her minister. By 1730, the Weston church had replaced the practice of reading experiential narratives with a ceremony in which "serious Persons" of "orderly, good lives" assented to a standardized "Profession of Faith" that minister William Williams appended to the conclusion of a published sermon on youthful piety.[24]

Statistical evidence from the two largest collections of early-eighteenth-century relations reveals a rising tide of doctrinal professions. In Medfield, Massachusetts, theological statements did not appear in extant church admission narratives until after 1730, but, within a decade, one in three candidates included doctrinal beliefs in their testimonies. The proportion of church membership professors increased steadily in Haverhill, and relations containing doctrinal statements outnumbered others by a margin of four to one by

---

23. Appendix B, Haverhill, Mass., First Church, 171.

24. J[oseph] B[axter], *A Confession of Faith* ... (Boston, 1704), 1; Samuel E. Morison, ed., "The Commonplace Book of Joseph Green (1675-1715)," CSM, *Pubs., Transactions, 1937-1942,* XXXIV (Boston, 1943), 239-244; George Ernest Bowman, ed., "Records of the First Church of Scituate, Mass.," *Mayflower Descendant,* X (1908), 94; Mary Frances Peirce, comp., *Town of Weston: Births, Deaths, and Marriages, 1707-1850; Gravestones, 1703-1900; Church Records, 1709-1825* ... (Boston, 1901), 530. See also William Williams, "A Profession of Faith, Made at Admission into Communion," in *Divine Warnings to Be Received with Faith and Fear, and Improved to Excite to All Proper Methods for Our Own Safety and Our Families* ... (Boston, 1728), back matter: 1-4.

the time of Brown's death in 1742. Likewise, church admission narratives from Boston's venerable First Church reflected a sharp division in what had once been an integrated admission process. The church voted in 1712 to promote candidates to full communion after a meeting in which they were examined by the minister and elders on their knowledge of Reformed theology and church practices. By the late 1720s, parishioners such as John Cravath were drafting elaborate doctrinal statements on the reverse side of their admission testimonies. Samuel Thorn's 1740 relation contained a pair of lines breaking it into two sections, and the author underscored the growing importance of professing correct doctrine by writing "As to my *Belief*" beneath these markings.[25]

Church admission professions covered a wide range of doctrinal issues. "The Religion that I own and beleave," wrote one Boston woman, "is that which doath contained in the Sacret Scripure and is Explained in the Assembles Catisem and I beleave itt to bee the only Right and true way for as I was allways brought up in itt." Other candidates moved beyond a simple affirmation of the Westminster Confession to offering detailed expositions of complex theological issues. A few described the Trinitarian essence of the divinity and God's role in creating heaven and earth. Original sin, too, figured prominently in many relations. "I am convinced that my first parents fell from that Estate wherein they were created by sinning against God," declared Stephen Dow of Haverhill, "and that I and all men are fallen in and with them, and deserve God's wrath and curse, both in this life and that which is to come." One Lynn End (now Lynnfield), Massachusetts, woman defined God's "double Covenant" with humanity—the covenant of works broken by Adam and Eve in their disobedience and the "Covenant of Grace made with the second adam jesus X [Christ]." Others, such as Haverhill's Rebecca Corlis, framed the doctrine of redemption bluntly: "I believe Jesus † [Christ] came into the ☉ [world] to save Sinners of whom I am chief." Without an "interest" in Christ, candidates asserted, they would be undone forever.[26]

A renewed vocabulary of Christian obligation emerged in early-eighteenth-

25. Pierce, ed., *Records of the First Church in Boston*, CSM, *Pubs.*, XXXIX (1961), 127; Appendix B, Boston, First Church, 3, 12; Douglas L. Winiarski, "Gendered 'Relations' in Haverhill, Massachusetts, 1719–1742," in Peter Benes, ed., *In Our Own Words: New England Diaries, 1600 to the Present*, I, *Diary Diversity, Coming of Age*, Dublin Seminar for New England Folklife, Annual Proceedings 2006–2007 (Boston, 2009), 66–67.

26. Appendix B, Boston, First Church, 4; Appendix B, Haverhill, Mass., First Church, 36, 50, 101; Kenneth P. Minkema, ed., "The Lynn End 'Earthquake' Relations of 1727," *NEQ*, LXIX (1996), 493. For other Haverhill relations citing the *Shorter Catechism Agreed upon by the Reverend Assembly of Divines at Westminster* (1647) (Cambridge, Mass., 1682), see Appendix B, Haverhill, Mass., First Church, 1, 113, 171, and 200. More than a dozen editions of the *Shorter Catechism* were published in New England before 1740.

century relations. Absent in seventeenth-century oral testimonies, the word "duty" appeared more than two hundred times in the Haverhill narratives. "I have now ventured to offer myself to God and this Church," Sarah Pattee asserted in a typical formulation, "sensible it is my Duty to Shew forth the Lords Death." Mary Weed was among the one in five Haverhill candidates who justified their decision to join the church by citing Jesus's "plain Command" in Luke 22:19, *"Do this in Remembrance of me."* Others resorted to contractual language to describe the meaning of church fellowship. "I depend upon the mercy of God in and through Christ for Salvation and Desire to Comply with the terms upon which it is promised," stated Ebenezer Buck. "I hope I can truly say I am willing to throw down the weapons of my Rebellion and am desirous to obey all christs Commandments." Over and over again, the men and women of Haverhill arrived at the same conclusion in their relations: joining the church was an obligation, a requirement placed on all believers, regardless of the state of their souls.[27]

Among the duties cited most frequently in church admission testimonies, none was more important than participating in the Lord's Supper. As one Boston man carefully explained to the Old South congregation, "thare are too Sacraments Baptism and the Lords Supper, and I Belive that it is the Duty of all in obedience to Christ Command to Pertake of them." Such statements reflected the burgeoning interest in sacramental theology among clergymen. During the latter decades of the seventeenth century, New England ministers responded to a perceived decline in church affiliations by elevating the status of the Lord's Supper. Ministers persuaded their parishioners to observe the sacrament at regular intervals. Tapping into the broader currents of a transatlantic consumer revolution, churches appropriated funds to purchase matching sets of silver communion vessels to replace their motley assortment of pewter and ceramic jugs, flagons, tankards, caudle cups, and beakers. Clergymen instituted Thursday lectures in which they discoursed on the meaning and significance of the Lord's Supper. One Congregational minister even developed a set liturgy for the "Celebration of the Eucharist"—complete with staging rubrics.[28]

27. Appendix B, Haverhill, Mass., First Church, 22, 179, 220. The argument in this paragraph draws on Hall, *Faithful Shepherd*, 257–260.

28. Appendix B, Boston, Third (Old South) Church, 9; "Directories and Forms, of Diverse Administrations," Westborough, Mass., Congregational Church Records, 1724–1808, microfilm, Westborough Public Library, Westborough, Mass. On the rise of sacramental theology, see, especially, E. Brooks Holifield, *The Covenant Sealed: The Development of Puritan Sacramental Theology in Old and New England, 1570–1720* (New Haven, Conn., 1974). See also Philip D. Zimmerman, "The Lord's Supper in Early New England: The Setting and the Ser-

Between 1690 and 1730, scores of books on the Lord's Supper streamed from the Boston press. Widely printed and distributed by regional peddlers and booksellers, the works of what has come to be known as New England's sacramental renaissance included theological treatises and preparatory devotional manuals written by notable transatlantic divines. The libraries of clergymen and middling laymen often included books on the Lord's Supper. Medfield minister Joseph Baxter, for example, owned copies of Boston clergyman Samuel Willard's *Some Brief Sacramental Meditations* and English divine Thomas Doolittle's *Treatise concerning the Lords Supper.* Lists of books lent to parishioners even by obscure rural clergymen, such as Christopher Sargeant of Methuen, Massachusetts, and Peleg Heath of Barrington, Rhode Island, suggest that these volumes circulated widely among the laity. They were so pervasive that Joseph Green discovered several sacramental treatises at the house where he boarded during the weeks before he joined the Roxbury church.[29]

Concern for the performance of the Lord's Supper developed into a dominant theme in relations composed during the first quarter of the eighteenth century. Evidence from churches in eastern Massachusetts confirms Increase Mather's 1708 observation that "many of the Lords People in *New-England*" read sacramental literature. One Medfield man paused in his relation to reflect on what he read in a book that examined the "sin and danger" of neglecting the sacrament. Elsewhere, he learned from a manual that those who "live in the neglect of the lords Super live a scandelous life." Several Haverhill candidates claimed to have been "stirred up" or "quickned" by sacramental sermons in which John Brown expounded on the "Meaning and Benefits of the Lords Supper." Mehetabel Johnson, in particular, drew encouragement to join the church from three published sacramental works that she cited by title in her 1727 relation, including Cotton Mather's popular *Monitor for Communicants.*[30]

---

vice," in Peter Benes, ed., *New England Meeting House and Church: 1630–1850,* Dublin Seminar for New England Folklife, Annual Proceedings 1979 (Boston, 1979), 130–133; Benes and Zimmerman, *New England Meeting House and Church, 1630–1850: A Loan Exhibition Held at the Currier Gallery of Art, Manchester, New Hampshire* (Boston, 1979), 83–100; Barbara McLean Ward, "'In a Feasting Posture': Communion Vessels and Community Values in Seventeenth- and Eighteenth-Century New England," *Winterthur Portfolio,* XXIII (1988), 1–24; and Mark A. Peterson, "Puritanism and Refinement in Early New England: Reflections on Communion Silver," *WMQ,* LVIII (2001), 307–346.

29. Holifield, *Covenant Sealed,* 197–224; Joseph Baxter, "A Catalog of Books," n.d. [circa 1745], CL; Christopher Sargeant, "Books Lent 1736," commonplace book, 1727–1788, MHS; Peleg Heath, diary and memorandum book, 1728–1746, box 1, Heath Family Collection, 1729–1865, Rhode Island Historical Society, Providence, R.I.; Morison, ed., "Commonplace Book of Joseph Green," CSM, *Pubs., Trans., 1937–1942,* XXXIV (1943), 240.

30. Increase Mather, "An Advertisement, Directed to the *Communicants* in the Churches

Prospective church members often timed their admissions to coincide with the celebration of the Lord's Supper. Although the Plymouth church administered communion once every two months, more than half of the men and women who affiliated during Ephraim Little's pastorate completed their propounding periods just one week before the next scheduled sacrament. Admissions recorded in the sermon notebooks of Newton, Massachusetts, layman William Hides reveal an even more pronounced trend, as do notations in the diary of Stonington, Connecticut, deacon Manasseh Minor. Benjamin Woods began preparing for the "holy ordinance" of the Lord's Supper in December 1726, noting his desire to participate the "next time it is administred" in his extensive devotional journal. Winter sacramental celebrations were infrequent, however, and so the prominent Marlborough, Massachusetts, civil magistrate elected to wait several months before closing with the church. Woods consulted with minister Robert Breck the following February and submitted a pair of relations for himself and his wife. A flurry of journal entries followed, as Woods labored to "prepare Myself for the Sacrament of the Lords supper." After renewing their personal covenants, the Woods were admitted to full communion on February 19, 1727—one week before the Marlborough church observed the Lord's Supper.[31]

Even as lay men and women recognized the importance of their sacramental obligations, many hesitated for fear of participating unworthily. After commemorating the "Broken" body and "Blood of Christ" for the first time, Woods lamented that he had been "Lifeless and Dull" while at the Lord's Table, and he prayed for divine mercy lest "Either Temporall or spiritual Judgments follow me for My Eating and Drinking unworthyly." The first entry of Daniel King's devotional diary, composed on the day he joined the Marblehead, Massachusetts, church, also betrayed grave misgivings and acute feelings of unworthiness about his fitness to participate in the Lord's Supper. "I hope My heart was upright," King reflected, "but Alass how Cold and lifeless." "I mourn that My soul was not Inflamed with Love to My savour who has done and suffered

---

of *New-England*," in Tho[mas] Doolittle, *A Treatise concerning the Lord's Supper* ..., 20th ed. (Boston, 1708), misc. back matter, [4]; Appendix B, Medfield, Mass., First Church, 18; Appendix B, Haverhill, Mass., First Church, 124, 148, 194.

31. Douglas Leo Winiarski, "All Manner of Error and Delusion: Josiah Cotton and the Religious Transformation of Southeastern New England, 1700–1770" (Ph.D. diss., Indiana University, 2000), 151n; William Hides, notebooks, 1652–1816, 4 vols., IV, Feb. 6, May 8, June 19, July 10, 27, Sept. 18, Nov. 13, 1715, Mar. 4, 11, Apr. 29, May 6, 1716, Mss 653, NEHGS; Hides, sermon notebook, 1717–1720, Aug. 3, Oct. 12, Nov. 9, 1718, Feb. 1, Oct. 29, 1719, June 26, Aug. 21, 1720, MHS; Frank Denison Miner, with Hannah Miner, [eds.], *The Diary of Manasseh Minor, Stonington, Conn., 1696–1720* (n.p., 1915), 20–150; Woods, journal, [8, 23–24].

so much for worthless sinners," he complained. Many lay men and women set apart a "day of preparasion" before each sacrament, but few ascended to the mystical heights achieved by devotional virtuosos such as the poet-clergyman Edward Taylor of Westfield. Instead, most plodded from month to month, hoping, as Woods and King both expressed in their journals, that God would "Give me Grace Better to prepare for the next Communion."[32]

Provincial clergymen provocatively balanced invitations to receive the ordinance with dire warnings of judgment. Only a handful of ministers followed Solomon Stoddard in asserting that the Lord's Supper was a converting ordinance, but virtually all of them believed that participating in the sacrament was a "Plain and Positive" duty incumbent on all of their parishioners. Newton minister John Cotton, great-grandson and namesake of the prominent puritan divine and brother-in-law of Haverhill minister John Brown, maintained that Jesus's sacrifice on the cross was an "unspeakabell Gift" that placed all Christians under great obligations to commemorate his death and resurrection. Cotton even promised that earnest seekers "who aright draw Near unto God shall find it Good for them." Communicating at the Lord's Table mortified sin and offered "foretasts of futer Joy an happyness." He admonished his audiences "not to be slothfull" in the "bisnis" of attending the sacrament. "The way is wide," Cotton assured his Newton congregation, and there "is roome anufe [enough] for all." Church members "that have a place at the lords table shall have a place In heaven," he concluded, as he urged his parishioners to "Endeaver to fill up the rome [room] that God and Christ hath prepared."[33]

Even as ministers counseled everyone to perform their sacramental duties by joining the church, they repeatedly warned their parishioners to prepare carefully for the Lord's Supper. Only true visible saints could participate worthily, argued Boston minister Samuel Willard; everyone else risked their own damnation. Commencing at the outset of the 1692 Salem witchcraft outbreak and continuing over the next two years, Samuel Parris's sermon series on 1 Corinthians 11 mixed "Cordials," in which he pressed his congregants to embrace their sacramental duties, with "corrosives," dire warnings of the "corporal and outward judgments," including "Sicknesses, Deaths, Sorrows

32. Woods, journal, [27]; Daniel King, diary, 1730–1767, [1], photostat, MHS; Miner, [ed.], *Diary of Manasseh Minor*, 24. For similar examples, see Erik R. Seeman, *Pious Persuasions: Laity and Clergy in Eighteenth-Century New England*, Early America: History, Context, Culture (Baltimore, 1999), 95–106. On Taylor's sacramental mysticism, see Charles E. Hambrick-Stowe, *The Practice of Piety: Puritan Devotional Disciplines in Seventeenth-Century New England* (Chapel Hill, N.C., 1982), 208–217.

33. [Cotton Mather], *A Monitor for Communicants ...* (Boston, 1714), 1; Hides, notebooks, III, Dec. 19, 1714, Feb. 13, June 5, 1715, Jan. 22, Mar. 11, 1716.

troubles and calamities" that would be visited on those who approached the communion table unworthily. John Brown voiced similar concerns in a sacramental lecture that he published in 1729. Full church members who failed to examine their hearts before communion, ignored the sacrament collection box, or engaged in immoral pursuits, the Haverhill minister argued, were deceived in their duty. Whether "carelessly, wittingly or willingly unprepared," they left themselves open to divine wrath. Or, as Robert Breck of Marlborough explained in a published sacramental sermon that Benjamin Woods summarized in his journal, those who "eat and drink unworthily" jeopardized their bodies and brought peril to their souls.[34]

The specter of 1 Corinthians 11:29—"For he that eateth and drinketh unworthily, eateth and drinketh damnation to himself, not discerning the Lord's body"—cast a long shadow during the early decades of the eighteenth century. John Brown and his colleagues regularly invoked this text in their sacramental sermons and publications. Hundreds of relations conformed to the same pattern. "I have had a Grate desire for sum time to Gine [join] to the Church," recalled a Plymouth candidate, "but i have been under feers Least i shold Cum unworthly and so eat and drink my one [own] damnation." A Medfield man worried that "if I should come unworthily to the Lords Table it would be far worse for me in the day of Judgment than if I had never come." One in three Haverhill church membership candidates quoted or cited 1 Corinthians 11:29 as a source of "discouragement," "exceeding dread," or a "matter of Terror" that clouded their decision to join the church, while scores of others deployed a less specific language of "unworthyness" to vent their fears of joining the church and attending the Lord's Supper. Seldom cited in seventeenth-century oral testimonies, 1 Corinthians 11:29 ranked among the top five most frequently quoted biblical passages in relations composed during the period between 1690 and 1740.[35]

Designed to stimulate church affiliation, the renaissance in sacramental theology placed prospective church members in a precarious position. It was

34. Holifield, *Covenant Sealed*, 203; James F. Cooper, Jr., and Kenneth P. Minkema, eds., *The Sermon Notebook of Samuel Parris, 1689–1694*, CSM, *Pubs.*, LXVI (Boston, 1993), 50, 306; John Brown, *Our Great King to Be Served with Our Best ...* (Boston, 1729), 18; Robert Breck, *Two Discourses ...* (Boston, 1728), 63. For Woods's sermon notes, see journal, [87].

35. Anonymous relation, n.d. [early eighteenth century], Individual Manuscripts Collection, PHM (for the full text of this relation, see Appendix C); Appendix B, Medfield, Mass., First Church, 11; Appendix B, Haverhill, Mass., First Church, 70, 83, 109, 227. For statistical data, see Winiarski, "Gendered 'Relations,' in Haverhill," in Benes, ed., *In Our Own Words*, I, 73–74; and Winiarski, "All Manner of Error and Delusion," 409–410. The argument here and in the paragraphs that follow draws on David D. Hall, *Worlds of Wonder, Days of Judgment: Popular Religious Belief in Early New England* (New York, 1989), 156–161.

the duty of all believing Christians to join the church and participate in the Lord's Supper, but to do so unworthily meant courting damnation. Even long-standing communicants, such as Jabez Fox of Falmouth, Maine, reached with "trembeling" hands to "take the sacred Bread," "fearing I have Eat and drank Damnation to myself." In his preparatory meditations, Fox longed for "Sweet Communion" with Christ, only to discover himself in a "poor lifeless fraim" or struggling against "stupid Lethergy" as he prepared to "receive the Elements." The Lord's Supper remained a constant terror to his dying day. On one occasion, he worried that God would "single me out in some very remarkable manner" and strike him dead as he approached the communion table. "I was afraid" to participate, Fox acknowledged in a candid entry inscribed in his personal prayer notebook, "and afraid not to do it."[36]

For many potential church members, the situation seemed hopelessly untenable. Although some recognized that the "dreadfull" words of 1 Corinthians 11:29 were "not Intended to drive men from the Sacraments but from their Sins," many more experienced acute anxiety when faced with the prospect of performing their duties at the Lord's Table. In a colorful example, one Medfield man glossed 2 Kings 7:4 in his relation. The biblical passage described the plight of four lepers who were forced to choose between starving in the famine-ridden city of Samaria or begging for sustenance among the invading hordes of enemy Syrians. Comparing himself to the lepers, the candidate reasoned that he "must needs die" if he stayed away from Christ, whom he interpreted as the typological successor of the Syrians; yet he also knew that if he came unworthily to the Lord's Table—the enemy encampment—he would perish anyway. Haverhill's Hannah Hutchins, too, "tho't of the Case of the Lepers" and applied the moral of the biblical story to her own situation. "If I sit still I shall perish," she complained, but "if I come I can but perish." In the end, no one exposed the conundrum with greater precision than Hutchins's neighbor Mary Sanders: "I Sin in Coming unworthily and I sin in staying away unworthily."[37]

Ministers were well aware of the paradox of the sacraments, and they encouraged, cajoled, pleaded, and threatened their parishioners to embrace their obligation to participate in the Lord's Supper. In later years, Hannah Carter appeared as a confident, pious matron, but as a young woman she was terrified at the prospect of joining the church in full communion. During the

36. Jabez Fox, prayer book, n.d. [circa 1730s–1755], 80, 88–89, Maine Historical Society, Portland.

37. Minkema, ed., "Lynn End 'Earthquake' Relations," *NEQ*, LXIX (1996), 490; Appendix B, Medfield, Mass., First Church, 62; Appendix B, Haverhill, Mass., First Church, 115, 195.

FIGURE 6 Joseph Badger, *Mrs. Richard Kent (Hannah Gookin).* Circa 1746. Oil on canvas, 127 × 101.6 cm. Courtesy, Yale University Art Gallery, New Haven, Connecticut

spring of 1714, Carter wrote to her cousin Cambridge minister William Brattle and voiced her apprehension regarding her fitness for the Lord's Supper. In his response, Brattle attempted to minimize the threat of judgment, assuring his anxious kinswoman that approaching the sacrament with a truly contrite and repentant heart would protect her from consuming her own damnation. Participating in the Lord's Supper with the full knowledge that a person was "burthen'd with the vilness of our hearts" was a clear sign, he reasoned, that "we are in our way to come to that Ordinance, And that we shall not eat and drink damnation to ourselves." Brattle chastised Carter for neglecting her Christian duty, even as he sought to alleviate her fears of unworthiness. "I must entreat your fears lest you offend God by not coming," he wrote. "Pray to God that he would help you over your difficulties; and be not at rest till you have communion with God in all his holy appointments." Carter joined the Charlestown church exactly one month after Brattle penned his response.[38]

---

38. William Brattle to Hannah Carter, May 27, 1714, typescript, Old Safe Manuscript Collection, 8/8/32, NEHGS; James F. Hunnewell, ed., "The First Record-Book of the First

Concerns over the dangers of participating in the Lord's Supper also surfaced in lay correspondence. Shortly after his own admission to full communion in 1696, Roxbury schoolmaster Joseph Green sent letters to his siblings and their spouses aggressively exhorting each to be "speedy in joining the church." Green's stern epistles demonstrated a close familiarity with the prevailing tropes of scrupulosity that structured lay discourse. "It may be [you] will object and say you are not fit," the aspiring clergyman cautioned one sister before explaining that "your unfitness does not at all excuse your neglect of that duty." "If you do not live up to your baptismal engagement" by joining the church in full communion, Green warned another sibling, "then your baptism will rise up against you at the great day." Neither bashfulness nor a scrupulous concern for personal sin was a sufficient reason for holding back. "I hope you will not delay," Green concluded, "for delays are dangerous."[39]

Sarah Whittelsey detected strong reservations in her sister, Katherine Brewer, during a visit to Springfield, Massachusetts, in 1734. Although she was pleased to find her sibling in good health, Whittelsey remained deeply concerned for Brewer's soul. "Shee is in much Excesice [exercise] in hir sperit," the younger sister related in a letter to her brother, clergyman Nathaniel Chauncey of Durham, Connecticut. Although Brewer was the widow of Springfield's recently deceased minister, she had neglected her sacramental duties. Whittelsey "got but littil out" of her during her visit. After encouraging Brewer to pour out her fears in a pastoral conference with Stephen Williams, one of the most seasoned ministers in the Connecticut Valley, Whittelsey appealed to Chauncey to help their sibling overcome her anxieties about the Lord's Supper. "I hope you Wil talk with sister and preswad [persuade] hir to hir deuty," she concluded. Brewer lived for another two decades, but she never summoned the courage to join the Springfield church in full communion.[40]

Paralyzed by fear, many scrupulous lay men and women followed Brewer's path and elected to hang back from the communion table. The Haverhill relations were littered with evidence of delay and neglect. "Many Years ago I had a Desire to join with the Church," lamented one congregant, "But I tho't twas

Church in Charlestown, Massachusetts," *NEHGR*, XXIV (1870), 7. See also John Lowell, *The Laudable Character of a Woman* ... (Boston, 1758), 25–30.

39. Morison, ed., "Commonplace Book of Joseph Green," CSM, *Pubs., Trans., 1937–1942*, XXXIV (1943), 226–227.

40. Sarah Whittelsey to Nathaniel Chauncey, Apr. 11, 1734, box 1, Chauncey Family Papers, 1675–1928, YUA. Katherine Brewer's name does not appear on the earliest roster of Springfield church members or on the list of men and women admitted to full communion before her death in 1754. See Theo. W. Ellis, comp., *Manual of the First Church of Christ and Names of All the Members: From the Year 1735 to Nov. 1, 1885* (Springfield, Mass., 1885), 54–64.

time eno' for me Yet." Others proceeded cautiously, electing to "Live a Litle Longer In the neglect" of the ordinances or to stay away "till I was better prepared." Still others tried to persuade themselves that appearing at the Lord's Supper was not an essential Christian duty. As Sarah Herriman of Haverhill stated, "I thought I could live as good a life without coming to that ordinance as with it."[41]

■ For those who managed to surmount their fears of eating and drinking damnation at the communion table, the decision to apply for the privileges of full church membership initiated an almost desperate quest to purify their souls. Confession of sin played a central role in this preparatory process. During the fortnight propounding period, candidates cleansed their consciences by mending fences with other church members and unburdening their hearts of hidden sins. Scores of relations penned by John Brown and his parishioners in Haverhill concluded with a refrain similar to the one that Thomas Johnson, Jr., placed at the end of his narrative: "I desire all whom Ive wronged or injured at any time to forgive me and I desire to forgive all that have injured me at any time as I expect to be forgiven of God." Participation in the Lord's Supper constituted an act of Christian reconciliation and personal reformation.[42]

Brown used Haverhill's church admission practices to enforce moral discipline among his flock. Many candidates acknowledged their innate depravity in the opening lines of their relations, and a few confessed to one or more specific sins at the time they joined the church in full communion. Several women acknowledged that they had been "left to fall by sinful uncleanness" when their first child was born less than six months after marriage. Haverhill's male candidates, on the other hand, decried their excessive drinking, Sabbath breaking, evil speeches, vain company, and loose living. Taken together, these were the same sins identified in countless jeremiads. From these well-known published sermons, lay men and women understood that God would afflict their bodies, families, and communities if they did not reform their sinful ways.[43]

41. Appendix B, Haverhill, Mass., First Church, 38, 100, 112, 220. On lay scrupulosity, see Edmund S. Morgan, "New England Puritanism: Another Approach," *WMQ*, XVIII (1961), 241–242; and Hall, *Worlds of Wonder*, 281n.

42. Appendix B, Haverhill, Mass., First Church, 130. See also Mark Valeri, "Forgiveness: From the Puritans to Jonathan Edwards," in Laurie F. Maffly-Kipp, Leigh E. Schmidt, and Valeri, eds., *Practicing Protestants: Histories of Christian Life in America, 1630–1965*, Lived Religions (Baltimore, 2006), 35–48.

43. Appendix B, Haverhill, Mass., First Church, 165. For a statistical analysis, see Winiarski, "Gendered 'Relations' in Haverhill," in Benes, ed., *In Our Own Words*, I, 73–76.

Prospective church members realized that no sin, however small, could remain hidden from God's omniscient gaze. Occasionally, the impending dread of eating and drinking judgment at the Lord's Supper unearthed long-buried transgressions. An extraordinary example unfolded during the fall of 1728, when Elizabeth Blanchard applied for membership in the Medford, Massachusetts, church. According to minister Ebenezer Turell, Blanchard gave a "very good account of herself" during a preliminary pastoral conference. She discoursed competently on a variety of doctrinal topics, and Turell propounded her for full membership the following day. On the Sabbath before Blanchard was to be admitted to the sacrament, however, Turell preached a sermon on the dangers of lying that dramatically affected the young woman. The following Saturday afternoon, she appeared at the Medford minister's parsonage and unburdened her soul of a dark secret that she had harbored for eight years.[44]

In 1720, while living with her parents in the interior farming village of Littleton, Massachusetts, Blanchard and her two sisters began to mimic the bizarre behavior of the afflicted women of Salem Village. Blanchard would swoon and appear to fall into a trance. She performed sleight-of-hand tricks, told fortunes, and appeared unexpectedly at the tops of trees, in ponds, and atop the roof of the barn. The Blanchard sisters claimed that they had been bewitched by Abigail Dudley, the wife of the town clerk and selectman. Tales of the afflicted girls generated considerable consternation in Littleton, but, in an unexpected turn of events, Dudley died of complications following the birth of her thirteenth child. The witchcraft furor quickly died down, and the incident was all but forgotten until Turell smote Blanchard's conscience in his 1728 sermon. She admitted that the entire episode had been a hoax, and she wept bitterly in the pastor's study, "bewailing and lamenting her egregious folly." Together, minister and candidate drafted a relation that contained an elaborate confession of her sin. The next day, Blanchard stood in the Medford meetinghouse with bowed head as Turell recounted the entire sordid affair before the assembled congregation and admitted his repentant parishioner to full communion.[45]

In addition to confessing a variety of sinful acts, propounded candidates pored over their Bibles seeking evidence that buttressed their hesitant deci-

44. "Detection of Witchcraft," MHS, *Colls.*, 2d Ser., X (Boston, 1823), 17.

45. Ibid., 7–10, 17–19; Medford, Mass., Congregational Church Records, 1712–1773, 131, Medford Town Clerk's Office, Medford, Mass. On the Littleton witchcraft incident, see Richard Godbeer, *The Devil's Dominion: Magic and Religion in Early New England* (Cambridge, 1992), 226–227.

sions to approach the communion table. Scripture reading was the cornerstone of private piety in early New England. Easily obtained from urban booksellers or traveling peddlers, Bibles were presented as gifts, bequeathed in wills, or borrowed from neighbors. Middling families typically owned at least one copy, along with assorted sermons, psalters, catechisms, and devotional tracts. Lay men and women who could not sign their names nonetheless had learned to read and study the scriptures. Deacon John Tuck of Hampton, New Hampshire, read his Bible from cover to cover twelve times over a three-decade period. Each reading took the greater part of a year, as he noted with pride in his journal the start and finish dates. As one young man versified on the front pages of his personal Bible: "God give him / grace, therein to look / To look and Read and / take Delight / and understand with / all his might." Most people viewed the Bible as a guide to proper conduct—a "perfect rule of faith and practice," as many Haverhill parishioners stated in their relations.[46]

Biblical passages played a central role in church admission testimonies. The 235 Haverhill narratives referenced more than 160 different biblical texts in 971 scriptural citations—an average of more than four citations per relation. Candidates in Medfield and other churches in New England averaged slightly more (see Table 8). These references may be organized into several distinct classes. The Bible provided a stock of literary images that were often woven into patterns of thought and speech. Applicants likened themselves to the "Foolish Virgins" in Matthew 25, reiterated "Joshua's resolution to serve the Lord," and prayed fervently in the words of Hosea 6:4 that they might be counted among Christ's "jewels" at the last day. Stricken with illness during the fall of 1719, one Haverhill woman "tho't with the Psalmist" that there was "no fleeing from God's presence." Reflecting on how she had "Shamefully neglected" her duty at the communion table, a Lynn End woman explained that she had "dwelt in the tents of Kedar and Sojourned In Meseck"—an obscure allusion to Psalm 120:5. Eighteenth-century New Englanders, in short, expressed themselves in a rich biblical idiom and embroidered their relations with vivid scriptural imagery.[47]

46. Appendix B, Haverhill, Mass., First Church, 220; Gloria L. Main, "The Standard of Living in Southern New England, 1640–1773," *WMQ*, XLV (1988), 129, 133; Joseph Dow, *History of the Town of Hampton, New Hampshire, from Its Settlement in 1683, to the Autumn of 1892*, ed. Lucy Dow, 2 vols. (Salem, Mass., 1893), II, 1017–1018; Willard Goldthwaite Bixby, comp., *A Genealogy of the Descendants of Joseph Bixby, 1621–1701, of Ipswich and Boxford, Massachusetts* ... (New York, 1914), 63. For the scattered financial accounts of one rural Bible peddler, see Richard Sanborn, account book, 1725–1761, Henry Francis du Pont Winterthur Library, Wilmington, Del.

47. Appendix B, Haverhill, Mass., First Church, 6, 37, 73, 169; Minkema, ed., "Lynn End 'Earthquake' Relations," *NEQ*, LXIX (1996), 486.

Colorful biblical allusions aside, most prospective church members cited one or more "Encouraging" biblical "Promises," as they were often called, as support for their decision to join the church. The most frequently cited scriptural passages revolved around two themes: God's boundless mercy in pardoning human sin and Jesus's generous invitation to eat and drink his body and blood. Candidates elected to close with the church after reading and studying Matthew 11:28, in which Jesus bids the heavy laden to come to him for rest; Isaiah 55:1–9, in which the faithful are exhorted to buy bread and wine without price; and Isaiah 1:18, in which the prophet speaks of crimson sins cleansed by divine mercy. Men and women in other congregations emphasized similar passages, such as Jesus's comforting promise to the people of Capernaum in John 6:37 or his command to the disciples during the Last Supper in Luke 22:19. These five texts accounted for more than 40 percent of all biblical citations in the Haverhill relations and nearly a third in the Medfield documents. Often the subject of sacramental lectures and devotional literature, the small stock of encouraging biblical verses was well known to prospective candidates. At least one aspiring church member, Newton layman William Hides, recorded the texts cited in the relations of his neighbors and relatives. Through a solemn and careful consideration of familiar scriptures, church membership applicants sought to convince themselves, their pastors, and their fellow parishioners that they were worthy to receive the Lord's Supper.[48]

To the last, provincial New Englanders remained ambivalent about their decisions to join the church. Knowledgeable in Reformed doctrine and encouraged by scriptural promises, most lay people nonetheless feared the sacramental obligations that came with church membership. Even those who mustered the courage to consult with their ministers, draft their relations, and prepare for admission by resolving disputes with neighbors and family members continued to worry that they were not "Duly prepared" to participate in the Lord's Supper. "I am still afraid" went the standard refrain in the Haverhill narratives. Other candidates frankly admitted that they were "not without fears yet" or had "not quite got rid of my fears." Something needed to change, to tip the scales in favor of embracing sacramental duty, to convince the scrupulous that "delaying may be more dangerous and Sinfull." Without

48. Appendix B, Haverhill, Mass., First Church, 24, 143; Hides, notebooks, III, Feb. 6, May 8, June 19, July 10, 27, Sept. 18, Nov. 13, 1715, Mar. 4, 11, Apr. 29, May 6, 1716; Hides, sermon notebook, July 14, Dec. 22, 1717, Mar. 2, June 22, Aug. 3, Oct. 12, Nov. 9, 1718, Mar. 8, Aug. 2, 1719, June 26, Aug. 21, 1720. Haverhill and Medfield data derived from content analysis of sources in Appendix B. For comparative examples from seventeenth-century oral relations, see Cohen, *God's Caress*, 189–199.

a loud call from the heavens, judgment-fearing New Englanders had little incentive to take up their Christian obligations.[49]

THE LOUD CALLS OF DIVINE PROVIDENCE

Shortly before eleven o'clock on the night of October 29, 1727, the townspeople of Haverhill were roused out of their homes by a "Mighty Earthquake." New England had experienced violent tremors a century earlier, but this event, which "shook the houses as if theye would have fell down" for about two minutes, was "beyound what was ever known in this Land." The Great Earthquake of 1727 rattled cupboards and chimneys, collapsed basement walls, and threw down stone fences from Maine to Philadelphia. Ships tossed dangerously in Boston harbor; a bell tolled of its own accord in Guilford, Connecticut; and clocks stopped as far away as New York City. Bostonians poured into the streets, fearing that "their houses would Fall upon their heads." A terrified Nantucket captain reportedly boarded his ship, convinced that the island was sinking. Near the epicenter in Newbury, Massachusetts, a new spring gushed from a hillside, and large fissures erupted in the ground, spewing cartloads of fine sand that smelled suspiciously of brimstone. One New Hampshire man even claimed to have heard the sound of distant trumpets "immediatly after the first Rumbling." For many men and women, the day of judgment had never seemed closer. Residents in Methuen, a new town carved from Haverhill's west parish, were "possest with fears that It was the Great Day of the Son of mans appearing in the Clouds of Heaven." It was, according to one clergyman, a "Night never to be forgotten."[50]

In Haverhill, John Brown was "full of Company, *rain* or *shine*," during the days and weeks that followed. His parishioners required constant attention, "some Days from Morning till 8 a Clock at Night, without so much as time to take any bodily refreshment." Despite the fatigue of ceaseless pastoral counseling, the Haverhill clergyman rejoiced in the knowledge that he was guiding his church through an explosion of piety unprecedented in town history. The

---

49. Appendix B, Haverhill, Mass., First Church, 60, 133, 198; Appendix B, Boston, First Church, 5, 10.

50. "Diary of Rev. Samuel Dexter, of Dedham," *NEHGR*, XIV (1860), 202; Andrew Sigourney, memoranda in *La Sainte Bible* ... (Amsterdam, 1687), Oct. 29, 1727, Andover-Harvard Theological Library, Harvard Divinity School, Cambridge, Mass.; J. R. Flynt, ed., "Letter from Jabez Delano of Dartmouth," *NEHGR*, VII (1853), 136; Joshua Coffin, *A Sketch of the History of Newbury, Newburyport, and West Newbury, from 1635 to 1845* (Boston, 1845), 198–199; *Letter-Book of Samuel Sewall*, MHS, *Colls.*, II (1888), 232; Sargeant, commonplace book, 18. See also *Boston Gazette*, Nov. 6, 13, 1727.

earthquake instantly roused Brown's congregants to attend to their Christian duties. A staggering 202 people joined the Haverhill church during the twelve months following the initial tremors. In towns throughout the Merrimack Valley, the aftershocks "much awakened" the "Minds of People." One newspaper reported "20, 30, and 40 Persons" admitted to full communion in a single day. Baptisms increased dramatically, with numerous adults and whole families receiving the sacrament at the same time. Long-standing sinners under censure for a variety of moral infractions finally stepped forward to confess and reconcile with the church.[51]

Church admissions "occasioned by the terrible Earthquake" soared in towns across northern New England. In Massachusetts, more than forty people affiliated with the Malden church during a brief two-month burst of activity; one hundred men and women flooded the Salisbury church during the six months following the initial shocks. Churches in New Hampshire and Maine tripled the average number of new communicants in 1728, while admissions in Essex County and Boston increased between five and eight times the average annual rate. So many people joined the Second Church of Newbury (now West Newbury), Massachusetts, that minister John Tufts was forced to list their names on a separate leaf of his record book, which he neatly divided into groups by sex and marital status.[52]

The men and women who streamed into churches across New England in the aftermath of the Great Earthquake of 1727 participated in one of the broadest currents of eighteenth-century popular piety. Convinced that a sovereign God controlled every facet of daily life, they sought to make a *"happy* Improvement" of divine afflictions and calamities by deepening their private and public devotional performances. Rededicating themselves to the traditional

---

51. John Brown, "Appendix," in John Cotton, *A Holy Fear of God, and His Judgments ...* (Boston, 1727), 4–5; Raymond, comp., "Records of First Parish, Haverhill," II, 53–64; *New-England Weekly Journal* (Boston), Nov. 27, 1727.

52. Bradford, Mass., First Church of Christ Records, 1682–1806, 1824, 28 (quote), CL (available online at NEHH); Deloraine Pendre Corey, *The History of Malden, Massachusetts, 1633–1785* (Malden, Mass., 1899), 506–507n; JCH, 197; West Newbury, Mass., First Congregational Church Records, 1698–1797, [20], Essex County Manuscripts Collection, 1639–1959, PEM. Church admission statistics for Essex County, Boston, and northern New England may be found in *Contributions to the Ecclesiastical History of Essex County, Mass.* (Boston, 1865), 290; Cedric B. Cowing, "Sex and Preaching in the Great Awakening," *American Quarterly*, XX (1968), 632–634; Philip J. Greven, Jr., "Youth, Maturity, and Religious Conversion: A Note on the Ages of Converts in Andover, Massachusetts, 1711–1749," *EIHC*, CVIII (1972), 124; Elizabeth C. Nordbeck, "Almost Awakened: The Great Revival in New Hampshire and Maine, 1727–1748," *Historical New Hampshire*, XXXV (1980), 27–30; and George W. Harper, *A People So Favored of God: Boston's Congregational Churches and Their Pastors, 1710–1760* (Lanham, Md., 2004), 182.

practices of piety, they withdrew to their bedchambers to pray and meditate, pore over their Bibles, and lead their families in daily prayers. Congregations enacted ritual days of fasting and covenant renewal. Hundreds of small slips of paper bearing prayers for the afflicted were tacked to meetinghouse doors. Providential events generated what Cotton Mather and many of his contemporaries called *"GOOD IMPRESSIONS"* that drove people into the church. During moments of personal pain and corporate calamity, the demands of Christian duty overwhelmed the perceived dangers of consuming damnation at the Lord's Table. From earthquakes and Indian raids to epidemics and sudden deaths, God's "rod" of temporal correction goaded the frightened, the scrupulous, and the slothful into action.[53]

■ New England meetinghouses thronged with anxious parishioners during the weeks following the initial earthquake. Speaking to a spontaneous assembly that gathered in Boston the following morning, Cotton Mather noted with grim pleasure that he saw no one sleeping in the pews. "'Tis a Congregation of *Hearers,* that I am this Time speaking to," he observed wryly. The shocks threw the town into a "general Consternation," reported Old South clergyman Joseph Sewall. Benjamin Wadsworth also described his auditors as "Very Still and quiet." A fast-day meeting in Salem several days later produced what one diarist called the "greatest concourse ever seen here at once." "I felt much Enlargement In prayer and my Affections [were] warm in all the services of the Day," Dedham minister Samuel Dexter summarized, the "People seem'd very Attentive."[54]

The aftershocks persisted for months, prompting the publication of two dozen sermons and theological treatises. Many of these works embraced the latest scientific theories to explain the causes of the recurrent tremors. Several ministers attributed the earthquakes to volatile *"Sulphurious, nitrous, fiery* and *mineral Particles"* that collided in subterranean caverns and exploded into shock waves that ripped across the surface of the land; others sent detailed reports to the Royal Society in London. But, even as they sought

53. Thomas Prince, *Earthquakes the Work of God and Tokens of His Just Displeasure...* (Boston, 1727), [ii]; [Cotton Mather], *Boanerges: A Short Essay to Preserve and Strengthen the Good Impressions Produced by Earthquakes...* (Boston, 1727), 3; "Letter from Rev. Benjamin Colman to His Daughter, Mrs. Jane Turell," *NEHGR,* XV (1861), 317.

54. [Cotton] Mather, *The Terror of the Lord* (Boston, 1727), 19; Hill, *History of the Old South Church,* I, 422; Benjamin Wadsworth, diary and account book, 169[3]–1737, Nov. 2, 1727, MHS; George A. Ward, "Extracts Copied, Some Twoscore Years Ago, from Interleaved Almanacs of James Jeffrey, Esq....," *EIHC,* II (1860), 65; "Diary of Rev. Samuel Dexter, of Dedham," *NEHGR,* XIV (1860), 202.

natural causes, clergymen readily acknowledged that the earthquakes were "surprizing," "amazing," and, above all, "Supernatural." "Let it be how it will," remarked Portsmouth, New Hampshire, clergyman William Shurtleff, "all will agree that it is an awfull and affecting instance of the Wonderfull Power, and Majesty of God." Only an atheist could believe that the earthquakes had occurred by *"blind Chance"* or the "meer unguided *Motion* of *Matter*," concurred Mather and James Allin of Brookline. Since they subverted the regular order of nature, the violent shocks invited contemplation on the "grand EFFICIENT" that had conjured such calamitous forces from the deep places of the earth.[55]

In looking to what Boston minister Thomas Foxcroft called a "higher Principle" beyond "second Causes" as the source of the earthquakes, ministers and lay people invoked a rich storehouse of folk wisdom, biblical stories, natural philosophy, and Reformed theology. For nearly a century, New Englanders had filled their diaries and correspondence with news of violent storms and natural disasters, Indian raids and sea deliveries, neighborhood illnesses and sudden deaths. Some even constructed elaborate chronologies of prodigies and omens, hoping to glean a pattern in the Lord's dealings with his New England plantations. Culled from learned and popular books, fueled by biblical exemplars and local superstitions, and shared by educated ministers and their parishioners, the lore of wonders provided a powerful incentive for hearkening to the *"loud Calls"* of divine providence.[56]

Observers interpreted the earthquakes as the latest in a series of ominous events that had plagued New England during the previous year. Several clergymen attempted to establish causal connections with meteorological events of the preceding hot summer, which had produced violent thunderstorms that destroyed barns, split trees, damaged meetinghouses, and killed several

55. Prince, *Earthquakes the Work of God*, 10; Williams, *Divine Warnings*, 10; Benjamin Colman, *The Judgments of Providence in the Hand of Christ* ... (Boston, 1727), iii; John Barnard, "Earthquakes Under the Divine Government ...," *Two Discourses Addressed to Young Persons* (Boston, 1727), 78; William Shurtleff to Thomas Prince, Nov. 20, 1727, Miscellaneous Bound Manuscripts, MHS; James Allin, *Thunder and Earthquake, a Loud and Awful Call to Reformation* ... (Boson, [1727]), 17; Mather, *Terror of the Lord*, 11; Thomas Foxcroft, *The Voice of the Lord from the Deep Places of the Earth* ... (Boston, 1727), 22. On the role of natural philosophy in sermons published after the 1727 earthquake, see William D. Andrews, "The Literature of the 1727 New England Earthquake," *EAL*, VII (1973), 281–294.

56. Foxcroft, *Voice of the Lord*, 24; Allin, *Thunder and Earthquake*, 4. On the lore of wonders in early New England, see Hall, *Worlds of Wonder*, 71–116. See also Peter Lockwood Rumsey, *Acts of God and the People, 1620–1730*, Studies in Religion, II (Ann Arbor, Mich., 1986), 117–142; Ross W. Beales, Jr., "The Smiles and Frowns of Providence," in Peter Benes, ed., *Wonders of the Invisible World: 1600–1900*, Dublin Seminar for New England Folklife, Annual Proceedings 1992 (Boston, 1995), 86–96; Seeman, *Pious Persuasions*, 149–154; and Matthew Mulcahy, "The Port Royal Earthquake and the World of Wonders in Seventeenth-Century Jamaica," *EAS*, VI (2008), 391–421.

people and numerous farm animals. Others associated the earthquakes with a recent "strange and general *Sickness*," a rash of fires and peculiar accidents, renewed threats by pirates and Indians, and the death of George I. In Sudbury, Massachusetts, fears of impending doom escalated when residents witnessed a shooting star in the heavens, a well-known bad omen in English folk culture. And few ministers failed to comment on the aftershocks as foreshadowing the death of the illustrious Cotton Mather the following February. All of these signs pointed to a single truth: God was "Wroth" with New England.[57]

Ministers advanced interpretations of the earthquakes that were at once both threatening and hopeful. Some declared the shocks to be a "Strange work" of God's "vindictive justice" provoked by a sinful people, while others contended that they demonstrated his "Extensive" benevolence. In a sermon preached one week after the initial tremors, Westborough minister Ebenezer Parkman exhorted his congregants to consider both the "Mercies and judgments of the Lord." The earthquake had been a dire warning, to be sure, but most ministers argued that God would take pity on his backslidden people if they would "abound more and more in those things that are pleasing unto God." A "Time of Terror," as John Danforth reminded his parishioners in Dorchester, Massachusetts, should be a "time of Prayer." The only way to avoid providential catastrophe, predicted one New Hampshire minister, was to be "watchful and carefull in the performance of our Duty." The earthquakes were as much an opportunity as a threat to God's chosen people in New England.[58]

All across the region, lay men and women responded to the earthquake by elevating and accelerating their devotional practices. "The minds of the people throughout the Countrey seem to be generally, and deeply impress'd" by the shocks, stated one clergyman. "Peopel seme to be mightily Afected with the late Earthquak," agreed a Dorchester resident. "I pray it may have such an Impresion upon us as to Awaken us out of our carnal security and quicken us to fly to Christ whear we shall be safe." Samuel Sewall enclosed samples of sand

57. Woods, journal, [67, 71]; Colman, *Judgments of Providence,* iv–v; Williams, *Divine Warnings,* 31–34; Prince, *Earthquakes the Work of God,* 23, 40–41; Foxcroft, *Voice of the Lord,* 20–21 (quotes); Louise Parkman Thomas, transcr., "Journal of the Rev. Israel Loring," no. 12188, 18, 21, SA.

58. Anonymous, sermon notes, 1727, 134, 140, 149, Dorchester, Mass., First Church Records, 1727–1784, CL (available online at NEHH); Jonathan Edwards, "Impending Judgments Averted Only by Reformation," in *WJE,* XIV, *Sermons and Discourses, 1723-1729,* ed. Kenneth P. Minkema (New Haven, Conn., 1997), 223; Ebenezer Parkman, sermon on Ps. 101:1, Nov. 9, 1727, MS Am 883, HL; William Cooper, sermon on 1 Thess. 4:1, Nov. 12, 1727, Samuel Cooper Papers, 1718–1798, Huntington Library, San Marino, Calif.; Nicholas Gilman, sermon notebook, Nov. 16, 1727, Nicholas Gilman II Papers, 1700–1784, MHS.

from the eruptions in Newbury with copies of published earthquake sermons in letters that he sent to prominent ministers and relatives. During the winter of 1728, as the aftershocks continued unabated, an Ipswich cobbler composed a set of doggerel verses that reiterated the crucial themes of ministerial literature:

> A third time tharefor god doth Speak
> in a most dreadful waye
> The Earth he causes for to Shake
> Lets Learn What God doth Say
> Our houses he doth cosuse [cause] to Shake
> Lets Learn What God doth Say.

A few earnest lay people continued to mark the anniversary of the earthquakes years later. "We are generally become a New People," William Bradbury of Salisbury summarized in a letter to a relative; "evil Practices are generally Abandoned, Religion Seems to be the Main Business."[59]

Of the 235 relations from John Brown's parish in Haverhill, just under half were composed in the wake of the earthquake. Twenty-eight candidates, roughly one in four men and women, addressed the earthquake in their testimonies. Most followed the lead of Brown and his ministerial colleagues and characterized the earthquakes as God's "awfull and Dredfull voice" that was "calling aloud" to the people of Haverhill to repent of their sins and join the church—before it was too late. Hannah Ford admitted that she had been waiting until she was "more fit" to participate in the Lord's Supper, "but now under the Great Earthquake I tho't the day of Judgment was come and I was in great Horror." Likewise, Judith Dow believed that she would be "surely damned if God should take me away" during the aftershocks. "God has [been] pleased to stir me up very much by these Earthquakes," concurred her father-in-law, Samuel Dow, when he joined the Haverhill church several months later. "I tho't what would become of me had I been swallowed up by them." The "late earthquake seemed extraordinary surprising and awakening to me," remarked Martha Roberds, "a loud call after God had been warning so long, to awaken us out of security." The Great Earthquake of 1727 proved to be the defining "quickning" event in the lives of an entire generation of Haverhill men and

---

59. Shurtleff to Prince, Nov. 20, 1727; Ebenezer Clapp, comp., *The Clapp Memorial: Record of the Clapp Family in America* ... (Boston, 1876), 382–383; *Letter-Book of Samuel Sewall*, MHS, *Colls.*, II (1888), 232; Samuel Brown, account book, 1727–1771, Chicago History Museum, Chicago; Ellen R. Glueck and Thelma S. Ernst, transcr., "Diary of Experience (Wight) Richardson, Sudbury, Mass., 1728–1782," typescript, 1, NEHGS; JCH, 197.

women, many of whom continued to cite the "Loud Calls of Divine providence" in relations written years after the shocks abated.[60]

Brown believed that a great moral reformation was under way in Haverhill. Many of the town's "loose Livers" had been "bro't to their Knees, humbled to the dust, melted into tears," and resolved to live a new life. Among the conscience stricken were two men who previously had been censured by the church. Less than a month after the first shocks, Richard Messer and Daniel Roberds were restored to communion after confessing their sins of fornication, intemperate drinking, profane swearing, and neglecting the Sabbath. In addition, Brown was pleased to discover "Family Worship set up even in the most unlikely Houses." Young Mary Ela, for example, hailed from a notoriously impious clan. Although she did not mention the earthquake in her December 1, 1727, relation, the tremors must have played a crucial role in her decision to affiliate. Five days earlier, Ela's mother had also joined the Haverhill church and presented Mary and her eight siblings for baptism. During the six months following the initial shocks, moreover, Brown baptized seven children of Henry Saunders and Samuel Burbank, six of John Tibbets, and five of Ebenezer Buck, Jonathan Haseltine, and John Lad as well as sixteen adults from families with no previous ties to the Haverhill church.[61]

Although no lives were lost in the Great Earthquake of 1727, despite widespread property damage, New Englanders living along the northern frontier and especially in John Brown's Haverhill parish were not so providentially fortunate a decade later, when their children began dying at an alarming rate. The scourge was diphtheria, or what was commonly called the "throat distemper." The headstones in Pentucket Cemetery tell a grim story of the epidemic that ravaged Haverhill for two years beginning in the fall of 1735. Set in a single row were markers for the 4 children of James and Margaret McHard, each of whom succumbed to the disease in July 1736. The following year, James and Jemima Holgate buried 4 children in a single month. Ebenezer Buck commissioned one gravestone to memorialize the deaths of his 2 adolescent children.

60. Appendix B, Haverhill, Mass., First Church, 48–49, 73, 105, 166, 170, 178, 191. For similar examples, see Minkema, ed., "Lynn End 'Earthquake' Relations," *NEQ*, LXIX, 483, 486, 490–491, 494; Appendix B, Medfield, Mass., First Church, 65. For the full text of Ford's relation, see Appendix C.

61. Brown, "Appendix," in Cotton, *Holy Fear of God*, 5; Confessions of Richard Messer and Daniel Roberds, Nov. 26, 1727, Disciplinary Cases, 1729–1739, Haverhill, First Congregational Church Records; Appendix B, Haverhill, Mass., First Church, 65; Raymond, comp., "Records of First Parish, Haverhill," II, 56, 101–102, 107, 112, 116, 123, 125. On the Ela family, see Richard P. Gildrie, *The Profane, the Civil, and the Godly: The Reformation of Manners in Orthodox New England, 1679–1749* (University Park, Pa., 1994), 81, 95–96.

FIGURE 7 McHard Family Gravestones, Pentucket Cemetery, Haverhill, Massachusetts. 1736. Photograph by the author

Other victims, including 2 of Brown's children, lay scattered throughout the cemetery. The Haverhill minister kept detailed mortality statistics during the crisis. Between November 1735 and December 1737, a total of 256 children from 140 families were lost to the throat distemper. Most victims were under ten years of age. Scores of Haverhill families were entirely bereft of children.[62]

The diphtheria epidemic, which spread across New England and continued to impact towns sporadically into the 1750s, was the latest in a series of maladies that arose with increasing regularity and virulence during the early decades of the eighteenth century. Previous generations of New Englanders had enjoyed generally robust health. Initially isolated from global patterns of dis-

62. "Haverhill Inscriptions; Pentucket Cemetery," *Essex Antiquarian*, XII (1908), 1, 3–6, 9–10, 13, 15–16, 18; John Brown, *The Number of Deaths in Haverhil ...* (Boston, 1738), 1–3. See, in general, Ernest Caulfield, *A True History of the Terrible Epidemic Vulgarly Called the Throat Distemper, Which Occurred in His Majesty's New England Colonies between the Years 1735 and 1740* (New Haven, Conn., 1939).

ease exchange and settled by relatively young, well-nourished families, the region's insular farming towns and small seaport communities maintained impressively low background morbidity levels during the first five decades of settlement. By the start of the eighteenth century, however, exploding population densities, proliferating settlements, expanding trade networks, and escalating warfare on the northern frontier placed families in increasing contact with dangerous pathogens. Periods of heightened mortality were common, especially in emergent mercantile centers such as Boston, Salem, New London, and New Haven. By 1740, morbidity rates had increased, life expectancy had declined, and infant mortality was on the rise.[63]

An elaborate culture of death took shape amid episodes of crisis mortality. Ministers expounded on the need for the living to sanctify the deaths of friends, family members, and neighbors in a profusion of published funeral sermons. The earliest Boston newspapers broadcast reports of sudden deaths—women carried away in childbirth, healthy men struck down in their prime by an apoplectic fit—while diarists filled their journals and correspondence with reports of dying townspeople and relatives. Family members, neighbors, and ministers gathered around the deathbeds of loved ones and listened as the afflicted repented of past sins, expressed hope of eternal salvation, and offered pious exhortations. Funeral expenses increased sevenfold, as wealthy families distributed scarves and rings to pallbearers, financed the publication of broadside elegies, and sponsored lavish celebrations on behalf of the dead. Ornate gravestones depicting iconic winged skulls replaced the plain-style wooden posts of the seventeenth century. Collectively, the richly expressive puritan *ars morendi* kept the specter of mortality fresh in the minds of young and old.[64]

63. On the demographic history of early New England, see John Demos, "Notes on Life in Plymouth County," *WMQ*, XXII (1965), 270–272; Kenneth A. Lockridge, "The Population of Dedham, Massachusetts, 1636–1736," *Economic History Review*, 2d Ser., XIX (1966), 318–344; Philip J. Greven, Jr., *Four Generations: Population, Land, and Family in Colonial Andover, Massachusetts* (Ithaca, N.Y., 1970), 175–221; and Susan L. Norton, "Population Growth in Colonial America: A Study of Ipswich, Massachusetts," *Population Studies*, XXV (1971), 433–452. Maris A. Vinovskis provides a helpful summary in "Mortality Rates and Trends in Massachusetts Before 1860," *Journal of Economic History*, XXXII (1972), 195–202. For patterns of disease exchange, see Mary J. Dobson, with David Hackett Fischer, *From Old England to New England: Changing Patterns of Mortality*, Oxford University, School of Geography Research Paper, no. 38 (Oxford, 1987), 5–64; and Dobson, "Mortality Gradients and Disease Exchanges: Comparisons from Old England and Colonial America," *Social History of Medicine*, II (1989), 259–297.

64. Peter Benes, *The Masks of Orthodoxy: Folk Gravestone Carving in Plymouth County, Massachusetts, 1689–1805* (Amherst, Mass., 1977), 33–56; David E. Stannard, *The Puritan Way of Death: A Study in Religion, Culture, and Social Change* (New York, 1977), 96–134; Gordon E. Geddes, *Welcome Joy: Death in Puritan New England*, Studies in American History and Culture, XXVIII (Ann Arbor, Mich., 1981), 102–153; Hambrick-Stowe, *Practice of*

No providential dispensation played a larger role in stirring men and women to join the church than the deaths of parents, siblings, spouses, children, neighbors, and ministers. Nearly one in four relations submitted by Brown's parishioners in Haverhill were punctuated by grief and loss. "I have been awakened to my duty by sundry Instances of sudden Death of late which are loud calls to me to come to prepare," Margaret McHard mourned, after burying her four children during the throat distemper epidemic. The "Sudden Death of my Brother," Hannah Roberds acknowledged, "was very Surprising and awakening to me, and gave me a more realizing View of Judgment, and a Solemn motive to prepare myself not knowing but I might be called as Suddenly." Sarah Singletary offered a similar testimony after God "Opened the Grave for my Near Relations" four times in a single summer. Several Haverhill candidates narrated a succession of deaths. A sermon preached at the 1718 funeral of Thomas Barnard, the longtime minister of the neighboring north parish in Andover, quickened William Whittier to begin praying in secret and renewing his family devotions, but these good impressions eventually "wore of[f] in a greate mesuer." During the decade that followed, Whittier was "greatly awakned and made sencable of my lost and undun Estate" by the deaths of his mother and father. But it was not until the 1727 earthquake that God's insistent loud calls finally overcame Whittier's fears of unworthiness. Scores of relations from other communities in New England followed comparable scripts. These were the events that transformed the scrupulous and the slothful alike into ardent seekers of the Lord's Supper.[65]

In addition to the rising tide of dangerous epidemics, a host of lesser maladies and misfortunes ranging from pleurisy and piles to burns and broken bones perennially incapacitated family members. These "languishments" and "low conditions," as they were commonly called, could last for weeks, creating seasons of poor health that disrupted work routines, hampered social intercourse, and curtailed private and public religious duties. Accidents and

---

Piety, 219–241; Stephen C. Messer, "Loud Sermons in the Press: The Reporting of Death in Early Massachusetts Newspapers," *Historical Journal of Massachusetts,* XVII (1989), 38–51; Hall, *Worlds of Wonder,* 204–210; Messer, "Individual Responses to Death in Puritan Massachusetts," *Omega: Journal of Death and Dying,* XXI (1990), 155–163; Seeman, *Pious Persuasions,* 44–78; Steven C. Bullock and Sheila McIntyre, "The Handsome Tokens of a Funeral: Glove-Giving and the Large Funeral in Eighteenth-Century New England," *WMQ,* LXIX (2012), 305–346; Bullock, "'Often Concerned in Funerals': Ritual, Material Culture, and the Large Funeral in the Age of Samuel Sewall," in Martha J. McNamara and Georgia B. Barnhill, eds., *New Views of New England: Studies in Material and Visual Culture, 1680–1830,* CSM, *Pubs.,* LXXXII (Boston, 2012), 181–211.

65. Appendix B, Haverhill, Mass., First Church, 145, 190, 204, 231. For statistical evidence, see Winiarski, "Gendered 'Relations' in Haverhill," in Benes, ed., *In Our Own Words,* I, 69.

illnesses fit neatly within the puritans' providential theology of affliction. Sermons, funeral elegies, and devotional tracts described sin as a palpable, physical force that, in the words of Scituate minister Nathaniel Eells, provoked God to "send his Curse upon us, and curse us in our bodies, and in our Souls, in our families, in our Enjoyments, and in our imployments." Eells charged his congregants with improving affliction through prayer and meditation, thus transmuting divine judgment into spiritual gain. God appointed "losses, crosses, disappointments and bereavements" to "drive us off from our sinfull courses," he remarked in a 1740 sermon, "and so drive us to religious practices." To those who failed to heed the warnings of such "Speaking providences," the Scituate minister offered a sharp rebuke. Failure to reform in the face of divinely appointed affliction brought further damage to the sufferer's estate, credit, family, and body as well as to their soul.[66]

Letters circulated among the descendants of the famous Pilgrim Myles Standish reveal the extent to which lay men and women in New England embraced clerical pronouncements on the providential origins of illness and accidents. Each epistle related news of sickness within the family and inquired after the health of distant relatives. Much of the correspondence emphasized the need to improve such difficult trials. During the spring of 1717, Lois Calking informed her sister of an illness suffered by their brother, Israel Standish. He endured patiently, she reported, often praying that God would not remove his illness until "it had accompleshed the eand for which it was sent." Other family members offered similar religious advice to afflicted kin. "Sister I am glad to hear you are in Such a mesure Recovered from dangerous Sickness," wrote Samuel Standish. "Wee may take notise of the power and goodness of God in Sparing and delivering us. He can help in the greatest difficoulties. He bringeth down to the grave and bringeth up." Standish urged his sister to learn from God's "deallings toward us" during periods of sickness and affliction. "Our duty is to be quiet and Submissive under all gods dispensations," he concluded. Still other letters spoke of family deaths as "Solemn warnings" and "tokens of our mortalite" to be improved for the benefit of the living. As Sarah

66. Rose Lockwood, "Birth, Illness, and Death in 18th-Century New England," *Journal of Social History*, XII (1978), 114; Nathaniel Eells, sermon on Ps. 77:6, Apr. 20, 1740, CSL; Eells, sermon on Gen. 43:14, Aug. 5, 1733, CL. On the puritan theology of affliction, see Douglas L. Winiarski, "Lydia Prout's Dreadfullest Thought," *NEQ*, LXXXVIII (2015), 362–363; and Hall, *Worlds of Wonder*, 197. See also Elaine Forman Crane, "'I Have Suffer'd Much Today': The Defining Force of Pain in Early America," in Ronald Hoffman, Mechal Sobel, and Fredrika J. Teute, eds., *Through a Glass Darkly: Reflections on Personal Identity in Early America* (Chapel Hill, N.C., 1997), 370–403; and Ben Mutschler, "The Province of Affliction: Illness in New England, 1690–1820" (Ph.D. diss., Columbia University, 2000), 21–55.

Standish advised her children in 1697, God is the "athar [author] and giver Of al the marcys we have and do injoy."[67]

Candidates for church membership regularly characterized illnesses and accidents as providential visitations from God—punishments for failing to perform their Christian duties, especially their unwillingness to appear at the communion table. Hannah Ingals of Haverhill acknowledged that she had "Lived a great while careless of my Duty" until a "time of Sickness," when "God was pleased" to "Set my sins in order before me in a very terrible manner." When Mary Fiske of Braintree endured a protracted period of illness, she worried that God "was calling my sins to rememberance." A painful riding accident impelled one Medfield woman to "consider how I had misimproved [the] sabbathe, and had not improved the word of God aright." In the east parish of Windsor, Connecticut, Ann Fitch believed that God had visited her with illness as a "warning to me to prepare for death, and that if I did not improve it, another severe sickness of which I should not recover would come and that in a little time." Phineas Northrop elected to join the church in Milford, Connecticut, shortly after he "experienced the goodness of God in raising me from a very dangerous sickness and Low state."[68]

In an age in which the Galenic system of bleedings and purgings did more harm than good, lay men and women frequently sought to combat illness by making vows to God. Scriptural warrant for the practice came from Psalm 50: 14–15: "Offer unto God thanksgiving; and pay thy vows unto the most High: And call upon me in the day of trouble: I will deliver thee, and thou shalt glorify me." Numerous church admission candidates described sacred contracts in which they pledged to carry out their sacramental duties in exchange for divine protection or restored health. "It plesed god to veset me with sickness abought a year agoo and I was brought so low by it that I thought I should dye," explained Edward Clark of Haverhill in what was a typical case. Fearful that he had "sind greatly in neglecting" the Lord's Supper, Clark "promised that if god wold Spare me I wold offer myself to the Church." "Brot near to death" during a dangerous illness, one Connecticut woman promised that she

67. Sarah Standish to James and Mary Cary, Nov. 11, 1697, Standish Families Collection, 1656–1748, PHM, Lois Calking to Mary Cary, May 11, 1717, Josiah Standish to James and Mary Cary, June 18, 1728, Samuel Standish to James and Mary Cary, Oct. 30, 1730.

68. Appendix B, Haverhill, Mass., First Church, 118; Relation of Mary Fiske, July 17, 1693, Miscellaneous Church Papers, 1693–1857, Medfield Historical Society, Medfield, Mass.; Appendix B, Medfield, Mass., First Church, 16; Kenneth P. Minkema, ed., "The East Windsor Conversion Relations, 1700–1725," *CHS Bulletin*, LI (1986), 33; Relation of Phineas Northrop, n.d., Ser. II, box 14, Strong Family Collection, 1667–1925, MSS 1198, YUA (I thank Ken Minkema for sharing his transcription of this document).

would "neglect God no longer" and "Join myself to the church" if he would "raise me up." James Stewart of Rowley, Massachusetts, voiced a similar vow as he lay bleeding to death at the gates of Quebec during the ill-fated Phips expedition of 1690. The sparing mercies that Ann Currier experienced after she suffered a broken bone reminded her of the promises that she had uttered at the time of her "Sudon axedence [accident]." On her recovery, she presented herself for full communion in Boston's Old South Church. "When God was pleased to lay his hand on" Benjamin Phinney's children, the Barnstable, Massachusetts, layman was "ready to make promises that if God would be pleased to restore them I would not neglect to bring them under the wing of the covenant." And one frightened Haverhill women promised to "lead a new Life" by joining the church if God spared her from the 1727 earthquake.[69]

John Comer recorded several vows in his diary during the devastating Boston smallpox epidemic of 1721. As the death toll mounted, residents fled to the countryside, and doctors initiated the controversial practice of inoculation, the "coal of conviction" began to glow in Comer's once-cold soul. The rapid demise of several friends and acquaintances, he wrote, "put me on the duty of self-examination and crying to the Lord." He initiated an intensive devotional regimen that included fasting, secret prayer, and the contemplation of religious literature. Later that summer on his seventeenth birthday, Comer inscribed the first of two vows in his diary. He resolved "that if the Lord saw meet to visit me with the small pox (which I in no way expected to escape) and would raise me up again, I would study the advancement of his glory; and walk in the observation of all gospel duties, even to the commemoration of his dying love at his holy table." In return for divine protection from the epidemic, Comer promised to train for the ministry and join the church in full membership. The vow bore almost immediate fruit, as a dying grandfather bequeathed five hundred pounds for his education several days later. Comer removed to Cambridge, where he prepared to enroll at Harvard College.[70]

During the fall of 1721, the disease, by a "strange and undiscovered way," visited the family with whom Comer boarded. It was the only family in the

69. Appendix B, Haverhill, Mass., First Church, 25, 73; Appendix B, Hebron, Conn., First Church, 6; Relation of James Stewart, Jan. 23, 1699, Mss C 77, NEHGS; Appendix B, Boston, First Church, 4; Relation of Benjamin Phinney, n.d. [adm. June 30, 1717], Lemuel Shaw Papers, 1648–1923, microfilm, reel 1, MHS (for the full texts of Hannah Ford's and Benjamin Phinney's relations, see Appendix C).

70. C. Edwin Barrows and James W. Willmarth, eds., *The Diary of John Comer*, Rhode Island Historical Society, *Collections*, VIII (Providence, R.I., 1893), 20–21. On the 1721 smallpox epidemic, see Amalie M. Kass, "Boston's Historic Smallpox Epidemic," *Massachusetts Historical Review*, XIV (2012), 1–51.

neighborhood to be stricken. The puzzling movement of the epidemic distressed the young scholar, who wondered if he had displeased God by moving out of Boston to the relative safety of Cambridge. He imagined himself as the biblical figure Jonah, "flying from the presence of the Lord" in the smallpox-ridden city. Profoundly apprehensive about contracting the disease, Comer once again resumed his devotional routines. During a meditational walk along the Charlestown road, he made his second vow. With hat in hands, Comer renewed his promise to prepare for the ministry, if God saw fit to grant him composure of mind at the "instant that I know the small pox is broke out upon me." "Let this be a token to me of my life for thy goodness' sake," he prayed. Almost immediately, Comer wondered whether he had uttered an unlawful petition. Perhaps, he worried with mounting alarm, God would be offended by his bargaining.[71]

Events reached a climax in November. While worshipping in the New North meetinghouse in Boston, Comer was overpowered by the disease as he sat near a young man that "smelt exceedingly strong" of the contagion. Stricken with terror, he could think only of the "gashly countenance of death" and despaired of any hope of his salvation. Then, they appeared: the first skin eruptions that signaled the onset of smallpox. At the moment Comer was told of his symptoms, however, his fears suddenly vanished and a "miraculous beam of comfort darted into my soul." He suffered through a mild case during the next several weeks but eventually was restored to health.[72]

Comer understood why his life had been spared while nine hundred others perished during the devastating smallpox epidemic. The "prayer-hearing God," he wrote, had listened and responded to his vows. He realized that diligent labor on his part was now required to meet his devotional obligations. During the next decade, he pored over theological works, grappled with issues of infant baptism, studied at Yale College, and was ordained pastor of a Baptist congregation in Providence, Rhode Island. Most important, he fulfilled his initial vow on February 17, 1723, when he was received into full membership in the Cambridge church. Ever since his recovery, he had considered himself obligated to "serve God in a more eminent manner." Comer knew that he had the "vows of God lying on me to serve him in the ways of his Holy Institutions and more especially in the commemoration of his dying love at his table."[73]

Sworn promises to God were powerful weapons in the daily struggle against

71. Barrows and Willmarth, eds., *Diary of John Comer*, R. I. Hist. Soc., *Colls.*, VIII (1893), 22.

72. Ibid., 23–24.

73. Ibid., 24–25; Sharples, ed., *Records of the Church of Christ at Cambridge*, 92.

afflictions and calamities, but they were not to be made lightly. Many candidates who described the practice in their relations also lamented that they had failed to make good on their promises. Although he hailed from one of Haverhill's most prominent families, Nicholas White feared coming unworthily to receive the Lord's Supper until he fell gravely ill in 1718. He uttered a solemn "promes that if it should pleas god to spare my life I would spend my time better of the futer" by joining the church. White hesitated for more than a year after being restored to health, until a friend warned him that those who were not "Carefull to perform their vows Expose themselves to the severe rath of god." Frightened by his neglect, White quickly closed with the Haverhill church later that summer.[74]

Closely allied to Congregational votive practices was the tradition of posting prayer bills for the sick, the injured, or the dying. Each week, lay men and women delivered dozens of these small slips of paper to their ministers, tacked them to the meetinghouse door, or deposited them in special boxes, where they were collected and read during Sabbath meetings. Prayer bills were among the most ubiquitous religious texts of the period, although few of them have survived. Several ministers, including Jonathan Edwards, scavenged their parishioners' notes for scrap paper. Cotton Mather organized his weekly schedule of pastoral visitations around "Bills putt up in our Congregation." Diarists both prominent and obscure posted prayer notes. Boston magistrate Samuel Sewall described dozens of petitions that he submitted on behalf of individuals ranging from Massachusetts governor William Shute to enslaved African Americans. He composed public prayers for himself, his family, and distant kinfolk as well as neighbors, Harvard College students, and native American converts. Unlike New England's restrictive church admission requirements, the practice of submitting public prayer requests was open to anyone, including travelers, slaves, and criminals.[75]

Undoubtedly the best known prayer bill was the 1697 statement in which Sewall repented of his involvement in the Salem witchcraft trials. The Boston magistrate penned his famous confession shortly after experiencing the "reiterated strokes of God upon himself and family," afflictions that included the death of his sixth child and his wife's stillborn delivery less than a month earlier. As with many church admission testimonies, Sewall and his contempo-

74. Appendix B, Haverhill, Mass., First Church, 223.

75. Worthington Chauncey Ford, ed., *Diary of Cotton Mather,* American Classics, 2 vols. (1911–1912; rpt. New York, 1957), II, 108. On the history of the prayer bill tradition, see Douglas L. Winiarski, "The Newbury Prayer Bill Hoax: Devotion and Deception in New England's Era of Great Awakenings," *Massachusetts Historical Review,* XIV (2012), 55–61.

raries turned to prayer to assuage their grief when confronting death. Nearly one-quarter of all prayer bills beseeched God to "sanctifi his holy and afflictin hand" in taking away parents, spouses, siblings, and children. Often the bereaved begged for the strength to "behave themsellves sutably undder the various dispensations of god towards them." In cases where languishing family members hastened toward their final dissolution, they asked God to comfort and support them through the "Dark Hour" of their "grate and Last Chang."[76]

Most prayer bills were composed in response to illnesses and accidents. During one of the several peaks of morbidity that punctuated the early eighteenth century, Mather recalled seeing hundreds of such notes posted on the doors of the Old North meetinghouse. In Northampton, Edwards's parishioners catalogued an extensive list of maladies and misfortunes. Many found themselves in low circumstances owing to a variety of dangerous diseases, which included cancers, consumption, pleurisy, the long fever, and the throat distemper. Other petitioners had been burned in fires, almost drowned in river accidents, crushed under falling trees, or injured during Indian raids. Families frequently sought the assistance of the congregation in the hope that the prayer-hearing God "would be pleasd to appear" for the recovery of sick, wounded, and afflicted members. "Exersised with Exeding pain," Joel Clark spoke for many of his contemporaries when he, along with his parents, asked the Northampton congregation to pray that "god would ese him of the pain that he labours under and Spaer his Life and restore his health." When Sewall inquired whether he should put up a note for a sick neighbor, the man "seeme'd very desirous of it; and said he counted it the best Medicine." The practice of submitting prayer notes was so closely associated with petitions for recovery from illness and injury that Edwards and other eighteenth-century ministers gauged the health of their communities based on the number of monthly bills they received from their parishioners.[77]

A related category of protective prayers involved petitions on behalf of men gone to sea or mustered into military service. Pious laymen such as Sewall penned thanksgiving prayers in response to a safely completed voyage. Like-

76. Thomas, ed., *Diary of Samuel Sewall*, I, 367; Stephen J. Stein, ed., "'For Their Spiritual Good': The Northampton, Massachusetts Prayer Bids of the 1730s and 1740s," *WMQ*, XXXVII (1980), 271, 273; Elizabeth Everton, prayer bill, n.d., microfilm, reel 6, Cotton Mather Papers, 1636–1724, MHS.

77. [Cotton Mather], *The Bostonian Ebenezer . . .* (Boston, 1698), 8; Stein, ed., "'For Their Spiritual Good,'" *WMQ*, XXXVII (1980), 275, 283; Thomas, ed., *Diary of Samuel Sewall*, II, 863; Jonathan Edwards, *A Faithful Narrative of the Surprizing Work of God . . .* (London, 1737), in *WJE*, IV, *The Great Awakening*, ed. C. C. Goen (New Haven, Conn., 1972), 205; Jonathan Townsend, diary, 1749, Townshend Family Collection, 1482–1952, MSS 114, New Haven Museum and Historical Society, New Haven, Conn.

wise, relatives of the Cape Cod mariner John Bursley asked the Barnstable congregation to intercede that God's goodness might affect his heart follow- ing his miraculous deliverance from a "violent storm at sea." Others, however, focused on the more tangible benefits of communal prayer. One of Mather's parishioners, a mariner named Benjamin Elton, desired prayers that "God would Bless and prosper him and in Safety Returne him" while he was bound to sea. Petitions offered by the families of Northampton soldiers embarking on the 1745 attack on the French fortress at Louisbourg asked God to preserve their lives, maintain their health while abroad, grant them victory in the up- coming campaign, and, above all, return them safely home.[78]

The longest Northampton prayer bill, written in the form of a letter by Ephraim Marble, balanced the dual demands of sanctifying past afflictions and seeking protection from future ones. Born in southeastern Massachu- setts, Marble had moved to a remote corner of the Connecticut River town of Sunderland during the early 1740s. There, he experienced a string of crip- pling losses, including the deaths of his wife and several children, "Bodyly Indispositions," and a 1746 fire that destroyed his house and a weaving shop stocked with looms, tackle, tools, Indian corn, grain, and almost everything else he needed for the "Suport of Life." Facing the onset of winter, Marble appealed to Edwards's parishioners for aid. He requested prayers from the Northampton congregation that God would "Sanctifie" his misfortunes and allow him to see the "holy and wise providence" in laying "his hand heavy uppon me." But Marble also took the opportunity to beg for material necessi- ties from Edwards's generous parishioners, on whose charity he, as a "Stranger in these parts," was entirely reliant to survive the winter.[79]

Provincial New Englanders did not sit idly by as disease and illness rav- aged family members. The continual round of agues, fevers, and fluxes threw families back on the limited resources of physicians, healers, midwives, and informed neighbors. Prayer bills, healing vows, and even the act of joining the church were common responses to afflictions that most people readily inter- preted as acts of divine chastisement.

■ Less than twelve hours after the great earthquake struck just a few miles away in Newbury, John Brown called for a day of public fasting. On the morn-

---

78. *Letter-Book of Samuel Sewall*, MHS, *Colls.*, II (1888), 264; [Elizabeth Bursley], prayer bill, n.d. [circa 1720s], West Barnstable, Mass., Congregational Church Records, 1668–1807, photostats, AAS; Ford, ed., *Diary of Cotton Mather*, I, 62–63n; Stein, ed., "'For Their Spiri- tual Good,'" *WMQ*, XXXVII (1980), 276–277.

79. Stein, ed., "'For Their Spiritual Good,'" *WMQ*, XXXVII (1980), 280.

ing of Monday, October 30, 1727, people from all parts of town poured into the Haverhill meetinghouse. Many came from a distance of more than six miles, despite having only a few hours' notice. Two days later, the town held a second fast, with full meetings morning and afternoon. Neighboring minister Joseph Parsons of Bradford delivered a pair of potent sermons to what Brown called the "most affected" congregation "that ever I saw." The following day, the Haverhill parishioners crossed over the Merrimack River to Bradford for another day of religious exercises. By the end of the week, Brown had met with thirty parishioners seeking to affiliate with his church. Among the awakened men and women was Sarah Smith, who later remarked in her church admission testimony that Parsons's fast-day sermons "shewing that God is a mighty and terrible God," in particular, had "been very quickning to me."[80]

Ritual days of fasting and humiliation had long been a staple among the public ordinances of puritan worship. Seventeenth-century ministers and magistrates had called for dozens of general fasts when confronted with a wide variety of afflictions, including disruptions in the natural order, perceived threats to the social fabric, and news of political and military reversals in England and Europe. Congregations held fasts in response to epidemics, droughts, and ecclesiastical disputes. Participants abstained from food and dressed in plain clothes. Rising early for private meditation or family prayer, they spent the remainder of the day in the meetinghouse listening to sermons on the necessity of moral reformation. Much of the ritual work of fast days was social in nature. Collective rites of confession, humiliation, and repentance bonded congregations together and restored the order of communal fellowship. In the face of natural disasters such as the 1727 earthquake and the throat distemper epidemic, fast days provided opportunities for parishioners to rededicate themselves to a disciplined, godly life in the hope of averting impending divine wrath. In addition to Boston's seven Congregational churches, many of the "Country Towns" kept days of "*extraordinary* Fasting and *Prayer*" within the first week after the initial shocks, including parishes located at a considerable distance from the epicenter such as Brookline, Dorchester, Sudbury, and Weymouth. As the Milton, Massachusetts, minister Peter Thacher explained several days after the earthquake, fast days were "Offencive" as well as "Defencive" weapons against the "Spiritual Adversiries" that would provoke God to bring ruin on his chosen New England people.[81]

---

80. Brown, "Appendix," in Cotton, *Holy Fear of God*, 4; Appendix B, Haverhill, Mass., First Church, 207.

81. "Diary of Rev. Samuel Dexter, of Dedham" *NEHGR*, XIV (1860), 202; Prince, *Earthquakes the Work of God*, [ii]; Anonymous, sermon notes, 1727, 146, Dorchester First Church

John Brown and his colleagues tended to view fast-day rituals as opportunities for their parishioners to prepare for death and divine judgment. But others understood the broader applications of collective acts of repentance. When Lieutenant Governor William Dummer declared a day of fasting and humiliation in March 1728, he emphasized the need for "importunate Supplications to Almighty GOD," not only to avert impending divine judgments but also to confer "all needful Blessings" on a repentant people. Published as the aftershocks continued to ripple across the region, Dummer's proclamation suggested that collective rituals of contrition would promote "gracious Government," safeguard English religious liberties, maintain peace within the empire, ensure the good health of the colony, provide for a plentiful harvest, and even "protect our *Merchandize* and *Fishery* from the Rapine of *Pirates*."[82]

On the day of the general fast, March 21, 1728, several hundred Haverhill parishioners stood in silence as Brown read the church covenant aloud and delivered a fast-day lecture. An infrequent occurrence among provincial churches, covenant renewal ceremonies dated back to the early years of the puritan settlements but received renewed attention during the Reforming Synod of 1679. Standing with heads bowed and arms upraised, the men and women of Haverhill affirmed their shared commitment to the principles of the church covenant and renounced the "provoking *evils* that have brought the Judgments of God upon *New-England*": "Lukewarmness in Religion," "Sabbath Breaking," "Contentions in Churches," "carelessness about Schools," "needless Lawsuits," "Fornication," "Covetousness," and "Rash Censuring and Promise-Breaking." Brown envisioned the ceremony as one component in a broader campaign in which his parishioners rededicated themselves to their regular religious duties, including Sabbath worship, family prayer, private devotions, and even business dealings and social relations, all of which they pledged to enact with the *"Glory of God"* as the highest aim.[83]

When Brown paused to consider the motives for engaging in covenant re-

---

Records. See also Allin, *Thunder and Earthquake*, title page; John Danforth, *A Sermon Occasioned by the Late Great Earthquake* ... (Boston, 1728), title page; Cotton, *Holy Fear of God*, title page; Thomas, transcr., "Journal of the Rev. Israel Loring," no. 12188, 15; Thomas Paine, *The Doctrine of Earthquakes* ... (Boston, 1728), preface. On fast-day practices, see Richard P. Gildrie, "The Ceremonial Puritan: Days of Humiliation and Thanksgiving," *NEHGR*, CXXXVI (1982), 3–16; Hambrick-Stowe, *Practice of Piety*, 100–103; and Hall, *Worlds of Wonder*, 169–172.

82. *Boston Gazette*, Mar. 18, 1728.

83. John Brown, *Solemn Covenanting with God, One of the Best Means to Prevent Fatal Declensions* ... (Boston, 1728), 24, 35. On the Reforming Synod of 1679, see Hall, *Faithful Shepherd*, 242–244; Foster, *Long Argument*, 227–230; and Gildrie, *The Profane, the Civil, and the Godly*, 19–40.

newal, his fast-day sermon turned in a decidedly practical direction. "What will become of us if we Live as strangers to his Covenant?" he wondered aloud. If his people turned away from their religious obligations while under the "threatning amazing *Judgments*" of the earthquakes, they would inevitably provoke God to visit them with more fearful calamities, especially "in *this Life*." He would "pour out his Fury" on their families, or conspire by "some other strange work to make an end of you." But, "if we will now cordially consent to God's Covenant, and all as one with our Wives and little ones and Servants enter into Covenant with the Lord our God, and keep it as we have been instructed," Brown continued, "how happy shall we be!" As with the lieutenant governor's fast-day proclamation, Brown believed that "all manner of Blessings" would follow acts of heartfelt repentance, reformation, and covenantal renewal. Collective ritual was one of the best means not only to "prevent Declensions" but also to avert future catastrophes and "derive the best of Blessings" in this world.[84]

By the 1720s, covenant renewal ceremonies had developed into an important tool through which Congregational ministers expanded the reach of their churches. At one such event in Taunton, Massachusetts, more than three hundred young adults—an entire generation of townspeople—were taken into the church on a single day in 1705. Similar seasons of ingathering occurred in the upper Connecticut Valley from the 1680s through the 1730s, where Northampton clergyman Solomon Stoddard developed new preaching tactics to goad his parishioners into joining the church. These "harvests" of new church members, as they came to be called, occurred in the surrounding communities as well. In the east parish of Windsor, Connecticut, church membership candidates described how they had experienced their "first Considerable Convictions" during the "time of the Last great Stir amongst us in this place." Recurrent periods of intensified religious concern made a strong impression on the young Jonathan Edwards—Stoddard's grandson and future colleague. Written in 1716, when he was only twelve, Edwards's earliest surviving letter described the surge of church admissions and pastoral conferences that he witnessed during a "very remarkable stirring and pouring out of the Spirit of God" in Windsor.[85]

84. Brown, *Solemn Covenanting with God*, 12, 15, 24–27, 29.
85. Jonathan Edwards, *A Faithful Narrative of the Surprizing Work of God* (London, 1737), in *WJE*, IV, *The Great Awakening*, ed. Goen, 146; Relation of Job Phelps, Oct. 30, 1724, Timothy Edwards Manuscript, circa 1720–1725, private collection (I thank Kenneth Minkema for sharing his transcription of this manuscript); Edwards to Mary Edwards, May 10, 1716, in *WJE*, XVI, *Letters and Personal Writings*, ed. George S. Claghorn (New Haven,

The most famous of these Connecticut Valley awakenings erupted in Northampton during the spring of 1735, after Edwards began preaching enlivened sermons on the moral failings of the rising generation and exhorting his parishioners to devote their Sabbath evenings to what he called "social religion," or neighborhood meetings. Renewed attention to moral reform and devotional discipline, in turn, sparked a powerful religious awakening in Northampton. "There was scarcely a single person in the town, either old or young, that was left unconcerned about the great things of the eternal world," Edwards remarked in his *Faithful Narrative of the Surprizing Work of God,* a short pamphlet published in London for which he received international acclaim. In less than six months during the summer of 1735, he reported, 160 new communicants swelled the Northampton church. Downriver in the small village of Suffield, 120 people stepped forward to join the church—so many that minister Ebenezer Devotion started keeping a separate list of the "Names of those who to a Judgement of Charity have been Converted." Eventually, the unusual religious stir spread to three dozen other parishes from central Massachusetts to coastal Connecticut.[86]

Church admission testimonies dating from the Connecticut stirs of the 1730s diverged in several ways from relations in eastern Massachusetts. Although a few candidates in Benjamin Pomeroy's Hebron, Connecticut, parish continued to describe the importance of "Loud Calls," "providential dealings and dispensations," and healing vows, they exhibited none of the scruples regarding the Lord's Supper as did their counterparts in places such as Haverhill. Nor did they cite the same encouraging biblical passages that appeared with overwhelming regularity elsewhere in New England during this period. Instead, prospective church members in Hebron were preoccupied with seek-

---

Conn., 1998), 29. See also Minkema, ed., "East Windsor Conversion Relations," *CHS Bulletin,* LI (1986), 45, 50, 54. For the Taunton event, see Anne S. Brown and David D. Hall, "Family Strategies and Religious Practice: Baptism and the Lord's Supper in Early New England," in Hall, ed., *Lived Religion in America: Toward a History of Practice* (Princeton, N.J., 1997), 58. On Stoddard's "harvests," see Thomas A. Schafer, "Solomon Stoddard and the Theology of the Revival," in Stuart C. Henry, ed., *A Miscellany of American Christianity: Essays in Honor of H. Shelton Smith* (Durham, N.C., 1963), 328–361; and Paul R. Lucas, "Solomon Stoddard and the Origin of the Great Awakening in New England," *Historian,* LIX (1997), 741–758.

86. Edwards, *Faithful Narrative* (1737), in *WJE,* IV, *Great Awakening,* ed. Goen, 148, 150, 157; *Records of the Congregational Church in Suffield, Connecticut (Except Votes), 1710–1836* (Hartford, Conn., 1941), 22. The literature on the so-called little awakening in Northampton is extensive. See, in particular, Patricia J. Tracy, *Jonathan Edwards, Pastor: Religion and Society in Eighteenth-Century Northampton,* American Century Series (New York, 1979), 109–122; and George M. Marsden, *Jonathan Edwards, A Life* (New Haven, Conn., 2003), 150–169.

ing "good Satisfaction of my conversion" and were more fluent in narrating "what God has done for my Soul." "Sometime Last summer I began to be more Concernd for my soul than ever I had been before," asserted Rachel Root. Her relation vacillated between extremes of despair and joy before concluding with the "hope that God has begun his work in my soul which shall be Carried on to perfection." Other Hebron candidates alternately described "distressing fears of hell" and elevated feelings of being "ravishd" by divine love. On balance, the men and women of Hebron emerged from the stirs of the 1730s more confident of their religious experiences than people in other parts of New England. As one woman revealed toward the end of her relation, "besure I think there is a great Change in me. I am not sure it is conversion, but I think I delight more in God in his word and ways, than I used to do." Testimonies such as these afforded a glimpse of what Edwards, Pomeroy, and their colleagues for the first time called "a remarkable revival of religion."[87]

Together, the earthquake and Connecticut Valley awakenings marked an important transitional moment in the history of New England Congregationalism. In both cases, churches in towns such as Haverhill and Suffield admitted exceptionally large cohorts of new communicants—between ten and twenty times the annual average (Chart 1). But some evidence suggests that New Englanders had begun to think about the "wonderful work of God" in regionally specific ways. Lay men and women in the towns of the Connecticut Valley increasingly arrived at the belief that their religious lives moved in unexpected, disorderly, spasmodic shifts that conformed only to God's surprising plan for his faithful saints. As one of Edwards's parishioners recognized in a diary entry composed during the 1735 awakening in Northampton, the search for "spiritual light" turned out to be "far different from what I conceived it to be." Religion had become, in Edwards's words, a "strange thing" "beyond God's usual way of working."[88]

For a time, John Brown, too, believed that "we were going into a *New World*" and that he would live to see the *"Coming of the Day of GOD."* In contrast to Edwards and the transatlantic readers of his *Faithful Narrative*, who rev-

87. Appendix B, Hebron, Conn., First Church, 1–2, 4, 8, 10–11, 13 (for the full text of Rachel Root's relation, see Appendix C); Thomas Milner, *The Life, Times, and Correspondence of the Rev. Isaac Watts, D.D.* (London, 1834), 546. See also Edwards, *Faithful Narrative* (1737), in *WJE*, IV, *Great Awakening*, ed. Goen, 155–156.

88. Edwards, *Faithful Narrative* (1737), in *WJE*, IV, *Great Awakening*, ed. Goen, 144; M. X. Lesser, "Preface to the Period," in *WJE*, XIX, *Sermons and Discourses, 1734–1738*, ed. Lesser (New Haven, Conn., 2001), 16n; Edwards to Benjamin Colman, Nov. 6, 1736, in William Williams, *The Duty and Interest of a People among Whom Religion Has Been Planted* ... (Boston, 1736), in *WJE*, IV, *Great Awakening*, ed. Goen, 121.

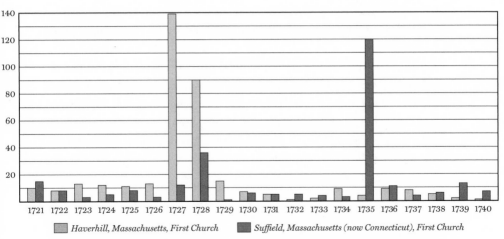

Legend: ☐ *Haverhill, Massachusetts, First Church*   ■ *Suffield, Massachusetts (now Connecticut), First Church*

CHART 1 Admissions to Full Communion in Haverhill, Massachusetts, and Suffield, Massachusetts (now Connecticut), 1721–1740. Drawn by Rebecca L. Wrenn

eled in reports of the "Great Conversions" in Northampton, however, Brown elected to highlight the conventional responses of his parishioners. Although Brown claimed to have witnessed what he called "Symptoms of *Conversion*," he reported only a *"General Reformation"* of manners along with a dramatic surge in church admissions in Haverhill and the surrounding towns. Unlike the Hebron relations, each of the 116 church admission testimonies that he penned on behalf of his parishioners during the twelve-month period following the initial shocks conformed closely to the generic conventions that had prevailed in Haverhill since the beginning of Brown's pastorate.[89]

At the close of the March 1728 covenant renewal ceremony, Brown prayed for healing in the broadest sense—of broken bodies, withered crops, damaged buildings, divided communities, and sundered covenants with God. In the towns and villages of eastern Massachusetts, ritual responses to temporal afflictions such as the Great Earthquake of 1727 and throat distemper epidemic that soon followed reflected a practical piety organized as much around what Brown and other clergymen called the outward or temporal lives of their congregants as it was oriented toward garnering assurance of salvation. His parishioners persisted in the belief that the performance of religious duties and, especially, the elevation of those routines in response to the loud calls of

---

89. Brown, "Appendix," in Cotton, *Holy Fear of God,* 5–7; Grace Denny to Thomas Prince, 1738, Thomas Prince Letters, 1721–1738, David M. Rubenstein Rare Book and Manuscript Library, Duke University, Durham, N.C.

divine providence helped to ensure the health of their bodies, the security of their frontiers, and the success of their agricultural, commercial, and military enterprises.[90]

Ritual observances could make an uncertain world of pain, strife, and upheaval more livable. But, if earthquakes and Indian raids, sudden deaths and epidemics did not impel people to attend to their religious duties, the imperatives of family life often did. For anxious young parents, family concerns soon overshadowed perennial fears of receiving the Lord's Supper unworthily, as they struggled to amass a spiritual patrimony that would safeguard the health and safety of their progeny.

I WAS BORN IN A LAND OF LIGHT

Several years before the Great Earthquake of 1727, an elderly woman stood in the Haverhill meetinghouse and listened as John Brown read her relation to the assembled congregants. "I Desire to be thankful that I was born in a Land of Light and Baptized when I was Young," he explained on behalf of his aging parishioner. She cited her pious upbringing and the "Good Education by My Father" but lamented that she had taken "but little Notice of it" as a child. Like many of her scrupulous contemporaries, she had considered coming to the Lord's Supper for many years but remained fearful of her unworthiness to participate in the sacrament. During the months leading up to Brown's ordination, she had reconsidered her "Delays and fears." She had been awakened by reading a book that described the sufferings of Jesus, studying encouraging biblical passages, and listening to the Haverhill minister's sacramental sermons. Finally, she resolved to offer herself to the church in full communion. It was the "Eleventh hour." In the sixty-seventh year of her age, Hannah Duston, the most famous woman in New England, had finally joined the Haverhill church.[91]

Brown paused partway through Duston's relation to note that she wished to express thanks to God for her "Captivity." During the pastoral conference in which the Haverhill minister drafted her church admission testimony, Duston had described this event as the "Comfortablest time that ever I had"—the most uplifting event in her long life. It was a seemingly strange choice of words. This brief departure from the conventional language of her relation recalled

90. Brown, *Solemn Covenanting with God,* 35.

91. Appendix B, Haverhill, Mass., First Church, 51. For the complete text of Duston's relation, see Winiarski, "Gendered 'Relations' in Haverhill," in Benes, ed., *In Our Own Words,* I, 78.

the traumatic events of March 15, 1697, when Haverhill was devastated by a Wabenaki war party. Recovering from childbirth a few days earlier, Duston had watched in horror as her infant daughter was bludgeoned to death by the raiders. She was dragged into the wilderness, only to rise up two weeks later to kill ten of her Indian captors with the help of her midwife and a young man from Worcester. Returning to Boston with their scalps neatly folded in cloth that was purportedly woven on her own loom, Duston received the accolades of elites, gifts of pewter from distant colonial leaders, and a handsome bounty from the Massachusetts General Court. Cotton Mather preached a sermon on her exploits and published several accounts of her captivity.[92]

During the nineteenth century, Duston's remarkable tale of violence and re-demption was memorialized in works of prose, poetry, paint, and bronze. But lingering ambiguities surrounding the moral rectitude of her bloody assault on her native American captors obscure rather than illuminate her religious biography. Viewed alongside her physically abusive father and a sister exe-cuted for infanticide, Duston has often been portrayed as a woman of suspect moral virtues who resisted the softening influences of the church until she was well into her sixties. Brown knew her by another name. In his "Catalogue of Kindnesses," he referred to the notorious Indian killer as "Mother Duston." Haverhill's unique collection of church records reveals a figure strangely at odds with the famed captive. Although the records of Brown's predecessors were destroyed in a subsequent Indian raid, a fragmentary baptismal register from the 1690s indicates that Duston and her husband, Thomas, presented three of their last four children for baptism shortly after their births. The only missing child born during this period was Martha, the infant killed during the 1697 attack. To secure this privilege, either Hannah or her husband must have affiliated with the Haverhill church through a ritual known as owning the covenant sometime before 1694 and probably earlier.[93]

92. Appendix B, Haverhill, Mass., First Church, 51. See also "Journal of the Rev. John Pike," NHHS, *Collections*, III (Concord, N.H., 1832), 48; Thomas, ed., *Diary of Samuel Sewall*, I, 372–373; Alden T. Vaughan and Edward W. Clark, eds., *Puritans among the Indians: Ac-counts of Captivity and Redemption, 1676–1724* (Cambridge, Mass., 1981), 161–164. An illus-tration of the Duston tankard, a gift from Maryland governor Francis Nicholson, appears in Augustus W. Corliss, comp., *A Genealogical Record of the Corliss Family of America* ... (Yar-mouth, Maine, 1875), facing 207.

93. John Brown, account book, 67; Laurel Thatcher Ulrich, *Good Wives: Image and Reality in the Lives of Women in Northern New England, 1650–1750* (New York, 1980), 234–235; David W. Hoyt, "The Duston Family of Haverhill," *EIHC*, XLVI (1910), 350–351; Ray-mond, comp., "Records of First Parish, Haverhill," II, 87–88. Studies that build on Ulrich's account of Duston's "long journey to the house of the Lord" (234) include Kathleen M. Brown, "Murderous Uncleanness: The Body of the Female Infanticide in Puritan New En-

The Dustons were far from religious outsiders. Although Thomas was a relative newcomer to town, his wife was the daughter of the early Haverhill pioneer Michael Emerson. The church affiliation strategies of Emerson's children and descendants form a coherent and persistent pattern over more than a century. Hannah, her three siblings, and their spouses all appear to have owned the covenant shortly after marriage, and they later joined the Haverhill church in full communion. They presented their children for baptism in a regular and orderly fashion. All but two of Duston's nineteen children, nieces, and nephews grew up, married, and affiliated with one of several local Congregational churches. Adding the descendants of Robert Emerson—Duston's first cousins and their children—doubles the tangled genealogical web of churched families. Roughly one in ten people admitted to full communion during Brown's two-decade pastorate were direct descendants of the Emerson brothers or related by marriage. The Duston-Emerson clan, in other words, formed the core of the Haverhill church. At the time that Brown began compiling his "Catalogue of Kindnesses," Mother Duston was its undisputed matriarch.[94]

Relations survive for more than two dozen of Duston's siblings, children, nieces, nephews, grandchildren, cousins, and their spouses. These remarkably uniform texts suggest that most New Englanders did not conceive of church membership as an individual response to a personal conversion crisis. Instead, they yoked their covenantal duties to life-course transitions, broader patterns of social maturation, and strategies of family preservation. Joining the church was a duty incumbent on all people that entailed distinct benefits and advantages—both spiritual and temporal—for young adults who were facing pres-

gland," in Janet Moore Lindman and Michele Lise Tarter, eds., *A Centre of Wonders: The Body in Early America* (Ithaca, N.Y., 2001), 77–94; and Teresa A. Toulouse, *The Captive's Position: Female Narrative, Male Identity, and Royal Authority in Colonial New England* (Philadelphia, 2007), 73–119. The most detailed account of Duston's captivity remains Kathryn Whitford, "Hannah Dustin: The Judgment of History," *EIHC*, CVIII (1972), 304–325. For nineteenth-century memorials, see Ann-Marie Weis, "The Murderous Mother and the Solicitous Father: Violence, Jacksonian Family Values, and Hannah Duston's Captivity," *American Studies International*, XXXVI, no. 1 (February 1998), 46–65; Barbara Cutter, "The Female Indian Killer Memorialized: Hannah Duston and the Nineteenth-Century Feminization of American Violence," *Journal of Women's History*, XX, no. 2 (Summer 2008), 10–33; and Lauren Lessing, "Theatrical Mayhem in Junius Brutus Stearn's *Hannah Duston Killing the Indians*," *American Art*, XXVIII, no. 3 (Fall 2014), 76–103.

94. Information on the church affiliation strategies of the Duston-Emerson families is based on a comparison of published genealogies with the Haverhill, Suffield, and West Newbury church records cited in Appendix A. See Hoyt, comp., "Duston Family," *EIHC*, XLVI (1910), 350–353; and Charles Henry Pope, comp., *The Haverhill Emersons: Part First* (Boston, 1913), 13–56.

sures of family formation for the first time. Women, especially, understood church affiliation as an extension of parenting responsibilities.

During the early decades of the eighteenth century, a practice that had once served to safeguard the purity of New England's gathered churches of visible saints evolved into a rite of passage that consolidated the religious status and social power of core parish families and projected that authority across the generations. "God saith that the Children of the Righteous upon the account of their parent have no more cause to hope for being Saved on that account than the Children of the Wicked," a New Hampshire man acknowledged at midcentury. Then, he added, "but God reward the Children of the Righteous often times on account of their Parents tho' not Eternal Salvation yet with the good things of this Life."[95]

■ It was not Hannah Duston's notoriety as an Indian captive but her advanced age that distinguished her from other members of the Haverhill church. John Brown indicated as much when he wrote "AEtat 67" next to the signature at the bottom of her relation. Fewer than 10 percent of all church membership candidates during the provincial era had reached the age of retirement and were considered old by eighteenth-century standards (see Table 1). Although New Englanders had been trained from childhood to prepare for death with diligence, anxieties about salvation appear to have fallen with greater weight on those who found themselves "on the very brinke of eternity."[96]

95. [Emily Hoffman Gilman], ed., *A Family History in Letters and Documents, 1667–1837 . . .*, 2 vols. (Saint Paul, Minn., 1919), I, 62–63. This section builds on the pioneering scholarship of David D. Hall on religion and the family in Brown and Hall, "Family Strategies and Religious Practice," in Hall, ed., *Lived Religion in America*, 41–68; and Hall, "From 'Religion and Society' to Practices: The New Religious History," in Robert Blair St. George, ed., *Possible Pasts: Becoming Colonial in Early America* (Ithaca, N.Y., 2000), 148–159. See also Gerald F. Moran and Maris A. Vinovskis, "The Puritan Family and Religion: A Critical Reappraisal," in Moran and Vinovskis, eds., *Religion, Family, and the Life Course: Explorations in the Social History of Early America* (Ann Arbor, Mich., 1992), 26–27; Mary Macmanus Ramsbottom, "Religious Society and the Family in Charlestown, Massachusetts, 1630 to 1740" (Ph.D. diss., Yale University, 1987), 88; and Mark A. Peterson, *The Price of Redemption: The Spiritual Economy of Puritan New England* (Stanford, Calif., 1997), 70–71.

96. Appendix B, Haverhill, Mass., First Church, 51; Seeman, *Pious Persuasions*, 35. On old age and retirement in early New England, see John Demos, *Past, Present, and Personal: The Family and the Life Course in American History* (New York, 1986), 139–185; Lisa Wilson, *Ye Heart of a Man: The Domestic Life of Men in Colonial New England* (New Haven, Conn., 1999), 171–185; and Kenneth P. Minkema, "Old Age and Religion in the Writings and Life of Jonathan Edwards," *Church History*, LXX (2001), 674–704. For comparative church membership data, see Greven, "Youth, Maturity, and Religious Conversion," *EIHC*, CVIII (1972), 133; Gerald F. Moran, "Conditions of Religious Conversion in the First Society of Norwich, Connecticut, 1718–1744," *Journal of Social History*, V (1972), 334; and Gerald Francis Moran,

FIGURE 8 *Anne Pollard at One Hundred Years of Age.* 1721. Oil on canvas by unknown artist, 70.7 × 57.7 cm. Courtesy, Massachusetts Historical Society, Boston

Men and women over the age of sixty formed an ambiguous religious co-hort. On the one hand, elderly church members often were venerated for their ancient virtue. Their ranks included unusual figures like centenarian Anne Pollard, whose 1725 portrait captured the stolid piety of the oldest surviv-ing member of the Winthrop fleet. A handful of virtuosos, including Samuel

"The Puritan Saint: Religious Experience, Church Membership, and Piety in Connecticut, 1636–1776" (Ph.D. diss., Rutgers University, 1974), 280.

Sewall and the portraitist Thomas Smith, occasionally took to meditating in graveyards or employing skulls as *memento mori* devotional aids. A few aging diarists started marking the passage of time during their advancing years by taking stock of their birthdays and the deaths of neighbors, townspeople, and former companions, while others assiduously compiled personal town death registers. "I find Old Age coming upon Me like an Armed Man," Plymouth magistrate Josiah Cotton confided in his personal memoirs on his sixtieth birthday, "And it is time for Me to think of being Unclothed for Another, Rather than being Advanced in this World." As the elderly Boston housewright John Barnard labored "to quicken my pac[e], and to make Redy" for the day of reckoning, he pledged to "set death before me, every day" and regularly pondered the question "if I dy this night is my soule safe?"[97]

At the same time, ministers chided sluggish parishioners like Hannah Duston, especially when they chose to hold back from the communion table into their advanced years. "It seems as if those that were grown up" and did not join the church "could not be saved," lamented Mary Johnson of Haverhill. Two middle-aged parishioners from the east parish in Windsor, Connecticut, feared that they had "out-stayed" their day of grace after hearing minister Timothy Edwards preach that God granted his mercy only to those under thirty years of age. "I am afraid God has been very Angry with me for delaying So long to Come to this Ordinance," admitted Duston's sister-in-law, Hannah Emerson. All Christians were duty bound to "shew forth the Lord's Death in the Sacrament of his supper," she acknowledged, "Especially for such as are in Years as I am."[98]

There was an unusual tone of urgency in the relations of candidates that had been favored with a "long day of grace" and yet "tarried to the 11th hour" before closing with the church. Men and women like Samuel Dow, who had neglected his "Duty so long, till old Age, till my understanding and Memory and strength is decayed," worried especially about continuing to avoid their sacramental responsibilities during the "little time I have to live." As they prepared for their "Poor carcase" to disintegrate into "meat for the worms," their relations increasingly emphasized issues of eternal salvation. Duston was one among several elderly Haverhill parishioners who pleaded with God to safeguard their immortal souls. Whereas younger candidates voiced healing vows

97. Thomas, ed., *Diary of Samuel Sewall*, I, 364; Roger B. Stein, "Thomas Smith's Self-Portrait: Image / Text as Artifact," *Art Journal*, XLIV (1984), 316–327; JCH, 289–290; Seeman, *Pious Persuasions*, 30–31.

98. Appendix B, Haverhill, Mass., First Church, 69, 123; Minkema, ed., "East Windsor Conversion Relations," *CHS Bulletin*, LI (1986), 27, 45.

and begged for sparing mercies, Haverhill octogenarian Peter Green hoped that "when I Shall go from hence and be here no more I may dwell at Gods right hand where is fulness of joy and pleasures forever more."[99]

At the other end of the life-course, youths formed a small proportion of all church admissions. In most towns, fewer than twenty percent of all prospective church members were under twenty, although this figure increased in places such as Haverhill during sporadic periods of religious awakening (see Table 1). Throughout the latter decades of the seventeenth century and into the early decades of the eighteenth, evangelizing the rising generation emerged as a special concern of parents and ministers. Covenant renewal ceremonies brought entire generations of young people into the church. Many of the larger New England towns sponsored prayer societies for young men and women. Catechism classes played an increasingly important role in the weekly pastoral activities of clergymen.[100]

To be sure, a few young men and women were renowned for their precocious theological knowledge or exacting devotional routines. Stories of these pious prodigies developed into a relatively well-defined literary genre. John Brown filled his poignant account of the devastating throat distemper epidemic in Haverhill with reports of children who prayed and meditated during their final hours, dutifully answered catechetical questions, perused religious books, and confronted death with patience and resignation. Two decades earlier, Samuel Sewall helped to publish the dying testimony of a nine-year-old Boston girl named Elizabeth Butcher in a short pamphlet that went through three editions and more than a thousand copies. Cotton Mather and other ministers excerpted the religious writings of their young parishioners or extolled their exceptional piety in published funeral sermons and elegies. That most examples of early piety come from published accounts of adolescents who died young, however, indicates just how unusual they were. Although some godly youths, such as the Boston apprentice brazier John Coney, man-

99. Appendix B, Medfield, Mass., First Church, 10, 19; Appendix B, Haverhill, Mass., First Church, 47, 49, 92.

100. For additional data, see Moran, "Conditions of Religious Conversion," *Journal of Social History*, V (1972), 334–335; James Walsh, "The Great Awakening in the First Congregational Church of Woodbury, Connecticut," *WMQ*, XXVIII (1971), 552; Greven, "Youth, Maturity, and Religious Conversion," *EIHC*, CVIII (1972), 126–127; Moran, "Puritan Saint," 301–306; Moran, "Religious Renewal, Puritan Tribalism, and the Family in Seventeenth-Century Milford, Connecticut," *WMQ*, XXXVI (1979), 246–247; William F. Willingham, "The Conversion Experience during the Great Awakening in Windham, Connecticut," *Connecticut History*, XXI (1980), 44; and Minkema, "Old Age and Religion," *Church History*, LXX (2001), 688–689. On the emergence of prayer societies, see Ramsbottom, "Religious Society and the Family in Charlestown," 207–209.

aged to bear their "worldly Cross" with equanimity during their "Pilgrimage in this World," a far greater number of their contemporaries detoured through an adolescent counterculture rife with intemperate drinking, illicit sensuality, gaming, and loose talk.[101]

Religious and civic leaders recognized youth as a *"chusing time,"* and many young people chose rebellion over obedience. They gathered for frolics in barns, mills, and outbuildings, went night walking at taverns, coupled with sexual partners after training days or husking bees, or met in a variety of clandestine spaces to read titillating literature. Few young men and women managed to escape from this flourishing subculture. Their ranks included future clergymen such as Joseph Green of Salem Village, who lamented an adolescence spent in the pursuit of "faiding vanitys and pleasures of this world," including fowling, fishing, dancing, drinking, and card playing. Likewise, the aspiring but melancholic Maine minister Joseph Moody devoted much of his anguished devotional diary to lamenting a failed courtship and bewailing his inability to control his autoerotic impulses. Even Cotton Mather's son, Creasy, fathered an illegitimate child. Adolescent rebellion was neither unusual, nor isolated, nor restricted to the unchurched or the ungodly.[102]

Premarital intercourse ranked among the most pervasive forms of rebellious behavior among young people. Rising rates of bridal pregnancy suggest that sex among unmarried men and women was a common aspect of eighteenth-century courtship in an era that witnessed a gradual loosening of social surveillance and regulation. More than three dozen Haverhill residents appeared before the Essex County magistrates during Brown's pastorate to answer charges of bearing children out of wedlock or within seven months of marriage. Fined in the civil courts, many of these same individuals were forced

101. Brown, *Number of Deaths in Haverhil*, 1–69; Peterson, *Price of Redemption*, 92–95; Laurel Thatcher Ulrich, "Vertuous Women Found: New England Ministerial Literature, 1668–1735," *American Quarterly*, XXVIII (1976), 22–23; William Cooper, *The Service of God Recommended to the Choice of Young People* ... (Boston, 1726), 41, 80.

102. Morison, ed., "Commonplace Book of Joseph Green," CSM, *Pubs., Trans., 1973–1942*, XXXIV (1943), 237–238; Brian D. Carroll, "'I Indulged My Desire Too Freely': Sexuality, Spirituality, and the Sin of Self-Pollution in the Diary of Joseph Moody, 1720–1724," *WMQ*, LX (2003), 155–170; N. Ray Hiner, "Cotton Mather and His Children: The Evolution of a Parent Educator, 1686–1728," in Barbara Finkelstein, ed., *Regulated Children / Liberated Children: Education in Psychohistorical Perspective* (New York, 1979), 36–38; Benjamin Colman, *Early Piety Again Inculcated from Those Famous Words of Solomon* ... (Boston, 1720), 33 (quote). On the rise of provincial youth culture, see Ross W. Beales, Jr., "In Search of the Historical Child: Miniature Adulthood and Youth in Colonial New England," *American Quarterly*, XXVII (1975), 379–398; Hiner, "Adolescence in Eighteenth-Century America," *History of Childhood Quarterly*, III (1975), 253–280; and Roger Thompson, "Adolescent Culture in Colonial Massachusetts," *Journal of Family History*, IX (1984), 127–144.

to "acknowledge with shame" their "sin of Fornication or Uncleaness before marriage" before joining the Haverhill church in full communion. Brown's parishioners inevitably initiated disciplinary proceedings in a small number of cases where one or both partners had already affiliated with the church before their sexual indiscretions. The Haverhill minister also baptized a dozen "spurious" children of these unions. Many men and women disciplined for fornication hailed from prominent families, including several members of the Duston-Emerson clan and Elizabeth Main, the wife of a Harvard College graduate and the minister of Rochester, New Hampshire.[103]

Few writings from the early eighteenth century embodied the competing alternatives of youthful piety and adolescent rebellion better than the diary and commonplace book of Joseph Prince. While his older brothers Nathan and Thomas—the future minister of Boston's Old South Church—were studying at Harvard College, Joseph remained on his father's large estate in the coastal farming village of Rochester, Massachusetts. He spent his days raking and mowing hay, carting stones and animal dung, clearing, fencing, and plowing fields, slaughtering livestock, and cutting timber. Prince also prepared to follow in his father's footsteps as a civil magistrate. During the 1710s, he began recording an "Acompt of the books that I red out." Spanning nearly a decade, the unusual list of more than four dozen titles was impressive. The titles at the beginning of Prince's account were heavily weighted toward sermons and devotional tracts. In addition to reading the Bible from Genesis to Revelation twice over a period of seven or eight years, Prince examined classic works of practical divinity, hagiographies of prominent English saints, and Cotton Mather's *Wonders of the Invisible World*.[104]

As he entered his twenties, Prince's reading tastes shifted in significant

103. Appendix B, Haverhill, Mass., First Church, 137; Raymond, comp., "Records of First Parish, Haverhill," II, 105, 109, 114, 119, 122, 126, 128. See also the Confessions of Daniel and Elizabeth Bradley, Dec. 6, 1730, Elizabeth Main, Jan. 7, 1733, Richard Messer, Nov. 26, 1727, Daniel Roberds, Nov. 26, 1727, Disciplinary Cases, 1729–1739, Haverhill First Congregational Church Records. For premarital pregnancy rates, see Daniel Scott Smith and Michael S. Hindus, "Premarital Pregnancy in America, 1640–1971: An Overview and Interpretation," *Journal of Interdisciplinary History*, V (1975), 537–570. A calendar of Essex County bastardy cases involving Haverhill residents may be found in Melinde Lutz Sanborn, *Lost Babes: Fornication Abstracts from Court Records, Essex County, Massachusetts, 1692–1745* (Derry, N.H., 1992).

104. Joseph Prince, diary and commonplace book, 1705–1728, MS copy, [11], Frederick William Prince Papers, 1580–1988, Mss 310, NEHGS. For an annotated list of Prince's "Acompt," see Douglas L. Winiarski, "The Education of Joseph Prince: Reading Adolescent Culture in Eighteenth-Century New England," in Peter Benes, ed., *The Worlds of Children, 1620–1920*, Dublin Seminar for New England Folklife, Annual Proceedings 2002 (Boston, 2004), 61–64.

ways. Grown to physical maturity and in the twilight of his adolescence, yet still suffering through a period of protracted family dependence as he waited for his inheritance, he turned his attention to a broader range of subjects. Later entries included works of law, natural philosophy, geography, and world history as well as advice literature on polite speech and penmanship. At the same time, Prince repeatedly turned from his education to distinctly adolescent, illicit, and impious pursuits. He developed a fascination with judicial astrology, poring over works pertaining to the zodiac and a controversial book on the occult arts of fortune-telling and divination. Prince appears to have been especially concerned with gathering information for an astrological natal chart. His diary includes tables relating to the planets that ruled each hour of the day and personal information that might have been used by a local conjurer to cast predictive horoscopes on his behalf.[105]

In time, Prince's reading interests turned to women, courtship, and sex. Both he and his brother Nathan perused pornographic books such as *The English Rogue* and *The London Jilt*, which arrived in Boston in surprising numbers through the transatlantic book trade. One text that Joseph excerpted in his commonplace book, an unidentified volume on "Court Arts," included thinly veiled misogynistic verses that attempted to explain "Woman's Natuer" through the astrological categories of the "slippery fish," Pisces. Even more instructive was the "Witty Epigram on the Efects of the Love of Venus" that Prince also copied: "Cupid is V[u]lcan's Son Venus his wife / No wonder then He gets Lain all his Life." Interestingly enough, he appears to have been perusing the smutty limericks at about the same time he joined the Sandwich, Massachusetts, church in full communion.[106]

Provincial youth culture provoked ministers to excoriate the pride and lust of the rising generation in scores of sermons and pamphlets. The discourse of these jeremiads, in turn, seeped into numerous church admission testimonies, as potential communicants lamented that they had squandered the "opportunities and advantages" or failed to make "better improvement" of their godly upbringing. Many young people acknowledged that they were prone to "neglect and delay." In a particularly evocative example of this trope, Rowley lay-

105. Prince, diary and commonplace book, [8, 10–11, 22]. On the various uses of astrology in eighteenth-century America, both licit and illicit, see T. J. Tomlin, *A Divinity for All Persuasions: Almanacs and Early American Religious Life,* Religion in America (New York, 2014), 29–54.

106. Prince, diary and commonplace book, [10, 21]; Roger Thompson, "The Puritans and Prurience: Aspects of the Restoration Book Trade," in H. C. Allen and Thompson, eds., *Contrast and Connection: Bicentennial Essays in Anglo-American History* (Athens, Ohio, 1976), 51; Sandwich, Mass., First Church Records, 1692–1853, Mss 638, NEHGS.

man Nathaniel Brown remembered his lusty bachelor days, during which he lived with a group of young men and "minded not anything of Religion a great while, neither praying nor asking gods blessing on our meat." He pursued a wild life for several years and was "much for company and merriment" until his elder brother and mother died a week apart during the winter of 1683. Brown soon contracted a serious illness and vowed to reform and "serve the Lord better if I should live." Although he found more comfort in religious observances than in his former entertainments, Brown continued to hold back from joining the church for more than a decade, thinking "I would do more after marriage."[107]

Brown's frank acknowledgment of the life-course transition that prompted his decision to close with the Rowley church resonated with many young people. Scores of church membership candidates admitted to having been stirred up to religious duties as children, only to watch their youthful convictions wear away as the "cares and troubles of the ☉ [world]" burst in on them. Despite receiving "good Consels and Instrucions" from her parents, a Medfield woman admitted that the Devil had been busily telling her that there would be "time enough here after to seek and seecuer an Intrest In Jesus Christ." More frequently, adolescents simply assumed that they were "too young to serve the LORD." Mary Merrill of Haverhill initially believed that she was not capable of "understanding the nature and End" of the Lord's Supper as a youth but "tho't If I lived to Years of adult age I would not neglect this Duty." "I thot I had more need to seek to get something of this world first," Haverhill's John Bayley summarized, "and it would be time eno', for the other after."[108]

Although adolescence remained a vaguely defined stage in the physical, social, and religious development of provincial New Englanders, just about everyone reached a crucial turning point sometime after their twentieth year. Benjamin Phinney of Barnstable spoke for many members of the rising generation when he recalled in his 1717 relation that he had met with "new duties and new difficulties" after God brought him into a "married State." "I began to flatter myself that when I Come to be Settled in the World I should have more time to mind the Business of Religion," echoed a Freetown, Massachu-

---

107. Appendix B, Medfield, Mass., First Church, 6, 46, 62; Relation of Nathaniel Brown, Apr. 18, 1699, Mss C77, NEHGS. For a sample of provincial jeremiads preached against the sins and vanities of the rising generation, see Gildrie, *The Profane, the Civil, and the Godly,* 104–109.

108. Appendix B, Haverhill, Mass., First Church, 11, 148, 189; Appendix B, Medfield, Mass., First Church, 34; Relation of Daniel Bliss, Oct. 4, 1730, Ser. II, folder 229, Emerson Family Papers, 1699–1939, MS Am 1280.235, HL.

setts, woman several decades later, "But when I Come to Settle in a family I found my Cares greate and my Time les than before." Entering into the "married estate," as Mary Rockwood of Medfield candidly explained, brought unrelenting "sorrowes, troubles, and afflictions"—events that frequently wrenched young adults from the carefree slumbers of adolescence.[109]

■ The opening words of Hannah Duston's 1724 church admission testimony—"I Desire to be thankful that I was born in a Land of Light"—reflected the central place of the family in shaping early-eighteenth-century Congregational piety. Nearly half of all candidates in Haverhill started their relations with a narrow range of stock phrases relating to their religious pedigree. References to their birth in New England—a divinely favored land of light—were most common, followed by expressions of thanksgiving for growing up under the means of grace. Duston and a few others emphasized that their parents had presented them for baptism as infants or provided them with a religious education. Mary Eaton's 1727 testimony was unusual only insofar as she catalogued all of the tropes that appeared with varying frequency in the relations of other prospective Haverhill church members. "I desire to be thankful that I was born in a land where the Glorious gopel is so plentifully preached," she began, "where we injoy the prevelidge of having the bible which Contain[s] gods will and our duty, that I was babtized in infancy, [and] that I have had the advantage of a good Education from my parents."[110]

Statements of religious pedigree instantly conveyed important information to the assembled congregation that the candidate had been raised within the community of the godly. By the turn of the eighteenth century, these credentialing statements appeared with increasing frequency in church admission testimonies from Boston to the Connecticut Valley. They also separated written relations from the oral narratives of New England's founding generation. During the decades following the puritan Great Migration, church membership candidates were far more likely to complain of the deficiencies of their religious upbringing. Some frankly admitted that they had been "brought up ignorantly," under "popery," or in a "place where there was bad examples" in England. Among the more than 350 extant relations composed between 1690

109. Relation of Benjamin Phinney, n.d. [circa June 30, 1717]; J. M. Bumsted, ed., "Emotion in Colonial America: Some Relations of Conversion Experience in Freetown, Massachusetts, 1749–1770," *NEQ*, XLIX (1976), 101; Appendix B, Medfield, Mass., First Church, 90. For the full texts of Phinney's and Rockwood's relations, see Appendix C.

110. Appendix B, Haverhill, Mass., First Church, 51, 62. For statistical evidence, see Winiarski, "Gendered 'Relations' in Haverhill," in Benes, ed., *In Our Own Words*, I, 64–66.

and 1740, by contrast, only one prospective communicant—an English emigre raised in Newfoundland who joined the Medfield church in 1721—questioned his religious heritage.[111]

Candidates' repeated references to their religious upbringings were a sign of the times, an index of the waxing authority of the family in a developing colonial society, and a marker of the increasingly tribal nature of Congregational culture. Increase Mather of Boston famously proclaimed that salvation sprang from the "loins of godly parents." Other clergymen likened the "little commonwealth" to nurseries of a godly society. Ministers compared the Gospel to the milk of nursing mothers, and this striking motif appeared in gravestone iconography beginning late in the seventeenth century. Some clergymen referred to their adult parishioners as "church-children," descendants of families in which one or both parents had affiliated in full communion. Around 1700, most Congregational ministers started keeping separate lists for baptized children in their record books. Families, too, began creating private birth registers in their diaries and account books, or they listed genealogical events in the front of their Bibles. Even the spatial organization of provincial meetinghouses and burial grounds symbolized the increasing authority of clan and kin in religious affairs. During the early decades of the eighteenth century, informal family burial plots developed in most town cemeteries, while family pew boxes replaced the gender-segregated benches of an earlier era.[112]

Church affiliation in towns like Haverhill followed generational cycles, as the children of established families came of age and took their place within a dense network of kin and neighbors. Scions of core parish families consistently joined at earlier ages than transient townspeople and newcomers, who rarely formed lasting ties to religious institutions. Between 1674 and 1700,

111. Selement and Woolley, eds., *Thomas Shepard's Confessions*, CSM, *Pubs., Colls.*, LVIII (1981), 93, 115, 125; Appendix B, Medfield, Mass., First Church, 74.

112. Edmund S. Morgan, *The Puritan Family: Religion and Domestic Relations in Seventeenth-Cenutry New England*, rev. ed. (New York, 1966), 143, 168, 182; John Demos, *A Little Commonwealth: Family Life in Plymouth Colony* (New York, 1970), [xix]; *Plymouth Church Records*, CSM, *Pubs.*, XXII (1920), 158; Allan I. Ludwig, *Graven Images: New England Stonecarving and Its Symbols, 1650–1815* (Middletown, Conn., 1966), 155–160; Karin Wulf, "Bible, King, and Common Law: Genealogical Literacies and Family History Practices in British America," *EAS*, X (2012), 467–502; Ian W. Brown, "The New England Cemetery as a Cultural Landscape," in Steven Lubar and W. David Kingery, eds., *History from Things: Essays on Material Culture* (Washington, D.C., 1993), 140–159; Robert J. Dinkin, "Seating the Meetinghouse in Early Massachusetts," in Robert Blair St. George, ed., *Material Life in America, 1600–1800* (Boston, 1988), 407–418. Edmund Morgan first introduced the concept of "Puritan tribalism" in the *Puritan Family*, 161–186, then tempered his initial negative assessment in *Visible Saints*, 136–138. For a summary and critique, see Moran and Vinovskis, "Puritan Family and Religion," in Moran and Vinovskis, eds., *Religion, Family, and the Life Course*, 13–32.

nearly three-quarters of all church members in Stonington, Connecticut, hailed from a pool of less than two dozen families. Relatives of diarist Manasseh Minor alone accounted for one in ten new communicants. In New Haven, more than 80 percent of all admitted men and women between 1668 and 1758 came from prominent church families. Between one-quarter and one-third had siblings in full communion; 60 percent grew up in a family in which one or both parents were members; and half produced progeny that eventually joined the church.[113]

When prospective church members gave thanks to God for "loyns" that had "folen in such pleasant places as under the means of the gospel," or when they acknowledged that the "Lines" of their "habitation" had been "Laid out in a Land of Light," they claimed church membership as a birthright, a privilege that they would soon seek to pass down to their own children. Joining the church required prospective communicants to close with Christ "on his own terms." It meant taking "God as the portion of my Soul." As one Boston merchant remarked in a Bible inscription written for posterity, it meant allowing God to "choose your inheritance" and to "carry this coppie before the Court of heaven and Earth." Drawn from deeds and probate records, the stock phrases that lent structure to early-eighteenth-century church relations and other devotional writings resonated with the emerging life experiences of young adults who were marrying, starting families, inheriting property, building homes, improving farms, completing apprenticeships, and assuming a wide variety of adult responsibilities.[114]

Samuel Prince, father of the rebellious adolescent Rochester diarist, drew up a set of instructions that he intended to pass on to his children after his death. The documents triangulated among a cluster of literary allusions that combined mercantile discourse with the conventions of probate records and marriage vows. "I do with all my power accept of thee for my Lord and King," Prince wrote in his personal covenant, "for my head and husband, my only portion, to love honor and obey thee, to cleave unto thee through all changes

---

113. Moran, "Puritan Saint," 174–188, 342–343; Harry S. Stout and Catherine Brekus, "A New England Congregation: Center Church, New Haven, 1638–1989," in James P. Wind and James W. Lewis, eds., *American Congregations*, I, *Portraits of Twelve Religious Communities* (Chicago, 1994), 32–34. See also Moran, "Religious Renewal, Puritan Tribalism, and the Family," *WMQ*, XXXVI (1979), 250–253; and Stephen R. Grossbart, "Seeking the Divine Favor: Conversion and Church Admission in Eastern Connecticut, 1711–1832," *WMQ*, XLVI (1989), 731–732.

114. Appendix B, Boston, Third (Old South) Church, 7; Appendix B, Medfield, Mass., First Church, 46, 49; Relation of Phineas Northrop, n.d., Strong Family Collection; Minkema, ed., "Lynn End 'Earthquake' Relations," *NEQ*, LXIX (1996), 486; "Two Old Bibles," *EIHC*, VI (1864), 160.

and conditions of peace or trouble, joy and sorrow, riches or poverty, prosperity or adversity, and to take my lot with thee as it falls, and this unto death." But Jesus was more than an eligible marriage suitor. Switching metaphors, Prince suggested that Christ was also his family's spiritual patrimony—literally, their inheritance. Turning to the language of probate courts, Prince drafted a letter of advice "under hand and seal" in which he exhorted his children to "renounce the world with all its vanities and delights" and "choose Christ for your portion." Later in Prince's instructions, Jesus assumed the role of a steadfast business partner and financier who propounded the terms of eternal salvation, served as "surety to pay all our debts and enrich us with his treasures," and ratified his covenant in heaven.[115]

Even as he rejected the world as "none of my portion," Prince recast his Lord and Savior in his own image: a patriarch who controlled his family's patrimony, a well-connected merchant and prosperous bondholder, a probate officer and civil magistrate. That he kept his personal covenant and instructions to his children in his desk, folded up with his will and other important legal documents, was telling. Coming of age and assuming adult status within the hierarchical world of provincial New England stood as powerful metaphors for salvation itself. The benefits that accrued to anyone willing to submit to Christ as husband, enter into commerce with God, and choose a heavenly portion were extensive. Prince hinted that those who used "all means and endeavors" to live up to the "terms" of his "Holy Covenant" could expect not only to be sustained "through faith unto salvation" but would earn God's "wages" and "special favor" in this world: aid in the performance of religious duties, succor in times of adversity, and temporal prosperity.[116]

During the early decades of the eighteenth century, social maturation was a painfully slow process that was tied to complex strategies of family preservation. Aging patriarchs sought to settle their children in proper marriages and transfer the land necessary for them to attain a flourishing economic competency. Fathers subtly controlled the lives of their children by providing them with gifts of property and dowries of movable goods in return for respectful service during their years of retirement. As material standards of living rose and undivided lands in many towns grew scarce during the eigh-

115. Samuel Prince, memorandum, 1685, box 3, Pulsifer Family Papers, 1680–1890, Mss 1071, NEHGS. On the prevalence of marital imagery in puritan sermon literature, see Michael P. Winship, "Behold the Bridegroom Cometh! Marital Imagery in Massachusetts Preaching, 1630–1730," *EAL*, XXVII (1992), 170–184; and Richard Godbeer, "'Love Raptures': Marital, Romantic, and Erotic Images of Jesus Christ in Puritan New England, 1670–1730," *NEQ*, LXVIII (1995), 355–384.

116. Prince, memorandum, 1685, Pulsifer Family Papers.

teenth century, middling families at times found it difficult to settle their sons and daughters. Young men often attained the independence of adulthood at a maddeningly slow pace. Eldest sons labored for years under the close supervision of their fathers as they angled for a larger portion of their inheritance and an opportunity to work their own land. Middle children, on the other hand, might have married at earlier ages, but they frequently faced a more precarious existence outside the comfortable surroundings of their natal towns, while youngest sons found themselves saddled with responsibilities to care for their aging parents.[117]

Once established in their own households, husbands and their wives faced daunting new challenges. The early years of family formation were fraught with anxiety and tension, as the loud calls of divine providence came quickly and often. Even as couples reached the peak of their mental and physical potential, they watched helplessly as their parents, siblings, relatives, and neighbors suffered and died. Mothers endured the pain of childbirth roughly every other year for much of their adult lives. Most women experienced at least one stillbirth, miscarriage, or delivery complication during their reproductive years. Completed families typically included between six and ten children, but one in three would die young as mortality rates steadily increased during the early decades of the eighteenth century. Warfare, crop failures, business reversals, and neighborhood squabbles continually threatened to unmake the orderly

117. In this and the two paragraphs that follow, I attempt to summarize an extensive body of scholarship on the family life-course in early New England by historical demographers and social historians. Foundational articles include Daniel Scott Smith, "Parental Power and Marriage Patterns: An Analysis of Historical Trends in Hingham, Massachusetts," *Journal of Marriage and the Family,* XXXV (1973), 419–428; John J. Waters, "Patrimony, Succession, and Social Stability: Guilford, Connecticut in the Eighteenth Century," *Perspectives in American History,* X (1976), 131–160; Thomas R. Cole, "Family, Settlement, and Migration in Southeastern Massachusetts, 1650–1805: The Case for Regional Analysis," *NEHGR,* CXXXII (1978), 171–185; and Waters, "Family, Inheritance, and Migration in Colonial New England: The Evidence from Guilford, Connecticut," *WMQ,* XXXIX (1982), 64–86. See also classic community studies by Demos, *Little Commonwealth;* Greven, *Four Generations;* Kenneth A. Lockridge, *A New England Town: The First Hundred Years: Dedham, Massachusetts, 1636–1736,* enlarged ed. (New York, 1985); Paul Boyer and Stephen Nissenbaum, *Salem Possessed: The Social Origins of Witchcraft* (Cambridge, Mass., 1974); Robert A. Gross, *The Minutemen and Their World* (New York, 1976); Tracy, *Jonathan Edwards;* and Douglas Lamar Jones, *Village and Seaport: Migration and Society in Eighteenth-Century Massachusetts* (Hanover, N.H., 1981). For monographs on the family and economy, see Jackson Turner Main, *Society and Economy in Colonial Connecticut* (Princeton, N.J., 1985); and Daniel Vickers, *Farmers and Fishermen: Two Centuries of Work in Essex County, Massachusetts, 1630–1853* (Chapel Hill, N.C., 1994). For cultural histories of family life, see Ulrich, *Good Wives;* Wilson, *Ye Heart of a Man;* Judith S. Graham, *Puritan Family Life: The Diary of Samuel Sewall* (Boston, 2000); and Gloria L. Main, *Peoples of a Spacious Land: Families and Cultures in Colonial New England* (Cambridge, Mass., 2001).

world of farmers, artisans, merchants, and mariners. Parents worried about the future, not just for their own souls, but for the health, safety, success, and salvation of their progeny.

A large family created its own problems. Multiple children exposed the household to perennial sickness and stretched the resources of the family to the breaking point. Middling yeomen worked ceaselessly to make ends meet. They rented land and hired day laborers to wrest their economic competency from the soil. Younger men in this stage of their lives started at the bottom rungs of the social ladder. Only with good fortune and the passage of time did fathers marshal the resources necessary to expand their landholdings and purchase the material possessions that supported a comfortable standard of living. But it was at just this point that the family life cycle turned again, as aging patriarchs shifted their attention to retirement and the establishment of the rising generation.

The rhythms of church affiliation correlated closely with these broader patterns of social maturation. Religious duties remained the peculiar responsibility of married adults who, in the words of the Cambridge *Platform*, had "grown up unto years of discretion." Men in the rural farming villages and the port towns of New England married in their mid-twenties; women did so several years earlier. In both cases, the mean age at admission to full communion lagged between five and ten years behind (Table 1). More than two-thirds of all prospective church members in Haverhill were married, and in many towns this figure was even higher. By the time they joined the church, most candidates had already made the transition to adulthood, starting families, acquiring or inheriting land, amassing a middling estate, and serving in a town office. Husbands and wives, moreover, frequently made their decision to affiliate together. More than one in four married women and nearly one in three married men joined the Haverhill church on the same day as their spouse. A few churches went so far as to allow these co-covenanting spouses to submit a joint relation of faith.[118]

118. Walker, comp., *Creeds and Platforms of Congregationalism*, 224. Data on co-covenanting spouses in Haverhill based on sources cited in Appendix A. See also J. M. Bumsted, "Religion, Finance, and Democracy in Massachusetts: The Town of Norton as a Case Study," *JAH*, LVII (1971), 823–824; Greven, "Youth, Maturity, and Religious Conversion," *EIHC*, CVIII (1972), 126–129; Moran, "Conditions of Religious Conversion in the First Society of Norwich," *Journal of Social History*, V (1972), 334–335; Walsh, "Great Awakening in the First Congregational Church of Woodbury," *WMQ*, XXVIII (1971), 552; Moran, "Puritan Saint," 310–316; and Stout and Brekus, "New England Congregation," in Wind and Lewis, eds., *American Congregations*, I, 30–32. Daniel Scott Smith summarizes marriage data in "The Demographic History of Colonial New England," *Journal of Economic History*, XXXII (1972), 176–177. The earliest surviving example of a joint church admission testimony ap-

Young parents affiliated with the church as part of a broader protective family strategy designed to ensure that their children would be raised in the gospel land of light. Baptism was the key. The close correspondence between church membership and family formation was particularly evident in parishes such as Chilmark, Massachusetts, and Berwick, Maine, where ministers kept a single running chronicle of church affairs, rather than separate lists of admissions, baptisms, and church votes. "John Chamberlane and Hannah his wife were received to full communion," wrote minister Thomas Cheever of Rumney Marsh (now Revere), Massachusetts, on July 21, 1717, in what was a typical example. One week later, he recorded the baptism of the Chamberlane's five children on the next available line in his record book. Of the more than one hundred families that affiliated with the Harwich, Massachusetts, church between 1700 and 1740, three-quarters presented at least one child for baptism within a month's time. A similar study of 446 parents from 340 families in Beverly, Massachusetts, between 1702 and 1765 found that 52 percent brought children for baptism the same day that they covenanted with the church, an additional 15 percent did so within a few weeks, and 12 percent were expecting their first child at the time they were propounded to full communion.[119]

Once affiliated with a church, parents carried their children to the baptismal basin with a regularity that eventually rivaled colonial Virginia, where an inclusive Anglican parish system ensured widespread rates of infant baptism. In Haverhill, 79 percent of all children baptized between 1694 and 1740 were younger than one year old (Table 2). In other towns, including Hingham, Northampton, and Suffield, Massachusetts, the proportion of children baptized within the first year of life soared to more than 90 percent by 1740. These figures marked a significant upturn from seventeenth-century Connecticut, where restrictive church membership requirements impelled more than two in five families to wait until after the birth of their third child before closing with the church and parents were likely to present at least two chil-

---

pears to be the 1737 relation of Rachel and Edward Foster (Appendix B, Sturbridge, Mass., First Church, 9). See also the 1721 relations of James and Mary New, which were composed on a single sheet of paper (Appendix B, Medfield, Mass., First Church, 74–75).

119. Charles Edward Banks, ed., "Diary of Rev. William Homes of Chilmark, Martha's Vineyard, 1689–1746," *NEHGR*, XLIX (1895), 413–416, L (1896), 155–166; Joseph Crook Anderson II, ed., *Records of the First and Second Churches of Berwick, Maine*, Maine Genealogical Society Special Publication, XXXIII (Rockport, Maine, 1999), 1–51; James F. Cooper, Jr., and Kenneth P. Minkema, eds., *The Colonial Church Records of the First Church of Reading (Wakefield) and the First Church of Rumney Marsh (Revere)*, CSM, *Pubs.*, LXXII (Boston, 2006), 229; Winiarski, "All Manner of Error and Delusion," 423; Anne Speerschneider Brown, "'Bound Up in a Bundle of Life': The Social Meaning of Religious Practice in Northeastern Massachusetts, 1700–1765" (Ph.D. diss., Boston University, 1995), 69n.

TABLE 1 Number, Age, and Marital Status of Men and Women Admitted to Full Communion in Selected Eighteenth-Century New England Churches

Church	N			% of Total		Annual Average		Under 20 (%)	
	Men	Women	Total	Men	Women	Men	Women	Men	Women
Hampton, N.H., First Church									
1697–1740	224	417	641	34.9	65.1	5.1	9.5	4.4	16.8
1741–1744	70	73	143	49.0	51.0	17.5	18.3	20.6	45.5
1745–1766	60	108	168	35.7	64.3	2.7	4.9	6.9	44.0
Haverhill, Mass., First Church									
1694–1740	193	319	512	37.7	62.3	4.1	6.8	8.2	26.8
1741–1744	8	29	37	21.6	78.4	2.0	7.3	0.0	36.0
1745–1774	20	40	60	33.3	66.7	0.7	1.3	0.0	10.8
Hingham, Mass., First Church									
1718–1740	100	129	229	43.7	56.3	4.3	5.6	2.1	0.9
1741–1744	25	50	75	33.3	66.7	6.3	12.5	19.0	17.0
1745–1787	97	181	278	34.9	65.1	2.3	4.2	3.2	10.1
Medfield, Mass., First Church									
1697–1740	125	179	304	41.1	58.9	2.8	4.1	5.0	8.2
1741–1744	29	41	70	41.4	58.6	7.3	10.3	28.0	25.0
1745–1769	22	34	56	39.3	60.7	0.8	1.4	5.3	3.3
Norwich, Conn., First Church									
1700–1740	74	132	206	35.9	64.1	1.8	3.2	1.4	4.3
1741–1744	35	61	96	36.5	63.5	8.8	15.3	15.6	23.1
1745–1778	29	43	72	40.3	59.7	0.9	1.3	0.0	9.4
Sandwich, Mass., First Church									
1695–1740	92	165	257	35.8	64.2	2.0	3.6	1.5	13.0
1741–1744	10	20	30	33.3	66.7	2.5	5.0	0.0	35.3
1745–1784	57	139	196	29.1	70.9	1.4	3.5	2.0	9.7
Suffield, Mass. (Conn. after 1749), First Church									
1710–1740	141	168	309	45.6	54.4	4.5	5.4	13.5	18.4
1741–1744	102	129	231	44.2	55.8	25.5	32.3	30.4	51.8
1745–1793	23	55	78	29.5	70.5	0.5	1.1	4.5	18.0
Westborough, Mass., First Church									
1724–1740	48	77	125	38.4	61.6	2.8	4.5	2.1	17.9
1741–1744	12	16	28	42.9	57.1	3.0	4.0	9.1	20.0
1745–1782	64	103	167	38.3	61.7	1.7	2.7	0.0	5.6

Note: Age and marital status figures based on known data only. Age cohorts may not sum to 100 percent as a result of rounding. Date ranges delimited by extant church records and ministers' pastorates. The "Married" column includes a small number of widows and widowers.

Source: Appendix A.

20–39 (%)		40–59 (%)		60 and Over (%)		Mean Age		Married (%)	
Men	Women	Men	Women	Men	Women	Men	Women	Men	Women
70.6	68.5	21.1	12.7	3.9	2.0	33.3	28.9	76.3	70.2
46.0	50.0	25.4	4.5	7.9	0.0	35.0	22.4	52.9	29.2
86.2	52.7	5.2	2.2	1.7	1.1	27.2	22.3	40.7	41.1
65.3	54.4	22.4	16.5	4.1	2.3	32.3	28.0	71.1	67.0
75.0	64.0	12.5	0.0	12.5	0.0	29.4	23.5	50.0	56.0
94.1	86.5	5.9	2.7	0.0	0.0	28.6	25.0	60.0	62.5
72.2	77.6	18.6	18.1	7.2	3.4	35.7	33.2	73.7	80.8
61.9	68.1	19.0	12.8	0.0	2.1	31.2	30.1	72.0	64.8
75.5	75.0	13.8	11.9	7.4	3.0	34.8	30.1	75.8	73.1
65.3	74.1	24.8	17.1	5.0	0.6	35.5	30.5	75.2	72.6
60.0	58.3	8.0	13.9	4.0	2.8	28.5	28.4	28.6	47.5
89.5	86.7	0.0	6.7	5.3	3.3	28.3	28.9	80.0	61.8
75.7	85.2	18.6	10.4	4.3	0.0	34.3	29.3	87.8	82.6
71.9	71.2	6.3	3.8	6.3	1.9	30.8	25.6	58.8	41.7
62.5	75.0	25.0	15.6	12.5	0.0	37.0	30.6	76.9	76.7
67.6	72.4	23.5	13.0	7.4	1.6	36.2	30.2	78.0	76.5
90.0	64.7	10.0	0.0	0.0	0.0	30.3	21.9	80.0	33.3
70.0	77.9	22.0	11.5	6.0	0.9	37.3	29.5	91.1	73.3
58.6	65.3	24.1	16.3	3.8	0.0	33.0	29.6	68.3	72.9
59.8	44.7	8.7	2.6	1.1	0.9	27.2	21.8	47.5	28.2
72.7	74.0	22.7	6.0	0.0	2.0	31.9	28.4	95.6	66.0
87.2	68.7	10.6	13.4	0.0	0.0	30.0	28.0	87.5	81.8
63.6	66.7	27.3	13.3	0.0	0.0	32.9	26.3	66.7	56.3
93.2	91.0	6.8	3.4	0.0	0.0	29.7	26.6	87.5	79.6

TABLE 2 Age of Children Presented for Baptism in Selected New England Churches to 1740

Church	N	Less than 1 Year (%)	1–2 Years (%)	3–15 Years (%)
Hampton, N.H., First Church (1696–1740)	1236	72.2	8.2	19.7
Haverhill, Mass., First Church (1694–1740)	1357	78.8	8.9	12.2
Hingham, Mass., First Church (1718–1740)	742	94.3	3.5	2.2
Medfield, Mass., First Church (1697–1740)	884	72.9	7.6	19.6
Norwich, Conn., First Church (1701–1740)	1047	79.7	10.5	9.8
Sandwich, Mass., First Church (1694–1740)	476	48.3	10.5	41.2
Suffield, Mass. (now Conn.), First Church (1710–1740)	883	93.7	3.1	3.3
Westborough, Mass., First Church (1724–1740)	328	86.3	8.2	5.5

Note: Data excludes adult baptisms (aged sixteeen and over) and children whose birthdate remains unknown. Age cohorts may not sum to 100 percent as a result of rounding. Date ranges delimited by extant church records.

Source: Appendix A.

dren at their first baptismal event. During John Brown's pastorate, by contrast, 79 percent of all Haverhill families presented their children singly and in order, beginning with the eldest. In many churches, including Suffield, and Westborough, Massachusetts, and Norwich, Connecticut, this figure was even higher; and in Hingham the rate of individual baptismal presentations approached 100 percent (Table 3).[120]

These baptismal figures suggest that provincial New Englanders were growing more insistent about access to the sacrament during the early decades of the eighteenth century. As the overall health of the region declined, anxious parents pressed their ministers to baptize sick and dying children in their own homes—and often on a weekday. Private baptism, however, was

120. Minkema, "Old Age and Religion," *Church History*, LXX (2001), 698–699; Moran, "Puritan Saint," 163–164. See also Brown, "'Bound Up in a Bundle of Life,'" 245. For comparative data from Virginia, see John K. Nelson, *A Blessed Company: Parishes, Parsons, and Parishioners in Anglican Virginia, 1690–1776* (Chapel Hill, N.C., 2001), 211–213, 242–244, 328.

TABLE 3 Total Number of Children Presented at First Family Baptismal
Presentation in Selected New England Churches to 1740

Church	Families (N)	Number of Children Presented (%)			
		1	2	3	4+
Hampton, N.H., First Church					
(1696–1740)	336	64.3	14.0	10.4	11.3
Haverhill, Mass., First Church					
(1694–1740)	259	79.4	8.0	4.9	7.7
Hingham, Mass., First Church					
(1718–1740)	201	97.5	1.0	1.0	0.5
Medfield, Mass., First Church					
(1697–1740)	221	67.0	11.8	7.7	13.6
Norwich, Conn., First Church					
(1701–1740)	290	78.6	12.4	4.8	4.1
Sandwich, Mass., First Church					
(1694–1740)	122	40.2	10.7	18.9	30.3
Suffield, Mass. (now Conn.),					
First Church (1710–1740)	205	96.1	2.9	0.5	0.5
Westborough, Mass., First Church					
(1724–1740)	70	82.9	14.3	2.9	0.0

Note: Date ranges delimited by extant church records.
Source: See Appendix A.

a controversial innovation. In 1716, for example, Middleborough, Massachusetts, church members considered Nathaniel Winslow's request to have his
child baptized in his "own house by reason of Its weaknes." Minister Peter
Thacher rejected his plea, asserting that "Baptism was not Necessary to salvation." During the next several decades, similar requests surfaced in many
towns. The Westborough church debated the issue of private baptisms the
following decade, as did the Bradford ministerial association to which John
Brown belonged. The Haverhill minister conducted his first midweek, private baptism for a dying infant during the summer of 1729. Most eighteenth-
century church record books contain an entry written sometime between 1710
and 1740 in which a clergyman agreed to perform baptismal ceremonies in a
"more private way" on behalf of children that were "dangerously sick and not
capable of being carried forth to Publick."[121]

121. Middleboro, Mass., First Congregational Church Records, 1707–1821, frame 101, CL
(available online at NEHH); Westborough Congregational Church Records, 17–18; Brad-

The rise of private baptisms during the first half of the eighteenth century was one of several important ecclesiastical reforms through which ministers and lay people worked to align church affiliation practices with the imperatives of family formation. The most famous of these innovations was the ritual that later critics would deride as the "Halfway Covenant." During the contentious Synod of 1662, clergymen from across the puritan colonies agreed to allow the children of full church members to present their offspring for baptism without passing through the test of a relation. By 1700, most New England churches had adopted the practice of *"owning the Covenant,"* which rapidly expanded to serve a variety of needs. In Dorchester and Reading, Massachusetts, the custom developed during the 1670s into mass ceremonies for adolescents and young adults. Covenant owners soon emerged as an entirely new class of affiliated parishioners in churches such as Boston's Old South. Of the more than two hundred people who owned the covenant in Norwich between 1717 and 1740, fewer than one in five progressed to full church membership. Over time, the rite evolved as a proving ground for newcomers, families with limited ties to the church, and socially disenfranchised native American servants and enslaved African Americans.[122]

Covenant owners affiliated at earlier ages than those who joined as full church members. In Haverhill, women did so in their late teens and early twenties; men in their mid-twenties. A larger proportion of adolescents and a more balanced ratio of men and women chose this distinctive method of affilia-

---

ford Ministers' Association, Records, 10; Raymond, comp., "Records of First Parish, Haverhill," I, 127; Upham, ed., *Records of the First Church in Beverly,* 189 (quote); Richard A. Wheeler, *History of the First Congregational Church, Stonington, Conn., 1674–1874* ... (Norwich, Conn., 1875), 218 (quote). On the rise of private baptisms during the 1720s and 1730s, see Holifield, *Covenant Sealed,* 192; and Brown, "'Bound Up in a Bundle of Life,'" 53–56. For a sample of churches that addressed this issue during the early decades of the eighteenth century, see Sharples, ed., *Records of the Church of Christ at Cambridge,* 112; Warren Brown, *History of Hampton Falls, N.H.,* 2 vols. (Concord, N.H., 1900–1918), II, 104; L. Vernon Briggs, *History and Records of the First Congregational Church, Hanover, Mass., 1727–1865* ... (Boston, 1895), 121; *Historical Catalogue of the First Church in Hartford, 1633–1885* (Hartford, Conn., 1885), 204; and Henry S. Nourse, ed., *The Birth, Marriage, and Death Register, Church Records and Epitaphs of Lancaster, Massachusetts, 1643–1850* (Lancaster, Mass., 1890), 289.

122. Walker, comp., *Creeds and Platforms of Congregationalism,* 314; Robert G. Pope, *The Half-Way Covenant: Church Membership in Puritan New England* (Princeton, N.J., 1969), 206–238, 272–276; J. M. Bumsted, "Revivalism and Separatism in New England: The First Society of Norwich, Connecticut, as a Case Study," *WMQ,* XXIV (1967), 596–597. See also Ross W. Beales, Jr., "The Half-Way Covenant and Religious Scrupulosity: The First Church of Dorchester, Massachusetts, as a Test Case," *WMQ,* XXXI (1974), 465–480; and Katharine Gerbner, "Beyond the 'Halfway Covenant': Church Membership, Extended Baptism, and Outreach in Cambridge, Massachusetts, 1656–1667," *NEQ,* LXXXV (2012), 281–301. On the origins of the phrase "Halfway Covenant," see Part 5, note 27, below.

tion (Table 4). More than half—and in some churches nearly three-quarters—of all married covenant owners affiliated together. Many co-covenanting parents brought children to be baptized on the same day or within a few weeks. Since half of all covenant owners in Haverhill were single, they were prepared to raise their children in the gospel land of light as they moved into the married estate. Even in churches where relatively few people embraced the new practice, the ritual innovation of owning the covenant promoted a culture of greater inclusivity that helped to ensure broad participation in the life of the church.[123]

In the end, the same family concerns that drove men and women to affiliate as covenant owners continued to dominate their religious practices as adults. Diarists such as John Paine worried constantly about the health of their households and communities. Like many of his contemporaries, the Cape Cod deacon wrote in his religious journal intermittently—roughly twice a year between 1695 and 1718—and most of the entries reflected his attempts to come to terms with the rigorous challenges of family life. The deaths and illnesses of his children, servants, and neighbors precipitated two out of every three meditations; his wife's childbirth travails accounted for the other third. The dual imperatives of preparing diligently for salvation and employing the means of grace to protect the lives of loved ones appeared side by side in the journal—often competing for space in a single entry. In Paine's several birthday meditations, the deacon envisioned his life as a solitary "Earthly pilgramage" toward a heavenly destination. Each year, as he looked back down the road that he had traveled, Paine bewailed his sinful failings. Only God's free grace preserved the ever-wandering pilgrim, "for it is not in man that walketh to direct his own Steps." Paine also begged God to preserve his family. "Spare us one year longer" was his constant refrain. In times of recurrent hardship, pious parents never worried solely about their eternal estates, nor did they question the salvation of their dying children. Preparation for salvation and protection from misfortune—early-eighteenth-century theology spoke to both the soteriological yearnings and temporal needs of provincial New England's weary parents.[124]

■ Hardships affecting men came at irregular intervals—a mill accident, an epidemic, a military campaign, a business reversal—but women like Haverhill's Mother Duston suffered the dangers and difficulties of childbirth every

---

123. Data on co-covenanting spouses derived from sources cited in Appendix A.

124. "Deacon John Paine's Journal," *Mayflower Descendant,* IX (1907), 50, 97, 99. For a similar argument, see Wilson, *Ye Heart of a Man,* 132–139.

TABLE 4 Number, Age, and Marital Status of Men and Women Owning the Covenant in Selected New England Churches to 1740

Church	N			% of Total		Annual Average		Under 20 (%)	
	Men	Women	Total	Men	Women	Men	Women	Men	Women
Hampton, N.H., First Church (1713–1740)									
	38	39	77	49.4	50.6	1.4	1.4	17.6	35.5
Haverhill, Mass., First Church (1694–1740)									
	144	196	340	42.4	57.6	3.1	4.2	22.1	51.1
Medfield, Mass., First Church (1697–1740)									
	96	120	216	44.4	55.6	2.2	2.7	30.4	42.3
Norwich, Conn., First Church (1700–1740)									
	113	134	247	45.7	54.3	2.8	3.3	3.1	15.5
Suffield, Mass. (now Conn.), First Church (1710–1740)									
	139	139	278	50.0	50.0	4.5	4.5	23.1	35.6
Westborough, Mass., First Church (1724–1740)									
	29	19	48	60.4	39.6	1.7	1.1	0.0	42.9

Note: Age and marital status figures based on known data only. Age cohorts may not sum to 100 percent as a result of rounding. Date ranges delimited by extant church records. The "Married" column includes a small number of widows and widowers.

Source: Appendix A.

twenty months, on average, during their reproductive years. The anticipated "Extremity" of labor marked a period of intense anticipation and trepidation, for a "Terrible hard and Tedious Travail" frequently placed the mother in serious peril. Although statistically infrequent, the prospect of dying during labor, widely broadcast in the image of mother and child entombed together, weighed heavily on the minds of all New England goodwives. Childbirth, as one woman grimly observed, was like passing "thro' a death."[125]

Women's experiences in childbirth, coupled with their roles as caregivers raising large families, explains the preponderance of young mothers among the ranks of church members. Cotton Mather once quipped that there were "three *Maries* to one *John*" in full communion. Joseph Baxter's 1697 roster of Medfield church members included twenty-five men and forty women. Three decades later, Nathan Stone counted thirty-nine men in the Harwich church, the "women about double." Although more than two-thirds of all communicants in Northampton were men at the time of Solomon Stoddard's ordi-

125. Margaret Higginson to Margaret Sewall, Jan. 21, 1724, box 2, Curwen Family Papers, 1637–1808, AAS. See also Daniel Scott Smith and J. David Hacker, "Cultural Demography: New England Deaths and the Puritan Perception of Risk," *Journal of Interdisciplinary History*, XXVI (1996), 380–383; and Ulrich, *Good Wives*, 126–132.

20–39 (%)		40–59 (%)		60 and Over (%)		Mean Age		Married (%)	
Men	Women	Men	Women	Men	Women	Men	Women	Men	Women
73.5	58.1	8.8	6.5	0.0	0.0	26.3	24.7	51.4	48.7
69.9	47.2	8.1	1.7	0.0	0.0	25.5	21.2	54.2	39.8
58.7	52.6	10.9	5.2	0.0	0.0	25.9	22.7	53.1	52.1
92.8	84.5	4.1	0.0	0.0	0.0	28.9	23.6	92.0	90.2
73.8	61.9	3.1	2.5	0.0	0.0	24.8	22.4	64.0	59.4
96.0	57.1	4.0	0.0	0.0	0.0	27.7	21.6	100.0	73.7

nation in 1677, the trend had nearly reversed by 1706. That same year, Sudbury clergyman Israel Loring catalogued the members of his church before his ordination, two-thirds of whom were women. In most New England towns during the period from 1670 to 1740, women made up more than 60 percent of all church membership candidates.[126]

Maternal mortality also afforded ministers a grim symbol for theological reflection. Several prominent clergymen endorsed childbirth as an important edifying event in a woman's life. Mather described the grievous yoke placed on women in Genesis, noting that Eve's curse might be transmuted into a bless-

126. Cotton Mather, *Ornaments for the Daughters of Zion; or, The Character and Happiness of a Vertuous Woman* ... (Cambridge, Mass., 1692), 44; Gerald F. Moran, "'Sisters' in Christ: Women and the Church in Seventeenth-Century New England," in Moran and Vinovskis, eds., *Religion, Family, and the Life Course*, 85–90; Medfield, Mass., Congregational Church Records, 1697–1866, 10, Medfield Historical Society; Bowman, ed., "Records of the First Parish in Brewster," *Mayflower Descendant*, VI (1904), 215; Minkema, "Old Age and Religion," *Church History*, LXX (2001), 701; Israel Loring, "List of Church Members," Nov. 20, 1706, no. 15094, SA. Comparative data from eastern Connecticut may be found in Moran, "Conditions of Religious Conversion," *Journal of Social History*, V (1972), 332–333; William F. Willingham, "Religious Conversion in the Second Society of Windham, Connecticut, 1723–43: A Case Study," *Societas*, VI (1976), 115–116; and Grossbart, "Seeking the Divine Favor," *WMQ*, XLVI (1989), 706–707.

ing, if only pregnant women would "look up to a dear Saviour" during their moments of distress. "The Approach of their *Travails*," he explained in a 1710 pamphlet addressed to midwives, "proves to them an Occasion and an Excitement for those Exercises of *Piety*, that Secure to them, and prepare them for, Eternal *Blessedness*." Mather even encouraged women to meditate on their own death in labor. "For ought you know, your *Death* has enterd into you," he warned, "and you may have conceived That which determines but about Nine Months more at the most, for you to Live in the World." The Boston divine advocated observing a battery of rituals in preparation for the lying-in period that followed a successful delivery. The main provision of such practices was to prepare the mother's soul for impending judgment, should the worst befall her before, during, or immediately after her travail. A woman's *"Pregnant Time,"* Mather concluded, "should be above all a *Praying Time*."[127]

Dread of childbirth was a recurring concern in women's devotional writings long after they had affiliated with the church. Eight of the nine entries in the extraordinary journal kept by Boston gentlewoman Lydia Prout between 1702 and 1716 were written during the months surrounding the births and deaths of her children. Prout repeatedly acknowledged being "full of doubts and fears about death" as each of her pregnancies drew to a close. She turned to traditional devotional practices, including Bible study, Sabbath worship, private meditation, and covenant renewal, during these dangerous periods in her life because she believed that the "prayer hearing god" would appear in her hour of need, bless the "fruit of my womb," "deliver me in due time with safety," and "bless our family and dwell in it." For Prout, who buried four children and her mother during the years she wrote in her journal, ritual provided a crucial bulwark against the "murmuring" and "unruly" thoughts that continually plagued her mind.[128]

Prout's contemporaries voiced identical fears and engaged in comparable protective practices. Five months pregnant, Mather's sister Jerusha Oliver wrote in her journal that she was of a "very fearful disposition naturally, and am much afraid of Death, and therefore afraid what will be the issue of my being with Child." Accordingly, she bolstered her devotional routines during the weeks before her travail, hoping that she might "obtain the victory over Death, and over my fears of Death." Boston minister Benjamin Colman's

---

127. [Cotton Mather], *Insanabilia; or, An Essay upon Incurables* ... (Boston, 1714), 43; [Mather], *Elizabeth in Her Holy Retirement* ... (Boston, 1710), 2, 6–7, 22. See also Ulrich, "Vertuous Women Found," *American Quarterly*, XXVIII (1976), 20–40.

128. Winiarski, "Lydia Prout's Dreadfullest Thought," *NEQ*, LXXXVIII (2015), 360, 413–414, 416–417, 420.

daughter, Jane Turell, raised a special prayer of thanksgiving after God "appear'd for me in such an Hour of Distress and Danger" when she was forced to deliver her child alone. Worried that she would die suddenly during her impending labor, Sarah Goodhue of Ipswich penned a secret letter to her family and friends in which she exhorted them to improve on her experiences and prepare themselves for death. A quarter century later, Margaret Cary marked the births of each of her children with a standard refrain: "This day God was pleased to appear for me in a wonderful manner, in a time of great difficulty and distress, and made me the living mother of a living and perfect child." In each of these cases, the cadence of women's literary activities reinforced the close correspondence between reproductive concerns and the practices of piety.[129]

Cary's brief meditations incorporated the stock language of prayer bills. In a typical example composed during the 1720s, Ebenezer and Sarah Eastman of Haverhill requested that "Gods name May be praised in this Congregation for his Goodness to hir in presarvinge hir from the dangers of Childe birth and makinge hir the livinge mother of a livinge Childe." After passing through the "Perils of Child Birth," new mothers sought to pay their vows to God by submitting prayers of thanksgiving, especially on the day they were well enough to return to the meetinghouse. Thanksgiving requests for "Safe Deliverance in Chilld bead" sometimes included additional healing petitions that God would preserve the life of an unusually sickly infant and restore mothers suffering through a difficult lying-in period to a "perfect measure of health again." Although they accounted for only 11 percent of all extant manuscript notes, childbirth prayers were undoubtedly the most common. In 1744, Medfield diarist Nathan Plimpton recorded ten public prayer requests in which a mother "returned thanks for Deliverance," a figure representing almost two-thirds the total number of recorded births in town that year. Of the more than twelve hundred prayer requests that Westfield minister John Ballantine recorded in his diary later in the century, more than 40 percent were voiced on behalf of a young mother recently "raised from Childbearing." By the time that Martha Ballard began keeping her diary in 1785, the phrase "living mother of a living child" had appeared so often in weekly prayer bills that the

---

129. Cotton Mather, *Memorials of Early Piety; Occurring in the Holy Life and Joyful Death of Mrs. Jerusha Oliver* ... (Boston, 1711), 28; Benjamin Colman, *Reliquiae Turellae, et Lachrymae Paternae* ... (Boston, 1735), 102; *The Copy of a Valedictory and Monitory Writing Left by Sarah Goodhue* (Portland, Maine, 1805), in David D. Hall, ed., *Puritans in the New World: A Critical Anthology* (Princeton, N.J., 2004), 181–187; [Caroline G. Curtis], ed., *The Cary Letters: Edited at the Request of the Family* (Cambridge, Mass., 1891), 60.

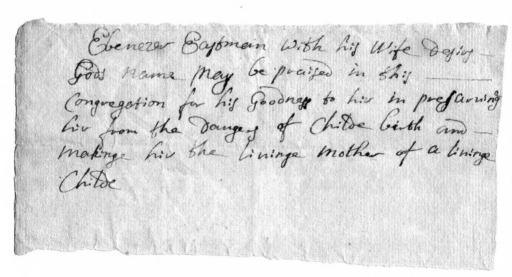

FIGURE 9 Ebenezer Eastman, Prayer Bill. Circa 1714–1729.
Courtesy, Congregational Library and Archive, Boston

prominent Maine midwife occasionally incorporated it into her reports of successful deliveries.[130]

Martha Coit's reflections on "gods gracious dealings with me in the times of sharp travil in Childe bareing" ranks among the most poignant examples of this prominent trend in female piety. For the first decade following her marriage to a pious New London, Connecticut, shipbuilder in 1667, Coit and her family enjoyed relatively good health. Although her first five pregnancies culminated in live births, she suffered repeated disappointments and bereavements between 1679 and 1692, including the deaths of two children, a breached delivery, and three stillbirths. Taking stock of her declining reproductive fortunes in 1688, Coit decided to record a few words "for memory unto my own Speritual Comfort" and the "edefiecation and incoragement of my ofspring." Poring over her Bible, she listed close to three dozen encourag-

---

130. Ebenezer Eastman, prayer bill, n.d. [circa 1714–1729], Personal Records, 1719–1745, Haverhill First Congregational Church Records; Andrew [surname unknown], prayer bill, n.d. [early eighteenth century], pt. 3, no. 1, MS Am. 1506, Boston Public Library; Anne Williams, prayer bill, n.d. [circa 1710s], reel 6, Cotton Mather Papers; Stein, ed., "'For Their Spiritual Good,'" *WMQ*, XXXVII (1980), 282; Nathan Plimpton, diary, 1744, MHS; George H. Ballentine, ed., *Journal of Rev. John Ballantine, Minister of Westfield, MA, 1737–1774* (Bowie, Md., 2002), CD-ROM, Aug. 14, 1743; Laurel Thatcher Ulrich, "'The Living Mother of a Living Child': Midwifery and Mortality in Post-Revolutionary New England," *WMQ*, XLVI (1989), 31. For examples from Ballard's diary, see *The Diary of Martha Ballard, 1785–1812*, ed. Robert R. and Cynthia MacAlman McCausland, Maine Genealogical Society, Special Publication no. 10 (Camden, Maine, 1992), 147, 176, 319, 321.

ing scriptural texts, including numerous verses from the Psalms in which God vowed to uphold the chosen people of Israel. Coit likened such comforting biblical promises to medicinal cordials. They buoyed her spirits, strengthened her faith, and gave her the courage to endure the pains of childbirth.[131]

Coit eventually identified these scriptural passages themselves as wondrous signs from God that she would survive her biennial ordeals. Biblical verses sprang to mind so often in moments of travail that she began to actively meditate while in labor. During her penultimate pregnancy, Coit once again languished in a "dangerous Condition," for her infant had "com wrong." As midwives and neighbors worked to turn the baby in the womb, Coit cast her thoughts toward the scriptures. She was rewarded in her meditation with the promise of Psalm 50:15, a classic healing vow text in which God pledged to deliver those that call on him in a day of trouble. The verse, she later recalled, "Came unto me with such soporting Confidence as if the lord had Spoaken unto me in pertickeler: I will [deliver] thee." God's promise was "soon made good unto me" as she was "delivered beyond all expectation" of a stillborn infant.[132]

Reflecting on her childbirth experiences allowed Coit to see the larger patterns of God's dispensations toward her. The physical pain of childbirth threatened to make her mistrust God, but devotional disciplines banished her fears as each "soar travil" approached. Over time, she dwelt less on postpartum bodily affliction and more on promises of divine mercy. Improving her experiences through meditation and writing, in turn, appeared to have had direct temporal benefits. Her final pregnancy in 1692 resulted in a quick delivery of a "liveing Childe." Coit hoped that God would "give me yet cause and grounds to hope in his mercy," praying, in the words of Hebrews 13:5, that "he will never leave me nor forsake me." Throughout two decades of painful pregnancies, Martha Coit had learned a difficult lesson: "trust in the lord att all times." Trusting in "thiss god" and keeping his mercies always in view meant something more than hoping for her eternal salvation. Coit's frank admission that God had delivered her ten times in childbirth suggests that she envisioned the traditional practices of piety as techniques for coping with the pains of childbirth.[133]

131. "The Experience of Gods Goodness towards Martha Coit," Mar. 15, 1688, [1], box 17, Gilman Family Papers, 1659–1935, YUA. My transcription of Coit's narrative differs in several places from that presented in Coughlin's *One Colonial Woman's World*, 41–44. For genealogical information, see F. W. Chapman, *The Coit Family; or, The Descendants of John Coit . . .* (Hartford, Conn., 1874), 16–17.

132. "Experience of Gods Goodness towards Martha Coit," Mar. 15, 1688, [2].

133. Ibid., [1–3].

During the weeks following a successful delivery, many young mothers watched in horror as their newborns suffered and died at an appalling rate. Of all children born in eighteenth-century New England, 10 to 30 percent died within a year. All parents cared deeply for their children and mourned their passing; but mothers bore special responsibility for the health of their families, and they exhibited a greater range of emotional depth in their religious writings following the death of a child. In Haverhill, only a handful of men mentioned bereavements of any kind in their church admission testimonies, and most of these references came in the wake of the "deaths of maney young parsons [persons]" during the devastating throat distemper epidemic of the 1730s. Nearly one in four married women, by contrast, cited at least one death; and they commented on a greater range of events, including the loss of parents, siblings, servants, and neighbors. The largest group, however, consisted of young mothers who were awakened to their sacramental duties through the sore stroke of divine providence in taking away their offspring. "God has been pleased to bereave me of several Children," lamented Abigail Rue, "which made me think what Need I had to provide for my own Soul." "The Death of my Children was very awakening to me," concurred Mehetabel Eaton after losing twins in 1726, and she envisioned the threatening words of Ezekiel 5:8—"Behold, I, even I, am against thee, and will execute judgments in the midst of thee in the sight of the nations"—poured out against her.[134]

Young mothers took the lead in affiliating with New England churches for a variety of reasons, not least of which was to express thanks for a safe delivery. As one Haverhill woman noted in her 1728 relation, "I've had before now a general knowledge that twas a Duty to come to the Lords Table, and sometimes Made great promises to myself of coming up to it, particularly when I was sick after the birth of my child." During the latter half of the seventeenth century, literary images of the virtuous Christian mother supplanted those of Eve in the published writings of New England ministers. Clergymen extolled the piety of pious goodwives in a profusion of published sermons, funeral elegies, and memorials. Church membership offered a limited measure of autonomy and indirect power, particularly within the family. When ministers preached on the subject of conversion, they often employed feminine imagery.

---

134. Appendix B, Haverhill, Mass., First Church, 1, 63, 192. See also Winiarski, "Gendered 'Relations' in Haverhill," in Benes, ed., *In Our Own Words*, I, 67–69. For data on infant mortality in provincial New England, see Vinovskis, "Mortality Rates and Trends in Massachusetts," *Journal of Economic History*, XXXII (1972), 200. On women as healers, see Rebecca J. Tannenbaum, *The Healer's Calling: Women and Medicine in Early New England* (Ithaca, N.Y., 2002).

The idealized saints of clerical literature were meek and submissive brides of Christ. Numerous relations of faith written both by men and women concluded with the candidate's yearning desire to be found clothed with a "Wedding Garment" on the day of judgment.[135]

Gendered work routines contributed to the dominance of female church members. Colonial women watched over their children in the home, cared for them while they were sick, and nurtured their religious development. Anecdotal evidence indicates that mothers regularly took the lead in educating their children in matters of religion. Several eighteenth-century diarists and autobiographers acknowledged that their mothers had taught them to read and pray. While Samuel Prince diligently worked to settle his son, Joseph, on a suitable farm, his wife, Mary, provided the wayward youth with gifts of Bibles and religious books as well as pious admonitions. In a particularly evocative passage, Reading minister Richard Brown extolled the virtues of his "pious and prudent" mother, who "traveled in Birth with me again" to have Christ "formed in me" through her tireless "instructions, admonitions, warnings, reproofs and exhortations." As the prominent merchant John Saffin summarized in a funeral elegy for his wife: "The Education of her Children young, / She knew full well, did unto her belong." Church affiliation thus constituted an extension of women's child-rearing duties.[136]

Baptismal records provide the most important statistical index of female piety in provincial New England. Most church record books list children under their father's names, but men alone rarely were responsible for presenting their children. One exception was Nicholas Noyes of Salem, who recorded the "Parents Account" under which he baptized each child. Of the 1,032 children listed on the Salem baptismal register between 1718 and 1740, 63 percent were presented by their mothers alone, and an additional 28 percent

135. Appendix B, Haverhill, Mass., First Church, 82, 188. This paragraph summarizes earlier studies of female piety in early New England, including Ulrich, "Vertuous Women Found," *American Quarterly*, XXVIII (1976), 20–40; Margaret W. Masson, "The Typology of the Female as a Model for the Regenerate: Puritan Preaching, 1690–1730," *Signs: Journal of Women in Culture and Society*, II (1976), 304–315; Gerald F. Moran, "'The Hidden Ones': Women and Religion in Puritan New England," in Richard L. Greaves, ed., *Triumph Over Silence: Women in Protestant History* (Westport, Conn., 1985), 126–133; and Amanda Porterfield, *Female Piety in Puritan New England: The Emergence of Religious Humanism*, Religion in America (New York, 1992), 116–153.

136. Winiarski, "Education of Joseph Prince," in Benes, ed., *Worlds of Children*, 48–50; Eaton, *Genealogical History of the Town of Reading*, 53; Caroline Hazard, ed., *John Saffin His Book (1665–1708): A Collection of Various Matters of Divinity, Law, and State Affairs Epitomiz'd Both in Verse and Prose* (New York, 1928), 84. For a similar argument, see Gerald F. Moran, "The Great Care of Godly Parents: Early Childhood in Puritan New England," in Moran and Vinovskis, eds., *Religion, Family, and the Life Course*, 130–134.

TABLE 5 Church Affiliation Status of Parents at First Baptismal Presentation
Event in Selected New England Churches to 1740

Church	Families (N)	Both Parents (%)	Father Only (%)	Mother Only (%)
Hampton, N.H., First Church (1696–1740)	296	30.1	16.2	53.7
Haverhill, Mass., First Church (1694–1740)	239	47.7	14.6	37.7
Medfield, Mass., First Church (1697–1740)	193	37.8	25.9	36.3
Norwich, Conn., First Church (1701–1740)	215	42.3	16.3	41.4
Sandwich, Mass., First Church (1694–1740)	110	24.5	20.0	55.5
Suffield, Mass. (now Conn.), First Church (1710–1740)	171	53.8	30.4	15.8
Westborough, Mass., First Church (1724–1740)	62	69.4	21.0	9.7

Note: Data excludes adult baptisms; baptismal presentations by nonresidents, grandparents, and masters of indentured servants and enslaved men and women; and families whose first baptismal presentation took place in another town or before church records begin. Percentages may not sum to 100 percent as a result of rounding. Date ranges delimited by extant church records.

Source: Appendix A.

were presented jointly by both parents. Fewer than one in ten appeared under the account of their fathers. In nearby Haverhill, both parents had owned the covenant or joined the church in full communion in roughly half of all cases in which they presented their first child for baptism. Among the remaining families, mothers outpaced fathers as the sole affiliated family member by more than 20 percent. Women in Norwich and Hampton were close to three times more likely to be the only spouse affiliated with the church at the time a family first appeared at the baptismal basin. In most parishes, the overall proportion of women who bore responsibility for presenting their children for baptism—either alone or jointly with their husbands—seldom dipped below 75 percent (Table 5).[137]

Within the household's religious economy, mothers were the chief providers. A few candidates made this point explicit in their relations. After more

137. Richard D. Pierce, ed., *The Records of the First Church in Salem, Massachusetts, 1629–1736* (Salem, Mass., 1974), 58–83, 304 (quote 58).

than a decade of periodic afflictions following her marriage in 1684, one Medfield woman was ready to conclude that "God was contending with me because I neglected to bring my children to the ordinance of baptisme." The 1727
earthquake convinced Abigail Staples that she had "Lived in the neglect of
my duty in that I have not brought my Children to baptism." In similar fashion, Elizabeth Emerson, the wife of Hannah Duston's nephew, had "walked
in Darkness, ready to Despair" for many years before joining the Haverhill
church. She was especially "concerned about my children and desirous that
they might be baptized." Desiring to "Do all my Duty" and assuage God's anger
for neglecting her maternal responsibilities, Emerson finally closed with the
church and presented three children for baptism during the fall of 1725. Timo-
rous, lax, or unusually scrupulous husbands could afford to hang back from
the communion table for fear of eating and drinking their own damnation.
No such option was readily available for godly women responsible for the religious upbringing of their children.[138]

As time passed and families grew, many husbands eventually found their
way into the church, but young mothers remained the driving engine of Congregational culture throughout the provincial period. As a result of their
pervasive experiences of affliction and the pressing needs of caring for their
families, women dominated the ranks of full church members and covenant
owners. Pious mothers took the lead in presenting their children for baptism,
providing them with a religious education, and raising them in the land of
gospel light.

■ Setting aside the sensational details of her Indian captivity, Hannah
Duston's religious biography flowed through broader channels in New England's evolving Congregational culture. Although she scrupulously held back
from the communion table until she was nearly seventy years old, Duston
had been affiliated with the Haverhill church for at least three decades and
perhaps as much as a half century before joining in full communion in 1724.
She and her husband had undoubtedly owned the covenant as young parents.
They had presented their children for baptism in a regular and orderly fashion. Duston made charitable contributions to support her minister. She was
part of an extensive kinship network of affiliated families. She was well versed
in Reformed theology and regularly read religious literature. For Duston and
thousands of anxious parents like her, church affiliation had become a mea-

138. Appendix B, Medfield, Mass., First Church, 9; Appendix B, Haverhill, Mass., First
Church, 68, 210.

sured decision based on a calculus of personal experience, social maturation, family strategies of protection and preservation, and female piety.

Tax lists, land records, and other census rosters of Haverhill households reveal the pervasive nature of this increasingly inclusive Congregational parish system. In 1710, the Massachusetts General Court issued an order requiring all towns to provide their militias with snowshoes to help defend their settlements against wintertime raids by native Americans. Only 15 percent of the forty-five Haverhill snowshoe men, as they were called, were listed as full church members when Joshua Gardner was ordained one year later. Yet more than 70 percent of these men and their wives previously had affiliated with the Haverhill church by owning the covenant and presenting at least one child for baptism. Three decades later, at the end of John Brown's quietly successful pastorate, more than 87 percent of all households listed on Haverhill's earliest tax list belonged to one of the town's four Congregational parishes (Table 6). More than three-quarters of the children born to these 226 families had been baptized as infants. Among the remaining families, a handful were Quaker dissenters; the rest were recently married couples, most of whom joined the church during the next decade as their families grew.[139]

Across New England, Congregational hegemony expanded dramatically during the final decades of the seventeenth century and the first decades of the eighteenth. In Charlestown, Massachusetts, the proportion of affiliated households grew from roughly half to nearly three-quarters between 1658 and 1677. Of the 105 families that were taxed in 1680 to build Hingham's stately Old Ship meetinghouse, 90 percent had previously joined the church and presented children for baptism. One or both spouses were full members or covenant owners in 83 percent of the identifiable households appearing on a pair of Medfield rate lists from 1717 and 1718. Even in newly established parishes such as Westford, Massachusetts, rates of affiliation rose quickly to include almost two out of every three families. Admitted at significantly younger ages than their peers elsewhere in New England, the members of Jonathan Edwards's church in Northampton included "almost all our adult persons" on the eve of the powerful awakening events of 1735.[140]

High rates of household affiliation, as Edwards indicated, were not the result of unusual seasons of ingathering, such as the religious awakening that

139. Church affiliation data for the Haverhill snowshoe men and baptismal data for families appearing on the town's early tax lists are drawn from sources cited in Appendix A.

140. Edwards, *Faithful Narrative* (1737), in *WJE*, IV, *Great Awakening*, ed. Goen, 157. For church affiliation trends in Charlestown and Northampton, see Ramsbottom, "Religious Society and the Family in Charlestown," 168; and Tracy, *Jonathan Edwards*, 229–230n.

TABLE 6 Religious Affiliation by Household in Selected New England Towns and Parishes to 1740

Town or Parish	Total Households	Congregational (%)	Other/No Affiliation[a] (%)
Andover, Mass., North Parish (Tax List, 1740)	149	96.0	4.0
Beverly, Mass. (Map, 1700)	61	86.9	13.1
Charlestown, Mass. (Tythingman's List, 1677)	220	64.1	35.9
Hampton, N.H., First Parish (Tax List, 1732)	159	95.0	5.0
Haverhill, Mass., First Parish (Tax List, 1741)	226	87.2	12.8
Hingham, Mass., First Parish (Tax List, 1680)	105	89.5	10.5
Lebanon, Conn., First Parish (Tax List, 1733)	139	93.5	6.5
Medfield, Mass. (Tax List, 1718)	81	82.7	17.3
New Haven, Conn., "Nine Squares" (Map, 1724)	115	71.3	28.7
Newbury (now West Newbury), Mass., Second Parish (Map, 1729)	174	87.4	12.6
Norwich, Conn., First Parish (Tax List, 1730)	141	76.6	23.4
Salem (now Danvers), Mass., Salem Village (Tax List, 1695)	93	52.7	47.3
Sandwich, Mass., First Parish (Minister's Census, 1730)[b]	123	43.9	56.1
Suffield, Mass. (now Conn.) (Land Division, 1713)	88	86.4	13.6
Westborough, Mass. (Minister's Census, 1724)	26	88.5	11.5
Westford, Mass. (Tax List, 1731)	84	61.9	38.1

Notes:

[a]Limitations in available church records make it difficult in many cases to identify with precision the household affiliation patterns of families who did not belong to the Congregational church. This comprehensive category, therefore, includes Anglican and Quaker families and families that established no formal ties to any religious society.

[b]The Other/No Affiliation figure, in this case, includes only unaffiliated Congregational families. Although the town of Sandwich included a large population of Quakers throughout the eighteenth century, none of them are listed on Benjamin Fessenden's "Names and Numbers of the Heads of Familys."

Sources: Appendix A; Mary Macmanus Ramsbottom, "Religious Society and the Family in Charlestown, Massachusetts, 1630 to 1740" (Ph.D. diss., Yale University, 1987), 168–169.

followed the Great Earthquake of 1727 or the various Connecticut Valley stirs and harvests. Instead, towns with extensive colonial tax records reveal robust participation figures over time, even as small numbers of families appeared and disappeared from the yearly rate lists. Households with ties to Andover's north parish, for example, exceeded 90 percent in all but two years of John Barnard's ministry between 1719 and 1740. Benjamin Lord's Norwich congregation enjoyed slightly lower yet still impressive rates. Between 75 and 80 percent of all families appearing on a series of annual tax lists during the 1730s were represented by one or both parents. As was the case in Haverhill, recently married couples without children formed the majority of unaffiliated families; these parents closed with the church in overwhelming numbers as their young families expanded. Of the 110 households appearing on all of the Norwich tax lists between 1730 and 1739, 91 percent eventually affiliated. Each week, as they mounted their pulpits, Barnard and Lord looked out across a sea of familiar faces sitting in the benches and pews of their respective meeting-houses—families that they had known for years through their repeated participation in the public ordinances; families dominated by baptized and cate-chized children and their parents who had assented to the church covenant or joined the church in full communion.[141]

The only exceptions to this pattern emerged in parishes with restrictive church admission standards, such as Salem Village or New Haven, Connecti-cut. Several of these more conservative congregations were located in the Old Colony region of southeastern Massachusetts, where ministers and lay people rejected the practice of owning the covenant into the 1730s. In the small coastal village of Sandwich, lax and scrupulous parents alike held out for years before affiliating with the church. The average age of both male and female candidates lagged several years behind their contemporaries in towns elsewhere in New England. Fewer married couples joined together as part of a coherent family strategy to provide for the religious needs of their children. As a result, the burden of affiliation fell with even greater weight on young mothers. Without the option to own the covenant, their families suffered. Ex-cluding the town's substantial population of Quakers, only 44 percent of the 123 families recorded on a 1730 census by minister Benjamin Fessenden had previously affiliated with the Sandwich church. Among those parents who did, almost one-third brought four or more children to their first baptismal pre-sentation; 41 percent of all children baptized in Sandwich were between the

---

141. Data on church affiliation trends in Andover, Mass., and Norwich, Conn., was derived from sources cited in Appendix A.

ages of three and fifteen (see Tables 2–3). More than half of all children born to the families on Fessenden's roster remained unbaptized. That many of these children died outside the protective watch of the church must have weighed heavily on their parents, who continually struggled with feelings of unworthiness.[142]

A final example brings the picture of widespread Congregational authority into sharper relief. Just across the Merrimack River from Haverhill lay the farming district of Newbury's second parish (now West Newbury). Here, too, family church affiliation patterns remained strikingly high during the first quarter of the eighteenth century. Of the fifty-one families that were taxed to build the second parish meetinghouse in 1696 and remained in the village during the next several decades, two-thirds had established formal ties to the church through one or both spouses by 1700 and 92 percent by 1715. During the 1710s, however, the village suffered through a protracted conflict over the location of the meetinghouse. Frustrated parishioners on the east side of town petitioned the Bishop of London to build Queen Anne's Chapel. In response, village leaders decided to divide the second parish in half, and they commissioned a surveyor to map the location of each household in 1729. The resulting "Plan of the West Parish or Newbury new Town" displayed 184 carefully labeled buildings and three meetinghouses (Map 2). Despite the presence of small clusters of Quaker and Anglican dissenters, adherence to the Congregational establishment and regular participation in the life of the church predominated. In total, 87 percent of all households appearing on the 1729 map had previously affiliated with the second parish church through one or both spouses. In her later years, as Hannah Duston walked from the Haverhill ferry to her daughter's house on the Merrimack River, she would have passed an unbroken string of Congregational families.[143]

In hinterland communities such as Haverhill, Andover, and Newbury, the Congregational establishment ruled as it had done for nearly a century. Few lay men and women might have been devotional virtuosos, yet there were even

142. On resistance to extended baptismal practices in the Old Colony, see Pope, *Half-Way Covenant*, 200–201. For church affiliation practices and baptismal data from Salem Village, see Larry Gragg, *A Quest for Security: The Life of Samuel Parris, 1653–1720*, Contributions to American History (Westport, Conn., 1990), 81n; and Benjamin C. Ray, "Satan's War against the Covenant in Salem Village, 1692," *NEQ*, LXXX (2007), 71–79. I examine the case of New Haven, Conn., in Part 5.

143. Additional data on church affiliation in the second parish of Newbury derived from sources cited in Appendix A. Brown's map is illustrated in Peter Benes, *Old-Town and the Waterside: Two Hundred Years of Tradition and Change in Newbury, Newburyport, and West Newbury, 1635–1835* (Newburyport, Mass., 1986), 62. See also Benes, *New England Prospect: A Loan Exhibition of Maps at the Currier Gallery of Art* (Boston, 1981), 60.

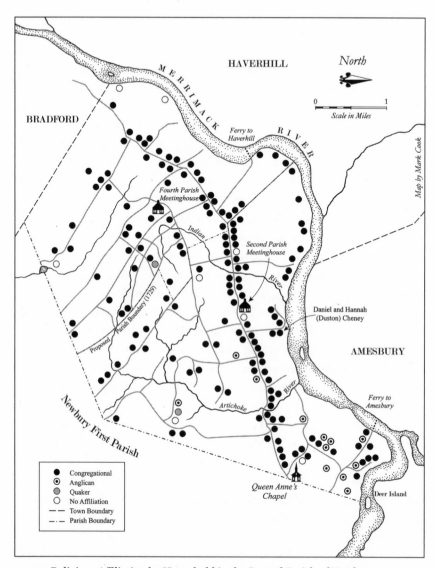

MAP 2 Religious Affiliation by Household in the Second Parish of Newbury, Massachusetts, 1729. Drawn by Mark Cook

fewer places where heterodoxy or apathy reigned. Conservative towns such as Sandwich and Salem Village were the exceptions, not the rule. Only in Rhode Island or in large port towns such as Boston, New Haven, or New London did Anglicans, Quakers, Baptists, and other dissenting sects compete with the descendants of the puritans for household affiliations. Instead, a broadly inclusive, parish-based, tribal Congregational culture dominated provincial New England. This was Mother Duston's religious world. This was the gospel land of light.

THAT I MIGHT WALK ANSWERABLE TO MY PROFESSION

John Brown rarely found himself in the public eye. He produced only a handful of published works during his life. One of them was the sermon that he preached in the small coastal village of Arundel (now Kennebunkport), Maine, at the ordination of Thomas Prentice in 1730. Brown's discourse that day was hardly a remarkable performance. It was one of numerous ordination sermons that issued from the Boston press during the early decades of the eighteenth century, as provincial clergymen attempted to consolidate their professional authority.[144]

Brown began his address with an extended comparison between the settlers of Arundel and the Israelites who sojourned with Moses in the wilderness. It was an apt comparison, he believed, for the small group of migrating families had recently formed themselves into an "Ecclesiastical Body." Brown knew that taming the Maine frontier would be difficult. Like the wandering Israelites, many of the Arundel pioneers would be sorely tempted to "excuse themselves from Religion" when faced with the daunting challenges of clearing the land, raising livestock, marrying and starting families, and providing for their progeny. "The Cares of the World," summarized the Haverhill minister, "are apt to choak the Word, and never more than in a new Plantation." Prentice's congregation had not removed to the northern frontier "meerly upon Worldly Views." Nor had they settled in a "Land of Darkness." Maine was, after all, part of Massachusetts, the gospel land of light. Brown challenged the people of Arundel to imitate both the "Example of *Israel*" and "of our Fathers in their

144. On the rise of published ordination sermons and the professionalization of the Congregational ministry during the early decades of the eighteenth century, see J. William T. Youngs, Jr., "Congregational Clericalism: New England Ordinations Before the Great Awakening," *WMQ*, XXXI (1974), 481–490; and Harry S. Stout, *The New England Soul: Preaching and Religious Culture in Colonial New England* (New York, 1986), 162–164.

Infant State in this Land" by making religion the "first and principal" order of business.[145]

The manner by which the Israelites "walked in the Wilderness" and "kept on in their walking after God" during their desert wandering provided an organizing metaphor for the Haverhill minister's argument. In a conventional ordination sermon about becoming a faithful people, Brown's central trope was one of motion. To "walk as Children of Light," he asserted, meant not only adhering to biblical statutes, upholding divine worship, and observing the Sabbath but also glorifying God with their bodies and making their "Members as Instruments of Righteousness." In raising their families, educating their children, and caring for the poor and afflicted, the Arundel pioneers needed to work toward cultivating "Intire Holiness" in all their activities. Attending to the affairs of religion was the "best way to Entail a Blessing on Posterity," he concluded, for God promised to reward those who walk in such an "Obedient and Holy" manner with "Temporal good Things."[146]

The godly "walk," as one Boston minister succinctly explained, was a "metaphor meaning a person's moral course, the usual tenor of our conversation and of our conduct in public." In eighteenth-century religious discourse, the concept of a godly walk was synonymous with what Brown called the upright "Carriage" of a people, or what his contemporaries frequently termed their "conversation." New England clergymen had long echoed the injunction to walk closely with God. Popular devotional treatises such as Lewis Bayley's *Practice of Piety Directing a Christian How to Walk that He May Please God* and Arthur Dent's *Plain Man's Pathway to Heaven* emphasized the performance of religious duties as a necessary, although not sufficient, precondition for salvation. In a 1714 sermon on "Well-Steering the *Course of Our Life,*" Cotton Mather connected the concept of a godly walk with *"The Whole Duty of Man,"* an allusion to Richard Allestree's popular guidebook to ethical behavior. Indeed, every sermon notebook kept over an extended period by a New England lay person during the provincial period included multiple entries for ordinary sermons in which ministers expounded on the concept of the godly walk. The trope derived from Genesis 17:1, which paired the terms of the Abrahamic covenant with God's command to *"walk before me, and be thou perfect"* in upholding its terms. It was the bedrock of practical divinity—a

145. John Brown, *Ordination Sermon Preach'd at Arundel* ... (Boston, 1731), 6, 13–15, 26, 29.

146. Ibid., 8, 16, 19, 24. For additional examples from Brown's published works, see *Divine Help Implored Under the Loss of Godly and Faithful Men* ... (Boston, 1726), 20; *Solemn Covenanting with God,* 6, 9–10, 18, 22, 24, 26, 32–33, 35; and *Our Great King,* 9.

branch of Reformed theology that blended guidelines for religious practice with exhortations for good works.[147]

Among the more than two thousand pages of sermon manuscripts that survive from the four-decade pastorate of Medfield minister Joseph Baxter, the dominant metaphor that lent shape to the Christian life was "walking in the ways of holinesse." "Christians should look well to their walk while they are here in this world," he explained in a typical sermon, "and see to it that it be Good, and Right." They should walk "accurately," "exactly," and "very circumspectly." On other occasions, Baxter spoke of walking in the "light of Gods countenance," in the "fear of the Lord," and "strictly in his ways." The Medfield minister urged his parishioners to "ponder" the course of their feet and consider the "good path which they have been walking in." They needed to "turn their feet into the way of Gods Testimonies," especially while suffering under the lash of divinely appointed affliction. At times, Baxter envisioned salvation as a heavenly country that mirrored New England's proprietary townships. Those who aspired to obtain a "good Title" to its undivided lands, he maintained, needed to "walk in the way which leads unto it" while in this world. To do so, the faithful needed to walk, not "loosely" in the flesh, but "closely" with God, "denying all ungodlinesse, and worldly lusts, and livingly wholly, righteously, and godly."[148]

Baxter's sermons on godly walking, at times, threatened to overwhelm the traditional Reformed theological distinction between divine grace and good works. The Christian life was "busie, and active," he explained, and "He that runs in a race, and desires to get the Goal will strain himself." Emphasizing

147. Corrigan, *Prism of Piety,* 95; Brown, *Ordination Sermon,* 6; Cotton Mather, *A Life of Piety Resolv'd Upon* ... (Boston, 1714), 3, 8. On the related concept of a "conversation," see Gildrie, *The Profane, the Civil, and the Godly,* 2–3; and Jane Kamensky, *Governing the Tongue: The Politics of Speech in Early New England* (New York, 1997), 5. On the broader context of "holy living," see John Spurr, *The Restoration Church of England, 1646–1689* (New Haven, Conn., 1991), 279–330. Stephen Foster traces the rise of practical divinity in *Long Argument,* 65–107.

148. Joseph Baxter, sermon on Prov. 9:12, n.d. [circa 1697–1745], sermon on Matt. 18:20, n.d. [circa 1697–1745], sermon on Heb. 11:16, Mar. 9, 1732, sermon fragments, n.d. [circa 1697–1745], box 2, folders 3, 5–6, 10–12, 16, Baxter-Adams Family Papers, 1699–1889, MHS; Baxter, sermon fragments, n.d. [circa 1697–1745], Mortimer Rare Book Room, Smith College Library, Northampton, Mass.; Baxter, sermon fragments, n.d. [circa 1697–1745], Medfield Historical Society. Medfield minister Joseph Baxter left behind one of the largest collections of eighteenth-century sermon notes. Scattered among seven research archives in New England, the individual folded sheets—once neatly pinned together to form sermon booklets—have devolved into a jumble of mostly undated sermon fragments spanning Baxter's long ministerial career (1697–1745). Whenever possible, here and in the notes that follow, I have provided citations for specific pages bearing sermon texts or dates and approximate folder locations within general collections for undated sermon fragments.

works, the Medfield minister exhorted his parishioners to "press toward perfection" and strive to obtain their heavenly "Portion" using all the means at their disposal. More commonly, Baxter described salvation as a reward paid by God for the diligent performance of religious duties. "Their Everlasting Good will be promoted, and advantaged" by "walking in the ways of holinesse," he argued. The Bible provided rules by which godly walkers could order "every affaire, in their whole worke, and walke." It was the "light of their feet, and the lamp of their paths." Yet he nonetheless maintained to "walk according to the rule of Gods word" also required divine grace. Like all of his contemporaries, the Medfield minister recognized that even the most zealous saints who were "sincere in their whole walk" would "sometimes stumble" as a result of their sinful natures. God alone led his people in the "paths of Righteousnesse," and thus the faithful needed to "walk depending upon him for his direction, and influence." Or, to be more precise, Jesus went before them, showing them "step by step how they should walke." To live a "holy, and spiritual Life" was to tread in his steps.[149]

Salvation was not the only incentive to godly walking. In one of the few apocalyptic allusions in his massive sermon corpus, Baxter paradoxically suggested that the "dissolution of the world" was imminent and, for this reason, Christians should aim at being "Holy in their whole walk, and conversation." Curiously, he then proceeded to extol the "Great Positive Blessings" and temporal benefits of a holy walk with God. Pursuing holiness in every action, he continued, was "greatly beneficial, and advantageous unto Persons with respect to this world." "Holy Persons," especially, were often spared by God during periods of providential affliction and "Great temporal destruction." Those who walked closely with God lived in the hope that "Their outward, and temporal Good, and profitt will be promoted, and advanced." A "well ordered conversation," in short, was the "surest way to enjoy the greatest Good, and happiness" while in this world.[150]

Baxter's colleagues frequently paused in their weekly sermons to consider the earthly "advantages" that derived from an "upright walk in the ways of religion." In a potent synopsis of the ideal of the godly walk, Boston minister Benjamin Wadsworth published a 1707 treatise entitled *The Blameless Chris-*

149. Baxter, sermon fragments, n.d. [circa 1697–1745], Medfield Historical Society; Baxter, sermon on Jas. 1:22, n.d. [circa 1697–1745], sermon fragments, n.d. [circa 1697–1745], box 2, folders 6–7, 12, 19, Baxter-Adams Family Papers; Baxter, sermon fragments, n.d. [circa 1697–1745], Mortimer Rare Book Room, Smith College Library; Baxter, sermon fragment, Dec. 6, 1732, MS Am 1397, HL.

150. Baxter, sermon fragments, n.d. [circa 1697–1745], box 2, folders 10, 19, Baxter-Adams Family Papers; Baxter, sermon fragments, n.d. [circa 1697–1745], Medfield Historical Society.

tian; or, Rules, Shewing How Christians Should Walk. "Practical Christianity,"
he maintained, was the "most *pleasant* and *profitable life,* that any person can
live." By walking "according to their profession" in their outward lives, godly
men and women "yield revenues of Glory to their glorious Maker" and "take
the best course that can be, to promote their own *external, internal,* and *everlasting welfare;* and the best course also, to benefit those about them." Wadsworth was unusually frank about the types of benefits that accrued to "sincere
practical Christians." Those who strove to live blameless lives in their *"whole
carriage"* could expect to gain *"personal advantage"* in their worldly affairs as
well as "secret spiritual joy" and, potentially, assurance of their future estate.[151]

To square their practice with their profession, godly walkers needed to adhere steadfastly to a biblical code of ethics and a comprehensive devotional
regimen, from praying in secret to participating in the public ordinance of the
Lord's Supper. Sober Christians, Wadsworth continued, exhibited a *"studious,
diligent, industrious"* disposition as they followed honest callings in their
worldly affairs. Temperate in their desires for *"Creature Enjoyments,"* they
were *"meek and humble"* in relations with neighbors, accepted their social station with equanimity, and endured affliction and misfortune with a stoic resignation. Under the heading of righteous carriage, Wadsworth coupled standard
biblical injunctions against murder, adultery, and false witness with fiduciary
responsibilities for honesty in business dealings, charity to the needy, and forbearance and tenderness toward neighbors. His was a comprehensive social
vision that applied equally to civil magistrates, ministers, parents, children,
and servants.[152]

Wadsworth's sermon outlined a civic piety that encompassed almost all
of the themes that appeared with regularity in correspondence, prayer bills,
devotional journals, and various published works during the early decades
of the eighteenth century. Elegists turned to the metaphor of godly walking
when praising the virtues of the pious dead. To cite one example among many,
a 1739 newspaper obituary described Boston deacon, magistrate, and militia officer Samuel Checkley as a "close Walker with GOD," a shorthand phrase
that encapsulated his steadfast attention to religious duties. The concept was
so closely intertwined with daily devotional practices that Benjamin Colman
published extracts from the religious writings of deceased merchant Grove

151. Peter Thacher, sermon on Prov. 3:17, July 30, 1704, Notes on Sermons Delivered in
Boston, 1704–1705, MS SBd-83, MHS; Benj[amin] Wadsworth, *The Blameless Christian; or,
Rules, Shewing How Christians Should Walk* ... (Boston, 1707), [i], 3, 54.

152. Wadsworth, *Blameless Christian,* 15, 19, 22.

Hirst under the title "A Walk with GOD." In their diaries and correspondence, Samuel Sewall and other leading provincials reminded themselves to "walk with a right foot" or "walk humbly, and watchfully," especially during periods of personal affliction or providential misfortune. Prayer bills expressing thanks for safe travel or deliverance from childbirth often ended with the petitioner vowing to "walke in Some Good measure according to the mercyes" received. And when Benjamin Woods of Marlborough and Daniel King of Marblehead joined their respective churches, they begged God for the grace to "walk worthy" of their high professions.[153]

One in four church membership candidates in Haverhill closed their relations with a nearly identical phrase, requesting that fellow parishioners "pray that I might walk answerable to my Profession." Similar concluding statements appear in relations from Boston, Lynn End, and the east parish of Windsor, Connecticut. The implication was not only that upright moral behavior was possible in this world—whatever the limitations of original sin—but also that a "steadfast" and "methodical" walk with God had consequences both in this life and in the next. Listening to their minister preach on this theme in his weekly sermons, Joseph Baxter's Medfield parishioners, in particular, infused their church admission testimonies with reflections on the temporal implications of walking "circumspectly" and with "exceeding *Accuracy*" during their earthly pilgrimage.

> I doe humbly offer myselfe to this church that I may enjoye all the ordinances of Christ, earnestly begging the prayers of all Gods People that I may be enabled to walke as becomes all those that doe enter into solemne engagements to be the lords.

> [I] earnestly beg the prayers of Gods People that I may be enabled to glorifie God while I am in the world, and to walk so as that I may be found at the right hand of the Lord Jesus Christ in the great day of the Lord.

> I Do Humbly offer myself to this Church to be admitted to that Ordainnance, and I Do Humbly and Ernestly aske youre prayers for me, that I may be found with my Weding Garment on; and that God would Enable me So to Walk Before Him in this world as that at last I may Be found of my Judg in peas [peace].

153. *Boston Weekly News Letter,* Jan. 4, 1739; Benjamin Colman, *A Funeral Sermon Preached upon the Death of the Truly Vertuous and Religious Grove Hirst Esq....* (Boston, 1717), 47; Thomas, ed., *Diary of Samuel Sewall,* I, 370; *Letter-Book of Samuel Sewall,* MHS, *Colls.,* II (1888), 3; Stein, "'For Their Spiritual Good,'" *WMQ,* XXXVII (1980), 281; Woods, journal, [24]; King, diary, [1].

I desire the Prayers of Gods People to God for me that He would prepare me, and strengthen me by his grace that I may come so as to find acceptance with God, and have my soul benefitted and so come to hate sin with a perfect hatred, and forsake every way of sinning, and particularly my own iniquity, and walk answerable to the profession which I make, and serve my Generation according to the will of God, and at last finish my course with Joy.[154]

■ Walking answerable to the high calling of a church admission relation was no simple matter. The practices of piety were "burthensome," as one prospective church member candidly acknowledged. There were complex theological doctrines to master, Bible passages to memorize, religious books to read, and lengthy sermons to notate, study, and discuss. Parents struggled to resign themselves to God's will during periods of affliction and bereavement. People made excuses for not attending the sacrament. Sins of the flesh tempted young people. Some parents neglected to present their children for baptism in a timely manner. Always, temporal affairs threatened to overwhelm religious discipline. "You Complain of the hurries of the World," wrote one minister in a 1737 letter to a Connecticut woman, "but I hope you will overcoom that, for everyone that is born of God overcometh the world. But allas that is no eassy thing to do because our hearts are Earthly and in Love with it."[155]

Many aspiring godly walkers during the provincial period failed to live up to the disciplined ideals outlined in their relations. Their devotional lives were punctuated with intermittent gaps and lapses as well as rededications and renewals. Richard Hazzen of Haverhill was a case in point. Composed while completing his second degree at Harvard College, his 1722 relation might have been among the longest that John Brown received during his two-decade pastorate, but it generally conformed to the conventions of the genre. So did the profession of beliefs that Hazzen composed for his wife when she joined the church shortly after the 1727 earthquake. During the next decade, the couple

154. Appendix B, Haverhill, Mass., First Church, 161; Prince, memorandum, 1685, Pulsifer Family Papers; Ford, ed. *Diary of Cotton Mather,* I, 73, 402; Cooper, *Service of God Recommended,* 33; Appendix B, Medfield, Mass., First Church, 8, 71, 90, 105. See also Appendix B, Boston, First Church, 3 (for the full text of Rebecca Coburn's relation, see Appendix C); Minkema, ed., "Lynn End 'Earthquake' Relations," *NEQ,* LXIX (1996), 498; Minkema, ed., "East Windsor Conversion Relations," *CHS Bulletin,* LI (1986), 54.

155. Appendix B, Hebron, Conn., First Church, 4; Anonymous to Hannah Morse, Dec. 7, 1737, Jonathan Edwards and Jonathan Edwards the Younger Papers, 1737–1793, Presbyterian Historical Society, Philadelphia. For examples of parents who struggled with grief and resignation, see Winiarski, "Lydia Prout's Dreadfullest Thought," *NEQ,* LXXXVIII (2015), 381–389.

had eight children, two of whom died during the devastating diphtheria epidemic in 1737. Hazzen remained active in politics throughout his life, serving briefly as a schoolmaster and town clerk before embarking on a career surveying roads, township boundaries, and individual landholdings in the rapidly expanding settlements on the northern frontier. He eventually settled on an extensive farm located in the Timberlane district of Haverhill (now Hampstead, New Hampshire), where he became a church leader during the years before his death from a riding accident in 1754.[156]

Best known for his work surveying the contested boundary between Massachusetts and New Hampshire in 1741, Hazzen later led an expedition to chart the Atlantic coastline from the Merrimack River in Massachusetts to the Saint Croix in Maine. On both trips, the Haverhill surveyor kept travel diaries that reveal the contours of his daily religious activities. Despite his high-ranking status, there are some surprising lapses in Hazzen's devotional practices. Baptismal records are lacking for several of his children. Nor was Hazzen entirely scrupulous in observing the Sabbath while traveling abroad. During his 1741 surveying trip, he reported several occasions on which he and his crew worked on Sunday hauling equipment and making measurements, rather than observing a day of rest. Only the perfunctory concluding words of Hazzen's official journal indicated any effort to improve the providential significance of his perilous but ultimately successful surveying expedition through the snowbound Berkshires: "Came to Haverhill about Eight or Nine O'Clock, after a journey of Thirty Seven days, all in perfect Health through God's goodness to us."[157]

Returning from his voyage to the mouth of the Saint Croix a decade later, Hazzen spent several months at home plotting measurements on a detailed map. Assisted by his two daughters, he worked tirelessly on his plan from sunup to well after sundown—as "Long as I could See," he confided in his diary. Neighbors came and went, sharing news, borrowing draft animals, or performing various jobs. They sought his assistance measuring their property and writing legal documents. Hazzen attended town meetings. He fenced his fields. There were days when "Nothing Remarkable hapned," and others when they did. On one occasion, he discovered the grave of a young woman "killd by Indians more than 50 years ago" in one of his fields—a chilling reminder of

156. Appendix B, Haverhill, Mass., First Church, 103–104; Harriette Eliza Noyes, *A Memorial History of Hampstead, New Hampshire*, II, *Congregational Church, 1752–1902* (Boston, 1903), 311–313; *SHG*, VI, 186–191; Brown, *Number of Deaths in Haverhil*, 3.

157. Henry A. Hazzen, ed., "The Boundary Line of New Hampshire and Massachusetts," *NEHGR*, XXXIII (1879), 332.

Haverhill's violent past. During the three months that he assiduously "Drawed the plan," Hazzen recorded only a handful of entries in his diary regarding his religious practices. He and his wife attended church sporadically during the winter months, owing to the distance they lived from the meetinghouse in the north parish of Haverhill (now Plaistow, New Hampshire). But the surveyor was far from an impious man. He occasionally commented favorably on sermons that he heard and spent Sabbaths at home reading godly literature and praying with his family when the weather was inclement. Hazzen's surveying diaries serve as important reminders that no New Englanders—no matter how devout or disciplined—spent more time prostrating themselves in their closets than working in their fields, shops, wharves, or homes.[158]

Tensions between worldly and spiritual affairs appear on the pages of an account book kept by four generations of the Graves family of Guilford, Connecticut. For more than a century, John Graves and his descendants recorded their finances and other important information in a haphazard collection of accounts, receipts, and lists. Scattered across more than two hundred pages of financial records were notes relating to genealogy, military service, newspaper subscriptions, and the tenures of indentured servants. The Graves men kept receipts for haying, plowing, carting wood, and keeping tavern along the Boston Post Road. They recorded gifts disbursed at the weddings of their daughters and family items divided in estate settlements; and they reckoned accounts with scores of neighbors for purchases of shoes, livestock, Indian corn, liquor, and a host of other household commodities.[159]

Sparse entries regarding religious matters fit untidily within the Graves's sprawling social and economic world. John III interlineated prayers and scriptural citations—including one for Matthew 11:28, the quintessential encouraging sacramental verse in church admission testimonies—between financial entries. His father recorded religious expenditures as well. A drum that the elder Graves purchased for seven shillings in 1713 was used to summon the Guilford townspeople to worship, and his house served as a place of entertainment between morning and afternoon Sabbath exercises. Most important, John, Jr., kept a record of his modest religious library. The two dozen works of divinity included Bibles and psalm books, exegetical treatises, sacramental literature, devotional tracts, jeremiads, election sermons, and a weather-beaten copy of John Bunyan's *Pilgrim's Progress*. These few entries, however,

158. Richard Hazzen, journal, 1750–1751, [29–30, 39], Mss C 1091, NEHGS.
159. Annie Kelsey Maher, ed., "'John Grave: His Booke': The Diary of a Connecticut Citizen in 1679 ...," *Connecticut Magazine*, X (1906), 18–24. See also *Making Ends Meet: Financing Every-Day Life for a Madison Family, 1685–1865* (Madison, Conn., 2006).

represented the only links between the account book and the broader religious practices of the Graves men, who were communicants and deacons in the Guilford church.[160]

As the economy of New England expanded during the first half of the eighteenth century, men like Richard Hazzen and John Graves, Jr., began to reimagine the "business of religion" in contractual terms. Religious musings could turn up in seemingly odd places. An Ipswich shoemaker penned a poem on the 1727 earthquake on a scrap of paper bearing financial calculations that he inserted into his account book. Newton layman William Hides practiced writing the opening words of countless deeds—"to all people to whom these Presents shall"—on the waste pages of the same journals in which he recorded weekly sermon notes. Rebecca Davis of Haverhill composed her relation on the back of an order for three barrels of hard cider. Tropes drawn from the world of commerce also worked in the opposite direction, lending structure to the prayers and meditations of pious lay men and women. Such was the case when the prominent Marlborough magistrate Benjamin Woods prayed that he might "Do as the wise Merchant to buy the goodly pearl of Great price to secure my own soul." Even ministers such as Joseph Baxter occasionally cast religious practice in the language of exchange. Those who resolved to work toward their salvation, he mused in a theological notebook, "must make it the standing Rule, and Principle" of their lives "never to do anything but what we can give a good account of." Making a "frequent, and Impartial account of our own lives and actions," he believed, was "no more than every Steward does, who looks over his Books, and adjusts his accounts himself, before He presents them to his Lord." Baxter reminded himself to engage in morning and evening meditations as a way of reckoning his soul accounts with God.[161]

The structure of lay devotional writings drew inspiration from financial records. The most common forms of personal religious writings that survive between 1680 and 1740 were not introspective journals; they were rather rules, covenants, and resolutions. Lay people seemed more willing to list and quantify their religious lives than to narrate them. Samuel Prince's personal covenant belonged to this tradition, as did the roster of biblical passages that comforted Martha Coit during labor and the "scriptur efidenses [evidences]

160. Maher, ed., "'John Grave: His Booke,'" *Connecticut Magazine*, X (1906), 23; John Graves et al., account book, 1678–1797, I, 160, 259, 280, 287, CSL.

161. Baxter, sermon fragment, n.d. [circa 1697–1745], box 2, folder 17, Baxter-Adams Family Papers; Samuel Brown, account book; Hides, notebooks, I, [23]; Appendix B, Haverhill, Mass., First Church, 46; Woods, journal, [12, 42]; Baxter, notes for sermons, 1676–1832, [6], MS Am 807, HL. On the prevalence of commercial metaphors in provincial religious discourse, see Valeri, *Heavenly Merchandize*, 157–161.

for heven" that the Hull, Massachusetts, elder John Loring enumerated on a single sheet of paper before his death in 1714. Among the earliest personal writings of the celebrated Northampton clergyman Jonathan Edwards was a list of seventy resolutions that governed every aspect of his life, from satisfying physical needs to managing social interactions. Plymouth magistrate Josiah Cotton, too, encumbered his memoirs with numerous lists that blended temporal and religious concerns, private and public business, and personal and familial duties. He compiled biblical passages to guard against character failings, observations on the proper conduct of husbands and wives, resolutions for administering his duties as a county court justice, rules for the temperate consumption of spirituous liquors, and religious advice for his children. In August 1724, Cotton recorded a "particular Account of a Weeks Transactions, even to the Most Minute Articles therein," only to discover how "much precious time runs waste, or is spent in Trifles."[162]

Written for the edification of his children, John Gardner's tattered devotional journal provides an extended example of the ups and downs of a godly walk. The pious Salem merchant and militia officer ranked among the very few disciplined provincials who attempted to record daily religious meditations. He began compiling the "remarkable Dispensation of Gods dealing to me" on his thirty-sixth birthday, June 3, 1717. The first entry, which sketched his life up to that time, drew heavily on the conventions of church admission testimonies. Gardner gave thanks to God for being "Born in A land of light" and descended from religious parents. He recalled a familiar story of parental advice and religious training, youthful vanities and temptations, providential deliverances, and fleeting moments of religious elevation. He joined the Salem church in 1703—an event that registered positive commentary in his journal but, like so many of his contemporaries, reflected no sustained spiritual crisis.[163]

Although Gardner claimed to have faced "nue Cares and nue Duties with respect to things in the world" when he changed his "Condission from A Singel to A married State," his family and temporal affairs were unusually prosperous. At the time he started keeping his devotional journal, Gardner had al-

162. Prince, memorandum, 1685, Pulsifer Family Papers; "Experience of Gods Goodness towards Martha Coit," Mar. 15, 1688, [1–3]; John Loring, religious notes, n.d. [before 1714], no. 12159, 1, SA; Jonathan Edwards, "Resolutions," in *WJE*, XVI, *Letters and Personal Writings*, ed. Claghorn, 753–759; JCH, 130, 136, 144–145, 147–148, 151, 170 (quote), 174–175, 177–182. For a similar argument, see Bruce Tucker, "Joseph Sewall's Diary and the Rhythm of Puritan Spirituality," *EAL*, XXII (1987), 3–18.

163. Gardner, journal, I, 1, II, 9, Ward Papers; Pierce, ed., *Records of the First Church in Salem*, 189.

ready inherited a small farm in what later became Salem's middle parish (now Peabody), which he aggressively expanded through the steady acquisition of adjacent tracts. After filling a variety of minor town offices, Gardner served several terms as Salem's representative to the Massachusetts General Court. Occasionally humbled by recurrent periods of sickness and affliction, Gardner nonetheless gave thanks to God for his providential good fortune. The "Grate preserver" had protected him from a dangerous riding accident as a youth and shielded him from harm during the bloody counterattack against the native American and French forces that almost destroyed Haverhill in 1708. All but one of Gardner's seven children were alive, and each had been baptized immediately after birth.[164]

Gardner's religious worldview mirrored his temporal affairs. Recognizing that he abounded in material comforts, he praised God for providing him with "time and lesur [leisure] In an Espesial maner to Pray and Read and meditat on the Futer world." Prosperity itself might initially have impelled Gardner to begin keeping a devotional journal. "Since it has plesed God thus to Bless me," he wrote in his initial autobiographical entry, "I think it my duty from this tim forward to the End of my Days to set apart one day in the year Solemly and searously to bless and prays God." It filled him with wonder to consider his good fortune that he was a rational being, endowed with a healthy body and a mind capable of understanding the truths of the Bible. The purpose of such a privileged life, he concluded, was to improve his God-given faculties. The Christian life involved answering the "End for wich I was maid" and improving the "talant Commited to me that God may have Glory And I may have peas [peace] and joy in that day when I shall be Called to an account." For a man of Gardner's station, this meant working for the good of Salem and the colony. Refusing or neglecting to serve his generation ranked among the foremost sins he could imagine. Gardner knew that he would receive correction for his temporal failures in the form of worldly afflictions meted out by an "angry Judg," but he took solace in also knowing that Jesus, like a faithful bondholder or creditor, provided surety for his immense spiritual debts. "Every title" of his place in heaven had been "paid and answered for by my Grat lord and master."[165]

Gardner's meditations disclosed more attention to temporal needs than preoccupation with assurance of salvation. He even cast the latter in terms of

164. Gardner, journal, I, 3, Ward Papers. For genealogical information, see Frank Augustine Gardner, comp., *Gardner Memorial: A Biographical and Genealogical Record of the Descendants of Thomas Gardner, Planter* ... (Salem, Mass., 1933), 67–80.

165. Gardner, journal, I, 3, 9, II, 20, 22–23, Ward Papers.

the former. Following a day of private devotions in February 1718, he penned a long journal entry in which he entreated God to provide him with various blessings and favors. The structure of Gardner's narrative said as much about his worldly ambition as his religious inheritance. If heaven "be my portion," Gardner wrote, then "I have all things, and shall have all things." Did he desire health? In Christ was the "fisission [physician] of sol and body." Did he desire wealth? In heaven he would enjoy "Durable Richis and righteousness." Did he desire public honor? "Hear it is that I may be mayd A King and A preast." Did he desire noble employment? "Hear I may belong to the Janaral [General] Assembly of the furst born whos names are riten in heaven." Salvation, as Gardner imagined it, made eternal and permanent his achievements in temporal affairs. Even fleeting knowledge of his eternal destination, fittingly enough, was the "beginning of heaven hear on erth." For Gardner, the way to heaven ran through this world—through his household, through Salem, and through New England. Serving in local government, practicing his piety with diligence, and raising his family in the land of gospel light were consequential actions.[166]

As Gardner strove to "mak relidgon my main bisness," he often fell prey to what he called an "over love to this Presant world." Metaphors drawn from his daily affairs anchored his religious meditations, but worldly business also occupied too much of his time and thought. It was his prevailing temptation, as Gardner admitted on one occasion. He wrote frequently of his desire to "walk humbly befor God" through an exacting and disciplined piety, only to find himself wandering and straying in duty. Although he believed that he had been created to serve the glory of God, the Salem magistrate too often was preoccupied with the material things that had been "lent to me" during his brief, but prosperous, life. On February 19, 1718, business demands forced him to cut short his meditation on the joys of heaven. For more than a week, Gardner was "diverted by Compani" and "worldly bisness," forced to "rob one day to pay another." Several months later, the demands of the planting season impelled him to put down his pen for two months. "The spring is Cum," Gardner lamented, and it is "my Duty to see that my family Eat not the bred of Eidelness." Even the godliest of walkers spent long periods of their earthy pilgrimage harried by temporal affairs.[167]

Benjamin Trumbull of Lebanon, Connecticut, framed the tension between earthly and heavenly concerns succinctly in his commonplace book when he

166. Ibid., II, 18.
167. Ibid., I, 9–10, II, 8, 15, 23.

exhorted himself and others to be "Adventurers for another World." Conjuring images of joint-stock ventures and land speculation schemes, his musings underscored the ties that bound religion and the business of everyday life. Throughout the provincial period, the rhetoric of conversion, divine grace, and regeneration mingled with protective healing vows, strategies of family preservation, and professions of orthodox doctrine. Church membership served a variety of needs, and the rhythms of affiliation fit unevenly within the lives of godly walkers and their families. Most New Englanders remained preoccupied with the outward practices of piety—and with good reason. Church membership professors believed that their devotional routines would make a difference in this world and, perhaps, in the next. Although Trumbull and many of his contemporaries recognized that life in the here and now was a mere "circulation of mean Actions," the metaphor of a diligent "Walk" with God did as much to assist pious New Englanders in constructing meaningful worlds as to transcend them.[168]

■ On December 2, 1742, John Brown opened his narrow account book and began jotting down a few business transactions with his neighbors. He had been hiring his parishioners and purchasing their commodities for more than two decades. Commencing with the "Catalogue of Kindnesses" that he started recording on the day of his ordination, Brown's account book had expanded to include hundreds of exchanges with scores of Haverhill townspeople. But on this day, Brown's faculties faltered. He paid James Cushing, his colleague in Haverhill's north parish, one pound and ten shillings for a hog, reconciled an existing debt with a neighbor, sent two pounds to Boston for "Necessaries," and ordered seven and a half yards of calico. Subsequent entries were less precise: three shillings and five pence "To Rum at Foster's," ten and six "To Spinning," five pounds "To Cotton," three "To Mrs. A.," seven "To Webster." Brown's elegant handwriting grew ragged and uneven. He died a few hours later, "having just compleated the 46th Year of his Age, and the 24th of his Ministry."[169]

Unassuming in life, Brown was largely forgotten in death. Long since lost, his gravestone in Haverhill's Pentucket Cemetery once described him as a man "greatly esteemed in this life for his learning, piety and prudence." Likewise, an obituary published in Boston's *Weekly News-Letter* praised the dutiful clergy-

168. Albert E. van Dusen, ed., *Adventurers for Another World: Jonathan Trumble's Common-place Book* (Hartford, Conn., 1983), 23, 25.

169. John Brown, account book, 114; *Boston Weekly News-Letter*, Dec. 23, 1742.

man as a "Gentleman of good natural Parts," an accomplished divine, a profit-able preacher, and a faithful steward to his congregation. Brown's brother-in-law, Josiah Cotton of Plymouth, extolled his kinsman as an "able Minister of the Gospel" and a "Sedate, Solid, Steady Religious Person." Such laudatory language was the conventional stock of funeral sermons, but Brown's obitu-arists went a step further. Cotton also described the Haverhill minister as an "Opposer of Enthusiasm and Disorder." According to the Boston prints, Brown was a "hearty Friend to the Growth of substantial and undefiled Reli-gion" and a staunch critic of the "Uncharitableness, and Irregularities, which so much prevail in the Land at this present Day."[170]

The defensive tone of Brown's obituaries seems out of place at first, for the Haverhill minister had never faced any serious opposition from his parish-ioners. Even still, he must have realized during his final years that his min-istry was growing increasingly out of step with the interests of his congre-gants, especially those among the rising generation. The times were changing rapidly. Between 1741 and 1742, churches throughout New England admitted more men and women than in any other period of the century, excepting only the powerful awakenings that followed the Great Earthquake of 1727. Unlike this earlier revitalization period, however, the men and women that swelled the ranks of full church members during the 1740s differed in significant ways from earlier generations. They were much younger, on average; men formed a larger proportion of this new cohort of communicants; and, since most were unmarried at the time they joined the church, the demands of raising a family in the land of light figured less prominently in their affiliation strategies. Their relations struck a decidedly different tone as well. Candidates admitted to full communion during the early 1740s expressed greater confidence about their spiritual estates. Fewer people acknowledged their fears of communicating at the Lord's Table or described church membership as a Christ-commanded duty encumbered with terms and obligations. Whereas candidates earlier in the eighteenth century cited the formative influence of published sacramen-tal works, the rising generation now claimed to have been stirred to join the church through the powerful oratory of a new generation of preachers, many of whom traveled widely throughout the region as itinerant ministers. They narrated dramatic conversion experiences in which they lay prostrate at the gaping maw of hell before being miraculously redeemed—often by words from scripture that leapt to mind in their darkest hour. A few even claimed to have

---

170. [Leverett Saltonstall], "An Historical Sketch of Haverhill …," MHS, *Colls.*, 2d Ser., IV (1816; rpt. Boston, 1846), 142; *Boston Weekly News-Letter*, Dec. 23, 1742; JCH, 326.

received revelatory communications from the Holy Spirit through dreams and other visionary phenomena. Soon, many of these young church members would begin to question the fitness of their ministers; within a few years more, thousands would abandon the Congregational establishment altogether.

For a time, Haverhill remained unaffected by the growing maelstrom. Brown continued to admit men and women to full communion as he had done throughout his career, and the relations that he penned during the months leading up to his death remained relatively unchanged. But he also took steps to insulate his congregation from the alarming ecclesiastical conflicts that were emerging in neighboring towns. In February 1742, he facilitated the publication of a small pamphlet written by a neighboring minister named Joseph Seccombe. The Kingston, New Hampshire, clergyman lamented the "awful *Delirium*" that had gripped his parish during the recent religious stir. Although Seccombe acknowledged that all Christians yearned to be *"filled with the Spirit,"* he feared that too many exhibited an "excessive fondness for *Trances*" and "unutterable Raptures and Extasies." Brown undoubtedly approved of Seccombe's exhortation to "regulate these Desires by the Rules of the Spirit in the Word of God" and make "Use of appointed Means."[171]

John Brown did not live to witness the dissolution of the steady religious culture that he had labored quietly and persistently to create throughout his career. But his successor, Edward Barnard, and longtime colleagues in the Bradford ministerial association certainly did. As they turned to assess blame for the ecclesiastical strife that plagued their once-tranquil parishes during the 1740s, they seized on a single cause: the celebrated itinerant Anglican evangelist, George Whitefield. New England had entered an era of great awakenings. The gospel land of light would never be the same.[172]

171. [Joseph Seccombe], *Some Occasional Thoughts on the Influence of the Spirit* . . . (Boston, 1742), i–ii, 3, 12; John Brown to Thomas Foxcroft, Feb. 20, 1742, Thomas Foxcroft Papers, 1690–1770, Mark and Llora Bortman Collection, HGARC. For relations composed in Haverhill during the early 1740s, see Appendix B, Haverhill, Mass., First Church, 9, 32, 66.

172. *A Letter from Two Neighbouring Associations of Ministers in the Country* ... (Boston, 1745), 2–7; Bradford Ministers' Association, Records, [48].

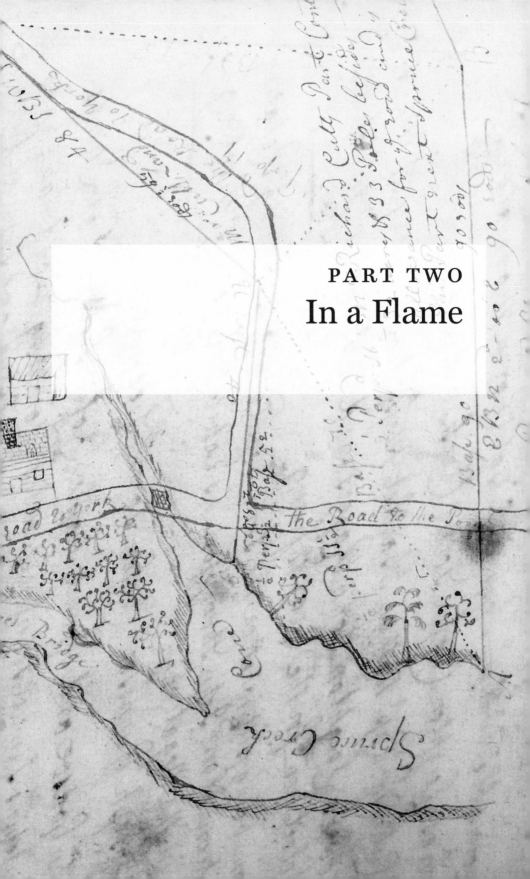

PART TWO

In a Flame

Nathan Cole halted momentarily to catch his breath. He had been running for miles beside his wife, who sat astride their only horse. Earlier that morning, October 23, 1740, a messenger had appeared suddenly at the Coles's farm in Kensington (now Berlin), a small, rural parish that straddled the boundaries of Farmington and Wethersfield, Connecticut, bearing news that the famed Anglican evangelist George Whitefield planned to preach in neighboring Middletown at ten o'clock. Cole immediately threw his tools to the ground, saddled his horse, and summoned his wife. At first, they attempted to ride together. But the horse quickly tired, and Cole was forced to dismount. Instructing his wife to sit in the saddle, he "bid her ride as fast as she could and not Stop or Slack" as he sprinted behind. Alternately riding and running, the Coles covered the twelve-mile distance in little more than an hour. "We improved every moment to get along," he later explained, "as if we were fleeing for our lives." Although it was the harvest season, they saw not a soul at work in the fields. Everyone was gone.[1]

Partway through their journey, the Coles paused to look up at Prospect Hill, a small but steeply pitched and wooded knob that rose above the Upper Houses parish of Middletown (now Cromwell) about three miles from their destination. It was a scene they would never forget. At first, the high land appeared to be cloaked in mist thrown up from the nearby Connecticut River. As the Coles approached closer, they were amazed to discover that the apparent bank of fog was, in fact, a vast cloud of dust. Hundreds of riders were thundering down the rutted cart path that served as the main thoroughfare from Hartford and the upriver towns. Their horses formed a steady stream, each scarcely "more than his length behind another, all of a Lather and foam with

1. NCS, 92–93.

sweat, their breath rolling out of their nostrils every Jump." The summer in New England had been unusually hot and dry, and dust billowed in enormous clouds that obscured both hill and highway.[2]

Slipping into line, the Coles proceeded to the center of town, where local residents had erected a makeshift scaffold for Whitefield's performance. In sight beyond the Middletown meetinghouse were ferries loaded to capacity, with "Oars Rowed nimble and quick," carrying visitors across the river from the opposite shore. *"The land and banks over the river looked black with people and horses,"* Cole later wrote. He estimated that a crowd of perhaps four thousand had gathered, a figure that nearly equaled the entire population of Middletown, which was well on its way to becoming the largest inland port between New York and Boston. Whitefield appeared "almost angelical" as he mounted the platform. A "Slim, slender, youth" with a "bold undaunted Countenance," he "looked as if he was Cloathed with authority from the Great God." Cole trembled as he spoke.[3]

The opening pages of Nathan Cole's "Spiritual Travels" rank among the most widely reprinted autobiographical narratives in early American history. His seemingly unschooled prose lends an air of populist immediacy and authenticity to a unified, transatlantic event that scholars have called the Protestant Evangelical Awakening; however, many interpreters have overlooked that Cole composed his account more than two decades after the events he described. He was no rustic. Nor was he a stranger to religion in 1740. Cole readily acknowledged that he had been a full member of the Kensington church for nearly a decade before Whitefield's first New England preaching tour. A late addition to his autobiographical narrative—added to the original manuscript almost as an afterthought—his artful account of the events in Middletown served instead as the prologue to a polemic in which he justified his later decision to abandon New England's Congregational establishment.[4]

2. Ibid., 93.

3. Ibid., 93; Evarts B. Greene and Virginia D. Harrington, *American Population Before the Federal Census of 1790* (1932; rpt. Gloucester, Mass., 1966), 58.

4. See, especially, Harry S. Stout, "Religion, Communications, and the Ideological Origins of the American Revolution," *WMQ*, XXXIV (1977), 519–520. Studies that emphasize Cole's account of Whitefield's preaching at Middletown and overlook or minimize his earlier and later religious experiences include Edwin Scott Gaustad, *The Great Awakening in New England* (New York, 1957), 53–55; J. M. Bumsted and John E. van de Wetering, *What Must I Do to Be Saved? The Great Awakening in Colonial America*, Berkshire Studies in History (Hinsdale, Ill., 1976), 76–77; W. R. Ward, *The Protestant Evangelical Awakening* (Cambridge, 1992), 287; Mark A. Noll, *The Rise of Evangelicalism: The Age of Edwards, Whitefield, and the Wesleys*, A History of Evangelicalism: People, Movements, and Ideas in the English-Speaking World, I (Downers Grove, Ill., 2003), 107; Thomas S. Kidd, *The Great Awakening: The Roots of Evangelical Christianity in Colonial America* (New Haven, Conn., 2007),

Driven by an almost Manichean juxtaposition of birth and death, light and dark, good and evil, converted and unregenerate, Cole's account of Whitefield's Middletown sermon severed ties with the past with a violence that was almost palpable. In contrast to the angelical itinerant standing boldly atop the scaffold, he imagined the road to Middletown choked with strife and upheaval: riders clouded by dust, obscured by shadows, stifled by sweat, harried by the press of time, and swallowed in a dark mass of hats, shirts, and horses. "Every horse seemed to go with all his might to carry his rider to hear news from heaven for the saving of Souls," he wrote, and "it made me tremble to see the Sight, how the world was in a Struggle." Cole described a society in turmoil waiting to be born again.[5]

For Cole, Whitefield's unexpected arrival in Middletown marked a decisive break with the past and propelled him into an uncertain religious future. Once he had lived in a land of gospel light, an orderly universe of bounded parishes, settled ministers, devotional ordinances both public and private, and rhythms of piety that pulsed through the life-course of earnest believers and their core parish families. Whitefield directly repudiated the ideal of the godly walk. Inspired by the touring evangelist's innovative preaching style, native-born New England itinerants began crisscrossing the region. These "whitfeldarians" or "rideing ministers," as Cole described them, attacked infant baptism, family upbringing, doctrinal knowledge, devotional routines, and healing vows as a "Sandy Foundation" on which to build hopes for salvation. Thousands of Cole's contemporaries responded to their powerful sermons, protracted religious meetings, and other new measures to promote religion. The era of "great awakenings" that began with Whitefield's 1740 tour quickened the pace of religious life in New England and broke down the parish boundaries that had delimited the Congregational establishment for more than a century. "New Converts," as they came to be called, examined their lives for evidence of a discrete conversion experience and imagined themselves as participants in an interconnected religious phenomenon—"a Revival of Religion"—that was rapidly spreading from town to town throughout the Atlantic world.[6]

88–89; and John Howard Smith, *The First Great Awakening: Redefining Religion in British America, 1725–1775* (Lanham, Md., 2015), 127–128.

5. NCS, 93.

6. Nathan Cole, "An Appeal to the Bible," Nathan Cole Papers, 1722–1780, I, 6, CHS; Daniel Rogers, sermon on Matt. 7:21–23, May 3, 1741, box 2, Sermons, 1724–1784, NHHS; NGD, 231; Thomas Foxcroft to Jonathan Dickinson, Dec. 16, 1741, Charles Roberts Autograph Collection, Haverford College Library, Haverford, Pa.; Ross W. Beales, Jr., ed., "'Our Hearts Are Traitors to Themselves': Jonathan Mayhew and the Great Awakening," *Bulletin of the CL*, 1st Ser., XXVII, no. 3 (Spring / Summer 1976), 8.

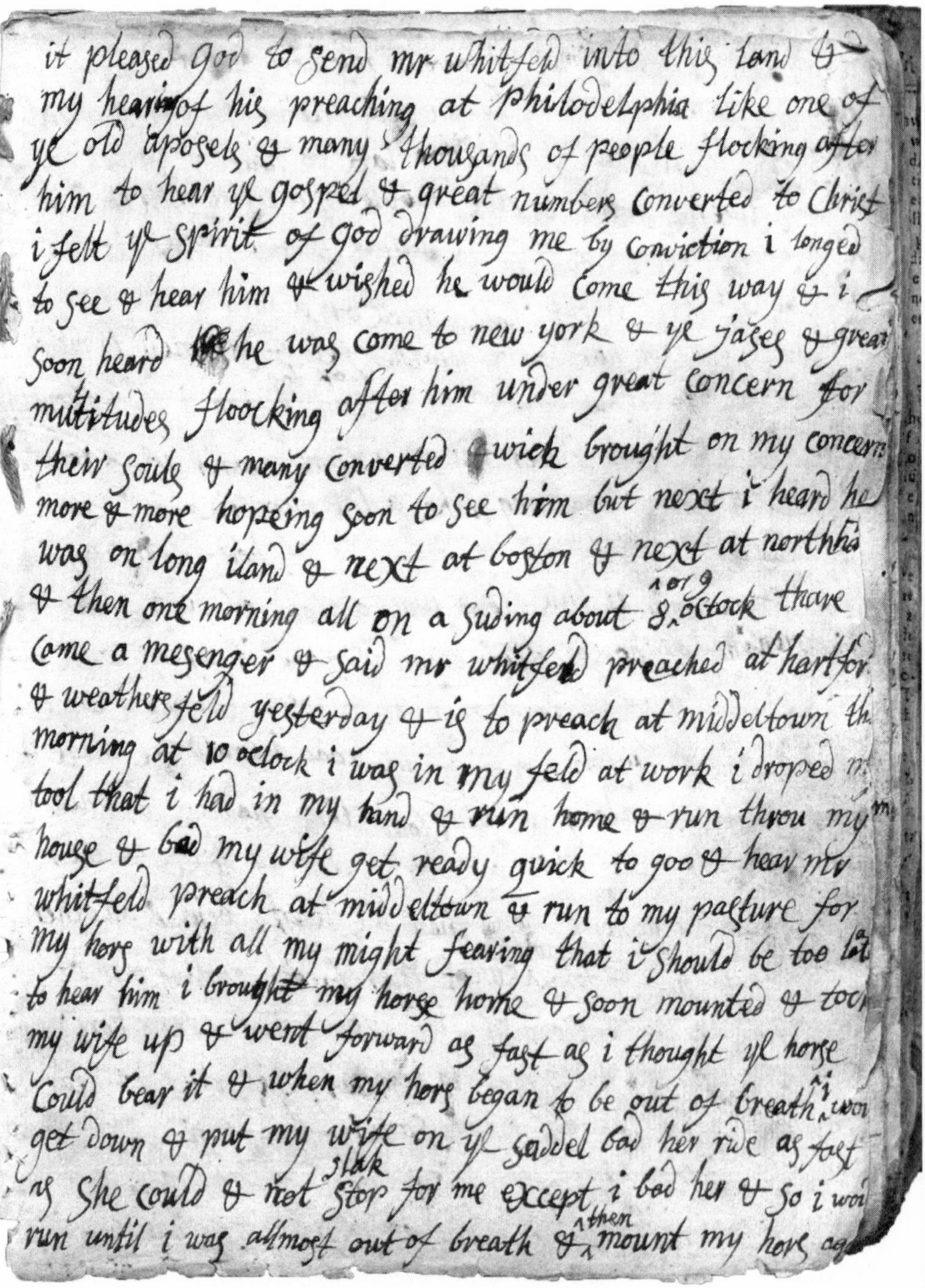

it pleased god to send mr whitfeld into this land &
my hear of his preaching at Philodelphia like one of
ye old aposels & many thousands of people flocking after
him to hear ye gospel & great numbers Converted to Christ
i felt ye spirit of god drawing me by Conviction i longed
to see & hear him & wished he would Come this way & i
soon heard he was come to new york & ye Jases & great
multitudes flocking after him under great Concern for
their souls & many Converted wich brought on my concern
more & more hopeing soon to see him but next i heard he
was on long iland & next at boston & next at northhā
& then one morning all on a suding about 8 oclock thare
Come a mesenger & said mr whitfeld preached at hartfor
& weathersfeld yesterday & is to preach at middeltown th
morning at 10 oclock i was in my feld at work i droped n
tool that i had in my hand & run home & run throu my
house & bad my wife get ready quick to goo & hear mr
whitfeld preach at middeltown & run to my pasture for
my hors with all my might fearing that i should be too la
to hear him i brought my horse home & soon mounted & too
my wife up & went forward as fast as i thought ye horse
Could bear it & when my hors began to be out of breath i wo
get down & put my wife on ye sadel bad her ride as fast
as She could & not stop for me except i bad her & so i wo
run until i was allmost out of breath & then mount my hors ag

FIGURE 10 Nathan Cole's Description of George Whitefield Preaching in
Middletown, Connecticut. "Spiritual Travels" Record Book, 1722–1780.
Courtesy, Connecticut Historical Society, Hartford

Writing from South Carolina to a Boston clergyman on the eve of his first New England tour, Whitefield boldly proclaimed that "Great things" were "doing in America." His earlier preaching in Savannah, Georgia, had been attended with "wonderful power," and recent labors in Charleston had undoubtedly turned "some poor Sinners from darkness to light." Letters from Philadelphia several weeks later carried similar reports of a burgeoning intercolonial awakening. "Surely our Lord intends to set the whole world in a flame," Whitefield concluded triumphantly. And in many New England congregations that is precisely what happened, as impassioned new converts like Nathan Cole rejected the inherited traditions of the godly walk and raced to blow up the foundations of their former religious lives.[7]

THEY BUILD UPON A SANDY FOUNDATION

Nathan Cole was not the only person to describe George Whitefield's visit to Middletown, Connecticut. The touring evangelist himself wrote rather laconically about the affair in the journal that he published later that year. After commenting briefly on the unusual piety of local clergyman William Russell, Whitefield tersely noted that he had preached to an assembly of about four thousand people before moving on to the town of Wallingford. Likewise, the *Boston Weekly News-Letter* listed his Middletown sermon as only one in a string of preaching performances in central Connecticut. Whitefield's more zealous traveling companion, the former Harvard College tutor Daniel Rogers, offered a more detailed description in his diary. He recorded Whitefield's sermon text and asserted that the audience was "much mov'd."[8]

A few who stood among the throng saw things differently. "The Famous Enthusiast Mr. Whitefield was along here, making a great Stir and noise," complained Middletown physician John Osborn in a letter to his father. In his professional opinion, Whitefield's emotive preaching style worked like an insidious disease, propagating contagions of fear and trembling throughout the audience person by person. "His discourse came out exactly to my expectation," the "learned man" and reputed Deist continued. Much like Whitefield's published sermons, several of which Osborn had perused with disgust, the Middletown lecture was little more than a "heap of confusion Railing, Bombast, Fawning, and Nonsense." "Expecting to See and hear good Ora-

---

7. George Whitefield to Benjamin Colman, July 4, 1740, tipped in Benjamin Dorr, *A Historical Account of Christ Church, Philadelphia: From Its Foundation, A.D. 1695, to A.D. 1841 ...* (New York, 1841), following 188, Huntington Library, San Marino, Calif.

8. *GWJ*, 479; *Boston Weekly News-Letter*, Nov. 6, 1740; DDR, Oct. 23, 1740.

tory," Osborn felt "basely cheated" by Whitefield's sermon, "unless distorted motions, Grimaces, and Squeeking voices be good Oratory."[9]

Positive or negative, contemporary reports of Whitefield's first New England preaching tour tended to focus on his physical appearance and rhetorical style, rather than the doctrines and arguments of his sermons. It was not his theology that "gained him such a multitude of hearers," observed Boston superior court justice Paul Dudley, for Whitefield's preaching seemed to be "much like that of the old English Puritans." Similarly, Harvard College tutor Henry Flynt detected little that was original in Whitefield's "old new England and puritanick way of thinking" and spent more time grousing about his commanding oratorical skills. Plymouth, Massachusetts, magistrate Josiah Cotton, too, passed quickly over the content of his sermons and marveled instead at his energy in preaching "every Day in the Week with great Zeal and Earnestness." After witnessing one of Whitefield's sermons, one Connecticut clergyman frankly admitted that he was not a "very polite or correct preacher," but his powerful extemporaneous sermons were carefully calculated to rouse "Stupid and thotless Sinners" in "this Dead and frozen Age."[10]

Cole understood not only the force of Whitefield's innovative preaching techniques but also his influence on local ministers. "After Mr. whitfeld went through the land like an angel," he noted in one of his later theological manuscripts, a zealous coterie of New England clergymen "stept into gods way and went forth in the same spirit thundering along through the land like sons of thunder." Often working together in teams, they crisscrossed the region preaching two or more sermons each day of the week. The distinctive mark that "god was with them," Cole asserted, was the simple fact that they "could not be pestered" with preaching from written sermon notes. Extemporaneous

9. John Osborn to Samuel Osborn, Nov. 17, 1740, MS Ch A 4.6, Boston Public Library; Franklin Bowditch Dexter, ed., *Extracts from the Itineraries and Other Miscellanies of Ezra Stiles, D.D., LL.D., 1755–1794* ... (New Haven, Conn., 1916), 395.

10. B. Joy Jeffries, [ed.], "Diary of Paul Dudley, 1740," *NEHGR*, XXXV (1881), 29; Edward T. Dunn, ed., "The Diary of Tutor Henry Flynt of Harvard College, 1675–1760," 3 vols., typescript (Buffalo, N.Y., 1978), 1453; *JCH*, 310–311; William Gaylord to Eleazar Wheelock, Nov. 24, 1740, in Richard L. Bushman, ed., *The Great Awakening: Documents on the Revival of Religion, 1740–1745*, Documentary Problems in Early American History (New York, 1970), 39. Studies that emphasize Whitefield's preaching innovations, marketing strategies, and charismatic personality over his purportedly derivative theology include Harry S. Stout, *The Divine Dramatist: George Whitefield and the Rise of Modern Evangelicalism*, Library of Religious Biography (Grand Rapids, Mich., 1991), 38; and Frank Lambert, *"Pedlar in Divinity": George Whitefield and the Transatlantic Revivals, 1737–1770* (Princeton, N.J., 1994), 19–20. For a more balanced treatment and assessment of Whitefield's accomplishments over the course of his long career, see Thomas S. Kidd, *George Whitefield: America's Spiritual Founding Father* (New Haven, Conn., 2014).

speech combined with relentless travel transformed puritan plain-style homiletics into the inspired performances of those whom the Kensington artisan had begun to call "whitfeldarians."[11]

At the same time, Cole's account also indicated just how radical the theological content of Whitefield's sermons struck some members of his audiences. The same event that might have appeared commonplace to Whitefield, empty raillery to John Osborn, or traditionally "puritanick" to other observers, initiated a remarkable period of turmoil in Cole's religious life. "My hearing him preach," Cole later recalled, "gave me a heart wound." More than mere sound and gesture, Whitefield's preaching was assaultive, incendiary, and corrosive. "My old Foundation was broken up," he continued, "and I saw that my righteousness would not save me." Drawing on the parable of the two builders in Matthew 7:26, Cole's erosional metaphor signaled an explicit repudiation of the ideal of the godly walk. As thousands of other New Englanders would soon discover, Cole realized to his great dismay that he had "built his house upon the sand."[12]

Cole perceived Whitefield's Middletown sermon as something qualitatively different both in style and content from the preaching under which he had lived for three decades in the gospel land of light. Descended from a prominent core parish family of Farmington, Connecticut, he had constructed his personal faith on what he had once thought to be the sturdy footing of his family upbringing, devotional duties, doctrinal knowledge, and healing vows. Following his breakneck ride to Middletown, Cole began quarreling in his mind with God over the meaning of the Calvinist doctrine of election. Whitefield had convinced him that devotional duties were inconsequential to a God who had "decreed from Eternity who should be saved and who not." For nearly a year, Cole struggled to resolve the theological misgivings unleashed by Whitefield's sermon. And this was only the start of his spiritual travels.[13]

■ Arriving in Newport, Rhode Island, in October 1740, Whitefield encountered a culture that had grown accustomed to periodic seasons of heightened religious concern. The religious awakening that enveloped British North America, however, differed from regional precursors owing to the attention that publishers heaped on the Anglican itinerant. Whitefield was a calculating entrepreneur who developed sophisticated marketing strategies to ensure the success of his various preaching excursions throughout the colonies.

11. Cole, "Appeal to the Bible," Nathan Cole Papers, I, 6.
12. Dunn, ed., "Diary of Tutor Henry Flynt," 1453; NCS, 93.
13. NCS, 94.

Correspondence with colonial clergymen and prominent merchants stimulated public demand for his oratorical skills and created an expansive support network that provided financial and logistical assistance during his travels. Together with his personal secretary William Seward, Whitefield shrewdly exploited a wide variety of print media as well. Newspapers chronicled his preaching engagements, advertised the publication of his sermons and travel journals, reported his pulpit successes, printed his correspondence, and announced his future itineraries. Benjamin Franklin and other booksellers scrambled to hawk his popular *Journals* and other commodities, including the itinerant's mezzotint portrait. Whitefield, in short, capitalized on a midcentury consumer revolution and engineered the first modern religious awakening in the Atlantic world.[14]

Self-promotion paid handsome dividends during Whitefield's first New England circuit. He traveled from Newport to Boston, then out and back to the eastward settlements in New Hampshire and Maine. After another week in Boston, he struck out for Northampton, Massachusetts, before working his way down the Connecticut Valley through Middletown and along the coast back to New York. Over the course of forty-six days, Whitefield delivered upwards of one hundred sermons in forty-one different towns as well as numerous informal discourses and public prayers. His sermons drew thousands of eager listeners from distant communities. So many people crowded into Boston's New South meetinghouse that the gallery cracked, generating a panic that killed five and injured many others. In the days that followed, Whitefield held forth on Boston Common to crowds estimated at between twenty and thirty thousand people, a figure that almost doubled the population of the entire city.[15]

Whitefield spoke in a direct, flamboyant, and emotive manner that blended English theater techniques with the warm pietism of John and Charles Wesley's Holy Club of Methodists at the University of Oxford, where Whitefield had studied during the 1730s. In place of the textual expositions, doctrines, and applications of traditional puritan sermons, Whitefield kept his homilies short and to the point. Tightly organized around a few key headings, they focused on vivid scriptural metaphors, colorful biblical characters, or well-known stories and parables. Whitefield personalized his sermons by subdividing his application into exhortations that targeted specific groups such

14. Lambert, *"Pedlar in Divinity,"* 52–94; Lisa Smith, *The First Great Awakening in Colonial American Newspapers: A Shifting Story* (Lanham, Md., 2012), 102–111.

15. *GWJ*, 451–483; Stout, *Divine Dramatist*, 113–132. Tax assessor Benjamin Walker, Jr., estimated the total population of Boston at 16,528. See Benjamin Walker, Jr., "Account of the Town of Boston," Dec. 14, 1742, diaries, 1726–1749, MHS.

as youths, women, slaves, or old men. Above all, he sought to connect with his listeners by preaching outdoors without formal sermon notes. Extemporaneous speech and dramatic voice modulation, punctuated by extravagant bodily gestures and frequent tearful outbursts, rounded out a repertoire of preaching strategies calibrated to elicit strong emotional responses.[16]

New Englanders had never seen anything like it. The rhetorical power of Whitefield's gospel labors soon persuaded other clergymen to adopt his emotive oratorical style. A little more than a month after Whitefield's departure, the fiery New Jersey Presbyterian Gilbert Tennent arrived in Boston, hoping to "blow up the divine fire lately kindled there." Whereas Whitefield captivated his audiences with his theatrical sermon performances, Tennent bludgeoned his listeners with multiple sermons preached over a period of several days in a single location. Transforming the traditional three-day Scottish communion season into a protracted religious meeting, he harangued assemblies in long discourses that began in the morning and ended in candlelight. Tennent preached eight sermons during a brief stay in Plymouth on his return trip to New Jersey in the spring of 1741; New London magistrate Joshua Hempstead attended six of his lectures on a pair of consecutive weekdays; Sarah Osborn claimed to have witnessed twenty-one sermons in Newport; New Haven gentlewoman Sarah Pierpont heard eighteen "Soul-Searching Sermons" in less than seven days; and Boston merchant Isaac Smith traveled with Tennent and recorded hearing an astonishing fifty-six sermons in just three weeks. The volume, intensity, and duration of these meetings, rather than the artfulness of his preaching, distinguished Tennent's labors from Whitefield's. According to the aspiring Whitefieldarian Daniel Rogers, Tennent spoke in a "Surprizing manner" with "great Power and Authority," and his rousing sermons "Shocked" his audiences. "Great Concern seemed immediately to follow his preaching" wherever he traveled, concluded one Connecticut minister.[17]

16. Eugene E. White, "The Preaching of George Whitefield during the Great Awakening in America," *Speech Monographs*, XV (1948), 33–43; Stout, *Divine Dramatist*, 38–44.

17. *Letters of George Whitefield for the Period 1734–1742* (Edinburgh, 1976), 221; *The Diary of Joshua Hempstead: A Daily Record of Life in Colonial New London, Connecticut, 1711–1758 . . .*, rev. ed. (New London, Conn., 1999), 371; Samuel Hopkins, *Memoirs of the Life of Mrs. Sarah Osborn . . .* (Worcester, Mass., 1799), 45; Ebenezer Parkman, "Memoirs of Mrs. Sarah Pierpont," n.d. [circa 1754], [70], box 2, Parkman Family Papers, 1707–1879, AAS; Isaac Smith, diaries, 1739–1744, Mar. 9–31, 1741, Smith-Carter Family Papers, 1669–1880, microfilm, reel 1, MHS; DDR, Feb. 13, 15, 1741; David Jewett to Benjamin Colman, May 29, 1741, Colman-Jenks Collection, 1651–1809, MHS. For Tennent's early career and New England tour, see Milton J. Coalter, Jr., *Gilbert Tennent, Son of Thunder: A Case Study of Continental Pietism's Impact on the First Great Awakening in the Middle Colonies*, Contributions to the Study of Religion, XVIII (Westport, Conn., 1986), 55–89.

Few could match Tennent's endurance, for, as Rogers frankly admitted, preaching three times in a day seemed beyond his "Natural Strength"; nevertheless, Tennent's sojourn in New England established a pattern for those who followed. After touring with Whitefield and Tennent, Rogers decided to set out on an ambitious month-long preaching circuit of northern New England during the summer of 1741 (Map 3). No sooner had he returned to his native Ipswich, Massachusetts, when he departed again, this time for the Old Colony. In one month, Rogers delivered forty sermons in twenty parishes. Along the way, he encountered Eleazar Wheelock, the minister at Lebanon Crank (now Columbia), Connecticut, who was already at work on a similar errand. Together, the two riding ministers preached their way to Boston. Both men were, as one colleague put it, "much in Itinirant Labours" during the next two years. In addition to his initial tour of southeastern New England, Wheelock preached in at least twenty other towns in 1741 and 1742, and he received invitations from nearly a dozen more. Rogers chronicled six major circuits in his diary during this same period, as he ranged widely across central and southeastern Massachusetts, eastern Connecticut, and the northern New England frontier.[18]

Wheelock and Rogers were only the best documented examples among a prominent cohort of native-born itinerants that crisscrossed New England during the three years following Whitefield's 1740 tour. Samuel Buell spent nearly a year on the road after graduating from Yale College in 1742, moving steadily across the region from Northampton and the small hamlets of central Massachusetts to Boston and down east Maine. The Bethlehem, Connecticut, clergyman Joseph Bellamy, too, traveled extensively in 1741 and 1742, delivering an estimated 458 sermons in 213 parishes. Equally ubiquitous were young Connecticut firebrands Andrew Croswell of Groton's north parish (now Ledyard), Jedidiah Mills of Stratford's Ripton Society (now Huntington), Benjamin Pomeroy of Hebron, Yale College student David Brainerd, and a host of other, lesser known New England clergymen. So many of the principal itinerants descended on Hartford and the surrounding towns during the spring and summer of 1741 that minister Daniel Wadsworth complained of "much Talk and running after new preachers" among his parishioners. "Steady christians," he grumbled, "generally dislike these new things set afoot."[19]

18. DDR, Oct. 11, 1741; John Graham to Eleazar Wheelock, Feb. 12, 1742, no. 742162, *EWP.*

19. Mark Valeri, *Law and Providence in Joseph Bellamy's New England: The Origins of the New Divinity in Revolutionary America*, Religion in America (New York, 1994), 19; George Leon Walker, ed., *Diary of Rev. Daniel Wadsworth, Seventh Pastor of the First Church of*

MAP 3 Daniel Rogers's Itinerant Preaching Tours, 1741–1742. Drawn by Mark Cook
All tours start and end in Ipswich, Massachusetts.

Ministers of a more cautious bent, including Northampton's Jonathan Edwards, traveled sporadically and by invitation only. Indeed, pulpit exchanges appear to have increased during the early 1740s. The North Hartford ministerial association passed a resolution in June 1741 encouraging members to set up frequent weekday lectures to "promote Religion and the Saving Conversion of souls." Commanding orators, such as Wheelock and Bellamy, received dozens of invitations from distant ministers, many of whom they had never met. The "Utmost Importunity" with which local clergymen begged their traveling colleagues to visit their parishes underscored the waxing power of the Whitefieldarians. "I Cant be denied of you," pleaded Peter Thacher of Middleborough, Massachusetts, in a hastily written note sent to Wheelock during his 1741 tour of southeastern New England. "I wont take A denial from You." The following week, a group of parishioners in Boston playfully threatened to confine him in the New North meetinghouse if he refused to stay and preach another day.[20]

Whitefield was pleased to learn that colleagues in New England had adopted his preaching techniques. Thomas Smith, the minister in Falmouth, Maine, delivered his first unscripted sermon less than one week after traveling to see Whitefield during the fall of 1740. Rogers abandoned his carefully crafted sermon notes and began jotting down brief outlines on scraps of paper less than a year later. Edwards developed a similar outlining technique early in 1742. Wheelock did so as well, although he eventually learned to preach "wholly memoritor." So did a number of little-known pastors and recent college graduates, including Edwards's student Samuel Hopkins, Daniel Bliss of Concord, Massachusetts, Josiah Crocker of Taunton, Massachusetts, and Connecticut ministers Jonathan Parsons and Philemon Robbins. Reduced to a single, folded sheet of paper, Robbins's sermons, in particular, consisted entirely of loosely numbered headings, sentence fragments, and individual keywords that cascaded down the page in a disorderly fashion that subverted the

---

Christ in Hartford, with Notes by the Fourteenth Pastor, 1737-1747 (Hartford, Conn., 1894), 65, 72–73. On the emergence of native-born itinerants, see Harry S. Stout, *The New England Soul: Preaching and Religious Culture in Colonial New England* (New York, 1986), 200–201.

20. Hartford North Association, Records, 1700–1800, I, 28, Connecticut Conference Archives, United Church of Christ (currently on deposit at CL; available online at NEHH); Peter Tha[ch]er to Eleazar Wheelock, Nov. 2, 1741, in Bushman, ed., *Great Awakening*, 43; EWD, 239. Similar letters of invitation to Joseph Bellamy and Jonathan Edwards may be found among the Joseph Bellamy Papers, Case Memorial Library, Hartford Seminary, Hartford, Conn.; in Richard Webster, transcr., "Letters to Joseph Bellamy from Aaron Burr, David Brainerd, etc., and Other Papers concerning Mr. Bellamy," 1739–1787, microfilm, Presbyterian Historical Society, Philadelphia; and in *WJEO*, XXXII, *Correspondence by, to, and about Edwards and His Family.*

traditional plain-style organizational schema, with its careful doctrinal exposition neatly dissected into numbered headings.[21]

Modified sermon notes proved to be the perfect vehicle for New England's new riding ministers. Compact, portable, and easily memorized, they liberated itinerants to deliver multiple lectures in various communities over an extended period. The most prominent itinerant preachers recycled two-thirds of their sermons during their travels. Each repeat performance offered new opportunities to hone the theatrical aspects of their delivery. Robbins wrote the word "amplify" on several sermons that date to the early 1740s. His notations might have included cues to raise the pitch of his voice. Composed with large gaps between underlined headings, abbreviated sermon notes created space for impromptu speech and provided visual markers that helped the speaker return to the basic flow of the sermon after extemporaneous digressions. Powerful delivery increasingly took precedence over measured composition as the Whitefieldarians strove to engage the affections of their audiences.[22]

The diary of Marston Cabot, the unassuming pastor of the north parish in Killingly (now Thompson), Connecticut, reveals the process through which Whitefield's preaching innovations penetrated even the most remote corners of New England. Ordained in 1730, Cabot was a diligent but sickly clergyman who suffered from a chronic digestive ailment that frequently left him bedridden. He often reported in his diary that he had "Sett a Vomiting" shortly after rising in the morning or "lost my breakfast" on the way to Sabbath meetings. In November 1741, Cabot received word that Eleazar Wheelock had arrived in his isolated hilltop parish. He immediately dispatched a brief preaching invitation to the touring Whitefieldarian. Wheelock obliged with three sermons delivered to the "vast attention" of the Killingly congregation. Deeply impressed, Cabot started to experiment with Wheelock's emotive sermon style

21. *GWJ*, 470; William Willis, ed., *Journals of the Rev. Thomas Smith, and the Rev. Samuel Deane* (Portland, Maine, 1849), 95; Douglas L. Winiarski, "Jonathan Edwards, Enthusiast? Radical Revivalism and the Great Awakening in the Connecticut Valley," *Church History*, LXXIV (2005), 738. The argument in this paragraph builds on Donald Weber, *Rhetoric and History in Revolutionary New England* (New York, 1988), 22–27. For additional examples of modified sermon notes, see Rogers, sermons, 1739–1787; Rogers, Sermons, 1724–1784; Wilson H. Kimnach, "General Introduction," in *WJE*, X, *Sermons and Discourses, 1720–1723* (New Haven, Conn., 1992), 62–63, 115–124; Eleazar Wheelock, sermons, 1734–1778, *EWP;* Samuel Hopkins, journal, 1741–1744, 44–45, 51, 56, box 322, SGC II; Hopkins, sermons, 1744–1800, Samuel Hopkins Papers, 1740–1800, Huntington Library, San Marino, Calif.; Daniel Bliss, sermons, 1743, Emerson Family Papers, 1699–1939, Ser. II, part A, folder 230, MS Am 1280.235, HL; Samuel Hopkins Emery, *The Ministry of Taunton, with Incidental Notices of Other Professions*, 2 vols. (Boston, 1853), I, 381–382; and Jonathan Parsons, sermons, 1737–1759, WCL.

22. Weber, *Rhetoric and History*, 26–27.

just one week later. Although he never dispensed with written sermon notes, the frail clergyman preached with greater emotional intensity, or what he called "freedom and liberty." "I find by Experience Lively preaching makes diligent hearing," he explained shortly after Wheelock's departure. "May I be filled more and more with that holiness and Zeal that becomes God's House!"[23]

During the next year, Cabot paid close attention to his own emotional temperament while in the pulpit, noting occasions on which he felt "Divine Warmth" and "Zeal." He also used his diary to track the impact of his "pungent" addresses on his parishioners. "May my Words go from the heart and reach the heart," he prayed in February 1742. His parishioners responded. More than sixty men and women presented themselves for admission to full communion in his small church; strangers from neighboring communities attended his meetings; and the entire town seemed to "thirst after the Word." In pastoral conferences at his home, Cabot encountered dozens of people who claimed to have "received light by some Sermons I'de lately delivered." The Killingly minister had never felt so alive.[24]

For a "poor and feeble" country parson plagued by a debilitating illness, preaching success clearly signaled that he had been quickened by God's Holy Spirit. "I am more and more confirmed," Cabot concluded a week after Daniel Rogers visited his parish, "Were it not for a divine power I could not go through the Services I am called to." Watching itinerants such as Wheelock and Rogers and adopting their preaching tactics, Cabot became convinced that God had fitted him as an "Instrument of Good to the Souls of men." To zealous Whitefieldarians, preaching, properly understood, meant becoming one of God's inspired "Oracles."[25]

■ There was more to the sermons of George Whitefield, Gilbert Tennent, and New England's riding ministers than mere oratorical pyrotechnics. Theologically, their sermons represented a narrowing of traditional preaching themes. Whereas provincial clergymen spoke on a broad range of issues—redeeming time, improving providences and afflictions, upright moral behavior, preparation for salvation—the Whitefieldarians trained their sights on election and

23. Marston Cabot, "Memorabilia," 1740–1745, May 4, 1740, Nov. 15–22, 1741, May 30, 1742, Mss A 1999, NEHGS; Cabot to Eleazar Wheelock, n.d. [Nov. 15, 1741], no. 741900.1, *EWP; EWD*, 240.

24. Cabot, "Memorabilia," Jan. 10, Feb. 7, Mar. 7–14, Aug. 8–15, Sept. 26, Nov. 21, 1742. See also *Manual of the Congregational Church in Thompson, Conn., 1730–1901* (Worcester, Mass., 1901), 28–29.

25. Cabot, "Memorabilia," July 18, Aug. 15, Sept. 26, Nov. 21, 1742. See also DDR, Sept. 22, 1742.

conversion and massed their impassioned preaching rhetoric in a frontal assault on the entrenched ideals of the godly walk and the prevailing conventions of church admission relations.

Published in London and Boston before his first American tour, the Anglican evangelist's celebrated early sermon, *The Nature and Necessity of Our New Birth in Jesus Christ,* drew a sharp line between the doctrine of the new birth and a godly conversation. Whitefield maintained that most people were orthodox Christians, at least in their beliefs. "But then tell them, They must be REGENERATE, they must be BORN AGAIN, they must be renewed in the very *Spirit,*" he chided, and "they are ready to cry out with *Nicodemus,* 'How can these things be?'" Investing hope for eternal salvation in outward religious observances or professions of belief, Whitefield continued, was a fatal mistake. To be *"in Christ,"* one must also testify to an "inward Change" wrought in the heart. Born of water in baptism, the gracious Christian must be born again, or transformed into a *"new Creature."* Thus, Whitefield urged his readers not to depend on a profession of beliefs or the mere observance of sacramental duties but to press forward to a *"thorough, sound* Conversion."[26]

Gilbert Tennent upbraided established church members for their religious laxity. The only sermon that he published from his extended visit to Boston roundly condemned *"old secure Professors."* They were like the Pharisees described in the gospel of Matthew: strict and punctual in their devotional practices, zealous and diligent in praying publicly or with their families, and honest in their worldly dealings. Many of these dutiful hypocrites would never enter the *"invisible"* kingdom of heaven, even though they were full members of the "visible Church" in New England. The means of grace were not in themselves sinful, Tennent argued; rather, too many *"Formalists"* pursued them for the wrong reasons. Some performed their devotional duties "meerly by the Force of a *religious Education"* or out of a slavish fear of damnation; others hoped to "obtain Credit" among their neighbors by appearing pious; and a few mistakenly believed that assiduously practicing religious duties might "do something towards the purchasing of God's Favour for them." In short, Tennent asserted, "They endeavour to grow in Grace, before they get Grace." Without conversion, New England's church membership Pharisees who contented themselves with their "dead dry Round of Duties" made no more progress toward salvation than a "turnspit Dog in a Wheel."[27]

26. George Whitefield, *The Nature and Necessity of Our New Birth in Christ Jesus, in Order to Salvation ...* (London, 1737), 2, 5, 18, 22.

27. Gilbert Tennent, *The Righteousness of the Scribes and Pharisees Considered ...* (Boston, 1741), 2–4, 11–13, 16.

During the months following Whitefield's and Tennent's preaching tours, local clergymen grew increasingly acerbic in their attacks on the godly walking. A Boston minister threatened damnation on the diligent, but purportedly unconverted, church members in his congregation who lead upright moral lives, prayed in secret, promoted family devotions, and participated in the Lord's Supper. While visiting Jonathan Edwards in Northampton, Yale College student Stephen Williams, Jr., reported hearing a sermon in which an unassuming ministerial candidate argued that church membership "Professors who had no internal divine principle would be Cast into outer Darkness." Solomon Williams aggressively sought to cut away the props supporting the hopeful assurance of the professors in his Lebanon, Connecticut, parish. A person's "Good Qualities and outward Virtues," he asserted, were of no help; worldly power and family relations ultimately achieved nothing; and assenting to the "Truth of the Gospel" was not enough. Philemon Robbins even accused those who observed only the "Forms of Religion" of committing acts of "spiritual fornication" that justly exposed them to God's wrath. Eleazar Wheelock argued in one of his sacramental sermons that all outward practices including the Lord's Supper were an "abomination" without an "inward Conformity" to God. "God's anger Burns hotter" against such hypocrites, he thundered on another occasion. Full church members who made an "External profession" yet lacked grace were "fit for nil but Everlasting Burnings."[28]

Other notable itinerants, such as Andrew Croswell, were even less restrained. When the Plymouth minister invited him to participate in the Lord's Supper and deliver a suitable sacramental sermon, the zealous riding minister responded with a torrid discourse on Matthew 11:28. Instead of promising rest to his weary and heavy-laden auditors, Croswell excoriated the church's full members. "I have been at Communion with you, today," he fulminated, and "I doubt not, but if you were to die tonight, 3 quarters of you would be damned to Hell." Croswell did not intend for his incendiary remark to be perceived as uncharitable, for he had discovered an equal number of dead souls among his own congregation in the north parish of Groton. Indeed, he, too, "knew no more, really, of Jesus Christ, than the beast I rode on" until he heard Whitefield and Tennent preach on the necessity of conversion. Like Nathan Cole and many others Whitefieldarians, Croswell discovered that he had "ever

28. Joshua Bowles, commonplace book, 1737–1776, 55, Mss C 1649, NEHGS; Stephen Williams, Jr., diary, 1742–1747, Dec. 2, 1742, Stephen Williams Family Papers, 1742–1815, MS 1430, YUA; Solomon Williams, sermon fragment, n.d. [circa early 1740s], JWC; Philemon Robbins, sermon on Rev. 2:21, Aug. 8, 1742, Robbins Family Papers, 1724–circa 1803, CHS; Eleazar Wheelock, sermons on Matt. 5:23–24, Feb. 20, 1741, and Matt. 3:10, Apr. 1741, *EWP*.

built on a false foundation." "I tell you now," he shouted at the Plymouth congregation, "that a man may live in all the commandments and ordinances of the Lord blameless, and yet go to Hell at last." Foremost among the fingered hypocrites was a group of *"Old grey headed Sinners"* seated nearest the pulpit, which included the town's most prominent church officers and community leaders. "You unconverted sinners," he railed the following day in a sermon on the miseries of hell, "GOD hates every one of you, as he does the Devils and damned Spirits in hell, and to one degree worse, inasmuch as they have never sinned against redeeming love and grace as you have."[29]

In the Connecticut Valley, where clergymen had been engineering church membership stirs and harvests for more than two generations, Jonathan Edwards and his most accomplished student, Joseph Bellamy, appear to have narrowed the theological focus of their sermons for several years before Whitefield's visit. Following the religious stirs of the 1730s, both clergymen minimized the importance of doctrinal knowledge, baptism, youthful religious training, upright moral conversations, the smiles of divine providence, and social status. All marks of a godly walk were untrustworthy signs of inward grace, or, worse, Pharisaical pretenses that prevented convicted sinners from pressing forward to conversion. Writing to Whitefield in February 1740, Edwards encouraged him to visit Northampton but expressed concern that the town would not live up to its emerging transatlantic reputation. "We who have dwelt in a land that has been distinguished with light, and have long enjoyed the gospel, and have been glutted with it, and have despised it," Edwards complained, castigating his parishioners, "are I fear more hardened than most of those places where you have preached hitherto."[30]

Shortly after Whitefield passed through Northampton the following fall, Edwards began praying that he might become "fervent, as a flame of fire in my work." Throughout the winter of 1741, he upbraided the formal professors in his congregation and relentlessly hammered away at the dangers of hypocrisy. In one extended sermon series, he compared full church members to the stony ground hearers in the parable of the sower in Matthew 13. Many

29. "Extracts from the Manuscripts of Josiah Cotton, Esq.," [1–2], Cotton Families Collection, PHM; JCH, 329. See also Leigh Eric Schmidt, "'A Second and Glorious Reformation': The New Light Extremism of Andrew Croswell," *WMQ*, XLIII (1986), 214–244.

30. Ava Chamberlain, "Brides of Christ and Signs of Grace: Edwards's Sermon Series on the Parable of the Wise and Foolish Virgins," in Stephen J. Stein, ed., *Jonathan Edwards's Writings: Text, Context, Interpretation* (Bloomington, Ind., 1996), 3–18; Valeri, *Law and Providence in Joseph Bellamy's New England,* 22–33; Jonathan Edwards to George Whitefield, Feb. 12, 1740, in *WJE*, XVI, *Letters and Personal Writings*, ed. George Claghorn (New Haven, Conn., 1998), 80.

who had joined the church in Northampton during the religious awakening that had gripped the Connecticut Valley during the 1730s, he warned, had become puffed up with pride. "Han't we been too much like a cake not turned," Edwards quipped, "religious as to the external duties" but inwardly destitute of inward grace. On other occasions, he divided his audience into "servants of God" and "professors of godliness." The latter could speak only of "pretenses to experience a work of conversion." Edwards went so far as to align "Christless" church members with unredeemed Indian captives who had been forced to convert to Catholicism.[31]

Not only did Edwards vehemently condemn "God's visible people" for their alleged torpor; he singled them out for especially gruesome punishments. God had reserved the "lowest place in hell" for "quiet and secure" church members, Edwards argued in "Sinners in Zion," which he preached only a few weeks after Whitefield's departure from Northampton. Hypocritical professors who "attend God's ordinances and make a show of being God's worshippers" would receive ten times the wrath meted out on those who were "visibly of Satan's kingdom." "When the light that is in men is darkness, how great is that darkness," Edwards noted ominously. "And when they live in wickedness in the midst of great light, that light is like to be turned into the blackness of darkness indeed."[32]

Edwards's caustic attacks on unconverted church members culminated in his homiletic masterpiece, *Sinners in the Hands of an Angry God*. Originally preached in Northampton but made famous during a visit to Enfield, Massachusetts (now Connecticut), on July 8, 1741, Edwards's sermon drew its overwhelming rhetorical force from two dozen evocative literary images, a stark juxtaposition of terror and hope, an intensely personal tone, escalating emotional appeal, and pulsating rhythm. Equally crucial to *Sinners*'s success, moreover, was the audience to whom the Northampton minister appealed halfway through the sermon. Who were the subjects of God's everlasting punishment? Whose feet would slide inexorably into the gaping maw of hell, drawn by the irresistible pull of their sinful natures? Who were the figures

31. Jonathan Edwards to George Whitefield, Dec. 14, 1740, in *WJE*, XVI, *Letters and Personal Writings*, ed. Claghorn, 87; Ava Chamberlain, "The Grand Sower of the Seed: Jonathan Edwards's Critique of George Whitefield," *NEQ*, LXX (1997), 376–377; and Edwards, "Bringing the Ark to Zion a Second Time," in *WJE*, XXII, *Sermons and Discourses, 1739–1742*, ed. Harry S. Stout and Nathan O. Hatch, with Kyle P. Farley (New Haven, Conn., 2003), 259, "God's Care for His Servants in Time of Public Commotions," 354–355, 357.

32. Edwards, "Sinners in Zion," in *WJE*, XXII, *Sermons and Discourses, 1739–1742*, ed. Stout and Hatch, 268, 278–279.

creeping across the "pit of hell on a rotten covering"? Against whose heart was the "bow of God's wrath" bent?[33]

The outwardly wicked justly deserved to be cast into the lake of eternal fire, but Edwards had a more specific target in mind. "God's visible people"—full church members who could not testify to a work of grace on their hearts—ran the greatest risk of inciting divine wrath.

> Thus are all you that never passed under a great change of heart, by the mighty power of the Spirit of God upon your souls; all that were never born again, and made new creatures, and raised from being dead in sin, to a state of new, and before altogether unexperienced light and life (however you may have reformed your life in many things, and may have had religious affections, and may keep up a form of religion in your families and closets, and in the house of God, and may be strict in it), you are thus in the hand of an angry God; 'tis nothing but his mere pleasure that keeps you from being this moment swallowed up in everlasting destruction.

Living carefully, performing devotional duties, and reading bodily health as a sign of divine favor were merely ways that those whom he called "natural" sinners descended into a kind of spiritual indolence. God was under no obligation to preserve Christless church members from eternal destruction, he asserted. Turning to address his audience directly, Edwards proclaimed that the "bigger part of those that heretofore have lived under the same means of grace, and are now dead, are undoubtedly gone to hell." His words stunned the communicants in the Enfield assembly, for he had aimed all of the literary weapons for which *Sinners* is justly famous—including the sermon's most enduring image of the loathsome spider dangling "over the pit of hell"— directly at them. Anyone who had not been born again, "however moral and strict, sober and religious they may otherwise be," would suffer eternal tor-

---

33. Jonathan Edwards, *Sinners in the Hands of an Angry God* (Boston, 1741), in *WJE*, XXII, *Sermons and Discourses, 1739–1742*, ed. Stout and Hatch, 407, 411. On Edwards's rhetorical strategies in *Sinners*, see Edwin H. Cady, "The Artistry of Jonathan Edwards," *NEQ*, XXII (1949), 61–72; Annette Kolodny, "Imagery in the Sermons of Jonathan Edwards," *EAL*, VII (1972), 172–182; Robert Lee Stuart, "Jonathan Edwards at Enfield: 'And Oh the Cheerfulness and Pleasantness . . . ,'" *American Literature*, XLVIII (1976), 46–59; Thomas J. Steele and Eugene R. Delay, "Vertigo in History: The Threatening Tactility of 'Sinners in the Hands,'" *EAL*, XVIII (1983–1984), 242–256; Rosemary Hearn, "Form as Argument in Edwards' 'Sinners in the Hands of an Angry God,'" *CLA Journal*, XXVIII (1985), 452–459; and Edward J. Gallagher, "'Sinners in the Hands of an Angry God': Some Unfinished Business," *NEQ*, LXXIII (2000), 202–221.

ment under the wrath of God, Edwards concluded. "We know not who they are, or in what seats they sit."[34]

New England's most active Whitefieldarian, Daniel Rogers, sounded similar warnings from Maine to southern Connecticut. He noted numerous occasions in his diary when he directly attacked "formal Professors" in his sermons, prayers, and lectures. Delivered in Boston and towns throughout eastern Massachusetts during the early 1740s, Rogers's sermon on Matthew 7:21 cataloged the many "false grounds" that pious people "build their hopes upon." Too many church members mistakenly associated divine election with the religious privileges of their youth—the tribal benefits handed down from "pious Ancestors," imparted by godly parents, or conferred through infant baptism. Others experienced emotional "Enlargement and Affection" by performing private and family devotional duties, attending Sabbath exercises and weekly lectures, and "Especially upon their Communicating in the Sacrament." A third group rested content in their knowledge of essential Reformed doctrines. Some, Rogers contended, even believed that "moral Goodness" would secure their eternal estate. Those who claimed to be free from "open Scandalous Sins," did "nobody any harm," or were "just and honest in their dealings," the Ipswich itinerant warned, "dont doubt of going to Heaven." All were mortally wrong.[35]

Rogers's list challenged nearly all the generic conventions of the traditional relation of faith formula. Being born and brought up in a land of light counted for nothing for those who lacked saving grace. A "head of knowledge of Spiritual things" was useless, or worse, without the inner illumination of God's Holy Spirit. Communicants who drew comfort from the renaissance in sacramental theology entertained false hopes of salvation. All aspects of an outwardly pious conversation were equally suspect, unless founded solidly on the rock of the new birth. "Wo unto you Pharisees," Rogers warned, "Those who build their Hopes upon any of these Grounds will be miserably disappointed in the Day of Judgment." His message was clear: godly walkers would not inherit the kingdom of God. In time, they would learn to their eternal misfortune that "They build upon a Sandy Foundation."[36]

Rogers was in a "cold dull Frame" when he delivered this sermon in Bos-

---

34. Edwards, *Sinners in the Hands of an Angry God*, in *WJE*, XXII, *Sermons and Discourses, 1739–1742*, ed. Stout and Hatch, 404, 407–409, 411, 416.

35. DDR, Mar. 1, 1742; Bowles, commonplace book, 60; Rogers, sermon on Matt. 7:21–23, May 3, 1741, box 2, Sermons.

36. Bowles, commonplace book, 60; Rogers, sermon on Matt. 7:21–23, May 3, 1741, box 2, Sermons.

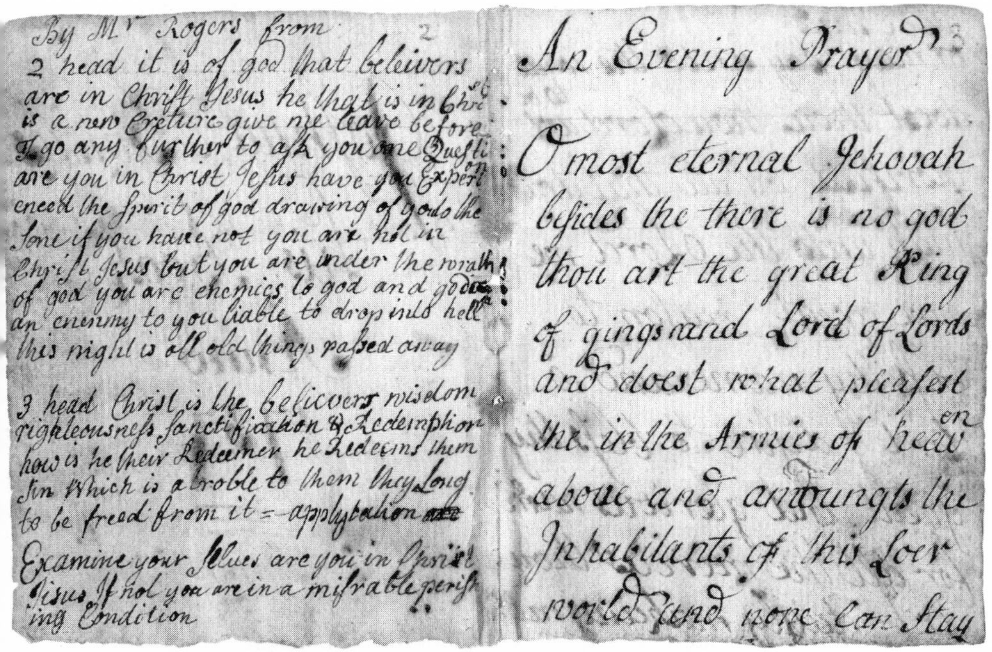
By Mr Rogers from
2 head it is of god that beleivers
are in Christ Jesus he that is in Chri
is a new Creture give me leave before
I go any further to ask you one Questi
are you in Christ Jesus have you Experi
enced the spirit of god drawing of you to the
Sone if you have not you are not in
Christ Jesus but you are under the wrath
of god you are enemies to god and god
an enemy to you liable to drop into hell
this night is all old things passed away

3 head Christ is the beleivers wisdom
righteousness sanctification & Redemption
how is he their Redeemer he Redeems them
sin which is a troble to them they Long
to be freed from it — applycation
Examine your selves are you in Christ
Jesus if not you are in a misrable perish
ing Condition

An Evening Prayer
O most eternal Jehovah
besides the there is no god
thou art the great King
of Kings and Lord of Lords
and doest what pleasest
the in the Armies of heaven
above and amoungst the
Inhabitants of this Lower
world and none Can Stay

FIGURE 11 Sermon Notes from Joshua Bowles's Commonplace Book. 1741. Image courtesy of the New England Historic Genealogical Society, Boston, *www.AmericanAncestors.org*

ton's New North meetinghouse on May 3, 1741, but his preaching had a dramatic impact on at least one member of his audience, a young artisan named Joshua Bowles. In later years, residents remembered hearing the master cabinetmaker praying audibly as he walked the streets of Copp's Hill, but he spent more time as a young man reading and reciting set prayers and studying the "advice of a Very Sick and weak Parent" that he had written down at the time of his father's death in 1737. When Gilbert Tennent arrived in Boston three years later, Bowles converted his pocket journal of family devotions into an informal sermon notebook. He recorded the scriptural texts from eighteen of Tennent's performances in Boston. During the next ten months, he summarized numerous sermons by local ministers and visiting itinerants, jotting the speakers' names, texts, doctrines, and other information on nearly every blank space in his tiny book. The stark division between the carefully lined, cautiously written formal prayers and the haphazard, increasingly diminutive handwriting of his sermon notes at once encapsulated the frenetic energy of the Boston awakening and registered the distinctiveness of the religious experiences reported by a new generation of men and women who had begun to distance themselves from the piety of their puritan ancestors.[37]

Bowles's sermon notes soon crowded out his older devotions, and many of these entries bore the peculiar marks of the Whitefieldarians' new preaching style and uncompromising theology. Generations of New Englanders had regularly produced detailed weekly sermon notes that they studied in private. Most surviving examples before 1740, however, were composed by older parishioners, and they usually reflected sermons delivered in a single location over an extended period of time by established clergymen. The notes hurriedly scribbled by the nineteen-year-old Bowles, by contrast, embodied the movement of its author. Although he composed most of the entries while sitting in the New North meetinghouse, Bowles appears to have ventured across town to hear lectures by prominent Boston preachers such as the aging Brattle Street pastor William Cooper. He also took notes on several sermons delivered by touring Whitefieldiarians, including Daniel Rogers. The pace of his writing, moreover, accelerated during the weeks following a traumatic accident in May 1741 when he almost drowned. Here, Bowles's personal experiences dovetailed with the Whitefieldarians' imprecatory rhetoric, as he imagined himself descending "right down to hell."[38]

The impact of these sermons on the young craftsman was profound. Nearly half of the sermons that Bowles recorded in his commonplace book emphasized the immediacy of hell, the urgency of conversion in a time of great awakenings, and the dangers of resting secure in routine religious duties. He also appears to have responded to the innovative oratorical techniques of visiting riding ministers. Bowles captured only fragments of a sermon by Rogers on the nature of the "new Creture," but his sparse notes included an outstanding example of the Ipswich itinerant's direct appeal to the audience. He summarized numerous sermons in the first person. On two occasions, he reported being "stired up" by sermons that "came home to me"—a clear sign that Bowles was actively engaged in applying the message of these performances to his own situation.[39]

Church admission relations composed during the 1740s reflected candidates' emerging fascination with Whitefieldian oratory. "God has of his great

37. DDR, May 3, 1741; Bowles, commonplace book, 23, 61–64. See also Thomas M. Farquhar, *The History of the Bowles Family* ... (Philadelphia, 1907), 188–189.

38. Bowles, commonplace book, 25–26, 45, 49. On the practice of sermon note-taking, see Meredith Marie Neuman, *Jeremiah's Scribes: Creating Sermon Literature in Puritan New England* (Philadelphia, 2013), 59–100.

39. Bowles, commonplace book, 2, 60, 64.

mercy ben pleased by the powerful preaching of his servants which of late has ben sent among us to convince me of my wretched estate both by nature and by practis," explained a young woman who joined Boston's Old South Church shortly after Tennent's departure in April 1741. In New Haven, one prospective church member presented a relation to minister Joseph Noyes in which "she mentioned the Names of several Ministers, whom she supposed had been Instrumental of her Conversion." Susanna Hinsdale of Medfield, Massachusetts, credited a stirring sermon on Amos 6:1—the terrifying sinners in Zion text—in which Tennent "shewed the dreadful danger of our being at ease in a natural, and unregenerate estate" as the turning point that prompted her to examine her soul and determine whether she had been "thoroughly wrought upon, and brought into a new estate." During a nine-month period in 1741, Sudbury, Massachusetts, minister Israel Loring recorded pastoral conferences with more than fifty prospective communicants. Almost half described potent sermons that had brought them "Under Convictions and Awakenings." Several congregants recalled a powerful lecture on 1 Thessalonians 5:19 that Loring "delivered with life and flame" at a private meeting. One woman cited Whitefield's visit to Sudbury in October 1740. Others spoke of being "Quickned to Duty by many Sermons," or cited the "powerful preaching of the Word as the Means of their Convictions."[40]

Although most church membership candidates continued to emphasize the importance of orthodox doctrine and the benefits of a pious family pedigree in their relations, some injected novel elements into the genre that drew on what they had heard in the sermons of itinerant preachers. Only a handful of lay men and women referenced the dangers of hell in relations composed before 1740, but, for those galvanized by Whitefield, Tennent, and their itinerating New England colleagues, the danger was imminent, inevitable, and desperately real. Threats of eternal damnation increasingly supplanted tales of providential affliction in the narratives of young converts. One Sudbury candidate, Loring noted, desired to be admitted to full communion after declaring that what he saw in hell "made him thoughtful and Concerned about himself." Parishioners in Boston's Old South Church evocatively imagined themselves perched on the "brinck of hel" or wondered why God had not already thrown them "down to Hell." In Medfield, prospective communicants lamented that they "could merit nothing but hell, and damnation" or "should have been in

40. Appendix B, Boston, Third (Old South) Church, 3; *Boston Weekly Post-Boy*, Oct. 5, 1741; Appendix B, Medfield, Mass., First Church, 58; Louise Parkman Thomas, transcr., "Journal of the Rev. Israel Loring," no. 12192, 12–13, 29, SA.

hell long ago," and they begged Jesus to "save me from hell." One woman even replicated the vertiginous metaphors of Edwards's *Sinners in the Hands of an Angry God* when she acknowledged "my danger of hell" and imagined herself "dropping down into the place of misery."[41]

In church admission testimonies and diaries, letters and sermon notebooks, lay men and women zealously embraced Whitefield's powerful new oratorical style as well as his sustained assault on the sandy foundations of faith. Within months of his departure, many New Englanders readily acknowledged that they were living in extraordinary times. "In the latter end of the yer 1741," Mary Dodge of Ipswich later summarized, "began a gloris reviel [revival] of the work of god," which "was at first begun a yer befor by the rev Mr. Whitefield and Mr. Tennant as the means."[42]

AN EXTRAORDINARY WORK ON FOOT IN THE LAND

Two days after Nathan Cole's breathless ride to Middletown, Connecticut, Boston merchant Samuel Phillips Savage arrived in Providence, Rhode Island, eager to see and hear George Whitefield. A few weeks earlier he had sat in rapt attention in Charlestown and Boston, listening as the touring evangelist delivered his classic homily, "The Lord our Righteousness," on two consecutive days. For a cosmopolitan Boston merchant who hailed from one of the town's wealthiest and most pious clans, Whitefield's sermon "threw down all my Foundation." Like Cole, Savage became convinced that he had been lulled into a "Carnal Security of my own power." Convicted in sin and struggling to accept the doctrine of election, Savage set off for Providence, where he planned to speak with Whitefield about the state of his soul.[43]

On Sunday, October 26, 1740, Savage and another young Bostonian named John Walley, Jr., stood among the vast multitude that had gathered for Whitefield's performance. But he never appeared. The following Tuesday an equally large crowd assembled in Taunton, and once again Whitefield did not arrive. At the time, he was nearly 100 miles away and hastening quickly to New York. Savage was disconsolate. So was Marston Cabot, the frail Connecticut minister, who also waited in vain among the Providence throng. Diarists Josiah Cotton and Joshua Hempstead reported similar events in Plymouth and Norwich,

---

41. Thomas, transcr., "Journal of the Rev. Israel Loring," no. 12192, 8; Appendix B, Boston, Third (Old South) Church, 3, 6; Appendix B, Medfield, Mass., First Church, 21, 37, 42, 53.

42. Mary [Dodge] Cleaveland, diaries, 1742–1762, I, [20], box 2, JCP.

43. *GWJ*, 472; Samuel Phillips Savage to [George Whitefield], Nov. 3, 1741, SSP II.

FIGURE 12 John Singleton Copley, *Samuel Phillips Savage*. 1764.
Oil on canvas, 125.7 × 99.1 cm. Private collection. Courtesy, Frick Art
Reference Library Photoarchive, New York

Connecticut. "I suppose you have heard that Mr. Whitfield has disappointed many thousands in these parts," Walley concluded in a letter to his father in Boston, adding that the "greatest part of the people were quite dissolved into Tears" on receiving the "News that he was not to come."[44]

Why had they gathered? What reason was there for thousands of eager listeners in towns located nearly one hundred miles away from Hartford and Middletown to hope for a sudden visit from the celebrated evangelist? The answer lies in the Boston prints, which tracked Whitefield's arrivals and departures as if he were a transatlantic merchant vessel. More than 275 news items on religion dominated the colonial newspapers in 1740. Most of them charted Whitefield's movements. The accompanying lists of dates, towns, and preaching engagements were more than just news. Whitefield's media campaign ensured large audiences wherever he traveled and, thus, helped to fashion his first American preaching tour into an intercolonial phenomenon.[45]

Three weeks earlier, itineraries published in the *New England Weekly-Journal* and the *Boston Weekly News-Letter* informed readers that Whitefield planned to swing into Rhode Island and southeastern Massachusetts after preaching in the upper Connecticut Valley. One version placed him in Providence and Taunton, just as Savage's and Walley's letters suggested. After consulting with fellow itinerants Eleazar Wheelock and Benjamin Pomeroy during his visit to Hartford, however, Whitefield suddenly changed his plans. Instead of preaching his way down to the Old Colony, he set off directly for New York. Although Whitefield immediately notified correspondents in Boston about the change in his itinerary, the news arrived too late for the assembled throngs in towns across southeastern New England.[46]

Epistolary reports of the disappointed crowds not only manifested the power of the public prints in shaping lay responses to Whitefield's ministry; they also help to explain the frenetic drama that punctuated the opening paragraphs of Cole's "Spiritual Travels." One town's loss was another's gain. Whitefield's last-minute decision to cut short his New England tour brought him uncharacteristically unannounced to Middletown. Messengers arrived "on a Sudden" at Cole's farm with news of Whitefield's imminent public appearance. Samuel Phillips Savage had planned his trip to Providence several weeks in

44. Savage to [Whitefield], Nov. 3, 1741, SSP II; John Walley, Jr., to John Walley, Sr., Oct. 30, 1740, Old Safe Manuscript Collection, NEHGS. See also *GWJ*, 480–481; Cabot, "Memorabilia," Oct. 26, 1740; and *Diary of Joshua Hempstead*, 364; and JCH, 310.

45. Smith, *First Great Awakening in Colonial American Newspapers*, 36–37, 102–103, 149; Lambert, *"Pedlar in Divinity,"* 103–110.

46. *Boston Weekly News-Letter*, Oct. 16, 30, 1740; *New-England Weekly Journal* (Boston), Oct. 14, 1740; *GWJ*, 479.

advance; Cole had little more than an hour's notice. He and his wife, along with thousands of others, scrambled pell-mell to the Middletown meeting-house to take advantage of an unexpected opportunity that must have seemed heaven-sent.[47]

The two dramatic images—thousands gathering in silent anticipation in Providence waiting for a preacher who would never appear, and thousands more coursing to Middletown at breakneck speed—were two sides of the same coin. Quite possibly the most distinctive feature of New England's era of great awakenings was the spectacular way the Whitefieldarians moved their audiences, both spiritually and physically. Rhetorical artistry and an uncom-promising assault on the godly walk accounted for the former. Epistolary and newspaper reports of dramatic preaching successes produced the latter. Whitefield's performances set people in motion and accelerated the pace of religious life. Together, these two factors ultimately burst the parish bound-aries that defined New England's Congregational culture, as lay men and women like Cole began to imagine themselves as participants in an unfolding cosmic drama that transcended the local and the particular.[48]

The stunning events that erupted in the small village of York, Maine, and reverberated across the coastal towns and interior farming villages of north-ern New England one year after Whitefield's visit in 1740 were among the most talked about events in colonial history. In dozens of letters, diary entries, and newspaper accounts, observers described, praised, ridiculed, and lamented the remarkable religious awakening that ensued. Savage, in particular, re-ceived no fewer than eight favorable reports from the northern frontier dur-ing the winter of 1742. As the Boston merchant and his contemporaries shared news about the religious stirs in York, the neighboring town of Portsmouth, New Hampshire, and communities across New England, they began to piece together these seemingly spasmodic and disjointed regional events into a sin-gular phenomenon: "a Revival of Religion."[49]

■ York had been on George Whitefield's itinerary from the start. No sooner had he arrived in Boston when local papers began broadcasting his plans for a

47. NCS, 92.

48. The argument in this section draws on Timothy D. Hall, *Contested Boundaries: Itin-erancy and the Reshaping of the Colonial American Religious World* (Durham, N.C., 1994), esp. Chapter 3; and T. H. Breen and Hall, "Structuring Provincial Imagination: The Rhetoric and Experience of Social Change in Eighteenth-Century New England," *AHR*, CIII (1998), 1411–1439.

49. Beales, ed., "'Our Hearts Are Traitors to Themselves,'" *Bulletin of the CL*, 1st Ser., XXVII, no. 3 (Spring/Summer 1976), 8.

trip to the northern frontier. York's venerable pastor, the aging Samuel Moody, welcomed the touring evangelist into his pulpit on October 2, 1740. Whitefield later noted in his published journal that he preached with "little or no terror, but almost all consolation," and his conciliatory sermon was received with joy by the York congregants. Their "hearts looked plain and simple," and "tears trickled apace down most of their cheeks." Whitefield was back in Boston a few days later, and the *American Weekly Mercury* reported that he had preached to the "Satisfaction of his hearers."[50]

Whitefield's northern swing propelled York into the public eye, and the towns along his route soon emerged as established destinations for the riding ministers who trailed in his wake. Gilbert Tennent delivered more than forty sermons during his three-week journey from Boston to York during the winter of 1741. "There were in Time of Sermon," he wrote in a letter to his brother, "such Out-cries that my Voice had like to be drowned." He claimed to have wounded the consciences of hundreds of men and women during his brief trip to the eastward settlements. In addition to organizing protracted meetings, the New Jersey itinerant traveled with an entourage of zealous disciples. Newbury, Massachusetts, diarist Joseph Goodhue spent several days in York with Tennent, visiting "frome hous to house" and seeking solace for his unconverted soul. The "Work of the Lord" in New Hampshire and Maine, Goodhue later noted, was "marvelos to mee."[51]

Daniel Rogers arrived in York six months later. Like his Presbyterian counterpart, Rogers preached in every town along the northern frontier. The families of the farmers, artisans, merchants, and grandees who sat in pews from Portsmouth to North Yarmouth, Maine, he asserted, had been a "loose dead People for a long Time." Still, Rogers managed to preach with "Freedom and Power" to large and very attentive assemblies in most of the parishes that he visited. People followed him about the countryside. After visiting Moody's parish in York, Rogers set off for Wells in the company of "near 30 Horse." That evening he preached to the "largest Congregation" that had ever assembled in that meetinghouse. Despite his earnest labors, however, Rogers acknowledged at the conclusion of his tour that a "Gracious work of God" had only just "begun in this Place."[52]

50. *Boston Weekly News-Letter*, Oct. 2, 1740; GWJ, 467 (quotes); *American Weekly Mercury* (Philadelphia), Oct. 16, 1740.

51. "A Copy of a Letter from the Reverend Mr. *Gilbert Tennent* to his Brother *William*," *Weekly History* (London), no. 9 (June 6, 1741), 1; Joseph Goodhue, diary, 1745–1765, [12], PEM (I thank Erik Seeman for sharing his research notes on the Goodhue diary).

52. DDR, Aug. 24, Sept. 1, 4, 1741.

Whitefield, Tennent, and Rogers sowed the seeds of a formidable religious awakening on the northern frontier, but the task of reaping the bountiful harvest of souls fell to local clergymen. In his extensive diary, the Durham, New Hampshire, minister Nicholas Gilman charted the rapid emergence of what he called "Experimental preaching" during the summer of 1741. A decade earlier, Gilman had aspired to all the trappings of a genteel country pastorate. Scion of a prominent Exeter, New Hampshire, clan, Gilman filled his youthful correspondence with rhetorical flourishes and classical allusions, and he moved easily from family news to discussions of medicine, mathematics, and Newtonian science. His personal library blended expensive multivolume biblical commentaries, sermons, and devotional guides with works by Ovid and Herodotus and treatises on gentlemanly comportment. His ascension to full communion in the Exeter church in 1724 registered only a brief notice in his diary.[53]

Gilman's latitudinarian theological sensibilities were especially evident early in 1740, when he began preaching to a small congregation in the neighboring town of Durham. Later that summer, he read all fifty-four sermons in the first volume of archbishop John Tillotson's multivolume *Works*—nearly eight hundred pages in all. His religious musings during this period emphasized the rationality of faith, moral virtue, and the steady course of the godly walk, or what he called the gradual "Increas and indefinite progress of the Saints Knowledge in a future State of Blessedness." The longest entries in his diary consisted of meditations on personal and family health, which he frequently paired with healing vows and prayers to sanctify divine afflictions. He composed family prayers for mornings, evenings, and mealtimes, and he engaged in extensive catechetical exercises with his children. Gilman's carefully scripted sermons, moreover, reflected a personal desire to "Improve My Time more wisely than heretofore, and husband the fleeting moments of Life to the best advantage."[54]

Attending Whitefield's outdoor preaching performances in Hampton, New Hampshire, changed everything. Almost immediately, Gilman questioned whether he had ever experienced the new birth. He dropped his daily Tillotson readings and refocused his studies toward classic seventeenth-century treatises on soteriology by Thomas Shepard, Joseph Alleine, and Solomon Stod-

---

53. NGD, 55, 120, 376–380; [Emily Hoffman Gilman] Noyes, comp., *A Family History in Letters and Documents, 1667–1837* ... (Saint Paul, Minn., 1919), I, 23–27, 34–37.

54. NGD, 63, 97; Nicholas Gilman, "Meditations Prayer Wise," n.d., Nicholas Gilman Papers II, 1700–1784, MHS, "A Morning Prayer for a Family," n.d. For Gilman's early sermon notes, see Nicholas Gilman Papers, 1694–circa 1900, MHS.

dard as well as John Bunyan's *Pilgrim's Progress*. He pored over Whitefield's published autobiography, letters, sermons, and travel journals. A few months later, he perused Gilbert Tennent's impassioned sermon series, the *Espousals*, along with John Wesley's controversial sermon on *Free Grace*, "over again and again." By the spring of 1741, Gilman was reading Jonathan Edwards's *Faithful Narrative of the Surprising Work of God* at Northampton and praying that he might behold more of God's majesty in his own isolated corner of Christendom.[55]

Gilman also recorded religious intelligence from abroad. As early as June 1740, he observed that Whitefield had become the subject of much conversation in Exeter, and he encountered news of a "great Reformation" in Philadelphia in the *Boston News-Letter* later that month. Reports of Tennent's powerful preaching in Boston reverberated across the northern frontier the following year, and Gilman set out to witness the surprising events for himself. As he traveled, he learned more about the growing religious spirit that seemed to be sweeping across the Atlantic world. Boston minister Benjamin Colman shared accounts of Whitefield's successes in England. Gilman visited Daniel Rogers and was impressed by the "Sweetness of the Communion of Saints" in Ipswich. Travelers passing through Durham brought news of distant religious awakenings. Collectively, all signs indicated that a dramatic "Work of the Lord" was rapidly closing in on New England's northern frontier.[56]

Although he often prayed for "more plentifull effusions of the Holy Spirit" in Durham, Gilman was not content to wait for a miraculous shower of divine grace. During the spring and summer of 1741, he attempted to stimulate greater religious zeal among his neighbors. Like many of his colleagues, Gilman consciously altered his preaching techniques after witnessing Whitefield and Tennent. His sermons assumed a more threatening tone. They were longer and occasionally extemporaneous. He labored to elevate the emotional pitch of his sermons, as he begged God to "Inflame My Soul" and animate his preaching. In his diary, Gilman began keeping track of his internal disposition—or what he called his emotional "Frame"—during his sermon performances as well as the outward effects of his preaching on his parishioners.[57]

Soon, small groups of men and women began appearing at Gilman's house to discourse about their soul concerns. He spent whole days visiting and "conversing with persons under awakenings" and savored these meetings with

55. *GWJ*, 466; NGD, 142–145, 147–149, 152–153, 156–160, 163, 165, 168, 172, 177, 179, 181, 183, 186–190 (quote 189), 193–194, 197, 199.

56. NGD, 123, 207, 209.

57. Ibid., 195–196, 217.

"Experienced" Christians. Gilman also established a special prayer society for young men that met several nights each week. An extension of these informal pastoral counseling sessions involved recommending suitable reading materials. In 1741, Gilman lent more than three dozen different books to nearly sixty people, including his parishioners in Durham, family members, and colleagues. A few of these works were Bibles, catechisms, and works of history; others were classic puritan tracts on grace and regeneration. The largest group, however, consisted of recent works by Whitefield, Tennent, and Jonathan Edwards.[58]

Gilman honed his oratorical skills as well, lecturing by candlelight every Thursday in Exeter. On several occasions, these evening meetings elicited impassioned responses from his audiences. Gilman was delighted to discover that his own zeal had helped to create "more of a Relish" for religious conversation among his neighbors in Exeter and his new parishioners in Durham, to which he relocated permanently in October 1741. For the next two months, he preached, expounded, exhorted, counseled, and prayed almost nightly. Twice in November 1741, the evening assemblies in Durham thrilled to the powerful cadences of Edwards's *Sinners in the Hands of an Angry God,* which their zealous ministerial candidate read from the recently published edition. Gilman also witnessed the first of many future incidents of his Durham parishioners falling to the ground and crying out in terror. "I bless thee My Lord for thine Assistance in those publick exercises," Gilman wrote, "So that Instead of being tir'd I Seem much refreshd thereby." The Durham minister's powerful late-night meetings achieved their desired effect. By December, he was preaching to thronged assemblies and declaring that large numbers of his parishioners had been "bro't under great awakenings."[59]

Gilman received occasional news throughout the summer of 1741 that colleagues in neighboring towns had been similarly stirred up and were actively encouraging what he called new "Measures to Promote religion." The Durham minister was one of several regional clergymen who had begun to experiment with Whitefield's preaching techniques. Earlier that spring, Simon Frost, a prominent merchant from Kittery, Maine, wrote to Samuel Phillips Savage in Boston informing him that ministers in Portsmouth and New Castle, New Hampshire, as well as the surrounding parishes in southern Maine "Seem to be more lively, and preach more awakening Sermons and the People are more rouz'd and convinc'd that Religion consists of Something more than a Form."

58. Ibid., 180, 197, 212; Nicholas Gilman, "Books Lent," 1741, Nicholas Gilman Papers II.
59. NGD, 181, 214, 228–231.

The settlements on the northern frontier had been kindled for a powerful religious awakening. All that was needed was someone to strike the flame.[60]

■ Most observers agreed that the catalyst of the York awakening was an obscure pastor from Biddeford, Maine, named Samuel Willard. According to Kittery physician Edmund Coffin, Willard spent nearly a week traveling among the coastal communities and preaching stirring sermons at "every town as he came." Willard arrived in York on October 8, 1741, and "God was pleased in a most wonderful manner to set home his word by his spirit on the hearts of the hearers." One visiting Boston merchant was amazed by what he encountered on his arrival in town two days later. During the next six weeks, he recorded daily religious events in a remarkable travel narrative entitled "A Jornal of a Fue Days at York." In the middle of one of Willard's evening lectures, the entire congregation cried out in distress. Some wondered whether the Son of Man had returned to earth; others called for "Rocks to hide them" in "Resemblance of the Judgment Day." So loud was the disturbance that Willard was forced to pause and wait for the congregants to compose themselves. The Biddeford minister eventually resumed his sermon, although "there was talking allmost the whole time of praying, and Preaching," which the Boston merchant found "very Surprising." Following Willard's electrifying sermon, members of the awakened assembly remained in the meetinghouse until midnight, exhorting and praying over convicted sinners with such fervor that the anonymous diarist could hear them from his lodgings a quarter of a mile away.[61]

As news of the "marvellous work" at York traveled southward, the seacoast town attracted a "great concourse of people," including ministers, pious visitors, and curiosity seekers. Willard had no sooner returned to Biddeford when minister John Rogers, brother of Daniel, the prominent Ipswich, itinerant, arrived in town with a large contingent of parishioners from Kittery's Middle Parish (now Eliot, Maine). More than a half dozen New England clergymen preached from Samuel Moody's pulpit in York during the next several weeks. Some were ministers or schoolmasters from neighboring parishes in Maine

60. NGD, 194; Simon Frost to Samuel Phillips Savage, Apr. 15, 1741, SSP I. The parallels with the famous "new measures" of the nineteenth-century revivalist Charles Grandison Finney are striking. See also Charles E. Hambrick-Stowe, *Charles G. Finney and the Spirit of American Evangelicalism*, Library of Religious Biography (Grand Rapids, Mich., 1996), 38–39. For a similar comparison, see Frank Lambert, *Inventing the "Great Awakening"* (Princeton, N.J., 1999), 91–92.

61. Joshua Coffin, *A Sketch of the History of Newbury, Newburyport, and West Newbury, from 1635 to 1845* (Boston, 1845), 210; Douglas L. Winiarski, "'A Jornal of a Fue Days at York': The Great Awakening on the Northern New England Frontier," *Maine History*, XLII (2004), 62–63.

or New Hampshire. Others, such as Josiah Cotton, the Congregational minister of Providence, Rhode Island, had traveled a considerable distance. Visiting colleagues assisted Moody in transforming the sporadic preaching of fiery itinerants like Whitefield, Tennent, and Rogers into a series of nightly meetings that lasted for more than a month.[62]

Events moved at a breathless pace. Day after day, the anonymous Boston merchant attended one religious meeting after another. He heard a total of twenty-two sermons preached by eight ministers during the fourteen days that he spent in York. Most occurred during evening worship exercises that lasted deep into the night and were attended by powerful somatic outbursts. Parishioners sighed and groaned; bodies contorted and eyes flooded with tears as the York townspeople listened to the forceful preaching of traveling clergymen. While some fell to the floor under the weight of their sins, others burst into peals of laughter and cries of joy as they emerged into the light of the new birth. Several men and women even fell into rapturous "Transports of Joy"—unusual trances in which their bodies lay insensible on the ground while their souls allegedly traveled to heaven, met with Jesus himself, and were allowed to read the names of the elect inscribed in the Book of Life.[63]

Religious exercises spilled outside the meetinghouse. Awakened men, women, and children exhorted their neighbors from the steps of the church, and boisterous psalm singing erupted in the streets. York's several taverns stood empty for days, and the author of the "Jornal" observed a marked decrease in "Profain Cursing and Swaring." A guilt-stricken woman fell down in the street and pleaded for forgiveness from a man whom she had wrongly accused of fathering her child. Wealthy families seeking to emulate the primitive communalism of the apostolic churches shared food and lodging with less fortunate neighbors, visitors, and strangers. Groups of pious young people gathered in the houses of convicted sinners who languished in spiritual darkness, such as Moody's famously melancholic son, Joseph. The York clergyman and his colleagues were active in these venues as well, visiting with distressed parishioners and delivering extemporaneous sermons, exhortations, prayers, and discourses to spontaneous assemblies that often numbered in the hundreds. Even a fashionable dinner party hosted by Mary Bulman, wife

---

62. Coffin, *Sketch of the History of Newbury*, 210; William H. Montague, ed., "Letter from Rev. Arthur Brown," *NEHGR*, VI (1852), 264; Winiarski, "'Jornal of a Fue Days at York,'" *Maine History*, XLII (2004), 66–73.

63. Winiarski, "'Jornal of a Fue Days at York,'" *Maine History*, XLII (2004), 73; *South Carolina Gazette* (Charleston), Mar. 6, 1742. For a more detailed discussion of these visions, see Part 3, section starting at note 77, below.

of a prominent York doctor, was consecrated to the cause of the awakening. Here, the visiting Boston diarist and a group of genteel companions spent the evening singing psalms and discussing the remarkable religious stir in town. Nearly all of these activities took place in the middle of the week and at the height of the harvest season.[64]

This was an awakening the likes of which was "never seen in New England," Edmund Coffin proudly announced, and he boasted that the "conversion of those at Northampton according to Mr. Edwards' account is not comparable to this." Coffin's comparison with Jonathan Edwards's *Faithful Narrative of the Surprising Work of God* might have been overstated, yet extant sources suggest that large numbers of men and women were involved in the York awakening during the fall of 1741. One newspaper correspondent stated that nearly 150 people had been affected by Willard's preaching, or roughly 10 percent of the town's total population. The author of the "Jornal" witnessed the admission of ten new communicants on November 22. That forty more had been propounded to full communion and would have joined the church within the next few weeks suggests that York experienced the largest church membership surge in the history of the eastward settlements.[65]

Coffin believed that the "finger of the Lord" was at work in stirring the dry bones at York, an assessment that was echoed by the visiting Boston merchant, who hoped that the "Good and Great work" of the Holy Spirit would shortly increase throughout the region. Sparked at York, the religious conflagration quickly spread south to Portsmouth. On November 25, 1741, the day before the anonymous author of the "Jornal" returned to Boston, William Shurtleff's parishioners in the town's south parish observed a day of fasting and prayer for the "Effusion of God's Spirit on them." Nearly two dozen men and women cried out during Shurtleff's sermon, including several who had previously been "struct at York." The Portsmouth minister and his colleagues continued to preach, pray, exhort, and discourse with the affected members of the assembly into the early hours of the morning. The "Blessed Work incresd in a most swift and amazing Manner" during the next several days, as regional clergymen kept up a steady barrage of sermons from morning to midnight. New Castle minister John Blunt, in particular, "Preached like a man Inspired."

64. Winiarski, "'Jornal of a Fue Days at York,'" *Maine History*, XLII (2004), 69.

65. Coffin, *Sketch of the History of Newbury*, 210–211; *South Carolina Gazette*, Mar. 6, 1742; Winiarski, "'Jornal of a Fue Days at York,'" *Maine History*, XLII (2004), 70. Population estimate for York based on Sybil Noyes, *Genealogical Dictionary of Maine and New Hampshire* (Portland, Maine, 1928–1939), 31–32; and Greene and Harrington, *American Population Before the Federal Census of 1790*, 29.

According to one report, between two or three hundred people could be heard crying out in distress at one time. Terrified men and women waved their arms, wrung their hands, and clutched their breasts. In all, perhaps as many as one thousand people—"Young and Old, Rich and poor, White and black"—were "deeply wounded" during the furious three-day event.[66]

Within weeks, the burgeoning religious awakening engulfed the northern frontier. "The works of God amongst us are wonderful," Blunt pronounced in a December 1741 letter to Samuel Phillips Savage. The New Castle minister welcomed the awakening as it "spread far and wide and fast." Early in January, Simon Frost informed Savage of the "great work that is going on" in Kittery. That same week, Falmouth clergyman Thomas Smith returned home from a journey to Portsmouth, "where I have been to observe and affect myself with the great work of God's grace." A religious stir broke out in his parish less than a month later. By the end of the year, Smith had admitted more than four times the average annual number of new communicants. In the twelve months following Samuel Willard's meteoric preaching tour, the churches in Berwick, Kittery, North Yarmouth, Scarborough, and Wells all received more new members and covenant owners than in any single year in their respective histories. By the spring of 1742, every town north of the Piscataqua River and many of the coastal parishes in New Hampshire were ablaze.[67]

■ News of religious events in northern New England coursed through epistolary networks at an astonishing pace. Edmund Coffin dispatched his "short representation of the mighty work of God" to his father in Newbury just two days after visiting York. One week later, the Cambridge shopkeeper Joseph Bean "herd this Evening of the wonderful operations of the Spiret of God upon pepels harts doun at York of late which made me for to go and rasel [wrestle] verry hartily and fervently with God for them and for the more abundant outpowrings of his Spiret on all parts." Early in November, Durham minister

---

66. Coffin, *Sketch of the History of Newbury*, 211; Winiarski, "'Jornal of a Fue Days at York,'" *Maine History*, XLII (2004), 65; Samuel Phillips Savage to Gilbert Tennent, Feb. 2, 1742, SSP II; William Parker to Richard Waldron, Nov. 28, 1741, Miscellaneous Bound Manuscripts, MHS; Julius Herbert Tuttle, comp., "The Glasgow-Weekly-History, 1743," MHS, *Proceedings*, LIII (1919–1920), 209; Savage, "Extract from a Letter from Piscataqua," n.d. [Dec. 3, 1741], SSP I; Ebenezer Parkman, commonplace book, 1721–1779, 88–89, Ebenezer Parkman Papers, 1718–1789, MHS.

67. John Blunt to Samuel Phillips Savage, Dec. 22, 1741, SSP I, Simon Frost to Savage, Jan. 6, 1742; Willis, ed., *Journals of the Rev. Thomas Smith, and the Rev. Samuel Deane*, 102. For church admission statistics in northern New England, see Elizabeth C. Nordbeck, "Almost Awakened: The Great Revival in New Hampshire and Maine, 1727–1748," *Historical New Hampshire*, XXXV (1980), 37.

Nicholas Gilman declared that a "Glorious Work of God" was under way in the surrounding towns, and his son soon forwarded news of the "Marvellous work" in Portsmouth to a cousin in Haverhill, Massachusetts.[68]

Savage relayed news of the "great shaking at York" in a letter to Gilbert Tennent in New Jersey. Another member of the Brattle Street Church, John Loring, sent a detailed report of events in Portsmouth to his father, Israel, who proceeded to read his son's epistle aloud to his parishioners in Sudbury. The elder Loring likely passed the news on to his colleague Ebenezer Parkman in nearby Westborough. Parkman then notified Jonathan Edwards, who subsequently sent the information on to Joseph Bellamy in western Connecticut. By the spring of 1742, reports of the "wonderful work of God" along the northern frontier were circulating in New York, Charleston, London, and Glasgow. Identical letters appeared in towns more than one hundred miles apart. "You have doubtless heard of the wonderful out-powring of the Spirit of God of late at Piscataqua," an ebullient Jonathan Mayhew summarized in a letter to his brother on Martha's Vineyard, "such an one as, perhaps, has not been known since the Days of the Apostles." Shortly thereafter, Mayhew set off for York, "induced to go by an earnest Desire I had to see, and get a right understanding of Affairs there with Respect to Religion."[69]

The York awakening served as catalyst for towns throughout northern New England and beyond. Ministers who visited the eastward settlements during those tumultuous weeks returned to their parishes refreshed and eager to

68. Coffin, *Sketch of the History of Newbury*, 210; Joseph Bean, diary, 1741–1744, 85, Mariam Coffin Canaday Library, Bryn Mawr College, Bryn Mawr, Pa.; NGD, 226; [Noyes], comp., *Family History in Letters and Documents*, 38–39.

69. John Blunt to Samuel Phillips Savage, Oct. 22, 1741, SSP I; Savage to Tennent, Feb. 2, 1742, SSP II; John Loring to Israel Loring, Dec. 9, 1741, Nathan Stone Papers, 1726–1832, MHS; Thomas, transcr., "Journal of the Rev. Israel Loring," no. 12192, 40; Ebenezer Parkman to Jonathan Edwards, December 1741, *WJEO*, XXXII, *Correspondence by, to, and about Edwards and His Family*, no. B7; Edwards to Joseph Bellamy, Jan. 21, 1742, in *WJE*, XVI, *Letters and Personal Writings*, ed. Claghorn, 99; Stephen Williams, diaries, 1715–1782, 10 vols., typescript, IV, 3, Storrs Library, Longmeadow, Mass. (available online at *http://www .longmeadowlibrary.org/stephen-williams-diary-available-online/*); Foxcroft to Dickinson, Dec. 16, 1741, Charles Roberts Autograph Collection; George Whitefield, *A Vindication and Confirmation of the Remarkable Work of God in New-England*... (Glasgow, 1742), 29; *South Carolina Gazette*, Mar. 6, 1742; Tuttle, comp., "Glasgow-Weekly-History," MHS, *Procs.*, LIII (1919–1920), 204–205; Jonathan Mayhew to Zechariah Mayhew, Dec. 26, 1741, no. 14, Mayhew Papers, 1648–1774, Mark and Llora Bortman Collection, HGARC; Beales, ed., "'Our Hearts Are Traitors to Themselves,'" *Bulletin of the CL*, 1st Ser., XXVII, no. 3 (Spring / Summer 1976), 5. For identical copies of a letter from an anonymous Portsmouth resident to a friend in Boston, see also Savage, "Extract from a Letter from Piscataqua," n.d. [Dec. 3, 1741], SSP I; and [Eleazar Wheelock], "A Copy of a Letter from Portsmouth," Dec. 3, 1741, no. 81513, Joseph Bellamy Papers. Ebenezer Parkman copied a similar missive into his commonplace book (89–90), Ebenezer Parkman Papers.

engineer religious stirs of their own. After participating in the "great and glorious work" at York, Josiah Cotton arrived in Providence, where he discovered his congregation in the grip of a powerful awakening. One year later, he was preaching several days a week to small groups of parishioners who gathered in the woods near his parsonage. Josiah Crocker, a young Harvard College graduate, visited York in February 1742 and carried the coals of the Maine awakening to Martha's Vineyard, where Indian missionary Experience Mayhew soon reported that religious meetings were "attended with much of God's presence." Following his ordination at Taunton later that spring, Crocker successfully ignited a powerful religious awakening that was modeled, in part, on the "remarkable and plentiful *Out-pouring* of the HOLY SPIRIT" that he had "Opportunity to see" in York.[70]

The currents of religious excitement flowed in both directions. Parishioners in Hopkinton, a small town in central Massachusetts, traveled nearly one hundred miles to York and invited Samuel Moody to preside over a day of fasting for the outpouring of the Holy Spirit in their parish. When the aging York clergyman arrived in September 1742, Hopkinton minister Samuel Barrett changed his mind and promptly closed his pulpit, fearing, as one of his colleagues put it, that Moody's preaching was "replete with odities." Undaunted, the York minister moved on to the neighboring towns of Concord, Framingham, Grafton, Upton, and Westborough, Massachusetts.[71]

Moody's itinerating labors left a deep impression on Grafton minister Solomon Prentice. In January 1743, he threw open the doors of his meetinghouse to anyone who "might Come and Hear." Over the next four days, Prentice and several neighboring colleagues preached from morning until late at night — five sermons per day, according to one account — with "Little Sleep or other Refreshment." Eager pilgrims flocked to attend the "Grafton Exercises," as the unusual protracted religious meetings came to be called, with many traveling on foot over distances of nearly twenty miles. The carefully staged event was a resounding success. "The work of God seems to prevail greatly amongst us," stated David Hall, minister of the neighboring town of Sutton.

70. Josiah Cotton (of Providence, R.I.) to Eleazar Wheelock, Dec. 17, 1741, no. 741667, *EWP;* Cotton to Wheelock, Dec. 16, 1742, case 8, box 22, SGC I; Experience Mayhew to Thomas Foxcroft, May 18, 1742, Thomas Foxcroft Correspondence, 1729–1759, Firestone Library, Princeton University, Princeton, N.J.; Josiah Crocker, "An Account of the Late Revival of Religion at Taunton, Continued" *CH,* no. 95 (Dec. 22, 1744), 342.

71. Nathan Stone, Jr., to Nathan Stone, Sr., Oct. 2, 1742, Nathan Stone Papers. See also Joseph Tracy, *The Great Awakening: A History of the Revival of Religion in the Time of Edwards and Whitefield* (1842; Edinburgh, 1976), 210; and Ross W. Beales, Jr., ed., "Solomon Prentice's Narrative of the Great Awakening," MHS, *Proceedings,* 3d Ser., LXXXIII (1971), 137.

Hundreds of people were visibly in great distress, and Prentice's meetinghouse was "filled with Lamentations and loud Shreeks and groans." "I have Seen So much of the *blessed Fruits* of *frequent Preaching*, Yea *Day after day*," the Grafton minister wrote, "that I can'nt but heartyly Recommend the Practice to all who are true Friends to the Cause of Christ and would be Promoters thereof in a Season of the Holy Spirit Blowing round about them." The religious gales in his own parish suggested an apt metaphor, and he exhorted his colleagues to spread their sails like the "Sea-faring Tribe" of New England mariners. "O that we could arise!" he continued, "for Surly the work (greatly) belongs unto us."[72]

As religious intelligence rippled outward from York and Portsmouth, ministers began to assemble reports from across New England into a larger understanding of the Whitefieldian awakening as a unified regional and even transatlantic event. Boston clergyman Thomas Foxcroft initially puzzled over the "Affair at York" in a letter that he sent to a colleague in New Jersey. "These Things are very surprizing," he concluded, since "no natural Cause seems to have had any the least hand in making the Difference between these Places and others." Always circumspect in his public pronouncements, Foxcroft declined to press his argument to its logical conclusion. But Jonathan Mayhew never hesitated. After visiting York and receiving news from his brother of an awakening on Martha's Vineyard, Mayhew seized on a clear interpretation. "I hear (and desire with my whole Soul to bless God for it)," he wrote to his brother during the spring of 1742, "that there is a Revival of Religion at the Vine Yard." Viewed from the vantage point of more than two centuries of evangelical revivalism, Mayhew's language appears conventional, but his letter was among the first to describe New England's scattered great awakenings as an interconnected phenomenon—"a Revival of Religion"—that transcended locality. The unusual religious stirs that gripped the northern New England frontier during the fall and winter of 1741–1742 convinced many clergymen that sporadic occurrences in distant towns were part of a grand scheme and even, perhaps, elements of God's rapidly unfolding cosmic plan.[73]

Consider the letter that Eleazar Wheelock sent to fellow Whitefieldar-

72. Beales, ed., "Solomon Prentice's Narrative," MHS, *Procs.*, 3d Ser., LXXXIII (1971), 137–139, 140; Francis G. Walett, ed., *The Diary of Ebenezer Parkman, 1703–1782* (Worcester, Mass., 1974), 88–89; David Hall, diaries, 1740–1789, Jan. 7, 1743, MHS.

73. Foxcroft to Dickinson, Dec. 16, 1741, Charles Roberts Autograph Collection; Beales, ed., "'Our Hearts Are Traitors to Themselves,'" *Bulletin of the CL*, 1st Ser., XXVII, no. 3 (Spring/Summer 1976), 8. For a similar argument, see Michael J. Crawford, *Seasons of Grace: Colonial New England's Revival Tradition in Its British Context*, Religion in America (New York, 1991), 180.

ian Joseph Bellamy shortly after he returned home from a highly success-ful preaching tour of southeastern New England in December 1741. While in Boston, he had lectured at the Brattle Street meetinghouse and undoubtedly received news of the religious stirrings that had begun at York. Meanwhile, Bellamy had delivered a rousing series of sermons in the town of Walling-ford, Connecticut, near Middletown. Wheelock enclosed a report of events in Portsmouth with his own letter, in which he distilled his recent tour, Bellamy's work in Wallingford, the awakening on the northern frontier, and religious news from several neighboring towns in eastern Connecticut into a single phe-nomenon. "The work of the Lord spreads gloriously in the land," Wheelock began. "We hear almost Every week of its being spread into one place and another where it has not before been." After listing more than a dozen towns in which the work had been "very great," Wheelock declared that nearly three hundred members of his own "dear flock" in the Lebanon Crank Society had been converted. He closed his letter wondering aloud which "valiant" Con-necticut magistrates were "friends of this work." Then, in one of the earliest references to a phrase destined to dominate all future discussions of the re-vivals, he encouraged Bellamy to consider a plan through which the "Breth-ren, whom the word calls New Lights" might meet together to agree on the defining characteristics of an authentic revival. Not only did he consider the "work" singular but those who supported it as well.[74]

During the next two years, the Whitefieldarians labored ceaselessly to con-nect local reports of religious awakenings with events from abroad. Already by the fall of 1741, English and Scottish ministers were broadcasting revival news in serialized publications such as the *Christian's Amusement*, the *Weekly History*, and the *Glasgow-Weekly-History*. On March 5, 1743, a similar maga-zine—the *Christian History, containing Accounts of the Revival and Propaga-tion of Religion in Great Britain and America*—issued for the first time from the Boston press. Interestingly enough, the origin of the first religious maga-zine in the colonies owed much to the events on the northern frontier. Brattle Street clergyman William Cooper appears to have been its first advocate. Writ-ing just two weeks before he departed Boston to assist in stoking the powerful revival in Portsmouth, Cooper encouraged "those who have been conversant in this work, in one place or another" to transmit their reports to Jonathan Edwards, so that they could be "compiled into a narrative" that traced the

74. Webster, transcr., "Letters to Joseph Bellamy," 12–13; Wheelock, "Copy of a Letter from Portsmouth," Dec. 3, 1741, Joseph Bellamy Papers. On Wheelock's correspondence net-work, see John Fea, "Wheelock's World: Letters and the Communication of Revival in Great Awakening New England," AAS, *Proceedings*, CIX (1999), 99–144.

"beginning, progress, and various circumstances" of "this surprising dispensation." Although Edwards never took up the task, one of Cooper's traveling companions eventually did.[75]

After witnessing "daily Displays of the infinite and all conquering Grace of God in the Conversion of sinners" on the northern frontier, Thomas Prince, Jr., seized on the idea of producing a magazine that would communicate revival intelligence from New England to a broad reading public. As Prince's father, who assisted in the publication of his son's magazine, explained in a letter to William McCulloch, editor of the *Glasgow-Weekly-History,* the stated purpose of the *Christian History* was to "give an Account of the Revival and Propagation of Religion in *England, Scotland* and *America.*"[76]

Over the course of its two-year publishing run, the *Christian History* printed more than two dozen revival narratives by New England ministers, each of which conformed to a set of instructions appearing in a printed circular letter by the elder Prince. William Shurtleff's account of the *"Revival of Religion* at PORTSMOUTH" was a case in point. He began with a brief history of the town that emphasized the residents' preoccupation with frivolous diversions and "sumptuous and elegant Living." Portsmouth from its inception had been a heterogeneous religious community, and even the Congregational church members in his parish, Shurtleff lamented, contented themselves with the "empty *Form"* of outward religious duties. First Whitefield, then Tennent, and finally local ministers succeeded in "shaking off their heavy Slumbers." On one "remarkable Day" in November 1741, hundreds of people cried out in distress. Meetings increased along with the rising zeal of the townspeople. Since that time, Shurtleff, continued, "Our *Assemblies* were *always throng'd,* and the Number of *Communicants* from Time to Time *greatly increase'd.*"[77]

75. William Cooper, preface to Jonathan Edwards, *The Distinguishing Marks of a Work of the Spirit of God* (Boston, 1741), in *WJE,* IV, *Great Awakening,* ed. C. C. Goen (New Haven, Conn., 1972), 224. On the crucial role of information networks in the development of transatlantic evangelicalism, see Susan Durden [O'Brien], "A Study of the First Evangelical Magazines, 1740–1748," *Journal of Ecclesiastical History,* XXVII (1976), 255–275; Susan O'Brien, "A Transatlantic Community of Saints: The Great Awakening and the First Evangelical Network, 1735–1755," *AHR,* XCI (1986), 811–832; O'Brien, "Eighteenth-Century Publishing Networks in the First Years of Transatlantic Evangelicalism," in Mark A. Noll, David W. Bebbington, and George A. Rawlyk, eds., *Evangelicalism: Comparative Studies of Popular Protestantism in North America, the British Isles, and Beyond, 1700–1990,* Religion in America (New York, 1994), 38–57; Lambert, *Inventing the "Great Awakening,"* 143–179; and Jennifer Snead, "Print, Predestination, and the Public Sphere: Transatlantic Evangelical Periodicals, 1740–1745," *EAL,* XLV (2010), 93–118.

76. Thomas Prince, Jr., to Thomas Prince, Dec. 7, 1741, John Davis Papers, 1627–1846, MHS; Prince, to William McCulloch, May 7, 1743, box 10, Park Family Papers, 1701–1929, MS 384, YUA.

77. Thomas Prince, *It Being Earnestly Desired by Many Pious and Judicious People* (Bos-

The Portsmouth clergymen devoted the second half of his narrative to what Prince in his circular letter called a *"Rise, Progress, and Effects of this Work among You to the Present Day."* Here, Shurtleff emphasized the general moral reformation that ensued, as once profane sailors and merchants laid aside their *"worldly Spirit"* of cursing, drinking, dancing, and singing *"profane* and *obscene Songs."* He commented on the power of the revivals among the young people in town and carefully acknowledged occasional instances in which the zeal of some participants had gone too far. The residents of Portsmouth had been "Sharers in those heavenly Showers," through which God was "watering *these northern Colonies."* Events in Portsmouth, Shurtleff concluded, were of a piece with "the Revival of Religion" that was spreading rapidly throughout the Atlantic world.[78]

Personal correspondence and published reports in newspapers and magazines, such as Prince's *Christian History,* transformed local events into a broader regional, intercolonial, and, ultimately, transatlantic phenomenon. The diffusion of revival news helped to create an overwhelming mood of expectation. Ministers and lay people began to imagine the revivals as an almost physical phenomenon that was propagated from town to town like an epidemic. Arthur Browne, Portsmouth's Anglican rector and an outspoken critic of the revivals, nonetheless spoke for many of his contemporaries when he described the York revival as an "extraordinary work on foot in the Land." News arrived daily of "its prevailing in neighbouring Towns," he complained, "and indeed there seems to be a prospect of its becoming general" throughout the province. Collectively, epistolary exchanges and published revival narratives in magazines convinced an emerging reading public that they were witnessing a unified work of the Holy Spirit. As Daniel Rogers proclaimed triumphantly in a diary entry written at the height of the revivals on the northern frontier, *"The Work is the Same in Every Place."*[79]

The revival of religion that exploded in York and Portsmouth between October and December 1741 conformed to what quickly became a widespread pattern. The diaries and correspondence of ministers across New England re-

ton, 1743); William Shurtleff, "Revival of Religion at Portsmouth . . . ," *CH,* nos. 48–49 (Jan. 28–Feb. 4, 1744), 383–384, 387. On the development of published revival narratives as a genre, see Crawford, *Seasons of Grace,* 183–90; and Lambert, *Inventing the "Great Awakening,"* 125–150. For an important corrective to these arguments, see Fea, "Wheelock's World," *AAS, Procs.,* CIX (1999), 100–113.

78. Prince, *It Being Earnestly Desired;* Shurtleff, "Revival of Religion at Portsmouth," *CH,* nos. 48–49 (Jan. 28, 1744–Feb. 4, 1744), 383, 390–391.

79. Montague, ed., "Letter from Rev. Arthur Brown," *NEHGR,* VI (1852), 264; DDR, Oct. 26, 1741.

veal the same sequence of events: a period of careful preparation and mounting interest followed by peaks of intensive itinerant preaching, attacks on the ideal of the godly walk, protracted revival meetings, surges in church membership, and the exportation of revival intelligence to distant communities. The difference in these local events lay, not in the details or even the personalities involved, but in their timing. Towns experienced revival seasons as ministers and lay people actively engineered the requisite conditions. New England's earliest great awakenings occurred in Boston and the Connecticut Valley during the spring and summer of 1741. Ministers in the western counties of Connecticut reported similar developments at about the same time. Revival activities crested in northern New England during the fall of 1741 and in central Massachusetts several months later. The awakenings that gripped the Old Colony and Cape Cod during the spring of 1742 were distinguished only by their lateness. "Blesd be the lord, that the gloryes work of his grace that hath ben going on the in land, is now apring [appearing] amongs this people," exclaimed Sandwich minister Francis Worcester. "This is a harvest day." Yet, by the time Worcester penned these words in April 1742, the tide of public opinion had turned decisively against the very revival phenomena that had been praised in places like York and Portsmouth only a few months earlier.[80]

York remained a key outpost of the Whitefieldian revivals for several years. During the summer of 1742, Samuel Moody and a group of clergymen took the audacious step of ordaining Daniel Rogers as an itinerant preacher with no settled parish—the first ordination of its kind in the history of New England's Congregational churches. The Ipswich revivalist returned to York, Portsmouth, and the hinterland communities of northern New England on numerous occasions during the 1740s, and his travels brought him into frequent contact with the network of clerical and lay elites who had assembled in York during the fall of 1741. Rogers, moreover, was not the only riding minister to target the northern frontier. Other Whitefieldarians, including Nicholas Gilman and Samuel Buell, and various unlettered exhorters kept the revival fires in Maine and New Hampshire flickering well after the flames had been quenched elsewhere in New England. Buell's ambiguous assessment of the situation was suggestive. "On the morrow," he wrote from Boston in an April 1742 letter to Eleazar Wheelock, "I Set out for old York" carrying "Letters and invitations to Preach from all Parts." "An effectual Door is open Daily for my Preaching," he declared, "But there are many adversaries."[81]

---

80. Francis Worcester, "The Church Record to Be Cept," 1735–1745, 3, John Davis Papers.

81. Samuel Buell to Eleazar Wheelock, Apr. 20, 1742, in Bushman, ed., *Great Awakening*, 44.

NEW CONVERTS

George Whitefield's departure from New England in October 1740 left Nathan Cole in near despair. Soon thereafter, Cole later explained in his "Spiritual Travels," "I began to think I was not Elected." For nearly a year he was beset by thoughts of writhing in "Hell fire for ever and ever." Nothing seemed to ease his distress, neither food nor drink, sleep nor work. Cole confessed secret adolescent sins to his parents and made resolutions to "forsake every thing that was Sinfull," but Satan relentlessly unmasked his false hope in the performance of religious duties. Experienced Christian friends and neighbors encouraged him to trust in God for deliverance, but still Cole continued to slide into black despair. "I went month after month," he later recalled, "mourning and begging for mercy."[82]

One night as he sat alone in his bedchamber languishing from a "Mortal disease," staring into the fire, and contemplating suicide, Cole experienced a sudden vision of his own body hanging in the open air before God. He lost consciousness, and, when he returned to his senses, Cole perceived a miraculous change in his heart. "I was set free," he wrote, "my distress was gone." He fell to his knees praising God. Cole's wife burst into the room and inquired after the nature of his distress, but the Kensington artisan could not answer for he was "swallowed up in God." Cole claimed to see with new eyes. It seemed to him as if "all things became new, A new God; new thoughts and new heart."[83]

Almost immediately Cole confronted a second vision. He perceived with his new spiritual eyes the "form of A Gospel Church," a house built "4 square" with a chimney at the west end. The first floor had been divided into rooms for the minister and his family. Outside, Cole gazed on a verdant land of hills and valleys, highways and brooks. A shimmering choir of angels hovered above the meetinghouse crying "the Glory of the Town, the glory of the Town." Passing strangers paused to marvel at the building. Sunlight radiated through the upper windows, illuminating the figure of a large man—a minister—who stood praying with his hands lifted toward the heavens. A small group of worshippers had gathered, and a "Solemn sweet Countenance sat upon their Faces." Although Cole spent many years puzzling over the meaning of this second vision, two things were immediately apparent. This was not the Kensington Society meetinghouse, and the praying figure was certainly not William Burnham, the man under whose ministry Cole had lived and worshipped for three decades.[84]

82. NCS, 94.
83. Ibid., 95–97.
84. Ibid., 97–98, 121. Cole appears to have been describing the meetinghouse erected in

Although Cole acknowledged that he had been "called a member of this old Church" in Kensington since the early 1730s, he chose to dismiss his previous religious experiences in a single sentence in his autobiography, berating himself for attempting to earn salvation through "my own works such as prayers and good deeds." But even this terse statement was telling, for it ignored his admission to full communion, an event that most New Englanders considered an important milestone in their religious, if not social, maturation. Cole had once consulted with Burnham, stood propounded for a fortnight, and drafted a written relation of faith to be read on the day he covenanted with the Kensington church in full communion. Three decades later, as he composed his "Spiritual Travels" during the 1760s, Cole understood what he could not have seen during the months following Whitefield's visit to Middletown. His powerful conversion experience marked a dramatic break with the past—a new birth—in which he repudiated the religious experiences that had precipitated his decision to affiliate with the Kensington church.[85]

Unlike his puritan progenitors a century earlier, Cole no longer conceptualized the doctrine of conversion as an extended process in which hopeful saints haltingly passed through a series of stages and cautiously prepared for salvation through the practices of piety. He did not perceive in Whitefield's Middletown sermon a call to elevate his devotional duties, improve providential good impressions, or grow in grace. Instead, the touring Anglican clergyman had struck at the foundations of Cole's faith and unleashed grave uncertainties about the proper order of the Congregational establishment. Whitefield exhorted Cole to stand fast on the necessity of the new birth alone. If neighbors and ministers like Burnham could not testify to having experienced such a miraculous transformation, then their churches "were not in a gospel order."[86]

Thousands of New Englanders like Cole experienced the Whitefieldian awakening as a sudden and dramatic rupture with the past rather than a resurgence of traditional puritan piety. Between 1741 and 1744, children, adolescents, and unmarried young adults joined Congregational churches in unprecedented numbers, thus undermining the meaning of membership as an index of family maturation and social status. Small numbers of native and enslaved African Americans joined the ranks of these new converts, a fact that some revival observers proclaimed was a harbinger of the coming millennium.

Middletown during the 1750s by members of Ebenezer Frothingham's Separate Congregational church. See Dexter, ed., *Extracts from the Itineraries and Other Miscellanies of Ezra Stiles*, 273.

85. NCS, 92, 103.

86. Ibid., 103.

Far from an ingathering of the unchurched or the notoriously sinful, revival meetings were dominated by long-standing church members—"ould Christions" like Cole who discovered that they had been building their hopes for salvation on a foundation of sand. In their church records and gravestones, their prayer bills and courtship letters, New Englanders during the early 1740s actively embraced the message of the Whitefieldarians and consciously, publicly, and, in some cases, permanently rejected the prevailing conventions of the godly walk.[87]

■ Church membership demographics provide the strongest measure of the degree to which lay men and women experienced New England's era of great awakenings as a disruption in the established order. Repudiating the religious duties associated with the ideal of the godly walk opened the doors of the church to anyone who could demonstrate an experimental knowledge of the new birth. Itinerants and local ministers favorable to revival innovations exhorted their audiences not to delay. They gloried in their preaching successes, frequently reporting the specific numbers of people that had experienced conversion as a direct result of their sermons. "The Lord is gathering in his Elect everywhere," proclaimed Samuel Phillips Savage in a letter to his brother, "O may the Lord grant you may not be left when so many are on the Wing to the New Jerusalem."[88]

Although the timing differed from region to region, churches across New England admitted record numbers of new communicants in 1741 and 1742. The largest gains came in Boston's Old South, Brattle Street, and New North churches, Ipswich, Middleborough, Newbury, Suffield, and Wrentham, Massachusetts, Lyme and Stonington, Connecticut, and Hampton, New Hampshire. Admissions in each of these congregations approached and frequently exceeded one hundred during these years. Overall, perhaps as many as 60 percent of all New England churches admitted more than twice the yearly number of communicants, and at least one-quarter grew at a rate between

---

87. Benjamin Cary to Eleazar Wheelock, Sept. 10, 1742, no. 742510, *EWP.*

88. Samuel Phillips Savage to Arthur Savage, Apr. 20, 1741, SSP II. For statistical reports of conversions by itinerants, see John Lee to Eleazar Wheelock, May 7, 1741, no. 741307, *EWP,* Wheelock to the Lebanon North Parish Church, n.d. [July 11, 1741], no. 743900.1, Benajah Case to Wheelock, Oct. 25, 1741, no. 741575, Wheelock to Daniel Rogers, Jan. 18, 1742, no. 742118; EWD, 237–239; Coffin, *Sketch of the History of Newbury,* 211; *Boston Weekly Post-Boy,* Oct. 5, 1741; William Allen, "Memoir of Rev. Eleazar Wheelock, D.D., Founder and First President of Dartmouth College," *American Quarterly Register,* X (1837), 12; Webster, transcr., "Letters to Joseph Bellamy," 12; and Hopkins, journal, 27, 29, 31–33, box 322, SGC II. For a different perspective, see Christopher Grasso, *A Speaking Aristocracy: Transforming Public Discourse in Eighteenth-Century Connecticut* (Chapel Hill, N.C., 1999), 89–96.

five and ten times the annual average. In the small village of Berwick, Maine, more than ninety new communicants swelled the church roles, exceeding the annual rate of admissions by a factor of more than eleven.[89]

Accounts of awakened communities regularly reported the involvement of "great Men both high and low" or "different Ages and Sexes," but clear patterns soon emerged. Few revival observers failed to take note of what Jonathan Edwards called the "strange alteration" among young people "all over New England." Their "night revels are changed into privet meetings for Religious Exersises," Ivory, Sr., and Ann Hovey of Topsfield, Massachusetts, explained in a letter to their son, and their "disscorses when they meet togather at other times is moch altered." By the fall of 1741, references to awakened youths had become so ubiquitous that revival proponents coined a pair of phrases to describe this distinctive cohort of church membership candidates. They called them "new converts" or "Young Christians."[90]

89. George W. Harper, *A People So Favored of God: Boston's Congregational Churches and Their Pastors, 1710–1760* (Lanham, Md., 2004), 182; Ipswich, Mass., Records of the First Church of Ipswich, 1739–1805, 9–10, microfilm no. 39, PEM; Edith R. Wills, transcr., "Newbury, Mass., Records of the Third Church of Christ (Unitarian)," 90–96, Mss C 1805, NEHGS; Thomas Weston, *History of the Town of Middleboro, Massachusetts* (Boston, 1906), 658–663; J. Richard Olivas, "Great Awakenings: Time, Space, and the Varieties of Religious Revivalism in Massachusetts and Northern New England, 1740–1748" (Ph.D. diss., University of California–Los Angeles, 1997), 524; *Records of the Congregational Church in Suffield, Conn. (Except Church Votes), 1710–1836* (Hartford, Conn., 1941), 52–57; Old Lyme, Conn., First Ecclesiastical Society and Congregational Church Records, 1731–1874, 36–40, microfilm no. 74, CSL; North Stonington, Conn., Congregational Church Records, 1727–1887, 9–10, microfilm no. 317, CSL; Hampton, N.H., Records of the First Congregational Church, 1667–1902, 36, 38, 40, 42, 44, microfilm, reel 1 (Watertown, Mass., 1986), NEHGS; Joseph Crook Anderson II, ed., *Records of the First and Second Churches of Berwick, Maine,* Maine Genealogical Society Special Publication, XXXIII (Rockport, Maine, 1999), 53–58.

90. Ebenezer Prout to Samuel Phillips Savage, Mar. 10, 1741 [1742], SSP I; Winiarski, "Jonathan Edwards, Enthusiast?" *Church History,* LXXIV (2005), 738; Jonathan Edwards, *Some Thoughts concerning the Present Revival of Religion in New-England* (Boston, 1742), in *WJE,* IV, *Great Awakening,* ed. Goen, 326; Ivory, Sr., and Anne Hovey, to Ivory Hovey, Jr., Mar. 29, 1742, Hovey Family Papers, 1734–1901, PHM; EWD, 237. For a sample of references to "new converts" and "young Christians," see Coffin, *Sketch of the History of Newbury,* 211; Winiarski, "'Jornal of a Fue Days at York,'" *Maine History,* XLII (2004), 69; Foxcroft to Dickinson, Dec. 16, 1741, Charles Roberts Autograph Collection; Case to Wheelock, Oct. 25, 1741, no. 741575, EWP; and Jonathan Edwards to James Robe, May 12, 1743, in *WJE,* XVI, *Letters and Personal Writings,* ed. Claghorn, 110. The phrases appeared in both pro- and antirevival publications during the period, including Charles Chauncy, *The New Creature Describ'd, and Consider'd as the Sure Characteristick of a Man's Being in Christ . . .* (Boston, 1741), 39; Edwards, *Distinguishing Marks,* in *WJE,* IV, *Great Awakening,* ed. Goen, 267; [Chauncy], *A Letter from a Gentleman in Boston to Mr. George Wishart . . .* (Edinburgh, 1742), in David S. Lovejoy, ed., *Religious Enthusiasm and the Great Awakening,* American Historical Sources: Research and Interpretation (Englewood Cliffs, N.J., 1969), 76; Andrew Croswell, *A Letter from the Revd Mr. Croswell, to the Revd Mr. Turell, in Answer to His Direction to His People* (Boston, 1742), 12; and Chauncy, *Seasonable Thoughts on the State of*

Between 1741 and 1744, the mean age at admission to full communion in parishes across New England plummeted. Peter Thacher's Middleborough church witnessed one of the largest disparities. Men admitted during the revival season were, on average, more than twelve years younger than their pre-awakening fathers, brothers, and neighbors; the mean age for women dropped by more than five years. More than one in five men and one in four women admitted to the Middleborough church during the revival were under the age of twenty, compared to 3 and 9 percent, respectively, before 1740. The new converts even included a pair of children aged seven and nine. Nor was Middleborough unique. Nearly all of the communities for which social historians have generated detailed church affiliation statistics demonstrate a significant downturn in the mean and median ages of both men and women. Even in towns that enjoyed only a moderate increase in membership, such as Haverhill and Medfield, where John Brown and Joseph Baxter downplayed or dismissed Whitefield's revival measures, the average age at admission for both men and women declined sharply (see Table 1, above).[91]

Most young converts continued to hail from prominent core parish families and were well versed in the social meanings of church membership. But other variables suggest that the revivals subverted traditional patterns of affiliation. Since the 1670s, men had seldom outnumbered women at the celebration of the Lord's Supper. During the early 1740s, however, a growing number of male converts narrowed the gap. The relative youthfulness of revival participants brought a large influx of single men and women. In previous decades, 75 per-

---

Religion in New-England ... (Boston, 1743), 249, 275; as well as in numerous revival reports published in the *CH*.

91. Douglas Leo Winiarski, "All Manner of Error and Delusion: Josiah Cotton and the Religious Transformation of Southeastern New England, 1700–1770" (Ph.D. diss., Indiana University, 2000), 418–421. See also J. M. Bumsted, "Religion, Finance, and Democracy in Massachusetts: The Town of Norton as a Case Study," *JAH*, LVII (1971), 828–830; James Walsh, "The Great Awakening in the First Congregational Church of Woodbury, Connecticut," *WMQ*, XXVIII (1971), 550–551; Philip J. Greven, Jr., "Youth, Maturity, and Religious Conversion: A Note on the Ages of Converts in Andover, Massachusetts, 1711–1749," *EIHC*, CVIII (1972), 132; Gerald F. Moran, "Conditions of Religious Conversion in the First Society of Norwich, Connecticut, 1718–1744," *Journal of Social History*, V (1972), 336; Kevin Michael Sweeney, "Unruly Saints: Religion and Society in the River Towns of Massachusetts, 1700–1750" (B.A. thesis, Williams College, 1972), 136, 162, 164, 166, 168, 170; Gerald Francis Moran, "The Puritan Saint: Religious Experience, Church Membership, and Piety in Connecticut, 1636–1776" (Ph.D. diss., Rutgers University, 1974), 280; William F. Willingham, "Religious Conversion in the Second Society of Windham, Connecticut, 1723–43: A Case Study," *Societas*, VI (1976), 112–113; Willingham, "The Conversion Experience during the Great Awakening in Windham, Connecticut," *Connecticut History*, XXI (1980), 41–43; and Stephen R. Grossbart, "Seeking the Divine Favor: Conversion and Church Admission in Eastern Connecticut, 1711–1832," *WMQ*, XLVI (1989), 705–706.

cent of all prospective church members had previously established independent households; young revival converts, by contrast, were much more likely
to be living with their parents and waiting to inherit or acquire taxable property, marry and start a family, or serve the town in a variety of leadership positions. Although they might have been religiously precocious, new converts
lacked the qualities of social maturation that distinguished earlier generations
of prospective church members.[92]

The Connecticut Valley village of Suffield perhaps best exemplified the
strikingly different patterns of church affiliation that swept across the region.
Following the death of minister Ebenezer Devotion in April 1741, parishioners encouraged neighboring clergymen and their itinerating colleagues
to stoke the revival fires that Whitefield had ignited during his brief visit to
Suffield the previous October. Several prominent riding ministers visited the
pastorless congregation, including Joseph Bellamy, Jedidiah Mills, Benjamin
Pomeroy, and Eleazar Wheelock. Northampton, Massachusetts, minister
Jonathan Edwards also took special interest in the Suffield church, for many
of his own parishioners retained close familial ties to the small hamlet downriver. In addition to delivering a powerfully awakening sermon in town a few
days after Devotion's funeral, Edwards sent a long letter to Suffield resident
Deborah Hathaway in June 1741. Like many of the sermons that he preached
in Northampton during these same months, his pastoral epistle drew a sharp
distinction between "old experiences" and "renewed experiences, new light,
and new, lively acts of faith and love." Edwards encouraged Hathaway and
the other young women in town to be "earnest and violent for the kingdom of
heaven" by setting up private meetings, exhorting one another, and ceaselessly
striving for conversion.[93]

Later that month, Edwards returned to Suffield at the request of the deacons to officiate at the Lord's Supper. He arrived on July 5, 1741, just three
days before he preached *Sinners in the Hands of an Angry God* across the river
in Enfield, and promptly admitted 97 new members. The Suffield sacrament
was a spectacular event—quite possibly the largest church admission ritual

92. Cedric B. Cowing, "Sex and Preaching in the Great Awakening," *American Quarterly*,
XX (1968), 630–633; Bumsted, "Religion, Finance, and Democracy," *JAH*, LVIII (1981), 823–
824, 828; Walsh, "Great Awakening in the First Congregational Church of Woodbury," *WMQ*,
XXVIII (1971), 549–551; Moran, "Conditions of Religious Conversion in the First Church of
Norwich," *Journal of Social History*, V (1972), 338–339; Willingham, "Religious Conversion
in the Second Society of Windham," *Societas*, VI (1976), 112.

93. Jonathan Edwards to Deborah Hathaway, June 3, 1741, in *WJE*, XIV, *Letters and Personal Writings*, ed. Claghorn, 91, 93. On revival events in Suffield, see Winiarski, "Jonathan
Edwards, Enthusiast?" *Church History*, LXXIV (2005), 692–701.

ever observed in colonial New England. Neighboring minister Peter Reynolds of Enfield presided over the sacrament in Suffield two months later and admitted 79 new communicants, which raised the total number to a staggering 176, or more than fifteen times the annual average. Of this group, 3 in 4 had been born Suffield and raised in households where one or both parents were full members. Ninety percent had been baptized as infants and placed under the watch of the congregation. Nearly half of the women and a quarter of the men were still in their teens—or even younger. Overall, 71 percent were under the age of twenty-five. The mean age of the Edwards and Reynolds cohorts, moreover, dropped by 9.9 and 8.5 years for women and men, respectively. More than two-thirds were unmarried.[94]

Among the people that Edwards admitted to the Lord's Supper in Suffield were three enslaved African Americans. Perhaps one-quarter of the town's black residents joined in full communion during the revival years. The presence of racial outsiders among the ranks of new converts presented a strikingly visual disruption in prevailing patterns of affiliation. Only a handful of enslaved or free blacks or native Americans had joined any New England church before 1740, although they constituted between 2 and 4 percent of the total population. Indeed, the concept of enslaved or indentured church members held little meaning in a culture that had previously associated religious affiliation with family formation and social maturation. English masters occasionally presented their native and African American servants for baptism, and a few Indians and free blacks owned the covenant during the decades between 1700 and 1740. Informal social pressures, however, effectively barred them from full membership.[95]

The Whitefieldian revivals initially appear to have had a mixed impact on the well-established Indian communities of the Old Colony and Martha's Vineyard, where native Christians had been worshipping in churches led by indigenous preachers for more than half a century. But the situation differed considerably in the larger native enclaves of Connecticut and Rhode Island. Regrouping from the devastating wars and epidemics of the seventeenth century, traditionalist leaders had actively resisted the incursion of English missionaries. As a result, the Mohegans, Narragansetts, Niantics, and Pequots

---

94. Winiarski, "Jonathan Edwards, Enthusiast?" *Church History*, LXXIV (2005), 698–699.

95. For different perspectives on church affiliation among native Americans and enslaved African Americans in early New England, see Linford D. Fisher, *The Indian Great Awakening: Religion and the Shaping of Native Cultures in Early America* (New York, 2012), 84–106; and Richard J. Boles, "Race and Colonial Congregational Churches: Some Surprising Findings," *Bulletin of the CL*, 2d Ser., IX, no. 1 (Spring / Summer 2012), 2–10.

continued to practice ancestral religious traditions well into the eighteenth century. The renowned Indian preacher Samson Occom spoke for many native Americans when he acknowledged in his 1768 autobiographical narrative that he had been "Born a Heathen and Brought up In Heathenism," in direct contrast to English church membership candidates who had been raised in the land of light. Occom's parents "Livd a wandering life" and "Strictly maintain'd and follow'd their Heathenish Ways, Customs and Religion," with only tenuous ties to the ministers and Indian agents who occasionally visited their villages to preach, distribute blankets, or conduct a few weeks of school.[96]

By 1740, the Algonquians of southern New England presented a large mission field. Clergymen in New London County, Connecticut, redoubled their efforts to evangelize Indian communities in the wake of Whitefield's first New England tour. They were joined by Gilbert Tennent, Daniel Rogers, Eleazar Wheelock, David Brainerd, Samuel Buell, Jedidiah Mills, and other zealous Whitefieldarians. During the summer of 1741, Occom later recalled, these "Extraordinary Ministers" generated a "great Stir of Religion in these Parts of the World both amongst the Indians as Well as the English." John Owen and Andrew Croswell sent a petition to the Connecticut General Court in which they acknowledged that the Pequots had languished in "heathenish Darkness" until September 1741, after which more than fifty men and women had regularly attended religious meetings in their parishes in Groton. The new native converts demonstrated an "Uncommon concern about theire Souls, a teachable Spirit and tempar, and a great Aptness to Receive light and knowledge." By January 1742, Wheelock was writing excitedly to Rogers about a "Great Work" among the Mohegans, Niantics, and Pequots, with "Many of them Converted and the Rest mostly under Concern."[97]

96. Joanna Brooks, ed., *The Collected Writings of Samson Occom, Mohegan: Leadership and Literature in Eighteenth-Century Native America* (New York, 2006), 52. On the persistence of ancestral religious practices among native Americans in eastern Connecticut and Rhode Island, see Douglas L. Winiarski, "Native American Popular Religion in New England's Old Colony, 1670–1770," in Joel W. Martin and Mark A. Nicholas, eds., *Native Americans, Christianity, and the Reshaping of the American Religious Landscape* (Chapel Hill, N.C., 2010), 100.

97. Brooks, ed., *Collected Writings of Samson Occom,* 52–53; John Owen and Andrew Croswell to the Connecticut General Assembly, May 6, 1742, Connective Archives: Indians, Ser. I: 1661–1748, I, 238, CSL (I thank Linford Fisher for sharing his transcription of this document); Wheelock to Rogers, Jan. 18, 1742, no. 742118, *EWP*. See also William S. Simmons, "Red Yankees: Narragansett Conversion in the Great Awakening," *American Ethnologist,* X (1983), 253–271; John Wood Sweet, *Bodies Politic: Negotiating Race in the American North, 1730–1830* (Baltimore, 2003), 102–140; Rachel Wheeler, *To Live upon Hope: Mohicans and Missionaries in the Eighteenth-Century Northeast* (Ithaca, N.Y., 2008), 93–104; and Fisher, *Indian Great Awakening,* 65–83.

For the first and only time in early American history, Indians joined English churches in significant numbers. "I was one that was Imprest with the things we had heard," Occom remembered. "These Preachers did not only Come to us, but we frequently went to their meetings and Churches." At least twenty Mohegans joined David Jewett's church in the north parish of New London (now Montville), Connecticut. The new Indian converts included Occom's mother and aunt, several descendants of the prominent seventeenth-century sachem Uncas, and Samuel Ashpo, who, along with Occom and several other Mohegans, eventually gravitated toward Wheelock's parsonage to become the first cohort of scholars at Moor's Indian Charity School, which later evolved into Dartmouth College. Between 1675 and 1740, no native Americans affiliated with any of the three English churches at Stonington, but more than 10 percent of the 185 men and women admitted to full communion during the revivals lived at the nearby Pequot reservation. A table that George Griswold appended to the report that he sent to the *Christian History* included thirteen Niantics among the more than 100 new converts in the east parish of Lyme, or roughly 10 percent of the entire Indian community.[98]

An even more unusual sequence of events unfolded in Westerly, Rhode Island, where New England Company for the Propagation of the Gospel missionary Joseph Park had been laboring fruitlessly among the Narragansetts for nearly a decade. Visits from Tennent and other riding ministers during the spring and summer of 1741 persuaded him to change the tenor of his preaching. Park began to *"contend for the Faith"* and "speak with more Boldness" in his sermons. Working in concert with colleagues, English lay men, and recent native converts among the neighboring Pequots and Mohegans, Park organized religious meetings and revitalized the Indian school. Near the end of January 1742, he and his Indian parishioners attended protracted revival meetings in Stonington, and, *"from that Time the Indians* were generally stirred up to seek after eternal Life." Park gathered a church in Westerly, and, although the fourteen founding pillars were English, Narragansetts soon began attending. "There was not above *ten* or *twelve Indians* that used to come to Meeting at all," the young missionary reported, but "there is now *near*

98. Brooks, ed., *Collected Writings of Samson Occom*, 53; Montville, Conn., Congregational Church Records, 1722–1909, 30, microfilm no. 78, CSL; Richard A. Wheeler, *History of the First Congregational Church, Stonington, Conn., 1674-1874 ...* (Norwich, Conn., 1875), 231, 235–236; North Stonington Congregational Church Records, 9–10; George Griswold, "An Account of the Revival of Religion at Lyme East Parish ...," *CH*, no. 66 (June 2, 1744), 109–110; Jonathan Parsons to Benjamin Colman, Dec. 16, 1741, in Jonathan Edwards, *The Distinguishing Marks of a Work of the Spirit of God ...* (London, 1742), 75.

an Hundred that come very constantly." So many native converts joined the Westerly church in full communion during the six-month period beginning in August 1743 that Park felt compelled to submit two letters to the *Christian History* detailing the "wonderful Work of GOD in *this Place.*"[99]

African Americans also embraced the opportunities provided by the revivals to enhance their social status through church affiliation. In many churches, the practice of owning the covenant declined among whites during the early 1740s but not among enslaved and free blacks. As a result, the proportion of African American covenant owners soared from less than 1 percent to more than 40 percent in towns such as Plymouth and Medfield. The number of candidates propounded to full membership increased, too. Between 1694 and 1740, the Middleborough church had admitted only one black woman, but six joined during the next four years. As much as one-quarter of the enslaved populations of the south parish in Reading (now Wakefield) and Suffield, Massachusetts, joined in full communion during the revival years. Although they constituted less than 1 percent of all admissions in Boston's nine Congregational churches before 1740, blacks accounted for more than 3 percent of all new converts admitted between 1741 and 1744. Fervent revival congregations such as the Brattle Street and Old South churches saw the ratio of African American church members rise even higher. Even a single new black communicant struck some New Englanders as a significant departure from past affiliation practices, especially in towns with small enslaved populations. When Caesar Long applied for membership in Hampton during the spring of 1741, minister Ward Cotton noted that he was the "first of that Color that ever belonged to this Church."[100]

It was the symbolism of African American converts, above all else, that

99. Joseph Park, "An Account of the Late Propagation of Religion at Westerly and Charlestown in Rhode-Island Colony ...," *CH*, nos. 26–27 (Aug. 27–Sept. 3, 1743), 203, 209; Park, "Westerly and Charlestown in Rhode-Island Colony ...," *CH*, no. 55 (Mar. 17, 1744), 22.

100. *Plymouth Church Records, 1620–1859*, CSM, *Publications*, XXII (Boston, 1920), 511, 523–525; Medfield, Mass., Congregational Church Records, 1697–1860, Medfield Historical Society, Medfield, Mass., 29–30; Weston, *History of the Town of Middleboro*, 658–664; James F. Cooper and Kenneth P. Minkema, eds., *The Colonial Church Records of the First Church of Reading (Wakefield) and the First Church of Rumney Marsh (Revere)*, CSM, *Publications*, LXXII (Boston, 2006), 145–147; *Records of the Congregational Church in Suffield*, 54, 56–57; Robert J. Dunkle and Ann S. Lainhart, transcr., *The Records of the Churches of Boston and the First Church, Second Parish, and Third Parish of Roxbury, Including Baptisms, Marriages, Deaths, Admissions and Dismissals* (Boston, 2001), CD-ROM; Hampton Records of the First Congregational Church, reel 1, 36. Population figures derived from Walker, Jr., "Account of the Town of Boston"; Greene and Harrington, *American Population Before the Federal Census of 1790*, 58; and Josiah H. Benton, Jr., *Early Census Making in Massachusetts, 1643–1765* ... (Boston, 1905), 13.

drew the attention of most revival proponents. Leading figures such as White-field and Jonathan Edwards defended the institution of slavery, but they also actively preached to blacks and eagerly reported their successes. New England's riding ministers viewed the conversions of enslaved men and women as a sign of God's extraordinary work. Edwards listed "poor Negroes" behind "new converts," "formerly esteemed" professors, and Indians—the "wretched people and dregs of mankind"—as evidence of the "wonderful work of God that has of late been carried on in the land." Among the more than one thousand people "deeply wounded and Awakened" during the Portsmouth revival, a widely circulated report singled out "8 or 10 negros" that had been "made Free in our Lord Jesus." More than thirty people cried out in distress during a sermon that Wheelock preached in Taunton during his fall 1741 tour, but he took care to note that "almost all the negroes in the town" had been "wounded." Wheelock's occasional traveling companion, Daniel Rogers, regularly preached to mixed audiences of blacks and whites, and he prayed fervently that God would "call more of the poor negroes to the Knowledge of his Son." By the time that Josiah Cotton wrote to Wheelock in December 1742 to describe the revival in Providence, enslaved African Americans had emerged as some of the "warmest Christians" in New England. Cotton declined to comment on candidates who hailed from established families and instead focused his report to Wheelock on a motley assortment of unlikely new converts: regular Baptists, Quakers, unchurched families that "never came to Meeting," an "underwitted Young Man," and a "Poor Negro Servant Woman."[101]

"Ethiopia has stretched out her hand," declared an exuberant William Cooper in his preface to Edwards's 1741 Yale College commencement address. The strangeness of this revival world turned upside down served as a strong rebuke to those whom Cooper called "formal" church membership professors.

101. Edwards, *Some Thoughts concerning the Present Revival of Religion,* in *WJE,* IV, *Great Awakening,* ed. Goen, 291, 329–330; Savage, "Extract of a Letter from Piscataqua," n.d. [Dec. 3, 1741], SSP I; EWD, 238; DDR, Mar. 27, May 17 (quote), 27, June 16, 1741, Jan. 6, 26, Feb. 3, Mar. 12, 16, 29, Apr. 21, May 4, 6, 9, Oct. 27, Dec. 22, 1742; Cotton (of Providence, R.I.) to Wheelock, Dec. 16, 1742, case 8, box 22, SGC I. On Whitefield's and Edwards's attitudes toward slavery, see Stephen J. Stein, "George Whitefield on Slavery: Some New Evidence," *Church History,* XLII (1973), 243–256; Allan Gallay, "The Great Sellout: George Whitefield on Slavery," in Winifred B. Moore, Jr., and Joseph F. Tripp, eds., *Looking South: Chapters in the Story of an American Region,* Contributions in American History, no. 136 (Westport, Conn., 1989), 17–30; Kenneth P. Minkema, "Jonathan Edwards's Defense of Slavery," *Massachusetts Historical Review,* IV (2004), 23–59; and Kidd, *George Whitefield,* 97–100, 108–112, 188–203, 261–262. See also Joanna Brooks, *American Lazarus: Religion and the Rise of African-American and Native American Literatures* (New York, 2003), 21–41; and Richard A. Bailey, *Race and Redemption in Puritan New England,* Religion in America (New York, 2011), 116–122, 125.

John Lee, the king's attorney for New London County, cast native American conversions in almost millennial terms in order to critique his lifeless neighbors and fellow parishioners. "They live much nearer GOD than the English do," Lee explained in a letter that was published in a Boston newspaper, "they not having so many Streams to sip at, live much nearer the Fountain." The Indians' "Joy is more pure and spiritual than commonly is to be observed among the English, and less of the Mixture of humane Passion," he added, before ending his account on an exultant note, praising God for breaking down the "middle Wall of Partition" that separated whites from native Christians.[102]

For many young converts, witnessing enslaved African Americans and "christian indians wonderfully fill'd" with the Holy Spirit and worshipping in English meetinghouses was an affecting sight that signaled the dawning of a new day. In York, Maine, Daniel Rogers encountered a woman who told him that she "had a View of the Coming of the Kingdome of God, and particularly of the Negroes being bro't into It." A chance encounter with a black man "full of the love of Christ" prompted Joseph Bean to pray in his diary that God might pour out his spirit on the "poore negros." "Wether bond or free white or black," the young Cambridge shopkeeper wrote, "it is all the same." Deborah Prince, daughter of Boston's Old South minister, devoted a considerable portion of a 1743 letter to informing relatives in London about the "Vast numbers" of Indians who had emerged "out of darkness" into the light of the gospel. "This is the Lord's doing," she wrote excitedly, quoting the famous passage in Psalm 118 regarding the stone that the builders rejected, "and it is marvellous in our eyes."[103]

Although their numbers remained small, the sudden emergence of native and African Americans among the ranks of revival converts disrupted prevailing patterns of affiliation, especially when viewed as part of a larger movement involving vast numbers of young adults, adolescents, and children. For a brief period between 1741 and 1744, church membership had ceased to serve as a badge of family status or social maturation.

▪ Young converts, Indians, and enslaved African Americans might have attracted the largest share of attention during the revivals of the early 1740s,

102. Cooper, preface to Edwards, *Distinguishing Marks of a Work of the Spirit of God*, in *WJE*, IV, *Great Awakening*, ed., Goen, 219–220; *Boston Weekly Post-Boy*, Aug. 30, 1742.

103. Barbara E. Lacey, ed., *The World of Hannah Heaton: The Diary of an Eighteenth-Century New England Farm Woman* (DeKalb, Ill., 2003), 13; DDR, Apr. 30, 1743; Bean, diary, 139; Benjamin B. Wisner, *The History of the Old South Church in Boston* ... (Boston, 1830), 111–112.

but, as Nathan Cole's "Spiritual Travels" narrative suggests, they were not the Whitefieldarians' largest constituency. According to Middleborough minister Peter Thacher, "very moral and blameless" church members were often the first to respond to caustic sermons delivered by Whitefield, Tennent, and their New England counterparts. Despite strong ties to the church, these earnest men and women renounced their former participation in the Lord's Supper as a mere delusion. In the wake of a powerful fast day sermon by neighboring minister Josiah Crocker, Thacher confronted a considerable number of "Professors" whose "Lamps went out: they discover'd there was no Oil of true Grace in them." As the revival spread throughout his parish, the Middleborough minister visited with scores of communicants who now questioned their eternal estates. Charged by Crocker to examine their hearts, many godly walkers discovered to their dismay that they had never truly experienced the new birth. They "find they built on the Sand," Thacher summarized in a letter to the *Christian History,* "rested in their Duties," and were "meer Hypocrites."[104]

Identifying long-standing church members who were caught up in the revivals is difficult, since their names, unlike those of new converts, seldom appear on membership lists. But some evidence hints that they might have made up as much as two-thirds of the total number of revival participants. In addition to the more than 150 people that he admitted to full communion in 1741 and 1742, Thacher counted more than 200 existing Middleborough church members who had repudiated their former pious conversations. One account of the Portsmouth revival placed the number of awakened souls at 1,000, although it is likely that fewer than 200 joined either of the town's two Congregational churches. Wheelock claimed to have converted 300 of his own parishioners in the Lebanon Crank Society (now Columbia, Connecticut), but his fragmentary church records list fewer than 100 new members during the revival years. Thomas Prince and John Webb, the ministers of Boston's Old South and New North churches, counseled more than 2,200 people during the months following Gilbert Tennent's departure in March 1741; however, a careful accounting of the town's nine congregations yields a total of only 594 admissions to full communion during the next two years. In each of these cases, some of those under "deep Concern about their Souls" might have lived in other towns, never passed through the new birth, turned against the revivals, or been barred from communion for various reasons. As Prince explained in the *Chris-*

104. Peter Thacher, "Revival of Religion at Middleborough Continued," *CH,* no. 64 (May 19, 1744), 90–92. See also Thacher, "Revival of Religion at Middleborough ...," *CH,* no. 52 (Feb. 25, 1744), 414.

tian History, most of the people whom he counseled during the revivals "had been in *full Communion* and going on in a Course of Religion *many Years.*"[105]

Stories of these distressed "old professing" Christians appear regularly in a wide range of sources. Reports from York highlighted the wrenching experiences of prominent church members. Newbury diarist Joseph Goodhue placed his hope for salvation in the performance of outward religious duties after he joined the church in 1739. Traveling with Tennent and talking with the awakened residents of York conspired to "cut of[f] these fals hops." God was pleased to shine into Goodhue's "Dark soul," filling him with "Wonder and Astonisment." The anonymous author of "A Jornal of a Fue Days at York" was surprised to discover "some that have been sober and reconed Godly, all there Days, are now in the Dark, and Complain of heardness of heart." Foremost among those in despair was the York church elder, Joseph Sayward, who remained deeply uncertain of his spiritual estate during the painful weeks before his death in December 1741. Another woman complained that Satan had tempted her to believe that she was in a "Damned condition" despite her frequent attendance at revival meetings. Of the many astonishing revival events that he witnessed in York during the fall of 1741, the anonymous diarist was especially struck by the sight of well-known church members who were "Exemplary in there Lives for Seriousness" condemning themselves as unconverted hypocrites.[106]

Daniel Rogers and other riding ministers regularly targeted church mem-

105. Thacher, "Revival of Religion at Middleborough Continued," *CH,* no. 64 (May 19, 1744), 91–92; Savage, "Extract from a Letter from Piscataqua," n.d. [Dec. 3, 1741], SSP I; Webster, transcr., "Letters to Joseph Bellamy," 12; Thomas Prince, "Accounts of the Revival of Religion in Boston, Continued," *CH,* no. 101 (Feb. 2, 1745), 391 (quotes); Tuttle, comp., "Glasgow-Weekly-History," MHS, *Procs.,* LIII (1919–1920), 196–197. Unfortunately, the records for Jabez Fitch's church in the north parish of Portsmouth are missing and the records for Wheelock's congregation are incomplete. I have estimated the Portsmouth figure by doubling the total number of admissions reported in William Shurtleff's south parish church, which was the site of the powerful revival events of December 1741. See Alfred Gooding, comp., "Records of the South Church of Portsmouth, N.H.," *NEHGR,* LXXXI (1927), 419–453. For the Lebanon Crank statistics, see *Catalogue of the Members of the Congregational Church, Columbia, Conn., 1720–1882* . . . (Willimantic, Conn., 1882), 11; and Columbia, Conn., First Congregational Church Files, 1737–1896, microfilm no. 461, CSL. For a similar argument, see Walsh, "Great Awakening in the First Congregational Church of Woodbury," *WMQ,* XXVIII (1971), 546–547n. For a different interpretation of the Boston data, see J. Richard Olivas, "Partial Revival: The Limits of the Great Awakening in Boston, Massachusetts, 1740–1742," in Carla Gardina Pestana and Sharon V. Salinger, eds., *Inequality in Early America,* Reencounters with Colonialism: New Perspectives on the Americas (Hanover, N.H., 1999), 75–77, 84n.

106. John Curtis to Eleazar Wheelock, Oct. 15, 1741, no. 741565, *EWP;* Goodhue, diary, [12]; Wills, transcr., "Newbury, Mass., Records of the Third Church of Christ," 89; Winiarski, "'Jornal of a Fue Days at York,'" *Maine History,* XLII (2004), 63, 69–70, 72.

bership professors in their audiences. One evening after delivering a rousing lecture in Abington, Massachusetts, Rogers remained at the meetinghouse and spoke to several affected parishioners. Many "Church Members were Shock't" by his sermon and now "thot their State bad," he recalled. Traveling through central Massachusetts with Samuel Buell during the spring of 1742, Samuel Hopkins observed a sermon that worked in a powerful manner on "formal professors" who were "shaken of[f] from their Sandy Foundations." Clergyman David Hall prayed with a neighbor whom the Sutton minister had previously esteemed for his piety and yet languished under great distress for his soul. The unnamed man condemned himself as a "self seeker" and complained that he had "never attain'd a real work of Conversion." Hall's colleague and close friend, Ebenezer Parkman of Westborough, was equally surprised when Bathsheba Pratt appeared unexpectedly at his parsonage for a pastoral conference. Like many of her contemporaries, Pratt was in great distress over the "hardness of her heart," even though "she had been a member in full communion above twenty years."[107]

The voluminous revival correspondence of Eleazar Wheelock includes a number of letters from distressed professors such as Hannah Huntington. A communicant in the Norwich, Connecticut, church since 1736, Huntington had traveled all the way to Boston to hear Whitefield preach. Four months later, she wrote to Wheelock worrying whether she was capable of walking "Worthy of the Vocation wherewith I am Called" and condemning herself as a "poor undone Creature." In a similar letter written a few months later, the future Windham, Connecticut, deacon Jonathan Martin wrote to thank Wheelock for his "painfull labors" during a visit to his parish. Although Martin had joined the Windham church more than a decade earlier, he now worried about the state of his soul and begged Wheelock to pray on his behalf "that I might be truly convartid and that I might not be decived in a mater of so grate concarne." Former tutors at Harvard College praised Enoch Ward as a "pious, worthy young man." The unassuming Plymouth schoolmaster had entertained great hopes of his eventual conversion at the time he affiliated with the Cambridge church in 1735, but reading Whitefield's sermons and the works of seventeenth-century divines subsequently convinced him that the "work was not throghly [thoroughly] wrought." Initially, Ward resolved to live a disciplined religious life through the outward practices of piety. By the spring of 1740, however, he was struggling to disentangle these "mechanical"

---

107. DDR, Oct. 26, 1741; Hopkins, journal, 31–32, box 322, SGC II; Hall, diaries, Mar. 26, 1742; Tracy, *Great Awakening*, 207.

devotions from authentic inward religious sensations. "All is gone," Ward complained in a letter to Wheelock, "Gods Spirit has forsaken me. I have griev'd him, and I fear It will never visit me again, My heart is hard. I cant pray. My mind is blind, and my Conscience is stupefied." Languishing in a poor state of health, Ward begged Wheelock to pray for his salvation. "I fear I am quickly going into Eternity," he concluded, "and I fear unprepared."[108]

Israel Markham reached an equally grim conclusion at the end of a long journal entry written during the early 1740s. He described his decision to join the Windham church ten years before as a measured choice based on "hed nollige [knowledge]" and his powers of "Rezon." Markham had corresponded with his future wife during their courtship about their obligations to serve God in a steady "Round of dutys," but Ann Spencer, like so many church membership candidates of her generation, remained fearful that she would "Eate and drank hur own dam[n]ation." Israel rejected the practice of owning the covenant and adhered instead to the more radical ideas of Northampton clergyman Solomon Stoddard, who had argued a half century earlier that the Lord's Supper was a "converting ordinense." One year after their marriage in 1733, the young couple conferred with Windham minister and future Yale College president Thomas Clap about their dilemma. "We told him we came not In as Converts," Markham later recalled, "for we knew not that we ware." After inquiring after their "outword life and conversations," Clap propounded the couple to full communion. Israel was admitted on July 18, 1734, one day before the birth of his first child. "I did as those I thought good men," he later noted. Ann followed him into the Windham church two months later.[109]

For the next several years, the Markhams lived contentedly in Windham, prospering in their temporal affairs. Israel "aspierd after knowledg." He settled into a daily course of Bible reading, studied learned books including John

108. Hannah Huntington to Eleazar Wheelock, Feb. 4, 1741, no. 741154, *EWP*, Jonathan Martin to Eleazar Wheelock, Apr. 27, 1741, no. 741277; *SHG*, X, 90; Enoch Ward to Eleazar Wheelock, May 28, 1740, no. 740328, *EWP*. For church membership data on these three individuals, see Stephen Paschall Sharples, ed., *Records of the Church of Christ at Cambridge in New England, 1632–1830* ... (Boston, 1906), 99; Norwich, Conn., First Congregational Church Records, 1699–1917, II, 209, microfilm no. 85, CSL; and *Records of the Congregational Church in Windham, Conn. (Except Church Votes), 1700–1851* (Hartford, Conn., 1943), 8.

109. [Israel Markham], confession, 1743–1745, [1–2], box 24, Benjamin Trumbull Papers, 1629–1867, MS 505, YUA; *Records of the Congregational Church in Windham*, 9. For genealogical information on Markham, see Carole Magnuson, comp., *Barbour Collection of Connecticut Town Vital Records*, LIV, *Windham, 1692–1850* (Baltimore, 2002), 240; and Francis Olcott Allen, *The History of Enfield, Connecticut*, 3 vols. (Lancaster, Pa., 1900), I, 385–387, 390, 392, 397–398, II, 1625–1626.

Locke's *Essay concerning Humane Understanding,* and took pleasure in disputing with neighbors on theological issues. He and Ann regularly attended weekly Sabbath exercises, prayed with their family, and baptized their children within days of their births. Israel assumed that they were "strong in the faith and all was well." He confidently believed that a "holly outword life"—reflected in "good works"—was the "best Evedense of a Inword saving faith."[110]

Sometime around 1737, Markham moved with his family to a farm in Enfield. Although he was soon elected constable and served the town in a variety of civic capacities, Israel was stymied in many of his "Desins of honer" and crossed in his "Temperriel afairs." Relations with even a few of his best friends soured; an infant daughter died in 1740. Then, in July 1741, Markham sat in terror with the Enfield congregation as Jonathan Edwards leveled the arsenal of *Sinners in the Hands of an Angry God* straight at unconverted men like him, who had foolishly placed "confidence in their own strength." Suddenly, it seemed as if his entire life had been wasted on mere external religious performances. In the fragmentary religious autobiography composed during the early 1740s, Markham set reason against his new religious experiences. "As I Grew In my hed I fell In My hart," he noted ruefully. Markham had for years been pursuing only the empty "forme of Relegion." He had conducted family prayers in a "cold formel Maner"; he and his wife had affiliated without ever experiencing the new birth. Even his former minister, Thomas Clap, now seemed, not a true spiritual guide, but a "preast." Temporal and religious affairs, Markham explained, had conspired to "pull down my pride" and expose the hypocrisy of his once confident faith.[111]

Responding to the instructions in Thomas Prince's circular letter, several ministers infused their published revival narratives in the *Christian History* with *"Remarkable Instances* of the Power and Grace of GOD" on men and women like Israel Markham—earnest Christians "who have been before in Repute for *Morality* and *Religion."* One account from Wrentham included a detailed description of an "honest, moral Liver" who cried out in distress after discovering that he had never experienced a "new and saving *Change"* on his heart. John Cotton of Halifax counted "several *moral* Persons and *Professors"* among his congregants who had been "dissetled from their Foundation." Portsmouth minister William Shurtleff, too, provided an extended description of a

110. [Markham], confession, [3, 5], Benjamin Trumbull Papers; *Records of the Congregational Church in Windham,* 21–22.

111. [Markham], confession, [1–3, 7], Benjamin Trumbull Papers; Edwards, *Sinners in the Hands of an Angry God,* in *WJE,* XXII, *Sermons and Discourses, 1739–1742,* ed. Stout and Hatch, 408.

"*steddy* Observer of the *Duties* of *divine Worship*, in his *Closet*, in his *Family*, and in *Publick*" who nonetheless had the "*corrupt Fountain* of *his own Heart* sufficiently laid open to his View" during the heady days of the revivals on the northern frontier. A number of church members in the north parish of Bridgewater (now Brockton) discovered the "*sandy Foundation of their own Righteousness*," wrote John Porter, "notwithstanding their blazing Professions." Published revival narratives from towns across New England struck similar notes. "The revival at first appeared chiefly among professors, and those that had entertained the hope that they were in a state of grace," Jonathan Edwards summarized in his account of revival events in Northampton. "Oh how were *Sinners* in *Zion* afraid," echoed Josiah Crocker of Taunton. Too many of his parishioners claimed to esteem the "*self-denying Doctrines*" contained in their catechisms, even as they "sunk into the very Dregs of *Formality*."[112]

By 1742, thousands of New Englanders—long-standing professors and new converts alike—had embraced the theological innovations of the Whitefieldarians and were prepared to cast off the inherited traditions of the godly walk. They demonstrated their commitment to Whitefield's experimental piety in a myriad of small ways. Zealous lay folk eagerly adorned their homes with mezzotint prints of Whitefield, and one wealthy Massachusetts family even commissioned a portrait of the touring evangelist. In graveyards across New England, hopeful images of smiling faces, hearts, and cherubs appeared alongside, within, or, occasionally, supplanted the classic winged skull motif that had dominated late-seventeenth-century funerary iconography. Meetinghouses were repainted in vibrant hues of sky blue; congregations adopted the moving hymnody of English clergyman Isaac Watts. Chastened by Whitefield's sandy foundations critique, Boston merchant Samuel Phillips Savage compiled a list of the "Marks of the Regenerate and the Unregenerate." Two of his criteria targeted godly walkers who "trust in their Own Righteousness" or "have long Enjoyed the Means of Grace but are nothing betterd there yet Continue still unchangd and reformd." And, in Westborough, church membership candidate Eli Forbush took the seemingly audacious step of writing his rela-

112. Prince, *It Being Earnestly Desired;* "The Account of the Late Revival of Religion at Wrentham Finished," *CH,* no. 32 (Oct. 8, 1743), 251, John Cotton, ". . . A General History of the Revival of Religion . . . at Halifax," *CH,* no. 33 (Oct. 15, 1743), 263, Shurtleff, "Revival of Religion at Portsmouth," *CH,* no. 49 (Feb. 4, 1744), 389, John Porter, "The Rev. Mr. Porter's Account of the Revival of Religion at Bridgewater Finished," *CH,* no. 51 (Feb. 18, 1744), 406; Jonathan Edwards to Thomas Prince, Dec. 12, 1743, in *WJE,* XVI, *Letters and Personal Writings,* ed. Claghorn, 116; Crocker, "Account of the Late Revival of Religion at Taunton," *CH,* no. 93 (Dec. 8, 1744), 324–325.

tion of faith in the form of a personal letter—the first known example in more than a century of practice.[113]

Revival rhetoric percolated down in a letter that Isaac Garfield sent from one of the most remote settlements in New England to his future wife during the fall of 1742. Unlike typical courtship missives, which focused on the practical considerations of marriage or were laced with romantic allusions to classical mythology, Garfield wrote with considerable urgency to inquire after the state of Mary Brewer's soul. "Seek now in a finding time," urged the young militia leader and early settler of Tyringham (now Monterey), Massachusetts, for the "Spirit of god Seems to be Striving with yong people." Then, in an anguished torrent of words infused with numerous biblical allusions, he upbraided both himself and his beloved for their sinful failings. "Wee have been asleep but our damnation Slumbreth not," Garfield lamented. "We have bin feeding on husks and are rady to perrish. O fearfull Estate for us to live only to heep up fuel for our own Everlasting burning even treasureing of wrath for the last day." He exhorted Brewer to "take large Steps daly" to ensure that she came to a "well grounded hope" in her salvation. The two young converts were married a few months later.[114]

Even the content of prayer bills momentarily shifted, as concerned family members and neighbors began submitting small slips of paper imploring God to speedily deliver convicted sinners from their spiritual darkness into the light of the new birth. Whitefield received a "ticket" requesting prayers on behalf of a young ministerial candidate who was "under apprehensions that he was not converted." Venturing over to the Brattle Street meetinghouse for a midweek lecture a few months later, Boston physician John Loring encountered the arresting sight of more than sixty notes of paper pinned to the doors, each requesting prayers for convicted sinners who had yet to experience the

113. Peter Benes, *The Masks of Orthodoxy: Folk Gravestone Carving in Plymouth County, Massachusetts, 1689–1805* (Amherst, Mass., 1977), 155–169; Benes, "'Distinguishing Signs of Truly Gracious and Holy Affections': Revival Motifs in Eighteenth-Century New England Gravestone Carvings," in Daniel W. Ingersoll and Gordon Bronitsky, eds., *Mirror and Metaphor: Material and Social Constructions of Reality* (Lanham, Md., 1987), 137–159; Benes, "Sky Colors and Scattered Clouds: The Decorative and Architectural Painting of New England Meeting Houses, 1738–1834," in Benes, ed., *New England Meeting House and Church: 1630–1850,* Dublin Seminar for New England Folklife, Annual Proceedings 1979 (Boston, 1980), 51–69; Benes, "Psalmody in Coastal Massachusetts and in the Connecticut River Valley," in Benes, ed., *The Bay and the River: 1600–1900,* Dublin Seminar for New England Folklife, Annual Proceedings 1981 (Boston, 1982), 117–131; Samuel P. Savage, "Marks of the Regenerate and the Unregenerate," n.d. [circa 1740s], SSP I; Appendix B, Westborough, Mass., First Church, 33.

114. Isaac Garfield to Mary Brewer, [Sept.] 27, 1742, I, Blandina Diedrich Collection, WCL.

ecstatic release of the new birth. Daniel Rogers received several prayer bills in which new converts in Ipswich gave "Thanks to God for the operation of his spirit with the Word." By the time that Thomas Prince wrote his "Account of the Late Revival of Religion in Boston" for the *Christian History,* reports of notes "put up in publick" for the unconverted had suddenly emerged as visible markers of a "wonderfully blest" revival season.[115]

TO WRITE SO FREELY OF YOUR OWN EXPERIENCES

"I was born Feb 15th 1711 and born again octo 1741." The terse opening sentence of Nathan Cole's "Spiritual Travels" not only signaled a sharp break with his religious past but it also provided an impetus to write. The Kensington artisan's dramatic account of George Whitefield's visit to Middletown, his subsequent conversion, and his early visionary religious experiences together form the prologue to a sophisticated literary work that Cole intended to publish or circulate in manuscript among his contemporaries. The original text survives in the form of a heavily revised draft prepared by a skilled copyist. Cole reviewed and corrected the manuscript, supplying missing words and additional material. The famous first line and his entire description of Whitefield's preaching were among these later insertions. Nathan Cole and other "experienced" Christians had a story to tell.[116]

For more than a century, puritan ministers had encouraged their parishioners to describe their religious experiences in writing, yet only a handful of seventeenth-century autobiographies, diaries, journals, religious poems, advice literature, and Indian captivity narratives have survived. Although provincial New Englanders wrote voluminously and often introspectively, they seldom told the kind of dramatic story that Cole recounted in the opening pages of his religious autobiography. Instead, godly walkers listed and catalogued; they resolved and covenanted. They infused their correspondence with pious counsel and marked religious time in annotated almanacs. Their prayer bills were relentlessly formulaic, as were most church admission testimonies composed between 1700 and 1740. The few lay men and women who kept

---

115. *GWJ,* 470; John Loring to Israel Loring, Dec. 18, 1740, Jan. 22, 1741, Nathan Stone Papers; *DDR,* July 8, 1741; Prince, "Accounts of the Revival of Religion in Boston, Continued," *CH,* no. 101 (Feb. 2, 1745), 391. For additional examples, see Samuel Phillips Savage to Gilbert Tennent, Jan. 30, 1742, SSP II; James R. Tanis, "A Child of the Great Awakening," *American Presbyterians,* LXX (1992), 128; and Douglas L. Winiarski, "The Newbury Prayer Bill Hoax: Devotion and Deception in New England's Era of Great Awakenings," *Massachusetts Historical Review,* XIV (2012), 72–73.

116. NCS, 92, 102.

devotional journals wrote sporadically, whenever sacramental occasions, life-course transitions, or remarkable instances of divine providence demanded. Their devotional writings shared much in common with the concurrent rise of financial ledgers. Most devout men and women early in the eighteenth century recognized that a full accounting of their spiritual estates awaited the "great day of reckoning."[117]

Whitefield's first New England preaching tour decisively changed the terms of popular religious discourse. Conjuring older debates among puritan divines regarding spiritist and preparationist models of conversion, the Anglican evangelist maintained that the elect received grace through a direct infusion of the Holy Spirit. "Regeneration is instantaneous," he argued during a heated debate with Anglican colleagues in Boston. Most prominent Whitefieldarians agreed that true Christians could pinpoint the precise moment of their conversions with a degree of certitude that perennially eluded godly walkers. Eleazar Wheelock aroused the ire of one colleague when he declared that "Christians generally knew the time of their conversion." Concord, Massachusetts, firebrand Daniel Bliss went a step further in his assertion that "every Person That is Converted must know it." How could a person be "brought out of Midnight Darkness into Noon Day-Light," wondered Philemon Robbins of Branford, Connecticut, "and not know there is a Change?" "We that are Calvinists," Andrew Croswell summarized, believe that "God doth in a Moment in the *twinkling of an Eye* reveal his Son to Sinners." As Kittery physician Edmund Coffin discovered during the weeks following the revival in York, the conversion experiences of young converts occasionally extended over a long period, but, more commonly, he asserted, the "Lord is pleased to make quick work of it," convincing and converting sinners in mere minutes or hours.[118]

For seventeenth-century puritans, conversion typically denoted an extended process that unfolded in stages during the saints' earthly pilgrimage. But, for eighteenth-century Whitefieldarians, the new birth was a momentous event that could be dated with accuracy and narrated with confidence. "I have

117. Benjamin Wadsworth, *The Great and Last Day of Judgment* ... (Boston, 1709), 130. On puritan devotional writing practices, see Part 1 and Charles E. Hambrick-Stowe, *The Practice of Piety: Puritan Devotional Disciplines in Seventeenth-Century New England* (Chapel Hill, N.C., 1982), 186–193.

118. *GWJ*, 458; EWD, 239; "An Ecclesiastical Council, 1743," *Historical Manuscripts in the Public Library in the City of Boston*, no. 2 (Boston, 1902), 3; Philemon Robbins, *A Plain Narrative of the Proceedings of the Reverend Association and Consocation of New-Haven County, against the Reverend Mr. Robbins of Branford* ... (Boston, 1747), 20; A[ndrew] Croswell, *Mr. Croswell's Reply to a Book Lately Publish'd* ... (Boston, 1742), 9; Coffin, *Sketch of the History of Newbury*, 211.

been *Illuminated*," a once-troubled Westborough professor boldly proclaimed in a long letter to Ebenezer Parkman, after examining her soul and inquiring "whether or no I were really regenerated." "I was sure that God had done some great thing for my soul," Cole concurred in his "Spiritual Travels" two decades later. Revival converts made a decisive break with their godly walking pasts as they learned to speak and write about their experience of the new birth.[119]

■ During the peak months of the New England revivals, a surprising number of prominent Whitefieldarians paused to take stock of whether they had been born again. Some reassessed their old devotional writings, while others penned new accounts of their conversion experiences. Harvard College student Joseph Emerson, noted on the flyleaf of his 1739 diary that it had been "Written before Convertion." Samuel Hopkins fronted his 1741 travel journal with an extended meditation on whether he had "pased the great Change of the new-Birth," and he reconsidered the issue in several other entries composed during the next three years. His traveling companion, the ubiquitous riding minister Samuel Buell, regularly recited a "Narrative of his Conversion" in the towns that he visited during his extensive preaching circuits. Several other graduates of Yale College, including Aaron Burr, David Brainerd, and, most notably, Jonathan Edwards composed autobiographical narratives that they shared with interested colleagues. Written during the fall of 1741 in response to an inquiry from Burr, Edwards's celebrated *"Account of his* CON-VERSION, EXPERIENCES, *and* RELIGIOUS EXERCISES" revised his episodic devotional diary and youthful religious resolutions manuscripts into a coherent narrative that recounted how he "met with that change, by which I was brought to those new dispositions, and that new sense of things, that I have since had." "I desire to bless God that he inclined you to write and especialy to write So freely of your own Experiences," Burr praised Edwards after perusing the Northampton minister's account of his "first conversion," before concluding "I think it has been much blessed to my Spiritual Good."[120]

119. Parkman, commonplace book, 92, Ebenezer Parkman Papers; Tracy, *Great Awakening*, 206–207; NCS, 97. On the transition from "puritan" to "evangelical" forms of devotional writing, see Catherine A. Brekus, "Writing as a Protestant Practice: Devotional Diaries in Early New England," in Laurie F. Maffly-Kipp, Leigh E. Schmidt, and Mark Valeri, eds., *Practicing Protestants: Histories of Christian Life in America, 1630–1965,* Lived Religions (Baltimore, 2006), 19–34.

120. Joseph Emerson, diary, 1739–1740, private collection (I thank Phyllis Cole for sharing her research notes on this manuscript); Hopkins, journal, 1 (quote), 36, 58, box 322, SGC II; NGD, 280; Samuel Hopkins, *The Life and Character of the Late Reverend Mr. Jonathan Edwards, President of the College at New-Jersey* (Boston, 1765), 23; Edwards, "Personal Narrative," in *WJE*, XVI, *Letters and Personal Writings*, ed. Claghorn, 790, 803; Aaron Burr to

Widely distributed and read throughout the British colonies, *A Short Account of God's Dealings with the Reverend Mr. George Whitefield* provided a literary model for the new religious autobiographies and conversion narratives produced by Edwards and his contemporaries. In it, the touring evangelist detailed his own crooked path to conversion while a student at the University of Oxford. Whitefield described himself as a diligent Anglican youth who pursued a regular round of devotional routines until Charles Wesley loaned him a copy of Henry Scougal's *Life of God in the Soul of Man*. He was especially struck by a passage in which the venerable Scottish divine warned "that some falsely placed religion in going to church, doing hurt to no one, being constant in the duties of the closet, and now and then reaching out their hands to give alms to their poor neighbors." Whitefield's religious life tilted dramatically from intensified periods of rigorous practice and scriptural study to a "state of quietism" in which he dressed in ragged clothes and nearly abandoned his devotional routines altogether. Satan relentlessly hounded him, stopping Whitefield's mouth in prayer and stilling his hand as he attempted to write about his religious melancholia. Finally, after seven weeks of "unspeakable pressure both of body and mind," Whitefield "was delivered from the burden that had so heavily oppressed me." This was the moment of his conversion.[121]

Evidence that New England's riding ministers consciously emulated Whitefield's autobiography and published journals is readily apparent in the diaries of Daniel Rogers. Before 1740, the former Harvard College tutor elected to record the weather and daily events on leaves of paper that he inserted be-

---

Jonathan Edwards, March 1741 [1742?], *WJEO*, XXXII, *Correspondence by, to, and About Edwards and His Family*, no. B6. For Brainerd, see John A. Grigg, *The Lives of David Brainerd: The Making of an Evangelical Icon*, Religion in America (New York, 2009), 10, 30. The literature on Edwards's "Personal Narrative" is extensive, but, see, especially, Kenneth P. Minkema, "Personal Writings," in Stephen J. Stein, ed., *The Cambridge Companion to Jonathan Edwards*, Cambridge Companions to Religion (New York, 2007), 48–52. Internal evidence from Burr's letter suggests that Edwards composed his "Personal Narrative" one year later than most scholars have assumed. Although the letter bears the date March 1741, it also mentions heavenly visions of the Book of Life, a controversial revival phenomenon that did not enter into public debates until the winter of 1742. For this reason, it appears more likely that Burr wrote his letter sometime in March 1741 and simply omitted the conventional "1741/42" from the dateline. If so, Edwards would have sent him his draft of his "Personal Narrative" on December 14, 1741, less than a month after Whitefield visited Northampton. The difference in chronology is important, for it suggests that Edwards participated in a broader trend in Whitefieldian revival discourse, rather than established that trend.

121. *GWJ*, 47, 53, 58. On the publication history of Whitefield's autobiography, see Hugh Amory, "The New England Book Trade, 1713–1790," in Amory and David D. Hall, ed., *The Colonial Book in the Atlantic World*, A History of the Book in America, I (Cambridge, 2000), 329.

tween the pages of an annual published almanac. After reading Whitefield's autobiography, traveling with him into the Middle Colonies, and embarking on his own career as an itinerant preacher, however, Rogers started compiling a new diary that closely mirrored that of the Anglican itinerant. As with Whitefield's published journals, each entry in Rogers's diary began with a heading in which he indicated the town that he was visiting. His writing grew more detailed and introspective, as he filled his diary with what Whitefield called "curious OBSERVATIONS" and "Edifying REFLECTIONS" on the state of religion in New England and detailed accounts of "what GOD has done for my Soul." During the winter of 1742, moreover, Rogers paused to consider "when I was Converted." He reviewed several incidents from his life but finally decided that he had been "Savingly wrot upon when I was a Child about Seven or Eight years old."[122]

No minister wrote about his conversion struggles during the revival years with greater pathos than Joseph Fish. His unusually candid journal deserves close attention as perhaps the most powerful example of the lengths the Whitefieldarians would go to repudiate their past religious lives and to confirm their experiences of the new birth. Fish had joined the church in Cambridge shortly after the Great Earthquake of 1727. Graduating from Harvard College a year later, he eventually secured a pastorate at the newly gathered church in the north parish of Stonington (now North Stonington), Connecticut. Fish's early sermon manuscripts suggest that he preached on conventional themes related to a "holy Conversation and Godliness." Legal and economic metaphors peppered his preaching during the 1730s. "Every vicious Action," he asserted on one occasion, would be "Tryd at the Bar of God," or what he called the "Great assize." Faithful Christians needed to live in this world acknowledging that they would one day have a "larger Account to settle with your Judge!" Fish admitted fifty-eight men and women to full communion during the first seven years of his ministry, and sixty more owned the covenant. Most of the families in his parish had affiliated with his church by 1740. They presented their children for baptism in an orderly manner and showered Fish with a steady stream of gifts, including food, tobacco, clothing, farm labor, access to draft animals, and hard currency.[123]

122. George Whitefield, *Journal of a Voyage from London to Gibraltar*, 6th ed. (Philadelphia, 1740), title page, 3; DDR, Jan. 4, 1742. For Rogers's interleaved almanacs, see Daniel Rogers, diaries, 1730–1785, Mss 652, NEHGS.

123. Sharples, ed., *Records of the Church of Christ at Cambridge*, 95; Joseph Fish, sermons, 1730–1736, 13, 27–29, CSL; "Benefactions for the Year 1739," in Fish, diary, 1739–1770, box 36, folder 68, Silliman Family Papers, 1717–1977, MS 450, YUA. On Fish's turbulent life and ministry, see *SHG*, VIII, 417–426; William S. Simmons and Cheryl L. Simmons, eds., *Old*

As riding ministers crisscrossed New London County preaching in the new Whitefieldian mode during the spring and summer of 1741, Fish turned inward and started recording his meditations. The earliest entries in his journal charted a steady decline into melancholia. Struggling to perform his private devotions, Fish labored under a "wretched Aversion to Duty, To examination To Prayer and Everything that is spiritually Good." The beleaguered clergyman felt as if an unseen force was pressing him down, clogging his religious sensibilities. Even worse were the moments in which he could feel nothing at all. "This flat Calm!" Fish complained. "This Cursed Case and Insensibility of my Soul!" He had become a *"poor, sleepy, Dead, Lifeless* Creature, Fit for nothing but to be Turned Into Hell, and Quickned by its Flames."[124]

The nadir came in November 1741. Fish managed to break through the "Hindrances" that stood in the way of his desire to meditate, "But never Did a more stupid soul Engage in such a Holy solemn Exercise." A torrent of self-loathing prose poured from his pen. Reading Thomas Shepard's classic work on conversion, *Sincere Convert,* on the subject of *"Carnal security,"* Fish found his case exactly described. He berated himself as the "Most *stupid, Insensible, Filthy* monster, That Crawls upon the earth." "I am in a Damnable state, and yet as Easy and secure as if There was no God to Fear, no Heaven to Loose nor Hell to Tremble at." If left to himself, Fish concluded, his soul would be destroyed as easily as if a thousand devils had been unleashed on him. "I Hate myself even like the Devil," he complained. For the next several weeks, Fish remained unable to pray, meditate, or write in his journal. He could do nothing, he later admitted, "but waste Away My Precious Time."[125]

After struggling for months to determine whether he had experienced the new birth, only to discover deadness in his heart, Fish did something unprecedented in the history of New England Congregationalism. On December 20, 1741, he laid aside his work in the ministry, fearing that by continuing to preach in an unconverted state he would be "Guilty of the Blood of precious souls." He notified his parishioners and colleagues in the New London ministerial association about his decision to "Retire from my office." For five weeks, Fish languished in "Egyptian Bondage and Slavery," unable to "Do anything to affect myself, Even to be Concerned about My soul that is in the Utmost Danger." "Satan has Me fast in his Chains," Fish lamented in a January 1742 medita-

---

Light on Separate Ways: The Narragansett Diary of Joseph Fish, 1765–1776 (Hanover, N.H., 1982), xix–xxxvii; and Joy Day Buel and Richard Buel, Jr., *The Way of Duty: A Woman and Her Family in Revolutionary America* (New York, 1984), 3–18.

124. Fish, diary, 6–8.
125. Ibid., 8–10.

tion. The traditional practices of piety—reading, praying, meditating, fasting, listening to sermons, conversing with neighbors and colleagues—provided no solace. Fish also experienced odd, insatiable hunger pangs. That he could feel "no higher Pleasure Than that of *Eating*" convinced him that he was *"more Brutish than Any man."* Fish was not tempted to commit heinous sins such as murder or blasphemy. Instead, Satan was continually distracting him from reading godly books, filling his mind with trifling and worldly thoughts, and, above all, seducing him with fantasies of "Perfect Ease and Quietude." Heaven appeared as if it was separated from him by an immense glass ceiling.[126]

Then, early in February 1742, Fish's tortured journey took yet another remarkable turn. As he reflected on the rapid sequence of events, Fish realized that a change had begun in him a few weeks earlier when he ceased upbraiding himself for sin and began prostrating himself "Continually at the Throne of Grace, begging for Relief." On his birthday, January 28, Fish suddenly found "Freedom of Speech and Abatement of Former Heaviness." He was almost persuaded to believe he had been saved, although he immediately lapsed back into a deep melancholia. Fish renewed his cries to God, entreating him to "force his passage into my Heart." This time, he suddenly discovered an "Uncommon Willingness to give myself wholly up to the Lord Jesus." It took several days before Fish was persuaded that Christ had "Indeed Releasd my soul from spiritual Death," but he eventually affirmed with confidence that this was the precise moment of his conversion. Fish soon found himself in a "Quite Different Frame" and "Things Appeard much brighter and Clearer." He hoped that he was *"building* for *Eternity"* on the *"Rock* of *Ages* and not upon the *sand."*[127]

Brimming with new confidence following his conversion, Fish threw himself back into his pastoral labors. The "Lord I Trust has Opend my mouth and brought me Again to his People," he confided in his journal. "Many have been awakened, And I Trust The Lord has given me some seals of My Ministry." Preaching lectures, recording church admission testimonies, examining candidates for communion, and counseling distressed parishioners occupied so much of his time during the spring of 1742 that he was forced to lay aside his occasional private days of fasting and thanksgiving. Parishioners responded to their minister's renewed zeal by joining the church in historic numbers. In June alone, more than one hundred new converts swelled the ranks of Fish's church, a figure that nearly doubled the total number of admissions during the

126. Ibid., 10–12.
127. Ibid., 13–15, 17.

previous decade. The large cohort included several native Americans as well as numerous adolescents and young children. Fish rejoined his colleagues in the New London ministerial association and itinerated in towns across southeastern New England with "Freedom, some Power and Success."[128]

Laypeople such as the Cambridge shopkeeper Joseph Bean also began to emulate Whitefield by writing their personal religious histories. Shortly after attending one of Gilbert Tennent's sermons in February 1741, he penned the "History of My Past Life to this Preasant Time" on the opening pages of a new devotional diary. Like Whitefield's published autobiography, Bean's account emphasized the limitations of his considerable religious training. Raised by godly parents and instructed in the principles of Christianity, the pious taverner's son had memorized his catechism and prayed regularly; he studied the Bible and read godly books each night. He practiced meditating during the day as he labored in his shop. As was the case with many godly walkers, Bean put off joining the church "untill I had arrived to a Prity good Estate" in his temporal affairs. Despite his exacting practices and observances, however, Bean had never experienced the new birth, as he learned to his great dismay after he followed Whitefield during the fall of 1740. Tennent's preaching, too, had stirred him from "Carnal Security." By the time he reached his twenty-second birthday on February 24, 1741, Bean had come to view his "prity Religious life" as self-serving vanity and lukewarm indifference. He knew that he lacked what Whitefield called the "one thing Nedeful": a "thorow and Sound and Saving Conversion unto God."[129]

During the next three years, Bean labored ceaselessly to examine the state of his soul for evidence of his conversion. He wrote in his diary almost every day. Most entries remained unconnected to the Sabbath exercises or episodic providential events that triggered the devotional reflections of an earlier generation of godly walkers. Instead, Bean relentlessly scrutinized the inward inclinations of his heart, or what he and many others of his generation called "my affections." He continued to read, meditate, pray, and renew his personal covenant, but he recognized that even the "Vary best dutys that I Perform are Corrupted and Defiled." He worried constantly that he would one day be engulfed "Eternally in the flams of hell." Most days, he reported "Clouds of Darkness hanging all round me," even after he affiliated with the Cambridge church during the summer of 1741. Unlike many of his reborn contemporaries, Bean

128. Ibid., 18, 21, 25; North Stonington Congregational Church Records, 9; New London Association, Records, 1709–1788, 97–98, Connecticut Conference Archives, United Church of Christ (currently on deposit at CL; available online at NEHH).

129. Bean, diary, 1, 4, 7–9, 12.

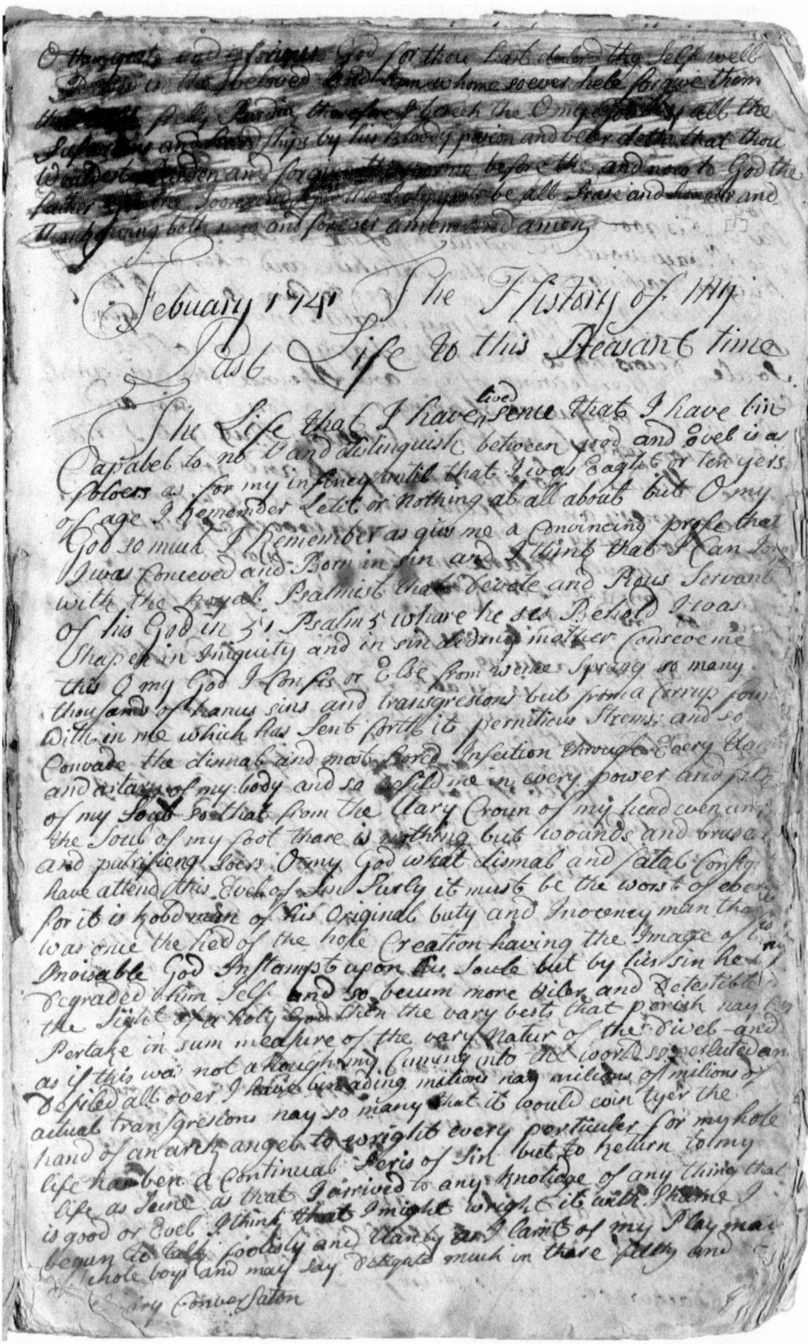

FIGURE 13 Joseph Bean, "The History of My Past Life to This Preasant Time." February 1741. Diary of Joseph Bean, 1741–1744, Manuscripts Collection, Special Collections Department, Bryn Mawr College Library, Bryn Mawr, Pennsylvania

never settled on a date for his conversion. For the rest of his life, long after he ceased writing in his diary, graduated from Harvard College, and received a call to serve the church in Wrentham, Massachusetts, Bean remained mired in what later observers called a "gloomy and melancholy state of mind," and he was "frequently tried with darkness, despondency, and the fiery darts of the wicked one."[130]

Bean's diary marks a turning point in the history of New England Congregationalism. It ranks among the earliest examples of a lay devotional diary whose author attempted to "date my yers from the new birth and from Christ being formed within me." Soon, a flood of new converts began daily charting the ups and downs of their emotional frames. Like Jonathan Edwards and Aaron Burr, Charlestown laymen Richard Kettell and Richard Devens exchanged letters during the fall of 1741 describing their recent religious experiences and attempting to establish the moment of their conversions. Sarah Prince, daughter of the minister of Boston's Old South Church, became "convinced that it is my duty to comit to writing My Experiences" two years later. Over a period of several months, Prince searched for evidence of her conviction, conversion, and sanctification. "Yes, Yes, Yes," she wrote in a breathless entry early in March 1744, "I think I can say (to God alone be the Glory) I have been experimentally convinced of these things." Hannah Heaton of New Haven's Northeast Society (now North Haven) composed a conversion narrative at the beginning of the sprawling four-hundred-page diary that she would keep for the next half century. So, too, did the impoverished Newport, Rhode Island, schoolmistress Sarah Osborn. Her daily ruminations on the state of her soul eventually expanded to fifty volumes and fifteen thousand pages. Others, including Edwards's wife, Sarah, future Separate Baptist elder Isaac Backus, and the Indian preacher Samson Occom recorded similar, although shorter, narratives. Looking back on his four-decade career as an itinerant revivalist, Andrew Croswell's brother Joseph remained convinced that he had been "made partaker of the glorious work of divine grace" on Friday, March 26, 1742, "at about an hour after two o'clock, P.M."[131]

130. Bean, diary, 15, 17, 23, 71, 177; Sharples, ed., *Records of the Church of Christ at Cambridge*, 145; "A Sketch of the Life of the Rev. Joseph Bean, the Third Pastor of the Church in Wrentham," *The Panoplist, and Missionary Magazine United*, n. s., II (1810), 483.

131. Bean, diary, 12; Richard Kettell to Richard Devens, Sept. 26, 1741, box 3, Richard Frothingham Charlestown Papers, 1634–1890, MHS, Devens to Kettell, Oct. 9, 1741; Sue Lane McCulley and Dorothy Z. Baker, ed., *The Silent and Soft Communion: The Spiritual Narratives of Sarah Pierpont Edwards and Sarah Prince Gill* (Knoxville, Tenn., 2005), 1–16, 17, 24–25; Lacey, ed., *World of Hannah Heaton*, 3–25; Catherine A. Brekus, *Sarah Osborn's World: The Rise of Evangelical Christianity in Early America* (New Haven, Conn., 2013), 4; William G. McLoughlin, ed., *The Diary of Isaac Backus*, 3 vols. (Providence, R.I., 1979),

The narrative structure of church admission relations also changed during the revivals. Throughout the preceding half century, the generic conventions governing these paper instruments had constrained lay men and women to situate their religious experiences within a narrow range of stock phrases, biblical texts, and providential events. Boston minister Thomas Prince, however, distinguished the relations of young converts who swelled the ranks of the Old South Church during the spring and summer of 1741 from those drafted by fearful godly walkers who covenanted in the wake of the earthquake of 1727. "People were *then* generally frighted," he explained in the *Christian History,* "yet very few came to me *then* under deep Convictions of their *unconverted* and *lost* Condition, in Comparison to what came *now.*" Preoccupied with performing their covenantal duties, the earthquake candidates narrated their experiences in the language of the sacramental renaissance, stating only that "they had such a Sense of their Duty to come to the *Lord's Table* that they dare not stay away any longer." Prince believed that a majority of the young converts stirred up by the preaching of Whitefield and Tennent, by contrast, "gave a more exact Account of the *Work* of the SPIRIT OF GOD on their Souls."[132]

Prince's parishioners struck a more confident tone in their relations. They seemed more convinced that something had happened to them. Harvard College student Samuel Fayerweather began his May 24, 1741, relation simultaneously praising God for casting his "lot in a land of Gospel Light" and lamenting his failure to live up to such an "unspeakable Priviledge." Then, his relation struck out in a different direction. Although he had always been "conscientious in keeping up a Form of Religion," Fayerweather acknowledged that he had been convinced by the preaching of "Faithful ministers" that the "Foundation I had been building my hopes of Salvation upon was false." Breaking forth in an unusually assertive tone, the young scholar proclaimed that "God has appeared for me, and delivered me." "O What reason have I to Lie down in the Dust, and admire the free and Soveraign Grace of God, that he should pluck me as a Firebrand out of the Burning," he continued, "and make me a Partaker of his Love, when most part of the world are Destitute of it." Fayerweather pressed on in the middle of his narrative to exhort "all young People to seek Christ in their early Days" and to "keep on Seeking, and dont rest short of Christ." Fayerweather's relation was as much a homily as a plea for admis-

III, 1523–1526; Brooks, ed., *Collected Writings of Samson Occom,* 51–58; *Sketches of the Life, and Extracts from the Journals, and Other Writings of the Late Joseph Croswell* ... (Boston, 1809), 7.

132. Prince, "Accounts of the Revival of Religion in Boston, Continued," *CH,* no. 101 (Feb. 2, 1745), 381, 395.

sion to full communion, for he little doubted that he had passed through the new birth.[133]

A similar tone of certainty pervades the testimony that saddler Samuel Belcher presented to Timothy Edwards, minister of the east parish in Windsor, Connecticut, later that summer. He claimed to have been "Cold and Dull in the things which Concerned my Eternal Salvation" until he heard Whitefield preach with great power on the doctrine of the new birth in October 1740. Initially, Belcher had been greatly stirred up by the touring evangelist's sermon, but he quickly returned to his sinful ways. His fears were renewed the following April after learning of the "Gloryous workings of the Spirit of God" in Eleazar Wheelock's awakened parish in Lebanon. When Wheelock and Benjamin Pomeroy preached a pair of stirring sermons in Windsor on July 6, 1741, Belcher felt "awakened up to Call upon God." Invoking the gravitational metaphors of *Sinners in the Hands of an Angry God*—which he likely heard Jonathan Edwards deliver several miles away in Enfield just days earlier— Belcher worried "what a Dreadfull thing it was to fall into the hands of an angry God," and he felt "such a Load of Guilt upon me that I thought it would Sink me Down to the Ground." Then, in a flash, Belcher's burdens vanished. "I felt as if my heart was Changed," he wrote in his relation, as he experienced a rush of "Joy and Comfort" that was "beyond Expression." Timothy Edwards later reported that more than seventy people in his parish had been converted during the summer of 1741. Belcher stood at the forefront of this impressive cohort of confident new members.[134]

The Fayerweather and Belcher narratives point toward a subtle, but important, emerging trend. Although older Congregational ministers continued to refer to church admission testimonies as relations, Whitefield adopted a different term. Wherever he went, he encouraged his audiences to recount their experience of the new birth. The shift in language percolated down so that many New England lay people and numerous clergymen began referring to "Experiences" read on behalf of prospective members. When Ebenezer Parkman wrote, somewhat uncomfortably, about a parishioner who "gave account of his Experiences and what he thought to be his Conversion," he did not have in mind the standard litany of familial credentials, providential afflictions,

133. Appendix B, Boston, Third (Old South) Church, 4. For the full text of Fayerweather's relation, see Appendix C.

134. Kenneth P. Minkema, ed., "A Great Awakening Conversion: The Relation of Samuel Belcher," *WMQ*, XLIV (1987), 125–126; *GWJ*, 478–479. See also Winiarski, "Jonathan Edwards, Enthusiast?" *Church History*, LXXIV (2005), 738; and Allen, "Memoir of Rev. Eleazar Wheelock," *American Quarterly Register*, X (1837), 12.

healing vows, doctrinal knowledge, or encouraging biblical texts. Instead, as Yale College student John Cleaveland explained, relating experiences meant sharing stories of friends, neighbors, and family members who had passed "out of Darkness into marvilous Lite." New Englanders had been experiencing religion all along; however, Whitefield succeeded in persuading many new converts that the only experience that counted was the new birth.[135]

But what did those experiences encompass? For ministers sympathetic to the revivals, conversion typically involved a protracted period of introspection in which they rejected their intellectual abilities, overcame their resistance to Reformed doctrines, and gradually discovered that they possessed a heart inclined to rely on the excellences of Christ for salvation. By contrast, lay men and women, including Nathan Cole, described their passage through the new birth as a sudden, violent supernatural intrusion involving physical distress, audible voices, and visionary phenomena. In a controversial passage that he struck from later editions of his published autobiography, Whitefield made plain the miraculous nature of the experience that he had placed at the center of his evangelical worldview: "Now did the Spirit of God take possession of my soul."[136]

135. Benjamin Bradstreet, *Godly Sorrow Described, and the Blessing Annexed Consider'd* ... (Boston, 1742), iii; Walett, ed., *Diary of Ebenezer Parkman*, 104; Ross W. Beales, Jr., ed., "The Diary of John Cleaveland, January 15–May 11, 1742," *EIHC*, CVII (1971), 168. On changing terminologies in New England church admission testimonies, see Douglas L. Winiarski, "Religious Experiences in New England," in Amanda Porterfield, ed., *Modern Christianity to 1900*, A People's History of Christianity, VI (Minneapolis, Minn., 2007), 210.
136. *GWJ*, 58.

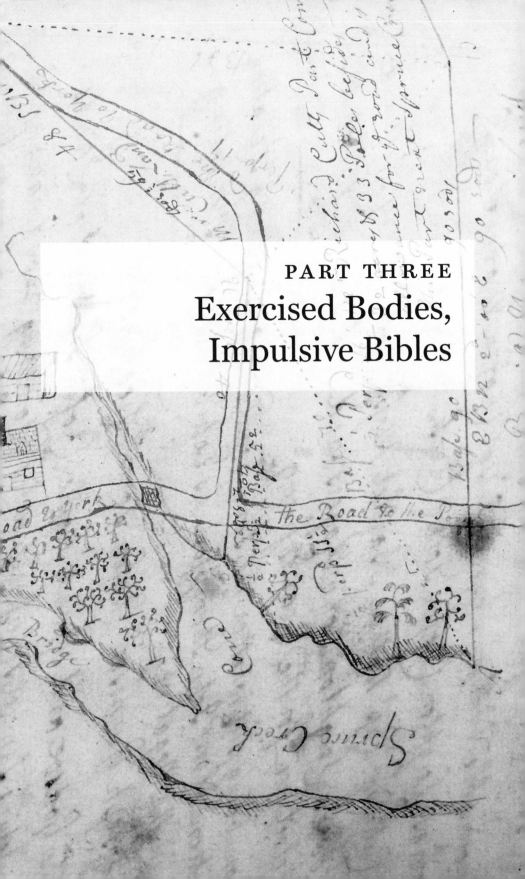

PART THREE
Exercised Bodies,
Impulsive Bibles

Martha Robinson stood defiantly before two of the most important men in New England with her fists "Doubled as if she would have Gone" at their faces in a hail of blows. Joseph Pitkin, a magistrate from Hartford, Connecticut, had witnessed the young woman's extreme agitation during a private interview the previous day at her home in Boston, but his traveling companion Timothy Dwight was shocked by Robinson's belligerence. The merchant, lawyer, and militia colonel from Northampton, Massachusetts, declared that he had never seen anything like it in all the "Days of his Life." Robinson initially received her two distinguished visitors with respect, as they sat down to discuss her distressing condition amid a crowd of people. Dwight had hardly opened the meeting with an invocation before Robinson's countenance changed to diabolic rage. She abruptly cut him off and blasphemously proclaimed that there was no God. Her voice then rose to a disdainful tone, as she upbraided Dwight and his fellow parishioners from Jonathan Edwards's famously awakened parish. "They Tell of Conversions" in Northampton, she sneered, "Conversion, Conversion, Conversion." "There is no Such thing. It is all a notion." In the spring of 1741, the two men had come face to face with a woman "Suposed to be possessed by the Devill."[1]

Robinson had been watching Pitkin for several days as he conducted business and lodged at a tavern across the street. Mistaking the Connecticut magistrate for a visiting clergyman, she approached him on the night before his

---

1. JPD, 55, 61. See also Kenneth P. Minkema, "'The Devil Will Roar in Me Anon': The Possession of Martha Roberson, Boston, 1741," in Elizabeth Reis, ed., *Spellbound: Women and Witchcraft in America*, Worlds of Women (Wilmington, Del., 1998), 99–119. On Pitkin and Dwight, see Benjamin W. Dwight, *The History of the Descendants of John Dwight of Dedham, Mass.*, 2 vols. (New York, 1874), I, 113–120; and Bruce Colin Daniels, *Connecticut's First Family: William Pitkin and His Connections*, Connecticut Bicentennial Series, XI (Chester, Conn., 1975), 20–23.

departure and appealed for pastoral counsel. Pitkin consented, and the two settled into an extended conversation in the company of several other young women. "She Told me she had been under Great Trouble in her mind," Pitkin later noted in a detailed report of his encounters with Robinson. For several months, she had been suffering through a "Strange kind of fitts." Pitkin prayed that God would sanctify their conversation, but the young woman interrupted, stating flatly that the "Devill is Disturbed at Your Coming" for "he knows You are a Good man and he hates all such." Immediately, she apologized for her forward speech. "It is now 15 weeks Since the Devil Began to speak in me," Robinson complained, "and he will Roar in me Anon."[2]

The young demoniac proceeded to narrate her unusual religious experiences. Martha was the fourth of Samuel and Mary Robinson's twelve children. Her mother was a full church member in Boston's Old South Church, but little is known about her father. Although he occasionally labored for the prominent civil magistrate and diarist, Samuel Sewall, the elder Robinson does not appear to have owned land or played an active role in town or church affairs. Baptized as an infant in 1717, Martha acknowledged being under considerable religious convictions at various times as a child, although she admitted that these fleeting soul concerns inevitably wore off, and she would "Grow as Light and vain as ever again." George Whitefield's arrival in Boston late in the fall of 1740 wrenched Robinson out of her protracted state of spiritual security. As she prepared to hear him preach for the first time, she begged God that "if ever he Designed my Conversion this might be the Time; and this man might be the Instrument." The touring evangelist did not disappoint, and Robinson was "peirced by the Word and pressed Down by Conviction" during one of his sermon performances. Pushing through the crowded meetinghouse to the pulpit, she informed Whitefield of her distress, whereupon he prayed tersely that God would set home her feelings of conviction to "saveing Conversion." Robinson might well have taken Whitefield at his word, for she joined the Old South Church several weeks later; but she omitted this important detail in her conversations with Pitkin. Like many other godly walkers, Robinson subsequently discovered that she built her initial hopes for salvation on a sandy foundation. Not long after that, she explained to Pitkin, the Devil entered into her body.[3]

2. JPD, 55–56.

3. JPD, 56; Robert J. Dunkle and Ann S. Lainhart, transcr., *The Records of the Churches of Boston and the First Church, Second Parish, and Third Parish of Roxbury, Including Baptisms, Marriages, Deaths, Admissions, and Dismissals* (Boston, 2001), CD-ROM, s.v. "Martha" and "Rob*"; *A Report of the Record Commissioners of the City of Boston, Containing Boston Births from A.D. 1700 to A.D. 1800* (Boston, 1894), 124; Hamilton Andrews Hill, comp., *An Historical Catalogue of the Old South Church (Third Church) Boston, 1669–1882*

By the time Gilbert Tennent visited Boston the following month, Robinson was languishing under strong convictions and struggling through dark periods of melancholy punctuated by fleeting glimpses of spiritual light. On the night of February 10, 1741, following Tennent's sermon on the vision of dry bones in Ezekiel 37, Robinson and several of her companions sought his pastoral advice. They found the New Jersey itinerant sitting with fellow Whitefieldarian Daniel Rogers and a group of colleagues in a nearby residence. Tennent led the young women into a separate room and inquired whether they would hearken to his words. "I Told him Yes," Robinson recalled in her conversation with Pitkin, "but before he had Said much to me or I to him, the Devil filld me with Such Rage and Spite against him That I Could have Torn him to peices and Should have Torn his Cloaths off if my frends had not held me." Rattled by the young woman's unprovoked verbal assault, Tennent retreated back into the main room of the house and promptly declared Robinson to be possessed by Satan. For several hours, the assembled ministers prayed with her and, according to some reports, Tennent attempted to perform a kind of exorcism ceremony. This was the first time the Devil had spoken through her, Robinson confessed. It would not be the last.[4]

In that moment, as she began to catalogue the various forms of demonic speech that had poured from her lips during her fits, Robinson exploded unexpectedly at Pitkin, shrieking as "Loud as her Voice would Cary." Recovering almost immediately, she begged the Hartford magistrate not to be alarmed at her outburst for the "Devil Endeavors to Scare everybody from me." Undaunted, Pitkin inquired whether his questions were offensive to her. "Not at all," replied the young woman, "but the Devil Cant Bear it." Their conversation resumed, and Pitkin once again offered pious counsel. But the more he spoke, the more her countenance transformed into the "most Dismall form of Rage," and the "Devill with her Tongue" suddenly "Broke forth in the most Hideous outcry Contradicting, Denying, and Mocking as if he would Spit in my face." This second outburst was so unexpected, according to Pitkin, that it "Seemd to Give the Blood a stop in my Veins for a Moment."[5]

In Robinson's demonic speech, modern readers might detect the sublimation of adolescent guilt, anxieties created by emergent social forces, family

---

(Boston, 1883), 40; M. Halsey Thomas, ed., *The Diary of Samuel Sewall, 1674–1729*, 2 vols. (New York, 1973), I, 521–522, 529, 543, 563, 566.

4. DDR, Feb. 9, 1741; JPD, 57. On Tennent's supernaturalism, see Jon Butler, *Awash in a Sea of Faith: Christianizing the American People*, Studies in Cultural History (Cambridge, Mass., 1990), 184.

5. JPD, 57.

tensions, or sexual desire. Local critics of the Boston revival, on the other hand, firmly believed that "Mr. Tenant put the Devil into her" through his lurid preaching on the terrors of hell. When he was gone, several townspeople asserted, Satan "woud Go out again." Others, including members of Robinson's extended family, buttressed their diagnosis of demonic possession with stories that drew on wonder lore stretching back through the centuries. The night before the altercation with Pitkin and Dwight, her aunt observed, a shadowy figure had emerged from their tavern, accompanied by preternatural noises "Like the Bleating of a Goat" and a "Violent, Gust of Wind" that nearly tore the roof off the Robinson's house. Pitkin remained unsure. His initial assessment was ambiguous. As he cautiously examined Robinson's "Suposed" condition, he learned to distinguish divine from diabolical intrusions. For him, the young woman's body had become the site of a cosmic struggle. Knowing the outcome of that battle depended on a close reading of physical and verbal signs. In the end, he elected to "Think of her State otherwise then I did at first" and concluded that Robinson had been possessed by two distinct spirits, Satan and the Holy Ghost. Despite her blasphemous outbursts, the young Boston convert was a monument of divine grace.[6]

Robinson's bodily and spiritual distress was unusual, to be sure, but far from unique. A rise in reports of wondrous supernatural phenomena coincided with the surge in church membership that crested across New England during the great awakenings of the early 1740s. In Sunderland, Massachusetts, rumors swirled that a member of the Gunn family had "made a league with the Devil" after falling into despair about the state of her unconverted soul and taking to excessive drink. Neighbors claimed to have heard Gunn conversing with Satan. "Don't make me a publick example," she shrieked one night from behind the door of her locked chamber. When concerned family members burst into the room, they found the woman lying dead on the floor with her bowels scorched in an unusual manner. Terrified townspeople believed that the Devil had killed her by setting the rum in her stomach on fire. Elsewhere in New England, rumors and accusations of witchcraft resurfaced. It seemed to many during the 1740s that Satan was perilously close at hand.[7]

---

6. Ibid., 55, 60–61, 63.

7. Edward Billing, diaries, 1743–1756, September 1750, Henry N. Flynt Library, Historic Deerfield, Deerfield, Mass. Billing dated this event to "About the year 1740." For reports of witchcraft, see William Stevens Perry, ed., *Historical Collections Relating to the American Colonial Church* (Hartford, Conn., 1873), III, 387; and David Hall, diaries, 1740–1780, Dec. 6, 1745, MHS. Elizabeth Reis offers a different perspective on the prevalence of demonic possession in eighteenth-century New England in *Damned Women: Sinners and Witches in Puritan New England* (Ithaca, N.Y., 1997), 164–193.

In addition to preaching vivid sermons on the realities of hell's torments, a few of the more zealous Whitefieldarians went so far as to compare secure professors and godly walkers with the demoniacs of old. "Let not any man value himself upon his profession," thundered Philemon Robbins of Branford, Connecticut, for those who did were "in a sense possess'd." The Devil, he asserted, dwelt in every secure, Christless sinner. Several notable new converts worried that they "hade a Divil in Me as some of old hade" or "seemed as one really possessed of the devil." Languishing in darkness for weeks as he struggled to determine whether he had been converted, the melancholic Stonington, Connecticut, clergyman Joseph Fish eventually concluded that his soul had been "possessed by the Devil, that strong man Armed." Satan was "too Strong for me," he lamented in his journal, "But the Lord Jesus Christ Appeard to Me to be Stronger than the Devil, And Well Able to Cast him out." Robbins agreed. For both ministers, passage through the experience that Whitefield called the new birth constituted an act of exorcism in which the Holy Spirit "awakens, Convinc's, and drives out" the Devil.[8]

Joseph Pitkin also chose to situate the sacred theater of spirit possession at the heart of the revivals. His account of Martha Robinson's religious experiences is an outstanding example of one layman's struggle to distinguish the converting work of the Whitefieldian awakenings from what opposers increasingly criticized as "enthusiasm," a highly derisive term reserved for deluded religious radicals who based their every action on revelatory communications that they mistakenly imagined to come from God. Pitkin, to the contrary, assumed that God worked in extraordinary ways and could inhabit the regenerate bodies of the faithful. On the pages of his journal, the Hartford magistrate labored to identify the visible and audible signs of the indwelling presence of the Holy Spirit. In so doing, he learned to define the seemingly ineffable conversion experience that had supplanted the ideal of the godly walk in the sermons of Whitefield and his New England supporters. Pitkin's analysis of the dual possession of Martha Robinson stands at the intersection of the three most controversial innovations of the revivals: exercised bodies, biblical impulses, and revelatory visions of the Book of Life.[9]

8. Philemon Robbins, sermon on Matt. 12:43–45, Aug. 4, 1742, Robbins Family Papers, 1724–circa 1803, CHS; J. M. Bumsted, ed., "Emotion in Colonial America: Some Relations of Conversion Experience in Freetown, Massachusetts, 1749–1770," *NEQ*, XLIX (1976), 102; Samuel Hopkins, comp., *The Life and Character of Miss Susanna Anthony* ... (Worcester, Mass., 1796), 23; Joseph Fish, diary, 1739–1770, 14–15, box 36, Silliman Family Papers, 1717–1977, MS 450, YUA.

9. David S. Lovejoy, *Religious Enthusiasm in the New World: Heresy to the Revolution* (Cambridge, Mass., 1985), 1–4.

PEIRCED BY THE WORD

Arriving in Boston at the height of an impressive revival season, Joseph Pitkin readily discerned the hand of God at work in Martha Robinson's case. Gilbert Tennent had recently returned to New Jersey, having delivered more than fifty sermons in town during his four-month preaching tour. Residents flocked to his rousing protracted meetings, and his preaching on the terrors of hell seldom failed to wound his hearers. Pitkin observed that the majority of families in Boston were under hopeful conviction and that many had been "Brot Saveingly Home" to Jesus. That month, eleven people joined the Old South Church. The surge in admissions marked the earliest phase of a potent revival that lasted well into the summer. Religious concerns no longer "Sneak into Corners, but Triumphed openly," Pitkin declared, and "Vice Sought where to hide its Head."[10]

To prove his point, Pitkin opened his narrative of Robinson's possession with a short description of an evening lecture that he attended on March 24, 1741, in which William Cooper, the minister of Boston's prominent Brattle Street Church, "Vindicated the Reality of the work of Gods Spirit." Every evening brought "new Instances of Convictions," he asserted, while each day witnessed more conversions. Cooper had made a similar pronouncement two days earlier, telling Robinson and her fellow parishioners in the Old South meetinghouse that they lived in a time of a "remarkable *Work of Grace*," a portentous moment in the history of Christianity that would be attended with singular success in the preaching labors of God's servants and the "surprizing Effusion of the Holy Spirit." "Lett the Pharisee and Publican Stand and fleer and Laugh [and] Deride it as they will," he exhorted Pitkin and the vast throng that packed the Brattle Street meetinghouse a few days later, "Yett Nevertheless it appears to be Shewn [a] Wonderful Work of God."[11]

During the earliest phase of New England's great awakenings, Cooper and his colleagues firmly believed that the Holy Spirit had descended on the Atlantic world in an unprecedented manner. For a brief time, nearly everyone agreed. Ministerial correspondence, including numerous accounts that were later published in the *Christian History,* spoke of an "extraordinary *Pouring out of the Spirit of God*" throughout New England. Local clergymen led their congregations in days of fasting for the "Effusion of his Blessed Spirit," and

10. JPD, 55; Hill, comp., *Historical Catalogue of the Old South Church,* 40–41. See also, DDR, Dec. 19, 21, 1740.

11. JPD, 55; William Cooper, *One Shall Be Taken, and Another Left ...* (Boston, 1741), 14; Andrew Eliot, annotated almanacs, 1740–1778, Mar., 24, 1741, MHS.

they invited riding ministers to come and preach, hoping that the "Lord is with you, and will send, you, full of his Spirit." In their weekly sermons and lectures, too, New England ministers exhibited a growing interest in the doctrine of the Holy Spirit. Leading revival luminaries, including Robinson's minister, Joseph Sewall, and outspoken critics, such as Charles Chauncy, published sermons on the subject during the early 1740s.[12]

Lay men and women framed the Whitefieldian revivals in a similar manner. Later in the spring of 1741, Sarah, the precociously pious daughter of Boston clergyman Thomas Prince, wrote excitedly to her cousin in London of the "Remarkable outpourings of the spirit of god in this town." "I long for the spirit of God," Sudbury, Massachusetts, goodwife Experience Richardson prayed during the winter of 1742 in the first of many intimate diary entries that she composed over the next half century. Devotional virtuoso Susanna Anthony, too, described herself as being jealous to have God's Spirit "dwelling in me," and another woman who belonged to the same prayer circle in Newport, Rhode Island, concluded a letter to Eleazar Wheelock wishing him the "Continual refreshing Preasence of the holy Spirit." One ardent revival participant even thanked a friend for offering pious advice "which I trust you gave from the Influence of God's Spirit on your Soul."[13]

New converts believed that God would "Send his holy Spirit" into the bodies of convicted sinners and open their "blind Eyes" or "Pour Down more Plentifull Effusions of the Holy Spirit on all People." A few devoted entire diaries to cataloging the "pleasant refreshing influences of the holy Spirit" and "Sweete Consolations of the blessed Spiret of God" almost daily. To experience conversion meant, in the language of the day, to be "filled with the holy Ghost," to come out "full of the Divine Spirit," to be "seiz'd with the *Spirit*," to be "Born anew by his almighty spirit," or to have a "marvellous Influx of the Divine Comforter." During peak periods of revival activity, witnesses claimed to have observed the Holy Ghost descending like a dove (Matthew 3:16) or a "mighty rushing Wind" (Acts 2:2) on awakened congregations, animating

12. Peter Thacher, "Account of the Revival of Religion at Middleborough Concluded," *CH*, no. 65 (May 26, 1744), 97; Chester Williams to Jonathan Edwards, Feb. 15, 1742, *WJEO*, XXXII, *Correspondence by, to, and about Edwards and His Family*, B8; Benjamin Pomeroy to Eleazar Wheelock, Nov. 17, 1742, case 8, box 24, SGC I. See also Joseph Sewall, *The Holy Spirit Convincing the World of Sin, of Righteousness, and of Judgment* ... (Boston, 1741); and Charles Chauncy, *The Out-Pouring of the Holy Ghost* ... (Boston, 1742).

13. Sarah Prince to Rebecca and Sarah Denny, May 15, 1741, no. 741315, *EWP;* Ellen Richardson Glueck and Thelma Smith Ernst, transcrs., "Diary of Experience (Wight) Richardson, Sudbury, Mass.," 1728–1782, 2, typescript, 1978, NEHGS; Sarah Anthony to Eleazar Wheelock, Sept. 26, 1744, no. 744526, *EWP*, Sarah Lifford to Wheelock, Oct. 17, 1742, no. 742567; Simon Frost to Samuel Phillips Savage, Jan. 6, 1742, SSP I.

the bodies of the faithful, filling them with unspeakable joy, and constraining them to praise God with uplifted voices. Even Massachusetts governor Jonathan Belcher hoped that the "Holy and Eternal Spirit of God" would take "full possession of my heart."[14]

Religious discourse among New England Congregationalists had not always been so saturated with pneumatological metaphors and imagery. The Whitefieldarians succeeded in reversing a theological trend that had curbed the doctrine of the Holy Spirit for more than half a century. Early English dissenters initially reveled in its operations. The same unstable religious climate that witnessed the birth of Quakerism also produced sophisticated treatises on the nature and inner workings of the triune God. Radical puritans and Quakers alike described the Holy Spirit as an indwelling presence that warmed the hearts of God's elect. Discerned through special spiritual faculties, it illuminated the saints' reading of the scriptures and occasionally propelled them into mystical raptures. Over the course of the seventeenth century, however, pneumatology receded from theological prominence, as New England ministers increasingly emphasized preparation for salvation, the orderly means of grace, tribalism, sacramental obligations, and the rational springs of the created cosmos. As a result, few relations of faith or diaries written between 1680 and 1740 described the third person of the Trinity as an indwelling vital presence. Instead, most lay men and women talked and wrote about the Holy Spirit as a comforting external presence that labored to awaken sinners to their Christian duties and could be grieved away by ignoring private devotional routines and public religious obligations.[15]

George Whitefield and his ministerial supporters labored to restore the emphasis on the Holy Spirit as an indwelling presence. In a famous but con-

---

14. Douglas L. Winiarski, "'A Jornal of a Fue Days at York': The Great Awakening on the Northern New England Frontier," *Maine History,* XLII (2004), 64; John Loring to Israel Loring, Dec. 31, 1742, Jan. 7, 1744, Nathan Stone Papers, 1726–1832, MHS; John Marsh to Eleazar Wheelock, June 11, 1742, no. 742361, *EWP;* Solomon Reed, diary, 1744–1745, Mar. 8, 1744, Solomon Reed Collection, 1743–1745, PHM; Joseph Bean, diary, 1741–1744, 30, Mariam Coffin Canaday Library, Bryn Mawr College, Bryn Mawr, Pa.; Samuel Hopkins, journal, 1741–1744, 47, box 322, SGC II; Ross W. Beales, Jr., ed., "The Diary of John Cleaveland, January 15–May 11, 1742," *EIHC,* CVII (1971), 167; *Boston Weekly News-Letter,* Dec. 8, 1743; Thomas Foxcroft to Jonathan Dickinson, Dec. 16, 1741, Charles Roberts Autograph Collection, Haverford College Library, Haverford, Pa; DDR, Apr. 25, 1743; Beales, ed., "Solomon Prentice's Narrative of the Great Awakening," MHS, *Proceedings,* 3d Ser., LXXXIII (1971), 142; Jonathan Belcher to Isaac Watts, May 20, 1741, Jonathan Belcher Collection, 1708–1950, box 1, Firestone Library, Princeton University, Princeton, N.J.

15. My argument in this paragraph follows John Corrigan, *The Prism of Piety: Catholick Congregational Clergy at the Beginning of the Enlightenment,* Religion in America (New York, 1991), 89.

troversial sermon delivered several times during his first New England tour, the Anglican evangelist declared that the indwelling presence of the Holy Spirit was the common privilege of the faithful. Lashing out against his critics, Whitefield asserted that born-again saints "no sooner mention the Necessity of our receiving the Holy Ghost in these last Days, as well as formerly; but we are look'd upon by some, as Enthusiasts and Madmen." In a brilliant reversal, he argued that "every Christian, in the proper Sense of the Word, must be an Enthusiast—That is, must be inspired of God, or have God in him." Human beings were a "Motly Mixture of Brute and Devil," Whitefield declared, in what became one of his most controversial pronouncements. New converts needed the Holy Spirit to enter their bodies "ere we can dwell with and enjoy God." Whitefield carefully warned his auditors that regeneration did not confer on the saints the power to work miracles, but he nonetheless concluded that the indwelling Spirit transmuted the dross material of human nature into the gold of God's elect.[16]

Jonathan Edwards also intensified his explorations on the nature of the Trinity during the revival years. Although Edwards had always described the Holy Spirit as an "indwelling vital principle," he tended to characterize the third person of the Godhead as a "temper and disposition" in his early writings. "Having the spirit of Christ" meant displaying virtuous fruits in outward behavior, including "love, joy, peace, long-suffering, gentleness, goodness, faith, meekness, temperance." Composed sometime between 1739 and 1743, Edwards's manuscript "Treatise on Grace" signaled an important theological shift. He began by dividing the "influence of God's Spirit" into common and special, or saving, grace. Whereas the former consisted of various "moral attainments" that were held in common by saints and sinners, the latter involved a peculiar operation on the hearts of the elect alone. Only "true saints that have communion with Christ" possessed a special faculty of understanding that provided a foundation for virtuous acts. The implantation of a "new heart" transformed natural persons into entirely new beings who "have the Spirit dwelling in them." This "resurrection," as Edwards termed it, came through an "immediate infusion or operation of the Divine Being upon the soul," an instantaneous conversion event that transformed the bodies of the faithful into "temples of the Holy Ghost." "Irrefragable to reason" but ridiculed as "enthusiasm, fanaticism, whimsy and distraction" by unbelievers, the "doctrine of a gracious nature being the immediate influence of the Spirit

16. George Whitefield, *The Indwelling of the Spirit, the Common Privilege of All Believers* ... (London, 1739), 4, 10, 17–18.

of God" had become an essential component of Edwards's emerging revival theology.[17]

Perhaps the most compelling example of the Whitefieldarians' burgeoning fascination with the doctrine of the Holy Spirit may be found in a pair of sermons on Romans 8:9 that Daniel Rogers preached before and during the revivals. Although he later stitched the two sets of notes together to form a single booklet, the latter discourse bore little resemblance to its predecessor. Like Edwards's early writings on the subject, the 1730s sermon included a series of tests for determining whether one possessed the "Spirit of Christ." According to Rogers, "Spiritually minded" people displayed their likeness to Jesus through their outward "Carriage and Behaviour." True Christians were faithful and fervent in their prayers and devotional routines, attended to sacramental duties with vigor, pursued fair and upright business dealings, shunned excessive worldliness, constantly performed good works, strove for peace in their communities, and patiently resigned themselves to providential afflictions. Evidence of a Christ-like temper "may be known best by the Effects of It in our Life and conversation," Rogers concluded. During the mid-1730s, godly walkers were still the chosen people of God.[18]

Performed in towns across New England during the early 1740s, Rogers's revival sermon drew a sharp boundary between internal motives and external actions. To possess the Holy Spirit within, he asserted, was to be "quickned by Him, to be regenerated—born again." True Christians were taught, led, and governed in every action by the indwelling Spirit. Many pious professors and godly walkers believed that the external "Assistance of the Spirit" was essential to salvation, Rogers warned; however, they "deny this Doctrine of the Spirit of Regeneration by him." Echoing the familiar refrain of the sandy foundation, he continued, "men may have bright parts, great natural and acquir'd abilities," but not know Christ. They "may have good Sense, and yet not discern Spiritual Things." Without an experimental knowledge of the new birth, they remained "Natural" and "mearly Rational" beings, little different from

17. Jonathan Edwards, *A Divine and Supernatural Light, Immediately Imparted to the Soul by the Spirit of God . . .* (Boston, 1734), in *WJE*, XVII, *Sermons and Discourses, 1730–1733*, ed. Mark Valeri (New Haven, Conn., 1999), 411; Edwards, "Treatise on Grace," in *WJE*, XXI, *Writings on the Trinity, Grace, and Faith*, ed. Sang Hyun Lee (New Haven, Conn., 2003), 153, 158, 160, 165, 176–177, 181, "Signs of Godliness," 488–489. On the importance of the Trinity in Edwards's incipient revival theology, see Amy Plantinga Pauw, *The Supreme Harmony of All: The Trinitarian Theology of Jonathan Edwards* (Grand Rapids, Mich., 2002), 151–181.

18. Daniel Rogers, sermon on Rom. 8:9, September 1735, May 18, 1740, Rogers Family Papers, 1614–1950, Ser. II, Subser. II, box 5B, New-York Historical Society, New York.

God's less-sentient creatures. Instead of urging his auditors to probe their outward behavior, Rogers concluded his revival sermon on a starkly Whitefieldian note: "Have we ever experienced the regenerating, renewing, Sanctifying operations of the Spirit of God"?[19]

It was a provocative question, but one with no clear answer. How could people make their bodies "meet temples" for the Holy Ghost, as Eleazar Wheelock proclaimed in one of his many assaults on the shortcomings of lifeless religious practices, or "labor to have Christ formed" in their bodies and possess the "Spirit abiding within 'em," as Philemon Robbins preached in several 1741 sermons? As an abstract theological principle, Whitefield's resurgent pneumatology resonated with Reformed sensibilities. As one Boston church membership candidate carefully explained in his 1742 relation, "all who make a profession of Religion" must do so from a "divine life or principle wrought within us by the holy Spirit." But what was this special sensory faculty that the Whitefieldarians positioned at the center of their theology? How did ordinary people experience the regenerating operations of the indwelling Spirit? What impact did the miraculous intrusion of the Holy Ghost have on the bodies of men and women like Martha Robinson, and how could an outsider like Joseph Pitkin detect and distinguish its presence from physical distempers, animal spirits, nerves, or worse, demonic possession?[20]

Determining whether one had been infused by the Holy Spirit proved to be no easy matter. Despite his technical writings on the subject, Edwards concluded that the principle of the indwelling Spirit was "ineffable," "inconceivable," and "infinitely above all our conceptions." He and his colleagues nonetheless challenged their audiences to search within themselves for this very "holy seed" of the new birth. Having repudiated the ideal of the godly walk and embraced Whitefield's stark concept of conversion as a discrete event, many ardent revival participants suddenly found themselves groping in the dark, their souls and bodies easily penetrated by spirits and devils. The wealthy Maine merchant Simon Frost expressed the conundrum succinctly in a 1742 letter to Samuel Phillips Savage, his Boston business partner, admitting that he was "at a Loss" to distinguish the "Operation of The Faculties of my Soul" from that of the "blessed Spirit." At the height of the Boston revival, how could one discern whether another person had been possessed by the Holy Spirit or

19. Ibid.
20. Eleazar Wheelock, sermon on Matt. 5:23–24, Feb. 20, 1741, *EWP;* Philemon Robbins, sermon on Col. 1:27, July 19, 1741, sermon on Rom. 8:10, Oct. 15, 1741, Robbins Family Papers, 1719–1850, MS 1169, YUA; Appendix B, Boston, First Church, 8.

by Satan? For sympathetic observers like Joseph Pitkin, there was only one way to know for certain: watch their bodies, listen to their words.[21]

■ From her first demonic outburst against Gilbert Tennent, Martha Robinson's violently exercised body was constantly on display. A few neighbors shunned her family after being "frighted out of their witts," but the Robinsons' home soon emerged as a gathering place for distressed sinners. Ministers assembled to preach, pray, and fast with her concerned family and neighbors. Inquiring what impact her outbursts "Comonly had upon those who Saw them" during these impromptu religious meetings, Pitkin was pleased to learn that "Some who were Secure were Throughly awakend by it, and had since Said they Had Reason to Bless God they had Seen her." Indeed, Robinson's "Strange kind of fitts" were a sight to behold.[22]

Like many people in the early modern period, Pitkin and other witnesses to Robinson's physical distress probably thought of her body, not as a fixed boundary between self and world, but as a porous site that remained open to the intrusion of forces ranging from epidemic disease to the Holy Spirit. At the same time, they granted words—especially those contained in the Bible—an autonomous force that is difficult to imagine in a modern age. When Robinson spoke of being "peirced by the Word" during one of George Whitefield's sermons and when a few of her more suspicious neighbors believed that Tennent had preached the "Devil into her," they gestured toward powerful religious experiences that were at once both spiritual and somatic.[23]

The extreme bodily agitation of convicted sinners drew more commentary—positive and negative—than any other aspect of the great awakenings in New England. During the fall of 1741, observers on the northern frontier had good reason to believe that the Holy Spirit had effected a "great Shaking" during the revival in York, Maine. Those in the "Pangs of the *new Birth*," wrote one skeptical newspaper correspondent, "generally appear to be in the greatest Agonies imaginable." Faces contorted, mouths were struck dumb, and bodies fell lifelessly to the floor. Some wept openly or shrieked in fear. The physical contortions of a distressed York woman proved so disruptive that even

21. Edwards, "Treatise on Grace," in *WJE*, XXI, *Writings on the Trinity, Grace, and Faith*, ed. Sang Hyun Lee, 184–185;

22. JPD, 55, 60. See also Eliot, annotated almanacs, Apr. 20, 1741.

23. JPD, 56, 60. On early modern conceptions of the body as a porous membrane, see Robert Blair St. George, *Conversing by Signs: Poetics of Implication in Colonial New England* (Chapel Hill, N.C., 1998), 115–204. My argument in this section builds on Susan Juster's discussion of early evangelicals' "porous sense of self" in *Disorderly Women: Sexual Politics and Evangelicalism in Revolutionary New England* (Ithaca, N.Y., 1994), 5.

sympathetic young converts consented to have her body gagged and bound with cords. Those who *"got thro"* the work of conversion burst out in peals of laughter, clapped neighbors on the back, sang boisterous hymns, kissed fellow parishioners, and loudly exhorted other persons to come to Christ. Nearly a thousand shrieking and writhing bodies filled the Portsmouth, New Hampshire, meetinghouse a few weeks later. "The whole Gallery was in Motion," explained William Parker, with "lifting up of hands, Clapping, wringing, Smiting the Breast" and making "Such a Sight of Distress as no words will Convey." It seemed to the Portsmouth merchant as if he were watching "two Armies Ingaged." Members of the congregation kept "dropping one after another by a Cause as Imperceptible" as "flying Bullets." To observers such as the anonymous author of the "Jornal of a Fue Days at York," the bodily manifestations attending protracted revival meetings were "amaising to Se, and hear." "In Short," concurred Parker, "Such a Congregation as this was never Seen before."[24]

Exercised bodies appeared wherever audiences embraced the innovative new measures engineered by Whitefield, Tennent, and New England's native itinerants. In addition to being "peirced," as Robinson described her embodied response to Whitefield's forceful oratory, revival participants were "lashed," "touched," "pricked," "shock't," "Wounded," "Quickned," and "Struck" by stirring preaching performances. The Whitefieldarians deployed "many Melting Expressions," and the hearts of their hearers were "warmed by the Word." Daniel Rogers believed that inspired preaching allowed the scriptures to "fall with Weight" on enlivened audiences, while a colleague hoped that the word of God would "take root" during his sermons. Yale College student John Cleaveland described a lecture that had "Some hold on me a Little whil," although "it Soon went off." On other occasions, he noted with a twinge of despair that he seemed to be "Seeled up Like a Stone," impervious to the penetration of God's word.[25]

24. John Blunt to Samuel Phillips Savage, Oct. 22, 1741, SSP I; *South Carolina Gazette* (Charleston), Mar. 1, 1742; William Parker to Richard Waldron, Nov. 20, 1741, Miscellaneous Bound Manuscripts Collection, 1741–1748, MHS; Winiarski, "'Jornal of a Fue Days at York,'" *Maine History*, XLII (2004), 62–66, 69.

25. JPD, 56; EWD, 239; Stephen Williams, diaries, 1715–1782, 10 vols., typescript, III, 379, Storrs Library, Longmeadow, Mass. (available online at *http://www.longmeadow library.org/stephen-williams-diary-available-online/*); Louise Parkman Thomas, transcr., "Journal of the Rev. Israel Loring," no. 12192, 17, 28–29, SA; Winiarski, "'Jornal of a Fue Days at York,'" *Maine History*, XLII (2004), 66–67, 72; DDR, Jan. 10, Mar. 3, Apr. 12, 1742; *American Weekly Mercury* (Philadelphia), July 16, 1741; Jonathan Parsons, sermon on John 17:6, Aug. 17, 1741, no. 84, Sermons, 1737–1761, WCL; Beales, ed., "Diary of John Cleaveland," *EIHC*, CVII (1971), 161, 163.

Vivid descriptions of bodies open or closed to the divine intrusion of the scriptures pointed toward a broader understanding of the nature of the indwelling presence of the Holy Spirit. Ardent revival participants took such metaphors literally. Many were convinced that inspired preaching transformed biblical texts into a "sensible," physical force that, in Rogers's words, was capable of creating "Marvellous Motion." An elderly Connecticut man put the matter succinctly when he informed Whitefield that he "'knew what I had preached in the morning was true,' for he had felt it." Or, as the frail Connecticut clergyman Marston Cabot explained, "plain and Earnest" preaching had a "desired effect" that ministers and their congregations could "see."[26]

The Whitefieldarians' firm belief that the "Lord was in the word" set the stage for Jonathan Edwards's remarkable performance of *Sinners in the Hands of an Angry God* in Enfield, Massachusetts (now Connecticut), on July 8, 1741. Edwards's gravitational imagery transformed his chosen biblical text into a potent dart that pierced the hearts of his audience and sent them careening into paroxysms of terror. Sitting in the Enfield meetinghouse alongside several colleagues, neighboring minister Stephen Williams described the "great moaning" and "crying out" that erupted "throughout the whole House." The outcries of the assembly grew so loud that Edwards was forced to stop speaking. Following a short prayer, the assembled ministers descended into the pews where they discoursed with small groups of frightened parishioners well into the night. The "power of God," Williams concluded, was "Amazing and Astonishing." Eleazar Wheelock, who was also in attendance, later claimed that more than a dozen people were instantly converted during the "Great assembly at Enfield."[27]

Edwards had carefully planned his performance. By the summer of 1741, he had mastered the art of inciting somatic responses to the preached word. In a letter published in the *Christian History* two years later, the Northampton minister explained that he had first encountered the exercised bodies of new converts during a lecture several months before his visit to Enfield. On this occasion, several "professors" were so "greatly affected with a sense of the greatness and glory of divine things" that they were "not able to conceal it" and cried out in distress. The "visible effect" of his preaching on their bodies proved contagious. After the lecture, he gathered the young people in a separate room of the house for a religious conference. Quickly, the same "affec-

26. DDR, Jan. 21, Apr. 10, 1742; *GWJ*, 478; Marston Cabot, "Memorabilia," 1740–1745, Jan. 31, 1742, Mss A 1999, NEHGS.

27. DDR, Dec. 21, 1742; Williams, diaries, III, 375–376; Eleazar Wheelock to the Lebanon North Parish Church, n.d. [July 11, 1741], no. 743900.1, *EWP*.

tion" that had gripped the Northampton professors was "propagated through the room." Converted and unconverted parishioners alike were overpowered, some with "admiration, love, joy, and praise" and others with terror and distress. In short order, the "whole room was full of nothing but outcries, faintings and such like."[28]

During the weeks that followed, these violent, embodied expressions of the new birth spread rapidly through the awakened families of Northampton. Edwards made a concerted effort to gather his young converts together in private to reinforce what he had preached in public. The children, he explained in his *Christian History* letter, were "greatly affected with the warnings and counsels that were given them, and many exceedingly overcome; and the room was filled with cries: and when they were dismissed, they, almost all of them, went home crying aloud through the streets, to all parts of the town." Edwards not only validated bodily exercises as authentic, he created space for convicted parishioners to enact their conversion struggles in somatic form. Throughout the summer of 1741, the Northampton revivalist concluded, "It was a very frequent thing to see an house full of outcries, faintings, convulsions and such like, both with distress, and also with admiration and joy."[29]

Edwards quickly recognized that the conversions that he witnessed in Northampton, Enfield, and the surrounding towns of the upper Connecticut Valley during the spring and summer of 1741 were qualitatively different from anything that he had experienced previously in his ministry, including the religious stir of the previous decade. They "were frequently wrought more sensibly and visibly," he later explained in the *Christian History*, "and more manifest by external effects of them." These "visible conversions (if I may so call them)," Edwards concluded, typically occurred during revival meetings, "where the appearances of what was wrought on the heart fell under public observation."[30]

Edwards's growing fascination with inciting a visible, embodied response in his audiences set the stage for the sermons that he delivered with devastating success during his week-long excursion to Enfield. Among the ninety-seven new communicants whom he admitted to the Lord's Supper across the Connecticut River in Suffield a few days earlier, many had already been similarly exercised. For weeks, rumors had circulated throughout the region that Suffield's young converts were falling into strange fits during religious meetings led by touring Whitefieldarians. One of these zealous new converts was

28. Jonathan Edwards to Thomas Prince, Dec. 12, 1743, in *WJE*, XVI, *Letters and Personal Writings*, ed. George S. Claghorn (New Haven, Conn., 1998), 117.

29. Ibid., 117–118.

30. Ibid., 119–120.

undoubtedly the deaf man mentioned in an unsigned letter by a traveling Boston merchant who attended the July 5 sacrament over which Edwards presided. Earlier that afternoon, the man's intense private devotions had been so boisterous that he could be heard at a distance of more than a mile from the Suffield meetinghouse. His shouts attracted Edwards and a large crowd. They discovered him in the "greatest agonies" with sweat running down his body in "Streams, heaving with his breast, and panting as if Just Expiring." For the anonymous Boston correspondent, the deaf man's outward physical symptoms clearly indicated that God was working to transform his unconverted soul, and he noted with pleasure that he was eventually "carryed thro' great distress to Considerable Joy."[31]

Edwards remained in Suffield and preached again the following day. Detained in town by bad weather, the Boston merchant had planned to watch the Northampton revivalist reprise his sacramental sermon, but he arrived at the meetinghouse late and witnessed only the effects of Edwards's performance. Following the lecture, two hundred people of all ages and both sexes retired to a nearby residence where a collective outcry erupted. The author's account of the cacophony was clinical. At a distance of a quarter of a mile, the noise sounded confused, but, as he entered the house, he discerned three ascending levels. The lowest pitch seemed like the "Sobs of bereaved Friends." Others engaged in "Groans and Screaches" that reminded the writer of "Women in the Pains of Childbirth." The most agitated members of the assembly exploded into "Houlings and Yellings, which to Even a Carnal Man might point out Hell." These bodily outbursts lasted for nearly three hours, during which time Edwards prayed with the convicted sinners until his strength was almost spent, then called for a group of laymen to counsel the distressed. In a short space of time, according to the Boston correspondent, nearly a score of people were "brought to different degrees of Peace and Joy, Some to Rapture."[32]

Edwards's sermons alone did not generate the religious awakening that ensued, for his preaching in Suffield and Enfield was part of a carefully orchestrated series of religious meetings in the adjacent towns of the Connecticut Valley. Edwards had arrived one week earlier to preach a weekday lecture for Stephen Williams in the neighboring Longmeadow parish of Springfield. Following his visit to Suffield, he set off for his father's parish in Windsor, where

31. Williams, diaries, III, 368–369; Douglas L. Winiarski, "Jonathan Edwards, Enthusiast? Radical Revivalism and the Great Awakening in the Connecticut Valley," *Church History*, LXXIV (2005), 737.

32. Winiarski, "Jonathan Edwards, Enthusiast?" *Church History*, LXXIV (2005), 738–739.

he witnessed a pair of lectures by fellow riding ministers Eleazar Wheelock and Benjamin Pomeroy. The following day, Coventry minister Joseph Meacham delivered an arresting sermon to a "Grave and Attentive" audience in Enfield. In the evening, Meacham and Williams crossed over to Suffield hoping to advance the "remarkable outpouring of the Spirit of God" that Edwards had ignited during the previous week. There, they met Wheelock and Pomeroy just arrived from Windsor. At about sunset, according to Williams, the assembled itinerants held an outdoor revival meeting that lasted deep into the night. Meacham and Wheelock took turns preaching and praying with the assembly, and the fruits of their labors were impressive. There was "considerable crying among the people," Williams confided in his diary, and "Screaching in the streets." The two ministers repeated their efforts the following morning, with similar results. Finally, on July 8, 1741, the four ministers ferried across the river, dined with colleague Peter Reynolds, and arrived at the Enfield meetinghouse just in time to hear Edwards deliver his "most awakening" lecture on Deuteronomy 32:35.[33]

Viewed against the backdrop of protracted revival meetings in the upper Connecticut Valley, Edwards's decision to preach his most terrifying sermon at Enfield must have been a calculated one. The grisly punishments that God would visit on secure professors were never far from his mind during these months. The entries in his theological notebooks from the early 1740s displayed a persistent preoccupation with the realities of hell's torments, and he composed no fewer than eight other sermons on hell in 1741 alone; nonetheless, his sermons from this period also reflected a wide range of pastoral concerns as well as a careful balance between themes of terror and hope. Edwards could have chosen a different tone for his visit to Enfield, but, after witnessing the ecstatic behavior of the Suffielders and gauging the temper of his audience, he elected to preach *Sinners in the Hands of an Angry God*. It was a deliberate attempt to evoke the dramatic physical manifestations that Williams recorded in his diary later that day.[34]

■ Neither Edwards, the anonymous Boston correspondent, nor any of the prominent Whitefieldarians who witnessed the revival events in Suffield and Enfield offered an interpretation of what they thought exercised bodies meant. They seemed to suggest only that extreme physical distress was somehow a

33. Williams, diaries, III, 373–375; Winiarski, "Jonathan Edwards, Enthusiast?" *Church History*, LXXIV (2005), 739.

34. Amy Plantinga Pauw, "Editor's Introduction," in *WJE*, XX, *The "Miscellanies" (Entry Nos. 833–1152)*, ed. Pauw (New Haven, Conn., 2002), 4n, 17–24.

prerequisite for or concomitant to the experience of the new birth. Other revival proponents, including Edwards's protégé and future biographer Samuel Hopkins, developed a more coherent assessment. The recent Yale College graduate arrived in Northampton six months later, fully expecting to witness glorious things in a town famous throughout the Atlantic world for its revival fervor. On his way, he passed through Suffield, where he heard "Strange accounts" of people "faling into fits and lying speechless" for hours at a time. "It seems to me," Hopkins noted in his journal, "that such may be the effects of Discoveries from the Spirit of God, and I rejoyce at it."[35]

Hopkins remained in Northampton for nearly a month, during which time he languished in a "senseless" frame as he tutored Edwards's four daughters. On New Year's Day, 1742, he begged God that he might become a "New-Man." Edwards returned bearing news of a religious awakening underway downriver in Hartford, but he departed again a few weeks later on an extended preaching tour of central Massachusetts. No signs of the revival appeared in Northampton until mid-January, when the young itinerant Samuel Buell arrived in town. As had been the case under Edward's ministry the previous spring, the Northampton parishioners exploded into bodily contortions under Buell's preaching. Hopkins reported seeing "wonderfull things" as the "spirit of God" descended on the town in a "remarkable manner."[36]

Puzzled by the behavior of the young converts in Northampton, Hopkins quickly learned to associate these "Strange things" with the work of the Holy Spirit as he rode with his former Yale College classmate through the isolated towns of central Massachusetts. Buell preached with authority, and his audiences alternately writhed in terror and leapt for joy. They were "Struck" in Western (now Warren), "cryed out" in Brookfield, and "bowed down under Convictions" in Leicester. Soon, Hopkins was counting the number of conversions that followed these somatic outbursts. Following one of Buell's sermons, the young riding minister explained, the "power of god came down in a wonderful manner." Nearly a dozen people were "crying out in distress all over the house and eight or ten were hopefully converted." For Hopkins, bodily distress marked the descent of the Spirit and signified its indwelling presence in the bodies of new converts.[37]

A detailed letter describing Buell's visit to Concord, Massachusetts, a few days after he parted company with Hopkins underscored the importance that lay men and women placed on bodily exercises during the revivals. Buell and

35. Hopkins, journal, 12–13, box 322, SGC II.
36. Ibid., 17, 22, 26–27.
37. Ibid., 30–33.

Concord minister Daniel Bliss preached for nine straight days—sometimes until two o'clock in the morning—hoping to rouse the passions of their audiences to the "highest pitch." Initially, Buell's sermons appeared to have little impact on the large assemblies; but, on the fifth day of his visit, more than three hundred were "visibly affected," and the noise of the outcries emanating from the meetinghouse became "inexpressibly great." "The effects Upon the Minds, or rather, bodies of the people," the anonymous correspondent reported, included "Sighing, groaning, crying out, fainting, falling down, praying, exhorting, singing, laughing, congratulation (or wishing each other Joy as they expres'd it) by shaking hands together, and by imbraceing each other, which was practic'd by different sexes, as well as others." Of these various somatic events, falling predominated, especially among women and children, who suddenly "drop'd down like persons in fits." Physical outbursts seldom occurred during meetings held in daylight, nor could those who suffered through them provide any "rational Account, of their distresses or Joys"; however, witnesses to the Concord revival firmly believed that exercised bodies were essential to the new birth. They esteemed all who languished in fits to be in a "damnable state," while joyous outcries afforded proof that an individual was "truly converted." In fact, the observer noted, "those Under concern, imagined, that the louder they Screem'd the sooner they should be converted."[38]

Daniel Rogers also learned to associate agitated bodies with the converting work of the indwelling Holy Spirit during his various preaching circuits. The boisterous revival that gripped his father's parish in Ipswich, Massachusetts, played a formative role in defining the meaning of somatic exercises for the young itinerant. During a meeting of young men in December 1741, one of Rogers's kinsmen preached in a lively manner, and the "Power of God came down" among the assembly. Arriving late, Rogers discovered the entire meeting in an uproar. Rogers's description mirrored accounts of Edwards's Enfield sermon six months earlier and prefigured reports from Buell's tour of central Massachusetts a few weeks later. But, in this case, the zealous Whitefieldarian pushed forward to a novel conclusion. This was one of the first instances in his diary in which Rogers explicitly noted that the "Children of God" in the meeting had been filled by the indwelling presence of the Holy Ghost.[39]

A similar scene unfolded in the Ipswich meeting house several days later. Following a pair of moving lectures by William Cooper of Boston, the congregation tarried in anticipation of the outpouring of the Spirit that had occurred

38. Anonymous to "Reverend Sir," n.d. [Mar. 31, 1742], Jonas Bowen Clark Collection, 1742–1810, 1831, CL.
39. DDR, Dec. 27, 1741.

earlier in the week. Rogers seized the initiative. Mounting the deacon's chair, he began to exhort the assembly. On this occasion, however, words failed, and he suddenly found himself unable to speak. Chastened, Rogers returned to his seat and confessed to the assembly that he was "quite empty of a Sense of Spiritual Things." The Ipswich parishioners sat in hushed silence for several minutes while he appealed to God for aid. According to his diary, Rogers suddenly felt empowered to apply some lessons from the parable of the prodigal son. He rose again and called on the "Prodigalls" in the pews to "come Away" to Christ. Instantly, he wrote, the "Spirit of God came down in an Astonishing manner." At first, only two or three people cried out in terror, but soon the power of the Spirit "Spread like fire." As many as four hundred of the estimated one thousand people in the meetinghouse started wailing at the same time. The din was so great that Rogers's voice could "not be heard half over the House." Hymn singing eventually quelled the commotion, but Rogers once again confided in his diary that extreme bodily distress marked the descent of the Spirit.[40]

Not only did the indwelling Holy Ghost exercise the bodies of new converts, it animated their tongues. The following night, Rogers, his brother Nathaniel, and Jedidiah Jewett of Rowley, Massachusetts, held a more intimate meeting among a group of young people that lasted until dawn. Nathaniel opened with an exhortation, and there was a "Sweet motion of the Spirit upon the Children." This "Influence went off" as quickly as it commenced, however, and Daniel worried that the "Spirit of God was quenched." Inexplicably, "He graciously return'd again," as several young women in the group began speaking, praying, exhorting, and narrating their own religious experiences by the "Immediate Help, or Influence of the Spirit of God."[41]

As the Ipswich revival deepened during the next few weeks, Rogers encountered scores of men and women who were "brim full of the Spirit" and manifested their unusual religious experiences in dramatic speech acts. During an evening meeting on February 1, 1742, the "Spirit of God came upon a Young Woman" from the neighboring Chebacco parish of Ipswich (now Essex), and she began to voice her concern for the unconverted in a "most earnest way of Speaking." With tears streaming down her face in agony, according to Rogers, she spoke and prayed continuously for almost ten hours. The following day, a young boy named William Harris felt the same rushing power of the indwelling Spirit, and he spoke to the assembly that had gathered in the Ipswich meetinghouse in a "most lively Affectionate manner." In a tell-

40. Ibid., Dec. 31, 1741.
41. Ibid., Jan. 1, 1742.

ing admission, Harris believed that it was the Holy Spirit that "Spake in Him" and that "if He thot It wasn't He would not speak a word more." Preaching at Chebacco later that week, Rogers met yet another inspired young woman who cried out under the weight of her sins. He proceeded to address her directly, and in a "few minutes She received Power from God." Like so many of Ipswich's revival participants, "Her Mouth was fill'd with the Praises of the Lord." In these and dozens of other diary entries composed during his travels across New England, Rogers consistently associated the indwelling presence of the Holy Spirit with exercised bodies and impassioned speech. People who prayed or exhorted in the "H.G."—as Rogers increasingly referred to the practice—did so seemingly with little control over their newly sacralized bodies.[42]

Learning to discern the "hopeful symptoms" of converting grace proved to be an educational experience for many Whitefieldarians. When Nicholas Gilman encountered violently agitated bodies in his Durham, New Hampshire, parish for the first time in September 1741, his initial diagnosis drew on contemporary medical discourse. In one early case, Gilman presumed that a woman who experienced bodily distress during a religious meeting was merely suffering from "Hysterick fits." Following the revivals in nearby York and Portsmouth, however, Gilman began to describe similarly exercised parishioners as being "under great awakenings." The previous summer, Benjamin Throop had also struggled to interpret the "Strange and unusual Opperations" that gripped his parishioners in the Bozrah parish of Norwich, Connecticut. "Stired up" by the sermons of visiting itinerants, young people and long-standing church members alike began fainting, screaming, and "falling down as Dead." Throop struggled to make sense of the unusual "Distortions and Convultions," but his parishioners easily recognized what was happening to their family members and neighbors. Several people informed Throop that the distressed had been "Mightily Comforted (and as the Term Now is) have Received Light or have Seen Christ." Although the Bozrah clergyman remained cautious in his own assessments, his parishioners readily pronounced them "Converted and Renewed Persons."[43]

By the spring of 1742, New England's native itinerants had heard so much shrieking and seen so much trembling and tumbling that many ceased to marvel at the somatic manifestations of the indwelling Holy Spirit. Rogers, for one, began to note only the rare occasions on which his preaching elicited

42. Ibid., Jan. 2–3, Feb. 1–3, 1742.
43. Hall, diaries, Feb. 8, 1741; NGD, 222, 231; Benjamin Throop, "Secret Interviews," 1741–1784, [4], CHS.

"no great visible Effects." His former traveling companion, Eleazar Wheelock, described his most successful preaching performances in terse diary entries patched together from a narrow cluster of stock phrases followed by a tally of the converted: audience "affected," "many stood trembling," "A great outcry," "A great deal of affection and sobbing," "great distress," "many wounded." The novelty might have worn off, but the religious experience that underwrote such increasingly commonplace revival events remained unchanged. In an evocative first-person example of this phenomenon, Timothy Sparhawk of Medfield, Massachusetts, described how the "spirit came powerfully upon me" as he listened to one particularly moving sermon in 1741. "I could not stand before him," Sparhawk explained in his church admission testimony, "but fell down under a sense of my sinfulness and misery." As one critic quipped, riding ministers who "pretend to an Extreordy shair of the spiret" labored to make their audiences swoon, "which they say, is a Shrude sign of their Conversion!"[44]

I THINK I HAVE THE SPIRIT OF GOD

Across the street from Martha Robinson's house, Joseph Pitkin sat in a Boston tavern, puzzling over her somatic outbursts and meditating on God's providential motive in permitting Satan to conscript her speech. Robinson's wildly contradictory demeanor troubled him the most. Although she behaved like a demoniac, Robinson also was a precociously pious young woman who appeared to be struggling in the throes of the new birth. She had requested Pitkin's prayers and pious counsel; she was an avid disciple of George Whitefield and Gilbert Tennent; and she had joined the Old South Church six months earlier. Could this possessed woman also be one of God's elect? Reexamining her strange fits, Pitkin seized on an unusual interpretation. He decided that Robinson's tongue had been "Interchangeably Used by two Different Spirits." Her soul was both the residence of Satan and the "Habitation of Christ by the Indwelling of the Spirit." As he grappled with this seemingly contradictory conclusion, Pitkin could hardly have missed the portentous double meaning of his lodgings, a venerable Boston establishment known as the Sign of the Lamb.[45]

---

44. DDR, Mar. 5, 1742; EWD, 237–239; William Allen, "Memoir of Rev. Eleazar Wheelock, Founder and First President of Dartmouth College," *American Quarterly Register*, X (1837), 17; Appendix B, Medfield, Mass., First Church, 98; "Extracts from the Interleaved Almanacs of Nathan Bowen, 1742–1799," *EIHC*, XCI (1955), 164.

45. JPD, 61–62. On the Lamb Tavern, see D. Brenton Simons, *Boston Beheld: Antique Town and Country Views* (Lebanon, N.H., 2008), 62–63.

To discern the signs of "Both the Spirit of Christ and Satan," the Hartford magistrate needed to attune his ear to the specific expressions that issued from Robinson's mouth during their interviews. The Devil occasionally recited words from Job, commanding Robinson to "curse God and die." More often, he spoke in what Pitkin called a "Tongue of flesh." He mocked and hissed, shrieked and fumed. Like earlier demoniacs, Robinson spouted words unfit for a person of her gender and social station, as was the case when the Devil "with her Voice" commanded Pitkin to "Holld Your Tongue" during a prayer. In more lucid moments, Robinson attributed other, more mundane speech acts to the power of Satan. The various forms of profane language that poured from her possessed mouth included rollicking tavern songs and "Tea Table Talk," the dominant idioms of both New England youth culture and refined Boston society.[46]

In counterpoint to Satan's blasphemous vernacular utterances, Pitkin also heard the voice of the Holy Spirit speaking through Robinson by turns in a distinct language that consisted of a string of direct quotations from scripture. This crucial discovery came midway through their first interview. Returning to her senses following her initial demonic outburst, Robinson warned Pitkin that Satan was prepared to "Roar Louder Yet, But what is this to the Hearing of him Roar in Hell forever"? Suddenly, the conversation veered in a new direction, as the young woman praised God for her miraculous salvation. "Blessed be God who has Delivered my soul as A prey from his Teeth," Robinson exclaimed. A torrent of words followed. The Devil "now Rages Knowing he Hath but a short time," she professed to Pitkin,

> but I have need of all this, and when the Devil Speaks all that is Bad in me then he would fain Impute it to me as my Sin. I Can freely Justifie God in all this. Yea I Can freely Justifie him in my Damnation; we were all overun with pride here among us and I among the Rest, but God is Righteous; and I Cant Tell how I Could have Done without this. But Though he Slay me yet I will I Trust in him; if I perish I will perish at the [feet of Christ for] none ever perished there: here am I Lett him Do with me as Seemeth him Good.

Pitkin instantly recognized the rhythms of her seemingly incoherent speech. Years of diligent Bible study had trained him to see that the possessed young woman's exclamation was cobbled together from a half dozen scriptural passages—Psalm 124:6, Revelation 12:12, Job 13:15, 2 Samuel 15:26—

46. JPD, 57–59, 62.

interspersed with a few of her own words and a key phrase from the relation of faith genre.[47]

Even more telling was the interpretation that Pitkin offered for Robinson's abrupt transformation. The following day he and Timothy Dwight listened as the young woman parried the Devil's command to fall down and worship him with another verbal outburst that combined words from Matthew, Deuteronomy, and Isaiah. "By this time," Pitkin explained, "it appeared to my Sattisfaction that Christ had Gott the Possession of her Soul by his Holy Spirit and had Dethroned Satan." He had made an astonishing discovery. Two invading spirits had conscripted Robinson's tongue. Pitkin praised the wisdom of God in permitting Satan to "Shew openly what are his words and what his Language is, in Clear Distinction from what the Spirit and Word of God Speaks."[48]

Robinson's verbal outbursts resonated with the conversion experiences of many revival participants. One boisterous, Maine man maintained that he was "Obliged to go out" of the York meetinghouse because he was so full of the Holy Spirit that he was "ready to Burst" and "could not refrain from Speaking out." Bodies that had been infused by the Holy Ghost and exploded into prayers, exhortations, and songs might have looked disorderly, acknowledged another observer, but they were "constrained" to speak by the "Influence of the Spirit." "Some with whom I have discoursed," acknowledged Jonathan Edwards, "have said that the Spirit of God, as it were, forces them to utter themselves thus, as it were forces out such words from their mouths, when otherwise they should not dare to utter them." The clearest sign of the indwelling of the Spirit, as Pitkin learned through his interviews with Robinson, were the words that emerged from the mouths of newborn saints. On nearly every occasion, they were direct quotations from scripture.[49]

Solomon Prentice, the zealous minister of Grafton, Massachusetts, observed the confluence of exercised bodies and ejaculatory biblical outbursts in one of his parishioners. The young woman of fourteen had experienced the pangs of conviction during a pair of stirring sermons preached by Samuel

---

47. JPD, 58. Robinson's reference to perishing at the feet of Christ, although not found in scripture, was a conventional phrase that appeared with regularity in relations from parishes in eastern Massachusetts before 1740. See, for example, Appendix B, Haverhill, Mass., First Church, 73, 82, 84, 96, 103, 141, 208.

48. JPD, 58–59, 62.

49. Winiarski, "'Jornal of a Fue Days at York,'" *Maine History*, XLII (2004), 66; Ebenezer Parkman, commonplace book, 1721–1779, 88–89, Ebenezer Parkman Papers, 1718–1789, MHS; Jonathan Edwards, *Some Thoughts concerning the Present Revival of Religion in New-England* (Boston, 1742), in *WJE*, IV, *The Great Awakening*, ed. C. C. Goen (New Haven, Conn., 1972), 482–483.

Buell during his tour of central Massachusetts in March 1742, and she expressed fears of dropping into hell at any moment. While in this distressed frame, her body shook uncontrollably, and her cries of anguish, which were audible at great distances from her house, were "en'o to make the Ears of all that heard to tingle." Then, in a flash, her doleful cries suddenly dissolved into sobs of joy as the young woman exclaimed, *"O My dear Saviour is Coming, is Coming! Behold how He Comes leaping over the Mountains and Skipping on the Hills, like a Lamb that had been Slain!" "O My B'loved, My B'loved! See how beautyfull and glorious He is! Come Look on Him, and with me admire Him! for He is altogether Lovely, The Chiefe of ten Thousands!"* Much like Robinson's Spirit-possessed utterances, the flood of words was a combination of several biblical passages, including Isaiah 4:2; Revelation 5:6; and, most importantly, the Song of Solomon 2:8, 5:10, and 5:16. Prentice was careful to note this peculiar feature of her conversion in an unpublished revival narrative that he penned two years later. That the young convert "describes her Beloved like *the Spouse* in the *Canticles*" he concluded, proved that she had been visited by the Holy Spirit and released from the bonds of sin.[50]

Extraordinary encounters with scripture did not originate during New England's era of great awakenings. For more than a century, Reformed exegetes had attempted to unlock the textual power of the Bible in a variety of ways. Seventeenth-century preaching manuals encouraged puritan clergymen to efface their own persona to allow the Holy Spirit to open scriptural truths directly to their audiences. In the intensely literate culture of early New England, biblical verses sprang to mind inexplicably, structuring the thoughts and patterning the speech of pious men and women. At the same time, some lay people carried this tradition too far. Enterprising parishioners resorted to divining the future from verses selected from a Bible opened at random; and, on certain occasions, the book itself became a kind of magical talisman. The immediate revelations of the notorious antinomian Anne Hutchinson, too, were neither unmediated prophecies nor precursors to the Quakers' freewheeling inner light. Instead, her inspired speech took the form of a collage of exact scriptural quotations transformed into a scathing critique of the Boston clergy. This highly subversive form of popular biblical exegesis, with deep roots in the soteriological underground of seventeenth-century English radical sectarianism, might have prefigured the phenomenon that resurfaced in Whitefieldian conversion narratives a century later.[51]

50. Beales, ed., "Solomon Prentice's Narrative," MHS, *Procds.*, 3d Ser., LXXXIII (1971), 136.

51. Lisa M. Gordis, *Opening Scripture: Bible Reading and Interpretive Authority in Puri-*

Ministers throughout the Atlantic world moved quickly to discredit comforting biblical texts that purportedly darted into the minds of new converts during their darkest hours of distress. They called them "impulses" or "impressions." Both terms were rooted in an empiricist epistemology that assumed that words constituted an external force that penetrated the body or were stamped on the mind like other sensory phenomena. At the same time, the notion of being impulsive and impressionable had strong, negative connotations, even in the eighteenth century. Scores of books and pamphlets published between 1741 and 1744 condemned the controversial practice of conflating instantaneous conversion with unusually strong impressions on the imagination. Both ministerial conventions that met in 1743 to assess the state of New England's great awakenings listed *"secret Impulses upon their Minds, without due Regard to the written Word,"* at the top of their lists of errors attending the revival. A year earlier, the Hampshire County ministerial association in western Massachusetts had approved a similar testimony that denounced "Impulses or Impressions made upon the Mind, either with Text of Scripture brought to the Mind, or without, as tho' they were immediate Revelations of some Truth or Duty." The prominent Newark, New Jersey, clergyman, Aaron Burr, spoke for many of his colleagues when he ranked biblical impulses at the head of the catalog of revival errors that he sent to Joseph Bellamy during the spring of 1742. "Thro' this door," he complained, "many errors have crept into the Church."[52]

Presbyterians in Scotland and the Middle Colonies, southern Anglicans, and New England Congregationalists seldom agreed on anything, but clergymen from all three denominations stood united in their distaste for biblical impulses. A growing number of these revival opponents, including Hampshire County ministers Benjamin Doolittle and William Rand, downplayed or conveniently ignored the scriptural component of conversion narratives

---

tan *New England* (Chicago, 2003), 13–36; David Cressy, "Books as Totems in Seventeenth-Century England and New England," *Journal of Library History,* XXI (1986), 92–106; David D. Hall, *Worlds of Wonder, Days of Judgment: Popular Religious Belief in Early New England* (New York, 1989), 23–27; Michael G. Ditmore, "A Prophetess in Her Own Country: An Exegesis of Anne Hutchinson's 'Immediate Revelation,'" *WMQ,* LVII (2000), 349–392. I borrow the phrase "soteriological underground" from Michael P. Winship, *Making Heretics: Militant Protestantism and Free Grace in Massachusetts, 1636-1641* (Princeton, N.J., 2002), 26.

52. *The Testimony of the Pastors of the Churches in the Province of the Massachusetts-Bay in New-England . . .* (Boston, 1743), 6; *The Testimony and Advice of an Assembly of Pastors of Churches in New-England . . .* (Boston, 1743), 11; *A Copy of the Resolves of a Council of Churches Met at Northampton* (Boston, 1742), 2; Richard Webster, transcr., "Letters to Joseph Bellamy from Aaron Burr, David Brainerd, etc., and Other Papers concerning Mr. Bellamy," 1739-1787, 19, microfilm, Presbyterian Historical Society, Philadelphia.

that attributed the new birth to supernatural impulses and impressions. Both assumed that when their parishioners spoke of receiving light, they were referring only to phantasms that penetrated the imagination and deluded individuals into thinking that they had received divine commands. Others set impulses in direct contrast to the eminently rational authority of scripture. For Saybrook, Connecticut, clergyman William Hart, "no Impressions or Impulses upon mens minds are to be regarded as coming from the *Spirit* of God, which are Contrary to *Reason* and *sound Judgment,* and inconsistent with *any Truth* of the *Gospel.*" Charles Chauncy agreed, asserting that those who claimed to be the "special favourites of GOD" disregarded the dictates of reason and threw aside the authority of the Bible. They suffered from an exaggerated sense of self; and the mistaken, unassailable notion that "GOD himself speaks inwardly and immediately to their souls" and through "impulses of his SPIRIT" sanctioned unsound religious principles, fostered ecclesiastical and social disorder, and, more often than not, led to immoral behavior and even licentiousness. Such people, Chauncy concluded, were beyond rational persuasion. "You had as good reason with the wind."[53]

■ A rising chorus of lay men and women unreservedly embraced biblical impulses, in spite of their ministers' efforts to contain them from the press and the pulpit. For the Connecticut diarist Hannah Heaton, piercing scriptural texts not only triggered her conversion but dominated each of the many periods of spiritual renewal that followed during the next five decades. Although Heaton began recording her religious experiences in 1752, the astonishing detail with which she recalled the intrusion of specific biblical verses that "prest upon my mind," "toock hold of my heart," or "followed me and kept sounding in my mind" a decade earlier testifies to the degree to which ardent new converts were "swallowed up" in scriptures during the Whitefieldian revivals and conflated such miraculous events with the indwelling presence of the Holy Spirit.[54]

The eldest of ten children, Heaton was born in the small village of Mecox, near the tip of Long Island, in 1721. Her earliest childhood memories were

53. [William Rand], *The Late Religious Commotions in New-England Considered* (Boston, 1743), 13–14; Benjamin Doolittle, *An Enquiry into Enthusiasm* ... (Boston, 1743), 27–31; William Hart, *A Discourse concerning the Nature of Regeneration* ... (N[ew] London, Conn., 1742), 35–36; Charles Chauncy, *Enthusiasm Descried and Caution'd Against* ... (Boston, 1742), in Alan Heimert and Perry Miller, eds., *The Great Awakening: Documents Illustrating the Crisis and Its Consequences,* American Heritage (Indianapolis, Ind., 1967), 232–233. See also Ann Taves, *Fits, Trances, and Visions: Experiencing Religion and Explaining Experience from Wesley to James* (Princeton, N.J., 1999), 27–28.

54. Barbara E. Lacey, ed., *The World of Hannah Heaton: The Diary of an Eighteenth-Century New England Farm Woman* (DeKalb, Ill., 2003), 10, 15, 18, 26.

filled with terrifying images. She suffered through "frightful dreams of danger death and destruction" at the hands of marauding Indians and their French allies, and she worried that she would burn in hell if captured and forced to convert to Catholicism. Heaton's world pulsed with providential wonders. When the aurora borealis appeared in the night skies, she imagined the ribbons of light as "shapes of men in the air in arms moving after each other"; a blood red sunset triggered doleful thoughts of Christ coming to judgment. To combat her fears, Heaton turned to a battery of devotional practices, including secret prayer and constant Bible study. Like many of her youthful contemporaries, however, she also "felt hurred to go frollicking" and, too often it later seemed, capitulated to the voices in her head that told her to wait to close with the church until after she was married. Neither a narrow escape from drowning nor recurrent illnesses softened her hardened heart.[55]

Heaton's earliest retrospective diary entry presented the figure of an unusually scrupulous and melancholy eighteenth-century godly walker. She also claimed to have learned little about how to obtain an "intrest in christ" during her early years. "I dont remember that i ever heard a word in them days about conversion work," Heaton later recalled. During the fall of 1740, however, she moved to New Haven, Connecticut, just in time to witness the preaching of George Whitefield and Gilbert Tennent. Their sermons on the "marks of an unconverted person" were such as she had never heard before. Convinced that her "nature must be changed," Heaton nonetheless persisted in her youthful vanities. She continued to attend "frollicks" and yearned for "fine cloaths and fashons." Back on Long Island, several members of Heaton's family languished deep in conviction, and pious letters from her sister and father made a "strong impression" on her mind. After several months in Connecticut, she returned home, where her father examined her, and she was "forst to tell my experiences as wel as i could." The elder Heaton chastised his daughter for her lassitude, and his words "took hold of my heart."[56]

On June 20, 1741, Heaton attended a revival meeting in the Mecox schoolhouse. Members of the assembly had been perusing Joseph Alleine's classic *Alarm to Unconverted Sinners,* but Heaton remained impervious to the religious conversations of her friends and neighbors. She described herself as "stupid and hardned and shut up," unable to concentrate on religious matters. Crossing a field later that night, Heaton paused and began thinking despondently that she might as well indulge in some sweet strawberries, since "no

55. Ibid., 3–4.
56. Ibid., 4, 6–7.

matter what i do its a gone case with me." Turning around, she walked back to the schoolhouse only to discover that the power of God had descended on the assembly. At one end of the room, a multitude of men and women were crying out in distress. Suddenly, Heaton felt a "great melting" in her soul. She wept bitterly and begged for divine mercy. Fearing that a just God had sealed her damnation, she trembled violently, and her "knees smote together." "It seemd to me," she later noted, that "i was a sinking down into hell." Heaton felt the floor give way. Collapsing to the ground, she lay prostrate for several moments "like a creature dead." Time slowed to a crawl, and she heard a voice calling to her in the words of Matthew 11:28. Instantly, Heaton saw Jesus—a smiling, "lovely god man"—"stand up in heaven" and stretch out his embracing arms. Weeping openly, the awakened young convert arose and strode about the room exhorting people to come to Christ.[57]

Returning home, Heaton felt transformed and exuberant. The very "moon and stars seemd as if they praisd god with me," she later wrote. "It seemd as if i had a new soul and body." Unable to sleep, she paced around her room for hours. She felt compelled to recite the Lord's Prayer and believed that she could affirm every word for the first time in her life. Her mind was enveloped in the scriptures, and she envisioned herself as the salt of the earth in the classic words of Matthew 5:14, her very body a sacralized city on a hill.[58]

As was the case with many young converts, a period of black despair followed Heaton's initial conversion experience, and she began to question her newfound assurance of salvation. Satan tempted her relentlessly during these months. He terrorized her during private prayer vigils and challenged her to question the state of her soul. Perhaps the Devil's most devastating ploy involved biblical impulses themselves. Shortly after Heaton received a "vew of the condecention of christ" in the form of words from Psalm 24 that leaped into her head, Satan appeared and told her that "he could fill my soul and bring places of schripture to me." In those moments, Heaton lamented, the Bible became a "seald book to me." The possibility that Satan could counterfeit the actions of the Holy Spirit plunged her into prolonged periods of despair.[59]

At the same time, Heaton also experienced unusual moments of illumination that were always accompanied by darting biblical verses. After listening to sermons by several riding ministers, scriptural passages were "imprest upon my mind," and she "felt the power of gods spirit" pulsing through her body. In

57. Ibid., 8–9.
58. Ibid., 10.
59. Ibid., 17.

some cases, the Holy Spirit spoke through her as a form of prophecy, as was the case when she divined the deaths of a pious neighbor and a local minister on the basis of impulsive biblical texts. When, in a "dark frame of mind," she married an unconverted man, chastening words from Isaiah 8:21 came to her "like a clap of thunder." Struggling in labor with her first child, Heaton suddenly received a liberating passage from Job 5:19 that "come to me with power" and promised a speedy delivery. Although the midwife chided her for speaking with such seemingly blasphemous confidence, "soon after their fears and tears was done away for i was delivered." Ostracized for her radical beliefs by neighbors in New Haven's Northeast Society (now North Haven) to which she and her husband moved during the early 1740s, Heaton received words from Luke that were "spoke to me with great power." "Methot i knew jesus then prayed for me for i was with him and did behold his glory," she wrote "and his spirit was in me a comforter."[60]

"I think i have the spirit of god," Heaton proclaimed on one occasion, but how could she be sure? Heaton turned to traditional devotional practices to assuage her fears of eternal damnation and prepare her soul for divine grace. Like the godly walkers of an earlier generation, she studied her Bible, catechism, and devotional books; renewed her covenant with God; and sought the pious counsel of ministers, neighbors, and family members. Still, biblical impulses dominated Heaton's early religious life. Over and over again, Heaton trod the same rutted course. Fear and distress gave way to raptures of joy and peace immediately after comforting scriptural passages darted into her head. In moments of uncertainty, scriptural texts "heald" her tormented soul, allaying her doubts and propelling her into visionary raptures. For the rest of her life, Heaton charted these periods of darkness and light in her diary, always connecting "sweet revivals" of divine grace with impulsive biblical texts.[61]

Heaton's experiences were anything but unusual. The vision that presaged Nathan Cole's conversion during the fall of 1741 was also accompanied by a voice that spoke to him in an "angry and Sovereign way" in direct quotations from Romans 9:21. After witnessing his own body hanging in the air before a judging God, Cole heaved his diseased body across the room, holding onto chairs for balance, until he stood before the table on which his great family Bible rested. Opening it, his eyes alighted on the parable of the vine and branches in John 15. The words, Cole explained in his autobiography, "spake to my very heart and every doubt and scruple that rose in my heart about the

60. Ibid., 12, 20, 22–23.
61. Ibid., 12, 19, 24.

truth of Gods word was took right off." Cole saw the "whole train of Scriptures all in a Connection," and he "felt just as the Apostles felt the truth of the word when they writ it." Every "leaf life and letter smiled" in his face. Hugging the book to his chest, Cole could find no language to describe his experience except the rapturous words of the Song of Solomon 5:16, *"he was altogether—lovely."*[62]

Sarah Edwards experienced a similar epiphany during the Northampton revival in January 1742. With her husband itinerating in central Massachusetts, she was forced to entertain several visiting preachers, including Samuel Buell. One morning, while Enfield minister Peter Reynolds was praying with her family, several lines from Romans 7 "came into my mind" and "occasioned great sweetness and delight in my soul." Edwards retired to her chamber to meditate, and the words were "impressed on my heart with vastly greater power." She thought she could hear God speaking directly to her. Then, in an instant, all of her anxieties vanished, and she knew with absolute certainty that she would never again be separated from the love of God. "I cannot find language to express, how *certain* this appeared," she later wrote, "the everlasting mountains and hills were but shadows to it." Edwards burst into tears, crying out in the language of the Song of Solomon. Through it all, the phrase "My God, my all; my God, my all" thundered over and over again in her mind. For the next two weeks, she basked in the "joyful presence of the holy Spirit," drinking "heavenly elysium" and speaking in the "sweet and instinctive language of my soul."[63]

Most conversion narratives penned during or shortly after the revivals were punctuated by biblical texts that darted into the minds of convicted sinners in their darkest hours to dispel their distress. Awakening sermons by itinerants Whitefield, Tennent, Eleazar Wheelock, and Jonathan Edwards convinced Sarah Prince of Boston that her precocious youthful devotions were "only the Common Work of the spirit of God and My own Imagination." Prince never fully trusted in the authenticity of her religious experiences and remained "ruffled and dejected" for several years because she assumed that "there must be a word of Promise bore in on the soul at the time of Conversion." Finally, during the fall of 1743, a passage from Isaiah "Came to my Mind with a Sweet Power," assuring her that "my heavenly Father wou'd not forget me, for I cou'd rest upon his Word." Impulsive scriptures regularly intruded with "uncommon

62. NCS, 96. For a similar argument, see Taves, *Fits, Trances, and Visions*, 68–70.

63. Sue Lane McCulley and Dorothy Z. Baker, eds., *The Silent and Soft Communion: The Spiritual Narratives of Sarah Pierpont Edwards and Sarah Prince Gill* (Knoxville, Tenn., 2005), 2–3, 5, 8, 10.

power" on the meditations and diary musings of Sarah Osborn and Susanna Anthony, and they punctuated the correspondence of ardent new converts throughout New England. Judging by the prevalence of darting biblical passages in the later religious autobiographies of enslaved African Americans, the popular conception of the indwelling Holy Spirit as a disembodied voice speaking in direct quotations from the scriptures that took shape during the 1740s might also account for the eager reception of Whitefieldian revivalism among enslaved New Englanders. As one minister acknowledged in the *Christian History,* conversion "Discoveries" generally were preceded by "some *Texts of Scripture:* Or if they had no Text of Scripture as they remember at first, there immediately came many flowing in upon their Minds."[64]

Descriptions of the new birth such as these frequently dripped with eroticism. From John Wollaston's portrait depicting Whitefield's ravishing power over his fawning female auditors, to Martha Robinson's demonic desire to tear off Tennent's clothes, to Heaton's soul-melting vision of Jesus standing with "arms open ready to receive me," revival discourse pulsed with a passionate heat that struck some critics as nakedly lascivious. "My heart burnt with love to christ," Heaton explained. But critics, such as the Marblehead, Massachusetts, magistrate Nathan Bowen, scoffed at such overheated statements and described the new converts as being "Infatuated" by religious concerns. Many opposers presumed that protracted revival meetings naturally produced "Licenciousness in the people."[65]

The sexual metaphors that appeared with increasing frequency in Whitefieldian revival discourse pointed to deeper theological divisions. Seventeenth-century puritan divines regularly employed marital metaphors in their sermons to describe the attraction of the Holy Spirit for the souls of his saints, which they often characterized as feminine and insatiable. But most clergymen presumed that such a union would not be consummated until Christ's return

---

64. McCulley and Baker, eds., *Silent and Soft Communion,* 19–20, 22; Hopkins, ed., *Life and Character of Miss Susanna Anthony,* 25; Josiah Crocker, "An Account of the Late Revival of Religion at Taunton, Continued," *CH,* no. 95 (Dec. 22, 1744), 346. See also Samuel Hopkins, *Memoirs of the Life of Mrs. Sarah Osborn . . .* (Worcester, Mass., 1799), 44, 49–50. On the fascination with biblical impulses among enslaved African Americans, see Frank Lambert, "'I Saw the Book Talk': Slave Readings of the First Great Awakening," *Journal of Negro History,* LXXVII (1992), 185–198; for later examples, see Vincent Carretta, ed., *Unchained Voices: An Anthology of Black Authors in the English-Speaking World of the Eighteenth Century* (Lexington, Ky., 1996), 41–43, 113–114, 120, 124–125.

65. JPD, 57; Lacey, ed., *World of Hannah Heaton,* 9, 13; "Extracts from the Interleaved Almanacs of Nathan Bowen," *EIHC,* XCI, 164, 168. See also Juster, *Disorderly Women,* 62–68; and Richard Godbeer, *Sexual Revolution in Early America,* Gender Relations in the American Experience (Baltimore, 2002), 240–243.

FIGURE 14 John Wollaston, *George Whitefield*. Circa 1742. Oil on canvas, 82.9 cm × 66.0 cm. © National Portrait Gallery, London

and the inauguration of the millennium. In the preparatory language of many relations of faith drafted before 1740, prospective church members hoped to be worthy receivers of the "wedding Garment when the Bridegroom appears." The budding prominence of the Song of Solomon in the ecstatic utterances of young converts, however, signaled a very different kind of religious experience. Hannah Heaton, Nathan Cole, Sarah Edwards, and Solomon Prentice's adolescent converts all turned to the book's rapturous verses when describing their fleeting moments of inner illumination. In York, Maine, Jonathan Mayhew witnessed the strange spectacle of new converts crying out in the words of the poem's narrator: *"Comfort me with Apples, stay me with Flaggons for I am sick of Love. This is my beloved and this is my Friend, O ye Daughters of Jerusalem!"* Half of the relations composed for parishioners in Boston's Old South congregation during the 1740s contained allusions to the "altogether Lovely" Christ; and, over the next thirty years, references to the Song of Solomon supplanted all other biblical texts except Matthew 11:28 that were cited in the church admission testimonies of candidates in Middleborough, Massachusetts, a town that had experienced one of New England's most powerful revivals.[66]

The attraction of this sexually charged imagery from the Song of Solomon proved irresistible, in part, because lay men and women were convinced that the Spirit of Christ had actually taken possession of their once-sinful bodies during their conversion experiences. "THE COMFORTER IS COME!" declared Sarah Edwards, after crumpling to the floor during one of her raptures. Edwards's sister-in-law, the New Haven gentlewoman Sarah Pierpont, explicitly associated exercised bodies with both sexual and marital metaphors of the indwelling presence of the Holy Spirit in her description of a wedding that took place in eastern Connecticut in February 1743. Previously, the bride

66. Appendix B, Haverhill, Mass., First Church, 147; Lacey, ed., *World of Hannah Heaton*, 9; NCS, 96; McCulley and Baker, eds., *Silent and Soft Communion*, 2–3; Beales, ed., "Solomon Prentice's Narrative," MHS, *Procds.*, 3d Ser., LXXXIII (1971), 136; Ross W. Beales, Jr., ed., "'Our Hearts Are Traitors to Themselves': Jonathan Mayhew and the Great Awakening," *Bulletin of the CL*, 1st Ser., XXVII, no. 3 (Spring/Summer 1976), 6; Appendix B, Boston, Third (Old South) Church, 3–4 (quote); Douglas Leo Winiarski, "All Manner of Error and Delusion: Josiah Cotton and the Religious Transformation of Southeastern New England, 1700–1770" (Ph.D. diss., Indiana University, 2000), 410. On marital imagery in puritan sermons, see Edmund S. Morgan, *The Puritan Family: Religion and Domestic Relations in Seventeenth-Century New England*, rev. ed. (New York, 1966), 162–163; Michael P. Winship, "Behold the Bridegroom Cometh! Marital Imagery in Massachusetts Preaching, 1630–1730," *EAL*, XXVII (1992), 170–184; and Richard Godbeer, "'Love Raptures': Marital, Romantic, and Erotic Images of Jesus Christ in Puritan New England, 1670–1730," *NEQ*, LXVIII (1995), 355–384. On the "feminine" soul in seventeenth-century puritan theology, see Reis, *Damned Women*, 93–120.

had suffered through seasons of "Distress about her soul," and, on the day of the ceremony, as the minister prayed for the betrothed couple, she collapsed to the ground. On recovery, she joined hands with her "earthly Husband," whereupon the "blessed Jesus" instantly "broke in upon her soul," and she united with her "Spiritual and Eternal Husband." The confluence of marital union and religious conversion was not lost on Pierpont, who concluded that the "Lord Jesus Christ condescended not only to be a Guest (but oh astonishing) was Himself the Bridgroom and seizd the bride for himself."[67]

Biblical impulses also provided a coherent theological framework for the exercised bodies of many revival converts. Few people discussed their somatic experiences of the new birth in their church admission narratives, diaries, letters, or memoirs. Those who did believed that they were reenacting events described in the Bible. Plymouth, Massachusetts, magistrate Josiah Cotton complained that many of his overzealous neighbors quoted "Scriptures like the Quakers" to justify their bizarre behaviors. Some asserted that the piercing cries attending the new birth reflected the physical pain promised to Eve in childbirth in Genesis 3:16. Others defended noisy revival meetings by comparing them to the shouts that rang out during the construction of the temple in Jerusalem in Ezra 3:3. One ingenious person attempted to excuse his laughter during a boisterous revival meeting by citing Abraham's incredulous response to God's initial promise of progeny in Genesis 17:17. Collapsing sinners in York cried for rocks to cover them in accordance with the actions of the figures mentioned in Revelation 6:16, and Heaton claimed that her knees smote together during her conversion like those of Belshazzar, the condemned Babylonian monarch described in Daniel 5:6. Even the ubiquitous watchwords of the revivals—"What must I do to be saved?"—had been plucked from the mouth of the Philippian jailer in Acts 16:30.[68]

To Cotton, such glib proof-texting seemed simpleminded and selfish. Revival converts justified their behavior through a "Partial Searching of the Scriptures." They ignored "Scriptures that Seem contrary" to their experiences and misapplied texts to support their "unusual and extraordinary Proceedings." Accounts of these intrusive biblical texts smacked of Quakerism, so much so that Cotton included biblical impulses in a fifteen-point list in which he compared the "former Quakers and present Enthusiasts." The fundamental

---

67. McCulley and Baker, eds., *Silent and Soft Communion*, 14; Ebenezer Parkman, "Memoirs of Mrs Sarah Pierpont," n.d. [circa 1754], box 2, [75–76], Parkman Family Papers, 1707–1879, AAS.

68. JCH, 338–339; Winiarski, "'Jornal of a Fue Days at York,'" *Maine History*, XLII (2004), 63; Lacey, ed., *World of Hannah Heaton*, 9.

errors of both, he explained in a letter to Boston minister Samuel Mather, "Seem to be Hearkening to and Pursuing immediate Motions which they take to be from the Spirit, although not founded on the Scriptures." Discouraging good works and a holy conversation, young converts relied instead on fleeting "Impressions," "Impulses," and other *"Sensations"* of inner joy for evidence of divine favor. To make matters worse, many revival participants accepted the somatic fruits of these *"Feelings"*—bodily exercises such as "Swelling, Foming, Falling down, and Crying out"—as authentic marks of the indwelling presence of the Holy Spirit. In their abuse of scripture, "uncouth Gestures," and "Odd and Unguarded Expressions," Cotton concluded, they had imbibed the "Quintessence of Quakerism."[69]

In comparing Plymouth's young converts to seventeenth-century Quakers and their controversial doctrine of the inward light, Cotton condemned the growing penchant of some lay men and women to collapse distinctions between Christ, the Word, or Logos, and the Holy Spirit. His seemingly odd comparison contained a kernel of insight. Joseph Pitkin and others well-versed in Reformed theology continued to describe the "Spirit and Word of God" as separate entities. But ardent new converts, captivated by Whitefield's theology of the new birth, seized on a different understanding of the nature of scripture and its power to penetrate the souls and bodies of the saints. One outspoken woman framed her position succinctly in a debate with Maine clergyman Nicholas Loring. "The word of god" revealed in the scriptures, Jane Drinkwater asserted, was "equal to god in power and glory." She even claimed that the word "was God" and had the "same Power as God." Loring and his colleagues were shocked by Drinkwater's "strange Opinions," yet lay fascination with the indwelling presence of the Holy Spirit continually threatened to collapse the divine *pneuma* and *logos* into a single entity.[70]

■ The Whitefieldarians' fascination with identifying the indwelling Holy Spirit through a careful examination of exercised bodies and impulsive biblical verses culminated in Benjamin Lord's 1743 account of the miraculous healing of a young convert named Mercy Wheeler. Daughter of a prominent Massachusetts family, Wheeler had achieved notoriety shortly after her parents

69. JCH, 331, 335–336, 338.
70. JPD, 62; Nicholas Loring to Thomas Foxcroft, Mar. 18, 1747, Foxcroft to Loring, Apr. 17, 1747, Thomas Foxcroft Papers, 1690–1770, Mark and Llora Bortman Collection, HGARC. For early Quaker theological categories, see Stephen W. Angell, "God, Christ, and the Light," in Angell and Pink Dandelion, eds. *The Oxford Handbook of Quaker Studies* (New York, 2013), 158–161.

moved to the new settlement of Plainfield, Connecticut, more than a decade earlier. In 1726, she contracted the "burning Ague," a debilitating malady that left her blind, bedridden, paralyzed in her limbs, and unable to speak. Wheeler wasted away on a diet of "thin, liquid food." Local physicians attempted numerous cures, and ministers frequently gathered with her family to pray for her physical redemption, but to no avail. When in 1732 her condition unexpectedly improved, local clergyman Samuel Stearns solicited a brief account of her afflictions that he published for the benefit of the young people in Plainfield. Wheeler's address was part of a popular genre of provincial religious literature in which invalids, precociously pious youths, and condemned criminals offered *"Warning from the Dead"* for worldly adolescents to repent and reform. Her statement drew on the ideal of the godly walk and the generic conventions of church admission testimonies. Although Wheeler mobilized a number of biblical passages in her admonitions, she described no impulsive encounters with scripture. Instead, she cited and quoted texts in an attempt to rouse others to practice their piety with greater diligence—to "seek and serve God with perfect Hearts," as she put it—to accrue divine favor.[71]

Wheeler slowly improved during the next decade. She sat up in bed, her vision returned, and she even ventured outside for brief periods. But she also suffered from periodic complications, including fits of pleurisy and two bouts with the dangerous throat distemper. Wheeler eventually learned to hobble about with crutches, but the weakness of her severely atrophied ankles prevented her from standing or walking unaided. She struggled to live with her afflictions until Wednesday, May 25, 1743, when a group of ministers led by neighboring clergyman Hezekiah Lord of Preston, Connecticut, once again visited her home to preach and pray for her deliverance. Shortly after the lecture, Wheeler was overcome by violent tremors that spread over her entire body, but especially in her hips, knees, and ankles. To the astonishment of the assembly, she suddenly *"rose up* and *walked* away among the People, with evident Sprightliness and Vigour." For the first time in sixteen years, Mercy Wheeler could walk. "Verily, This is the Power of God!" proclaimed her excited neighbors and family members.[72]

This later account of Wheeler's healing appeared in a pamphlet authored

71. Samuel Stearns, *An Address to the Young People … Given by Mercy Wheeler* (Boston, 1733), ii–iii, v, 8. My argument here and in the paragraphs that follow builds on Thomas S. Kidd, "The Healing of Mercy Wheeler: Illness and Miracles among Early American Evangelicals," *WMQ*, LXIII (2006), 149–170.

72. Benjamin Lord, *God Glorified in His Works, of Providence and Grace* (Boston, 1743), 36–37.

by Lord's cousin, Benjamin, the prominent minister of Norwich, Connecticut. Whereas Stearns's earlier tract focused on Wheeler's declining health as a providential warning to sinful youths, Lord recast her story as a conversion narrative. Although he frankly acknowledged that Wheeler had "made little, or no Discovery of her Conversion" during the 1730s, Lord nonetheless proceeded to narrate her earlier experiences as a dramatic rebirth. Drawing on conversations with Wheeler and two short narratives that she had written in the wake of the Whitefieldian revivals, Lord recounted how God had used her original illness to "send *his Holy Spirit*" to convince her of her "miserable State." Wheeler described herself languishing through a period of deep concern for weeks before the initial restoration of her sight, alternately buffeted by the terrors of hell and comforted by scriptural passages that "took Hold of me." In October 1732, several months after she wrote her address to the young people of Plainfield, words from Matthew 11:28 unexpectedly came to her mind. "It now appeared *real,*" she recalled, "that Christ was calling and inviting me to come unto him." In retrospect, this "notable Experience" of the "Power of God upon her Heart," Lord concluded in 1743, was her moment of *"saving Conversion."* [73]

Biblical impulses played an even more critical role in Lord's account of the decade of physical ups and downs that followed. When Wheeler suffered through a dangerous diphtheria infection in 1740, words from Isaiah 41:10 "came to Mind" with "great Power and Consolation." During the days leading up to her miraculous healing, Lord continued, Wheeler had experienced both a "painful Sense of her Infirmities" and the "Power and Sweetness of God's Word." She received impulses from James 1:4, Revelation 2:10, and, especially John 11:40, "If thou wouldst believe, thou shouldest see the glory of God." Wheeler understood these darting biblical passages as more than mere words of comfort, for they provided "Direction and Promise to her Mind." The latter text was "brought home" to Wheeler with such a "powerful Impression" that she "had a strong Perswasion, that she should be healed." During the next several days, Wheeler meditated intensively on Jesus's miracles and imagined herself as part of an unfolding biblical drama. By the time that Hezekiah Lord and his colleagues arrived to preach at her home, Wheeler was in a state of anticipatory excitement.[74]

The Preston minister preached from Isaiah 57, and his words sank into Wheeler's heart "as if the Lord did indeed set it home by his Spirit." She col-

73. Ibid., 14, 21–25.
74. Ibid., 28–32.

lapsed onto the ground trembling uncontrollably. Her involuntary shaking subsided shortly after the meeting, whereupon Wheeler burst out in the words of the spouse in the Song of Solomon. She "cou'dn't help talking about her Healing," Lord reported in his published account, and she said that "Christ was *willing* to heal her." Almost immediately, Wheeler confronted Satan's vernacular voice tempting her to disbelief. But this "Cloud of great Darkness" was quickly dispelled by John 11:40. "Under the Influence of this Word," Lord continued, Wheeler seemed to be *"wholly taken out of herself, into the Hands of God."* As she stood and walked unaided across the room for the first time in sixteen years, biblical impulses, including Jeremiah 31:3, sustained and supported her. Lord closed his narrative with several examples in which Wheeler repelled the temptations of the Devil through a succession of refreshing words from scripture that arose in her mind. Wheeler had been delivered from her *"bodily Evils"* by the indwelling power of the Holy Spirit, which had assumed the form of intrusive biblical texts. Her restored body constituted a *"visible* Seat *of the divine Wonders."* Lord concluded that she had been subject both to an *"extraordinary Deliverance by Providence"* and *"converting and saving Grace."*[75]

For inspired lay men and women like Hannah Heaton, Mercy Wheeler, or Jane Drinkwater, Whitefield's doctrine of the indwelling Holy Spirit was no abstract theological principle, and the Bible was anything but a dead letter. When new converts such as Sarah Edwards described their conversions as a "constant flowing and reflowing of heavenly and divine love, from Christ's heart to mine," they envisioned a steady stream of biblical texts that dropped into their minds without warning or meditation. In the minds of lay Whitefieldarians, the Word literally was the Holy Spirit, especially when it intruded with supernatural force during sermons, devotional exercises, or daily activities. The Bible was more than a simple rule for godly walking; the Holy Spirit was more than an external comforter and sanctifier. In a world suffused with supernatural power, the God of the apostolic age was close at hand. Through darting scriptural texts, a Bible opened at random, or a piercing sermon, the Holy Spirit could penetrate the bodies of the faithful at any moment, conscripting their voices and constraining them to cry out in impassioned praise. And, on rare occasions, he carried the saints to heaven in dreams, trances, and visions.[76]

75. Ibid., vii–viii, 33–35.
76. McCulley and Baker, eds., *Silent and Soft Communion,* 8. See also Hall, *Worlds of Wonder,* 244.

HIS NAME WAS IN THE BOOK OF LIFE

Martha Robinson's fits constituted Boston's first case of alleged demonic possession in half a century. This fact was not lost on Samuel Phillips Savage. At about the time that Joseph Pitkin interviewed Robinson for the first time, the wealthy merchant and pious Brattle Street Church parishioner recorded an unusual story about a "Woman who is now alive here, but desires to be nameless, Concerning Some Visions she had when in a Trance" five decades earlier. In September 1693, as the storm of "Inchantments" plaguing Salem Village was winding down, Margaret Rule, a young parishioner in Cotton Mather's congregation, was violently assaulted by Satan and his "cruel Spectres." For more than five weeks, "Evil-Angels" pinched and stuck her with invisible pins, distorted her joints, poured invisible brimstone down her throat, and scorched her skin with unseen sulfur. On one occasion, the demons reportedly pulled Rule's broken body up to the ceiling in full view of a crowd of astonished onlookers. All the while, the Devil stood nearby, demanding that she mark her name with her own blood in his massive book.[77]

Rule had struggled with doubts for months before the onset of her diabolic afflictions, and she sought solace among a prayer group of devout women who met weekly in Mather's study. At a gathering held during one of the brief periods of calm that punctuated her fits, Rule fell into a trance and lay for hours in a "Senceless Frame" with her eyes fixed open. When she awoke, according to Savage's notes, Rule described a vision in which she saw a glorious angel in "Shining Apparel." She never glimpsed the face of this shimmering *"Spirit, in White and bright Raiment,"* but he stood beside Rule's bed throughout her ordeal with witches and devils, encouraging her to maintain her faith, assuring her of a speedy deliverance, and exhorting her to look on Mather as her spiritual father.[78]

The Salem witchcraft trials were punctuated by divine as well as demonic visitations. At the outset of the conflict, a visiting clergyman reported that one of the afflicted women of Salem Village had travelled with a man in glittering robes to a "glorious place, which had no candles nor sun, yet was full of light and brightness." Eerily similar testimonies regarding the appearance of heav-

---

77. "Savage Papers, 1703–1779," MHS, *Procds.*, XLIV (1910–1911), 685; George Lincoln Burr, ed., *Narratives of the Witchcraft Cases, 1648–1706*, Original Narratives of Early American History (New York, 1914), 310–311, 313.

78. "Savage Papers," MHS, *Procds.*, XLIV (1910–1911), 685; Worthington Chauncey Ford, ed., *Diary of Cotton Mather*, American Classics, 2 vols. (1911–1912, rpt., New York, 1957), I, 175.

enly beings figured in the examinations of other accused witches. Later in the fall of 1692, Mather encountered a woman from Salem who informed him that she had been "strangely visited with some *shining Spirits,* which were *good Angels,* in her opinion." Undoubtedly the most sensational of these reports involved another member of Mather's congregation, a Maine war refugee named Mercy Short whose possession symptoms prefigured those of Margaret Rule. Short frequently took up her Bible while suffering in her fits and, according to Mather, turned directly to comforting passages "without ever casting her Eye upon" the book. Asked to explain this marvel, Short asserted that she had been led by the "Impulse" of a "Wonderful Spirit" who told her "How to Answer the Temptacions of the Diabolical Spectres" and promised that "shee should at last bee Victorious over Them." In one dramatic instance, Short repelled her tormentors' demand to sign the Devil's book by turning to Revelation 13:8. The text that "Darted into her Mind" described the salvation of the saints whose names appeared in the *"Book of Life of the Lamb."* Short proclaimed that she had seen her own name written on its pages.[79]

For Samuel Phillips Savage, the remarkable events in Boston during the Salem witch hunt foreshadowed Martha Robinson's dual possession almost fifty years later. Witnesses had flocked to view the possessed bodies of the afflicted women, and admissions in Mather's Old North Church soared. Fifty-five people, mostly young adults, joined in full communion after visiting Short's "Haunted Chamber," with peaks coinciding directly with her deliverance in March 1693 and Rule's affliction six months later. In addition, the two possessed women were themselves "savingly brought home unto God" and covenanted the following winter. Scores of young people had been "awaken'd unto some acquaintance with Religion," Mather concluded at the end of his account of Rule's possession. Reframing the episode in 1742, Savage knew precisely what had happened. He called it "a great Revival of the Work of God."[80]

Within a year of her deliverance from the grip of Satanic forces, Rule married the first of her three husbands, and she soon faded into obscurity. She worshipped quietly in the Old North meetinghouse for decades, hoping that

79. David D. Hall, ed., *Witch-Hunting in Seventeenth-Century New England: A Documentary History, 1638–1693,* 2d ed. (Boston, 1999), 288; Ford, ed., *Diary of Cotton Mather,* I, 172, 175; Burr, ed., *Narratives of the Witchcraft Cases,* 275–276, 283–284. See also Bernard Rosenthal et al., eds., *Records of the Salem Witch-Hunt* (New York, 2009), 173. On the possession of Mercy Short, see Mary Beth Norton, *In the Devil's Snare: The Salem Witchcraft Crisis of 1692* (New York, 2002), 176–182.

80. Burr, ed., *Narratives of the Witchcraft Cases,* 276, 322; "Savage Papers," MHS, *Procds.,* XLIV (1910–1911), 685. For admissions to the Old North church in 1693, see Dunkle and Lainhart, transcrs., *Records of the Churches of Boston.*

her painful ordeal would be forgotten in a culture that had grown increasingly uncomfortable with wondrous tales of witchcraft, demonic possession, and heavenly visions. During the Whitefieldian awakenings of the 1740s, however, the experiences of young converts like Martha Robinson brought the elderly onetime demoniac unexpectedly back into the public eye. An avid consumer of revival intelligence, Savage placed Rule's story alongside news of events such as Jonathan Edwards's preaching in the Connecticut Valley and the great awakenings along the northern frontier. But he also puzzled over the steady stream of letters that he received from his business partners, many of which described young converts who were "full of raptures" and experienced visions of heaven and hell during their conversions. At first, the Boston merchant dismissed the reports as the rantings of those who were "Easily mov'd." In secret, however, Savage longed to "feel like them." Such was the seductive power of their remarkable dreams, trances, and visions.[81]

Beginning in the fall of 1741 and continuing for months thereafter, young converts encountered demons and angels, Satan and Jesus. Like Mercy Short, many of these visionists believed they saw their names inscribed in the Book of Life. The well-publicized vision outbreak proved to be a source of consternation even to revival advocates, since such phenomena emerged directly out of the new converts' fascination with bodily exercises, biblical impulses, and, above all, the indwelling presence of the Holy Spirit. To an emerging chorus of critics, however, their strange fits brought to mind the "worm wood and the Gall" of the Salem witch hunt. Those who claimed to have been "seiz'd with the *Spirit*" were instead suffering under the afflictions of a new kind of "Spiritual Witchcraft." "I know not," summarized Salem's Anglican minister Charles Brockwell, in a 1742 letter to his superiors in London, "but this year for Enthusiasm may be as memorable as was 1692 for witchcraft."[82]

■ In March 1742, Eleazar Wheelock received an unusual manuscript conversion narrative from a parishioner in the neighboring town of Hebron, Connecticut, where his good friend and fellow riding minister Benjamin Pomeroy served as minister. Scrawled in an unschooled hand by an anonymous author

---

81. Samuel Phillips Savage, meditation, n.d. [circa 1742], SSP II. For genealogical information on Margaret Rule, see *A Report of the Record Commissioners of the City of Boston, Containing the Boston Marriages from 1700 to 1751* (Boston, 1898), 1, 16, 349; H. Minot Pitman, "Descendants of John Snelling," *NEHGR*, CVIII (1954), 180–181; Dunkle and Lainhart, transcrs., *Records of the Churches of Boston*, s.v. "Marg* Rule" and "Marg* Snelling."

82. "Extracts from the Interleaved Almanacs of Nathan Bowen," *EIHC*, XCI (1955), 165; *Boston Weekly News-Letter*, Dec. 8, 1743; Perry, ed., *Historical Collections Relating to the American Colonial Church*, III, 353.

who, by his or her own reckoning had "never Learnt to right nor spell," the 746-word testimony described a celestial spirit journey during which the entranced author was carried to the gates of heaven on the wings of a giant dove and shown his or her name written in blood in the Book of Life by Jesus himself.[83]

Like most revival testimonies, the Wheelock vision manuscript began with Whitefieldian oratory. Dramatically affected by a rousing sermon by Pomeroy on Isaiah 40, the narrator's soul was "filld with ravishing transport." So great was this mystical revelry that there seemed to be "but a thin paper wall that seperated me from perfect Glory." Suddenly, the visionist fainted, only to awaken at the foot of a rugged mountain that blocked the path to the heavenly land of Canaan. A giant dove materialized and carried the narrator to a great plain at the summit of the mountain. There, the writer confronted a fierce wild bull. A guardian figure appeared in this moment of danger—a heavenly angel of inexpressible beauty—who escorted the author safely past the raging bull and up to the gates of heaven where Jesus and God sat enthroned in glory. Around them stood "angels bowing and paying ther homage and adoration to them." Speechless in the presence of divine majesty, the visionist desired only to shrink into nothingness.[84]

Looking down on the frightened pilgrim, Jesus then opened a large book and "shewed me my name reten in Letters of blood." With a smile, he commanded the narrator to return to the world, and he pledged to supply his penitent sinner with grace sufficient to "withstand all temptation you shall mete with." The angel and the giant dove once again returned the traveler to the foot of the mountain. At once, a horrid vista unfolded, as the author saw the "mouth of hell open and the damed souls wallowing in the flames shreaking and houling." Satan rose out of the fire, and "he told me he would have me." Stricken in terror as the Devil grinned and gnashed his teeth, the narrator heard a voice shouting words from Isaiah 41:10, "be not dismayed I am thy God." Buoyed by the booming biblical impulses, the author summoned the courage to renounce Satan. The Devil plunged back into the flames with his "Ghashly crew," and the visionist's senses returned: "I found my body all disorderd with the Cramp."[85]

Stunning in its luxuriant details, the Wheelock vision manuscript was not an isolated example. Dozens of other young converts in towns across New

83. Douglas L. Winiarski, "Souls Filled with Ravishing Transport: Heavenly Visions and the Radical Awakening in New England," *WMQ*, LXI (2004), 46.

84. Ibid., 44–45.

85. Ibid., 45.

England experienced similar raptures involving visions of the Book of Life. The earliest reports of such conversion "Transports" had filtered down to Boston during the York revival in the fall of 1741. In addition to the "hideous Cryings and Yellings" that attended revival meetings on the northern frontier, the preaching of local ministers propelled the bodies of the York congregants into convulsive spasms of alternating fear and joy. Terrified parishioners were "struck to the Ground in an Instant"—like Paul on the road to Damascus, according to one account—where they "remaind for some Time wholly speechless." On reviving, the York visionists spoke freely with the assembled spectators about their unusual experiences. While their bodies lay insensible on the ground, Satan violently tormented their souls. They spoke of "frightful Shapes" that closely mirrored the imagery of sermons such as *Sinners in the Hands of an Angry God.* In each case, the entranced young converts ascended to a celestial city, where they stood in awe before Jesus sitting on a throne and watched as he wrote their names in the Book of Life. So vivid were these beatific images that the York visionists described the physical characteristics of the book and even the details of Christ's hand and pen.[86]

The following summer, Jacob Eliot—Wheelock's colleague and minister to the neighboring Goshen parish in Lebanon, Connecticut—recorded in his diary that Noah Chappel and Mary Webster "were at Night both in a kind of Trance and so remained for near 2 Days and 2 Nights." According to Eliot, the children occasionally cried out in terror, and they later confessed to having "sev'e conflicts with the Devil." At other times, however, they were "calm and still, with their eyes open seeming as if they w'r writing or reading." Puzzled by the children's disturbing behavior, Eliot took note of some of their peculiarities. During the forty-eight hours in which they lay together on the same bed, Chappel and Webster each kept "one spot between 'em" as their own, and, if "but a hair" dropped into their space, they quickly snatched the object up, although both appeared to have been blinded. Eliot's colleague in Lebanon's first parish, Solomon Williams, testified that they "seemed very Busie, and engaged in Pointing, and making Motions and Marks with their Fingers upon a Blanket or Pillow."[87]

86. Winiarski, "'Jornal of a Fue Days at York,'" *Maine History,* XLII (2004), 73; Beales, ed., "Our Hearts Are Traitors to Themselves," *Bulletin of the CL,* 1st Ser., XXVII, no. 3 (Spring/Summer 1976), 5–6; *South Carolina Gazette,* Mar. 1, 1742.

87. E. H. Gillett, ed., "Diary of Rev. Jacob Eliot," *Historical Magazine and Notes and Queries, concerning the Antiquities, History, and Biography of America,* 2d Ser., V (1869), 33; Solomon Williams, *The More Excellent Way; or, The Ordinary, Renewing, and Sanctifying Graces of the Holy Spirit, More Excellent Than All Extraordinary Gifts That Can Be Coveted or Obtained by Men* ... (New London, Conn., 1742), i.

Separated and carried back to their respective homes after they came to their senses, Chappel and Webster related identical stories. They both "pretended to be going to heaven," Eliot stated in his diary. "The Lad," according to Williams, traveled a *"great Race in a Narrow Road"* while entranced. Satan had attempted to hinder his progress, but Jesus appeared to bolster the boy's resolve. Looking back down the road, Chappel spied Webster coming after him. As he looked forward to the horizon, he saw a great city. Once inside the walls of this celestial metropolis, Chappel again encountered Jesus. This time, the savior presented him with the Book of Life. When Webster arrived, she found the young boy busily reading in a tome that was "bigger than any Book they had ever seen in the World." On its pages were listed in "Golden Capitals" the names of numerous local saints as well as those of George Whitefield, Eleazar Wheelock, and Benjamin Pomeroy.[88]

During the Ipswich revival in January 1742, Daniel Rogers participated in a late-night prayer vigil for a young boy named William Holland, who lay insensible for several hours. When he awoke, the youth told the crowd gathered at his bedside that his *"Spirit* had been drawn out and carried up to Heaven where He had a View of Xt [Christ] in Glory sitting at the right Hand of God" encircled by angels and saints. The heavenly chorus included his deceased grandfather. Jesus informed Holland that the "Day of Judgement was comeing," prophesied that the boy would die within three months, and commanded the young oracle to declare all that he had seen and heard to the people in Ipswich. Holland's spirit then beheld a terrifying "View of Hell as a Place of dreadfull Darkness full of Divels" until a guardian angel exhorted him not to be afraid. According to Rogers, Holland's stunning message "Exceedingly mov'd the People" and elicited a "great Tumult" among the assembly.[89]

Two weeks later and fifty miles away, Ebenezer Parkman witnessed the "strange condition" of Isaiah Pratt. For more than twenty-four hours his young parishioner lay in a cataleptic trance, "his pulse *exceeding slow*," according to the Westborough, Massachusetts, clergyman. A local doctor's bloodletting and the constant prodding of concerned friends and family members gradually brought Pratt back to his senses. The revived youth informed the astonished onlookers that he had not been asleep. Rather, he had "seen hell, and seen Christ." During this celestial audience, Jesus "told him his name was in the book of life." Interviewing Pratt two days later, Parkman learned more about his experiences. The young convert

88. Gillett, ed., "Diary of Rev. Jacob Eliot," *Historical Magazine, and Notes and Queries,* 2d Ser., V (1869), 33; Williams, *More Excellent Way,* i–ii.
89. DDR, Feb. 1, 1742.

informed me of his seeing (as he thought) the devil, who met him as he seemed to be in the way towards heaven, and told him that there was no room for him there; of his seeing hell, and hearing the most dreadful noise of roaring and crying; his seeing heaven, so wondrously happy a place as nobody could tell but those that were there; and Christ, who looked more pleasant than ever he had seen any man, and who had a great book before him, and in turning over the leaves of it, told him that his name was there, and showed it him; and that he had seen a great many more things, which were such great things that he could not speak of them.

Although Parkman initially embraced his parishioner's fantastic report, he quickly reversed his opinion and cautioned Pratt that prophetic utterances were not to be trusted. One month later, he led the Westborough congregation in a day of fasting and ritual humiliation, praying that "we be not carried away by the many snares, temptations, and delusions to which we are greatly exposed."[90]

Nowhere did the popular fascination with dreams, trances, and visions reach greater heights than in Nicholas Gilman's parish in Durham, New Hampshire. After witnessing the revivals in York and Portsmouth and praying for an effusion of the Holy Spirit among his own flock, Gilman finally broke through. On January 31, 1742, as he watched his parishioners scramble quickly for the meetinghouse door in the middle of Sabbath exercises, the disgruntled pastor suddenly felt "movd to tell em that if I coud See them flocking to Heaven as they were from Meeting it woud Make My Heart leap within me." The chastened parishioners returned to their pews, and Gilman resumed his preaching. At one point, the Durham minister was "constrained to cry with a loud voice, Glory to God on high, Glory to the Redeemer." His labors were amply rewarded, as the meetinghouse soon thronged with supernatural visitors. Stephen Busse observed two angels and a white dove "come down into the Meeting House overhead which He stedfastly beheld till prayer was done." Young Hubbard Stevens was amazed to spy a light "like an exceeding bright star about as big as a Mans fist" descend from the meetinghouse turret and alight on one of the crossbeams. Anointed by the Holy Spirit, "we held on thro the Night, Blessing and Praising, admiring and adorning God and the Redeemer, Sometimes Praying, then Singing, Exhorting advising and directing,

---

90. Joseph Tracy, *The Great Awakening: A History of the Revival of Religion in the Time of Edwards and Whitefield* (1842; Edinburgh, 1976), 204–205.

and Rejoycing together in the Lord." "These are the Lords doings," Gilman noted triumphantly, "and truly marvelous in Mine Eyes."[91]

During the next six months, Gilman's parishioners "fell into Visions and Spake out" at a startling rate. In all, more than a half dozen members of the Durham congregation had their hearts in heaven and were "wrapt Up in Divine Praises." Like their counterparts in eastern Connecticut and central Massachusetts, most of the visionists received their revelations while languishing in cataleptic trances. Foremost among them was a young woman named Mary Reed, who "lay Some time to appearance Breathless but her pulse beating." "My Soul is in heaven," she later told Gilman, and she warned her minister not to be in haste to bury her the next time she was taken up in such raptures, even if they lasted a fortnight. Like Martha Robinson, Reed suffered through protracted conflicts with Satan and was beset with blasphemous temptations. Other local visionists reported seeing her in heaven singing with the angels and praising God. In addition to witnessing descending doves, angels, and preternatural lights, the Durham oracles listened to celestial voices, received curing recipes, and conveyed messages to Gilman from the spirit world commanding him to read or preach from specific scriptural texts.[92]

The Durham minister was one of a handful of Whitefieldarians who nurtured the visionary experiences of his young converts. He corresponded with local clergymen and addressed the theological implications of dreams and visions in his weekly sermons. He interviewed and counseled his zealous converts, transcribed their visions, read these narratives to the Durham congregation, and allowed the young oracles to address the Sabbath assemblies directly. So seriously did Gilman take their prognostications, he even called church meetings and changed his sermon texts when commanded to do so by entranced parishioners. Mary Reed and the other visionists were never stigmatized in Durham. Instead, Gilman admitted all of them to full church membership shortly after his ordination during the spring of 1742.[93]

By then, similar reports were pouring in from all quarters of New England. Returning to New Jersey from New Haven, a horrified Jonathan Dickinson discovered "strange Appearances" at Horseneck (now Greenwich), Connecticut, in which a number of people had fallen into fits and beheld "wonderful visions." Stonington minister Joseph Fish decried the purported raptures of several zealous parishioners who had fallen into visions during worship exer-

91. NGD, 241–243.
92. NGD, 255, 257–258. See also DDR, June 5, 1742.
93. NGD, 241–275.

cises and laid senseless on the meetinghouse floor for hours. Fish later recalled that they awoke claiming to have seen their neighbors—living and dead—ascending to heaven or descending to hell; and, worse, they treated the living persons "as they were seen in *vision*." Tutor Henry Flynt even confided in his diary that visions had broken out among his students at Harvard College. African and native Americans, too, might have been drawn to protracted revival meetings because somatic and visionary phenomena resonated with traditional forms of religious expression in their communities.[94]

Across New England, young men and women testified to the same phenomena—the cataleptic trance, the heavenly journey, the temptations of Satan, the father and son enthroned, and, most important, the image of the Book of Life opened to the names of God's elect. Their behavior was shocking, grumbled Charles Brockwell. "Their groans, cries, screams, and agonies" excited "both laughter and contempt" among spectators. "They tell you they saw the Joys of Heaven, can describe its situation, inhabitants, employments, and have seen their names entered into the Book of Life and can point out the writer, character and pen." Newspaper reports from places as diverse as New Haven and Mendon, Massachusetts, told nearly identical stories of young converts who lapsed into trances and were transported to heaven. When revived, they entertained fascinated onlookers with vivid descriptions of the glories of heaven and the names appearing in the Book of Life. The highly visible and patterned nature of their experiences might even have contributed to the emerging fascination with deathbed portraits—the earliest examples of which date to this period—in which the arrangement of the body of the deceased bore a striking resemblance to accounts of entranced visionists.[95]

Ecstatic religious transports involving angels, Satan, Christ, and the Book of Life were not without precedent, as accounts of the Salem witchcraft trials indicate. Otherworldly visions had deep roots in the history of Christianity, especially among medieval Catholic mystics and the radical Protestant sects that flourished during the English Civil War. But the sheer numbers, expan-

94. Jonathan Dickinson to Thomas Foxcroft, July 27, 1742, Thomas Foxcroft Correspondence, 1729–1759, Firestone Library, Princeton University, Princeton, N.J.; Joseph Fish, *The Church of Christ a Firm and Durable House* (New London, Conn., 1767), 139; Edward T. Dunn, ed., "The Diary of Tutor Henry Flynt of Harvard College, 1675–1760," 3 vols., typescript (Buffalo, N.Y., 1978), 1458. For dreams and visions among native and African Americans, see William D. Pierson, *Black Yankees: The Development of an Afro-American Subculture in Eighteenth-Century New England* (Amherst, Mass., 1988), 65–86; and Anne Marie Plane, *Dreams and the Invisible World in Colonial New England* (Philadelphia, 2014), 154–171.

95. Perry, ed., *Historical Collections Relating to the American Colonial Church*, III, 353; *Boston Weekly Post-Boy*, Mar. 1, 1742; *Boston Evening-Post*, Mar. 14, 1743.

FIGURE 15 Attributed to Joseph Badger, *Portrait of a Dead Child, Thought to Be Elizabeth Royall.* Circa 1740. Oil on canvas, 29 × 24.25 in. Image courtesy of the New England Historic Genealogical Society, Boston, *www.AmericanAncestors.org*

sive geographical scope, and unusually heterodox theological implications of the vision outbreak of 1742 dwarfed previous incidents in New England, especially when set against the backdrop of a broader transatlantic revival that included incidents in places as far-flung as Scotland and South Carolina. That Daniel Rogers initially struggled to classify "what is called a Trance" and Samuel Phillips Savage reached back to events that took place a half century earlier suggests that even the most ardent Whitefieldarians had never witnessed anything like it before. Ebenezer Parkman admitted as much, confiding in his diary that visions "are now (blessed be God) more frequent, which heretofore were very rare." Gilman, too, noted that visions were the "Main Subject of Conversation" at the height of the revival in his small New Hampshire parish. Brockwell and other Anglican critics portrayed the "uncouth dreams" as a veritable epidemic of enthusiasm in which "Vissionaries young and old abound and think themselves obliged to exhibit their gifts of praying and expounding to all that will attend them." By the spring of 1742, stories of visionary phenomena had become so prevalent in New England that diarist Heaton simply assumed that a "person must be in a sort of trance and be carried to heaven and see wonders there and then be brought back again" before their conversion would be complete.[96]

▪ Reports of entranced young converts seeing their names written in the Book of Life exerted a power that extended well beyond the small number of documented incidents. Concerned local pastors meditated on outbreaks of dreams, trances, and visions. They made notes in their diaries, exchanged letters with colleagues, consulted the wisdom of venerable Reformed theologians in their libraries, and presided over public rituals intended to counter the divisive outbursts of enthused parishioners. Newspapers broadcast local eruptions of religious enthusiasm to a transatlantic reading public, while dozens of pro- and antirevival books, broadsides, and pamphlets kept the issue continually in the public eye. Visions soon emerged as a crucial battleground in an increasingly fractious print war between revival opposers and apologists. Widespread debates over the authenticity of visionary enthusiasm testified to the burgeoning radicalism of New England's awakened young converts.[97]

Although a few revival critics blamed the outbreak of visions on the Devil, who was thought to be capable of assuming the form of an "Angel of light," a more common oppositional strategy involved discrediting the growing popu-

96. DDR, Feb. 1, 1742; "Savage Papers," MHS, *Procds.*, 3d Ser., XLIV (1910–1911), 685; Tracy, *Great Awakening*, 205; NGD, 262; Perry, ed., *Historical Collections Relating to the American Colonial Church*, III, 353, 355; Lacey, ed., *World of Hannah Heaton*, 8. For a similar argument, see Elizabeth Reis, "Otherworldly Visions: Angels, Devils, and Gender in Puritan New England," in Peter Marshall and Alexandra Walsham, eds., *Angels in the Early Modern World* (New York, 2006), 282–296. On the controversial role of visions during the Cambuslang, Scotland, and Charleston, South Carolina, revivals, see Harvey H. Jackson, "Hugh Bryan and the Evangelical Movement in Colonial South Carolina," *WMQ*, XLIII (1986), 594–614; Leigh Eric Schmidt, "'The Grand Prophet,' Hugh Bryan: Early Evangelicalism's Challenge to the Establishment and Slavery in the Colonial South," *South Carolina Historical Magazine*, LXXXVII (1986), 238–250; Ned Landsman, "Evangelists and Their Hearers: Popular Interpretation of Revivalist Preaching in Eighteenth-Century Scotland," *Journal of British Studies*, XXVIII (1989), 120–149; Schmidt, *Holy Fairs: Scotland and the Making of American Revivalism*, 2d ed. (Grand Rapids, Mich., 2001), 145–153; and Roark Atkinson, "Satan in the Pulpit: Popular Christianity during the Scottish Great Awakening, 1680–1750," *Journal of Social History*, XLVII (2013), 344–370.

97. For a bibliography of sermons and pamphlets published in New England between 1741 and 1744 that condemned dreams, trances, and visions, see Winiarski, "Souls Filled with Ravishing Transport," *WMQ*, LXI (2004), 21n.

larity of dreams, trances, and visions on naturalistic grounds. Joseph Sec-combe, minister of the interior farming village of Harvard, Massachusetts, attempted to establish a direct connection between visionary experiences and bodily infirmities. Drawing on a trio of French theorists including René Descartes, he argued that dreams and visions were merely the workings of the imagination, a "lower Power of human Nature." According to continental physiologists, the human body contained a vast network of nerves—"little hollow Strings," in Seccombe's words, with a "Liquid, like Whey or moist Air in them"—that carried data from the sense organs to the brain. When the mind was agitated by a dream or an affecting sermon, the nerves caused people to "see and hear such and such Things, and converse with these and those Persons, when we do not." Embracing new developments in natural philosophy, revival critics like Seccombe attempted to distinguish the learned opinions of the clergy from the superstitious delusions of their errant flocks.[98]

Other polemicists questioned the authenticity of the revivals themselves by publishing lurid reports of enthusiastic excesses. "I could fill many Pages with the Accounts I have had of the *Trances* Persons have been in, from different Parts of the Country," Charles Chauncy declared in *Seasonable Thoughts on the State of Religion*. The Boston clergyman spent the summer of 1742 touring towns in Connecticut that had recently witnessed eruptions of visionary enthusiasm and compiling evidence for his massive oppositional tract. The literary product of his three-hundred-mile circuit through New England was an equally rambling exposé that combined eyewitness reports of revival errors interspersed with theological commentary culled from the works of seventeenth-century puritan divines. Among the most noteworthy examples in Chauncy's collection of *"Raptures* and *Extasies"* was an excerpt from a letter penned by a Connecticut correspondent who detailed the bizarre behavior of two women who "fell into a *Trance* together" while walking down the street in New Haven. For nearly a week, Chauncy reported, they lay like "Persons dead or asleep," during which time they traveled to heaven and saw their seats sitting empty among the blessed saints. Set off by quotation marks and authorized by Chauncy's extensive interviews with "Ministers, *and many other Gentleman, in the Country,"* this single report transcended *"meer Hear-say"* and assumed a factual authority that, in his opinion, revealed a disturbing trend. *"Visions* now became common, and *Trances* also," Chauncy summa-

---

98. Joshua Coffin, *A Sketch of the History of Newbury, Newburyport, and West Newbury, from 1635 to 1845* (Boston, 1845), 213; [Joseph Seccombe], *Some Occasional Thoughts on the Influence of the Spirit ...* (Boston, 1742), 7–8. See also Taves, *Fits, Trances, and Visions*, 28–30.

rized in a published letter to a Scottish correspondent later that year, "the Subjects of which were in their own Conceit transported from Earth to Heaven, where they saw and heard most glorious Things; conversed with *Christ* and *holy Angels;* had opened to them the *Book of Life,* and were permitted to read the names of persons there."[99]

While Chauncy trumpeted the objectivity and authority of his informants, a witness to the New Haven incident who called himself "Anti-Enthusiasticus" followed a different tack in an antirevival polemic entitled *The Wonderful Narrative; or, A Faithful Account of the French Prophets.* The author's identity has been the subject of scholarly debate, but the events that precipitated the publication of his controversial pamphlet were stated clearly on its final pages. Like many revival critics, Anti-Enthusiasticus expressed grave reservations about the recent outbreak of "VISIONS, or Representations to the *bodily Sight,* of *Christ* and the Devil" and "TRANCES, wherein the Subjects of them have a clear and distinct View of *Heaven* and *Hell; of the Process of the last Judgment; of the Book of Life,* with the Names of particular Persons wrote there." Such unusual appearances, the author concluded were not signs of the work of the Holy Spirit but rather evidence that the purported visionists were "under the Power of a *disturbed Imagination.*"[100]

To prove his case, the anonymous pamphleteer provided a detailed history of the French Prophets, a community of Huguenot refugees in England whose female preachers, apocalyptic theology, ritual attempts to raise the dead, and well-publicized trances and visions had aroused the ire of London clergymen during the 1710s. Anti-Enthusiasticus was convinced that the French Prophets were "either *Impostors,* or under the *Power of Delusion,*" but tarring a notorious sect that had collapsed a generation earlier was not his primary goal. Instead, *The Wonderful Narrative* furnished a long roster of fraudulent visionaries appearing in "almost every Age, from the Days of *Moses*"to contemporary times. The author glossed two dozen well-known heretics and radicals, including the early Christian mystics Simon Magus and Montanus, Mohammad, medieval Catholic saints, the militant Protestant prophets at Münster, and English sectarians and seekers ranging from *"Dooms-Day* SEDGWICK" to Anne Hutchinson and George Fox. Anti-Enthusiasticus concluded that the

99. Charles Chauncy, *Seasonable Thoughts on the State of Religion in New-England* ... (Boston, 1743), xxix, 127–128; [Chauncy], *A Letter from a Gentleman in Boston to Mr. George Wishart* ... (Edinburgh, 1742), in David S. Lovejoy, ed., *Religious Enthusiasm and the Great Awakening,* American Historical Sources: Research and Interpretation (Englewood Cliffs, N.J., 1969), 75–76. See also *Boston Weekly Post-Boy,* Mar. 1, 1742.

100. *The Wonderful Narrative; or, A Faithful Account of the French Prophets* (Boston, 1742), 97, 108.

young converts in New Haven, with their trances and visions of the Book of Life, were cut from the same cloth as all deluded zealots in Christian history. His message was clear: "Thus it has been with all *Visionaries*." Chauncy, who likely pushed *The Wonderful Narrative* through the Boston press, praised Anti-Enthusiasticus for speaking plainly on the dangers of visionary enthusiasm. "*Passion* seems to take the place too much in the room of reason," he quipped to a kinsman in Connecticut in a letter praising the pamphlet. "I fear in a multitude of cases an *overheated imagination* is taken for the influence of the *divine spirit*."[101]

Other clergyman dismissed hyperbolic reports of visionary enthusiasm, while promoting the revivals as an authentic outpouring of the Holy Spirit. Thomas Prince's printed directions had a sanitizing effect on the content of the narratives that appeared in the *Christian History*. His son's magazine included more than two dozen testimonies from faithful shepherds who claimed to have shielded their flocks from revival errors. "As to Trances and Visions," asserted John Porter, the fervent pastor of the north parish of Bridgewater (now Brockton), Massachusetts, "we have none, and I think have had none from the Beginning." John Cotton, a colleague of neighboring Halifax, also maintained that his parish had been free from trances and visions, although he admitted that "there was *one* or *two* that was something Visionary." Revival narratives penned by clergymen from Scotland to the Middle Colonies all conformed to a common script. Emphasizing the surge in conversions and the benefits of moral reformation, ministers throughout the Atlantic world labored to construct an image of the great awakenings shorn of all evidence of enthusiastic excess.[102]

Perhaps the best example of this more moderate position on dreams and visions may be found on the pages of Wheelock's vision manuscript itself. Shortly after he received the anonymous narrative, the Lebanon Crank minister began emending the text, perhaps with the hope of preparing a more suitable version for publication. In addition to correcting spelling and diction, Wheelock strategically worked to soften the literalism of the testimony, en-

---

101. *Wonderful Narrative*, 6, 59, 78, 103; "Original Letters of Dr. Charles Chauncy," *NEHGR*, X (1856), 333. On the authorship of *The Wonderful Narrative*, see Edwin S. Gaustad, "Charles Chauncy and the Great Awakening: A Survey and Bibliography," *Papers of the Bibliographical Society of America*, XLV (1951), 126–128.

102. John Porter, "The Rev. Mr. Porter's Account of the Revival of Religion at Bridgewater Finished," *CH*, no. 51 (Feb. 18, 1744), 407; John Cotton, "The Account of the Late Revival of Religion at Halifax in the County of Plymouth Finished," *CH*, no. 34 (Oct. 22, 1743), 267. For a similar argument and additional examples, see Timothy E. W. Gloege, "The Trouble with *Christian History*: Thomas Prince's Great Awakening," *Church History*, LXXXII (2013), 153.

casing it instead in the metaphorical language of a Bunyanesque meditation. Mountains that were steep and high in the original narrative only "seamd" that way in Wheelock's interlineated manuscript. Vivid descriptions of doves and angels became "inexpressible" under the clergyman's editorial hand. The author claimed to have gazed directly on heaven, but Wheelock tempered the narrative so that the anonymous visionist only "Supposd" this to be the case. Where the narrator reveled in the presence of divine majesty during a "ravishing transport" to heaven, Wheelock questioned the reality of the spirit journey altogether. As revised, the author sought only to "See More of the Glorious attributes of the incomprehensible God." Behind these alterations lay Wheelock's assumption that the visionist had not actually seen heaven, giant doves, Christ, or the Book of Life. Rather, these images merely had unfolded in the mind's eye during an unusually vivid meditation.[103]

A few earnest new converts paid close attention to the cautionary words of their ministers. During the peak months of the revivals, Joseph Bean's rapturous meditations verged on the visionary. Closing his store one night in the fall of 1741, the Cambridge shopkeeper set aside an hour for "Prayer and meditation and God was Pleased Verry graciously for to assest me." Elevated to a "heavenly frame," Bean's soul took flight, and he viewed "those Blessed mantions of Eternity." Elsewhere in the diary, Bean recounted startling meditations in which he confronted visions of the "immaculate lamb of God hanging upon the Cursed tree and with his arms widly Extended," sinners wallowing in the flames of hell, and even his own corpse being carried to the grave by a funeral throng. For a brief moment during a midday meditation in the spring of 1742, Bean saw a vision of heavenly bliss, with "God and Christ at his right hand and the burning throne with millions of shining angels in posters [postures] of adoration," and he longed to "Joyn in Consort with the hole assembly." And on several occasions, Bean even read his "name in the records of heaven the lams book of life." But, in each instance, Bean was careful to note that these were not out-of-body experiences. His raptures had been induced by his own devotional practices, not by supernatural transport, and he saw through the "Eye of fath," not his "bodily Eys." Endorsed by Protestant ministers on both sides of the Atlantic, this important distinction kept Bean's vivid meditations from spilling over into the kinds of enthusiastic revelries reported by Spirit-possessed new converts.[104]

Although Bean recognized his own role in stimulating visions of the Book of

103. Winiarski, "Souls Filled with Ravishing Transport," *WMQ*, LXI (2004), 44nn.

104. Bean, diary, 65, 79, 88, 171, 182. On the "eye of faith" in transatlantic revival discourse, see Schmidt, *Holy Fairs*, 148–149.

Life during private devotional exercises, other witnesses eagerly asserted that "Trances and Transports" issued directly from the "opperation of the Spiret of God!" Indeed, the visions experienced by impressionable young people replicated the vivid sermon imagery that characterized the revivals. For months before the first reported spirit journeys, itinerant preachers had thundered on the torments of hell and the glories of heaven. Primed by the Whitefieldarians to think of conversion as an embodied experience, many lay people welcomed the reports of dreams, trances, and visions. Ecclesiastical authorities confronted unusually stiff resistance to scientific and theological arguments that were designed to corral outbreaks of visionary enthusiasm. According to Yale College president Thomas Clap, students "exceedingly Condemned" a published pamphlet in which Solomon Williams criticized the heavenly visions of Noah Chappel and Mary Webster; and one of Jacob Eliot's parishioners upbraided him for refusing to pray with the entranced children in his parish. In central Massachusetts, Sudbury minister Israel Loring denounced "visions and Revelations" in a sermon preached less than a month after Isaiah Pratt of neighboring Westborough testified to seeing his name written in the Book of Life. Loring labored to convince his parishioners that alleged celestial encounters were "Vain and Imaginary" delusions, and "'Twas Justly to be feared that Some of them Were Diabolical." Most of his congregation, the Sudbury minister lamented glumly in his diary, were dissatisfied with his performance.[105]

The same markers that heralded the indwelling presence of the Holy Ghost among revival converts—exercised bodies and biblical impulses—also figured prominently in narrative accounts of dreams, trances, and visions. The anonymous author of the Wheelock vision manuscript heard a disembodied voice shouting words from Isaiah 41:10 that banished Satan and his "Ghashly crew." Anglican minister Ebenezer Punderson observed an entranced visionist in Norwich, Connecticut, who had been overcome with what he called a "Dumb Spirit." The man remained in a senseless condition for nearly a week, except for uttering a few blasphemous expressions, including the words attributed to Jesus in Matthew 28:10 and Mark 10:14. Verses from Luke ran in Mary Reed's mind all day before her first cataleptic trance in March 1742, and her subsequent raptures included revelations instructing Nicholas Gilman to read and preach from specific texts of scripture. Reed declared that these texts had been

---

105. "Extracts from the Interleaved Almanacs of Nathan Bowen," *EIHC*, XCI (1955), 169; Stephen Nissenbaum, ed., *The Great Awakening at Yale College*, American History Research (Belmont, Calif., 1972), 170; Gillett, ed., "Diary of Rev. Jacob Eliot," *Historical Magazine, and Notes and Queries*, 2d Ser., V (1869), 34; Thomas, transcr., "Journal of the Rev. Israel Loring," no. 12192, 51–52, SA.

sent to the Durham minister by the "Spirit of Christ." For his part, Gilman believed that her entranced scriptural "whispers" bespoke the "Language of a Soul actually in Heaven."[106]

The plot of these celestial journeys was heavily mediated by biblical tropes and imagery. References to names written in blood might have been borrowed from traditional Anglo-American witch-lore, but vivid descriptions of celestial cities and the Devil gnashing his teeth emerged straight from the pages of the King James Bible. The giant dove appearing in the Wheelock vision manuscript, especially, had direct textual roots. Doubtless the anonymous Connecticut visionist would have been familiar with synoptic accounts of Jesus's baptism in the Jordan River in which the Holy Spirit descended from the heavens in the form of a dove. Celestial avians appeared in reports from central Connecticut to the northern frontier. One of the Durham visionists spied a white dove enter the meetinghouse along with bright lights and angelic figures. Daniel Rogers recognized the parallel during a 1743 visit to his brother's parish in Kittery, Maine, where three men claimed to have seen a "Bird much larger than a Dove White as Snow, hovering at one of the upper Windows" of the meetinghouse. Rogers interpreted the strange event as a harbinger of the Holy Ghost, and he prayed in his diary that the Spirit might "descend from Time to Time upon the minsters and congregation in that House."[107]

Most important, the climax of each account—the traveler's audience with "God the father and God the son seated on a throne of Glory"—approximated Revelation 20. John's apocalypse described an angel that would descend from the heavens and chain Satan in a bottomless pit for a thousand years. Several verses later, the biblical narrator stood before a great white throne and watched as the Book of Life was opened, the resurrected dead were judged "according to their works," and the unregenerate were "cast into the lake of fire." For many young converts, the events described in Revelation appeared so real, so immediately accessible, that it seemed as if they could step right into the pages of the Bible.[108]

Aided by special illuminations of the indwelling Holy Spirit, visionists fervently believed that they were living in the last days, and they eagerly anticipated the appearance of the Son of Man descending from the clouds and

---

106. Winiarski, "Souls Filled with Ravishing Transport," *WMQ*, LXI (2004), 45; Kenneth Walter Cameron, ed., *The Church of England in Pre-Revolutionary Connecticut: New Documents and Letters concerning the Loyalist Clergy and the Plight of Their Surviving Church* (Hartford, Conn., 1976), 59; NGD, 257–258 (see also 264–265, 279, 300–301).

107. Winiarski, "Souls Filled with Ravishing Transport," *WMQ*, LXI (2004), 44; NGD, 243; DDR, Apr. 19, 1743.

108. Winiarski, "Souls Filled with Ravishing Transport," *WMQ*, LXI (2004), 44.

throwing open the Book of Life for all to see. Jesus informed Goshen's Mary Webster that the *"Day of Judgment was very near."* Noah Chappel concurred, asserting that he had seen only a single blank leaf, and, when that page was filled, the Day of Judgment would quickly follow. Echoing these apocalyptic pronouncements, an entranced youth from Mendon cautioned her neighbors that the "Book wanted but two Inches to be fill'd up" and that its author would appear in judgment over the earth in a short time. The Durham oracle, Mary Reed, voiced similar warnings. These were astonishing claims, for the young visionists' suggestion that God continued to inscribe the names of the faithful in the Book of Life and that he would do so until its pages were filled directly contravened New England's predestinarian orthodoxy.[109]

Revelatory experiences unleashed by Whitefield's innovative doctrine of the Holy Spirit threatened to propel radicals beyond the bounds of the Reformed theological tradition altogether. Visionists believed that they were separated from "perfect Glory" by only a "thin paper wall," and a few willingly tore down even this minimal barricade and proclaimed that they were "without Sin." One of them was a long-standing Ipswich church member named Lydia Halliday. Rogers discoursed with her just two days before he recorded the visionary ec- stasies of her young neighbor, William Holland, and he was horrified to dis- cover that she was "under a great Mistake as to Xtian [Christian] perfection in this Life." She cried out during worship exercises, declaring that the Spirit of Christ had already entered her body and that it "would never Come in any other manner." To Rogers, Halliday seemed out of her mind during her rap- tures. Behind her boisterous disruptions in the Ipswich meetinghouse, how- ever, stood her brazen confidence that the indwelling presence of the Holy Spirit had transformed her body into something "above All Saints and Angels." Halliday was among the first of many revival converts who passed through the new birth and on to an exalted state of sinless perfection. Try as he might, over the next several years Rogers failed to convince the zealous Ipswich goodwife of her "dangerous Errors." Halliday remained "fully Satisfied" of the truth of what Rogers derisively called her "false Light" and "Quakerish Delusions."[110]

Previous generations of godly walkers had plodded along a pilgrim's path, never certain of their own salvation, but radicals like Lydia Halliday, the Dur- ham oracles, and the author of the Wheelock vision manuscript discovered a shortcut to what a contemporary newspaper critic called an "infallible Assur- ance." The notion that entranced young men and women could peer into the

---

109. Williams, *More Excellent Way,* ii; *Boston Evening-Post,* Mar. 14, 1743; NGD, 264.

110. Winiarski, "Souls Filled with Ravishing Transport," *WMQ,* LXI (2004), 44; DDR, Jan. 29, Feb. 7, Mar. 14, 27, 1742.

Book of Life and read the names of God's elect rendered obsolete the classic morphology of conversion. As one revival observer candidly remarked, the "old Stingy puritan Doctrines" were "much out of Fashion with the most in these Days." Inspired by the miraculous operations of the indwelling Holy Spirit, young visionists discovered that they lived in a latter-day Pentecost, and they imagined themselves as direct participants in an unfolding cosmic drama that was rapidly drawing to its apocalyptic close.[111]

IF THIS BEE DELUSION LETT MEE HAVE MORE OF IT

As he stepped out of the Sign of the Lamb, mounted his horse, and set off for home, Joseph Pitkin paused to consider the significance of his conversations with Martha Robinson. The unusual events of the previous days, he later recalled, "filld up my Meditation" most of the way back to Hartford. He pitied Robinson for her afflictions and praised his own special role in her deliverance from the bondage of sin. In fact, Pitkin appears to have experienced a visionary epiphany of his own while on the road. As he pondered the unusual circumstances that had brought him to Robinson's home, he imagined Jesus speaking directly to him. "You whom I have Used and Treated from Your Birth with A Peculiar Care" as "my Special friend and favourite," the words that sounded in Pitkin's mind began, "I have now Brot You Safe here in A Dificult Season and have Cary'd You Through Your own Business according to Your Hearts Desire." He had witnessed powerful revival events and "Mett with Soul Reviveing Cordials in this Town." Now Jesus needed his help in letting a "poor opressed soul Know how faithfull and Good I have Been to You." The voice enjoined Pitkin to battle against the "Ruler of the Darkness of this World" and pledged that God would give him courage to assist Robinson in her struggles with Satan. Pitkin emerged from his riding reveries certain of his own salvation and confirmed in the knowledge that his conferences with Robinson issued from an immediate command handed down to him from on high.[112]

The notion that Jesus required a Connecticut civil magistrate to "Step in to the Help of the Lord Against the Mighty Adversary of Souls" undoubtedly would have struck most of his contemporaries as presumptuous. Nonetheless, hyperbolic statements of this nature seemed eminently plausible during the heady early months of New England's great awakenings. Ministers and

---

111. *Boston Weekly Post-Boy*, Sept. 28, 1741; Samuel Cooke to Thomas Foxcroft, May 15, 1745, Thomas Foxcroft Correspondence, 1714–1759, CHS.

112. JPD, 61–62.

lay people threw rhetorical caution to the wind and likened the revivals to events described in Revelation or the Acts of the Apostles. A few days after Jonathan Edwards preached *Sinners in the Hands of an Angry God*, for example, Eleazar Wheelock proclaimed that "people Everywhere throng together to hear the Word And I do Verily beleive these are the begining of the Glorious things that are Spoken Concerning the City of our God in the Latter Day." "It Seams that God is about to viset America in a Most Glorious manner," concurred the anonymous author of "A Jornal of a Fue Days at York" several months later. William Parker beheld "Marvellous things" in Portsmouth, New Hampshire, that were "without Parallel," excepting only biblical descriptions of the Day of Pentecost. "Our exalted Saviour has been riding forth in his Magnificence and Glory thro' divers Parts of our Land, in so triumphant a Manner," Thomas Prince announced in a published letter to George Whitefield, "as has never been seen or heard among us, or among any other People as we know of, since the Apostles Days." "It is the opinion of many eminent divines," Prince's daughter wrote to relatives in London, "that it is the dawning of that glorious day, when the whole earth shall be filled with the knowledge of the Lord as the waters cover the sea."[113]

As the millennial promise of the awakenings gave way to increasingly boisterous and disruptive revival meetings and as churches swelled with young converts who justified their experiences of the indwelling Holy Spirit on the basis of bodily distress, darting biblical texts, or visions of the Book of Life, most New England clergymen retreated from their initial assessments. An increasingly vocal chorus of ministerial opposers began condemning revival errors in scores of published sermons and pamphlets. Nearly 750 people from more than 125 towns across New England, including three royal governors, 146 Congregational ministers, and dozens of notable merchants, magistrates, and militia officers, subscribed to *Seasonable Thoughts on the State of Religion in New-England*, Charles Chauncy's ponderous antidote to the "Great disorders and irregularities" that the outspoken Boston revival opposer believed were flourishing everywhere. Connecticut enacted a law banning the practice of itinerant preaching. Ministerial associations passed denunciations. The public prints turned sour. And once-zealous Whitefieldarian riding ministers abandoned their preaching tours and other new revival measures. "The

113. JPD, 62; Wheelock to the Lebanon North Parish Church, n.d. [July 11, 1741], no. 743900.1, *EWP;* Winiarski, "'Jornal of a Fue Days at York,'" *Maine History*, XLII (2004), 72; Parker to Waldron, Nov. 20, 1741, Miscellaneous Bound Manuscripts Collection; Julius Herbert Tuttle, "The Glasgow-Weekly-History, 1743," MHS, *Procds.*, LIII (1919–1920), 204; Benjamin B. Wisner, *The History of the Old South Church in Boston …* (Boston, 1830), 111.

great awakening," Hartford minister Daniel Wadsworth predicted in September 1741, "seems to be degenerating into Strife and faction."[114]

■ It is not clear whether Joseph Pitkin shared the narrative of his encounters with Satan and the Holy Spirit in Boston after returning home to the Connecticut Valley, but news of Martha Robinson's dual possession undoubtedly reached the ears of Jonathan Edwards sometime during the spring of 1741. After all, she had railed against the alleged conversions in Edwards's parish in a demonic outburst directed against one of his closest friends and parishioners: Pitkin's traveling companion, Timothy Dwight. Boston taverner Josiah Sheldon might also have informed Edwards about the remarkable events in the Robinson household shortly after he sold the Sign of the Lamb and moved back to Northampton later that fall.[115]

Edwards's early reflections on the flourishing state of religion in New England suggest that he might have welcomed the news of another brand plucked from the burning. His sense of expectation during the six months following George Whitefield's 1740 preaching tour was almost palpable. Even as Pitkin sat down to interview Robinson, Edwards wrote excitedly to Benjamin Colman praising God for news of the revivals at Boston, Charlestown, and Cambridge. He trumpeted "God's Spirit wonderfully breaking forth" in towns along the Connecticut River, and he praised the work of his fellow riding ministers Eleazar Wheelock and Benjamin Pomeroy, whose itinerant labors had been "remarkably blessed." In his sermons and theological notebooks, Edwards anticipated the dawning of the "glorious state of the church" on earth. The miraculous work of the Holy Spirit seemed "so extraordinary, so much beside the settled course of things within the memory of all living, and in many things diverse from all that ever was heard." "If any in New England, ten years ago, had foretold such a change," Edwards mused, "it would have been perhaps as difficult to believe it, as to believe the great events foretold to

114. Chauncy, *Seasonable Thoughts on the State of Religion*, 1–18; "Original Letters of Dr. Charles Chauncy," *NEHGR*, X (1856), 333 (quote); George Leon Walker, ed., *Diary of Daniel Wadsworth, 1737–1747, Seventh Pastor of the First Church of Christ in Hartford, with Notes by the Fourteenth Pastor* ... (Hartford, Conn., 1894), 71. For a detailed analysis of the emerging "antirevival" faction in New England, see Frank Lambert, *Inventing the "Great Awakening"* (Princeton, N.J., 1999), 185–221. See also Edwin Scott Gaustad, *The Great Awakening in New England* (New York, 1957), 61–79; and Thomas S. Kidd, *The Great Awakening: The Roots of Evangelical Christianity in Colonial America* (New Haven, Conn., 2007), 156–161. For changes in newspaper reporting, see Lisa Smith, *The First Great Awakening in Colonial American Newspapers: A Shifting Story* (Lanham, Md., 2012), 25–37.

115. *A Report of the Record Commissioners of the City of Boston, Containing the Records of the Boston Selectmen, 1736 to 1742* (Boston, 1886), 320.

accompany the end of the world." He resumed the intensive studies of Revelation that he had begun during the 1730s. Rumors even surfaced that Edwards had pronounced the millennium already underway in Northampton. As he explained to Wheelock just days before his trip to Suffield and Enfield in July 1741, they were living in an "extraordinary day of God's gracious visitation."[116]

Edwards struck a more cautious tone in the letter that he sent to a former parishioner less than two months after his celebrated performance of *Sinners in the Hands of an Angry God*. For the first time, the Northampton revivalist admitted that the recent "great stir that is in the land" contained "mixtures of natural affection, and sometimes of temptation, and some imprudences and irregularities." Edwards vented even deeper misgivings ten days later in his Yale College commencement address on *The Distinguishing Marks of the Work of the Spirit of God*. To colleagues such as William Cooper of Boston, who wrote the preface to the published version of Edwards's sermon, the "dispensation of grace we are now under" was so unusual that he believed there had "not been the like since the extraordinary pouring out of the Spirit immediately after our Lord's ascension." But the return of the signs and wonders of the apostolic age gave Edwards pause. In the discourse that followed, he worked to disentangle authentic evidence of the Holy Spirit's indwelling presence from delusive enthusiasm. In his cautionary lecture at Yale, Edwards positioned his growing reservations regarding the New England revivals within an overarching framework that stressed the mixed results of divine dispensations in all eras of Christian history.[117]

Exercised bodies and piercing outcries figured prominently among what Edwards called the negative signs of the Holy Spirit's operation. Although he had worked aggressively to promote bodily distress in the towns of the upper Connecticut Valley earlier that summer, Edwards reversed his position in his Yale address and stated only that he had observed such phenomena at a distance. The work of the Holy Spirit was not to be judged by its somatic effects, he told the assembled scholars. The Bible provided no clear evidence that excessive emotionalism, loud verbal outbursts, or any other bodily agitations

116. Jonathan Edwards to Benjamin Colman, Mar. 9, 1741, in *WJE*, XVI, *Letters and Personal Writings*, ed. Claghorn, 88, Edwards to Eleazar Wheelock, June 9, 1741, 90; Edwards, "Importunate Prayer for Millennial Glory," in *WJE*, XXII, *Sermons and Discourses, 1739–1742*, ed. Harry S. Stout and Nathan O. Hatch, with Kyle P. Farley (New Haven, Conn., 2003), 369; Edwards, Miscellany 903, in *WJE*, XX, *"Miscellanies" (Entry Nos. 833–1152)*, ed. Pauw, 160; Chauncy, *Seasonable Thoughts on the State of Religion*, 372.

117. Jonathan Edwards to Moses Lyman, Aug. 31, 1741, in *WJE*, XVI, *Letters and Personal Writings*, ed. Claghorn, 97; William Cooper, preface to Edwards, *The Distinguishing Marks of a Work of the Spirit of God* (Boston, 1741), in *WJE*, IV, *Great Awakening*, ed. C. C. Goen (New Haven, Conn., 1972), 217.

were marks of the indwelling Holy Spirit. In a veiled allusion to the sermon that he had delivered only a few weeks earlier in Enfield, Edwards admitted that convicted sinners who imagined themselves in the "hand of God" and "hanging over a great pit" might crumple to the ground in fear, but the frailties of human nature easily accounted for such phenomena. Many notable biblical figures had endured physical distress—Edwards cited many of the key examples that appeared with regularity in conversion narratives, from the bride in the Song of Solomon to the Philippian jailor—yet the cause of their exercised bodies remained obscure. The same argument obtained for what Edwards called the "great ado" and noise that attended revival meetings. All were imperfect signs of the Spirit's presence that neither confirmed nor invalidated the experiences of purported young converts.[118]

Biblical impulses were even more suspect. In his travels, Edwards had encountered many "true friends of the work of God's Spirit" who nonetheless "erred in giving too much heed to impulses and strong impressions on their minds, as though they were immediate significations from heaven." They were misled in their "great divine discoveries," despite receiving many biblical "texts following one another, extraordinarily and wonderfully brought to the mind, and with great power and majesty." Darting verses from the scriptures had proven "more mischievous to the present and glorious work of God" than any other "erroneous principle." He went so far as to label biblical impulses as the one error that "will defend and support all errors." New converts who believed that their actions were "guided by immediate direction from heaven," Edwards ominously observed in *Some Thoughts concerning the Present Revival of Religion in New-England*, would inevitably become "incorrigible and impregnable" in their speech and actions. He dismissed the widespread belief among many revival participants that the Holy Spirit constrained the faithful to speak and exhort. And, in one 1743 sermon series, he characterized ministers who supported these disruptive new revival measures as "false prophets" and "ravening wolves" bent on devouring "true Christians." Edwards even criticized George Whitefield for adhering too much to biblical impulses during his visit to Northampton in 1740. All such pretended communications from the Holy Spirit, he concluded, were as "vain and empty as the wind."[119]

118. Edwards, *Distinguishing Marks of a Work of the Spirit of God*, in *WJE*, IV, *Great Awakening*, ed. Goen, 231–232, 235.

119. Ibid., 278, Edwards, *Some Thoughts concerning the Present Revival of Religion*, 432–433; Ava Chamberlain, "Brides of Christ and Signs of Grace: Edwards's Sermon Series on the Parable of the Wise and Foolish Virgins," in Stephen J. Stein, ed., *Jonathan Edwards's Writings: Text, Context, Interpretation* (Bloomington, Ind., 1996), 13; Edwards, *Copies of Two Letters Cited by the Reverend Mr. Clap* [Boston, 1745], in *WJE*, XVI, *Letters and Personal*

Edwards continued to sharpen his critique during the years that followed. Some people, he argued in his 1746 *Treatise concerning Religious Affections*, "suppose that they are expressly taught by some Scripture coming to their minds, that they in particular are beloved of God, or that their sins are forgiven, that God is their Father, and the like." Edwards well knew that the first comfort of many revival participants, or "what they call their conversion," frequently involved darting biblical texts. He had always maintained that a gracious understanding of God's word required a special "spiritual sense" that issued from the inner illumination of the Holy Spirit, but scriptures delivered by impression were of a wholly different stamp. The texts that leapt, dropped, ran, and thundered in the minds of young converts were external ideas, Edwards asserted, mere "sounds or letters" that Satan could paint in the minds of the credulous as easily as one "put ink upon paper." Too often the Devil's artful illusions deluded earnest seekers into overvaluing the "mystical meaning of the Scripture." Its parables, types, and allegories became a kind of oracle for actions that lay men and women mistakenly attributed to the will of God. Biblical impulses, in short, were "heat without light." To conflate their presence with the voice of God, Edwards concluded, was a "wretched delusion" as well as a "false and sandy foundation for faith."[120]

Dreams, trances, and visions assumed an increasingly sinister cast in Edwards's rapidly evolving revival theology. He had witnessed his parishioners in a "kind of ecstasy" in which they were "wrapped up even to heaven, and there saw glorious sights." But visionary enthusiasm, he explained in 1741 to the students at Yale College, was seldom an authentic sign of the work of the Holy Spirit. After Samuel Buell catapulted his Northampton congregation into enthusiasm and error, Edwards struggled to keep his congregants from "running wild." He later published an edited account of his wife's "high and extraordinary transports" but carefully excised all references to visionary phenomena. By the time he composed his *Treatise concerning Religious Affections*, Edwards

---

Writings, ed. Claghorn, 157; Edwards, Miscellany 1058, in *WJE*, XX, *"Miscellanies" (Entry Nos. 833–1152)*, ed. Pauw, 395. See also Edwards, "Keeping the Presence of God," in *WJE*, XXII, *Sermons and Discourses, 1739–1742*, ed. Stout and Hatch, 519–535. For Edwards's occasionally awkward relationship with Whitefield, see Ava Chamberlain, "The Grand Sower of the Seed: Jonathan Edwards's Critique of George Whitefield," *NEQ*, LXX (1997), 368–385; and Kenneth P. Minkema, "Whitefield, Jonathan Edwards, and Revival," in Geordan Hammond and David Ceri Jones, eds., *George Whitefield: Life, Context, and Legacy* (London, 2016), 115–131.

120. Jonathan Edwards, *A Treatise concerning Religious Affections* (Boston, 1746), in *WJE*, II, *Religious Affections*, ed. John E. Smith (New Haven, Conn., 1959), 217, 219–221, 223, 266, 268, 278. See also Stephen J. Stein, "The Quest for the Spiritual Sense: The Biblical Hermeneutics of Jonathan Edwards," *Harvard Theological Review*, LXX (1977), 99–113.

had come to identify "false discoveries and elevations"—entranced encounters with the Book of Life in particular—as clear evidence of a dangerous religious pride that had infected the churches of New England. "Those that have had visions and impulses about other things," he argued, "it has generally been to reveal such things as they are desirous and fond of." To countenance the desperate desires of those who sought to know whether their sins were forgiven or their "names are written in the Book of Life" would only stoke the fires of what he increasingly referred to in his writings as "evangelical hypocrisy."[121]

The unifying thread that bound together Edwards's increasingly vituperative assaults on purported manifestations of the Holy Spirit was his insistence—common among eighteenth-century ministers in New England—that miracles had ceased at the close of the apostolic age and that the biblical canon was closed. An early formulation of this theological position appeared in Edwards's trinitarian meditations early in the 1740s. Halfway through his manuscript "Treatise on Grace," the Northampton clergyman refined his original distinction between common and saving grace, complicating the binarism by adding two additional phrases: "gifts of the Spirit" and "grace of the Spirit." The former included all forms of biblical charismata described in the Acts of the Apostles and 1 Corinthians: healing, casting out demons, working miracles, prophecy, discerning spirits, and speaking in tongues. These, seemingly God-given gifts belonged to saints and sinners alike. Performed by Adam, Noah, Abraham, Moses, and Jesus's disciples, but also by notable biblical apostates including Balaam and Judas, they were, by definition, unrelated to the indwelling presence of the Holy Spirit. Extraordinary gifts, he explained in a 1748 sermon, arose in ancient times, when the church was "imperfectly furnished with the means of grace," to establish the Christian religion among nonbelievers. The close of the apostolic age, the completion of the scriptural canon, and the maturation of the church obviated the need for additional miracles and new revelations.[122]

---

121. Edwards, *Distinguishing Marks of a Work of the Spirit of God,* in *WJE,* IV, *Great Awakening,* ed. Goen, 237, *Some Thoughts concerning the Present Revival of Religion,* 331; Edwards to Thomas Prince, Dec. 12, 1743, in *WJE,* XVI, *Letters and Personal Writings,* ed. Claghorn, 121; Edwards, *Treatise concerning Religious Affections,* in *WJE,* II, *Religious Affections,* ed. Smith, 173, 318–319. On Edwards's emerging conservatism during the mid-1740s, see also Julie Ellison, "The Sociology of 'Holy Indifference': Sarah Edwards' Narrative," *American Literature,* LVI (1984), 479–495; Winiarski, "Souls Filled with Ravishing Transport," *WMQ,* LXI (2004), 29; Ava Chamberlain, "Self-Deception as a Theological Problem in Jonathan Edwards's 'Treatise concerning Religious Affections,'" *Church History,* LXIII (1994), 541–556; and Sandra M. Gustafson, *Eloquence is Power: Oratory and Performance in Early America* (Chapel Hill, N.C., 2000), 67–74.

122. Edwards, "Treatise on Grace," in *WJE,* XXI, *Writings on the Trinity, Grace, and Faith,*

Edwards returned to this theological distinction on numerous occasions during the 1740s. Because the Bible was a complete and perfect rule of faith and practice, he argued, people claiming to possess special knowledge of their individual election or future events on the basis of their "bright experiences" grossly abused scripture by making it "speak what it does not speak." This was especially true of those who claimed to have experienced visions of Jesus, angels, or "names in the book of life." Edwards also cataloged more mundane examples in which new converts who doubted of their salvation, soldiers who desired foreknowledge of their expeditions, or parents who worried over sick children mistakenly deployed biblical impulses as an oracle. "They say the Word of God is their rule," he maintained, but instead advanced "immediate revelations" that wrested the Bible off its original foundation. "The Apostle shows us a more excellent way," he concluded. "Such gifts as these are not to be desired on their own account: in themselves they are worthless." By the late 1740s, Edwards had grown emphatic on this issue. "No more gifts implying immediate revelations are to be expected" in contemporary times.[123]

Edwards's revival treatises, sermons, theological notebooks, exegetical writings, and personal correspondence demonstrate not only a creeping conservatism regarding the marks and signs of the indwelling Spirit but also a mounting distaste for what he called revival errors. Awakening events that once appeared to herald the dawning of a new age now struck him as an "extraordinary religious commotion." In a crescendo of increasingly bitter letters to Scottish colleagues, the Northampton clergyman regretted the "great decay of the work of God amongst us." His earlier millennial speculations turned to dark thoughts of impending apocalyptic warfare with false prophets who imitated the "great and wonderful works of God's Holy Spirit" through "counterfeit illuminations," "false affections," and "enthusiasm." He filled his "Images of Divine Things" notebook, especially, with meditations on themes of violence, corruption, instability, disorder, and, above all, failure. Types of revival errors included showy flower blossoms that "drop off and come to nothing," gold ore mixed with impure dross, wandering planets, swarming insects, devouring

---

ed. Sang Hyun Lee, 168; Edwards, "Extraordinary Gifts of the Spirit Are Inferior to Graces of the Spirit," in *WJE*, XXV, *Sermons and Discourses, 1743–1758*, ed. Wilson H. Kimnach (New Haven, Conn., 2006), 284. On the long history of debates involving miracles and continuing revelation, see Robert Bruce Mullin, *Miracles and the Modern Religious Imagination* (New Haven, Conn., 1996); and David F. Holland, *Sacred Borders: Continuing Revelation and Canonical Restraint in Early America*, Religion in America (New York, 2011), esp. 58–65, for Edwards's place within this theological tradition.

123. Edwards, "Extraordinary Gifts," in *WJE*, XXV, *Sermons and Discourses, 1743–1758*, ed. Kimnach, 301, 304–306, 308, 311.

beasts, and setting suns. In a telling admission, Edwards conflated several of these examples with "tall Christians" brought low by their pride, and he likened "young converts" to children in need of correction or bitter fruit that might never ripen.[124]

Many of Edwards's contemporaries puzzled over the changing tenor of the awakening, especially as seemingly bizarre reports of dreams, trances, and visions exploded across the country during the winter of 1742. As early as December 1740, Hartford minister Daniel Wadsworth read Whitefield's autobiography and wondered "what is it"? Ebenezer Turell, the minister of Medford, Massachusetts, cast the controversy in the form of a published dialogue in which he attempted to persuade his parishioners of the dangers of enthusiasm. *"What is the Work of GOD?"* the fictional neighbor inquired of his minister at the outset of Turell's debate. Although he had invited Daniel Rogers to preach to his congregants during the fall of 1741, Theophilus Pickering, minister in the Chebacco parish of Ipswich, soon turned on his itinerating neighbor in an open letter. "I am at a loss to understand that Distinction that you make betwixt the *ordinary* or *usual* Work of GOD in the Conversion of Sinners," Pickering complained, "and *that* Work wherein you are engaged which you emphatically call *This Work—This Work of God.*"[125]

Between the summer of 1741 and spring of 1742, ministers and magistrates across New England closed ranks and attempted to reassert control over their Spirit-possessed congregations. In some cases, the turnabout was almost instantaneous. The North Hartford ministerial association initially endorsed the practice of convening frequent weekday lectures but changed course only a few weeks after Edwards set out on his preaching tour of Suffield and Enfield in July 1741. After witnessing the outbursts of religious radicalism that ensued, the association met in August to debate a series of questions relating to "Sundry things attending this work which are unscriptural and of a dangerous Tendency." In an abrupt reversal, the assembled ministers, which included Edwards's aged father, Timothy, condemned itinerant preaching as a practice that was "destructive to the peace of the churches." Later that fall,

124. Jonathan Edwards to James Robe, May 12, 1743, in *WJE*, XVI, *Letters and Personal Writings*, ed. Claghorn, 108, Edwards to William McCulloch, Sept. 23, 1747, 239; Edwards, "Notes on the Apocalypse," in *WJE*, V, *Apocalyptic Writings*, ed. Stephen J. Stein (New Haven, Conn., 1977), 218; Edwards, "Images of Divine Things," in *WJE*, XI, *Typological Writings*, ed. Wallace E. Anderson and Mason I. Lowance, Jr., with David H. Watters (New Haven, Conn., 1993), 105, 108, 115.

125. Walker, ed., *Diary of Rev. Daniel Wadsworth*, 58; E[benezer] Turell, *Mr. Turell's Dialogue between a Minister and His Neighbour about the Times* (Boston, 1742), 4; Theophilus Pickering, *The Rev. Mr. Pickering's Letters to the Rev. N. Rogers and Mr. D. Rogers of Ipswich* ... (Boston, 1742), 2.

they expanded the range of "Scandalous" revival measures to include private lectures and traveling unusual distances on the Sabbath to "hear a Converted minister." The most ominous of the provisions stated that "no weight" would be given to the outcries, bodily convulsions, and, especially, visional discoveries of heaven and hell that frequently attended the "terrifying Language of Some preachers." The resolutions reflected the Connecticut ministers' desire to "maintain peace and unity among themselves and in the churches."[126]

Other ministerial associations whose members had once endorsed the revivals produced similar testimonies. In May 1742, Edwards and the Hampshire County association in western Massachusetts met to discuss "What may be Proper to Promote the Interest of Religion and Good Order in our Churches." Although they agreed that "there has been a very glorious and extraordinary Work of the Spirit of God, and revival of Religion of late in *New-England*," the members lamented the emergence of errors that had "cast a Blemish and Reproach upon it." In eastern Connecticut, the Windham County association drafted a resolution in which they condemned the "Disorder and Confusion" that had erupted as a result of the "Practice of Itinerant Preaching." They urged their colleagues, including notable Whitefieldarians Eleazar Wheelock and Benjamin Pomeroy, to be "Cautious in Giving their Opinions or Judgments concerning the Conversion of Particular Persons." A statement signed later in the year by nearly two dozen Connecticut clergymen went a step further, singling out "what Some call Trances, Visions, immediate Revelations and extraordinary Impressions or Impulses on their Mind" as especially dangerous errors. "Speciall Impressions of the Divine Spirit" were absolutely necessary for salvation, of course, but the ministers feared that "Instances of Irregularity and misconduct" too often stood in the room of "reall Godliness."[127]

Although a few radicals, including Samuel Buell, Andrew Croswell, and Daniel Rogers, continued to itinerate after the summer of 1742, nearly all of New England's most active riding ministers curtailed their travels in direct response to their colleagues' increasingly hostile assessment of revival innovations. Edwards appears to have left off itinerating before most of his contemporaries. Turning his pastoral attentions homeward, he proceeded to lead the Northampton congregation in that most conservative of godly walking rituals:

126. Hartford North Association, Records, 1708–1800, I, 28–29, Connecticut Conference Archives, United Church of Christ (currently on deposit at CL; available online at NEHH).

127. Hampshire Association, Records, 1731–1747, Forbes Library, Northampton, Mass., 38; *Copy of the Resolves of a Council of Churches Met at Northampton*, 2; Jacob Eliot to Joseph Meacham and Eleazar Wheelock, Aug. 25, 1741, no. 741475, *EWP*, Samuel Cooke et al., "We the Suscribers," n.d. [circa 1742], no. 742900.2.

public covenant renewal. When Wheelock returned from a contentious tour of southern Connecticut, he, too, began to question whether it was possible to distinguish the elect from hypocrites. He even hinted in an April 1742 letter to Joseph Bellamy that revival techniques—including "beating down" weak Christians with caustic sermons on the sandy foundations of faith—had actually hindered the work of the Holy Spirit. For his part, Bellamy later wrote about his decision to abandon the practice of itinerating as if awakening from a stupor. "Is it possible," he questioned, "that the Holy Ghost so regards me, as in connection with my words and voice, to bring up a crowded congregation to their feet, or prostrate them on the floor, with wailing or joy inexpressible? I have seemed able, at such moments of overwhelming excitement and agitation, to do anything I pleased with an audience." Then he paused and wondered whether inciting bodily exercises was consistent with God's work. "No, I fear not," he concluded. "I feel that it must be mere *animal* excitement." Bellamy set aside his itinerant labors and vowed to "go out thus no more."[128]

■ By 1743, only a handful of Whitefieldarians would have endorsed Grafton, Massachusetts, minister Solomon Prentice's bold pronouncement that "Persons in these Days have the Knowledge of the divine Spirit in greater Measures than the Prophets and Apostles had." As they reassessed the revivals, many Congregational clergymen soon found themselves at odds with scores of lay men and women who continued to trumpet the revivals as an unprecedented outpouring of the Holy Spirit.[129]

Boston merchant Samuel Phillips Savage received a steady stream of letters from his business partners during the early 1740s. Over time, interest in sharing religious intelligence might have declined among the members of this well-established epistolary network, and Savage's own letters increasingly emphasized the languishing state of his own soul rather than revival news from abroad. But not one of the seventeen surviving letters included even a single reference to revival errors or enthusiasm. This fact appears all the more striking when comparing Savage's incoming business correspondence with the brief notes that he received from his primary ministerial correspondent, John Blunt. Like so many of his colleagues, the New Castle, New Hampshire, clergyman initially greeted the revivals on the northern frontier with awe and joy, but he grew increasingly critical during the next twelve months. By the fall

128. Edwards to Prince, Dec. 12, 1743, in *WJE,* XVI, *Letters and Personal Writings,* ed. Claghorn, 121–125; Webster, transcr., "Letters to Joseph Bellamy," 15; Tryon Edwards, "Memoir," *The Works of Joseph Bellamy, D.D....,* 2 vols. (Boston, 1853), I, lxiii.
129. A *Result of a Council of Churches at Grafton* ([Boston, 1744]), 10.

of 1742, he was writing to Savage complaining of "hot Controversies," "Disputings," and "strange Itinerants," and he worried about the spread of "Antinomianism and familism." Savage's merchant contacts, by contrast, registered none of these concerns.[130]

The members of Savage's pious circle of business associates displayed a genteel regard for discretion that might have precluded the discussion of gossipy religious anecdotes. No such pretensions, however, marked the homespun narrative that Ivory Hovey, Jr., the minister of Rochester, Massachusetts, received from his parents in March 1742. Written in the unsteady hand of an aging country yeoman and church deacon from Topsfield, Massachusetts, Ivory, Sr., and Anne Hoveys' letter chronicled "a great Reviveal of Religon in Ipswich and in Rowley and in this Town." They praised minister John Emerson for preaching "Exeding Earnest and lively" sermons to unusually large congregations. Neighboring ministers visited Topsfield several times a week to promote evening prayer meetings. Public worship exercises were attended by dramatic bodily manifestations in which "there have bin sumtimes Six or Eight parsons [persons] Struck with Conviction and concern and have cried out." The awakened included members of their own family including their daughter, who lay "under concern about her soul and futer state." The Hoveys closed their letter urging their son to share revival news from Rochester and the surrounding towns in the Old Colony and begging prayers on behalf of the entire family.[131]

All of these topics were conventional by the emerging standards of revival discourse, yet, the Hoveys lived just a few miles away from of one of the wildest and most contentious revivals in New England history. During the previous three months, zealous new converts in the neighboring town of Ipswich had witnessed outbreaks of religious enthusiasm, including verbal outbursts, bizarre bodily behavior, a profusion of heterodox beliefs, mounting ecclesiastical discord, and ecstatic visionary phenomena. By March, troubling reports of the "Managements at Ipswich" had found their way into print and were widely debated among ministers and conservative laymen. Ignoring these tensions in their letter, the Hoveys remained firmly committed to spreading news of the "outpourings of the blessed Sperit of God in this remarkable day."[132]

---

130. John Blunt to Samuel Phillips Savage, Oct. 22, Dec. 29, 1742, SSP I. For correspondence from Savage's business partners, see David Jeffries to Savage, Jan. 29, 1742, Peter Cally to Savage, Feb. 10, 1742, Ebenezer Prout to Savage, Mar. 10, 1741 [1742], and Shippie Townsend to Savage, June 2, 1742, SSP I.

131. Ivory, Sr., and Anne Hovey to Ivory Hovey, Jr., Mar. 22, 1742, Hovey Family Papers, 1734–1901, PHM.

132. JCH, 333; Hovey and Hovey to Hovey, Mar. 22, 1742, Hovey Family Papers.

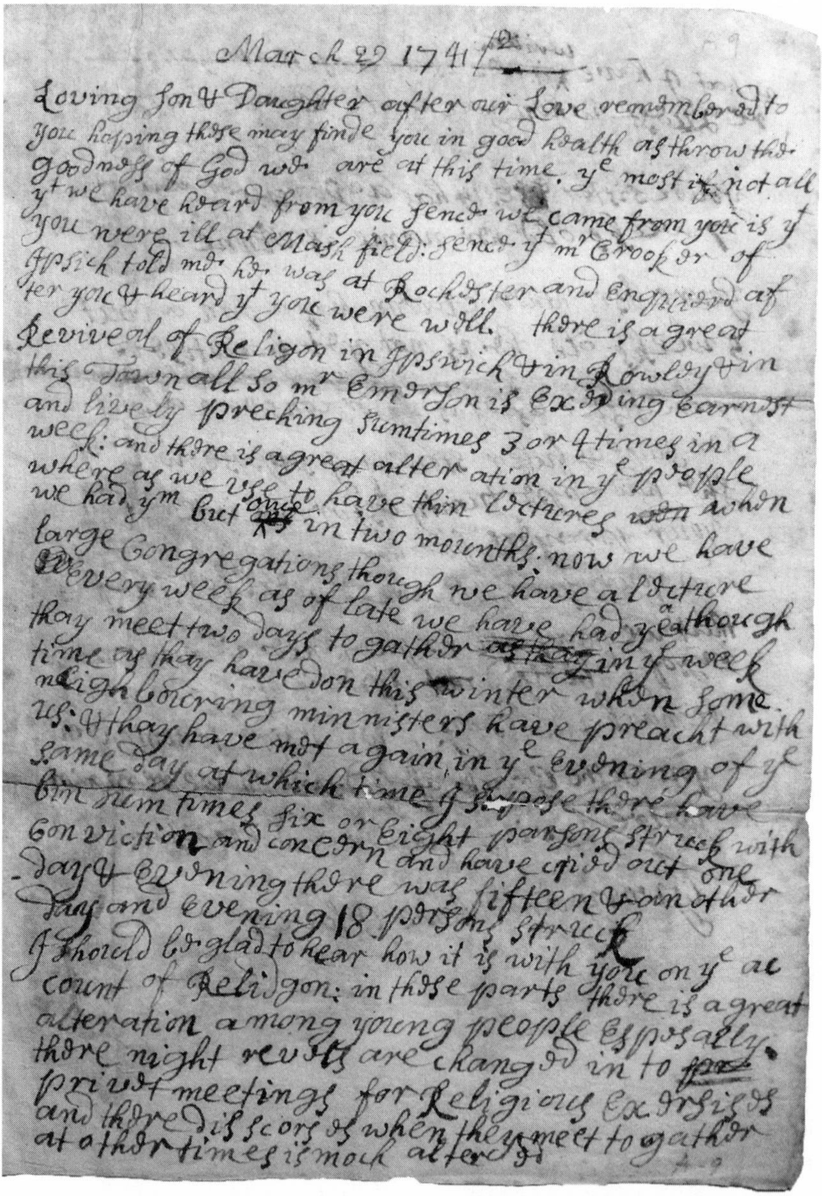

March 29 1741/2

Loving son & Daughter after our Love remembered to
you hoping these may finde you in good health as throw the
goodness of God we are at this time. ye most if not all
yt we have heard from you sence we came from you is yt
you were ill at Marshfield: sence yt mr Crooker of
Ipsvich told me he was at Rochester and enquired after you & heard yt you were well. there is a great
Revival of Religon in Ipswich & in Rowley & in
this Town all so mr Emerson is exceeding earnest
and lively preching sumtimes 3 or 4 times in a
week: and there is a great alteration in ye people
where as we use to have thin lectures won when
we had ym but once in two mounths. now we have
large Congregations though we have a lecture
every week as of late we have had yea although
thay meet two days to gather in ye week
time as thay have don this winter when some
neigbouring ministers have preacht with
us: & thay have met again in ye evening of ye
same day at which time I supose there have
bin sumtimes six or eight parsons struck with
conviction and concern and have cried out one
day & evening there was fifteen & in another
day and evening 18 parsons struck
I should be glad to hear how it is with you on ye account of Religon: in those parts there is a great
alteration among young people espesially.
there night revels are changed in to
privet meetings for Religious exersises
and there is scores of when they meet to gather
at other times is much altered

FIGURE 16 Ivory, Sr., and Anne Hovey to Ivory Hovey, Jr. March 29, 1742.
Hovey Family Papers. Courtesy, Pilgrim Hall Museum, Plymouth, Massachusetts

Preaching invitations sent to notable Whitefieldarians such as Wheelock and Joseph Bellamy provide another index of emerging lay radicalism. As ministers pulled back from itinerating and closed their pulpits to riding ministers, lay support appears to have grown more assertive. In addition to sharing local revival news and reflecting on the state of their souls in preaching invitations, lay men and women offered scathing indictments of their "Lukewarme" ministers and neighbors. Many of these lengthy missives were sent by zealous parishioners in direct opposition to the stated wishes of their local pastors. Lay correspondents likened their poor congregations to the struggling churches in Macedonia described in the Acts of the Apostles, or they boldly conflated the new converts in their parishes with "Gideons fleece," the tangible sign by which God presaged Israel's victory over its enemies in Judges 6. In New London, Connecticut, John Curtis begged Wheelock to "visit this vine" and "Rescue the Ark" of the Covenant from the "Captivity and Insults of the Philistines." Thomas Seymour informed Bellamy that many souls were "hovering like doves" in Hartford's second parish, but he also complained that "opposition arises as a bird of prey and they are scattered."[133]

Seymour's candid admission that he had "not half vented" himself in his strident letter of invitation captured much of the sense of alienation and betrayal—as well as the militant tone—that pervaded lay revival correspondence throughout the early 1740s. Over time, these individual efforts crystallized into elaborate petitions signed by dozens of disaffected parishioners. Daniel Rogers received several preaching requests in 1741 and 1742, each originating in parishes led by stern opposers. In the Chebacco precinct of Ipswich, a committee of eight leading men endorsed the revivals as an "Extraordinary Work of God" and pleaded with Rogers for a visit. "Some of us have made our Application to our Reverend Pastor," they declared in a postscript, but the recalcitrant Theophilus Pickering flatly rejected their request. Another example sent to Bellamy by a group of thirty-three Simsbury, Connecticut, laymen illuminated the strikingly oppositional nature of these letters. "We Cannot write to You in the Name of our Reverend Pasture," the petitioners explained, but they considered it "our Duty to Use Such means for our Souls Salvation." Signed by six women and eighteen men from the remote hamlet of Sharon, Connecticut, a similar invitation encouraged Wheelock to "bring any Servant of Christ with you who may be of Service to promote the work of the Lord." In "poor

---

133. Reuben Ely to Eleazar Wheelock, Mar. 4, 1741 [1742?], no. 741204, *EWP*, John Curtis to Wheelock, Oct. 15, 1741, no. 741575, Israel Gillet et al., to Wheelock, May 10, 1742, no. 742310, Joseph Safford to Wheelock, Mar. 30, 1742, no. 742230; Webster, transcr., "Letters to Joseph Bellamy," 11.

Wallingford," where the outspoken revival opposer Samuel Whittelsey condemned the revivals and locked the doors of the meetinghouse to interloping itinerants, layman Israel Johnson gladly pledged to host any riding minister who would "dare preach under such surcumstances." Collectively, petitions like these helped to establish a network of lay men and women who remained boldly engaged in the cause of Whitefieldian revivalism.[134]

The writings of John Lee provide a detailed view of deepening lay radicalism. The prominent lawyer from the east parish in Lyme, Connecticut, ranked among the most prolific revival reporters in all of New England. His glowing accounts of religious events in neighboring communities circulated widely, both in manuscript and in print, on both sides of the Atlantic. Lee's earliest letters to Wheelock rehearsed a typical set of revival themes. Writing in the wake of Gilbert Tennent's visit during the spring of 1741, he noted that the "Gloryous work in this place hath Increast in a most wonderful Manner." Religious concerns dominated daily conversations, especially in newly formed prayer societies. The town's clergymen had been "wonderfull Enlivened and stir'd up" by Tennent's rousing orations. They preached to vast assemblies, and their sermons were attended with great physical effects. Lee described entire congregations "Drounded in tears" and supplied detailed statistics on the numbers of convicted sinners and converted saints in his own parish. He documented the conversions of a wide range of people—notorious sinners, young children, and even the members of his own family—who had become "willing Captives to the Gosple." During his business travels through the eastern Connecticut uplands, he broadcast local revival intelligence, published a newspaper account of the spread of the gospel among native Americans, and zealously defended the work against accusations of excess in a highly publicized pamphlet debate with Medford minister Ebenezer Turell.[135]

By the fall of 1742, Lee had developed a reputation for his uncompromising revival zeal. As the itinerant preacher Benjamin Pomeroy later noted, Lee stood out as a "Peter" among "so many Judas's." His last letter to Wheelock struck a decidedly combative tone. The two men appear to have been out of touch for nearly a year, for Lee began the letter with a reference to renew-

134. Webster, transcr., "Letters to Joseph Bellamy," 12, 16–17; DDR, Feb. 3, 1742; Jacob Case et al., to Joseph Bellamy, Dec. 10, 1741, Joseph Bellamy Correspondence and Sermons, 1737–1800, CHS; Gillet et al., to Wheelock, May 10, 1742, no. 742310, *EWP*.

135. John Lee to Eleazar Wheelock, Apr. 20, May 7–8, Sept. 18, 1741, no. 741518.1, *EWP*. See also Lee to Wheelock, Dec. 5, 1740, in Bushman, ed., *Great Awakening*, 40–42; Lee to Wheelock, May 7, 1741, no. 741307, *EWP*, Lee to Wheelock, May 8, 1741, no. 741308.1, Lee to Wheelock, Sept. 18, 1741, no. 1741518; *American Weekly Mercury*, July 16, 1741; *Boston Weekly Post-Boy*, Aug. 30, 1742; Turell, *Mr. Turell's Dialogue*, 15–18.

ing their epistolary exchanges. During that time, Wheelock had tempered his ardor and curtailed his itinerating activities, but Lee remained keenly interested in local revival intelligence. His scrape with Turell a few months earlier might have revealed the "Dark Side of the Aspects of Divine providence," but it also steeled his resolve. He continued to pray that "God would again Send that Gloryous Sunshine to warm and refresh the frozen North." Lee stood ready to pass through a "thick of Divells for one Tast of the Love of Christ." Was Wheelock? "Dear Brother," he warned, "be Strong."[136]

In all, more than one hundred letters containing religious content penned by lay men and women have survived from the years between 1740 and 1744. The vast majority reflect a militant spirit unbroken by clerical pronouncements, public sphere exposés, ecclesiastical censures, or civil penalties. Many people became increasingly vocal revival supporters in the face of mounting criticism. For this radicalized cohort of new converts—men and women who dated their conversions to the descent of potent biblical impulses or believed that they had been carried to heaven in visions and shown their names in the Book of Life—the prospect that miraculous dispensations of the Holy Spirit ceased with the close of the apostolic age seemed absurd—even blasphemous.

Wheelock learned this lesson the hard way during his several visits to Voluntown, Connecticut. Passing through the tiny hill country hamlet during his preaching tour of southeastern New England during the fall of 1741, the prominent riding minister took note of the religious state of the community. Wheelock applauded the recent revival in the church, but he feared that the zeal of some new converts was "too furious." They "tell of many visions, revelations, and many Strong impressions upon their imagination," he groused. Some believed that the Holy Spirit had bestowed gifts on them to prophesy and exhort in public. Wheelock was dismayed by their stories, writing in his diary that "I never heard so many imaginations as young Christians tell of here in my life." Although he remained hopeful that a few conversions were authentic, Wheelock took particular care to admonish his audience for what he considered to be their gullibility, delusion, and errors.[137]

When Wheelock returned to Voluntown three years later, he encountered staunch resistance from an angry parishioner named Nathaniel French. Following Wheelock's sermon, the prominent Voluntown layman accosted the traveling preacher as he tarried at the meetinghouse door. Upset by Wheelock's stern critique of prophesying, speaking in tongues, and other miracu-

---

136. Benjamin Pomeroy to Wheelock, July 2, 1743, no. 743402, *EWP*, John Lee to Eleazar Wheelock, Nov. 29, 1742, no. 742629.
137. EWD, 237.

lous gifts of the Holy Spirit, French inquired whether the visiting clergyman would allow the Bible to determine the matter. On receiving his consent, French sprung his cleverly designed trap and proceeded to quote several passages from 1 Corinthians in which Paul favorably endorsed such practices as authentic manifestations of the Holy Spirit. Wheelock was astonished and concerned. Those "scriptures were not meant for these days," he explained, "wherein the Extreordinary gifts of the holy ghost were ceased from the church." Undaunted, French pressed the debate forward in a subsequent letter. "Since you do shew yourself so bold as to take away some of gods word from this generation," he countered sarcastically, "I desire you to go on if you dare and lett mee know how much of gods word must bee taken away: so that I may look over the little Remnant that you will leave and see whether I find any proof in that or no."[138]

French was one of Voluntown's leading residents: a selectman, founding church pillar, and deacon. During the previous decade, he had suffered through a series of misfortunes, including financial reversals, the deaths of his spouse and parents, and a fire that consumed his house. But never had he experienced a betrayal like this. "I must Say you are strangely fallen from what you seemed to bee two or three years agoe," he complained, before warning Wheelock to "take heed you have not the blood of Souls laid att your door" for hardening the hearts of his audience against the revivals. To French, God continuously revealed his will to the saints through immediate revelations. He could not help writing to warn Wheelock of his soul-damning change of heart. "I speak not my own words," the self-proclaimed oracle wrote, "butt what the lord teacheth mee." Ministers shunned French as one deluded by Satan, but the Voluntown deacon remained convinced that God had opened his eyes to "behold the things of his Spirit." "If this bee delusion," he brazenly proclaimed, "lett mee have more of it."[139]

■ As the weeks stretched into months following his visit to Boston during the winter of 1741, Joseph Pitkin reflected deeply on his providential encounter with Martha Robinson. On several occasions, he wrote to inquire after her

138. Nathaniel French to Eleazar Wheelock, Aug. 13, 1744, no. 744463, *EWP*.

139. Ibid. For biographical information on French, see Henry A. Hazen, *History of Billerica, Massachusetts, with a Genealogical Register* (Boston, 1883), 56; Lucy Hall Greenlaw, "Abstracts from the First Book of Bristol County Probate Records," *NEHGR*, LXIII (1909), 81; Carole Magnuson, comp., *The Barbour Collection of Connecticut Town Vital Records*, XXXIII, *Orange (1822–1850), Oxford (1798–1850), and Plainfield (1699–1852)* (Baltimore, 2000), 145–146; and Ellen D. Larned, *History of Windham County, Connecticut*, 2 vols. (Worcester, Mass., 1874), I, 243, 247, 250, 256, 258.

condition. Pitkin was pleased to hear that Robinson had been "Gradually Delivered" out of her demonic fits and ever since had "walked very Humbly and Circumspectly." Still, the Hartford magistrate remained concerned. What had she done, he wondered, to provoke God to visit her with such a sore affliction? When business affairs once again called him to Boston sometime in 1743, Pitkin stopped at Robinson's home to learn more about her possession experiences.[140]

Pitkin initiated the second interview by asking Robinson whether she remembered what had passed between them two years earlier. She answered in the affirmative and "Thankfully acknowledged her obligation" for his previous kindness in discoursing with her during a period of "Great Distress." What followed—at least as Pitkin later recorded it—was a strangely contrived series of questions and answers in which he reassessed Robinson's possession. Could she now affirm that her demonic speech was the "abhorrence of her Soul"? Yes. "Could you not Help Uttering those words with your Tongue"? No, she replied, "I was almost all Devil." Could she now be provoked to speak such words again? No, came her reply, not even "if I might have the world for it." How did she feel when Satan forced her to utter such horrid words? "I was Pressed," Robinson recalled, "as if my soul would be pressed out of my Body."[141]

The staccato questions and answers that structured the final lines of Pitkin's account of Robinson's possession contrasted with the earlier sections of his narrative. He seemed to be struggling to wrest an appropriate moral lesson from his interviews with the former demoniac. A narrative that began with the author's discovery of the indwelling Holy Spirit ended with an unsatisfactory directive to his readers that seemed to deny the supernatural origins of Robinson's diabolic and divine fits. Pitkin had entered into a cosmic drama in Boston. He had confronted the Devil directly and ascended to near visionary heights during his return trip to Hartford. Yet, here he was offering moral platitudes and exhorting his readers to maintain verbal order and mind their tongues, lest they become "Volluntary Slaves and vessels" of Satan. "Now my Hearty Desire," Pitkin concluded, "is that all who Se this Narrative be Excited to Devote their Souls and Tongues to the Service and Glory of God." Robinson appeared as a complex personality early in his account, but, by the end she possessed all the spontaneity of a stock character in a pastoral dialogue. The tone, structure, and content of these final paragraphs suggested that Pitkin had experienced yet another change of heart regarding his earlier assessment

140. JPD, 62.
141. Ibid., 63.

of Robinson's supposed condition. He appears to have given up his project to discern the voice of the Holy Spirit inside the body of one of Boston's most unusual young converts. By 1743, the Hartford magistrate seemed more interested in issues of deference, hierarchy, and order.[142]

Regardless of what she told Pitkin during their second interview, Robinson remained mired in acute distress during the next several years. In time, she would develop a reputation for disrupting public worship exercises with her corporeal and verbal explosions. During the summer of 1741, Daniel Rogers singled out "M. Robinson" among several people who fell to the ground during one of his preaching performances as a "poor Woman" in whom "Satan rag'd horribly." At about the time that Pitkin returned to Boston two years later, John Walley, Jr., attended a meeting at Robinson's home to pray on "Behalf of the Daughter of the Family, who has for several months been under Disorder of Mind, and 'tis to be feared is under strong Temptations and Delusions of Satan." Robinson even outlasted George Whitefield. During his controversial second tour of New England in 1744 and 1745, one Boston diarist described "Robinson's daughter" standing at the front of a vast assembly whose piercing outcries eventually drowned out Whitefield's voice.[143]

By the mid-1740s, the inspired performances of Spirit-possessed new converts such as Martha Robinson had given way to heated exchanges between ministers and parishioners. Sparked by itinerant preaching on the sandy foundations of faith, fueled by the riotous emotionalism of protracted meetings, and buttressed by a revelatory understanding of scripture, gifts of the indwelling Holy Spirit divided families, neighbors, congregations, and even ministerial associations. As the revivals unfolded, the work was increasingly manifested in perfectionist revelries, anticlerical raillery, special commissions to preach and exhort in public, and church schisms that threatened to overwhelm the churches of the Congregational standing order. Everywhere, it seemed to opposers and Whitefieldarians alike, "wild people" and "high pretenders" were conspiring to dismantle the New England way.[144]

142. Ibid., 63.

143. DDR, June 29, 1742; John Walley, Jr., journal, 1742–1751, 45–46, microfilm, MHS; Justin Winsor, ed., *The Memorial History of Boston, Including Suffolk County, Massachusetts, 1630–1880*, II, *The Provincial Period* (Boston, 1882), 239n.

144. Edwards, "Extraordinary Gifts," in *WJE*, XXV, *Sermons and Discourses, 1743–1758*, ed. Kimnach, 294, 303.

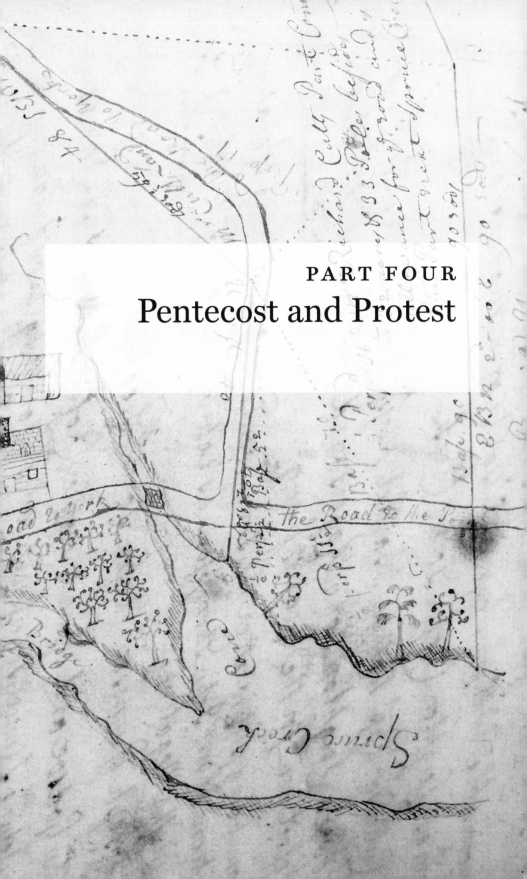

PART FOUR
Pentecost and Protest

Smoke billowed from the street outside the waterfront residence of the New London, Connecticut, merchant Edward Robinson. Parishioners departing the nearby Congregational meetinghouse that Sabbath afternoon early in March 1743 were surprised not only by the ascending plume but by the "great Noise and Out-cry" that issued from one of the "most publick Places in the town." Fearing the outbreak of a fatal conflagration, concerned residents poured into the streets where they witnessed a horrifying sight. A large crowd, perhaps as many as one hundred men and women, had gathered around a fire "into which they were casting a Number of Books, principally on Divinity, and those that were well-approved by *Protestant* Divines." As the pyre blazed, the assembled throng sang hallelujahs and consigned the souls of the books' "heretical" authors to the flames of hell. Over the din could be heard the loud voice of the self-proclaimed "Ringleader" of the New London bonfires: the "grand Enthusiast," James Davenport.[1]

The ardent Whitefieldarian from Southold, New York, had arrived in New London several days earlier. This was Davenport's third trip across the Long Island Sound in as many years. On his two previous preaching tours, Davenport had been arrested for disturbing the peace, declared non compos mentis by trial juries, deported from Connecticut, jailed in Boston, and barred from nearly every pulpit in Massachusetts. During the fall of 1742, he was roundly

1. "To the Publisher of the *Boston Post-Boy*," *Boston Weekly Post-Boy*, Mar. 28, 1743, in Richard L. Bushman, ed., *The Great Awakening: Documents on the Revival of Religion, 1740–1745*, Documentary Problems in Early American History (Chapel Hill, N.C., 1969), 52; Frances Marwaring Caulkins, *History of New London, Connecticut, from the First Survey of the Coast in 1612 to 1852* (New London, Conn., 1852), 456; *Boston Evening-Post*, Apr. 11, 1743. See also Francis L. Hawks and William Stevens Perry, eds., *Documentary History of the Protestant Episcopal Church in the United States of America …*, 2 vols. (New York, 1863–1864), I, 189; and Richard Webster, *A History of the Presbyterian Church in America: From Its Origin until the Year 1760 …*, ed. Joseph M. Wilson (Philadelphia, 1857), 204.

censured by an ecclesiastical council for his new revival measures and ceaseless itinerating. Given five months to repent of his errors, Davenport nonetheless appeared in New London to preside at the irregular ordination of a
layman named John Curtis over a newly gathered Separate Congregational
church. Even more peculiar was the setting for this event—an upstart theological seminary known as the Shepherd's Tent, whose members were well
practiced in the most radical innovations of the Whitefieldian revivals.[2]

Events in New London took an even more scandalous turn the following night. Informing his audience that "some of them made Idols of their
gay Cloaths," Davenport ordered the crowd to burn their finest possessions.
Women deposited their "Scarlet Cloaks, Velvet Hoods, fine Laces, and everything that had two Colours"; men dispatched their wigs and velvet collars.
Altogether, the value of the heap of finery was estimated in excess of several
hundred pounds sterling. The assembly prayed for a full discovery of God's
will in the matter. After several unsuccessful appeals, Davenport proclaimed
that the *"Things must be burnt,"* and, to "confirm the Truth of the Revelation," he removed his "Plush Breeches" and "hove them with Violence into the
Pile, saying, *Go you with the Rest.*" Bedlam erupted as the assembly dissolved
into confusion. A young woman snatched Davenport's pants from the fire and
thrust them back at the fiery itinerant with "much Indignation." One scoffer
sarcastically offered to burn Davenport alive, claiming that he had always idol-
ized the Southold revivalist. Even John Lee, the prominent lawyer and revival
correspondent from the neighboring town of Lyme, castigated Davenport for
abusing divine authority and declared that he was *"making a Calf"* of the so-
called idols. Stunned by the unexpected turn of events, Davenport retreated
to the Shepherd's Tent, where for weeks he pondered whether *"God had left
Him."*[3]

This was the strange story that occupied Alexander Hamilton as he sat in a
New London tavern drinking and socializing with the son of Timothy Green,
the town's prominent church deacon and printer, on the evening of August
26, 1744. Suffering from tuberculosis, which claimed his life a decade later,

2. *Boston Evening-Post*, Mar. 14, 1743. My analysis of Davenport's career and the New
London bonfires builds on earlier studies by Richard Warch, "The Shepherd's Tent: Educa-
tion and Enthusiasm in the Great Awakening," *American Quarterly*, XXX (1978), 177–198;
Harry S. Stout and Peter Onuf, "James Davenport and the Great Awakening in New London,"
JAH, LXX (1983), 556–578; and Robert E. Cray, Jr., "James Davenport's Post-Bonfire Min-
istry, 1743-1757," *Historian*, LIX (1996), 59–73.

3. *Boston Evening-Post*, Mar. 14, Apr. 11, 1743; "To the Publisher," *Boston Weekly Post-
Boy*, Mar. 28, 1743, in Bushman, ed., *Great Awakening*, 52–53; Thomas Skinner to Ebenezer
Turell, Mar. 12, 1743, Miscellaneous Bound Manuscripts, MHS.

the Scottish-born émigré and physician from Annapolis, Maryland, had been traveling for "health and recreation" through the northern colonies during the previous three months. Along the way, he recorded his observations on the "manners and character" of provincial Americans in a journal that he later revised into one of the most notable travel narratives of the eighteenth century. Hamilton's *Itinerarium* was a curious mélange of anthropology, natural philosophy, coffee house conversations, and popular wonder lore. Attuned to the quixotic, he populated the manuscript with a carnivalesque sideshow of colonial oddballs. From Annapolis to York, Maine, the touring physician encountered hordes of "inquisitive rusticks" who relished the opportunity to share their local knowledge with an illustrious southern gentleman. Hamilton crossed paths with drunken tavernkeepers, a hump-backed barber, promenading buxom belles, an effeminate falsetto singer, superstitious jack tars, a "topsy turvy" hermaphrodite, foul-smelling Mohawks, and a gentleman addicted to swearing by the Devil's name. He savored a glass of good wine with Narragansett sachem George Ninigret; watched with horror as an impoverished Maryland family hungrily consumed their plain fare without knives, forks, spoons, plates, or napkins; listened to lewd tales involving the humorously named "Captain Scrotum"; and witnessed the antics of an elderly Long Island man who vaulted his body six inches off the ground using only the muscles in his buttocks.[4]

Hamilton's account of the New London bonfires fit neatly into the cabinet of curiosities that he cataloged in his *Itinerarium*, yet he borrowed heavily from newspaper reports in crafting his narrative of the events. The Annapolis physician reviewed only the basic details of the conflagrations: Davenport's "enthusiastic rhapsodies," fires consuming the books of prominent divines and material finery, and the fanatical itinerant's breeches pulled from the pyre at the last moment. His only novel contribution to public discourse on the controversy was the sneering observation that Davenport "would have been obliged to strutt about bare-arsed" had he succeeded in offering up his breeches as an "expiatory sacrifise." Hamilton generally eschewed overtly moralizing judgments in favor of artful description in his *Itinerarium*, but this was one of the few moments where he let down his guard.[5]

---

4. *AHI*, 3, 20, 110, 124, 194, 199 (see also 6–8, 13, 18, 84–85, 92–93, 98, 128, 134). For Hamilton's life and literary works, see Elaine G. Breslaw, *Dr. Alexander Hamilton and Provincial America: Expanding the Orbit of Scottish Culture*, Southern Biography (Baton Rouge, La., 2008); and Robert Micklus, *The Comic Genius of Dr. Alexander Hamilton* (Knoxville, Tenn., 1990).

5. *AHI*, 161.

FIGURE 17 Alexander Hamilton, "Loquacious Scribble Esqr." From "The History of the Ancient and Honorable Tuesday Club: From the Earliest Ages Down to This Present Year." 1755. Courtesy, John Work Garrett Library, The Johns Hopkins University, Baltimore

Religion was the one subject that the ailing Scottish physician could not stomach. Shortly after arriving in the colonies in 1739, Hamilton jettisoned the moderate Presbyterianism espoused by his father—a noted professor of divinity at the University of Edinburgh—and embraced Maryland's genteel Anglicanism. He firmly believed that the practical aspects of religion—ethics, morality, tradition, hierarchy—provided a rational foundation for a stable society. Few colonials appear to have shared his sentiments. Instead, they seemed to be captivated with what Hamilton called "speculative points of religion." He vented his disdain for these "New Light bigotts" and "hair brained fanaticks" whenever he crossed their paths, whether he was ferrying across the Susquehanna River, riding the rough roads of New Hampshire, or dining in a tavern in Poughkeepsie, New York. The deluded followers of George Whitefield were everywhere the same: peculiarly obsessed with arcane theological controversies, strangely averse to "innocent amusements," and excessively prone to railing against their social betters. Hamilton had witnessed Whitefield's preaching in Annapolis in 1739. By the time he visited New London five years later, he had heard and seen enough of the "spirit of enthusiasm" that had infested the colonies.[6]

Hamilton demonstrated little interest in understanding why the New London bonfires had taken place or what the events might have meant to Davenport and his followers. His aversion to the recent New England revivals—"a stupid subject of discourse" of "little consequence to the benefit of mankind," he once grumbled—made it almost impossible to take the 1743 book-burning event seriously as anything other than an act of irrational madness. He paid little attention in his *Itinerarium* to the aftermath of the conflagrations or to their broader historical context. Hamilton surely knew that civil and ecclesiastical authorities had been burning books for centuries in carefully orchestrated rites of violence. During the 1650s, Davenport's puritan ancestors had consigned early Quaker books to the flames along with William Pynchon's heretical treatise on atonement, *The Meritorious Price of Our Redemption,* and the works of the infamous English Antinomian William Dell. Politically subversive pamphlets, moreover, were publicly burned in New England during the decades on either side of the revivals of the 1740s. What logic lay behind the New London bonfires? Was there a method to Davenport's purported madness?[7]

6. *AHI,* 8, 10, 23, 127. For a similar report from Annapolis, see Richard J. Cox, ed., "Stephen Bordley, George Whitefield, and the Great Awakening in Maryland," *Historical Magazine of the Protestant Episcopal Church,* XLVI (1977), 297–307.

7. *AHI,* 152; Philip F. Gura, *A Glimpse of Sion's Glory: Puritan Radicalism in New England, 1620–1660* (Middletown, Conn., 1984), 72, 309; Clyde Augustus Duniway, *The De-*

The New London book-burning incident was not a bizarre aberration. It was Whitefieldian revivalism in full flower; the most extreme expression of the new converts' commitment to exercised bodies, biblical impulses, visions, and other gifts of the Holy Spirit; and the pinnacle of Davenport's charismatic ministry. Interpreting this act of "wildest Enthusiasm" requires a close examination of the many ways awakened lay men and women translated the experience of the indwelling Spirit into action and how their inspired practices disrupted congregations and polarized communities. Among the ringleaders of the Whitefieldarians' crusade to restore the Pentecostal charismata of the apostolic age, the "Right Zealous" Mr. Davenport had no equal.[8]

THE LORD OPENED MY MOUTH

The "fanatick preacher" who served as the butt of Alexander Hamilton's satirical account of the New London bonfires descended from an eminent ministerial clan. Born in Stamford, Connecticut, around 1716, James Davenport rose rapidly to prominence at Yale College, where he distinguished himself as the youngest member of the class of 1732. He was an unusually sickly adolescent who suffered through a succession of maladies during the next several years, including a painful bout of gonorrhea. Guilt from youthful sexual dalliances and the divine chastisement that followed might have prompted Davenport to seek solace alongside his future brother-in-law, Eleazar Wheelock, and several later revival leaders in an informal religious society led by the controversial Quaker renegade David Ferris. Following graduation, Davenport preached for several years to a pair of small Presbyterian congregations at Hopewell and Maidenhead (now Lawrenceville), New Jersey. Eventually, he secured a call at Southold, a bustling hamlet near the tip of Long Island, where he was ordained in 1738.[9]

---

velopment of Freedom of the Press in Massachusetts (New York, 1906), 79, 115. On the New London bonfires as ritual, see David D. Hall, "Religion and Society: Problems and Reconsiderations," in Jack P. Greene and J. R. Pole, eds., *Colonial British America: Essays in the New History of the Early Modern Era* (Baltimore, 1984), 337. For a survey of early modern book-burning events, see Hans J. Hillerbrand, "On Book Burnings and Book Burners: Reflections on the Power (and Powerlessness) of Ideas," *Journal of the American Academy of Religion*, LXXIV (2006), 593–614. I borrow the phrase "rites of violence" from Natalie Zemon Davis, "The Rites of Violence: Religious Riot in Sixteenth-Century France," *Past and Present: A Journal of Historical Studies*, LIX (1973), 51–91.

8. Hawks and Perry, eds., *Documentary History of the Protestant Episcopal Church*, I, 189; Peter Benes, "'Pedlars in Divinity': Street Religion in Massachusetts and Rhode Island before 1830," in Benes, ed., *Life on the Streets and Commons, 1600 to the Present*, Dublin Seminar for New England Folklife, Annual Proceedings 2005 (Boston, 2007), 39.

9. *AHI*, 161; James Davenport to Stephen Williams, June 20, 1734, box 322, SGC II.

The early years of Davenport's career elicited few comments, positive or negative. But when word reached Southold of George Whitefield's impending northern tour, he and Jonathan Barber, a former Yale classmate and neighboring colleague, began to pray fervently for an outpouring of the Holy Spirit. Barber soon received an answer in the form of a pair of biblical impulses from Habakkuk and the Psalms. Convinced that a glorious work of God was imminent, Barber started visiting from house to house in his Long Island parish at Oyster Ponds, exhorting families to repent and prepare for the kingdom of heaven. When he arrived in Southold, he learned that Davenport had received a similar revelation from Psalm 115.[10]

Believing that God had called them to spread the good news, Davenport and Barber itinerated across Long Island. Biblical impulses guided their labors. In accordance with Jesus's instructions to his disciples in Mark 6, they traveled in tandem but without money, food, or change of apparel. On one occasion, they attempted to heal a sick woman as the apostles had done. Rumors of a *"great Commotion"* in Southold soon surfaced. Some reports suggested that Davenport had become distracted or even died, but Wheelock defended his brother-in-law, explaining that he had recently experienced a "most Wonderful Visitation of God" and "Lives a heaven." Even before Whitefield arrived in the northern colonies, many of Davenport's parishioners were reportedly *"under Soul-Concern."* According to Wheelock, who ventured down to Southold in April 1740 to investigate the rumors, there had been "many very Clear Convertions of Late in this Place."[11]

Davenport impressed Whitefield at their first meeting in New York later that spring. Although "He is looked upon as an enthusiast and a madman by many of his reverend pharisaical brethren," Whitefield noted, the Southold

---

The only modern biography of Davenport is Robert William Brockway, "The Significance of James Davenport in the Great Awakening" (Ph.D. diss., Columbia University, 1951). See also William B. Sprague, *Annals of the American Pulpit; or, Commemorative Notices of Distinguished American Clergymen of Various Denominations* ..., 9 vols. (New York, 1857–1869), III, 80–92; and Franklin Bowditch Dexter, *Biographical Sketches of the Graduates of Yale College*, 6 vols. (New York, 1885–1912), I, 447–450.

10. Charles Chauncy, *Seasonable Thoughts on the State of Religion in New-England* ... (Boston, 1743), 183–188.

11. Julius Herbert Tuttle, comp., "The Glasgow-Weekly-History, 1743," MHS, *Proceedings*, LIII (1919–1920), 196; Eleazar Wheelock to Sarah Wheelock, Apr. 26, 1740, no. 740276, *EWP*, Eleazar Wheelock to Sarah Wheelock, Apr. 28, 1740, no. 740278. For reports of Davenport's alleged insanity, see Eleazar Wheelock to Stephen Williams, May 22, 1740, no. 740322, *EWP*; Stephen Williams, diaries, 1715–1782, 10 vols., typescript, Storrs Library, Longmeadow, Mass., III, 363, 384 (available online at *http://www.longmeadowlibrary.org/stephen-williams-diary-available-online/*); Solomon Williams to Eleazar Wheelock, July 17, 1741, no. 741417, *EWP*; and John Blunt to Samuel Phillips Savage, Dec. 22, 1741, SSP I.

minister had been "highly honoured" in his gospel labors. Davenport remained on the road for the rest of the summer of 1740, preaching in the "open Air and High ways" to vast audiences in New Jersey and eastern Pennsylvania. Only occasionally did he return to his parish on Long Island. "Never did I before see the word come with Such power," he proclaimed in a letter to Wheelock, "or people so hungry after it." "I rejoice to hear that the LORD is with you," Whitefield wrote to Davenport. "I feel that I love you in the bowels of the dear Jesus, our ever blessed and glorious *Emmanuel*."[12]

In July 1741, Davenport crossed the Long Island Sound and began igniting religious revivals along the Boston Post Road from New London to New Haven. In contrast to Whitefield, Wheelock, and most of his itinerating peers, Davenport preached without the consent of the standing ministers in the towns that he visited. Parading through the streets with his arms outstretched and his head arched to the heavens, singing hymns at the top of his voice, he encouraged his listeners to follow him to the meetinghouse or to the fields, orchards, barns, or homes of sympathetic supporters. There, he often declined to preach altogether. Instead, Davenport opened his revival meetings with a short prayer before ceding control to gifted lay people who were constrained to speak by the Holy Spirit. Local ministers watched in horror as the traditional order of the Congregational meeting broke down into a chaotic jumble of songs, exhortations, prayers, and extemporaneous preaching. Witnesses claimed that as many as thirty people spoke at the same time "without any certain Order or Method." Some addressed the assembly from the pulpit; others stood in their pews or shouted down from the galleries. Davenport's meetings were punctuated by piercing outcries, exercised bodies, dramatic conversions, and ecstatic raptures. One newspaper report even suggested that he compelled his hearers to bark like dogs. Meanwhile, the Southold revivalist circulated through throngs screaming "Come to Christ." "Were you to see him in his most violent Agitations," scoffed one observer, "you would be apt to think, that he was a Madman just broke from his Chains."[13]

When he did preach, Davenport yoked the Whitefieldarians' practice of extemporaneous speech to the emerging popular fascination with immediate revelations of the Holy Spirit. During the summer of 1740, he received a

---

12. *GWJ*, 416, 487; James Davenport to Eleazar Wheelock, July 9, 1740, case 8, box 22, SGC I; *Letters of George Whitefield for the Period 1734–1742* (Edinburgh, 1976), 223.

13. *Boston Weekly Post-Boy*, Sept. 28, 1741; *The Diary of Joshua Hempstead: A Daily Record of Life in Colonial New London, Connecticut, 1711–1758* . . . , rev. ed. (New London, Conn., 1999), 374; *Boston Evening-Post*, July 5, 1742. See also *South Carolina Gazette* (Charleston), June 21, 1742.

biblical impulse from Matthew 10:19 urging him to *"Take no Thought what you shall say, for it shall be given you in that Hour."* Davenport discarded his sermon notes, and words came with power. The "Lord opened my mouth," he reported to Wheelock, "So that I Scarcely knew how to Shut it." The Southold itinerant brazenly declared that his every utterance issued from the "immediate impressions and directions of the Divine Spirit." Later observers recalled that he entered the pulpit with "no *Intention* what Subject to Preach upon" and prayed instead for God to "direct him to a Text, and put Words into his Mouth." The resulting discourses were, in the estimation of the New London civil magistrate Joshua Hempstead "without form or Comelyness." He had no "Text nor Bible visable, no Doctrine, uses, nor Improvement nor anything Else that was Regular." Preaching, prayer, and exhortation ran together in a "Confused medley," as Davenport chanted key phrases over and over in a hypnotic, singsong voice. He deployed lurid images of hell, blasted his audiences with threats of divine judgment, and struck fear into their hearts by repeatedly shouting the word *"Damn'd!"* These inspired, extemporaneous discourses lasted from two to an extraordinary twenty-four consecutive hours.[14]

To ministers and magistrates, former friends and new adversaries, Davenport appeared possessed or "touched in his brain." The public prints mercilessly tarred him during his several New England itinerations. But, an equal and perhaps even greater number of lay men and women praised him as a "wonderfull man of God." By almost any measure, Davenport was the single most successful riding minister of his generation. Lacking the advance publicity of Whitefield's tour, Davenport nonetheless succeeded in gathering crowds in excess of one thousand at Groton and Stonington, Connecticut, during the summer of 1741. His preaching emptied fields, wharves, and stores. "All hands have been hearing Mr. Davenport this week," Hempstead explained. Those who attended his meetings were profoundly affected. Audiences groaned, people cried out in distress, and bodily exercises multiplied. So did conversions. According to Andrew Croswell, three dozen people in his parish and more than one hundred in the surrounding towns had been "hopefully Converted in one Day" during Davenport's first tour of southern New England, "which Glorious Success surpasses even any that Mr. *Tennent* or *Whitefield* have recorded." His *"new Way"* of preaching was particularly effec-

---

14. Chauncy, *Seasonable Thoughts on the State of Religion,* 189, 197; James Davenport to Eleazar Wheelock, Oct. 5, 1740, no. 740555, *EWP;* Joseph Tracy, *The Great Awakening: A History of the Revival of Religion in the Time of Edwards and Whitefield* (1842; Edinburgh, 1976), 209; *Boston Weekly Post-Boy,* Aug. 10, 1741, Sept. 28, 1741; *Diary of Joshua Hempstead,* 401. See also Wheelock to Williams, May 22, 1740, no. 740322, *EWP.*

tive among native Americans, and several revival correspondents believed that he was the "Great instrument" in converting scores of Mohegans, Montauks, Narragansetts, Niantics, and Pequots.[15]

Every aspect of Davenport's singular ministry incited both curiosity and contempt. His "strange and unaccountable" penchant for singing in the streets was especially controversial. Sung to the tunes of popular ballads and tavern songs, laced with intruding biblical texts, and artfully designed to arouse the emotions during protracted revival meetings, Davenport's hymns accentuated the most radical aspects of the Whitefieldian new birth. The lyrics of one note-worthy example emphasized the descent and physical indwelling of the Holy Spirit, complete assurance of salvation, and, above all, the religious ecstasy that attended conversion:

> Down from above the blessed Dove
> Is come into my Breast,
> To witness God's eternal Love;
> This is my heavenly Feast.
> This makes me *Abba Father* cry,
> With Confidence of Soul;
> It makes me cry, My Lord, my God,
> And that without Controul.

Even warm supporters of revival innovations decried Davenport's penchant for singing in the streets. If *"Hymns* of meer humane Composure" were brought into public worship, Boston minister Benjamin Colman complained, "there will be no Bound to the soaring *Flights* of Men of *elevated* Wit and Piety, nor yet to the *Fancies* of others *of a lower Vein.*" Unlike the new practice of regular psalm singing, which many congregations debated during the two decades leading up to the revivals of the 1740s, Davenport's sacred street music remained outside the control of ecclesiastical authorities and unattached to the stated preferences of specific congregations.[16]

---

15. Tracy, *Great Awakening*, 209; DDR, Sept. 10, 1742; *Diary of Joshua Hempstead*, 375; *Boston Weekly Post-Boy*, Oct. 5, 1741; Chauncy, *Seasonable Thoughts on the State of Religion*, 199; Eleazar Wheelock to Daniel Rogers, Jan. 18, 1742, no. 742118, *EWP*. See also Williams to Wheelock, July 17, 1741, no. 741417, *EWP*.

16. *Boston Weekly Post-Boy*, Aug. 10, 1741; Alan Heimert and Perry Miller, eds., *The Great Awakening: Documents Illustrating the Crisis and Its Consequences*, American Heritage (Indianapolis, Ind., 1967), 202; Benjamin Colman, *A Letter from the Reverend Dr. Colman of Boston, to the Reverend Mr. Williams of Lebanon, upon Reading the Confession and Retrac-tations of the Reverend Mr. James Davenport* (Boston, 1744), 8. On Davenport's contribu-tions to Protestant hymnody, see Stephen A. Marini, "Rehearsal for Revival: Sacred Singing and the Great Awakening in America," in Joyce Irwin, ed., *Sacred Sound: Music in Religious*

Davenport's innovative hymnody was only one aspect of a much broader charismatic ministry. He drank deeply from the streams of direct revelation, believing that "GOD INSPIR'D HIM as he did the *ancient Prophets.*" "I would leave myself wholly with Him and live by faith on Him," Davenport declared in a 1740 letter to Wheelock, citing words from Jeremiah 26:14, "Let Him do with me as Seemeth Him Good." In fact, the Southold minister appealed to the indwelling voice of the Holy Spirit to direct his every action. Questioned by colleagues in Boston whether he placed too much weight on *"Impulses* and *Impressions,"* Davenport raised his eyes to the heavens and boldly prayed to God for an immediate answer. Words from scripture dropped into his mind, as he launched into a relation of his conversion experiences that lasted for nearly two hours. Whenever he explained his actions, grumbled Charles Chauncy, "he always exprest it in some such Language as that, GOD CALL'D ME, or GOD COMMANDED ME, or GOD IMPRESSED IT UPON MY MIND." Not surprisingly, most of his ministerial colleagues soon denounced his audacious claims to being led by the Spirit as "big with Errors" and "deeply tinctur'd with a Spirit of Enthusiasm."[17]

Equally perplexing to many was the strange story behind the entourage that accompanied the revivalist on his several New England preaching circuits. Shortly after Davenport received his calling to itinerate in 1740, Daniel Tuttle, son of the Southold deacon, urged him to expand the scope of his pastoral labors. Davenport weighed the idea carefully and decided to appeal to the scriptures. As he opened his Bible, the story of Jonathan smiting the Philistines in 1 Samuel 14 "cast up to him, without his having the least Thought of turning to it." He read and saw *"every Line, every Word in a new Light;* and the LORD caused it to make a STRONG IMPRESSION upon him." Together, Davenport and Tuttle set off for Easthampton, New York. Henceforth, Davenport thought of himself as a latter-day Jonathan; Tuttle, now his constant traveling companion, became known as his faithful *"Armour-Bearer."* Over time, the Southold revivalist expanded the concept to refer to any of his inner circle of disciples. Until the bonfire controversy at New London in 1743, he frequently cast himself in the role of King David. The towns that he visited emerged as types of Jerichos and his revival opponents, Pharisees and Philistines. Daven-

---

Thought and Practice, Journal of the American Academy of Religion Studies, L (Chico, Calif., 1983), 71–91.

17. Chauncy, *Seasonable Thoughts on the State of Religion,* 195, 198; Davenport to Wheelock, Oct. 5, 1740, no. 740555, *EWP; The Declaration of a Number of the Associated Pastors of Boston and Charles-Town Relating to the Rev. Mr. James Davenport, and His Conduct* (Boston, 1742), in Bushman, ed., *Great Awakening,* 50–51. See also Elisha Williams to Stephen Williams, July 1, 1742, Yale Letters, YUB.

port envisioned himself as a biblical figure participating in an unfolding cosmic drama, and he modeled his behavior accordingly.[18]

The most controversial component of Davenport's ministry was his "arbitrary and uncharitable" penchant for judging whether other people would be saved or damned. On the basis of a biblical impulse from 1 Corinthians 2:15, Davenport believed that the Holy Spirit had bestowed on him the apostolic gift of spiritual discernment, the power to peer directly into the souls of those with whom he spoke and to determine whether they would be counted among God's elect. He introduced this controversial practice while still in Southold. During the summer of 1740, Davenport divided the full church members in his congregation into two groups, basing his judgment solely on his spiritual gifts. He restricted the Lord's Supper and the right of baptism to those whom he designated as regenerate brothers, while mere "NEIGHBORS"—including one of the deacons and long-standing communicants of "blameless and regular Conversations"—were barred from the sacrament until such a time as they could provide credible testimony of experiencing the new birth. Davenport's imperious actions precipitated bitter disputes among his flock, although some parishioners continued to believe that their minister was guided by "REVELATIONS OF THE SPIRIT; and his *Words*, ORACLES."[19]

By the time he appeared in Connecticut during the summer of 1741, Davenport was actively exercising his gift of spiritual discernment on local ministers and urging a "general Separation *between the Precious and the Vile*." He created a "Mighty Ruffle" in New London when he declared minister Eliphalet Adams to be an "unconverted Man." A few days later, he pronounced the same judgment on Joseph Fish and his two colleagues in Stonington. Davenport publicly branded nearly every clergyman in southern Connecticut as *"carnal"* Pharisees and *"blind guides"* during his extended preaching tour that summer. In response to colleagues who closed their pulpits to his ministrations, Davenport's sermons grew increasingly "full of Rancour and Invective." He lashed out at opposing clergymen, condemning them as unconverted wolves in sheep's clothing. In New Haven, especially, he upbraided Joseph Noyes as the *"Devil incarnate"* and flatly stated that thousands of his deceased parishioners were now cursing him in hell for being the "Instrument of their Damna-

18. Chauncy, *Seasonable Thoughts on the State of Religion*, 196–197. On Tuttle, see Henry B. Hoff, comp., *Genealogies of Long Island Families: From the New York Genealogical and Biographical Record*, 2 vols. (Baltimore, 1987), II, 486–487, 489–490.

19. "At a Council of Ministers Conven'd at Southold," October 1742, Miscellaneous Collections: Personal Names, 1729–1972, Richard H. Handley Long Island History Room, Smithtown Library, Smithtown, N.Y.; Chauncy, *Seasonable Thoughts on the State of Religion*, 190.

tion." Davenport even encouraged his audiences facing opposition from their ministers to form separate meetings. *"Parish-Bounds are nothing,"* he proclaimed, asserting that he would willingly "go ten Miles on Foot to hear a private *Brother,* rather than an *unconverted Minister."* [20]

Davenport arrived in New Haven just in time to disrupt the start of the academic year at Yale College. The Hartford diarist and stern revival critic Daniel Wadsworth called his inspired and incendiary preaching the "most strange management and a pretence of religion that ever I saw." The trustees instantly passed a resolution imposing stern penalties on any student who followed Davenport's lead in condemning the college officials as "Hypocrites, carnall or unconverted Men." Jonathan Edwards's initial change of heart regarding the revivals came as a direct result of witnessing Davenport's unbridled zeal. He delivered his cautionary commencement address on the *Distinguishing Marks of a Work of the Spirit of God* one day later.[21]

■ "My heart Trembles for the Ark of God," warned Solomon Williams of Lebanon, Connecticut, in a letter that he dispatched to Eleazar Wheelock after watching Davenport's revival meetings in New London during the summer of 1741. "What shall we do if God Leaves his Ministers to pull down with one hand what They build With the other"? Members of the New Haven and Windham County ministerial associations went a step further, calling for a colony-wide synod to address the disorderly conduct of Davenport and his itinerating colleagues. Ecclesiastical and civil authorities branded the Southold interloper a "Haughty" and "arrogant" pretender and his purported gifts of spiritual discernment an "imperious and unwarrientable" usurpation of the "authority of the Most High."[22]

Responding to the Davenport insurgency, ministers from across the colony gathered in Guilford, Connecticut, on November 24, 1741. The resolutions

20. *Boston Weekly Post-Boy,* Aug. 10, Sept. 28, 1741; Williams to Wheelock, July 17, 1741, no. 741417, *EWP;* Chauncy, *Seasonable Thoughts on the State of Religion,* 153.

21. George Leon Walker, ed., *Diary of Rev. Daniel Wadsworth, Seventh Pastor of the First Church of Christ in Hartford, with Notes by the Fourteenth Pastor, 1737–1747* (Hartford, Conn., 1894), 72; Franklin Bowditch Dexter, ed., *Documentary History of Yale University under the Original Charter of the Collegiate School of Connecticut, 1701–1745* (New Haven, Conn., 1916), 351.

22. Williams to Wheelock, July 17, 1741, no. 741417, *EWP;* Eliphalet Adams, diary, July 14, 1741, box 1, Curtis Family Papers, 1695–1912, MS 684, YUA; Joseph Talcott to Samuel Lynde, Sept. 4, 1741, in Mary Kingsbury Talcott, ed., *The Talcott Papers: Correspondence and Documents (Chiefly Official) during Joseph Talcott's Governorship of the Colony of Connecticut, 1724–41,* 2 vols., CHS, *Colls.,* V (Hartford, Conn., 1896), II, 372; *Boston Weekly Post-Boy,* Aug. 10, 1741. See also Jacob Eliot to Joseph Meacham and Eleazar Wheelock, Aug. 25, 1741, no. 741475, *EWP.*

passed by the general consociation of clergymen praised the recent revivals as a "remarkable Work of God" but acknowledged the inevitability of "imperfections and imprudences," especially among those who were "most Zealous to promote it." The "Guilford Resolves," as the formal statement summarizing the proceedings came to be known, directly attacked Davenport's controversial practice of spiritual discernment. The ministers stated flatly there was "no way to Determine of the Conversion of any other person, but from his Christian Profession, life and Conversation." They rebuked parishioners who left their parishes to attend revival meetings in other towns, encouraged limitations on the formation of private prayer meetings, and recommended stringent standards for licensing preachers.[23]

The following May, four delegates from the Guilford conference presented a copy of the resolutions to the Connecticut General Assembly and urged the legislators to protect the peace and order of the colony's established churches. The representatives responded two weeks later with an "Act for regulating Abuses and correcting Disorders in Ecclesiastical Affairs," a landmark anti-itinerancy statute that withheld tax-supported salaries from any ordained clergyman who attempted to preach beyond the territorial limits of his parish without the consent of the settled minister and a majority of the church members. The statute also empowered local magistrates to banish interloping riding ministers from other colonies. The law elicited sharp criticism outside Connecticut—even from revival opposers such as Boston's Charles Chauncy—but it was strictly enforced and even strengthened during the next several years.[24]

None of the representatives sitting in Hartford during their May 1742 session could have ignored the fact that Davenport and his riotous revival meetings lay behind the draconian statute. On the same day that the Connecticut General Assembly passed the anti-itinerancy act, two prominent residents from Stratford's Ripton Society (now Huntington) begged for relief from the chaos that Davenport had unleashed in their community during his second

---

23. Samuel Whittelsey, "Resolves of the General Consociation," in Albert C. Bates, ed., *The Law Papers: Correspondence and Documents during Jonathan Law's Governorship of the Colony of Connecticut, 1741–1750*, 3 vols., CHS, *Colls.*, XI (Hartford, Conn., 1907), I, 5–7. See also Joseph Bellamy, "Resolves of the General Consociation Convened at Guilford," Nov. 24, 1741, no. 81659, Joseph Bellamy Papers, Case Memorial Library, Hartford Seminary, Hartford, Conn.

24. Charles J. Hoadley, ed., *The Public Records of the Colony of Connecticut, from October, 1735, to October, 1743, Inclusive* (Hartford, Conn., 1874), VIII, 454. For opposition to Connecticut's anti-itinerancy laws, see JCH, 340; "Original Letters of Dr. Charles Chauncy," *NEHGR*, X (1856), 334; Ebenezer Pemberton to Philip Doddridge, Dec. 16, 1743, Maggs 707, HM 22337, Huntington Library, San Marino, Calif.; and Caleb Smith to William Smith, Nov. 26, 1743, box 1, Smith and Robert Family Papers, circa 1741–1879, New-York Historical Society.

New England preaching tour. Arriving in Ripton earlier that month accompanied by the Hebron, Connecticut, itinerant Benjamin Pomeroy and a train of armor bearers, the Southold revivalist organized a protracted revival meeting. The Ripton petitioners maintained that Davenport's "wild and Extravigent transports of pretend Religious Zeal" menaced the peace of the community. They were appalled by his repeated use of the word "hell" in his sermons as well as his pronouncements of "damnation to all those that opposed there Eregoler [irregular] proseading." Women and children, especially, had been "deprived of the use of there Limbs" and "Rationol faculties." During the five-day meeting, Davenport had thrown the people of Ripton into the "utmost Confusion Contention heat and anger among themselves."[25]

The General Assembly responded swiftly by issuing an arrest warrant and summoning witnesses. Davenport and Pomeroy were brought to Hartford three days later and placed under house arrest. But, in an unusual turn of events, the Long Island itinerant railed against the governor and legislature in a sermon preached in the home of a supportive layman. Davenport's abusive conduct did little to persuade the sitting members of the assembly of his innocence. Declaring him a disturbed person "under the influences of enthusiastical impressions and impulses," they voted to deport Davenport from the colony. Later that night, a mob gathered to protest the magistrates' decision. Davenport fanned the flames of the incipient riot by invoking Jesus's words from the cross in Luke 23:34, *"Lord forgive them, for they know not what they do,"* and imploring God to smite his adversaries. Throughout the night, "shocking scenes of horror and confusion" unfolded in various parts of town, as "wild ungovernable" new converts, incited by Davenport's impending deportation, rallied in the streets and hurled threatening insults at the members of the assembly. Governor Jonathan Law hastily called out the militia, and the disturbance was eventually quelled with great difficulty.[26]

Banished from Connecticut, Davenport turned up in Boston just one month later. Benjamin Colman and a group of twelve prominent clergymen immediately issued a pamphlet condemning his irregular ministry. Although he was barred from every pulpit in the city, Davenport nonetheless held forth on Bos-

25. Joseph Blackleach and Samuel Adams, petition to the Connecticut General Court, May 27, 1742, Ecclesiastical Affairs, Ser. 1, 1658–1789, VII, 253a, Connecticut Archives, 1629–1856, CSL. See also *Boston Evening-Post*, June 7, 1742; and "Extract of a Letter from Hartford," *Boston Weekly News-Letter*, July 1, 1742, in Bushman, ed., *Great Awakening*, 45–46.

26. Hoadley, ed., *Public Records of the Colony of Connecticut*, VIII, 483; *Boston Evening-Post*, June 7, 1742; "Extract of a Letter from Hartford," *Boston Weekly News-Letter*, July 1, 1742, in Bushman, ed., *Great Awakening*, 49. See also Walker, ed., *Diary of Rev. Daniel Wadsworth*, 83–84.

ton Common and Copp's Hill for a fortnight and made excursions to revival strongholds in Ipswich and Concord. Everywhere he went, the Southold revivalist sowed discord, as audiences alternately thrilled to his inspired preaching performances or vilified him for his rabble-rousing rhetoric. Westborough, Massachusetts, clergyman Ebenezer Parkman described Davenport's sermon on Revelation 22:17 as a "very fervent" assault on "unconverted ministers." On other occasions, he was seen "running out into the street among the crowd, and crying out to them in an indecent voice." To his detractors, Davenport was a "Wonder of the Mobb, and the Scorn of the Wise and Sober." His "Stand in the Common," wrote one observer, was "nearer to Bedlam than Whitfields." "In a word," summarized Parkman, the Boston clergy concluded that he was "crazed."[27]

By the end of August 1742, Davenport's revival meetings had fomented numerous "Jangles and Quarrels" and "perpetrated divers Routs, Disturbances and tumultuous Disorders." He had declared a dozen Congregational clergymen in Boston and the neighboring towns to be "carnal and unconverted Men" who were "leading their People blindfold to Hell" and murdering "Souls by the Thousands." His "slanderous and reviling Speeches" goaded local magistrates into action. Arrested for disturbing the peace, Davenport refused bail and willingly suffered incarceration rather than desist from his gospel labors. "His Master Suffred" on the cross, he proclaimed on his way to the old stone prison house on Court Street, "Why not he?" Writing from his cell, Davenport's traveling companion and future participant in the New London bonfires, Michael Hill, asserted in a letter to a sympathetic Connecticut minister that the "Rage of the Clargy" against Davenport's work in "Blood[y] Boston" was "Beyond what you Ever saw." For his part, Davenport welcomed imprisonment as an opportunity to be refined in the furnace of affliction as "gold tried in the fire." The "Lord calls me to suffer as well as to do His will," he acknowledged, before adding that God had made his term in the Boston jail a precious cross to bear in the service of the Holy Spirit.[28]

With the exception of a few outspoken Whitefieldarians such as Daniel Rogers and Andrew Croswell, most of Davenport's former colleagues and

27. Tracy, *Great Awakening*, 209; "Extracts from the Interleaved Almanacs of Nathan Bowen, Marblehead, 1742–1799," *EIHC*, XCI (1955), 170–171. See also *Declaration of a Number of the Associated Pastors of Boston and Charles-Town* (Boston, 1742), in Bushman, *Great Awakening*, 50–51; *Boston Weekly News-Letter*, July 1, 1742; *Boston Evening-Post*, July 5 and Aug. 2, 1742; and DDR, July 20–Aug. 21, 1742.

28. *Boston Evening-Post*, Aug. 2, 23, Sept. 6, 1742; "Extracts from the Interleaved Almanacs of Nathan Bowen," *EIHC*, XCI (1955), 172; Michael Hill and James Davenport to Philemon Robbins, Aug. 30, 1742, Robbins Family Papers, 1724–circa 1803, CHS.

ministerial supporters eventually abandoned him. Davenport undoubtedly brushed aside the pamphlets published against him by revival critics, such as Charles Chauncy, but he must have been stung at the betrayal of his former confederates. Writing to his brother-in-law later shortly after he delivered his Yale College commencement address, Jonathan Edwards complained that Davenport "does more toward giving Satan and other opposers an advantage against the work of God than any one person." While Davenport was preaching on Boston Common, Gilbert Tennent published a letter sternly criticizing his *"enthusiastick Fooleries."* Even Whitefield recognized that the "dear man has been too imprudent." "As to the work in *this Town,*" Old South clergyman Thomas Prince later summarized, "It Seems to have a dreadfull Decline ever since Mr. *Davenport's* Journey Hither."[29]

Davenport's troubles continued unabated following his release from jail in Boston. Later in the fall of 1742, a council of four leading Presbyterian clergymen from New York and New Jersey gathered in Southold to assess a series of complaints that had been leveled against Davenport by his parishioners. Although they acknowledged that God had favored his preaching during the recent revivals, the ministerial council condemned the irregularities in Davenport's conduct that had greatly "hindered his usefulness and been the unhappy occasion of prejudicing many against the work of God that has been carried on in the Land." They rebuked him for abandoning Southold during his ceaseless preaching excursions and denounced his practice of "making impulses upon his Mind the Rule of his Conduct." The council also admonished Davenport for his unwarranted decision to suspend church privileges from those whom he had judged to be unconverted. They objected to his lusty hymn singing in the streets and his encouragement of disorderly public worship exercises.[30]

---

29. Richard Webster, transcr., "Letters to Joseph Bellamy from Aaron Burr, David Brainerd, etc., and Other Papers concerning Mr. Bellamy," 14, microfilm, Presbyterian Historical Society, Philadelphia; *Boston Evening-Post,* July 26, 1742, in David S. Lovejoy, ed., *Religious Enthusiasm and the Great Awakening,* American Historical Sources: Research and Interpretation (Englewood Cliffs, N.J., 1969), 109; Henry F. Jenks, ed., "Letters of the Rev. George Whitefield," MHS, *Procds.,* 2d Ser., X (1895), 300; Thomas Prince to William McCulloch, June 15, 1743, box 1, Park Family Papers, 1701–1929, MS 384, YUA. See also Jonathan Dickinson to Thomas Foxcroft, July 27, 1742, Thomas Foxcroft Correspondence, 1729–1759, Firestone Library, Princeton University, Princeton, N.J.; Stephen Williams to Eleazar Wheelock, Sept. 14, 1741, no. 741514, *EWP;* Charles Chauncy, *Enthusiasm Described and Caution'd Against ...* (Boston, 1742), i–viii; and Theophilus Pickering, *The Rev. Mr. Pickering's Letters to the Rev. N. Rogers and Mr. D. Rogers of Ipswich ...* (Boston, 1742), 18–20. For Croswell's support, see Andrew Croswell, *Mr. Croswell's Reply to the Declaration of a Number of the Associated Ministers in Boston ...* (Boston, 1742).

30. "At a Council of Ministers Conven'd at Southold," October 1742, Miscellaneous Collections: Personal Names.

To the council's shock and dismay, Davenport did not deny any of the charges against him. Nor did he repent of his purported errors. Instead, he attempted to justify the new measures that had led his congregation into the "utmost Confusion." As the council moved to censure the Southold minister, they also encouraged his parishioners to exercise patience in the hope that Davenport "might be convinc'd of his Mistakes and reform 'em." They proposed a deadline for initiating further disciplinary actions against the recalcitrant Whitefieldarian: March 1, 1743. Three days after it expired, Davenport set fire to the first pile of books in New London.[31]

■ As James Davenport reveled in disorder and persecution in Hartford and Boston, the revival that he had sparked in New London had taken a radical turn. By the fall of 1741, many of his devoted followers had grown dissatisfied with the sermons of their aging minister, Eliphalet Adams. On the same day that the general consociation of ministers met in Guilford, John Curtis and Christopher Christophers—both Yale College graduates and prominent New London merchants and magistrates—submitted a petition to the county court requesting the right to worship in a separate church. Citing Adams's opposition to the recent "abundant Effusions" of God's "Blessed Spirit," the aggrieved faction grounded their argument in the provisions of the 1689 Toleration Act, which granted limited legal protection to qualifying dissenters. Less than a week later, they absented themselves from the sacrament in an overt act of protest against Adams's ministry.[32]

Although the county justices initially denied their request, the "People who are Stiled New Lights" proceeded to gather a separatist church during the summer of 1742 under the leadership of an outspoken Whitefieldarian named Timothy Allen. Earlier that year, Allen had been deposed from his pastorate in the west parish of New Haven after declaring that reading the Bible in an unconverted state was as useless as perusing an "OLD ALMANACK." Later that fall, the dissenters renewed their appeal. This second petition included the names of ninety men and women, one-third of whom were full members in Adams's church. Other petitioners hailed from nearly a dozen towns in eastern Connecticut that had experienced powerful revivals. The list included

31. Jonathan Dickinson to Thomas Foxcroft, n.d. [circa fall 1742], Foxcroft Correspondence.

32. Christopher Christophers et al., "Memorial of Cr. Christophers," Nov. 24, 1741, box 81, New London County Court Files, 1691–1855, CSL; *Diary of Joshua Hempstead*, 380. See also Thomas Youngs to Caleb Smith, Nov. 18, 1742, Caleb Smith Correspondence, 1742–1761, New Jersey Historical Society, Newark (I thank John Grigg for sharing his transcription of this document).

white-hot itinerants such as Joseph Prince, the blind son of a prominent Old South Church family in Boston, who had taken to the road as a lay preacher; inquisitive seekers such as Ephraim Clark of Stonington and Noah Ely of Springfield, Massachusetts; and former Yale College students John Brainerd and Silas Brett, who had withdrawn from school following the suppression of revival activities the previous spring. This time, the dissenters were successful. On November 27, 1742, local magistrates administered the required oath of allegiance to a group of three dozen men. The tolerance extended by the court transformed New London into a haven for ardent Whitefieldarians from across the colony.[33]

With Curtis and Allen at the helm of their new church, the separatists took a further step toward ecclesiastical independence by establishing a theological seminary. Unlike its more prestigious rivals, Harvard and Yale Colleges, the Shepherd's Tent, as the upstart seminary was known, eschewed a formal curriculum of theological studies. Its sole educational mission was to translate the Whitefieldian experience of the indwelling Holy Spirit into practice. Candidates for admission to the Shepherd's Tent narrated their conversions in a daunting public spectacle that even a few of the most eager applicants failed. The men and women who successfully gained entrance to the exclusive group were expected to share their Spirit-inspired gifts of preaching, exhorting, and prophesying with the breakaway congregation. Gathering with scholars of the Shepherd's Tent in a small house on the edge of town, Allen, in particular, was "Swallowed up in God" for weeks before the bonfire incident. "My dear Brother," he wrote excitedly to Eleazar Wheelock, "when you are really in God, you have it all." Then, he exclaimed, "My soul Sees Oceans, boundless Oceans of Grace." Other members of the Shepherd's Tent experienced dreams, visions, and other immediate revelations. When David Brainerd visited New London early in February 1743, he discovered Allen and Curtis's congregation and seminary in "wild confusion, too long to mention."[34]

---

33. Merritt Smith to William Smith, July 15, 1742, box 1, Smith and Robert Family Papers; Chauncy, *Seasonable Thoughts on the State of Religion*, 215; Christopher Christophers et al., "Memoriall of C. Christophers," n.d. [circa November 1742], box 81, New London County Court Files; Herman Ely, comp., *Records of the Descendants of Nathaniel Ely ...* (Cleveland, Ohio, 1885), 21; Silas Brett to Eleazar Wheelock, Mar. 29, 1742, no. 742229, *EWP*, Timothy Allen to Wheelock, June 22, 1743, no. 743372. See also Peter S. Onuf, "New Lights in New London: A Group Portrait of the Separatists," *WMQ*, XXXVII (1980), 627–643.

34. Timothy Allen to Eleazar Wheelock, Feb. 27, 1743, no. 743177, *EWP*; Webster, transcr., "Letters to Joseph Bellamy," 24. See also *Diary of Joshua Hempstead*, 396–397, 399; and *Boston Evening-Post*, Mar. 28, 1743. For the location and physical appearance of the seminary, see James Lawrence Chew, "An Account of the Old Houses of New London," *Records and Papers of the New London County Historical Society* (New London, Conn., 1893), I, 94–95.

By the end of the month, the New London dissenters had an "unceasing Expectation" that "glorious Things" were "att the Door." They sent a delegation across the Long Island Sound with instructions to return with Davenport, whom they hoped would preside over Curtis's ordination. Languishing with a leg ailment that confined him to a chair, Davenport still managed to lead the New London separatists in a series of rousing revival meetings. Tinged with anti-Catholic allusions, one report suggested Curtis and his followers greeted him as a prophet equal with Jesus and that Davenport had to "check their Devotion, by telling them, he was not a God, but a Man." The separatists allegedly made "auricular Confessions" and were granted absolution by the visiting revivalist. The group prayed and fasted for divine direction, judging themselves to be in a "good Condition to do some memorable Exploits, to the lasting Honour of their Sect, and the Establishment of their Religion."[35]

On the night of March 6, 1743, Davenport received a divine command to "root out Heresy and pull down Idolatry." The bonfires began the next day. Although a few critics maintained that the dissenters indiscriminately had "burnt the old testament" itself, there appears to have been a clear logic to the books that they committed to the flames. In destroying "useful treatises" of "practical Godliness" by seventeenth-century English latitudinarians, the book-burners condemned the rote performance of religious duties. They dispatched Richard Allestree's best-selling *Whole Duty of Man;* devotional works by William Beveridge, William Dyer, and John Tillotson; and comforting treatises on the *ars moriendi* by Charles Drelincourt and William Sherlock. All of these authors minimized the sectarian theological squabbles of the English Civil War and emphasized the importance of upright moral behavior, the reasonableness of Christian doctrine, and the orderly nature of a salvation that was potentially available to all believers. Emblems of an inclusive, cosmopolitan Protestant sensibility best reserved for the privacy of home and family, their works were popular among Restoration Anglicans in the Middle and southern colonies and frequently imported by New England booksellers.[36]

35. Allen to Wheelock, Feb. 27, 1743, no. 743177, *EWP;* "To the Publisher," *Boston Weekly Post-Boy,* Mar. 28, 1743, in Bushman, ed., *Great Awakening,* 51–52.

36. "To the Publisher," *Boston Weekly Post-Boy,* Mar. 28, 1743, in Bushman, ed., *Great Awakening,* 52; Webster, transcr., "Letters to Joseph Bellamy," 28; Caulkins, *History of New London,* 456. My analysis here and in the paragraphs that follow draws on lists of specific books burned at New London. In addition to the works cited above, see also Skinner to Turell, Mar. 12, 1743, Miscellaneous Bound Manuscripts; Webster, *History of the Presbyterian Church in America,* 204; *Boston Evening-Post,* Mar. 21, 1743, Apr. 11, 1743; Hawks and Perry, eds., *Documentary History of the Protestant Episcopal Church,* I, 189; *Boston Weekly Post-Boy,* Mar. 28, Apr. 11, 1743; *Boston Gazette,* May 17, 1743; *AHI,* 161; and Isaac Backus, *A History of New England with Particular Reference to the Denomination of Chris-*

Davenport and his followers also struck a blow against an earlier generation of "able divines." The New London dissenters distanced themselves from
their puritan heritage by destroying Thomas Shepard's *The Sincere Convert,* a
classic soteriological work that Boston printer Daniel Henchman had repub-
lished the previous year as part of a coordinated effort among booksellers and
ministers to inoculate the reading public against Whitefield's new birth. Although clerical agonists Increase Mather, Samuel Willard, and Solomon Stoddard seldom agreed on ecclesiastical or sacramental matters, they all followed
Shepard in extending the meaning of conversion into a lifelong pilgrimage
toward growth in grace. For this reason, their works appeared on the pyre
alongside sermons and devotional works by notable English nonconformists
such as John Flavel, Matthew Henry, and Samuel Russel. And, in firing the
Bay Psalm Book, the earliest and most frequently reprinted book in British
North America, the separatists registered their profound alienation from the
orderly traditions of puritan worship.[37]

Lastly, Davenport sent a clear message to New England's ecclesiastical
establishment by burning the works of both revival opposers and moderate
supporters. One witness to the conflagrations overheard Davenport and his
followers exclaim that the authors would soon find themselves *"roasting in
the Flames of Hell"* unless they speedily repented of their errors in quenching
the work of the Holy Spirit. The roster of antirevival books and pamphlets was
extensive. Preached shortly after Davenport's visit to Boston in 1742, Charles
Chauncy's *Enthusiasm Described and Caution'd against* caricatured revival
enthusiasm as "properly a disease, a sort of madness." The book-burners also
consigned to the flames works by Boston ministers Benjamin Colman and
Joseph Sewall as well as those of John Barnard of Marblehead, Massachusetts—moderate revival supporters who had closed their pulpits to Davenport one year earlier. The same fate awaited the works of Jonathan Dickinson
of Elizabethtown (now Elizabeth), New Jersey, who had led the disciplinary
proceedings in Southold. The fiery revivalist Andrew Croswell, who joined in
with the leaders of the bonfires, might have been responsible for targeting the

tians Called Baptists, 3 vols. (Providence, R.I., 1777), II, 147. On the popularity of English
Latitudinarian books in eighteenth-century New England, see Norman Fiering, "The First
American Enlightenment: Tillotson, Leverett, and Philosophical Anglicanism," *NEQ,* LIV
(1981), 307–344.

37. Caulkins, *History of New London,* 456. On the publication of classic puritan devotional works during the 1740s, see Charles E. Hambrick-Stowe, "The Spirit of the Old
Writers: The Great Awakening and the Persistence of Puritan Piety," in Francis J. Bremer,
ed., *Puritanism: Transatlantic Perspectives on a Seventeenth-Century Anglo-American Faith*
(Boston, 1993), 277–291.

collected sermons of tutor Henry Flynt, for the two men had clashed at Harvard College the previous year. The roster of sacrificed volumes also had a distinctive regional focus. The dissenters burned an oppositional sermon by New London's Anglican clergyman, Samuel Seabury, along with "all that could be had" by their former minister, Eliphalet Adams. Works by at least five clergymen from coastal Connecticut found their way into the flames alongside a sermon by the outspoken Hartford opposer Daniel Wadsworth and Solomon Williams's cautionary pamphlet in which he criticized visions of the Book of Life. In short, the bonfires registered the dissenters' growing distance from the ideal of the godly walk and their frustration with the creeping conservatism of the New England clergy.[38]

Three weeks later, Curtis, Allen, Christophers, and three of Davenport's armor bearers appeared at the home of New London civil magistrate Joshua Hempstead to answer charges of profaning the Sabbath during the book-burning incident. They offered an intriguing defense of their actions. In what constituted the only supportive account of the incident, Davenport's most devoted followers declared that they were members of an independent religious society that previously had received a license from the county magistrates to "worship God according to their own consciences." The defendants claimed that the bonfires were part of a legitimate religious ritual that had been solemnized with hymns and prayers. Not only was there nothing immoral in destroying the "heretical books in their custody," but Curtis and the other dissenters asserted that their unusual activities were divinely sanctioned and "agreeable to the word of God."[39]

The defendants supplied additional information about the vision that Davenport had experienced on the night before the bonfires. He appears to have initiated the burnings after receiving a biblical impulse from Acts 19:19. The early Christian writer described the miracles of the Holy Spirit that attended Paul's mission work among the earliest churches of Asia Minor: dramatic conversions, faith healings, and speaking in tongues. Of particular significance for Davenport was the story of the Jewish magicians mentioned in verse sixteen. Previously, the sons of Sceva, the chief priest of Ephesus, had attempted to usurp Paul's authority by casting out demons in the name of Jesus. But when a possessed man "leaped on them, and overcame them," the

38. "To the Publisher," *Boston Weekly Post-Boy*, Mar. 28, 1743, in Bushman, ed., *Great Awakening*, 52; Heimert and Miller, eds., *Great Awakening*, 231; *Boston Evening-Post*, Apr. 11, 1743.

39. Caulkins, *History of New London*, 456. See also *Diary of Joshua Hempstead*, 401.

Jewish community was thrown into confusion. Stripped of their authority, the magicians gathered their books on the "curious arts" of exorcism and publicly burned them. Davenport undoubtedly persuaded his auditors at the Shepherd's Tent to envision the burned books in a similar manner. Casting them into the flames became a rite of repentance and exorcism, a communal cleansing of impure beliefs and practices. For revival radicals who believed, as the New London dissenters did, that immediate revelations and charismatic gifts of the Holy Spirit were as common in their own times as they were in the "Earliest ages of Christianity," Davenport's revelation made perfect sense.[40]

Hempstead found the book-burners guilty and fined each of them six shillings plus court costs. But the New London magistrate was not the only one to dismiss the defendants' arguments as groundless. One day before the trial, Jonathan Edwards and nine colleagues had arrived to "reclaim the people" from their errors. The assembly of clergymen made up an impressive roster of current and former Whitefieldarians, including itinerants Benjamin Pomeroy, Joseph Bellamy, and Samuel Buell as well as revival supporters from several neighboring towns. At the conclusion of the trial, Edwards delivered an afternoon lecture. Hempstead deemed the discourse "very Suitable for the times," as Edwards bore "Wittness against the prevailing disorders and destractions that are Subsisting in the Country by means of Enthusiasm." Hempstead's effort to conflate Davenport's seemingly bizarre actions with insanity was telling. To him, the bonfires had been perpetrated by a disorderly group of mentally unhinged persons.[41]

Edwards and his colleagues saw things differently. Although they were greatly alarmed by the "strange and surprising Transaction" at New London, the visiting clergymen declined to argue that Davenport was insane. Instead, they classified the bonfires as a gross error and the logical result of acting "under a Notion of a special and immediate Direction of the Holy Ghost." In a published statement written on behalf of the delegation, minister Benjamin Lord of Norwich, Connecticut, used the book-burning incident to condemn biblical impulses and impressions. Spurious revelations such as Davenport's call to pull down idolatry, he argued, were "altogether different from the true sanctifying and gracious Influences of the Holy Ghost." Even when attended

40. Christophers et al., "Memorial of Cr. Christophers," Nov. 24, 1741, box 81, New London County Court Files. For the book-burners' reference to Acts 19:19, see Caulkins, *History of New London*, 456.

41. Jonathan Edwards to Sarah Edwards, Mar. 25, 1743, in *WJE*, XVI, *Letters and Personal Writings*, ed. George S. Claghorn (New Haven, Conn., 1998), 104; *Diary of Joshua Hempstead*, 401.

by verses of scripture that came with "great Power," such immediate revelations were *"Mistakes* and *Delusions"*—the "grand Instrument" employed by
the Devil to delude God's people. James Davenport was not insane, Lord
concluded. He was a dangerous enthusiast. And, as the large assembly that
gathered for the New London bonfires clearly indicated, he was not alone.[42]

THEY CAN HARDLY BE NEIGHBOURLY OR PEACEABLE

Of the many clergymen whom Alexander Hamilton encountered during his
travels through the northern colonies, none impressed him more than William
Hooper. That Hamilton ranked the minister of Boston's West Church among
the "best preachers I have heard in America" was partly owing to his sense of
nationalistic pride. Hooper was both a fellow Scotsman and graduate of the
University of Edinburgh. Erected in 1737, his church reflected the genteel refinement of its first minister, from its stately spire to the green window cur-
tains and matching velvet seat cushions to the fashionable pulpit adorned
with a large sounding board and supported by fluted Doric pilasters. Hooper's
congregation included many of the city's "better sort," including wealthy Scottish merchants and the renowned portraitist John Smibert. Hamilton was so
taken with the "sollid sense, strong connected reasoning, and good language"
of Hooper's sermons that he attended religious meetings in the West Church
on each of the three Sabbaths that he spent in the city. The two men dined
together and toured Harvard College. Hamilton felt more at home with his
fellow Scotsman in Boston than anywhere else in the colonies.[43]

Visiting with Hooper provided ample opportunities to discuss the state of
religion in New England, for the West Church clergyman ranked among Boston's most outspoken revival opposers. Two years earlier, Hooper had published a signature polemic entitled *The Apostles Neither Imposters nor Enthusiasts*. His argument attempted to chart a middle course between infidels who
denied the authority of revealed religion and enthusiasts who reveled in "their
own Fancies and Dreams and Imaginations as the Inspiration of GOD." The
sages of the apostolic era, he maintained, were credible witnesses to Jesus's
miracles, crucifixion, and resurrection. They preached plain doctrines, championed morality, and demanded orderly worship practices. The "Truth of the

42. *Boston Gazette,* Apr. 12, 1743.

43. *AHI,* 130, 146. On Hooper and the West Church, see Charles W. Akers, *Called unto
Liberty: A Life of Jonathan Mayhew, 1720–1766* (Cambridge, Mass., 1964), 44–59; and John
Corrigan, *The Hidden Balance: Religion and the Social Theories of Charles Chauncy and
Jonathan Mayhew* (Cambridge, Mass., 1987), 114–125.

Christian Religion," Hooper continued, was "plain and certain," equally available to "every serious and considerate" believer.[44]

How different the apostles were from enthusiasts like James Davenport, who claimed to have "found another Way to Heaven, than that of a good and holy Life." Operating under the "Conceits of a warmed or over-weening Brain," enthusiasts mistakenly assumed that "every vain Notion that settles strongly in their Fancies" was a revelation from God. Enthusiasts were "rebellious and turbulent," ceaselessly obsessing over "idle Dreams and Chimeras" and railling against their critics. "And how base and unmanly is it," Hooper insisted, "to be guided neither by Scripture nor Reason, but to give ourselves up to the blind and mad Suggestions of an heated and disorderly Brain! Nothing more vilifies human Nature: It sinks it even below the Brutes that perish." Small wonder that Davenport heaped a copy of *The Apostles Neither Impostors nor Enthusiasts* on the New London bonfires one year later.[45]

Reflecting on his visit to Boston in his *Itinerarium,* Hamilton praised the inhabitants for their gaiety and cultural sophistication, but he followed Hooper in condemning the religious commotions. "The people here," he wrote, have lately been "much infested with enthusiasm from the preaching of some fanaticks and New Light teachers." Everywhere he traveled in New England, Hamilton heard stories of a "strange madness" attending the revivals. The most bizarre reports involved an obscure layman named Richard Woodbury from Rowley, Massachusetts. According to the aging magistrate Stephen Sewall, with whom Hamilton conversed on July 30, 1744, Woodbury claimed not only to have received absolute assurance of his election but also to have passed into a state of sinless perfection and physical immortality. He believed that he possessed the power to "save or damn whom he pleased," drank "healths to King Jesus," and vehemently condemned to hell anyone who questioned his charismatic authority. Woodbury had been itinerating in the towns straddling the border between Massachusetts and New Hampshire, where he could be heard uttering "blasphemous and absurd speeches."[46]

Hamilton was shocked by Sewall's report and would scarcely have given it credit had he not encountered a newspaper account confirming the details of Woodbury's itinerant activities on the same day. Abandoning the conventions of the disinterested travel narrative, Hamilton paused in his *Itinerarium* to offer a scathing indictment of Woodbury's eccentricities. The Rowley layman

44. William Hooper, *The Apostles Neither Impostors nor Enthusiasts* ... (Boston, 1742), 1, 5–6.

45. Ibid., 21, 27, 30, 45.

46. *AHI,* 120, 145.

was a remarkable instance of the "lengths of madness enthusiasm will carry men once they give it a loose [rein]," he admonished. Hamilton seemed to revel in the absurdity of Woodbury's excesses, asserting that his "ridiculous frolicks" would do more to bring people back to their senses through the power of ridicule. In Hamilton's telling, Woodbury served the same function that Davenport had performed in Hooper's sermon. For both men, biblical impulses and visionary phenomena stood well outside the boundaries of reasonable Christianity. At the same time, the charismatic elements of the revivals constituted a far more serious threat to the Congregational establishment than either was willing to admit. Between the publication of Hooper's pamphlet during the fall of 1742 and newspaper reports of Woodbury's activities two years later, a new cadre of enthusiasts had emerged to dominate the revival scene. The Whitefieldian awakening had entered a militant phase. In the van of the host of insurgent rebels stood outspoken men and women who fervently believed that the indwelling presence of the Holy Spirit sanctioned the disruption—and even, perhaps, the destruction—of all ecclesiastical hierarchies.[47]

■ The connection between religious enthusiasm and social protest was a complex one that operated on several levels. Ecclesiastical and civil discord often erupted simultaneously. In Connecticut, zealous Whitefieldarians convicted of violating the colony's anti-itinerancy law held forth from their jail cells in emulation of Davenport, thus dramatizing the opposition between the work of the Holy Spirit and that of godless civil magistrates. Fisticuffs broke out in the Providence, Rhode Island, meetinghouse as revival supporters and scoffers "collared one another, until the King's Attorney" arrived to suppress the incipient riot; Daniel Rogers heard several muskets fired outside the same building during one of his sermons a year later. Self-appointed defenders of orthodoxy in Wallingford, Connecticut, told the minister's son that they "stood Radey at any time with clubs, so that if any new lite minister came to preach, they would club him or stone him." When Samuel Hopkins arrived to deliver a weekday lecture in Suffield, Massachusetts, revival opposers staged a makeshift sit-in, occupying the meetinghouse for more than seven hours and forcing the young minister to preach at the home of a supportive layman. The reverse occurred several years later in Salem, Massachusetts, when prorevival parishioners effectively locked a visiting itinerant preacher into the pulpit by nailing the doors shut and instructing the constable to escort the local min-

47. Ibid., 120.

ister to his pew. Events such as these fomented endless quarrels and disturbances in towns throughout New England during the mid-1740s.[48]

Disorder had been part of the revivals from the beginning. Even the powerful awakening in York, Maine, had its dark side. Although some participants
experienced rapturous visions and joyful conversions, others spoke only of despair. One York man confessed that he had been "Sorely Tempted to Distroy
himself." The accelerated pace of religious meetings frequently bound the
community together in Christian love, but it also tore families apart. Another
woman who had been "much inlightened by the Spirit of God" was turned out
of her own house by her disapproving husband. Where the anonymous author
of a "Jornal of a Fue Days at York" witnessed emotional displays of primitive
Christian communalism, an Anglican gentleman whose letter was later published in the *South Carolina Gazette* saw only natural hierarchies subverted,
passions loosed, and social disorder unleashed. The anonymous newspaper
correspondent roundly condemned the cruel manner in which new converts
chided their neighbors who continued to struggle "under Darkness." Local
farmers had ceased working during the revival season and left their harvests
to rot in the fields. To him, the "merry Tricks and antick Gestures" that attended the nightly meetings seemed closer to a drunken frolic than a solemn
religious occasion.[49]

As the tide of revivals crested in 1742, opponents increasingly resorted to
ridiculing the new converts' ecstatic religious experiences. Eleazar Wheelock
described a group of scoffers in Providence that hired a man for twenty shillings to "come into the meeting house and fall down, which he did, and made
a great disturbance." Heated exchanges with touring riding ministers devolved
into personal attacks and, occasionally, ethnic slurs. Polemicists attacked their
religious opponents in broadsides, pamphlets, and the Boston newspapers
using many of the same strategies that had made London's Grub Street notorious a few decades earlier. Gossipy reports of revival excesses—masquerading
as news from the far corners of the British Empire—trafficked in the scandalous, the lurid, and the bizarre. Witty pundits writing under humorous pseudo-
nyms served up mock biographies of Whitefield, "infallible" medicinal recipes

48. Walker, ed., *Diary of Rev. Daniel Wadsworth*, 89; *Boston Evening-Post*, Aug. 23, 1742;
DDR, Oct. 9, 1742; Webster, transcr., "Letters to Joseph Bellamy," 16 (quote); Samuel Hopkins, journal, 1741–1744, 45–46, box 322, SGC II; John Higginson to Samuel Curwen, Aug.
20, 1745, box 3, Curwen Family Papers, 1637–1808, AAS.
49. Douglas L. Winiarski, "'A Jornal of a Fue Days at York': The Great Awakening on
the Northern New England Frontier," *Maine History*, XLII (2004), 65, 70; *South Carolina
Gazette*, Mar. 1, 1742.

for making new converts, directions for curing religious ills using a "Chinese Stone," and even a Swiftian essay entitled "A Modest Proposal for the Destruction of Reason." Laced with sexual innuendo and scatological references, doggerel verses on the revivals circulated widely both in printed broadsides and in manuscripts. Across New England, the tone of public religious discourse assumed a decidedly darker cast.[50]

New converts fought fire with fire. Enterprising Whitefieldarians produced mock prayer bills that simultaneously lampooned the foibles of opposing clergymen and parodied the conventions of Congregational prayer practices. During the summer of 1742, as James Davenport languished in a Boston jail, an "enthusiastick Zealot" slipped a "scandalous Note" into the stack of prayer bills scheduled to be read at a lecture in the Brattle Street meetinghouse. Instead of requesting prayers for the unconverted, the petitioner asked the assembly to pray for the Boston *"Arssosacahsiion [association] of Menesters,"* which the note derided as the *"Choase [choice] Cause of the present Parsaction [persecution] of X [Christ] in boston or spirittual Jerusalem."* The following year, parishioners in Newbury, Massachusetts, forged a prayer bill in the name of their unsuspecting minister, the aged and outspoken revival opposer Christopher Toppan. In what turned out to be an elaborate hoax, the fictitious Toppan thanked God for preserving his body during a recent riding accident. For several days after the mishap, Toppan allegedly pondered the cause of his misfortune, until a "Voyce came to me and Said, I Need nott Truble myself, it was that Devill did it, that Deseav'd all the people, and Now I hope that god will Enable me to Oppose that Great work of the Devill, and the Instruments of it more than Ever I Did." For the "new light men" in Newbury, who at the time were embroiled in a protracted dispute with their minister, the joke was obvious. Toppan had formed his opposition to the Whitefieldian revivals after hearkening to an imaginary voice inside his head. He comes across in the fraudulent prayer bill as much a deluded enthusiast as his scheming antagonists.[51]

50. EWD, 238; Lisa Herb Smith, "The First Great Awakening in American Newspapers, 1739–48" (Ph.D. diss., University of Delaware, 1998), 196, 224, 275, 358; J. A. Leo Lemay, "Joseph Green's Satirical Poem on the Great Awakening," *Resources for American Literary Studies*, IV (1974), 173–183. For additional examples of satirical poetry composed by revival opposers, see the Colman-Jenks Collection, 1651–1809, MHS.

51. *Boston Weekly News-Letter*, Aug. 19, 1742; *Boston Evening-Post*, Aug. 30, 1742; Anonymous, prayer bill, n.d. [circa 1743–1744?], "Miscellaneous Papers—Churches," Museum of Old Newbury, Newburyport, Mass.; Joshua Coffin, *A Sketch of the History of Newbury, Newburyport, and West Newbury, from 1638 to 1845* (Boston, 1845), 213. For an extended discussion of these incidents, see Douglas L. Winiarski, "The Newbury Prayer Bill Hoax: Devotion and Deception in New England's Era of Great Awakenings," *Massachusetts Historical Review*, XIV (2012), 53–86.

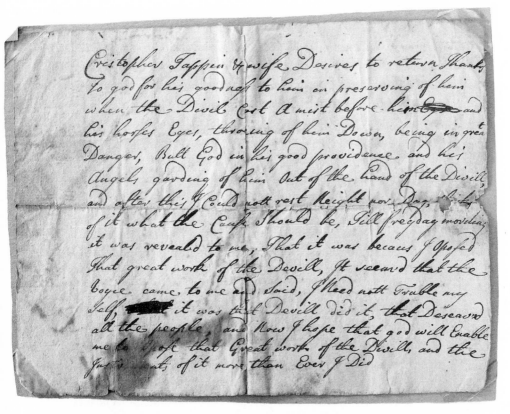

FIGURE 18 Fraudulent Prayer Bill Written in the Name of Christopher Toppan. Circa 1743-1744. From the collections of the Museum of Old Newbury, Newburyport, Massachusetts

Others conjured new threats. *"Ran-away on Saturday Night last,"* reported the *Boston Weekly-News Letter* in April 1742, an enslaved *"new convert"* named Pompey York, whom the advertisement described as *"very forward to mimick some of the Strangers that have of late been preaching about among us."* Grifters posing as itinerant preachers—including the notorious confidence man Tom Bell and an anonymous figure claiming to be the brother of Gilbert Tennent—appeared during the peak months of the revivals. A man in Norton, Massachusetts, reported that he had been robbed of some valuable garments by a smooth-talking traveler posing as "one of those called New-Light Preachers." Pickpockets preyed on unsuspecting worshippers at Whitefield's meetings. In Stratford, Connecticut, Jedidiah Mills mercilessly tarred his Anglican opponents, arguing that there was "no more holiness in a Church than under an oak tree." Following one lecture, according to several accounts, several auditors "put his doctrine in practice" by hurling dung into the recently constructed Saint Paul's church.[52]

For revival opposers such as Boston's Charles Chauncy, the social ramifications of an inspired laity were profoundly unsettling. Ever since Whitefield had ignited the passions of his impressionable followers with his "Doctrine of *inward Feelings*," Chauncy argued in a published letter to a Scottish correspondent, New England's houses of worship had been filled with confusion. Revival meetings featured unimaginable "Excesses and Extravangancies." The "Hubbub" included exhortations by children, women, and *"conceited young Men,"* all of which lasted well into the night. New converts railed against the unconverted, interrupted their ministers' sermons, and narrated their conversions with certain assurance of divine election. They exhorted on the streets and itinerated in neighboring parishes. In Chauncy's mind, the ecclesiastical and theological innovations of the Whitefieldarians were *"Affronts* to *common Decency."*[53]

A few clergymen reached deep into biblical history to explain the disorders that plagued their parishes during the revival years. According to the Northfield, Massachusetts, clergyman Benjamin Doolittle, "ENTHUSIASM" was the *"first,* or *Original Sin."* Eve's desire to know the *"Secrets of the most High"* through immediate revelations of the Holy Spirit inflamed her bodily passions and exposed her immortal soul to the temptations of the serpent. Born of pride and irrationality, enthusiasm irreparably tainted her descendants. The latest generation, Doolittle asserted, had imbibed the sins of their first parents by the gallon. Emboldened by their purported experiences of the new birth, an enthusiastic laity would grow ever more *"loud* and *boisterous,* and *threaten* what they will do; and begin *boldly to trample upon Authority,* in *Church* and *State,* and are not afraid to *speak evil of Dignities."* In short, Doolittle concluded ominously, enthusiasts "can hardly be neighbourly or peaceable."[54]

52. *Boston Weekly News-Letter,* Apr. 15, 1742; Steven C. Bullock, "A Mumper among the Gentle: Tom Bell, Colonial Confidence Man," *WMQ,* LV (1998), 240; NGD, 320; DDR, May 9, 1743; Williams, diaries, IV, 25; *Boston Evening-Post,* Apr. 30, 1744 (quote); *American Weekly Mercury* (Philadelphia), Jan. 15, 1745; Hawks and Perry, eds., *Documentary History of the Protestant Episcopal Church,* I, 197 (quote); *Boston Evening-Post,* Oct. 10, 1743. On the history of imposter pastors, see Thomas Kidd, "Passing as a Pastor: Clerical Imposture in the Colonial Atlantic World," *Religion and American Culture: A Journal of Interpretation,* XIV (2004), 149–174.

53. [Chauncy], *A Letter from a Gentleman in Boston to Mr. George Wishart* ... (Edinburgh, 1742), in Lovejoy, ed., *Religious Enthusiasm and the Great Awakening,* 75–78. For a similar argument, see Timothy D. Hall, *Contested Boundaries: Itinerancy and the Reshaping of the Colonial American Religious World* (Durham, N.C., 1994), 44–59.

54. Benjamin Doolittle, *An Enquiry into Enthusiasm* ... (Boston, 1743), 12, 33, 35.

Jonathan Edwards was quick to observe that effusions of the Holy Spirit had been attended with "manifold imprudences, and great and sinful irregularities" in all ages of Christianity, as Satan labored to counterfeit the "mark of the true Spirit." The seemingly chaotic aspects of powerful revival meetings, he argued in his September 1741 Yale College commencement address, were merely negative signs. Sutton, Massachusetts, clergymen David Hall went further. In an angry letter written several weeks later, he criticized Eleazar Wheelock for promoting many of the disorderly revival innovations attributed to Davenport, including violent preaching rhetoric and gestures, judging the souls of church members, encouraging bodily outbursts, and singing in the streets. "Surely brethren God is the Auther of order and not of confusion," Hall warned, paraphrasing 1 Corinthians 14:33. Edwards cited the same passage in *Some Thoughts concerning the Present Revival of Religion in New-England*. "Order is one of the most necessary of all external means of the spiritual good of God's church," he asserted. A church without order was "like a city without walls."[55]

Zealous Whitefieldarians vehemently disagreed. The Durham, New Hampshire, firebrand Nicholas Gilman, for example, sneered at colleagues who were "afraid of Confusion—and for keeping All in Peace." During a brief lull in the powerful Ipswich revival in January 1742, Daniel Rogers questioned his unusually silent auditors "whether this was better than what was call'd Confusion Some nights past." He pressed on to chastise the sluggish assembly for being too preoccupied with outward order in public worship. Extraordinary works of the Holy Spirit, Rogers maintained, inevitably produced "External Disorders, and we must be Willing that God Should carry on his Work in his own Way." "Where a Minister and his People are at Peace," another minister reportedly declared, "Satan is at the Head of it."[56]

According to Harvard tutor Henry Flynt, many riding ministers and new converts attempted to justify disorderly revival meetings by paraphrasing Matthew 10:34, "I came not to send peace on Earth but a sword." Their "maxim" agreed Edwards, was the "more division and strife, the better [the] sign." The Connecticut itinerant Andrew Croswell disparaged Edwards for

55. Jonathan Edwards, *The Distinguishing Marks of a Work of the Spirit of God...* (Boston, 1741), in *WJE*, IV, *The Great Awakening*, ed. C. C. Goen (New Haven, Conn., 1972), 226, 241; David Hall to Eleazar Wheelock, Sept. 23, 1741, no. 741523, *EWP*; Edwards, *Some Thoughts concerning the Present Revival of Religion in New-England* (Boston, 1742), in *WJE*, IV, *Great Awakening*, ed. Goen, 455.

56. NGD, 306; DDR, Jan. 12, 1741; Ebenezer Turell, *Mr. Turell's Directions to His People with Relation to the Present Times* (Boston, 1742), 11. For Rogers's growing radicalism, see Thomas S. Kidd, "Daniel Rogers' Egalitarian Great Awakening," *Journal of the Historical Society*, VII (2007), 111–135.

being "too timerous, or Cowardly in the Cause of Xt [Christ]," and he blasted his opponents in Boston for their slavish idolatry to ecclesiastical tranquility. "In Times past, there hath been *Order* in the Churches of Christ, instead of *Religion*," he explained in one of his many revival pamphlets. "The Truth is, God never works *powerfully*, but Men cry out of *Disorder:* for God's *Order* differs vastly from their *nice* and *delicate* Apprehensions of it." Croswell's Christology championed the revolutionary messiah who overturned the tables of the money changers and threatened the unrighteous with eternal judgment. The Whitefieldarians were Christ's lieutenants, charged to preach in places where their "company is not Desired" in order to expose and correct "Such Ministers as are Gross and Evident opposers of the Work of God." Willing agents of "blessed Confusions," Gilman, Rogers, and Croswell understood their revival activities as an apocalyptic holy war against the purported hypocrisy of the godly walk.[57]

■ Despite their seemingly chaotic nature, the religious commotions that roiled New England during the peak years of the Whitefieldian awakenings can be grouped into three broadly transgressive practices: railing against revival opposers, judging the religious experiences of others, and insisting on an "Inward Commission" to preach or exhort in public without clerical sanction.[58]

Heated speech had been a constant source of tension in the covenanted communities of seventeenth-century New England, but, by 1740, disputes involving verbal transgressions were on the decline in both the Congregational churches and the provincial courts. New England's era of great awakenings brought a new sense of urgency to the time-honored puritan practice of policing public discourse, as religious enthusiasts recovered the bombastic, railing style of public address that marked the sectarian controversies of the English Civil War. Charles Chauncy directed one of his earliest antirevival pamphlets at the dangers of an *"unbridled tongue,"* but his message went unheeded by militants such as Andrew Croswell, who resolutely refused to "muzzle" their

---

57. Edward T. Dunn, ed., "The Diary of Tutor Henry Flynt of Harvard College, 1675–1760," 3 vols., typescript (Buffalo, N.Y., 1978), 1478, 1480; Edwards, *Some Thoughts concerning the Present Revival of Religion*, in *WJE*, IV, *Great Awakening*, ed. Goen, 447; Andrew Croswell to Eleazar Wheelock, May 3, 1742, *WJEO*, XXXII, *Correspondence by, to, and About Edwards and His Family*; Croswell, *A Letter from the Revd. Mr. Croswell, to the Revd Mr. Turell in Answer to His Direction to His People* (Boston, 1742), 12; Croswell to Nathaniel and Daniel Rogers, Sept. 23, 1742, case 8, box 22, SGC I. See also Leigh Eric Schmidt, "'A Second and Glorious Reformation': The New Light Extremism of Andrew Croswell," *WMQ*, XLIII (1986), 222–223.

58. Windham Association, Records, 1723–1814, I, 121, Connecticut Conference Archives, United Church of Christ (currently on deposit at CL; available online at NEHH).

mouths. The indwelling presence of the Spirit taught many New Englanders to speak and act with what one Rhode Island woman aptly called a "holy boldness."[59]

David Brainerd, who famously uttered that Yale College tutor Chauncey Whittelsey had "no more Grace than this Chair," was but one soloist amid a riotous chorus of newborn saints who trumpeted their own conversions and scorned the security of their unconverted neighbors and the dead formalism of their conservative ministers. Whittelsey's first cousin was convicted of defaming Simon Backus, a clergyman from Newington, Connecticut, just one year later. "It was as bad for any people to Go to hear him preach as to Get Drunk," Josiah Whittelsey proclaimed, before adding that he could just as easily "Live with the Devil in the pulpit or hear him preach as Mr. Backus, for he was as fit for it." In the south parish of Reading (now Wakefield), Massachusetts, John Dammon and his wife served up similar fare to their minister, fulminating that "this Church and all Other Churches in the Land were but Baals Churches and the Ministers, but the Dragons Angels." When the New Haven gentleman and warm revival advocate James Pierpont read the Hampshire County ministerial association's 1742 pamphlet decrying biblical impulses and other revival irregularities, he burst out in a rage, declaring that it could not have been "more calculated to destroy the interest of Religion" if it had been "drawn up in the Cabinet Councel of Hell."[60]

The corrosive effects of heated revival discourse are well documented in the Goshen Society of Lebanon, Connecticut, where minister Jacob Eliot bewailed the rising audacity of his wayward flock. Several months after witnessing the celestial spirit journeys of Noah Chappel, Eliot discovered the young visionist praying between Sabbath exercises for the "old Damned Hypocrites"

59. Charles Chauncy, *An Unbridled Tongue a Sure Evidence, That Our Religion is Hypocritical and Vain* (Boston, 1741), 19, 44; Croswell to Wheelock, May 3, 1742, *WJEO*, XXXII, *Correspondence by, to, and about Edwards and His Family;* Samuel Hopkins, comp., *The Life and Character of Miss Susanna Anthony* ... (Worcester, Mass., 1796), 44. On the dangers of transgressive speech, see Robert Blair St. George, "'Heated' Speech and Literacy in Seventeenth-Century New England," in David D. Hall and David Grayson Allen, eds., *Seventeenth-Century New England,* CSM, *Publications,* LXIII (Boston, 1984), 275–322; and Jane Kamensky, *Governing the Tongue: The Politics of Speech in Early New England* (New York, 1997).

60. Jonathan Edwards, *An Account of the Life of the Late Reverend Mr. David Brainerd* (Boston, 1749), in *WJE*, VII, *The Life of David Brainerd,* ed. Norman Pettit (New Haven, Conn., 1984), 155; Confession of Josiah Whittelsey, Nov. 30, 1743, no. 81407, Joseph Bellamy Papers; James F. Cooper, Jr., and Kenneth P. Minkema, eds., *The Colonial Church Records of the First Church of Reading (Wakefield) and the First Church of Rumney Marsh (Revere),* CSM, *Pubs.,* LXXII (Boston, 2006), 190; Thomas Clap to Solomon Williams, June 8, 1742, case 8, box 21, SGC I.

in the congregation to be immediately cast into hell. Chappel was just the first of many outspoken critics of Eliot's ministry. Following a visit from James Davenport's armor bearers later that summer, Eliot soon found himself confronted by dozens of "saucy" and "impudent" parishioners who continually disrupted his worship services. One man publicly branded him a "Pope" and an opposer of the revivals before the large assembly that gathered to sing and exhort after Sabbath exercises. Others openly prayed for his imminent conversion or speedy removal from office. A woman appeared at his house and announced that the Lord, speaking to her in revelatory impulses, had forbid her to join the church. Another congregant voiced his hope that a plague might overspread the country, that the "children of God were safe and it might be the means of converting many." Even basic pastoral tasks proved arduous. Summoned to the bedside of a dying man one evening, Eliot was "admonished, affronted and abused" by the assembled mourners.[61]

Hot verbal disputes fueled conflict in parishes across New England. One notable case erupted in Suffield during the weeks following Edwards's stirring performance of *Sinners in the Hands of an Angry God*. Neighboring clergyman Stephen Williams of Longmeadow parish in Springfield reported the eruption of "Different opinions," "strange and unusuall things," and "confusions" during the summer and fall of 1741, as "carping" parishioners fell into "hurtful Exreams." "They Seem to have religion at heart," he wrote in his diary following a visit from several angry Suffield residents, "but I fear their zeal boils over." Most of the "strange rumours from Suffield" centered on the ordination of a young ministerial candidate named Ebenezer Gay. Appointed by a narrow margin and against the wishes of a vocal faction in the town's west precinct, Gay worked steadily to dampen the ardor of his fractious parishioners. He introduced new church admission practices, including written relations and a two-week propounding period. Although commonplace in eastern Massachusetts, the new standards for full communion in the Suffield church did not square with the dramatic conversion experiences of those who had witnessed the Holy Spirit descend on the Connecticut Valley.[62]

61. E. H. Gillett, ed., "Diary of the Rev. Jacob Eliot," *Historical Magazine and Notes and Queries, concerning the Antiquities, History, and Biography of America*, 2d Ser., V (1869), 33–34; Elisha Huntington to Jacob Eliot, Sept. 10, 1744, box 1, Jacob Eliot Family Papers, 1716–1945, MS 193, YUA.

62. Williams, diaries, III, 368, 398, 406, 409, IV, 5, 24; Marston Cabot to Ebenezer Gay, Jan. 11, 1742, Suffield, Conn., First Congregational Church Papers, 1741–1917, microfilm no. 1014184, GSU. On the Suffield conflict, see Douglas L. Winiarski, "Jonathan Edwards, Enthusiast? Radical Revivalism and the Great Awakening in the Connecticut Valley," *Church History*, LXXIV (2005), 712–727.

Within a few months of his ordination, contempt for the young Suffield minister had become open, widespread, and unusually brazen. When a visiting clergyman tried to convince the congregation that outward humility was a sign of a Christlike spirit, Noah Smith stood up and shouted that he preached a "Cursed Damnable Devilish Doctrine and a Doctrine that comes from Devils and a Doctrine that leads Souls down to Hell." Smith and two of his neighbors were found guilty of slander and fined for their outbursts. Another outspoken parishioner, Joseph Hastings, declared that Gay and a local magistrate had been persecuting the "Spirit of Christ." Like Daniel Rogers and Andrew Croswell, the brash layman envisioned ecclesiastical disorder as an emblem of divine favor. He openly prayed that the Suffield "Church was broke all to Peices, or that the Breaches in it were a great Deal Wider." Called before the church to account for his brash speeches, Hastings maintained that the divisions were, "not sinful Quarrellings," but rather a way of "separating Persons from Sin" by the "Operations of the Spirit of God."[63]

Hastings's desire to divide the Suffield church between newborn saints and unregenerate hypocrites gestured toward a second major source of ecclesiastical discord: spiritual discernment, perhaps the defining characteristic of James Davenport's inspired ministry. Impassioned new converts typically directed their heated speech against their unconverted neighbors and arrogated to themselves the ability to judge the souls of others. To both opposers and moderates, censorious judging ranked among the most dangerous errors of the day. For lay men and women such as Nathaniel Lothrop, Jr., however, condemning the unconverted was a holy act, a gift of inspired, ecstatic, and, at times, involuntary speech that issued directly from the indwelling presence of the Holy Spirit. Thumping his fist against his chest one cold Sabbath in January 1742, the zealous Norwich layman challenged revival "apposers to say that I have not got the sperit of god in me for I know that I have." Later that same day, shocked witnesses overheard Lothrop tell his own sister that it would be the "pleasentis sight that ever my Eyes saw" if Jesus descended on a cloud and commissioned the devils to drag her unconverted soul down to hell. The two audacious statements were theologically related. In Lothrop's mind, the indwelling Spirit provided complete assurance of his own salvation and conveyed the power to discern its presence in others.[64]

---

63. Hampshire County, Mass., Court of General Sessions of the Peace, 1734–1745, 101, microfilm no. 0886421, GSU; Suffield, Conn., Church Records, 1742–1836, June 29, 1743, CHS.

64. Statements of Joseph Reynolds, Thomas Grist, and Peter Huntington, Jan. 20–26, 1742, 3B–3C, "Papers Relating to the First Church in Norwich during the Ministry of Rev. Benjamin Lord, D.D.," 1742–1877, microfilm no. 656, CSL.

In the north parish of Groton (now Ledyard), Connecticut, Andrew Croswell's Anglican rival, Ebenezer Punderson, bemoaned the "Bewitching Enthusiasm" that had gripped local residents following Davenport's visit during the summer of 1741. The Groton revival had been marked by emotional conversions, somatic outbursts, "Screitchings Screamings, faintings, Convulsions, and Visions." The latter involved two "wild visionaries" who descended on Punderson's parsonage to "oppose me in my Ministrations." One spoke in the name of Jesus himself, while the other demanded to know whether the Anglican clergyman had been born again and had the "witness of the Spirit." Unsatisfied with Punderson's response, the "Demoniaks" heatedly branded him "Bellzebub the prince of Devills" and boldly declared both the clergyman and his congregation to be "unconverted, and going Straight Down to Hell." One of the unnamed visionists later burned £1,200 of his own property, including his account books, paper money, household possessions, and clothes. In an eerie precursor to events that unfolded only a few miles away in New London one year later, the Groton visionist nearly broke his "House almost to Pieces," noted town minister John Owen, before returning to his senses and begging forgiveness of those whom he had offended.[65]

Closely allied to verbal outbursts and discerning spirits were divine commands to preach and exhort. Hundreds of new converts spoke, prayed, exhorted, and even preached during revival meetings. A few of these gifted individuals—including the Salem baker Richard Elvins, Shepherd's Tent scholars Joseph Prince and Ephraim Clark, the Canterbury, Connecticut, lawyer Elisha Paine, and Andrew Croswell's younger brother, Joseph—managed to transform their brief appearances on the public stage into lifelong ministerial callings. Occasionally, newspapers took notice of their labors, as was the case with a vagabond named Samuel Green, who proudly hocked a printed "History" of his visions and revelations on the streets of Boston and Newport, Rhode Island, while proclaiming that he was an *"Emblem and Type of the Son of God"* and was *"as much inspired to preach as any of the Apostles."* But the vast majority of these impromptu "Pedlars in Divinity" were anonymous men, women, children, Indians, and African Americans whose brief gospel labors seldom elicited sustained or favorable reports from revival observers.[66]

65. Kenneth Walter Cameron, ed., *The Church of England in Pre-Revolutionary Connecticut: New Documents and Letters concerning the Loyalist Clergy and the Plight of Their Surviving Church* (Hartford, Conn., 1976), 58–59, 61; *Boston Weekly News-Letter*, Nov. 13, 1741.

66. *Boston Evening-Post*, May 31, July 12, 1742; Benes, "Pedlars in Divinity," in Benes, ed., *Life on the Streets and Commons*, 31. See also Elizabeth C. Nordbeck, "Almost Awakened: The Great Revival in New Hampshire and Maine, 1727–1748," *Historical New Hampshire*,

Few lay preachers and exhorters left letters or diaries in which they chronicled their activities. One notable exception was Reuben Ely, brother of one of the scholars who attended the Shepherd's Tent in New London. During the early months of the revivals in the upper Connecticut Valley, he wrote to Eleazar Wheelock complaining of "great oppositions" voiced by "strict moralists," "weak Christians," and "openly prophane" parishioners. Ely's list of offenders included his own pastor in the west parish of Springfield, Massachusetts. "A Lukewarme minister," he grumbled, "makes A people so." Ely started preaching "strict Godliness" to his slumbering neighbors. "It seames as tho they were fast asleep and the Devil had enclos'd them and buried them as it were in A drift of snow and they are afraid so much as to peek out and let the world know that they are on xts [Christ's] side." Neighbors believed that Ely was mad, but he justified his eager promotion of the work in his letter to Wheelock. "I long to be wheere God is," he explained, "that I may behold him face to face."[67]

Ely received his divine call to preach and exhort early in the revivals, but, for unlettered preachers such as Nathaniel Wardell, Jr., the decision to travel abroad on the Lord's work constituted a relatively advanced stage in their religious development. A tradesman originally from Braintree, Massachusetts, Wardell moved to Boston and received a commission in 1739 to erect a scale for weighing hay on the outskirts of town. The "Hay-weigher," as he came to be known, joined Mather Byles's Hollis Street congregation at the peak of the revivals, but he withdrew from communion and applied for admission to the Old South Church a few months later. The reasoning behind Wardell's abrupt change of heart remains unclear, although it likely stemmed from Byles's growing opposition to the work of the Holy Spirit. Affiliated with Boston's most prominent revival congregation, Wardell and his new wife presented their first child for baptism several months later.[68]

XXXV (1980), 43–44; Onuf, "New Lights in New London," *WMQ*, XXXVII (1980), 633n; C. C. Goen, *Revivalism and Separatism in New England, 1740–1800: Strict Congregationalists and Separate Baptists in the Great Awakening* (Middletown, Conn., 1987), 107–108, 115–123; and *Sketches of the Life and Extracts from the Journals and Other Writings of the Late Joseph Croswell* (Boston, 1809). My argument here and in the paragraphs that follow draws on Leigh Eric Schmidt, *Hearing Things: Religion, Illusion, and the American Enlightenment* (Cambridge, Mass., 2000), 41–47.

67. Reuben Ely to Eleazar Wheelock, Mar. 4, 1741 [1742?], no. 741204, *EWP*.

68. *Boston Weekly Post-Boy*, Mar. 28, 1743 (quote). For genealogical information on Wardell, see Annie Haven Thwing, *Inhabitants and Estates of the Town of Boston, 1630–1800, and the Crooked and Narrow Streets of Boston, 1630–1822* (Boston, 2001), CD-ROM, s.v. "Nathan*" and "Ward*"; Robert Francis Seybolt, *The Town Officials of Colonial Boston, 1634–1775* (Cambridge, Mass., 1939), 212; and Robert J. Dunkle and Ann S. Lainhart, transcr., *The Records of the Churches of Boston and the First Church, Second Parish, and Third Parish*

Wardell's religious radicalism deepened during the next several years. In August 1742, he hosted a lecture in his workshop in which James Davenport warned the audience not to attend the meetings of unconverted Boston clergymen who were "serving the Interest of Satan." Their *"Preaching to your Souls,"* the Long Island itinerant thundered, is as "Ratsbane *is to your Bodies."* Taking Davenport at his inspired word, Wardell soon turned against the Old South Church. According to Joseph Sewall and Thomas Prince, Wardell absented himself from communion in a "disorderly manner," despite solemnly promising to "walk with us in a due Submission to and attendance upon all the Orders and Ordinances of the Gospel." He openly renounced his church membership, declared that Sewall, Prince, and their parishioners worshipped in a "synogogue of Satan," and began preaching in his home and on the streets.[69]

Unlike Reuben Ely, the Boston hay weigher did not content himself with railing against clerical authorities. As the newspapers filled with reports of the New London bonfires during the spring of 1743, Wardell further shocked the members of his former church by baptizing two women by immersion in Boston harbor. When questioned about his "manner of dipping," Wardell answered defiantly that he was "not afraid of all the D—l's in Hell, nor all the Men upon the Earth." Condemning his actions as a "bold intrusion into the pastoral Office, without any regular Call or due Qualifications," Sewall and Prince sent a delegation to confront Wardell and urge him to confess his errors, but he adamantly refused and was suspended from communion on Christmas Day 1743. Wardell remained under church censure for five years, during which time he converted to Seventh-Day Baptist principles and closed his scales on Saturdays. Finally, during the summer of 1748, the Old South ministers led the church in a ritual of excommunication, hoping that this rare disciplinary action would impel the hay weigher to a serious consideration of his "hainous violations of God's Law." As Sewall pronounced the "awful sentence" in which the church threatened their former brother with "everlasting destruction," Wardell stood up and defiantly walked out of the meetinghouse.[70]

Women like Ann Gary formed a shadowy presence among the growing ranks of notable lay preachers and exhorters. Her story appears briefly in a

---

of Roxbury, Including Baptisms, Marriages, Deaths, Admissions, and Dismissals (Boston, 2001), CD-ROM, s.v. "Nathan*" and "Ward*."

69. *Boston Evening-Post*, Sept. 6, 1742; Hamilton Andrews Hill, *History of the Old South Church (Third Church]) Boston, 1669–1884*, 2 vols. (Boston, 1890), I, 540.

70. *Boston Weekly Post-Boy*, Mar. 28, 1743; Hill, *History of the Old South Church*, I, 540, 587–589. See also *Boston Evening-Post*, Feb. 14, 1743.

1743 letter in which the Enfield, Massachusetts (now Connecticut), minister Peter Reynolds reported to a colleague that his former parishioner had set out for Worcester and Boston on a preaching tour. "I Fear she will Wound Religion Much in Either of those Places," he worried. Similar examples of gifted women who usurped ministerial prerogatives peppered the diaries and correspondence of revival observers. Shortly after Jacob Eliot entered the Goshen meetinghouse one afternoon during the winter of 1742, an anonymous woman stood up, began to exhort the congregation, and refused to stop, despite the protests of her minister. A woman in Leicester, Massachusetts, contested a sermon delivered by visiting minister David Hall by singing hymns at the top of her voice as he preached. Andrew Croswell's revival meetings in Plymouth, Massachusetts, later that spring featured the labors of a "big-bellied Woman" who "straddled into the Pulpit" and preached for half an hour, "extending her Arms every Way." And at least two women from eastern Connecticut were among the "Newlight Exhorters" who attended the Shepherd's Tent and spoke at private meetings in New London during the weeks leading up to the bonfires.[71]

The best documented female preacher of the Whitefieldian era was Bathsheba Kingsley of Westfield, Massachusetts. For a period of more than a year beginning in the summer of 1741, Kingsley had been in a "continual Tumult, like the sea in a storm." She spent her days away from her home and family, visiting with her neighbors to discuss the state of their souls and proclaiming that she was doing God's work. As a female itinerant, Kingsley was "quite out of her Place to promote Religion," Jonathan Edwards remarked in a censuring statement signed by seven other colleagues in the Hampshire Association. She railed against "visible Christians in good standing," Edwards explained, and even prayed that her husband "might Go quick to Hell."[72]

Edwards and his colleagues branded Kingsley as a woman with a "weak vapoury Habit of Body." But the Westfield goodwife maintained that her preaching gifts flowed directly from the "gracious influences of the spirit of God." Following her conversion during Whitefield's 1740 tour, Kingsley ex-

---

71. Peter Reynolds to Eleazar Wheelock, Sept. 15, 1743, case 8, box 24, SCG I; Gillett, ed., "Diary of the Rev. Jacob Eliot," *Historical Magazine and Notes and Queries*, 2d Ser., V (1869), 34; David Hall, diaries, 1740–1789, Oct. 18, 1742, MHS; *South Carolina Gazette*, June 21, 1742; *Diary of Joshua Hempstead*, 396–397.

72. Jonathan Edwards, "Advice to Mr. and Mrs. Kingsley," Feb. 17, 1743, *WJEO*, XXXIX, *Church and Pastoral Documents*. See also Catherine A. Brekus, *Strangers and Pilgrims: Female Preaching in America, 1740–1845*, Gender and American Culture (Chapel Hill, N.C., 1998), 23–26; and Erik R. Seeman, *Pious Persuasions: Laity and Clergy in Eighteenth-Century New England*, Early America: History, Context, Culture (Baltimore, 1999), 169–171.

plained during her disciplinary hearing, she had been "almost wholly under the Government of a series of dreams, imaginations and sudden Impulses" that she interpreted as immediate revelations. The leadings of the Holy Spirit, in turn, authorized Kingsley to judge the religious experiences of others and infused her ministry with a sense of apocalyptic urgency. Kingsley believed that the revival in Westfield "depended on her, and that if she was not improved its Cause would sink." Thus, while some ministers branded her a deluded enthusiast, Kingsley characterized herself as an instrument of divine authority, a passive oracle "delivering messages from God." Although Kingsley bowed to the pressure of Edwards and his colleagues and promised to "submit to her husband" and "keep chiefly at home," other evidence suggests that the inspired preacher persisted in her unusual gospel labors and later withdrew from communion in the Westfield church.[73]

James Davenport's preaching set the Mohegan Indian Samson Occom on the path that ultimately lead to his career as a prominent preacher and missionary. Numerous other native and African Americans found an audience during the revivals as well. Stunned guests at a Boston dinner party discovered that the host's black servant had learned Whitefield's oratorical techniques; he preached with such authority that he "struck the Gentlemen to Heart." Yale College student John Cleaveland was exhorted by Pompey, his father's enslaved servant, during an evening meeting in Canterbury, Connecticut. In nearby Goshen, Jacob Eliot confronted a company of Indians who invaded his parish and attempted to exhort and sing hymns with his congregants. The following month, another converted black man preached to the Colchester, Connecticut, congregation in an orchard near the meetinghouse; strange reports circulated in the public prints that "two large monstrous black Snakes crept up his Back" as he spoke. Josiah Cotton recoiled at Croswell's decision to cede the Plymouth pulpit to several black children during a powerful series of revival meetings in March 1742. One of the boys castigated the "Grey headed sinners" in the congregation, telling them to "come away to the Lord Jesus Christ, you are in a few steps of hell." Later that day, another enslaved youth addressed the people from the top of the deacon's pew. "Oh Dear, O Dear, O Dear, beg pardon O Lord, O Dear Lord," he called out ominously with upraised arms, "send down a great sword. Cuttee, cuttee all hearts."[74]

73. Edwards, "Advice to Mr. and Mrs. Kingsley," Feb. 17, 1743, *WJEO*, XXXIV, *Church and Pastoral Documents;* Eleazar Wheelock to Stephen Williams, Apr. 22, 1743, no. 743272, *EWP.* See also Williams to Wheelock, Feb. 16, 1743, no. 743166.1, *EWP.*

74. Tuttle, comp., "Glasgow-Weekly-History," MHS, *Procds.,* LIII (1919–1920), 200;

To revival critics, such as the Cape Cod mariner Benjamin Bangs, the "people called *New Lights*" had provoked a great "deal of disturbance all over New England." Although Bangs was convinced that they acted strangely, their tactics were inspired by Whitefieldian itinerants, and their sense of calling emerged directly from the indwelling presence of the Holy Spirit. The indefatigable Elisha Paine, whose disorderly gospel labors Bangs denounced in his diary, adopted Gilbert Tennent's protracted meeting format. Over a period of five months in 1742, he delivered 244 sermons in parishes from central Massachusetts to Cape Cod. Repeatedly jailed for disturbing the peace, Paine followed James Davenport in refusing to be silenced in the "midst of wolves and dragons" and exhorted the faithful from his confinement. According to members of the Windham County ministerial association, he believed that he was authorized to preach the gospel on the basis of an "inward Call and Motion of the Holy Ghost." Or, as the Canterbury lawyer explained in a letter to his wife, he preached whenever and wherever he "felt the Spirit of the Lord come upon me."[75]

"New Prophets" provoked the ire of established clergymen. Proper training and ritual investiture through ordination were essential to the peace of the churches, most ministers asserted. "Ignorant and Superstitious Pretenders" such as Paine, by contrast, demanded that their followers "receive everything they Declare" in the "Name of God," since their charismatic authority rested on their purported "Inward Commission." Blind faith in inspired lay ministers, the Windham Association asserted, would inevitably result in "endless Divisions in the Christian Church." Paine once declared that he would rather have been "burnt at the Stake" than listen to the sermons of his former pastor in Canterbury. He allegedly denied the separate personhood of the Trinity and vented other "Dangerous Doctrines." Unqualified lay preachers threatened to "lead People away from Christ and the ordinary Methods wherein He Communicates his Grace to the Souls of Men." The Windham Association commanded their parishioners to "inviolably adhere" to ordained authorities,

---

Ross W. Beales, Jr., ed., "The Diary of John Cleaveland, January 15–May 11, 1742," *EIHC*, CVII (1971), 170; Gillett, ed., "Diary of the Rev. Jacob Eliot," *Historical Magazine and Notes and Queries*, 2d Ser., V (1869), 33; *Boston Weekly Post-Boy*, May 17, 1742; "Extracts from the Manuscripts of Josiah Cotton Esqr.," [4], Cotton Families Collection, PHM.

75. Dean Dudley, *History and Genealogy of the Bangs Family in America, with Genealogical Tables and Notes* (Montrose, Mass., 1896), 8; Windham Association, Records, I, 120; Isaac Backus, *A History of New England, with Particular Reference to the Baptists*, ed. David Weston, 2d ed. (1871; New York, 1969), 67–68n. See also Solomon Williams to Col. Wadsworth, Oct. 8, 1744, JWC.

lest God leave them perilously exposed to "Satanical Imitations of the work of God's Spirit."[76]

Marblehead, Massachusetts, magistrate Nathan Bowen saw the storm clouds brewing earlier than most of his contemporaries. "This Town seems Infatuated about what the people Call Religion," he grumbled as early as January 1742. A series of "Bewitching" itinerant preachers had enflamed the town with a "Hot Spirit of Enthuseasm" and transformed "Ignorant" fishermen, carters, cobblers, and laborers as well as "Common negros," "Babes and Sucklings," and "silly women" into a "Giddy Mobb" all too willing to act on their revelatory conversion experiences. "Who would pay Clergymen for preaching," Bowen protested, "when a Lay Brother or Sister, can by the Immediate Impulse of the Sperit Teach to better purpose, for nothing?" To his astonishment, Marblehead minister Simon Bradstreet encouraged such practices, but Bowen knew well their danger. "I should think they Tend directly to subvert the Good order in society," he asserted. Playing on the etymological connections between "Effusions" and "Confusions," Bowen characterized the revivals as a "Sea of fraud" and "Anerchy."[77]

Bowen's diary suggests that lay preachers and exhorters were wildly popular, and their many supporters ably defended their call to preach and exhort over and against the territorial claims of established clergymen. In a letter written sometime late in the 1740s, Newbury layman Joseph Goodhue crafted an alternative etiology of pastoral authority in his response to an anonymous published attack on the Salem baker-turned-itinerant preacher, Richard Elvins. Whenever ministers and their flocks pushed beyond the "dry and dead Forms" of worship, Goodhue maintained, they were censured as "Enthusiates or mad men." Conservative arguments in favor of ministers with "Accademial Learning" were based on the assumption that "human prudence" required learned shepherds to guide their fickle flocks in the post-apostolic age. Although Goodhue acknowledged that colleges were an important training ground for many clergymen, he feared that his opponent artificially separated book wisdom from the "spearite of God and Christian Experience." Such reasoning, he warned, was Satan's ploy to promote the work of unconverted ministers. For Goodhue, the simple logic that justified the inward calling of lay preachers was the same as that which grounded the boisterous outbursts and

---

76. *South Carolina Gazette*, June 21, 1742; Windham Association, Records, I, 120–122; *Letter from the Associated Ministers of the County of Windham, to the People in the Several Societies in Said County* (Boston, 1745), 7.

77. "Extracts from the Interleaved Almanacs of Nathan Bowen," *EIHC*, XCI (1955), 164–167, 169.

censorious judging of other new converts: "Unlarned Coman [common] and Eletror [unlettered] men may preach becase the spriate [Spirit] of God sterrs them up to it and theay have a mind to it."[78]

■ It was against a backdrop of rising clerical and legal censure and increasingly mobile and impassioned popular support for lay preaching that Richard Woodbury, the "mad enthusiast," stepped onto the public stage. The charismata of the revivals—gifts of inspired speech, spiritual discernment, and special commissions as well as exercised bodies, biblical impulses, and ecstatic visions—reached their apogee in his meteoric career. Born and baptized in Rowley, Massachusetts, in 1724, Woodbury appears to have been profoundly affected by James Davenport's labors in nearby Ipswich during the summer of 1742. Several months later, he turned up in Durham, New Hampshire, at the height of an unusual outbreak of dreams, trances, and visions. Minister Nicholas Gilman welcomed Woodbury into his home and allowed the gifted layman to exhort after his lectures. By the time that Alexander Hamilton arrived in Salem during the spring of 1744, the two men had begun itinerating extensively in northern New England. Wherever they went, Woodbury's confrontational style incited heated disputes, "great uneasiness," "Uproar," "Tummult," "Clamour," and "much ado." His prayers, sermons, and exhortations aggravated magistrates and lay elites and alienated even the most ardent prorevival ministers.[79]

With Gilman serving as his personal secretary, Woodbury spent the month of May 1744 dispatching "Monitory Letters" to revival opposers in Essex County, Massachusetts, and New Hampshire. Each followed a common script that began with the salutation "In the Name of the King of Kings and Lord of Lords," by which Woodbury announced his special commission to "perform great and Wonderful things" in God's name. Like Davenport, Woodbury struck a militant tone in his letters. He exhorted local ministers to "hear the Sound of the Trumpet and the Alarm of Warr" and "Approve Yourself a Faithfull Soldier of Your Lord and King." "Gird on Your Armour," Woodbury exhorted Samuel Webster of Salisbury, Massachusetts, "come forth and vindicate the Lords Quarrell." He also judged the spiritual estates of established clergymen. "If you have not experienced the Love of Christ in your own Soul,"

78. [Joseph Goodhue], statement on Richard Elvins, n.d. [circa 1747], Goodhue Family Papers, 1684–1858, box 5, PEM.

79. *AHI*, 120; *Vital Records of Rowley, Massachusetts, to the End of the Year 1849*, 2 vols. (Salem, Mass., 1928–1931), I, 236; NGD, 299–300, 326, 333. See also Clarke Garrett, *Origins of the Shakers: From the Old World to the New World* (1987; rpt. Baltimore, 1997), 131–134; and Seeman, *Pious Persuasions*, 133–138.

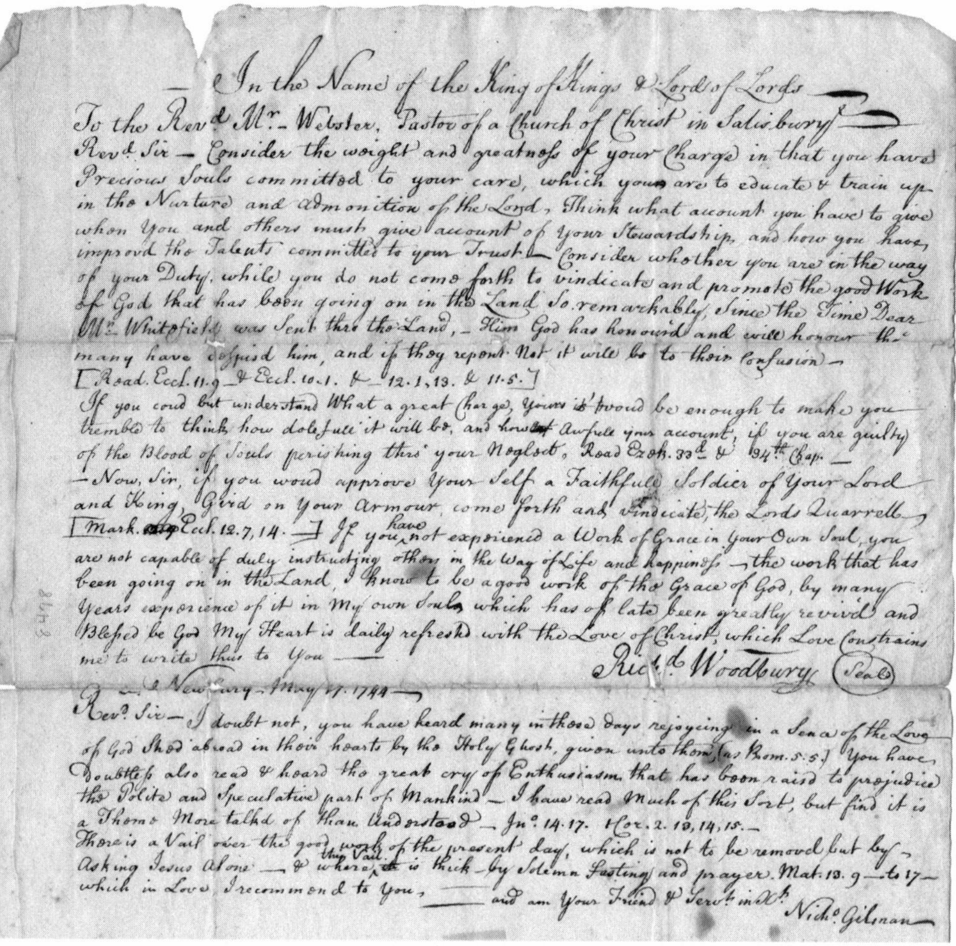
— In the Name of the King of Kings & Lord of Lords —

To the Revd. Mr.– Webster, Pastor of a Church of Christ in Salisbury —

Revd. Sir – Consider the weight and greatness of your Charge in that you have Precious Souls committed to your care, which you are to educate & train up in the Nurture and Admonition of the Lord, Think what account you have to give when You and others must give account of Your Stewardship, and how you have improved the Talents committed to your Trust — Consider whether you are in the way of your Duty, while you do not come forth to vindicate and promote the good Work of God that has been going on in the Land So remarkably, Since the Time Dear Mr. Whitefield was Sent thro the Land, – Him God has honourd and will honour tho many have despisd him, and if they repent Not it will be to their Confusion –
[Read. Eccl. 11.9 – & Eccl. 10.1. & – 12.1, 13. & 11.5.]

If you coud but understand What a great Charge, Yours is, twoud be enough to make you tremble to think how dolefull it will be, and how Awfull your account, if you are guilty of the Blood of Souls perishing thro' your Neglect, Read Ezek. 33d. & 34th Chap. —
— Now, Sir, if you woud approve Your Self a Faithfull Soldier of Your Lord and King, Gird on Your Armour, come forth and vindicate, the Lords Quarrell, [Mark. Eccl. 12.7, 14. —] If you have not experienced a Work of Grace in Your Own Soul, you are not capable of duly instructing others in the Way of Life and happiness, – the work that has been going on in the Land, I know to be a good work of the Grace of God, by many Years experience of it in My own Soul, which has of late been greatly revivd and Blessed be God My Heart is daily refreshd with the Love of Christ, which Love Constrains me to write thus to You —

Richd. Woodbury (Seal)

Newbury – May 17. 1744 –

Revd. Sir – I doubt not, you have heard many in these days rejoycing in a Sence of the Love of God Shed abroad in their hearts by the Holy Ghost, given unto them (as Rom. 5.5) You have Doubtless also read & heard the great cry of Enthusiasm that has been raisd to prejudice the Polite and Speculative part of Mankind – I have read Much of this Sort, but find it is a Theme More talkd of than Understood – Jno. 14.17. 1Cor. 2.10, 14, 15. –
There is a Vail over the good work of the present day, which is not to be removed but by Asking Jesus Alone – & where this Vail is thick – by Solemn Fasting and prayer. Mat. 13.9 – to 17 – which in Love, I recommend to you, — and am Your Friend & Servt. in Xt.

Nichs. Gilman

FIGURE 19 Nicholas Gilman and Richard Woodbury to Samuel Webster. May 17, 1744. Box 1, Robbins Gilman Family Papers, 1699–2009, Minnesota Historical Society, Saint Paul

he warned William Parsons of South Hampton, New Hampshire, "humble yourself before the Lord and Seek the Lord before it be too late." Gilman added a postscript to each letter defending the "Glorious work of Reformation that has been going on in the Land" and challenging his correspondents to embrace the title of "Enthusiast" as a badge of honor.[80]

80. DDR, May 2, 1744; Richard Woodbury and Nicholas Gilman to William Parsons, May 23, 1744, Nicholas Gilman Papers II, 1700–1784, MHS; William Stevens Perry, ed., *Historical Collections Relating to the American Colonial Church*, 5 vols. (Hartford, Conn., 1870–1878), III, 387; [Emily Hoffman Gilman], ed., *A Family History in Letters and Documents,*

Woodbury's incendiary missives heralded the emergence of a charismatic prophet. He imagined himself as a type of the white horseman described in Revelation 19:16 who wields the word of God like a sharp sword and makes war on the unrighteous. Gilman, sanctioned Woodbury's divine commission by conducting an irregular ordination ritual in which a company of laymen placed their hands on the Rowley itinerant and welcomed him as a "fellow Labourer in the Lords Vineyard." The Boston prints, by contrast, lampooned his "ridiculous and absurd" behavior. Woodbury uttered "blasphemous and profane" prophecies and drank healths to "King Jesus." Exhibiting what one report called a "strange Emotion," Woodbury frequently lapsed into trances during which he would roll on the floor and rail against revival opposers, crying out that they had crucified Christ.[81]

Although Woodbury's many critics labeled him a latter-day Antinomian, Daniel Rogers initially believed that he was "filled with the Holy Ghost," and his exhortations seemed "agreeable to the Word of God." On one occasion in May 1744, Rogers reported with approval that a score of the Rowley layman's followers "fell prostrate upon the Ground" and began praising God with trembling bodies. Two weeks later, Woodbury confronted a possessed Ipswich man named John Fowler, who complained that the "Devil had been in him for some years." Woodbury proceeded to perform an exorcism ceremony that involved a group of lay men and women stamping Satan out of Fowler's body and "down to Hell, with their Feet upon the Floor." Satisfied with the results, Woodbury "pronounced that the Devil Should never have power" over Fowler again. Then he declared that he had seen the possessed man's name written in the Book of Life. Other witnesses to Woodbury's late-night meetings in Ipswich, however, hinted that he manipulated his devotees. "When Woodbury Says Fall down ye Servants of God," wrote one critic, "they all fall down flatt upon their Faces and there lye till he bidds them get up." Another account suggested that his disciples bent to the ground and made crosses in the dust, before kissing and licking the earthen symbols as a token of their humility.[82]

Unquestionably, the most audacious pronouncement attributed to Wood-

---

1667–1837 . . . , 2 vols. (Saint Paul, Minn., 1919), I, 42; Arthur Gilman, comp., *The Gilman Family Traced in the Line of Hon. John Gilman of Exeter, N.H.* (Albany, N.Y., 1869), 61. See also NGD, 367–370; and Francis G. Walett, ed., *The Diary of Ebenezer Parkman, 1703–1782* (Worcester, Mass., 1974), 100.

81. DDR, May 25, 1744; *Boston Evening-Post*, July 30, 1744; Perry, ed., *Historical Collections Relating to the American Colonial Church*, III, 387.

82. DDR, Apr. 29, May 15, 25, 1744; Christian Wainwright to Lucy Dudley, June 20, 1744, box 3, Parkman Family Papers, 1707–1879, AAS; *Boston Evening-Post*, July 30, 1744; Perry, ed., *Historical Collections Relating to the American Colonial Church*, III, 383.

bury was the statement that his newly acquired religious authority included the Christlike "Power to bless and curse eternally" whomever he chose. The unusual salutations of his monitory letters as well as his revealing assertion that he could peer directly into the Book of Life to read the names of God's elect demonstrated his commitment to the doctrine of "Sinless Perfection in this Life." Salem magistrate Stephen Sewall informed Alexander Hamilton that Woodbury had proclaimed that "he was the same today, yesterday, and forever." Within a few years, he appears to have transmitted these unusually heterodox doctrines to Gilman's parishioners. Eventually, the Durham minister abandoned his pastoral duties altogether, ceding his pulpit to Woodbury and the ubiquitous blind itinerant and Shepherd's Tent scholar, Joseph Prince.[83]

"Poor Mr. Gilman of Durham is too far gone into the wilds of Enthusiasm to allow us any reasonable hopes of his return unless God should restore him to a Sound mind," one sympathetic minister lamented during the fall of 1746. When two Maine colleagues, Samuel Chandler and Jeremiah Wise, visited Gilman's former parish earlier that summer, they discovered the Durham congregation in almost complete chaos. As Wise started to preach, four or five members of the assembly began "twisting their bodies in all manner of unseemly postures." Others fell down, gestured wildly with their arms, groaned, cried out in distress, and sang bawdy songs. With his voice nearly drowned out by the noise of Woodbury's supporters, Wise attempted to still the assembly, whereupon Gilman stood up and asserted that perfection was "attainable in this life." Later that same evening, a young woman named Hannah Huckins informed the two ministers in a "boasting air" that she had passed through conversion and proceeded on to experience "justification and sanctification and perfection and perseverance," all in rapid succession. When Chandler questioned the orthodoxy of her claims, Huckins broke into divine praises and danced around the room in a rhythmic jig, shouting "Glory, glory, glory" and keeping time with her feet.[84]

Woodbury's perfectionist beliefs ultimately propelled him, Gilman, and their followers well beyond the boundaries of the Congregational establishment. Even Rogers broke with the former Durham clergyman in 1745, tell-

---

83. *Boston Evening-Post*, July 30, 1744; George Chandler, transcr., "Diary of the Rev. Samuel Chandler while at York, Me., and at Gloucester, Mass.," 1745–1746, 1749–1764, Apr. 2, 1746, Mss A 1079, NEHGS; *AHI*, 120. See also Perry, ed., *Historical Collections Relating to the American Colonial Church*, III, 387; and Wainwright to Dudley, June 20, 1744, box 3, Parkman Family Papers.

84. John Blunt to Benjamin Colman, Sept. 9, 1746, Letters to Benjamin Colman, 1693–1747, MHS; Joshua Coffin, "Religious Excitement One Hundred and Odd Years Ago," *NEHGR*, XV (1861), 23.

ing Gilman "plainly I thot He was out of the Way" with regard to Woodbury's doctrine of perfection and in laying down his pastoral duties. "He Seem'd to be Shock't," Rogers wrote in his diary. Two years later, an association of New Hampshire ministers censured Gilman for ceding his authority to the Rowley layman. Surveying the situation in Durham, the association's committee was horrified to learn that most of the congregation had separated from the church. Led by Woodbury, they gathered for worship in a private house, where they continued to practice "very disorderly vile and absurd things," including "profane singing and dancing, damning the Devil," and "spitting in Persons Faces whom they apprehended not to be of their Society." Gilman died less than a year later, but Woodbury held on in Durham into the 1750s. Arrested and jailed as a "Vagrant Person," Woodbury eventually returned to Rowley, suffered through a smallpox infection, and lived as a public charge for several years before his death in 1767.[85]

From ministers and magistrates to newspaper correspondents and travelers, nearly everyone who encountered Woodbury during the brief few years of his prophetic ministry concluded that he was either deluded or deranged. His "extravagancies," as Alexander Hamilton noted in his *Itinerarium*, "take all their first root from the labours of that righteous apostle Whitefield," who "sowed the first seeds of distraction in these unhappy, ignorant parts." The genealogy of the Durham "high flyers" stretched back to Whitefield's 1740 tour, of course, but a more direct line of descent led straight to James Davenport. His fascination with immediate revelations, gifts of the Holy Spirit, and ecclesiastical disorder fomented ecclesiastical strife across New England but especially among the small coastal settlements of southern Connecticut.[86]

HE WOULD AS SOON GIVE THE BREAD
IN THE SACRAMENT TO A DOG

Alexander Hamilton spent the morning of August 27, 1744, drinking tea and discussing the New London bonfires with deacon Timothy Green. Then he

85. DDR, Aug. 20, Dec. 12, 1745; "A Record of the Transactions of the Annual Convocation of Ministers in the Province of N: Hampshire," *New Hampshire Historical Society, Collections*, IX (1889), 7–8; William G. McLoughlin, ed., *The Diary of Isaac Backus*, 3 vols. (Providence, R.I., 1979), 149–150; Archibald Smith v. Richard Woodberry, 1747, no. 25924, Provincial Court Cases, circa 1670–circa 1771, New Hampshire Division of Archives and Records Management, Concord. See also Amos Everett Jewett and Emily Mabel Adams Jewett, *Rowley, Massachusetts: "Mr. Ezechi Rogers Plantation," 1639–1850* (Rowley, Mass., 1946), 144; and *Vital Records of Rowley, Massachusetts*, II, 29.

86. *AHI*, 120; Coffin, "Religious Excitement One Hundred and Odd Years Ago," *NEHGR*, XV (1861), 23–24.

set off for home along the Boston Post Road. As he entered the east parish of Lyme, Connecticut, Hamilton passed a small Indian village composed of about a dozen wigwams covered in bark mats. Had he paused to speak with the Niantics, Hamilton would have learned that almost all the native Americans in the region had recently been converted by James Davenport. He spent the entire day riding through a town that had experienced one of the largest, best-publicized, and most divisive revivals in all of New England. But Hamilton was moving quickly. Proceeding through the center of Lyme, he made his way down to the bank of the Connecticut River, where he hoped to find a ferry waiting to carry him across to Saybrook.[87]

Inclement weather and uncooperative tides conspired against his travel plans, and the Annapolis physician was forced to take refuge in the home of a Lyme resident named Timothy Mather, Sr. Hamilton's host boasted an impressive pedigree. He was the great-grandson of the puritan clergyman Richard Mather and, thus, a kinsman of Boston ministers Increase and Cotton Mather. The two men settled into a conversation about the "opinions lately broached here in religion," Hamilton reported in his *Itinerarium*. The touring physician praised Mather for criticizing George Whitefield's conduct in 1740, but he heaped contempt on the "rabble of clowns" that barged into the ferryman's house at the conclusion of their midday meal. To Hamilton's great irritation, the newcomers angrily began debating with Mather on "points of divinity as learnedly as if they had been professed theologues." Recording the incident several weeks later, the Scottish gentleman found it strange that so many New Englanders felt emboldened to hold forth on "justification, sanctification, adoption, regeneration, repentance, free grace, reprobation, original sin, and a thousand other such pritty, chimerical knick knacks as they had done nothing but studied divinity all their life time and perused all the lumber of the scholastic divines."[88]

To an outsider from Maryland, the altercation at the Lyme ferry pitted "lower class" "riff-raff" against their social betters. But Hamilton was mistaken. He had unwittingly stepped into a bitter religious dispute. The antagonists were far from marginal members of the community, for the leader of the rabble that invaded Mather's house that afternoon was the local church deacon, Reynold Marvin. The protracted quarrel that erupted in Lyme as a result of Marvin's blistering critique of a fellow church member epitomized the theological and ecclesiastical controversies that roiled New England's Con-

87. *AHI*, 162–163.
88. Ibid., 162–163.

gregational establishment during the era of great awakenings, from the rise of Whitefieldian oratory to dramatic conversions and debates over charismatic gifts of the Holy Spirit to inspired acts of social and ecclesiastical protest. Here, in the towns adjacent to New London, during the weeks and months following the 1743 bonfires, one of the best-documented church schisms of the eighteenth century unmasked Whitefieldian revivalism as a frontal assault on the gospel land of light and revealed the lasting scars inflicted on the Congregational establishment by James Davenport's incendiary itinerancy.[89]

■ The Lyme conflict began a year earlier with the gift of a large black gelding. In January 1743, Eleazar Wheelock journeyed to New London to visit the fledgling Shepherd's Tent. But, on this occasion, his travel plans foundered, and Wheelock suddenly was left without a horse. Reynold Marvin offered to provide one "out of that Plenty of Creature Comforts wherewith God hath Been Pleased to Bless me." A communicant in the Lyme church for more than a decade and recently elected deacon, Marvin was also a rising star in local politics. He descended from a prosperous family and served the town in a variety of civic capacities. On the surface, his generous donation appeared to be a charitable act on behalf of one of Wheelock's many lay supporters, but the men who witnessed the gift agreement signaled a deeper connection between Marvin and the surging currents of radical revivalism. At the bottom of the written instrument drawn up by the Lyme deacon were two other names: Michael Hill, principal financier of the Shepherd's Tent, and James Pierpont, a wealthy New Haven merchant and the brother-in-law of Jonathan Edwards. Both men ranked among James Davenport's closest companions and most vociferous supporters.[90]

Back in Lyme two months later—and only a few weeks after the book-burning incident had erupted just a few miles away—Marvin shocked the community when he branded Edmund Dorr, the father-in-law of his recently married daughter, an unconverted hypocrite. In Dorr's words, the Lyme deacon boldly pronounced that he had "no more reason to think me a tru" Christian than the "worst Indian" at Niantic and that "he would as Soon give the bread in the Sacrament to a dog as to me." On another occasion, Marvin railed against the "Sad Effects of Taking into the Church such unconverted Crea-

89. Ibid., 163.

90. Reynold Marvin, "Deacon Marvins Loan for a Hors to Mr. E Wheelock," Jan. 27, 1743, no. 743127, *EWP*. For genealogical information, see George Franklin Marvin, *Descendants of Reinold and Matthew Marvin* (Boston, 1904), 56–57. See also Bruce P. Stark, *Lyme, Connecticut: From Founding to Independence* ([Lyme, Conn.], 1976), 16–39.

tures" who "Knew not X [Christ]." When asked for specific examples, the deacon pointed straight at his kinsman. Three months later, Dorr presented a
formal complaint to Lyme minister Jonathan Parsons in which he accused
Marvin of bearing false witness and breaking covenant. The deacon pleaded
"Justification" and vindicated his treatment of Dorr. In a surprising turn of
events, his neighbors agreed. Acquitting Marvin of any wrongdoing, the Lyme
church members voted that his statements did "not amount to a censurable
evil." During the weeks that followed, Dorr later recalled, Marvin "waxed bold
in his errors and Sinfull Conduct," making it his "Common business to go
about and judge the Spiritual and invisible State of his fellow Xns [Chris-
tians]." The church's decision to endorse Marvin's gifts of spiritual discernment offers a rough measurement of the town's white-hot revival temperament. By 1744, Parsons and his congregants had developed a transatlantic
reputation for revival zeal that, at times, went too far.[91]

Lyme was a typical coastal village straddling the Post Road between New
York and Boston. Despite the emergence of traders, magistrates, ministers,
and military leaders during the first half of the eighteenth century, few families in Lyme managed to rise above the middling standard of living that prevailed throughout the region. Parsons presided over his quiescent coastal
parish for a decade following his ordination in 1731. Sabbaths were marked
by the familiar rhythm of baptisms, church admissions, fast days, and sacraments. He sent flowery, although ultimately unsuccessful, courtship letters to
Jonathan Edwards's sister, enhanced his small salary by arranging with the
New England Company to preach occasionally at nearby Indian settlements,
and borrowed books from Benjamin Colman in Boston. Parsons's preaching
accented the "Steady Xn [Christian] Course" of the godly walk. He was, by all
measures, an unremarkable parson living in an ordinary country town. No
evidence suggests that his parishioners were dissatisfied with his labors.[92]

91. Timothy Mather, Sr., "Arguments Offered by Edmund Dorr to Prove the Church Guilty
of Male Administration in the Case of Deacon Reynold Marvin," n.d. [circa 1743–1744], [1,
3, 8], JWC, Edmund Dorr, "Edmund Dorrs Complaint to the Church against Deacon Reynold
Marvin," Apr. 4, 1744, Solomon Williams, "Minutes of Evidence," n.d. [circa Sept. 2, 1746];
Old Lyme, Conn., Congregational Church Records, 1721–1876, 62, microfilm no. 5359, GSU.
92. Jonathan Parsons to Hannah Edwards, Jan. 29, July 29, 1730, box 28, Jonathan
Edwards Collection, 1696–1972, GEN MSS 151, YUB; Parsons to Benjamin Colman, Feb.
14, 26, 1734, box 1, Benjamin Colman Papers, 1641–1806, MHS (available online at *www
.masshist.org*); Parsons, sermon fragment, n.d. [circa 1730s], MSS 4711, Miscellaneous
Manuscripts Collection, Library of Congress (quote). See also Sprague, *Annals of the American Pulpit*, III, 47–52. Additional examples of Parsons's pre-1740 sermons may be found
among the special collections of Harvard Divinity School, MHS, NEHGS, and WCL. For the
early history of Lyme, see Stark, *Lyme, Connecticut*, 1–15; and Jackson Turner Main, "The

Whitefield's 1740 preaching tour of New England dramatically transformed the young clergyman's pastorate. Denouncing his former ministry as having been tinged with *"Arminian* Principles,"* Parsons embraced the Anglican evangelist's doctrine of the new birth and his innovative preaching tactics. He itinerated along an arc that stretched from the Connecticut Valley to central Massachusetts. Whole congregations were reduced to tears during Parsons's rousing lectures, reported John Lee, an avid revival correspondent from Lyme's east parish, in letters to Eleazar Wheelock. Drawing on the tactics of Gilbert Tennent, who stopped in Lyme during his return trip to New Jersey, Parsons soon emerged as a "sun of thunder" whose preaching shocked and unsettled young people and long-standing church members alike. "More awakening heart Searching Sermons I Never heard," Lee declared. Revival opposers branded Parsons a "hot Zealot" and a "mad fellow," but the Lyme lawyer realized that such insults would inevitably be heaped on "all Such as Dare be So bold as to break the Peace of the Carnally Secure."[93]

During a sermon deliverd on May 14, 1741, Parsons watched as the "Spirit of God fell upon the Assembly with great Power." Men and women began crying out and "praying with loud Voices under a Sense of their Sins." Parsons spent the ensuing weeks counselling his parishioners, often advising scores of them on a single day. More than one hundred new converts joined the Lyme church during the spring and summer of 1741. News of what Parsons called "our *Penticost"* spread rapidly through transatlantic epistolary and print networks as far away as London and Edinburgh.[94]

By the time James Davenport arrived in mid-August, the Lyme revival was in full swing. His armor bearer, Daniel Tuttle, later remarked that they received a warm welcome from Parsons and his parishioners, although they

---

Economic and Social Structure of Early Lyme," in George J. Willauer, Jr., ed., *A Lyme Miscellany, 1776-1976* (Middletown, Conn., 1977) 29–47.

93. Jonathan Parsons, "Account of the Revival of Religion at Lyme West Parish in Connecticut, Continued," *CH*, no. 68 (June 16, 1744), 123; John Lee to Eleazar Wheelock, Dec. 5, 1740, in Bushman, ed., *Great Awakening*, 42. For reports of Parsons's itinerations, see Williams, diaries, III, 356–357; Webster, transcr., "Letters to Joseph Bellamy," 16; Tracy, *Great Awakening*, 210; Nathan Stone, Jr., to Nathan Stone, Sr., Oct. 2, 1742, Nathan Stone Papers, 1726–1832, MHS; and *Diary of Joshua Hempstead*, 373, 384.

94. Jonathan Parsons to Benjamin Colman, Dec. 16, 1741, in Jonathan Edwards, *The Distinguishing Marks of a Work of the Spirit of God* (London, 1742), 72–73; Old Lyme Congregational Church Records, 36–40; Parsons, "Account of the Revival of Religion at Lyme West Parish in Connecticut, Continued," *CH*, no. 71 (July 7, 1744), 146. See also John Lee to Eleazar Wheelock, Apr. 20, 1741, no. 741270, *EWP*, Parsons to Wheelock, Apr. 21, 1741, no. 741271; Parsons to Benjamin Colman, Apr. 27, 1741, box 2, Colman Papers; and *American Weekly Mercury*, July 9–July 16, 1741.

were "Oppos'd By sume and that Publicly too." Filled with "Boldness and free-dom to Speak in the Cause of Our Lord and master," he and the Southold fire-brand converted a number of residents in a matter of days. Convinced that they were present-day Davids and Jonathans, Davenport and Tuttle used Parsons's parish as a staging ground for their assault on the walls of "JERICHO" across the Connecticut River in Saybrook. In an ominous turn of events, Davenport also exhibited his ability to judge the souls of saints and sinners in the pres-ence of the Lyme congregants. There is a "great union among us about him," Lee explained, except in his practice of condemning specific church members and praying in public for his own mother, whom he judged to be unconverted. The more radical members of Parsons's congregation, Marvin especially, un-doubtedly learned to recognize and value the practice of spiritual discernment during Davenport's tumultuous visit.[95]

According to Andrew Croswell, a fellow member of the New London County ministerial association, Parsons believed that "not one Minister whom he had seen was to be compar'd with Mr. *Davenport,* for living near to GOD, and having his *Conversation always in Heaven.*" Parishioners recalled the Lyme minister praising Davenport as a "holy Man" coequal in power and au-thority with Jesus's disciples. When Parsons inquired whether he should re-ciprocate by preaching in Davenport's parish on Long Island, the Southold revivalist was "Lead to Pray to the Lord that he would direck in that mater" and the "Lord did direck us to go." During the next several weeks, Parsons em-braced Davenport's *"new* Method" of preaching with an almost reckless aban-don. The young convert Hannah Heaton, who attended several of Parsons's sermons in Southold, recalled how he lashed out against "Carnal ministers." At least one Long Island clergyman took Parsons's warning to heart and "did Promis to Leav Preching until he was Converted."[96]

The following summer, Parsons hurried to Boston on learning of Daven-port's trial and incarceration. He remained in town for a fortnight, during which time he preached daily sermons on a wide range of conventional re-vival themes, including the new birth and justification by faith alone. When

95. Daniel Tuttle and James Davenport to Eleazar Wheelock, Aug. 24, 1741, no. 742474, *EWP;* Chauncy, *Seasonable Thoughts on the State of Religion,* 197; John Lee to Wheelock, Sept. 18, 1741, no. 741518.1, *EWP.*

96. Croswell, *Croswell's Reply,* 9; Joseph Higgins to unidentified clergyman, n.d. [circa December 1743], Mss C 1345, NEHGS; Tuttle and Davenport to Wheelock, Aug. 24, 1741, no. 742747, *EWP;* Parsons, "Account of the Revival of Religion at Lyme West Parish in Con-necticut, Continued," *CH,* no. 70 (June 30, 1744), 144; Barbara E. Lacey, ed., *The World of Hannah Heaton: The Diary of an Eighteenth-Century New England Farm Woman* (DeKalb, Ill., 2003), 12.

Thomas Foxcroft invited him to deliver a Thursday lecture, however, Parsons ignited a firestorm of controversy. Subsequently published as *Wisdom Justified of Her Children,* his sermon addressed Davenport's controversial injunction to separate from the churches of purportedly unconverted ministers. Parsons excoriated the "Bastards" among his ministerial colleagues whose fixation on good works and outward moral behavior had set their unwitting auditors on the "Road of Self-Righteousness." He inveighed against revival opposers who published tracts critical of the *"surprising* and *numerous* Conversions in our Land." Incessant "Paper-Quarrels," he asserted, had transformed New England into a "carping World." Parsons condemned several antirevival tracts by name, but the real target of his stinging portrayal of muttering polemicists might have been Charles Chauncy, who was actively gathering reports of *"Visions, Revelations, Enthusiasms,* and other Fooleries" to *"hide* the glorious Work of divine Grace under the Filth of human Imprudences." Waxing militant toward the end of his sermon, Parsons exhorted young converts, not to sit idle or keep silent, but rather to withdraw from churches led by corrupt and unconverted ministers.[97]

Within weeks Parsons was responding to outraged colleagues who savaged his now "famous *Sermon"* as an "injurious, abusive Discourse." Although the Lyme minister was stung by the public criticism, his unguarded references to established ministers as *"Wolves in Sheep's Cloathing"* who were actively leading people "along in the broad Way to Destruction" nonetheless reiterated the invectives that had spewed from Davenport's inspired mouth on Boston Common just a few weeks earlier. The preface to the published edition of *Wisdom Justified of Her Children* only added fuel to the fire. *"I did not aim at being a Man-Pleaser therein,"* Parsons wrote defiantly. Instead, he sought to awaken his audience to consider the *"great Importance of an* orthodox *Ministry."* Parsons believed that it was reasonable, justifiable, and, above all, "highly necessary" for new converts to separate from corrupt ministers. "I was then, and am still far from thinking that all the Churches" in Massachusetts had been blessed with converted ministers, he explained in an angry exchange with Ebenezer Turell of Medford, Massachusetts. "I pray God that I may never have my eyes so blinded as to imagine that Quietness in the Churches with a corrupt Ministry," Parsons concluded, "is better than the boldest meek Endeavours to alarm mankind of the Danger of the same tho' it shou'd stir up Strife." By 1742,

97. Jonathan Parsons to Ebenezer Turell, Nov. 8, 1742, John Davis Papers, 1627–1846, MHS; Jonathan Parsons, *Wisdom Justified of Her Children* ... (Boston, 1742), 15, 18, 30–31, 37, 45.

Parsons had arrived at the realization that overt acts of ecclesiastical disorder were necessary to stir up New England's sleepy and secure churches.[98]

Parsons's fiery lecture in Boston alienated most of his colleagues, including his close friend and former mentor, Benjamin Colman. In a brief but heated burst of letters, the two clergymen debated specific points of doctrine. To Parsons's dismay, one of Colman's letters fell into the hands of a Lyme parishioner named Joseph Higgins. Instead of delivering the document to his pastor, Higgins, a respected merchant and coastal trader, threatened to publish its controversial theological contents. Opposers in his congregation, Parsons noted warily, now had a "handle to lay hold of and improve" in their case against him for "preaching false Doctrines."[99]

▪ Reynold Marvin's acquittal during the summer of 1743 proved to be the decisive turning point. Shortly after the church dismissed Edmund Dorr's initial complaint, Joseph Higgins leaked a copy of a written grievance against Jonathan Parsons to an unnamed minister, perhaps Benjamin Colman or Charles Chauncy. The original complaint, drafted by Timothy Mather, Sr., charged Parsons with more than forty articles of clerical misconduct, including allegations that stemmed from James Davenport's sojourn in Lyme two years earlier. Mather accused his minister of breaking covenant with his congregation by "Going to Long Island, to preach without any Necessary Call, when he knew the Church was in Great Danger of being led away from the simplicity of the Gospel by the Enthusiastick Doctrines and Practices of Mr. Davenport." He also hinted that Parsons had attempted to implement many of Davenport's most extreme church practices. In addition to condemning unconverted ministers, Parsons began making "Unscriptural and unwarrantable" distinctions between "Chirch Members of Good standing." Following Davenport's lead, he reserved the exclusive "Appelation of Dear Brothers" for parishioners who could narrate their personal conversion experiences to his satisfaction.[100]

98. *Mr. Parsons Corrected* (Boston, 1743), 2; Jonathan Parsons to Benjamin Colman, Dec. 29, 1742, box 2, Colman Papers; Parsons, *Wisdom Justified*, i–ii, v, 41, 46; Parsons to Turell, Nov. 8, 1742, John Davis Papers. See also *Boston Weekly Post-Boy*, Mar. 7, 1743.

99. Jonathan Parsons to Benjamin Colman, n.d. [fall 1742], Colman-Jenks Collection; Parsons to Colman, Dec. 29, 1742, box 2, Colman Papers (quote).

100. Higgins to unidentified clergyman, n.d. [circa December 1743]. Higgins appears to have been a member of the Dorr-Mather faction, but, since he was not affiliated with the Lyme church, his name rarely appears in the records produced during the controversy. For information on Higgins, see Katherine Chapin Higgins, comp., *Richard Higgins: A Resident and Pioneer Settler at Plymouth and Eastham, Massachusetts, and at Piscataway, New Jersey, and His Descendants* (Worcester, Mass., 1918), 96–99.

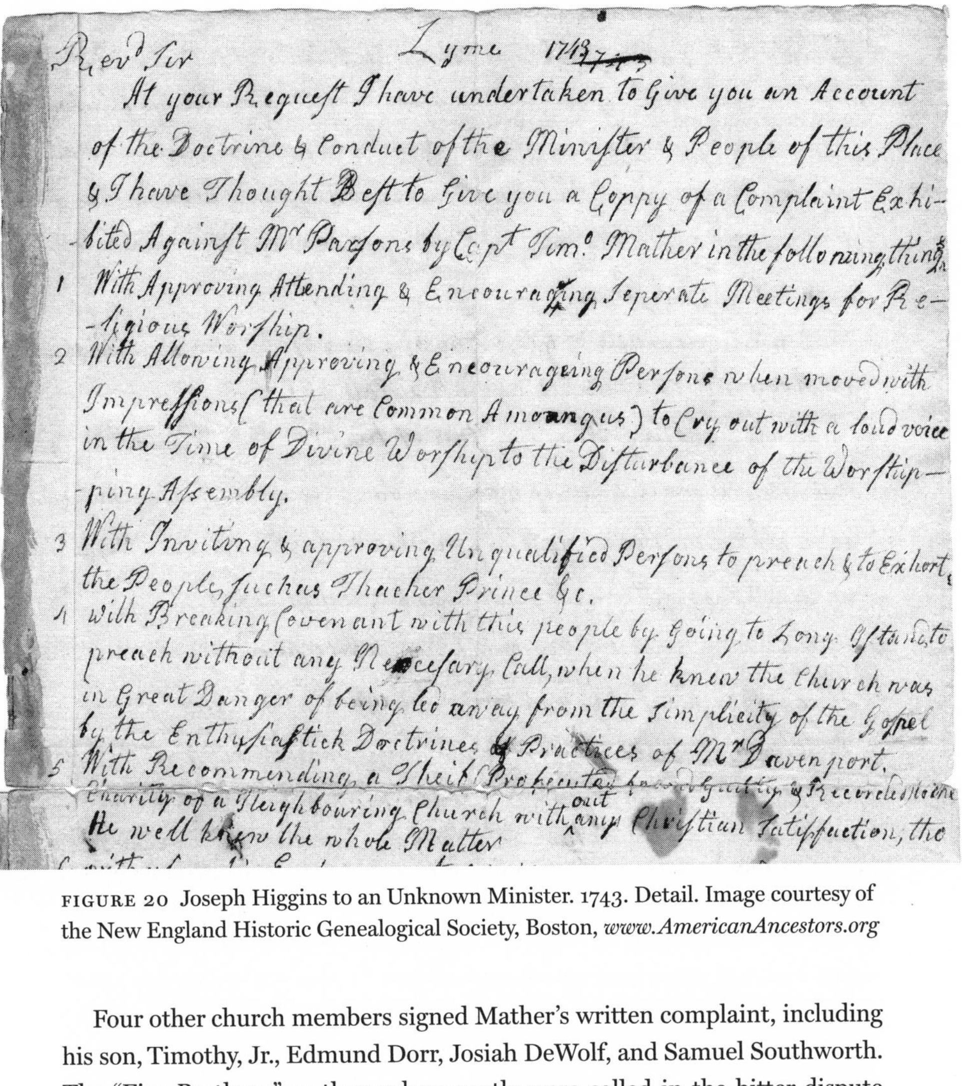
Rev.d Sir Lyme 1743

At your Request I have undertaken to Give you an Account of the Doctrine & Conduct of the Minister & People of this Place & I have Thought Best to Give you a Coppy of a Complaint Exhi-bited Against Mr Parsons by Capt Tim.o Mather in the following things

1 With Approving Attending & Encouraging Seperate Meetings for Re-ligious Worship.

2 With Allowing Approving & Encourageing Persons when moved with Impressions (that are Common Amongus) to Cry out with a loud voice in the Time of Divine Worship to the Disturbance of the Worship-ping Assembly.

3 With Inviting & approving Unqualified Persons to preach & to Exhort the People such as Thacher Prince &c.

4 with Breaking Covenant with this people by going to Long Island to preach without any Necessary Call, when he knew the Church was in Great Danger of being led away from the Simplicity of the Gospel by the Enthusiastick Doctrines & Practices of Mr Davenport.

5 With Recommending a Sheif Prosecuted found Guilty & Recorded in the Charity of a Neighbouring Church without any Christian Satisfaction, the He well knew the whole Matter

FIGURE 20 Joseph Higgins to an Unknown Minister. 1743. Detail. Image courtesy of the New England Historic Genealogical Society, Boston, *www.AmericanAncestors.org*

Four other church members signed Mather's written complaint, including his son, Timothy, Jr., Edmund Dorr, Josiah DeWolf, and Samuel Southworth. The "Five Brethren" as they subsequently were called in the bitter dispute that followed, accused Parsons of barring qualified communicants from the Lord's Supper, promoting grossly ignorant candidates to full church membership, and opening his pulpit to a motley assortment of disorderly and schismatical itinerants, including John Curtis, leader of the Shepherd's Tent seminary in New London. Even more shocking to the critics of the Lyme revival was Parsons's willingness to sanction the charismatic gifts of his parishioners. The aggrieved brethren protested that Parsons had allowed Deacon Marvin to assume the "Office of the Publick Ministry Contrary to the Gospel Rule" and "without any Call, Commission, or Qualification." For months, Marvin had been disturbing weekly worship exercises by interrupting Parsons's sermons, offering his own exposition of the Lyme minister's sermon texts, singing psalms, and exhorting the assembly after the meeting had concluded—all "against the known mind of some of the Brethren of the Church."[101]

Underwriting Parsons's new revival measures was a scorching indictment of the godly walk. The Lyme minister candidly condemned both himself and his colleagues for their past errors, asserting that sermons preached in New England before Whitefield's arrival were "Cursed and Damnable Stuff." Parsons's 1743 sermon series on Mark 12:34 featured a relentless catalog of hellish punishments awaiting hopeful professors who fell short of grace. An "External Conformity to the Gospel," he warned, "is noe Evidence that a person is a True Christian." Whereas previous generations of puritan ministers maintained that salvation sprang from the loins of godly parents, Parsons boldly declared that the genealogy of grace now ran through a lineage of "Whores and Witches," "Highway and hedge sinners," rakes and "hell hounds." Converted sailors, swearers, Sabbath breakers, drunkards, prostitutes, and whoremasters had more hope of going to heaven than full church members who merely lived honest lives and attempted to serve God through good works and devotional duties.[102]

If the several written complaints of the Five Brethren are to be trusted, Parsons had allowed the heat of his revival zeal to get the better of his pulpit rhetoric. But, once again, his bold pronouncements flowed directly from impressions that he interpreted as the indwelling presence of the Holy Spirit. Parsons preached ferocious sermons that drew on terrifying images of "hell flames" blazing from the mouths of those who discovered that they were not among the elect. Even moderate revival supporters observed that his sermons, which were delivered with great power, elicited bodily exercises and piercing outcries. But, the Lyme revivalist went a step further than nearly all of his fellow Whitefieldarians. In a manner that anticipated the unusual ministry of layman Richard Woodbury, he arrogated to himself not only the ability to

101. Joseph Higgins and Timothy Mather, Jr., "Complaint or Questions of Joseph Higgins and Timothy Mather Junr.," Aug. 28, 1746, JWC. See also Higgins to unidentified clergyman, n.d. [circa December 1743]; Timothy Mather, Sr., et al., "Articles of Complaint against Mr. Parsons," Aug. 24; 1744, transcr. Jonathan Parsons, JWC, and Anonymous, "5 Brethren's Complaint," n.d. [circa Sept. 2, 1746].

102. Higgins to unidentified clergyman, n.d. [circa December 1743]; Jonathan Parsons, Sermon on Mark 12:34, n.d. [circa 1743], no. 147, Miscellaneous Manuscripts Collection, WCL. See also Mather et al., "Articles of Complaint against Mr. Parsons," Aug. 24, 1744, JWC.

judge the eternal estates of others but also the power to save and damn. According to the Five Brethren, Parsons once said that he had the authority to kill or keep alive whomever he chose. "I will Increase your Damnation in hell," Higgins heard him exclaim. "I Expect to be a Witness against the Worst of you in the Day of Judgment." Parsons also fulminated against the conservative Connecticut magistrates who were responsible for passing the anti-itinerancy act of 1742, condemning their actions as a "Bloody Inquisition."[103]

True saints never considered others saved until they had narrated their conversion experiences, Parsons warned in one of his sermons. When critics attacked his church admission practices and purported gifts of spiritual discernment, Parsons fought back. The only thing rash about assessing the salvation of others lay in prematurely "Judging men converted" before they could publicly relate the precise moment of grace. Like other Whitefieldarians, he believed that conversion occurred instantaneously and was marked by a physical sensation that followed a brief period of distress. Certain knowledge of salvation was possible in this world, Parsons maintained, but it did not arise through disciplined devotional practices or reasoned argument. The regenerate mind "sees Grace and can as certainly distinguish it from a Counterfeit as it can know its own Perception," Parsons asserted in an exchange with Ebenezer Turell. Convicted sinners might experience the *"earnest* of the holy Spirit"—the powerful emotions that frequently attended potent preaching—but only true converts possessed what Parsons called the *"Seal* of the Spirit," an intuitive sense of the indwelling workings of grace that produced an infallible knowledge of personal salvation and an incontrovertible guide to action.[104]

Parsons claimed to care nothing for denominational distinctions or the territorial boundaries of the established Congregational churches, and he welcomed anyone who could testify to the indwelling presence of the Holy Spirit, including Quakers, Baptists, and Anglicans. Parsons eagerly endorsed the spiritual gifts of his congregants and prayed for the descent of other primitive charismata, including the "Miraculous Gift of Tongus." He also might have endorsed a version of controversial doctrine of entire sanctification proposed by John and Charles Wesley in London at about this time. For early Methodists,

103. Higgins to unidentified clergyman, n.d. [circa December 1743]; Tracy, *Great Awakening*, 210. See also Mather et al., "Articles of Complaint against Mr. Parsons," Aug. 24, 1744, JWC, and Anonymous, "5 Brethren's Complaint," n.d. [circa Sept. 2, 1746].

104. Higgins to unidentified clergyman, n.d. [circa December 1743]; Parsons to Turell, Nov. 8, 1742, John Davis Papers. See also Parsons, Sermon on Rom. 8:16, July 15, 1742, no. 123, Miscellaneous Manuscripts Collection.

conversion led to a second stage of regeneration that rendered the individual morally incorruptible and spiritually perfect. "Repentance is not necessary after Conversion," the Lyme pastor allegedly told his fervent parishioners. In a statement that reverberated in perfectionist circles across New England for decades, he proclaimed that "all Doubting in a Christian of his Good state was from the Devil."[105]

At the same time, Parsons actively and perhaps deceptively attempted to shield his radicalized parish from prying eyes. In the wake of the New London bonfires in March 1743, he criticized Davenport in a newspaper editorial, claiming that the Southold revivalist's practice of following the leadings of biblical impulses was an "Error of very dangerous Tendency." Several months after Deacon Marvin's acquittal, John Walley, Jr., a young ministerial candidate from Boston, passed through town and talked at length with Parsons about the "State of Religion among his People." The Lyme minister recounted a familiar story of revival meetings, convicted sinners, surges in church admissions, and the good fruits of moral reformation that ensued. He also claimed that his parish had been "free from Exhorters and Separations" and only briefly alluded to the "censorious Spirit which has so much prevailed thro' the Land." Clearly, Parsons was laboring to distance himself from Davenport and to put the best possible face on a worsening situation.[106]

The following year, Parsons penned a letter to the *Christian History* in which he acknowledged having a "very *extensive* and *personal* Acquaintance" with new converts during the "late Season of Grace," but he dismissed as groundless the rising chorus of complaints against enthusiasm in New England. There had been few instances of dreams, trances, and visions in Lyme, he maintained. His parishioners did not claim to possess infallible knowledge of their salvation, nor did they disparage good works or rail against unconverted ministers. Among the thousands that he had interviewed during pastoral conferences, Parsons claimed that he had "not met with a *Score* that pretended to *any* such Things." The few outcries that occasionally disrupted religious meetings had issued from the mouths of bitter revival opposers, rather than unlearned exhorters and rabble rousers. Parsons even declared that the *"new Converts"* in his parish judged their "Neighbours to be *uncon-*

---

105. Higgins to unidentified clergyman, n.d. [circa December 1743]. On the Wesleyan doctrine of sanctification and the "witness of the Spirit," see Ann Taves, *Fits, Trances, and Visions: Experiencing Religion and Explaining Experience from Wesley to James* (Princeton, N.J., 1999), 50–58.

106. *Boston Gazette*, May 17, 1743; John Walley, Jr., journal, 1742–1751, Sept. 28, 1743, microfilm, MHS.

verted" only in extreme cases in which the "Course of their Life is manifestly *carnal* or *vicious."* To confirm the truth of his assessment of the Lyme revival as a "wonderful Work of God's Grace," Parsons concluded his long narrative in the *Christian History* with an attestation signed by five parishioners.[107]

Perhaps the Lyme minister truly believed that he had been living by the intuitive motions of the Spirit rather than enthusiastic impulses. Or, perhaps he grasped more fully than his contemporaries the potential of print as a medium for crafting a public persona. Either way, Parsons ignored, elided, or, more likely, simply lied about the Marvin controversy in his published account of the Lyme revival. To an anonymous pamphleteer, who imagined that he could see through the *"Mazes"* of Parsons's empty rhetoric, the Lyme clergyman's seemingly measured pronouncements on revival errors were *"cunning wheedling"* falsehoods — *"down-right insincere Dealing"* designed to safeguard his reputation during a period of intense ecclesiastical discord and public scrutiny. The Five Brethren went a step further, denouncing Parson's letter to the *Christian History* as "utterly false."[108]

Meanwhile, Edmund Dorr, Timothy Mather, Sr., and the other members of the aggrieved faction redoubled their efforts to discipline Reynold Marvin and expose the minister who had shielded him from censure. During the spring of 1744, Dorr appealed to Parsons to reopen the case against Marvin. He buttressed his appeal with an eight-page statement in which he accused Parsons and the Lyme church of maladministration in their decision to acquit the deacon of false witness. The reason that Marvin had questioned the state of his soul, Dorr asserted, was simply because he had refused to "tell the time and relate the particular Circumstances of my Conversion." He argued further that the "work of judgeing the Spiritual and invisible state of men" was reserved to God and "Suspended till the great day" of Judgment. Condemned by prominent seventeenth-century New England divines down to Jonathan Edwards — whose works Dorr cited by title in his complaint — Marvin's "plainly forbidden" and "insufferably arrogant" sins demanded a public confession.[109]

But Dorr did not stop there. The aggrieved layman emphasized that he had made a "publick profession of religion" more than twenty-five years earlier. In the written relation of faith that he had submitted to Parsons's predecessor,

107. Parsons, "Account of the Revival of Religion at Lyme West Parish in Connecticut, Continued," *CH*, no. 70 (June 30, 1744), 140, 156, 161.

108. *Mr. Parsons Corrected*, 3, 5, 8; Joseph Fish, "Judgment of a Council against the 5 Brethren," Jan. 25, 1745, JWC. See also, Anonymous, "5 Brethren's Complaint," n.d. [circa Sept. 2, 1746], JWC.

109. Mather, "Arguments Offered by Edmund Dorr," n.d. [circa 1743–1744], [2–3], JWC.

Dorr solemnly swore to accept Christ in all his "offices as my prophet priest and king" and make "his Laws the rule of my obedience." Surely, Marvin knew that Dorr was one of Lyme's oldest and most esteemed church members. As for "whether my life Since has ben answerable to this my profession," Dorr left it to the world to judge. In contrast to Parsons, who railed against "false hearted Professors" and "Moral men" in his revival sermons, Dorr rooted his complaint in the ideal of a godly walk. Discrediting his "Solemn profession," Marvin, in effect, had called him a liar. Dorr charged the deacon with the "most inveterate malice" in slandering his good name before the entire Lyme congregation. What began as a debate over revival excesses threatened to explode into a civil case of defamation.[110]

By the summer of 1744, it had become abundantly clear to the Five Brethren that their arguments had fallen on deaf ears. The Lyme church had acquitted Marvin, refused to consider the initial complaint lodged by Timothy Mather, Sr., and ignored Dorr's appeal. The aggrieved laymen had turned to the New London County ministerial association for advice, but the assembled clergymen merely encouraged Parsons to take action. He, in turn, considered the matter closed and steadfastly refused to call another church meeting. Ensnared in bureaucratic inertia, the Five Brethren took matters into their own hands on August 24, 1744, just three days before Alexander Hamilton witnessed the altercation with the "rabble of clowns" in the home of Mather, Sr. In a second statement written on behalf of the aggrieved faction, the elder Mather condemned Parsons's irregular ministry in fourteen articles and demanded a hearing to "lay our grievances before the Church."[111]

For more than a century, Congregational churches had adhered to strict disciplinary procedures in matters of ecclesiastical controversy. The Cambridge *Platform* enjoined church members to settle their disputes in private before airing them in a public meeting. The danger lay in the promiscuous diffusion of unproven allegations—such as the articles of complaint exhibited by the Five Brethren—beyond the boundaries of the local community. On this issue, Parsons and his supporters had good reason to be concerned. After all, Joseph Higgins previously had impounded Parsons's correspondence with Benjamin Colman and forwarded a copy of the elder Mather's complaint to an

110. Ibid., [4–5].
111. Benjamin Lord, "Advice of the Association at New Concord to Edmund Dorr," June 12, 1744, JWC, Jonathan Parsons, "Church Vote Respecting Deacon Mr. Marvin's Withdrawal," June 13, 1744, Mather et al., "Articles of Complaint against Mr. Parsons," Aug. 24, 1744 (quotes); Old Lyme Congregational Church Records, 63; *AHI*, 163.

unnamed minister. Reports like these fueled Charles Chauncy's massive anti-revival exposé, *Seasonable Thoughts on the State of Religion in New-England*, a treatise to which Higgins, Mather, and at least one other member of Lyme's aggrieved faction had subscribed in 1743.[112]

At this point in the conflict, Parsons went on the offensive. He believed that the Five Brethren had violated gospel rule in airing their grievances against him in public. Yet, he also knew that the New London Association was unlikely to support any attempt to discipline his outspoken parishioners. Several months before the Lyme controversy began in 1743, Parsons withdrew from that body, as his conservative colleagues grew increasingly vocal in their opposition to the revival innovations. With the ecclesiastical establishment arrayed against him, Parsons seized on an unusual solution. On December 17, 1744, the Lyme church voted to renounce the Saybrook Platform, which granted ministerial associations the power to adjudicate local church disputes. Noting the vote in his record book, Parsons asserted that "none of the particular Churches are subordinate to each other." Ecclesiastical authority over "Matters of Scandal" properly belonged to church members and was to be determined by a "Major Vote of those present when properly Assembled for that End."[113]

In casting off the authority of the Connecticut religious establishment, Parsons hoped to convene an independent council of his own choosing to discipline the Five Brethren. The Lyme church voted to "demand Satisfaction" from the offending party just two days later. When Dorr and the Five Brethren refused to appear at a scheduled hearing, Parsons and his supporters promptly produced a document calling for a council to arbitrate the dispute. They charged Dorr, Mather, and their confederates with spreading false reports, disturbing the peace, and hindering the "Progress of the Gospel of our Lord Jesus Christ." In addition, Parsons's supporters contended that the dissenters' August 1744 articles of grievance had failed to provide precise details relating to the dates, times, and locations of the alleged offenses. On January 15, 1745, a council of five ministers and lay delegates—all of whom were warm

---

112. Matthew Griswold and Zechariah Marvin, "Churches Complaint against the 5 Brethren," Sept. 2, 1746, JWC; Parsons to Colman, Dec. 29, 1742, box 2, Colman Papers; Chauncy, *Seasonable Thoughts on the State of Religion*, 9, 13, 16. On puritan church discipline practices, see Emil Oberholzer, Jr., *Delinquent Saints: Disciplinary Action in the Early Congregational Churches of Massachusetts* (New York, 1956), 30–31.

113. Old Lyme Congregational Church Records, 74. See also New London Association, Records, 1709–1788, 105–106, 113–114, Connecticut Conference Archives, United Church of Christ (currently on deposit at CL; available online at NEHH); and William Hart, "Direction of the Association at Killingworth to Edmund Dorr," Oct. 2, 1744, JWC.

advocates of the Whitefieldian revivals—convened to offer their judgment in the controversy. Not surprisingly, they concurred with the Parsons faction, sternly censured the Five Brethren, and ordered them to make an immediate and public avowal of their sinful conduct.[114]

Dorr, Mather, and their allies initially requested time to consider whether they would comply with the advice of the council. Then they dug in. In a written rebuttal submitted to the church one month later, the Five Brethen decisively changed the terms of the debate. Previously, the Dorr faction had worked within well-established exegetical and theological parameters in pursuing their case against Marvin and Parsons. Now, they retreated to the language of English common law. "To Complain when he is injured," Dorr argued, citing the works of prominent jurists Giles Jacob and Edward Coke, is the "natural right of every freeborn Subject, provided he do it in a regular manner." The Five Brethren maintained that they had published their list of grievances only after consulting with a lawful court—the New London Association—which by the authority of the Saybrook Platform had a "regular jurisdiction in the matters of our Complaint." Thus, they concluded that their behavior throughout the entire affair had been unobjectionable and that the rump council that Parsons had assembled held no authority in their case.[115]

The dispute dragged on for another year. Although Dorr apologized for a few heated statements that he had uttered during the proceedings, the Five Brethren resolutely refused to retract their allegedly libelous complaints. Then, in a stunning turn of events, Parsons laid down his pastorate late in the fall of 1745 and abruptly left town. During the next year, he divided his time among revival splinter groups in Boston and Newbury. Parsons's unexpected departure left the Lyme church in turmoil and sapped the power of his supporters. Within weeks, the church had reversed its position and was writing to the New London Association requesting advice on issues that cut in several directions, including procedures for securing a new pastor and the legitimacy of sanctioning lay exhorters. The church also voted to "Refer all their subsisting Difficulties that were matter of Controversie" between the church and the Five Brethren to an independent council of four ministers. Dorr and his party finally agreed.[116]

114. Old Lyme Congregational Church Records, 72, 74; Fish, "Judgment of a Council against the 5 Brethren," Jan. 25, 1745, JWC.

115. Old Lyme Congregational Church Records, 77; Edmund Dorr, "Pleas of the 5 Brethren Before the Council in Their Defense," n.d. [circa 1745], JWC. See also Giles Jacob, *A New Law-Dictionary: Containing, the Interpretation and Definition of Words and Terms Used in the Law* (London, 1729), s.v. "defamation," "slander," and "libel."

116. Timothy Mather, Sr., and Josiah DeWolf, "The 5 Brethren's Complaint against the

The final showdown between the Lyme church and the Five Brethren occurred on September 2, 1746. Both groups kept to their original arguments and filed additional complaints that restated and summarized the grievances of the previous three years in exhaustive detail. The composition of the clerical delegation was evenly balanced between revival advocates and opposers, but neither faction could have been pleased with the final judgment. On the one hand, the assembled ministers reversed the decision of the 1745 council and proclaimed that Parsons's church had erred in acquitting Marvin in the first place and had subsequently failed in its duty to uphold the "Laws of Christ." They further urged the Lyme church to reconsider censuring the deacon for pronouncing Dorr unconverted. The council also rejected the church's complaint that the Five Brethren had violated gospel rule. At the same time, they acknowledged that the written complaints exhibited by Dorr and Mather contained nearly a dozen false articles. Admonishing the Five Brethren for their "Great Fault and Transgression," the council exhorted them to seek the forgiveness of God and the church. Confessions on both sides, the ministers concluded emphatically, would provide grounds on which to "bury all Past Offences, and Embrace Each Other In Christian Love."[117]

One day later, the Five Brethren submitted a written response to the council proceedings that revealed just how deep the fissure between the factions had grown and just how technically sophisticated they had become in arguing ecclesiastical matters. Writing on behalf of the group, Mather attempted to transform the greatest weakness of their argument—the purported "loose, and Uncertain" content of the August 1744 complaint—into a potential asset. Ironically, only one of the fifteen articles named the church as the offending party. The other allegations focused specifically on Parsons's revival excesses and mismanagement of the Marvin case. Since he had abandoned his congregation and moved to Newbury, Mather argued, the church no longer had grounds on which to prosecute the Five Brethren. "We Can't See that this Church has any more right to pursue us for publishing a false report of the minister of Newberry," he explained, "than the Church at New London has, yea or the *Bishop of London* or *Superintendant of Denmark*." It was Parsons's prerogative alone to seek redress. That he had not appealed to the New London Association or even attended the September 1746 council provided reasonable grounds for Mather's self-serving speculation that their former

---

Church," Sept. 30, 1745, JWC, Eleazar Mather, Nathaniel Matson, and James Marvin, "Questions to Be Proposed to the Reverend Consociation," June 17, 1746, Zechariah Marvin, "Church Vote," July 8, 1746 (quote).

117. Solomon Williams, "The Result of the Council," Sept. 2, 1746, JWC.

minister was satisfied with the state of affairs in Lyme, "otherwise he would doubtless have prosecuted us himself."[118]

Even if Parsons had returned to participate in the Lyme council, Mather continued, the decision of the assembled ministers would not have ended the controversy. Their judgment could not prevent the dismissed clergyman from filing a defamation suit against the Five Brethren in civil court. But the "Law abhors multiplicity of Lawsuits," he argued, "and tis a Maxim in the Law of England and we think in the Law of God and nature too, that no man Shall be twice endangered for the Same fact." The same legal principles that governed civil courts, in other words, equally applied to the ecclesiastical proceedings of the New London Association. The strong argument put forward by the Five Brethren mirrored the rise of technical pleas in the colonial courts during the middle decades of the eighteenth century.[119]

With this final statement, the bitter dispute finally came to a close. The damage sustained by both sides was irreparable. Repeated references to the Five Brethren and the Parsons faction as "Parties" amply testified to a fundamental breakdown in ecclesiastical order. The individuals at the center of the dispute were respected church leaders who were committed to mutually incompatible visions of religious fellowship. Marvin and Parsons drew on James Davenport's practice of spiritual discernment and other charismatic gifts of the Holy Spirit. Dorr, initially resisted these "fashionable" revival innovations and turned to the inclusive ideal of the godly walk. The Five Brethren were no less religious than Marvin, nor were they categorically opposed to the Whitefieldian revivals. Most of the antagonists had children who joined the Lyme church during the powerful 1741 revival. The willingness of both parties to step outside the traditional methods of adjudicating ecclesiastical disputes, moreover, signaled a critical breach of both communication and fellowship. Whereas Parsons's church committee relied on the Cambridge *Platform* in prosecuting their case against the offenders, the Five Brethren turned away from the theological treatises of "old celebrated divines" and voiced their complaints through a technical language of natural law, legal maxims, and actionable offenses. As the rancor deepened and intensified, both sides began to imagine the Lyme church, not as a mediating institution designed to preserve

---

118. Williams, "Result of the Council," Sept. 2, 1746, JWC, Timothy Mather, Sr., "5 Brethrens Pleas in Bar against the Councils Hearing the Churches Complaint," Sept. 3, 1746.

119. Mather, "5 Brethrens Pleas in Bar," Sept. 3, 1746, JWC. On the legal context of the dispute, see William E. Nelson, *Dispute and Conflict Resolution in Plymouth County, Massachusetts, 1725-1825*, Studies in Legal History (Chapel Hill, N.C., 1981), 26–44; and Bruce H. Mann, *Neighbors and Strangers: Law and Community in Early Connecticut*, Studies in Legal History (Chapel Hill, N.C., 1987), 137–161.

the corporate values of the community, but as an adversarial arena nearly indistinguishable from the civil courts in its disciplinary mechanisms and procedures. By 1746, Marvin and Dorr no longer spoke the same language, nor could they find an institutional forum in which to negotiate their differences.[120]

In the end, the acrimonious dispute that began with the deacon's vituperative assault on the unconverted soul of a fellow parishioner lasted for more than three years and involved nearly two dozen church meetings and councils, all without a final resolution. Collectively, the surviving petitions, pleas, complaints, letters, votes, depositions, and decisions produced by both parties totaled more than twenty thousand words. The residents of Lyme were still hotly debating the proceedings more than a decade later. Dorr might have won vindication from the 1746 council, but he never received the public satisfaction that he desperately craved. Marvin withdrew from communion in the Lyme church and remained beyond the reach of ecclesiastical discipline. Nor did the Five Brethren ever apologize to Parsons or the rest of the church for their loose complaints.[121]

Marvin was savaged in the public prints. Two weeks before the final church council, the *Boston Evening-Post* published a satirical account of the deacon's second marriage, which had taken place a mere three months after the death of his first wife. In addition to reprinting the couple's pious wedding vows as a "Pattern for all the NEW LIGHTS in the Country," the article included a humorous account of their betrothal. One stormy night earlier that summer, Marvin heard a noise that sounded like a cradle rocking. Loose clapboarding was to blame, but the deacon interpreted the event as a sign from God. "The Impulse was so strong upon his mind," the newspaper wag asserted, that he set out the next morning on a journey to Colchester to visit the widow Mary Kellog. Family lore maintained that he rode up to Kellogg's door and, without dismounting, bluntly informed her "It has been revealed to me by the Lord that you are to be my wife." To which the widow meekly replied, "The Lord's will be done." Similar tales regarding the deacon's alleged "eccentricities" and "revelations" circulated in Lyme for more than a century.[122]

120. New London Association, Records, 119; Mather "Arguments Offered by Edmund Dorr," n.d. [circa 1743–1744], [3], JWC.

121. *A Letter from a Gentleman in the Country, to His Friend in Boston, respecting Some Late Observations upon the Conduct of the Rev. Mr. Jonathan Parsons, while He Was Minister at Lyme in Connecticut* (Boston, 1757); Solomon Paine and Matthew Smith, petition to the Connecticut General Assembly, May 2, 1748, Ecclesiastical Affairs, Ser. 1, X, 29d, Connecticut Archives.

122. *Boston Evening-Post*, Aug. 18, 1746; Edward Elbridge Salisbury and Evelyn McCurdy

Jonathan Parsons was ordained over a Separate Congregational church in Newbury during the spring of 1746, although the precise details regarding his removal from Lyme remain unclear. Parsons's allies claimed that he made a suitable confession and received an orderly dismissal from a group of sympathetic colleagues who contended that he had been "injuriously treated, and much wronged in his character" and absolved him of any "censurable Evil." Critics, however, continued to assert that Parsons simply abandoned his pastorate in Lyme. Rumors of his past misconduct surfaced occasionally during the next decade. Even as he rose to prominence at the head of one of New England's largest and wealthiest separatist churches, Parsons never entirely escaped the charges of enthusiasm that dogged him in Lyme. To his many adversaries, he would always be remembered as a "Companion and Intimate of the famous Incendiary Mr. Davenport."[123]

LET HIM STAND UP IN THE DAY OF PENTECOST

Alexander Hamilton departed for Annapolis along the same road that had carried James Davenport to New Haven three years earlier. The Boston Post Road led him through the Connecticut parishes of several ministers whose books had been burned on the streets of New London. Following his encounter with Reynold Marvin and the "riff-raff" in Lyme, he stopped in Branford, Stratford, and Horseneck (now Greenwich)—all hotbeds of itinerant preaching and sites of extraordinary revival commotions. With the exception of a brief report involving a disturbing dream and a haunted house, however, Hamilton declined to comment on religious affairs during his last days in New England. The hurried final pages of his *Itinerarium* read as if the author had seen enough. "Farewell, Connecticut," Hamilton grumbled as he crossed into New York. "I have had a surfeit of your ragged money, rough roads, and enthusiastick people."[124]

He concluded his peregrinations several weeks later. In all, Hamilton had traveled more than 1,624 miles by land and water. His health had improved along with his spirits. Almost immediately Hamilton set to work transforming

---

Salisbury, *Family-Histories and Genealogies*, III, *Genealogical and Biographical Monographs on the Families of Lee and Marvin* ([New Haven, Conn.], 1892), 132–134.

123. Jonathan F. Stearns, *A Historical Discourse Commemorative of the Organization of the First Presbyterian Church in Newburyport* (Newburyport, Mass., 1846), 56; *Letter from a Gentleman in the Country*, 9; Moses Gerrish et al., to William Shirley, Aug. 4, 1749, XII, 726, MA. See also Franklin Bowditch Dexter, ed., *Extracts from the Itineraries and Other Miscellanies of Ezra Stiles, D.D., LL.D., 1755-1794* ... (New Haven, Conn., 1916), 293.

124. *AHI*, 163, 170.

his rough travel journal into a polished manuscript that he circulated among an emerging circle of literary wits in Annapolis. Curiously, he presented one copy to an Italian gentleman named Onorio Razolini, who had recently arrived in Maryland and later returned to Europe with the *Itinerarium*, where the manuscript slumbered for more than a century until it was sold to a rare books dealer in London. Hamilton's inscription on the flyleaf bore the date November 29, 1744. One month earlier, George Whitefield had returned to a land irreparably divided by Davenport's radicalism.[125]

■ "Some, I understand, are for burning not only the book I lately put out," quipped Charles Chauncy in a letter to his nephew, "but me also, had they the power in their hands." For Boston's "Old Brick," incidents like the New London bonfires all came back to the same source: George Whitefield. Chauncy's assessment of New England's great awakenings dimmed with each passing month. He initially characterized the Anglican itinerant as a vain man of "smaller talents" but soon conjured Whitefield as the "source of all our other disorder" and the author of the "late and present religious commotions." On receiving the news that Whitefield had shipped out of Liverpool and was heading back to New England for a second preaching tour, Chauncy could scarcely contain his distress. "I fear we shall again be thrown into disorder by the grand promoter of all the confusion that has been in the land," he wrote to his Connecticut kinsman. "I am in concern at the thought of a revival of the spirit that has been the occasion of so many difficulties in many of the Towns and churches." A second visit from Whitefield, he feared, "would give the finishing stroke to our religious constitution."[126]

Whitefield arrived in York, Maine, on October 26, 1744, and quickly converted the town into the hub of a vibrant revival network. Regional clergymen, riding ministers, Boston merchants, and "great crowds come out of the Country" once again descended on the coastal village. Whitefield met with admiring colleagues from as far away as eastern Connecticut. He listened with pleasure as local pastors described how he had "razed" their false foundations four years earlier, and he received dozens of letters from devoted followers from across New England. As he ascended Samuel Moody's pulpit to deliver the first of several sermons, Whitefield was pleased to learn that York and the

125. *AHI*, xxx–xxxi, 2, 199.

126. Edward M. Griffin, "Chauncy and *Seasonable Thoughts:* A New Letter," *American Notes and Queries*, XI (1972), 4–5; "Original Letters of Dr. Charles Chauncy," *NEHGR*, X, 333–335. See also Griffin, *Old Brick: Charles Chauncy of Boston, 1705–1787*, Minnesota Monographs in the Humanities, XI (Minneapolis, 1980), 71–93.

surrounding towns on the northern frontier had lately experienced an uncommonly powerful revival season. "I find they were favored with some glorious gales of the blessed Spirit about three years ago," he explained in an unpublished journal, "and other adjacent places catched the flame."[127]

Whitefield's evocative imagery effectively described the overheated religious temperament in New England, although not in ways that he had intended. Metaphors of combustion dominated public discourse during his extended second visit. "Mr. Whitefield expounds every morning at Boston," noted Westborough minister Ebenezer Parkman, the "Divisions on that occasion, I think, hotter than ever." "The furious Zeal with which you had So fired the Passions of the People," complained Harvard College president Edward Holyoke, "hath in many Places burn'd up the very Vitals of Religion." Reflecting on Whitefield's return, Plymouth civil magistrate Josiah Cotton lamented that "We are got into a Flame," and he prayed to God to "Extinguish the Fire that We may not be Consumed." On Whitefield's departure, Cotton reported that he had preached to "almost all Points of the Compass, and kindled a Fire amongst Ministers and People that will hardly be quench'd in Many Years."[128]

How different it all sounded. In 1740, the public prints had gushed with praise during Whitefield's initial fortnight in Boston, noting that his sermons were attended with "much of the divine Presence" and elicited "Great meltings" and "great Applause" among the vast crowds that thronged his daily meetings. The tragic collapse of the galleries in the New South meetinghouse generated news of "Disorder and Confusion" but no personal attacks on Whitefield or his character. Nor did Thomas Fleet, publisher of what soon emerged as the staunchly antirevival *Boston Weekly News-Letter,* criticize the touring evangelist. Instead, the overwhelming majority of New Englanders felt nothing but "unfeigned Esteem and Joy" for Whitefield during his first visit. Superior court justice Paul Dudley proclaimed that he was "admired and followed beyond any man that ever was in America," and Benjamin Colman went so far as to compare Whitefield to Martin Luther and John Calvin. With perhaps the notable exception of jealous Anglican colleagues—who grudgingly acknowledged that "he was the subject of all our Talk, and to speak against him was neither credible nor scarce safe"—no one uttered a cross word against the "Phoenix of the Episcopalians" in 1740. Even Charles Chauncy held his peace.[129]

---

127. *GWJ*, 523–524, 526.

128. Walett, ed., *Diary of Ebenezer Parkman,* 114; Edward Holyoke to George Whitefield, Feb. 20, 1745, 10, Edward Holyoke Papers, 1737–1744, MHS; JCH, 352, 362.

129. *New England Weekly-Journal,* Sept. 23, Oct. 7, 1740; *Boston Evening-Post,* Sept. 22, 1740; *Pennsylvania Gazette* (Philadelphia), Oct. 16, 1740; B. Joy Jeffries, [ed.], "Diary of Paul

Whitefield traveled extensively throughout New England for nearly a year, but reports of his second preaching tour were decidedly mixed. Although he generated "a buzz" wherever he went and remained the "Chief Subject of Conversation," Whitefield encountered determined ministerial opposition at every turn. Boston clergyman Andrew Eliot protested that "Ctians [Christians] are divided into Parties" over the evangelist's itinerant ministry, "their Sperits are roil'd and disturbed, Feuds and Animosities are got to a prodigious Heighth." The Barnstable, Bristol, Cambridge, First and Second Essex, Hampshire, Marlborough, Weymouth, and Western Merrimack ministerial associations in Massachusetts all roundly condemned Whitefield's second tour in published pamphlets. Colleagues in the North Hartford and New Haven associations in Connecticut followed suit, vowing to "Strike a fatal Stroke" against the popular preacher, as did the faculties of both Harvard and Yale Colleges. Congregational clergymen who once pleaded with Whitefield to visit their parishes now excoriated him as an interloper and disturber of the peace. More than 120 ministers closed their pulpits. Scores of hostile editorials appearing in the public prints contributed to one of the largest and most vitriolic newspaper debates in colonial history.[130]

Dudley, 1740," *NEHGR*, XXXV (1881), 30; Louise Parkman Thomas, transcr., "Journal of the Rev. Israel Loring," no. 12191, 2, SA; Perry, ed., *Historical Collections*, III, 347; JCH, 310; Griffin, *Old Brick*, 52.

130. W[illiam] Willis, ed., *Journals of the Rev. Thomas Smith, and the Rev. Samuel Deane* (Portland, Maine, 1849), 117; Walett, ed., *Diary of Ebenezer Parkman*, 119; Andrew Eliot to Stephen Williams, Apr. 15, 1745, case 8, box 22, SGC I; Samuel Whittelsey to Nathaniel Chauncy, Feb. 21, 1745, box 1, Chauncey Family Papers, 1675–1928, MS 135, YUA. For the ministerial associations, see *The Declaration of the Association of the County of New-Haven in Connecticut* ... (Boston, 1745); *The Declaration of Ministers in Barnstable County, Relating to the Late Practice of Itinerant Preaching* (Boston, 1745); *The Declaration of the Rector and Tutors of Yale-College in New-Haven, against the Reverend Mr. George Whitefield, His Principles and Designs* ... (Boston, 1745); *A Letter from Two Neighbouring Associations of Ministers in the Country to the Associated Ministers of Boston and Charlestown, Relating to the Admission of Mr. Whitefield into Their Pulpits* (Boston, 1745); *The Sentiments and Resolution of an Association of Ministers Convened at Weymouth* ... *concerning the Reverend Mr. George Whitefield* ... (Boston, 1745); *Some Reasons Given by the Western Association upon Merrimack River, Why They Disapprove of the Reverend Mr. George Whitefield's Preaching in the New-England Churches* ... (Boston, 1745); *The Testimony of an Association of Ministers Convened at Marlborough* ... *against the Reverend Mr. George Whitefield, and His Conduct, as Also the Testimony of a Number of Ministers in the County of Bristol, against the Said Gentleman* (Boston, 1745); *The Testimony of the North Association in the County of Hartford* ... *and an Address from Some of the Ministers in the County of Hampshire* ... (Boston, 1745); and *The Testimony of the President, Professors, Tutors, and Hebrew Instructor of Harvard College in Cambridge, against the Reverend Mr. George Whitefield and His Conduct* (Boston, 1744). For newspaper reporting during Whitefield's second New England tour, see Lisa Smith, *The First Great Awakening in Colonial American Newspapers: A Shifting Story* (Lanham, Md., 2012), 111–120, 149.

Only in Boston, the Old Colony, the hill country of eastern Connecticut, and along the northern New England frontier did Whitefield discover sympathetic colleagues who allowed him to preach from their pulpits. Even still, he faced opposition in these areas as well. An elderly man accosted him along the back roads of Plymouth County, sternly demanding to see his "Commission to go about preaching." In Exeter, New Hampshire, Whitefield fell into a heated dispute with minister John Odlin. A visitor who witnessed the altercation threatened to "go and take him bodily" out of the meetinghouse. Citing the "vast charge, expence and trouble" that Whitefield and his entourage would impose on his family, a taverner refused to provide lodgings during his visit to Lebanon, Connecticut. Even his strongest supporters were forced to admit that his presence fomented a "Spirit of Wrath Bitterness and Contention, Scorn and Derision" in churches where he had preached with power only a few years earlier.[131]

Jonathan Edwards minimized the "great uproar" that exploded during Whitefield's second New England tour. Writing in a letter to a Scottish correspondent, he blamed revival opposers for the "heat, violence and contention" that plagued the region. The "greatness of the fire" with which they sought to blacken Whitefield's name was entirely out of proportion to the circumstances, for the Anglican itinerant had "conducted himself much more modestly, wisely, and inoffensively than before," at least according to Edwards. Unlike his first visit, in which Whitefield relentlessly accosted secure professors, he preached with a considerable degree of caution in 1744 and 1745. His sermons emphasized God's "universal Love" to sinners and the necessity of an "honorable Walk." Whitefield spoke out against religious pride and extravagant emotional outbursts. He condemned ecclesiastical divisions; he pleaded with young converts to act in ways that would lend credibility to their church admission professions; and he generally avoided holding meetings in direct opposition to the stated wishes of local ministers. Whitefield even published apologies for his youthful revival exuberance. "I come to America not to raise, or foment Factions, Seperations, or Parties," he explained to Portsmouth, New

131. *GWJ*, 540, 555; Ebenezer Gray to Eleazar Wheelock, Jan. 24, 1745, no. 745124, *EWP*; Benjamin Colman to Solomon Williams, Apr. 12, 1745, case 8, box 22, SGC I. For Whitefield's preaching invitations, see *The Testimony of a Number of Ministers Conven'd at Taunton … in Favour of the Rev. Mr. Whitefield* (Boston, 1745); William Shurtleff, *A Letter to Those of His Brethren in the Ministry Who Refuse to Admit the Rev. Mr. Whitefield into Their Pulpits* (Boston, 1745); Nicholas Loring, *A Letter from the Reverend Mr. Nicholas Loring of North-Yarmouth in the County of York, to the Reverend Mr. Thomas Smith, of Falmouth, in the Same County …* (Boston, 1745); and *Invitations to the Reverend Mr. Whitefield from the Eastern Consocation of the County of Fairfield* (Boston, 1745).

Hampshire, minister William Shurtleff shortly after his arrival, "but simply to preach the dear Redeemer wheresoever he shall be pleas'd *plainly* to open a Door."[132]

By all accounts, Whitefield failed to capture the hearts of his New England audiences a second time. Edwards acknowledged that Whitefield had preached as often as he had done in 1740 to "commonly great and crowded congregations" but without "such remarkable effects, in awakenings and reviving religion." Most letters written in the wake of Whitefield's second tour concluded with news that local religious vitality was "upon the Decline" or at "low Ebb." Anglican clergymen who previously had suffered under the lash of Whitefield's stinging sermons now relished the opportunity to pounce on his preaching failures. "Multitudes flock after him," reported Boston's Timothy Cutler, "but without that Fervency and Fury as heretofore." After witnessing Whitefield preach in Providence and Newport, Rhode Island, rector James MacSparran concluded "Small numbers attend him now to w[ha]t did some years ago. There is a change somewhere, in him or them."[133]

The difference was James Davenport. During the peak years of the revivals between 1740 and 1744, the Southold itinerant and his fellow Whitefieldarians had stirred up thousands of lay men and women to believe and do extraordinary things. Assured of their divine election, new converts welcomed bodily distress and ecclesiastical discord. They sang hymns in the streets and championed dreams, trances, and visions. They lived by biblical impulses, judged the experiences of others, and claimed special commissions to exhort and preach. And they damned to hell all pretended Christians who questioned whether their boisterous new revival measures were authentic manifestations of the Holy Spirit. Whitefield had always been more cautious on these issues, but that mattered little to his many adversaries who now proclaimed that the

132. Jonathan Edwards to Friends in Scotland, n.d. [after Sept. 16, 1745], in *WJE*, XVI, *Letters and Personal Writings*, ed. Claghorn, 175–176, 178–179; Thomas Foxcroft, diary, Nov. 26–Dec. 13, 1744, Thomas Foxcroft Papers, 1690–1770, 1, 24, Mark and Llora Bortman Collection, HGARC; William Shurtleff to Benjamin Colman, Nov. 12, 1744, Letters to Benjamin Colman. For similar arguments, see Harry S. Stout, *The Divine Dramatist: George Whitefield and the Rise of Modern Evangelicalism*, Library of Religious Biography (Grand Rapids, Mich., 1991), 182–196; Thomas S. Kidd, *George Whitefield: America's Spiritual Founding Father* (New Haven, Conn., 2014), 178–187; and Kenneth P. Minkema, "Whitefield, Jonathan Edwards, and Revival," in Geordan Hammond and David Ceri Jones, eds., *George Whitefield: Life, Legacy, and Context* (London, 2016), 115–131.

133. Edwards to Friends in Scotland, n.d. [after Sept. 16, 1745], in *WJE*, XVI, *Letters and Personal Writings*, ed. Claghorn, 178; Chester Williams to Thomas Foxcroft, Dec. 18, 1744, Foxcroft Papers; Eliot to Williams, Apr. 15, 1745, case 8, box 22, SGC I; Perry, ed., *Historical Collections*, III, 388; Daniel Goodwin, ed., *A Letter Book and Abstract of Out Services Written during the Years 1743–1751 by the Revd. James MacSparran* (Boston, 1899), 25.

"Errors and Disorders" that roiled the country stemmed from his first New England preaching tour as well as his published journals and sermons, all of which were "Calculated to Stir up Divisions" and "create Jealousies in People about their Ministers." By 1745, public discourse had transformed Whitefield into a dangerous strolling vagabond whose incendiary sermons were the very *Engine of Enthusiasm.* He had emerged as the "great *Master-Builder* in the *Babel of Confusion* which has been erecting in the four preceding Years." As if to underscore the direct connection between the "grand Itinerant" and the "grand Enthusiast," several ministerial associations tarred Whitefield with the same charge that Benjamin Colman had famously leveled against Davenport during the summer of 1742: "deeply tinctured with *Enthusiasm.*"[134]

■ James Davenport followed Alexander Hamilton for more than one hundred miles during the Maryland physician's return trip to Annapolis. The ringleader of the New London bonfires was merely days behind, spurred by a call from his former parishioners in Hopewell and Maidenhead, New Jersey. He had preached as a ministerial candidate in the predominantly Scots-Irish parishes before his ordination at Southold in 1738. Now the New Siders allied with Gilbert Tennent's New Brunswick Presbytery sought his services again. Even as Hamilton sat down to consign Whitefield's "New Light biggots" to intellectual oblivion in his *Itinerarium,* Davenport's exodus to New Jersey marked the resurgence of one of British North America's most influential and successful Whitefieldarians. It was difficult, if not impossible, to keep the charismatic preacher down and harder, still, to corral the new converts that he left behind in New England.[135]

The New London bonfires of March 1743 tarnished Davenport's reputation and threw him into a protracted period of melancholy. The Boston prints reported during the weeks following the conflagrations that he had retracted his "strange Opinions." Davenport's closest disciples quickly abandoned him. Revival narratives published in the *Christian History* minimized or ignored his considerable role in sparking New England's era of great awakenings. Even Davenport's most fiery defenders, Andrew Croswell and Jonathan Parsons, distanced themselves from the events in New London in published newspaper editorials. To his many critics, Davenport seemed a broken man. Dismissed

134. Williams to Foxcroft, Dec. 18, 1744, Foxcroft Papers; *Boston Evening-Post,* Aug. 27, 1744, Feb. 4, 1745; *Testimony of the North Association,* 3, 6; *Sentiments and Resolution of an Association of Ministers,* 4. See also "To the Publisher," *Boston Weekly Post-Boy,* Mar. 28, 1743, in Bushman, ed., *Great Awakening,* 51.

135. *AHI,* 8.

from his pastorate in Southold, he rode dejectedly from town to town, forsaken by kin, colleagues, and once-devoted followers. "Mr. Davenport is very much alone in this world," New Haven gentlewoman Sarah Pierpont lamented in a letter to Eleazar Wheelock later that spring. But, in the next sentence Pierpont declared that Davenport had recently experienced a "great deal of Soul Satisfaction" as well.[136]

The troubled preacher also believed that his charismatic ministry had weathered the storm of public criticism intact. Languishing for several weeks at the Shepherd's Tent suffering with a "Cancry Humour" in his leg, Davenport struggled to make sense of a public ministry gone terribly wrong. In time, however, he arrived at a very different understanding of his role in the bonfires. Satan, he explained in a published letter to former traveling companion Jonathan Barber, had exploited his physical infirmities and duped him into believing that the Holy Spirit sanctioned his decision to burn the heretical books. Davenport now understood that he had been "under the powerful Influence of the false Spirit, almost one whole Day together, and Part of several Days." He attributed his extravagant actions on the streets of New London to an indwelling demonic presence.[137]

This interpretive position allowed Davenport to make a "free and full Confession" of his error, while preserving the theological framework that had structured his public ministry during the previous three years. In contrast to his armor bearers, who were wracked with guilt and remorse, Davenport once again was filled with rapture for nearly a month. Rising from his sick bed like Lazarus rising from the dead, he began receiving fresh biblical impulses that darted into his mind and comforted his afflicted soul. The words of the risen Jesus to Mary Magdalene and the women at the tomb in Mark 16:7, in particular, convinced Davenport that he would "stand up in the Day of Pentecost" and once again speak with power to the unconverted. Even as he warned Barber to take heed from his "terrible Fall," Davenport persisted in the same beliefs regarding the indwelling presence of the Holy Spirit that had precipitated the book-burning incident.[138]

Published in the Boston newspapers one year later, Davenport's sensational *Retractations* conveyed a similar ambivalence. On the one hand, he apolo-

---

136. *Boston Evening-Post,* Mar. 28, 1743; Sarah Pierpont to Eleazar Wheelock, May 30, 1743, no. 743330, *EWP.* See also Smith, *First Great Awakening in Colonial American Newspapers,* 144–147, 150; and Timothy E. W. Gloege, "The Trouble with *Christian History:* Thomas Prince's 'Great Awakening,'" *Church History,* LXXXII (2013), 139–140, 154.

137. James Davenport, *A Letter from the Rev. Mr. James Davenport, to Mr. Jonathan Barber* ... ([Philadelphia, 1744]), 3, 7.

138. Ibid., 4, 9, 11.

gized for his "misguided zeal" and repudiated many of the controversial aspects of the revivals, including censorious judging, urging separation from unconverted ministers, encouraging lay exhorters, singing in the streets, and *"following Impulses* or Impressions as a Rule of Conduct." He quoted the critical paragraphs of his published letter to Barber in which he attributed the *"horrid Action"* in New London to a *"false Spirit."* Yet, Davenport continued to believe that God had favored him with "special Assistance and Success" during his earlier preaching tours of New England. In a postscript, he even suggested that his decision to offer his confession to the public came as the result of an unusually intense period of renewal.[139]

Reactions ranged from outright dismissal to grudging acceptance. Plymouth magistrate Josiah Cotton drew predictable lessons from the downfall of the "famous New Light," noting in his family memoirs that the bonfire incident revealed the dangerous "Influence of an Enthusiastick Spirit, from which Good Lord deliver Us." "Mr. Davenport is truly very much altered," Jonathan Edwards countered in a letter to Wheelock, "he is now much fuller of the Spirit of God than he was in years past, when he seemed to have such a constant series of high elevations and raptures." But not all of Davenport's former colleagues were equally charitable. Benjamin Colman's reservations about his *Retractations* precipitated several tense exchanges with colleagues in eastern Connecticut. A letter that he published in response to the confession conjured the specter of Richard Woodbury, whose exploits in Essex County had received prominent attention in the newspapers several weeks earlier.[140]

None of these critics exposed the ambiguities of Davenport's public confession with greater precision than the author of an *Impartial Examination of Mr. Davenport's Retractions.* The anonymous revival opposer complained that Davenport's confession was "neither so *full* nor so *early* as might have been expected." His retraction read more like an endorsement of his irregular ministry than a refutation of his errors, especially the assertion that he had been possessed by a false spirit in New London. "Men should not lick themselves whole, by laying the Blame of their Sins on the Tempter," he quipped, "and it must needs grate on the Ears of a Christian, to hear him in the same Breath, boast of *special Assistance* and *Success*, in carrying on a glorious and wonder-

---

139. James Davenport, *The Reverend Mr. James Davenport's Confession and Retractions* (Boston, 1744), in Bushman, ed., *Great Awakening*, 53–55.

140. JCH, 354; Jonathan Edwards to Eleazar Wheelock, July 13, 1744, in *WJE*, XVI, *Letters and Personal Writings*, ed. Claghorn, 145; [Benjamin] Colman, *A Letter from the Reverend Dr. Colman of Boston, to the Reverend Mr. Williams of Lebanon, upon Reading the Confession and Retractations of the Reverend Mr. James Davenport* (Boston, 1744), 4.

ful Work of *divine Power* and *Grace*." After all, Davenport had been deluded by Satan for only a few days. By implication, he claimed to be "under the Influence of the true Spirit all the rest of the Time."[141]

Throughout the summer and fall of 1744, Davenport traveled through the towns of eastern Connecticut, openly confessing his mistakes during the New London bonfires to "those who had been Misled." Joseph Fish later recalled how he appeared in Stonington "broken and contrite, as I scarce ever saw exceeded or e'en equall'd." He apologized to Fish, whom he once branded unconverted, and offered a full recantation of his errors to a large assembly in Stonington's north parish meetinghouse. The "mask was thrown aside," Fish declared. No longer the "noisy, boisterous, rash and censorious" book-burner, Davenport bewailed his past conduct and exhorted Fish's congregation to take warning from the "errors which he had unhappily spread and promoted."[142]

Davenport preached for a short time in Plainfield, Connecticut, during the winter and spring of 1745 before declining health forced him to turn down a unanimous call to fill the town's vacant pulpit. In his letters to Whitefield, he acknowledged his "sad Blunder and misconduct" but also wrote of being "favoured with some refreshing Seasons and Special assistance." Although a few cautious friends and colleagues expressed renewed fears that Davenport would "come here about his high Horse, and sew the seeds of inthusiasm" in their parishes, the former fiery Whitefieldarian continued to moderate his public ministry. He resurrected his career among the New Jersey Presbyterians, published a few sermons and devotional tracts, and itinerated in Virginia before his untimely death in 1757.[143]

Like so many of his contemporaries, Davenport ultimately stepped back from the revivals, but a surprising number of lay men and women continued to testify to his powerful preaching in autobiographical conversion narratives penned during the next two decades. One factor united this eclectic cohort: all of them eventually separated from established Congregational churches. At the time that she wrote of Davenport's despondency, Sarah Pierpont and

141. *An Impartial Examination of Mr. Davenport's Retractations* ([Boston, 1744]), 1–2, 5.

142. Solomon Williams to Benjamin Colman, Sept. 17, 1744, JWC; Joseph Fish, *The Church of Christ a Firm and Durable House* ... (New London, Conn., 1767), 123–124.

143. James Davenport to George Whitefield, Jan. 15, 1745, no. 9, Davenport to George and Eleanor Whitefield, June 3, 1745, no. 10, Davenport to George Whitefield, May 31, 1746, no. 11, "Various Letters Addressed to George Whitefield, 1739–1768," Mss. II.c.9, Congregational Library, London; Carol F. Karlsen and Laurie Crumpacker, eds., *The Journal of Esther Edwards Burr, 1754–1757* (New Haven, Conn., 1984), 248. See also Davenport, *Meditations on Several Divine Subjects* (Boston, 1748); and Davenport, *The Faithful Minister Encouraged* ... (Philadelphia, 1756).

her husband, James, were worshipping with a group of breakaway new converts who had withdrawn from the New Haven church during the fall of 1741. She prefaced her oft-quoted account of the shattered revivalist with a scathing indictment of the dark state of religion in New England, its sleepy congregations dominated by the "enemies of religeon." In later years, Brookline, Massachusetts, layman and future separatist minister Nathaniel Shepard dated his conversion to a sermon that Davenport delivered on Boston Common during the summer of 1742. His dissenting colleague, Isaac Backus, penned a similar autobiographical narrative in which he credited the Long Island evangelist's powerful preaching as being "most blessed For my Conversion." Diarist Hannah Heaton heard Davenport preach eleven times in Southold and witnessed the power of God animating the bodies of his audiences. Memories of his sonorous voice booming above the multitudes and exhorting them to "come away to the lord jesus" later empowered her to break with the Congregational church in the Northeast Society of New Haven (now North Haven).[144]

Hartford clockmaker Seth Youngs perhaps best exemplified this emerging cohort of radical Whitefieldarians. In May 1741, the transplanted Long Islander received reports from family members in Southold who proclaimed that "God is a Discovering Rotten herted hipocrits to the world" through Davenport's controversial practice of separating converted brethren from mere neighbors. A covenant owner since 1736, Youngs had joined the Hartford church several months earlier. Almost immediately, however, he rebelled against his minister, the outspoken revival opposer Daniel Wadsworth. He sent several letters to Eleazar Wheelock urging the Lebanon Crank itinerant to preach in Hartford, and he prayed that God might "Destroy this Stronghold of Satan purefy the Sons of Levi and Gather in his Elect." Youngs and the members of his extended family retreated to his house for late-night religious meetings punctuated by bodily outbursts and powerful conversions. During the late spring of 1741, he spent a week traveling with Davenport on Long Island. He was the "most wonderfull man I think I Ever Se," Youngs proclaimed in a letter to Wheelock. "He Sems to have Intemate Communian with God," and "Thare is no oposition will prevent his preching when the lord Directs his way."[145]

144. Pierpont to Wheelock, May 30, 1743, no. 743330, *EWP;* Isaac Backus, *All True Ministers of the Gospel, Are Called into That Work by the Special Influences of the Holy Spirit ...* (Boston, 1754), in William G. McLoughlin, ed., *Isaac Backus on Church, State, and Calvinism: Pamphlets, 1754–1789,* John Harvard Library (Cambridge, Mass., 1968), 123; McLoughlin, ed., *Diary of Isaac Backus,* III, 1524; Lacey, ed., *World of Hannah Heaton,* 12–13.

145. Seth Youngs to Eleazar Wheelock, May 22, 1741, no. 741322.1, *EWP,* Youngs to Wheelock, July 1, 1741, no. 741401; *Historical Catalogue of the First Church in Hartford, 1633–1885* (Hartford, 1885), 30, 49.

As Davenport began his first assault on southern Connecticut during the summer of 1741, Youngs sought to prepare the way by disrupting weekly Sabbath exercises in Hartford. Youngs was among the numerous "distracted," "erroneous," and "crazy" parishioners whom Wadsworth repeatedly condemned on the pages of his diary, and he might have been the "very zealous" enthusiast with whom the Hartford minister conversed a few weeks after Youngs returned from his visit to Long Island. The following spring, Youngs listened as Davenport railed against the tyranny of the Connecticut General Assembly on the eve of his trial and deportation. Soon, the Hartford clockmaker was exhorting illegally on the streets. According to one observer, Youngs was "allmost Constantly imployed in Pleading his Masters Cause." Like the Southold preacher whom he deeply admired, he was incarcerated for violating Connecticut's anti-itinerancy act in August 1742. There, Youngs and his fellow radicals provoked an "ugly squabble" that resulted in "Considerable tumults and commotions." Within a few years, Youngs abandoned Hartford and began worshipping alongside the famous new convert Nathan Cole in a separatist congregation led by lay preacher Ebenezer Frothingham.[146]

In a few cases, whole communities remained mired in ecclesiastical controversies long after Davenport had reversed course. Lyme and New London were among the most noteworthy examples, but there were others. "We are in a dreadfully shattered posture," Nathaniel Hunting explained in a pair of letters to Benjamin Colman. During the weeks following the bonfires, his Easthampton parish on Long Island had been overrun with exhorters ranging from John Curtis and Davenport's armor bearers to obscure blacksmiths and plowmen from the Shepherd's Tent. "Imitating Davenport," the zealous interlopers admitted "none but converts" to their evening meetings. They preached "strange doctrines" regarding a coming apocalypse. And they were wildly popular. Hunting's own son "grew very warm" and began exhorting sinners "night and day privately, with a vehement voice," before he was overcome by exhaustion and fell into melancholia. His daughter-in-law became so "bigotted to Davenport" that she hardly ever spoke with Hunting. Other parishioners, stirred up by the renewed labors of the "Tent exhorters," heaped "Horrible slanders" against him. Nearly half of the communicants in Easthampton withdrew from communion; neighboring churches were similarly thinned. During the years

---

146. Walker, ed., *Diary of Daniel Wadsworth*, 68, 85, 90, 93; Caleb Smith to William Smith, Aug. 29, 1741, box 1, Smith and Robert Family Papers; Paine and Smith, petition to the Connecticut General Assembly, May 2, 1748, Ecclesiastical Affairs, Ser. 1, X, 29d, Connecticut Archives; Nathan Cole, "A Coppy of the Church Records," 1747–1777, 1, Nathan Cole Papers, I, CHS.

leading up to Hunting's death in 1746, the beleaguered minister continued to languish under the "bondage" of his parishioners' "censoriousness."[147]

In the postscript to his *Retractations,* Davenport warned that many of his most vocal supporters were "not alter'd in their Minds." In Easthampton, disaffected parishioners led by Hunting's son vowed to topple all churches led by unconverted clergymen and "erect new ones out of their new converts." They rejected Davenport's recantation as being "of no relation to ministers or churches on Long Island." Congregants in the north parish of Stonington were also "far from being pleas'd" with his change of heart. When they learned that their inspired leader had turned against "some of their darling principles and ways," minister Joseph Fish later recalled, they denounced Davenport as "cold, dead, and lifeless" and promptly rejected his conciliatory message. "He could by no means pluck up the errors which he had so deeply planted in their minds," Fish lamented. Many of Davenport's former disciples "remain'd stiff" supporters of revival innovations and "some waxed worse," the chastened Whitefieldarian lamented in an unusually candid 1746 letter. All of the towns that he had visited during his 1744 reconciliation tour of eastern Connecticut—Canterbury, Groton, Mansfield, New London, Stonington, and Preston—suffered through bitter church schisms during the years that followed.[148]

Although revival apologists and critics recoiled at the belligerence, antinomianism, and antisocial behavior of James Davenport and his followers, an inspired vanguard surged forward. Rather than ending New England's era of great awakenings, the New London bonfires served as a prelude to what was to come. During the next two decades, his disciples organized scores of breakaway Separate Congregational and Separate Baptist churches in which they attempted to institutionalize many of the Southold evangelist's most innovative, Spirit-centered beliefs, practices, and experiences. Exhausted from the ceaseless ecclesiastical commotions sparked during the Whitefieldian revivals, others sought shelter among the Church of England or simply turned away from religion altogether. Congregational hegemony in the gospel land of light teetered on the brink of collapse.

147. Nathaniel Hunting to Benjamin Colman, May 24, 1743, Colman-Jenks Collection, 1651–1809, MHS; Hunting to Colman, Oct. 18, 1744, Letters to Benjamin Colman.

148. James Davenport, *The Reverend Mr. James Davenport's Confession and Retractions* (Boston, 1744), in Bushman, ed., *Great Awakening,* 55; Hunting to Colman, Oct. 18, 1744, Letters to Benjamin Colman; Fish, *Church of Christ a Firm and Durable House,* 127–129; Davenport to Whitefield, May 31, 1746, no. 11, "Various Letters to George Whitefield." See also Williams to Benjamin Colman, Sept. 17, 1744, JWC.

PART FIVE
Travels

In the wake of George Whitefield's controversial second New England tour, John Lowell, the Congregational minister of the prosperous waterside parish in Newbury (now Newburyport), Massachusetts, commissioned a local limner to paint a composition above the fireplace in the dining room of his handsome, gambrel-roofed manse. During the second half of the eighteenth century, ornamental painting of all sorts—from marbleized wood paneling to elaborate plaster stenciling—had emerged as a powerful marker of gentility and refinement. Most surviving overmantel paintings featured landscapes, hunting scenes, distant views of bustling port towns, or fanciful mythological subjects. Lowell's was different. The aging clergyman purchased one of the first known figural compositions of its kind. Its subject was equally unusual: a council of ministers.[1]

The right half of the painted wood panel depicts a group of six bewigged clergymen, each wearing the distinctive Geneva bands of their office. A punch bowl and clay pipes spread across the table signify casual sociability, yet the large book, paper, and quills suggest that the figures are also engaged in ecclesiastical or theological discussion—perhaps even debate. Three ministers, each differentiated in their facial features, appear at the left. They sit at an elaborately fringed table facing three others whom the artist portrayed with less distinction, except for the central figure, who clasps the ivory handle of a walking stick. At the head of the table, tilted clumsily upward to evoke recession in space, sits a seventh figure, presumably Lowell himself. He gestures toward the paper while looking at the three ministers seated on the right.

1. Sarah Anna Emery, *Reminiscences of a Nonagenarian* (Newburyport, Mass., 1879), 205; John J. Currier, *"Ould Newbury": Historical and Biographical Sketches* (Boston, 1896), 451–452. On painted overmantels in early New England, see Nina Fletcher Little, *American Decorative Wall Painting, 1700–1850*, new ed. (New York, 1989), 25–65.

FIGURE 21 Unidentified artist, *Council of Ministers*. Circa 1744. Oil on wood panel, 77.3 × 106 cm. Harvard Art Museums / Fogg Museum, Gift of Dr. Francis L. Burnett and Mrs. Esther Lowell Cunningham, 1964.27. Imaging Department © President and Fellows of Harvard College, Cambridge, Massachusetts

A stone arch supported by a pair of Corinthian columns frames the council. Behind, a dense enclosure of trees recedes into a landscape scene that dominates the left half of the composition. Environmental elements complement the cluster of seated ministers. Three mountain peaks of descending height and ruggedness parallel three sailing vessels; two lines of three swans cruise along the placid waters of a river in perfect tandem. Although discolored over the years from smoke and age, the gentle clouds and soft atmospheric effects lend an aura of peace to the entire work. Despite the painting's awkward execution, a sense of harmony pervades the whole and is reinforced by a Latin expression painted in capital letters across the stone arch. According to one prominent nineteenth-century church historian, the words comprise a "famous motto of Christian Irenics" that would have been familiar to Protestants throughout the British Empire: *IN NECESSARIIS UNITAS. IN NON NECESSARIIS*

LIBERTAS. IN UTRISQUE CHARITAS, or "In essentials unity, in non-essentials liberty, in all things charity."[2]

Installed above the fireplace in the room where he composed his weekly sermons, counseled his parishioners, and dined with his colleagues, Lowell's overmantel reinforced his cosmopolitan sensibilities. An avid reader of advice literature and belles lettres, Lowell styled himself a man of "Learning Polite Taste and Virtue." He leavened his gossipy correspondence with amorous allusions, attempts at poetry, and "Phylosophical remarks" on natural phenomena and the latest medical news. Like many of his prosperous waterside neighbors who stood at the forefront of New England's burgeoning consumer revolution, Lowell drank tea, smoked socially, and traveled in style. The overmantel that graced his study trumpeted the prestige and honor of his ministerial calling. As both a symbol of refinement and an icon of civic virtue, it signaled to all who entered Lowell's parsonage that New England's established clergy stood united, despite the recent ugliness of the Whitefieldian revivals. But commissioning a painting of a harmonious council of ministers was also an act of wish fulfillment. The overmantel reflected Lowell's desire to see himself as he once was and should have still been but was no longer. Few Congregational ministers had experienced a revival season as tumultuous, wrenching, and fracturing as the beleaguered Newbury clergyman. The figure seated at the center on the right side of the table is likely Jonathan Parsons, the controversial former minister of Lyme, Connecticut, Lowell's chief antagonist during the final years of his life, and the principal cause of his rapidly disintegrating pastorate.[3]

Like many of his colleagues, Lowell had been "xtremly taken with the new Scheme" of the revivals, at least initially. He dined with Whitefield during the touring evangelist's excursion to York, Maine, in 1740 and opened the waterside meetinghouse for two stirring sermon performances that were thronged with people. A few months later, Lowell welcomed Gilbert Tennent into his pulpit. With his parishioners "going their visionary lengths" and flocking after itinerants, the Newbury clergyman reaped a bountiful harvest of nearly two

2. Philip Schaff, *History of the Christian Church*, VII, *Modern Christianity: The German Reformation*, 2d ed. (Grand Rapids, Mich., 1910), 650.

3. John Lowell to Joshua Brackett, Mar. 25, 1757, Spence and Lowell Family Papers, 1740–1958, Huntington Library, San Marino, Calif.; Lowell to Benjamin Colman, Sept. 2, 1728, Colman-Jenks Collection, 1651–1804, MHS; *SHG*, VI, 496–503. For the economic development of Newbury as well as critical scholarship on "A Council of Ministers," see Peter Benes with Gregory H. Laing and Wilhelmina V. Lunt, *Old-Town and the Waterside: Two Hundred Years of Tradition and Change in Newbury, Newburyport, and West Newbury, 1635–1835* ... (Newburyport, Mass., 1986), 8–28, 91.

hundred new converts, including seventy-six admitted to full communion on a single Sabbath. Then, at the height of one of the largest revivals in colonial history, Lowell abruptly reversed his position. On April 27, 1742, two of the region's most aggressive riding ministers, Daniel Rogers and Samuel Buell, "formed a Party, and took Possession" of the meetinghouse without Lowell's consent. He exploded in rage during a heated exchange with the two men the following day. Partisans on both sides spent the next several months sniping at one another in the Boston prints. Lowell's parish soon developed into a staging ground for some of the period's most remarkable revival events. During the spring of 1744, Richard Woodbury and Nicholas Gilman launched their monitory letter-writing campaign in the name of the King of Kings and Lord of Lords while visiting with supporters in Lowell's parish. By then, Lowell had closed his pulpit to all itinerating interlopers, including Whitefield, who was forced to preach in the fields during his second visit to Newbury in 1745.[4]

Lowell's efforts to curb the growing spirit of enthusiasm succeeded only in fomenting a "great Schism" among the "sudden Converts" in his parish. By the fall of 1743, thirty-eight brothers and perhaps an equal or greater number of sisters had protested by absenting themselves from the Lord's Supper. When an attempt to heal the breach through traditional means of collective fasting and prayer failed, Lowell demanded that the "Separatists" provide a written statement of their reasons for withdrawing from communion. In their reply, the aggrieved brethren blasted Lowell for condemning the revivals as a "day of temptation," rather than a "day of illumination." They complained that their minister had turned "cold and strange" toward itinerant preachers and refused to counsel convicted sinners in the throes of the new birth. Nor had Lowell spoken with the dissenters about their uneasiness. Instead, he had "spread our faults and slips abroad" during the 1742 meetinghouse controversy. "We are very much stumbled to reconcile your Conduct with a friend to the glorious work of God's Sovereign Grace which he has of late been displaying in such a wonderfull manner in our land," the disaffected church members concluded.[5]

4. Matthias Plant, diary, 1734–1748, Mar. 2, 1742, typescript, microfilm, PEM; William Stevens Perry, ed., *Historical Collections Relating to the American Colonial Church*, 5 vols. (Hartford, Conn., 1870–1878), III, 368; *Boston Evening-Post*, May 3, 1742. See also *GWJ*, 468, 549–550; Edith R. Wills, transcr., "Newbury, Mass., Records of the Third Church of Christ (Unitarian)," 90–96, Mss C 1805, NEHGS; DDR, Apr. 27–28, 1742; and *A Letter from Two Neighbouring Associations of Ministers in the Country, to the Associated Ministers of Boston and Charlestown, Relating to the Admission of Mr. Whitefield into Their Pulpits . . .* (Boston, 1745), 7.

5. Wills, transcr., "Newbury, Mass., Records of the Third Church of Christ," 18, 20, 22; Perry, ed., *Historical Collections Relating to the American Colonial Church*, III, 368; John

The Newbury separatists requested an orderly dismissal to form a new Congregational parish. After Lowell rejected their appeal and convened a disciplinary committee, they simply walked away. By the winter of 1744, the waterside faction had merged with another group of disaffected "schemers" from Christopher Toppan's neighboring church in Newbury's old town parish. They erected a new meetinghouse without the consent of the town or the Massachusetts General Court and invited Joseph Adams to serve as their pastor. The fiery Harvard College graduate and Newbury native had lately emerged as the *"principal* northern Itinerant," and he ranked among the most vitupera-tive Whitefieldarians of the period. Adams preached to the growing number of dissenters for the next six months; then he departed for the New Hampshire frontier. Searching for a suitable replacement, the Separates turned to Jonathan Parsons, who had laid aside his pastorate in Lyme after defending the inspired activities of Deacon Reynold Marvin. The breakaway congregation remained "independent of other Churches" for several years before voting in 1748 to affiliate with the Boston Presbytery, a loose coalition of Scots-Irish congregations scattered across northern and western New England.[6]

Despite financial hardships and legal harassment, Parsons's church blossomed into one of the largest and wealthiest religious societies in New England, even as Lowell's church fell into steep decline. During the quarter century following the bitter schism, the waterside parish minister admitted on average only two new communicants each year, while membership in Parsons's church expanded at a rate nearly five times greater. By 1750, his congregation exceeded one thousand souls. Six years later, the Presbyterians financed the construction of one of the most imposing meetinghouses in New England. Lowell's much smaller building, by contrast, was shattered by a lightning strike. The Boston newspapers scarcely took note of Lowell's death in 1767; but, when George Whitefield died unexpectedly in Parsons's home during his ninth New England preaching tour several years later, bells tolled

---

Lowell to Enoch Titcomb et al., Nov. 1, 1743, [Timothy Toppan and Titcomb] to John Lowell, Dec. 16, 1743, 2, 12, 23, 26, Newbury, Mass., First Church and Third Church Separation Documents, 1743–1746, CL.

6. Joshua Coffin, *A Sketch of the History of Newbury, Newburyport, and West Newbury, from 1635 to 1845* (Boston, 1845), 213; [Thomas Barnard], *A Letter from Mr. Joseph Adams, to the Rev. Mr. Thomas Barnard of Newbury, with Mr. Barnard's Answer Thereto* (Boston, 1743), 2; Jonathan F. Stearns, *A Historical Discourse, Commemorative of the Organization of the First Presbyterian Church, in Newburyport* ... (Newburyport, Mass., 1846), 57. For Adams's career, see the Epilogue as well as *SHG*, XI, 110–114. On the schism in Newbury's First Church, see Douglas L. Winiarski, "The Newbury Prayer Bill Hoax: Devotion and Deception in New England's Era of Great Awakenings," *Massachusetts Historical Review*, XIV (2012), 61–71.

for half an hour, ships in the harbor hoisted mourning flags, and six thousand people packed the Presbyterian meetinghouse to pay their respects. His remains were interred in the church crypt. Parsons was buried at his side a few years later, as was Joseph Prince, the famed blind itinerant, former Shepherd's Tent scholar, and book-burner. During the decades that followed, the Old South Presbyterian Church emerged as a popular Protestant pilgrimage site. It remains so to this day.[7]

During the period between 1745 and 1780, Congregational ministers found themselves engaged in a pitched battle to hold the center of a religious culture rapidly coming apart at the seams. Although most clergymen eventually sorted themselves into discernible "Connexions"—liberals and conservatives, rationalists and evangelicals, Unitarians and New Divinity men—the process took decades to complete. Reduced from the high calling of their office to a mere profession, divided and ossified into hostile theological camps, and repeatedly bested by a new generation of unlettered itinerants peddling innovative beliefs and practices, ministers of the Congregational establishment struggled to maintain uniformity, order, and participation among a combative laity who sought, in the words of one Newbury separatist, to worship "where they choose" and "pay where they attend."[8]

7. Wills, transcr., "Newbury, Mass., Records of the Third Church of Christ," 96–98; Newburyport, Mass., First Presbyterian Church Records, 1745–1861, 10–15, microfilm no. 893125, GSU; Stearns, *Historical Discourse*, 64; Charles Peirce et al., to William Shirley, June 1, 1749, MA, XII, 680; Benes, *Old-Town and the Waterside*, 149; *Boston Gazette*, Feb. 19, 1754; Currier, *"Ould Newbury,"* 437–438, 521; *Boston Evening-Post*, May 18, 1767; Franklin Bowditch Dexter, ed., *The Literary Diary of Ezra Stiles, D.D., LL.D.*, 3 vols. (New York, 1901), I, 79–81. On Whitefield's death and the Newburyport pilgrimage site, see Robert E. Cray, Jr., "Memorialization and Enshrinement: George Whitefield and Popular Religious Culture, 1770–1850," *Journal of the Early Republic*, X (1990), 339–361.

8. Dexter, ed., *Literary Diary of Ezra Stiles*, I, 250; Currier, *"Ould Newbury,"* 516. On the declining social status of Congregational clergymen after 1750, see James W. Schmotter, "Ministerial Careers in Eighteenth-Century New England: The Social Context, 1700–1760," *Journal of Social History*, IX (1975), 249–267. Notable biographies include Edmund S. Morgan, *The Gentle Puritan: A Life of Ezra Stiles, 1727–1795* (New Haven, Conn., 1962); Charles W. Akers, *Called unto Liberty: A Life of Jonathan Mayhew, 1720–1766* (Cambridge, Mass., 1964); Christopher M. Jedrey, *The World of John Cleaveland: Family and Community in Eighteenth-Century New England* (New York, 1979); Edward M. Griffin, *Old Brick: Charles Chauncy of Boston, 1705–1787*, Minnesota Monographs in the Humanities, XI (Minneapolis, Minn., 1980); Joseph A. Conforti, *Samuel Hopkins and the New Divinity Movement: Calvinism, the Congregational Ministry, and Reform in New England between the Great Awakenings* (Grand Rapids, Mich., 1981); Robert J. Wilson III, *The Benevolent Deity: Ebenezer Gay and the Rise of Rational Religion in New England, 1696–1787* (Philadelphia, 1984); John Corrigan, *The Hidden Balance: Religion and the Social Theories of Charles Chauncy and Jonathan Mayhew* (New York, 1987); Mark Valeri, *Law and Providence in Joseph Bellamy's New England: The Origins of the New Divinity in Revolutionary America*, Religion in America (New York, 1994); and Christopher Grasso, *A Speaking Aristocracy:*

The Whitefieldian revivals were the rock on which the ship of New England Congregationalism foundered. During the decades that followed, John Lowell and his more noteworthy contemporaries, including Jonathan Edwards, Ebenezer Parkman, and Ezra Stiles, clashed with contentious parishioners who claimed to experience religion differently and refused to bridle their tongues or even constrain their worship practices within the churches of the Congregational standing order. In a fractured religious culture increasingly dominated by zealous seekers and their revelatory experiences—"Spiritual Travels," as they were called in the language of the day—no clergyman could hope to unite an entire community as had been the case only a few decades earlier. Most lay men and women, to be sure, continued to tack back and forth between the varied theological positions outlined in the weekly sermons of their ministers. But many more set sail for distant, as yet unknown, experiential shores, blown by the gales of spirit possession, biblical impulses, heavenly visions, and immediate revelations into tempests of believers' baptism, universal salvation, perfectionism, and spiritual marriage. Still others, exhausted by the maelstrom of ecclesiastical strife, dismissed the Reformed traditions of their puritan ancestors, sought refuge in one of the region's rapidly expanding Anglican churches, or professed no religion at all.[9]

The transformation of New England Congregationalism during the second half of the eighteenth century mirrored broader forces of social change, as the once-puritan commonwealths took their place in a world marked by partisan politics, intellectual ferment, expanding consumer choice, growing ethnic diversity, and increased geographical mobility. Ecclesiastical discord was especially acute in the unstable new villages of the central New England uplands or in the recently opened settlements of the Berkshires, the Hampshire Grants, Maine, and Atlantic Canada. The few congregations that emerged unscathed were led by irenic ministers such as Ebenezer Gay of Hingham, Massachusetts, who resisted revival innovations and continued to foster inclusive church membership practices not only in his own parish but among those of his liberal South Shore colleagues. Elsewhere across New England, churches of the standing order fell into steep decline, as the land of light devolved into a competitive marketplace of denominations and sects.[10]

Transforming Public Discourse in Eighteenth-Century Connecticut (Chapel Hill, N.C., 1999). For broader intellectual histories of the period, see Conrad Wright, *The Beginnings of Unitarianism in America* (Boston, 1955); Alan Heimert, *Religion and the American Mind: From the Great Awakening to the Revolution* (Cambridge, Mass., 1966); and Henry F. May, *The Enlightenment in America* (New York, 1976).

9. NCS, 91.

10. Surveys of social and cultural change in eighteenth-century British North America in-

John Lowell's overmantel served as an ironic emblem of his era. It embodied the Newbury clergyman's desire for ministerial control over the centrifugal forces of Whitefieldian revivalism that had shattered his pastorate. But that mastery continually eluded him—and his contemporaries—during the second half of the eighteenth century. For once-godly walkers turned "Strict" Congregationalists and Separate Baptists, Anglicans and "Orminians," "Shaking-quakers" and Sandemanians, "new dispensationists" and "Nothingarians," no controversy seemed too minor and no debate over the authenticity of their experimental religion *non necessariis*.[11]

OUT OF THE FOLD

Throughout the 1740s and 1750s, Congregational ministers across New England squared off against troublesome parishioners bent on challenging their authority. Consider the case of the boisterous members of the Fay family of Westborough, Massachusetts. Ebenezer Parkman, the town's broad-minded pastor, wrote repeatedly in his diary about his tense encounters with Deacon John Fay, his sons James, Benjamin, and Stephen, and their sisters, spouses, and children. Collectively, the Fay clan plagued Parkman's ministry for a decade.

The difficulties began shortly after Jonathan Edwards visited Westborough

---

clude Jon Butler, *Becoming America: The Revolution before 1776* (Cambridge, Mass., 2000); and T. H. Breen, *The Marketplace of Revolution: How Consumer Politics Shaped American Independence* (New York, 2004). The argument presented in Part 5 builds on earlier studies that examine the fragility of the Congregational establishment after 1750, especially Stephen A. Marini, *Radical Sects of Revolutionary New England* (Cambridge, Mass., 1982), 11–59; Gregory H. Nobles, *Divisions Throughout the Whole: Politics and Society in Hampshire County, Massachusetts, 1740-1775* (New York, 1983), 75–106; Alan Taylor, *Liberty Men and Great Proprietors: The Revolutionary Settlement of the Maine Frontier, 1760-1820* (Chapel Hill, N.C., 1990), 123–153; David Jaffee, *People of the Wachusett: Greater New England in History and Memory, 1630-1860* (Ithaca, N.Y., 1999), 139–146, 191–199, 216–218; Elizabeth Mancke, *The Fault Lines of Empire: Political Differentiation in Massachusetts and Nova Scotia, ca. 1760-1830*, New World in the Atlantic World (New York, 2005), 109–137; and Shelby M. Balik, *Rally the Scattered Believers: Northern New England's Religious Geography*, Religion in North America (Bloomington, Ind., 2014).

11. For these groups, discussed in greater detail below, see Bennington, Vt., First Church Records, 1762–1820, 2 vols., I, 41, typescript, Bennington Museum, Bennington, Vt.; John Adams to Charles Cushing, Apr. 1, 1756, Adams Papers Digital Editions, MHS (available online at *www.masshist.org/publications*); Ruby Parke Anderson, comp., *The Parke Scrapbook, Including Records of the Separate Church, Preston, Conn., 1747-1800, by Rev. Paul Parke*, 3 vols. (Baltimore, 1965–), I, [162]; G. A. Rawlyk, *The Canada Fire: Radical Evangelicalism in British North America, 1775-1812* (Kingston, Ont., 1994), 66; and Franklin Bowditch Dexter, ed., *Extracts from the Itineraries and Other Miscellanies of Ezra Stiles, D.D., LL.D., 1755-1794* (New Haven, Conn., 1916), 105.

in January 1742 and delivered several "very awakening" sermons to large assemblies. All eight of John Fay's adult children and their spouses had previously joined the Westborough church in full communion, but Edwards threw them into deep distress. James, the deacon's eldest son, was troubled by Edwards's discourse on the destruction of Sodom and Gomorrah. Four days later, he informed Parkman that he saw "things in a new light, and that he is now converted." Later that week, Fay's grandson, Isaiah Pratt, was carried to heaven during a cataleptic trance and saw his name written in the Book of Life. The deacon "broke forth with a loud voice" on hearing the news, blessing God that he had lived to see such a marvelous effusion of the Holy Spirit in his family. The next day, Fay's youngest son, Stephen, appeared at Parkman's parsonage complaining of "great distress concerning his spiritual state." A church member since 1736, Stephen suddenly feared that "all he had done in religion was only to still his conscience."[12]

Casting off their former religious professions, the Fays embraced George Whitefield's concept of conversion as an instantaneous, somatic intrusion of the Holy Spirit. Parkman initially encouraged his parishioners' growing zeal, but he remained wary of the emotional tumults that the revivals had created. His cautionary lectures and sermons soon alienated the deacon and his inspired family. Shortly after Samuel Buell passed through Westborough on his way to York, Maine, and the northern frontier, eldest son James engaged Parkman in a heated debate over the infallible "assurance of every new convert." The crisis deepened later that fall, when another of the deacon's sons, Benjamin, invited James Davenport to preach at his home just days after the Southold, New York, revivalist had been released from jail in Boston. Then, in October 1742, Stephen broke through his "religious disquietments" and was "rapt in spiritual delight." Panting with "overbearing joy," he spoke to the Westborough congregation of God's "divine greatness" in saving his soul.[13]

The Fays' burgeoning radicalism strained their relationship with Parkman during the next several years. Within weeks of his "wonderful experiences," Stephen began railing against the Westborough minister's preaching. Wild evening revival meetings conducted in the homes of Deacon Fay and his chil-

12. Joseph Tracy, *The Great Awakening: A History of the Revival of Religion in the Time of Edwards and Whitefield* (1842; Edinburgh, 1976), 204–205. For Pratt's vision, see Part 3, note 90, above. For genealogical and church affiliation information, see George Henry Johnson, *One Branch of the Fay Family Tree: An Account of the Ancestors and Descendants of William and Elizabeth Fay of Westboro, Mass., and Marietta, Ohio* (Columbus, Ohio, 1913), 24–27; and Westborough, Mass., Congregational Church Records, 1724–1808, 2–3, 6, microfilm, Westborough Town Library, Westborough, Mass.

13. Tracy, *Great Awakening*, 206, 210–211.

dren elicited various sentiments from Parkman's parishioners. When the town was rocked by an earthquake in 1744, James's wife, Lydia, cried out and proceeded to lead a group of parishioners into the woods near the meetinghouse to pray between Sabbath exercises. Her outbursts proved so disruptive that a magistrate threatened to arrest her for disturbing the peace. Sister-in-law Martha Fay struggled to stifle her lamentations, which drew a throng of onlookers. When the Westborough minister exhorted the Fays to restrain themselves, they lashed out. Stephen and his wife, Ruth, "rak'd" his sermons in a "most unaccountable and intolerable" manner. Whenever Parkman encountered them about town, they always seemed to be in a "great Flame," a "dreadful passion," or an "indecent Temper." "'Tis Matter of Grief," the exasperated clergyman complained to Stephen, "that we are so Frequently in Jarrs."[14]

The tipping point between Parkman and the Fays came during the spring of 1743, when Stephen Fay encouraged the Canterbury, Connecticut, lawyer and incendiary lay exhorter Elisha Paine to preach in his home. Recently released from jail after being arrested for mimicking established clergymen, Paine barnstormed across central New England, vowing to promote ecclesiastical divisions wherever he went. Facing a direct attack on his pastoral authority, Parkman immediately dispatched a stern letter expressing his concern that Deacon Fay and the members of his family were in danger of being led astray by Paine's irregular and unlicensed ministry. He deployed a potent equestrian metaphor to convey his sharp condemnation of unchecked itinerant preaching. Comparing his Westborough parish to a heavenly pasture, Parkman implored Fay not to be "so impatient as to jump over the Sacred Fence" nor assist "any Stranger either to break over Christs Wall wherewith he has encompassed this holy Enclosure." Parkman's warning was clear: "Do not run out of the Fold of Jesus Christ."[15]

But the Fays refused to be bridled. By 1745, James Fay had stopped attending Sabbath meetings in Westborough. Two years later, he and his brother Stephen, along with the young visionist Isaiah Pratt, had pulled up stakes and moved to the frontier settlement of Hardwick, Massachusetts, where they began agitating against minister David White. During the summer of 1749, a church council led by Jonathan Edwards admonished the dissenters for their disorderly conduct. Parkman soon received the "sorrowfull News" that the

14. Ibid., 211; Francis G. Walett, ed., *The Diary of Ebenezer Parkman, 1703–1782* (Worcester, Mass., 1974), 96, 123, 131 (see also 96, 100).

15. Ebenezer Parkman to Elisha Paine and John Fay, May 19, 1743, Parkman Family Papers, 1707–1879, box 3, AAS. See also *Letter from the Associated Ministers of the County of Windham, to the People in the Several Societies in Said County* (Boston, 1745), 9.

Fays had organized an illegal Separate church in Hardwick that had siphoned off scores of White's parishioners. By the time of the American Revolution, the Fays and their extended kin had retreated to the wilderness of Bennington, Vermont. There, they encountered other separatists fleeing from established Congregational churches in Massachusetts and Connecticut.[16]

The children of Deacon John Fay were a different breed from the godly walkers of previous generations. The Fays were restless and restive, and they were not alone. Throughout New England, hundreds of zealous new converts leapt out of the sacred enclosures that had safely corralled religious life in the puritan commonwealths for a century, while thousands more refused to affiliate with the churches of the standing order. The earliest schisms erupted in New Haven, New London, and the eastern Connecticut uplands, where Paine and other renegade lay preachers capitalized on disparate sources of discontent, including perennial parish divisions, flagging support for revival innovations among established clergymen, and political concerns over the colony's virulent suppression of itinerant preaching. Soon, zealous Whitefieldarians were crisscrossing the region, sowing seeds of discord in a broad arch that stretched into Worcester County in central Massachusetts, down the Blackstone River Valley into Rhode Island and the Old Colony, and out onto Cape Cod. Similar disputes arose independently in Boston, the upper Connecticut Valley, Essex County, Massachusetts, and along the northern frontier. Even native American congregations supported by the New England Company were rent by separations. Often, the divisions were temporary, and disaffected church members returned to worship in the established churches. But, for the Fay clan and others like them, the acrimony was acute, the conflict long in duration, and the final break permanent.[17]

Perhaps as many as one hundred New England congregations fractured into competing factions between 1742 and 1760. But the Separate or "Strict Congregational" movement, as it came to be called, proved highly unstable. Most Separate churches collapsed under the weight of their founders' purify-

16. Walett, ed., *Diary of Ebenezer Parkman*, 130, 159, 207 (quote). See also Ebenezer Parkman, commonplace book, 1721–1779, 113–114, Ebenezer Parkman Papers, 1718–1789, MHS; Westborough Congregational Church Records, 80; Hardwick, Mass., Congregational Church Records, 1736–1786, 15, 19–21, microfilm no. 868519, GSU; and Lucius R. Paige, *History of Hardwick, Massachusetts, with a Genealogical Register* (Boston, 1883), 225–229.

17. For a map and list of Separate Congregational churches, see C. C. Goen, *Revivalism and Separatism in New England, 1740–1800: Strict Congregationalists and Separate Baptists in the Great Awakening* (Middletown, Conn., 1987), 114, 300–327. On the development of native American Separate churches, see Linford D. Fisher, *The Indian Great Awakening: Religion and the Shaping of Native Cultures in Early America* (New York, 2012), 107–135.

ing zeal. Others followed the logic of the Whitefieldian revivals a step further by restricting the sacrament of baptism to converted adult believers. The meteoric rise of Separate Baptist churches during the second half of the eighteenth century instilled a powerful lesson in the minds of new converts and their descendants: religious affiliation was a voluntary decision, not a marker of social status. "They seem always as tho' they had their Religion to chuse," grumbled one Connecticut clergyman. It was a revolution in the New England way.[18]

▓ The origin of the "many unhappy Divisions and Contentions" that plagued Westborough and scores of other towns throughout New England lay in the peculiarly mobile nature of the Whitefieldian revivals. At first, Ebenezer Parkman and his colleagues in the Marlborough ministerial association applauded the greater solemnity and zeal of their parishioners, and they hoped that revival meetings would eventuate in moral reformation. But, when their parishioners began flocking after itinerants, they changed their position. What most distressed Parkman about the Fay family was their hankering after pastures other than the "holy Enclosure" to which Christ had allotted them. On several occasions in 1745, Parkman sharply criticized James and Stephen Fay for "going away to other Towns on Lords Day." He carefully tracked the Sabbaths in which the Fays failed to appear in the Westborough meetinghouse as well

18. *Records of the Congregational Church in Canterbury, Connecticut, 1711–1844* (Hartford, Conn., 1932), 108; Isaac Stiles, *A Looking-Glass for Changlings; A Seasonable Caveat against Meddling with Them That Are Given to Change* ... (New London, [Conn.], 1743), 15. Congregational ministers typically referred to the men and women who withdrew from communion during the 1740s as "separatists." By about 1750, they appear to have settled on the term "Separates" to describe members of the breakaway churches that emerged from these schisms. In the argument that follows, I seek to preserve this important distinction. I restrict the category of "separatist" to aggrieved factions in the process of withdrawing from communion, typically during the brief but chaotic period between 1742 and 1748. "Separate" denotes dissenting communities of men and women who took the additional step of organizing new religious institutions: "Separate Congregational" and "Separate Baptist" churches. Of course, the leaders of these upstart congregations seldom referred to their churches as Separate. As numerous petitions and church missives in the JTC suggest, they simply presumed that they belonged to the "Church of Christ." Around 1780, the few remaining Separate churches embraced the phrase "Strict Congregational" to differentiate themselves from the mainstream Congregational churches. For examples of these terms at work in eighteenth-century texts, see Jonathan Edwards, *A Farewel-Sermon Preached at the First Precinct in Northampton* ... (Boston, 1751), in *WJE*, XXV, *Sermons and Discourses, 1743–1758*, ed. Wilson H. Kimnach (New Haven, Conn., 2006), 489; Wills, transcr., "Newbury, Mass., Records of the Third Church of Christ," 18; David Hall, diaries, 1740–1789, Sept. 25, 1748, MHS; Dexter, ed., *Extracts from the Itineraries and Other Miscellanies of Ezra Stiles*, 251; Anderson, comp., *Parke Scrapbook*, I, [31]; and S. Leroy Blake, *The Separates or Strict Congregationalists of New England* (Chicago, 1902), 158.

as the bitter disputes that invariably followed his efforts to coax his wayward parishioners back into the fold.[19]

In time, the practice of traveling to attend revival meetings in other towns crystallized into a clear choice, as lay men and women withdrew from their covenantal obligations to observe the Lord's Supper. For a brief time, these small groups of disaffected new converts enjoyed the support of prominent riding ministers. James Davenport incited his auditors to travel *"ten* or *twenty Miles* to hear a *converted* Minister, or even *set up private Meetings* among themselves," rather than attend Sabbath exercises led by purportedly unconverted clergymen in their home parishes. Davenport, Eleazar Wheelock, and Joseph Bellamy occasionally preached in the homes of leading separatists, and they maintained an active correspondence with dissenting factions across New England during the 1740s. By the end of the decade, Separate churches had ordained three other prominent Whitefieldarians, Andrew Croswell, Jonathan Parsons, and Daniel Rogers. Even Jonathan Edwards urged colleagues to proceed cautiously when dealing with fractious parishioners. Dissenters, he explained in a 1744 letter, ought to be left to their own consciences in the "manner or means of worship, or the society or worshippers."[20]

With growing numbers of disaffected church members swarming "as Bees," as one clergyman put it, ministers closed ranks and reluctantly brought the ecclesiastical machinery of the Congregational establishment to bear on the aggrieved factions. Between 1745 and 1760, disciplinary cases involving these *"disorderly Walkers"* and "Godly Strollers" glutted the record books of churches across New England. In Hardwick, David White called James Fay and his Pratt kinsmen to "give the reasons if any they have why they absented

19. Walett, ed., *Diary of Ebenezer Parkman*, 106, 123; Parkman to Paine and Fay, May 19, 1743, box 3, Parkman Family Papers.

20. Charles Chauncy, *Seasonable Thoughts on the State of Religion in New-England* . . . (Boston, 1743), 153; Jonathan Edwards to Elnathan Whitman, Feb. 9, 1744, in *WJE*, XVI, *Letters and Personal Writings*, ed. George S. Claghorn (New Haven, Conn., 1998), 128. See also William Allen, "Memoir of the Rev. Eleazar Wheelock, D.D., Founder and First President of Dartmouth College," *American Quarterly Register*, X (1837), 16–17; Richard Webster, transcr., "Letters to Joseph Bellamy from Aaron Burr, David Brainerd, etc., and Other Papers concerning Mr. Bellamy, 1739–1787," 16, 33–37, microfilm, Presbyterian Historical Society, Philadelphia; John A. Grigg, *The Lives of David Brainerd: The Making of an Evangelical Icon*, Religion in America (New York, 2009), 23–25, 39–40; Philemon Robbins, *A Plain Narrative of the Proceedings of the Reverend Association and Consociation of New-Haven County, against the Reverend Mr. Robbins of Branford* . . . (Boston, 1747), 3–44; Leigh Eric Schmidt, "'A Second and Glorious Reformation': The New Light Extremism of Andrew Croswell," *WMQ*, XLIII (1986), 225–226; and Elizabeth C. Nordbeck, "Almost Awakened: The Great Revival in New Hampshire and Maine, 1727–1748," *Historical New Hampshire*, XXXV (1980), 54–58.

themselves from the Publick worship of God." Most of the "Dissatisfied Brethren" followed Fay's lead and declared their "Noncompliance" with the high-handed measures. But a few dissenters, including Fay's nephew, Silas Pratt, submitted written statements defending their actions or agreed to testify before a church committee. Records of the Hardwick separatists' arguments have not survived, but reports from church meetings in other parishes reveal the depths of their commitment to the most radical innovations of the Whitefieldian revivals. To be sure, the schisms of the 1740s and 1750s sometimes erupted along preexisting socioeconomic fault lines, and the Separate movement later served as a proving ground for Revolutionary radicalism; yet dissenters seldom cited social, political, or economic issues to justify breaking fellowship with established churches. The roots of their ecclesiastical rebellion lay elsewhere—in the fertile soil of religious enthusiasm.[21]

Opposition to the "Late glorious work of Gods Rich, and free grace" ranked near the top of every list of separatist grievances. The aggrieved faction in Norwich, Connecticut, criticized Benjamin Lord for "denying the power of godliness" and refusing to defend the revivals. Eight disaffected members of the Needham, Massachusetts, church believed that they had been "Instrumentall in the hand of the Holy Spirit" by setting up prayer meetings and evening lectures to promote the "hapy Revivall" in town. But they withdrew from communion in 1747, after minister Jonathan Townsend and his supporters "Treated us very unchristianly," making a "mocke and Dirision" of the earnest new converts for "our Errors and delusions as they Called it." In Colchester, Connecticut, an unnamed man walked out of the meetinghouse during a sermon in which minister Thomas Skinner condemned the revivals as a "Spirit of Error." "I don't remember Sir," summarized a man from Newbury's Byfield

---

21. Hall, diaries, Sept. 25, 1746; *The Result of a Council of the Consociated Churches of the County of Windham* ... (Boston, 1747), 21; *Boston Weekly Post-Boy*, Oct. 12, 1741; Hardwick Congregational Church Records, 19–20. Studies that attribute the Separate movement to preexisting socioeconomic tensions include J. M. Bumsted, "Revivalism and Separatism in New England: The First Society of Norwich, Connecticut, as a Case Study," *WMQ*, XXIV (1967), 588–612; James H. Barnett and Esther D. Barnett, *On the Trail of a Legend: The Separatist Movement in Mansfield, Connecticut, 1745-1769* (Storrs, Conn., 1978); John W. Jeffries, "The Separation in the Canterbury Congregational Church: Religion, Family, and Politics in a Connecticut Town," *NEQ*, LII (1979), 522–549; Peter S. Onuf, "New Lights in New London: A Group Portrait of the Separatists," *WMQ*, XXXVII (1980), 627–643; and David W. Stowe, "'The Opposers Are Very Much Enraged': Religious Conflict and Separation in New Haven during the Great Awakening, 1741–1760," *CHS Bulletin*, LVI (1991), 211–235. On the restorationist impulse within the separatist movement, see James P. Walsh, "The Conservative Nature of Connecticut Separatism," *CHS Bulletin*, XXXIV (1969), 9–17. My argument in this section follows James F. Cooper, Jr., "Enthusiasts or Democrats? Separatism, Church Government, and the Great Awakening in Massachusetts," *NEQ*, LXV (1992), 265–283.

parish in his complaint against Moses Parsons, "that you ever So much as gave Thanks for Such an Unspeakable Favour to the World as Mr. Whitefield."[22]

Closely related to general debates over the nature of the revivals were conflicts between ministers and their parishioners involving the gifts of the Holy Spirit. One in five dissenters in the north parish of Stonington, Connecticut, criticized minister Joseph Fish for suppressing spontaneous prayers voiced by his parishioners during worship exercises and closing his pulpit to itinerants and lay exhorters. Several former church members in Westfield, Massachusetts, justified their separation on the grounds that "private Brethren had not liberty to exercise their Gifts and to speak when they were fill'd" with the Spirit. When the young Yale College graduate Nathaniel Draper boldly proclaimed he "could certainly tell who were Converted, and that there was no other Call to the Ministry but What was internal," the Windham County ministerial association revoked his preaching license and branded his purported gifts of spiritual discernment "unwarrantable and dangerous." "I cant see any Duty in settling in the Standing way," Draper later complained in a letter to a friend, "considering how much the Churches are corrupted universally."[23]

Draper's letter hinted at widespread dissatisfaction with the preaching doctrines of revival opposers, a third major class of grievances cited in extant disciplinary proceedings. Elisha Huntington, a deacon in the Goshen parish of Lebanon, Connecticut, declared that it would "mock God" to listen to the "Trash" and "old stories" delivered by minister Jacob Eliot in his weekly sermons, and he dared the church to "Call him to account for Absenting from the Publick worship." In parishes across New England, separatists rebelled against the preparationist theology of the godly walk, with its emphasis on stolid devotional duties. An outspoken enslaved woman from Cape Cod argued that Nathan Stone did not preach the "Doctrine of Grace." Separatists in the Scotland parish of Windham, Connecticut, upbraided Ebenezer Devotion

22. "Aggrieved Brethren" to John Odlin, n.d. [circa 1743], I, Blandina Diedrich Collection, WCL; Eleazar Kingsbury et al., to Jonathan Townsend, June 12, 1747, Mss C 5147, NEHGS; Frederic Denison, *Notes of the Baptists, and Their Principles, in Norwich, Conn., from the Settlement of the Town to 1850* (Norwich, Conn., 1857), 21; Thomas Skinner to Ebenezer Turell, Mar. 12, 1743, Miscellaneous Bound Manuscripts, MHS; Byfield (now Georgetown, Mass.), Parish Church Records, 1744–1826, 56, CL (available online at NEHH).

23. John H. Lockwood, *Westfield and Its Historic Influences, 1669–1919: The Life of an Early Town . . .*, 2 vols. (Springfield, Mass., 1922), II, 325; Windham Association, Records, 1723–1814, I, 140–141, Connecticut Conference Archives, United Church of Christ (currently on deposit at CL; available online at NEHH); Nathaniel Draper to John Cleaveland, Mar. 3, 1748, box 1, JCP. For data from the north parish in Stonington, see Douglas Leo Winiarski, "All Manner of Error and Delusion: Josiah Cotton and the Religious Transformation of Southeastern New England, 1700–1770" (Ph.D. diss., Indiana University, 2000), 285n.

for encouraging "poor Blind Sinners to Work in order to Obtain Salvation." In a neighboring parish, Abigail Smith separated "because the Pastor Preach'd that Some might be the Children of God and not know it, and that Assurance was not So Necessary in these days as in the days of the Apostles." Christopher Toppan, the aged minister of Newbury, aroused the ire of his parishioners when he hinted that God had an "easier way to Convert men" than through the terrors of hell, while colleague Timothy Pickering alienated new converts in the Chebacco Parish in Ipswich (now Essex), Massachusetts, when he asserted that sinners who "waited on God in the way of Duty" would have nothing to fear on the Day of Judgment. In each of these cases, the theological errors identified by the dissenters involved a softening of the hard edge of Whitefield's uncompromising conversionist theology.[24]

Separatists rejected ministers who refused to embrace the extemporaneous preaching techniques of the Whitefieldarians and continued to read from prepared sermon notes. Although the aggrieved brethren in the waterside parish of Newbury acknowledged that John Lowell was an orthodox theologian, they criticized the cautious tone of his sermons during a time of "great awakenings by the Spirit of God." The Newbury separatists craved "pungent" performances delivered with "more liveliness and fervour" than Lowell allowed. They desired to have the terrors of hell set before them and hoped to be "entertained" by accounts of "Conviction and Conversion" that were "fully handled" and "closely and Zealously applied." To their great disappointment, Lowell's sermons failed to slake their insatiable thirst for revival work. In an evocative statement that registered the new converts' fascination with somatic manifestations of the Holy Spirit, the separatists complained that his expositions seemed to "go all over without touching us." Lowell's preaching, in short, was "not So Suitable to our experience as we wished and longed for."[25]

For many dissenters, the powerful sermons delivered by unlettered lay preachers and exhorters provided a strong incentive to leave established churches. A Mansfield, Connecticut, separatist explained that "he could not

24. Elisha Huntington to Jacob Eliot, Sept. 10, 1744, box 1, Jacob Eliot Family Papers, 1716–1945, MS 193, YUA; George Ernest Bowman, transcr., "Records of the First Parish in Brewster, Formerly the First Parish in Harwich, Mass.," *Mayflower Descendant*, X (1908), 124; Scotland, Conn., Congregational Church Records, 1732–1915, 43, microfilm no. 345, CSL; Brooklyn, Conn., First Trinitarian Congregational Church Records, 1734–1912, 59, microfilm no. 143, CSL; "Meeting of a Council to Hear Charges against Rev. Christopher Toppan," Aug. 31, 1744, [2], Joshua Noyes Papers, 1740–1773, MHS; William Story, church council minutes, May 20, 1746, box 2, JCP.

25. [Toppan and Titcomb] to Lowell, Dec. 16, 1743, 17–18, 20–22, Newbury First Church and Third Church Separation Documents.

hear the voice of Christ under the dispensation of the gospel in this church, and was obliged to go out and seek it where it is to be heard." "The reason of my going to the Separate Meeting on The Sabbath Days," agreed a New Hampshire woman, "is because I found it more Profitable and the Word Explaind more clearly to my Understanding." No longer edified by their conservative, unconverted ministers, dissenters began to look beyond an institution that some now called the "Church of Antichrist."[26]

At the heart of the separatist impulse lay the ideal of a pure church purged of its mixed multitude of lukewarm professors and godly walkers. Several Norwich church members withdrew from communion after Benjamin Lord refused to require prospective communicants to narrate a discrete conversion experience. Likewise, Jeremiah Tracy criticized his neighbors for assuming that a mere profession of beliefs was "Evidence of a gracious State." Several outspoken dissenters, including an enslaved man named Pompey, rejected the Westfield church for admitting candidates that "had not Grace." Other separatists condemned the renaissance in sacramental theology and derided the practice of owning the covenant. "You make a half way Covenant," Sylvester Baldwin of Stonington complained to Fish in a statement that marked the entrance of this derisive phrase into the lexicon of American religious history. When asked whether the Hampton, New Hampshire, church was a "True Church of Christ," Ebenezer Sanborn and Hannah Palmer simply answered no.[27]

A handful of separatists defended their actions on the basis of emerging liberal political ideals involving liberty of conscience, but, more often than not, the indwelling Spirit provided the most powerful impetus to withdraw from communion. "My God Commanded Me to go from you and I know it," announced Edmund Hewit of Stonington, "And that is all my Reason." "I cant Come here," concurred a Mohegan Indian woman named Sarah Patak, "for God Calls to go and hear others." The Sturbridge, Massachusetts, dissenters, in particular, employed metaphors of inward illumination to bolster their testimonies: "God has given me to See" the truth of the gospel; he has "shown

26. Barnett and Barnett, *On the Trail of a Legend*, 13; "Church Records of Kingston Second Parish, East Kingston, N.H.," Congregational Church Records, 1739–1772, 77, typescript, NHHS; Scotland Congregational Church Records, 45.

27. Denison, *Notes of the Baptists, and Their Principles*, 21; Lisbon, Conn., Newent Congregational Church Records, 1723–1932, 29, microfilm no. 100, CSL; John H. Lockwood, *Westfield and Its Historic Influences, 1669–1919: The Life of an Early Town ...*, 2 vols. (Springfield, Mass., 1922), II, 325; North Stonington, Conn., Congregational Church Records, 1727–1887, 116, microfilm no. 317, CSL (see also 122, 124); Hampton, N.H., Records of the First Congregational Church, 1667–1902, 113, microfilm, reel 1 (Watertown, Mass., 1986), NEHGS.

me that you are not a Church of his"; he "Gave me to See the Sepperrates god was my god and thay was my people." Sarah Blanchard put it best when she explained to Sturbridge minister Caleb Rice that "inasmuch as you and I cant see alike, those things which to me are Soul-Satesfying reasons, are to you no reasons at all." "My dear friends," she continued, "I think I am bound to obey what God Says to me by his voice."[28]

In contrast to college-educated ministers, who placed their authority to interpret the scriptures in philology, the exposition of historical context, and a long tradition of learned exegesis, separatists treated the Bible as an oracle, a storehouse of tropes whose occult meanings disclosed not only the secrets of individual salvation but God's plan to purify the corrupt churches of his back-slidden New England plantations. The members of the Windham Association accused a group of Separates in Mansfield of holding a *"double Meaning to the Word of GOD, viz. a* literal *and a* spiritual." David Morse abandoned the Sturbridge church after the Holy Spirit directed him to ponder several scriptural texts on church government. In Norwich, John Griswold withdrew after the powerful words of Matthew 24:28 "weighed with him": "For wheresoever the carcase is, there will the eagles be gathered together." Two New Haven visionists even received a revelatory command to abandon Joseph Noyes's ministry after traveling to heaven in spirit and speaking with Christ himself. In 1746, a dangerous illness exposed Ebenezer Cleaveland to the temptations of Satan and threw him into a period of spiritual uncertainty. The Devil "bofited me," he explained in a letter to his brother, by "telling me that I never was Converted" and that the Canterbury Separate church "wold Come to nothing." In that very moment, however, the "words that the Aingel spake to the sheperds" in Luke 2:10 "Came to me with Grait Power" and convinced him that the breakaway congregation in which he now worshipped was "founded upon the verassity of God."[29]

28. North Stonington Congregational Church Records, 117, 120; Testimonies of Sarah Blanchard, Stephen Blanchard, John Corey, and Jonathan Perry, Apr. 5, 1749, Sturbridge, Mass., Separatist Congregational Church Records, 1745–1762, CL (available online at NEHH). For examples of separatists citing liberty of conscience, see Huntington to Eliot, Sept. 10, 1744, box 1, Jacob Eliot Family Papers; William G. McLoughlin, *New England Dissent, 1630–1833: The Baptists and the Separation of Church and State*, 2 vols. (Cambridge, Mass., 1971), I, 386–398; Edward Goddard, *A Brief Account of the Formation and Settlement of the 2nd Church and Congregation in Framingham* ([Boston], 1750), 4; and Douglas K. Fidler, "John Odlin of Exeter and the Threat to Congregational Peace and Order in Northern New England," *Historical New Hampshire*, LV, nos. 1–2 (Spring / Summer 2000), 17–19. On the emergence of "liberty of conscience" during the eighteenth century, see Chris Beneke, *Beyond Toleration: The Religious Origins of American Pluralism* (New York, 2006), 31–36.

29. *Result of a Council of the Consociated Churches*, 18; Testimony of David Morse, Apr. 5, 1749, Sturbridge Separatist Congregational Church Papers; Denison, *Notes of the Baptists,*

A few ministers struggled to understand the confusing "languague of Babel" that separatists used to justify withdrawing from communion, but ears attuned to the theological pitch of biblical impulses easily recognized the revelatory voice of the Holy Spirit in the dissenters' "very obscure" and "long and tedious" testimonies. Texts such as 2 Corinthians 6:17, "come out from among them, and be ye separate, saith the Lord," intruded on the minds of zealous new converts with supernatural force while they listened to sermons, prepared for the Lord's Supper, meditated in private, or worked about town. Hannah Heaton, the prolific diarist, withdrew from New Haven's Northeast Society (now North Haven) after God opened to her the secret meaning of the prophecy of the faithless shepherds in Ezekiel 34. While conferring about her revelation with minister Isaac Stiles, a prominent revival opposer, she saw as "plain as i could see the sun in a clear day" that his church was "out of the rules in gods word." A second impulse from Revelation 18:4, "Come out of her, my people, that ye be not partakers of her sins, and that ye receive not of her plagues," confirmed the truth of her vision. Heaton promptly "withdrew and never heard Mr. Stiles no more."[30]

In the end, many of the same revival innovations that new converts affirmed when relating their conversion experiences during the revivals of the early 1740s justified their decisions to withdraw from public worship just a few years later. Sarah Martin offered an extended meditation on the enduring power of biblical impulses in her 1749 testimony to the Sturbridge church. Like many separatists, she had not profited from the sermons of her minister. As a result, Martin preferred to stay at home on the Sabbath, studying her Bible and reading the works of "ould divines." The last time she attended the sacrament, she maintained, the words of 1 Kings 19:9 roared in her ears. Comparing herself to the backslidden people of Israel, Martin cried to God for solace but received no answer and remained as "darck as eygept." Martin was "tosed upon the waves of the sea," knowing that "our Spiritual fathers" abhorred separatism. For a year and a half, she vacillated, but, in time, biblical impulses banished all of her fears. A providential flip of the Bible resolved her concerns, as she unexpectedly opened her book to Ezekiel 34:12, a passage describing how God would gather his scattered sheep during dark times.

and Their Principles, 22; *Boston Weekly Post-Boy,* Mar. 1, 1742; Ebenezer Cleaveland to John Cleaveland, Feb. 11, 1746, box 1, JCP.

30. Thomas Skinner to Benjamin Colman, Feb. 14, 1743, Benjamin Colman Papers, 1641–1806, MHS (available online at *www.masshist.org*); Suffield, Conn., Congregational Church Records, 1742–1836, Feb. 17, 1748, CHS; Barbara E. Lacey, ed., *The World of Hannah Heaton: The Diary of an Eighteenth-Century New England Farm Woman* (DeKalb, Ill., 2003), 28.

Throughout her testimony, Martin repeatedly claimed to be able to see into the scriptures, to read between the lines of the verses that continually "dropt into my minde." "Whenever I was destrest to know which way to go," Martin declared to the Sturbridge church, "it would be intimated to me cry to God till he Show you."[31]

■ There was little in the Fays' family history that marked them as religious incendiaries. A founding pillar of the Westborough church, John Fay served as deacon for more than a decade before George Whitefield's first New England tour in 1740. He owned one of the first pew boxes in the meetinghouse and was one of Ebenezer Parkman's frequent dining companions and closest friends. Deacon Fay also served as the Westborough clerk, treasurer, and moderator of the town meeting. His eldest son, John, Jr., achieved a comfortable yeoman competency on his prosperous farm in the adjoining north parish. Benjamin, the youngest of the Fay children, served as one of two militia captains from Westborough during the Seven Years' War. His conventional 1741 church admission relation evinced none of the revival innovations evident elsewhere in New England. Even James and Stephen Fay prospered in the frontier settlements to which they migrated during the 1750s. The Fays emerged from the Whitefieldian revivals as outspoken and independent-minded religious enthusiasts, but they were also valued community members, indistinguishable from their Yankee neighbors.[32]

Strict Congregationalists hailed from every possible social station. Their churches included wealthy gentlemen and powerful town leaders such as Daniel Gilman of Exeter, New Hampshire, and James Pierpont of New Haven as well as less prosperous members of middling farm families, enslaved African Americans, and Indians. Young revival converts made up two-thirds of the Separate church in Stonington, yet the movement also attracted long-standing church members such as the noted Kensington artisan Nathan Cole. As with the Fays, the currents of radical religious dissent sometimes flowed through kinship networks, but the church schisms of the 1740s and 1750s could just as easily foment what one Cape Cod diarist called a "civil war at home." Scattered evidence suggests that Separates were predisposed to geographical mobility, and a disproportionate number later settled along New England's northern and western frontiers or migrated to Atlantic Canada. No single socioeco-

31. Testimony of Sarah Martin, n.d. [April 1749], Sturbridge Separatist Church Records.
32. Johnson, comp., *One Branch of the Fay Family Tree*, 20–28; Appendix B, Westborough, Mass., First Church, 31.

nomic or demographic variable explains why some people remained within the churches of the standing order while others rebelled.[33]

The one factor that united the Separates was their unwavering commitment to the most radical innovations of the Whitefieldian revivals. The earliest dissenters were, without exception, zealous new converts who repudiated their once secure lives and experienced powerful conversions during the early 1740s. They associated the indwelling voice of the Holy Spirit with biblical impulses and acknowledged that God continued to communicate with the faithful remnant of his people through new revelations—including dreams and visions. They felt constrained to improve their charismatic gifts of spiritual discernment and their special internal callings to preach, pray, and exhort in public. And they sought fellowship with others who embraced these innovative revival measures.

The experiences of the early Separate Congregational minister Isaac Backus and one of his parishioners underscores the religious origins of the movement. Born in Norwich in 1724, Backus exhibited an outwardly pious religious life until James Davenport preached on the "Dredful danger of delays" during his first tour of southern New England. Tormented by fears of eternal damnation, Backus wrestled with God as he watched friends and neighbors experience the joyful release of the new birth. Like many young converts, he was buffeted by frequent satanic temptations. Shortly after Davenport's departure, Backus began receiving biblical impulses he ascribed to the operations of the Holy Spirit. "Them words seemed to be Spok into my mind" from Mark 12: 34, he later wrote, telling him "thou art not far from the kingdom of God." On August 24, 1741, as he was mowing in the field, God "Shined into my heart," and Backus was "Swallowed up" in the admiration of "Divine glories." In a flash, the world was transformed. All nature appeared to him in a new light.[34]

Seasons of joy and terror followed, as Backus struggled to gauge the authenticity of his great change. Eventually, he received the "Sweet Sealings of the holy Spirit" and joined Benjamin Lord's church in full communion during the summer of 1742. Three years later, the Norwich church voted to end the practice of requiring written relations from prospective communicants. Backus

33. Fidler, "John Odlin of Exeter," *Historical New Hampshire*, LV, nos. 1–2 (Spring / Summer 2000), 16; Stowe, "Opposers Are Very Much Enraged," *CHS Bulletin*, LVI (1991), 228–229; Dean Dudley, *History and Genealogy of the Bangs Family in America, with Genealogical Tables and Notes* (Montrose, Mass., 1896), 8 (quote).

34. William G. McLoughlin, ed., *The Diary of Isaac Backus*, 3 vols. (Providence, R.I., 1979), III, 1523, 1525. See also McLoughlin, *Isaac Backus and the American Pietistic Tradition*, Library of American Biography (Boston, 1967), 1–56.

and a small group of radicalized new converts interpreted the change in admission procedures as a sign of creeping laxity in the Norwich church, a token that those who pledged to walk answerable to their professions possessed only the "form of Godliness." Soon the voice of the Spirit was commanding him to withdraw from communion. During the winter of 1745, Backus, his mother, and eleven church members abandoned Lord's church and ordained Jedidiah Hide over their newly gathered Separate church at Bean Hill.[35]

Soon after the Norwich schism, Backus received additional divine instructions to preach the word of God abroad. On several occasions, the Holy Spirit opened the will of God to him through texts that powerfully impressed themselves on his mind. Backus resisted the "hand of the Lord" that lay heavily on him; but a steady stream of biblical impulses drowned out all of his objections, and he was "much Confirmed" in his new calling. Backus itinerated across southeastern New England, visiting two dozen towns and preaching for several months to a group of Separates in Windham, Connecticut.[36]

By December 1747, Backus's travels had carried him to Titicut, a former Indian settlement straddling the border between Middleborough and Bridgewater, Massachusetts. Residents greeted Backus with caution until one afternoon, while dining at the home of a leading separatist, Backus received a powerful impulse in which "God Broake in upon my Soul" in words from John 4:35, and he beheld a vision of a vast field ripe for harvesting. Interpreting the intrusive biblical passage as a divine command, the Norwich itinerant was "Constrained by divine light Love and power" to offer his pastoral services to the Titicut congregation. The next day, he preached with power. "Divine truth seemed to flow thro' my Soul like a river," Backus recalled in his diary, and many sinners were "struck under Conviction."[37]

During the next several months, Backus continued preaching with "special Clearness." Like Davenport, he appealed to the Holy Spirit for direction in his extemporaneous addresses. Meanwhile, the Titicut Separates gathered a church, invited Backus to draft a confession of faith and covenant, and admitted more than two dozen men and women to full communion. On March 22, 1748, after listening to Backus narrate his conversion experiences and call to the ministry, several church members testified that they had received divine

35. McLoughlin, ed., *Diary of Isaac Backus*, I, 3, III, 1526. See also Benjamin Lord, "The Vote of the Church in 1745," Norwich, Connecticut, First Congregational Church Papers, 1660–1928, CSL; and Denison, *Notes of the Baptists, and Their Principles*, 20.

36. McLoughlin, ed., *Diary of Isaac Backus*, I, 4–5.

37. Isaac Backus to the Norwich Separate Church, Apr. 1, 1748, no. 295, *IBP;* McLoughlin, ed., *Diary of Isaac Backus*, I, 12, 15.

revelations endorsing him as their pastor. Ordained by a group of prominent Separate leaders from eastern Connecticut, Backus ministered to the dissenting community at Titicut for the next six decades.[38]

Backus's transit from an earnest new convert to a separatist dissenter resonated with the experiences of lesser-known men and women such as Edmund Williams, a husbandman from the neighboring village of Raynham. Most of the terse entries that Williams haphazardly inscribed in the margins of his yearly almanacs between 1742 and 1765 dealt with the care of his livestock and other business matters. He hired day laborers, dug for iron ore on his property, exchanged pasturage with neighbors, and bartered with peddlers for consumer goods. Williams also recorded astrological information considered essential to the yearly agricultural cycle. Although he occasionally noted major international events, most of his marginal notations dealt with lecture days, militia musters, and town meetings. Williams never mentioned the powerful revival that gripped Raynham in 1742, during which fifty new converts were admitted to full communion, but he recorded his annual ministerial, provincial, and county taxes. A decade later, Williams catalogued his farm animals: one horse, three cows, two swine, and fifteen sheep valued at nine pounds, eleven shillings. Both figures placed him roughly one-third down the economic scale—a respectable competency by the standards of the day.[39]

A closer look at Williams's marginalia reveals his rising interest in radical religious dissent. Williams and his wife affiliated with the Raynham church shortly after their marriage in 1737. During the next decade, they presented each of their first seven children for baptism. Signs that Williams was developing into something more than a typical godly walker surfaced in his almanacs as early as 1742. Obscure itinerants occasionally preached at his house. Two years later, Williams recorded an extended series of notes on a sermon that addressed the nature of conversion. In December 1744, he traveled to hear George Whitefield preach in Bridgewater during the Anglican evangelist's controversial second New England tour. During these years, Williams might have passed through a discrete conversion experience that impelled

---

38. McLoughlin, ed., *Diary of Isaac Backus*, I, 15 (quote), 34, 37–39.

39. Edmund Williams, diaries, 1742–1765, AAS; "Manuscript Memoranda," *NEHGR*, LXV (1911), 381. See also James A. Tilbe, Dorothy A. Newton, and Bonnie Lester, *If These Stones Could Speak: A History of the First Congregational Church of Raynham, U.C.C.* ([Raynham, Mass.], 1994), 86; and Marquis F. King, "Valuation of Raynham, Mass., 1746," *Maine Historical and Genealogical Recorder*, VII (1893), 44–45. On almanacs as diaries, see T. J. Tomlin, *A Divinity for All Persuasions: Almanacs and Early American Religious Life*, Religion in America (New York, 2014), 17.

him to question his earlier decision to join the Raynham church. Although he was elected deacon in 1750, he met with Backus one year later and informed the Titicut minister that he had "Come out from the Church" because "many things appeared wrong to him there." Backus noted in his diary that Williams's account of his tribulations in Raynham was "Considerable Satesfying."[40]

Williams's sporadic entries for 1753 and 1754 were markedly different from the terse notes he scribbled in the margins of his earlier almanacs. He tracked the activities of Backus and other prominent separatist ministers, the deaths of notable dissenters, and news of their legal and ecclesiastical trials. An adversarial tone emerged in these brief ruminations. On the flyleaf of his 1753 almanac, Williams repeatedly wrote the words "Wisdom is justified of all her children": the same biblical text that formed the basis of Jonathan Parsons's controversial defense of separatism a decade earlier. On March 22, 1756, Williams recited a satisfactory relation of his religious experiences in the Titicut meetinghouse and joined Backus's church in full communion. His strident correspondence during the 1760s and 1770s marked the ascendance of religious radicalism over the ideal of the godly walk.[41]

Similar stories of dramatic religious transformation are woven through the roster of more than 330 Connecticut Separates who signed a 1748 petition drafted by Canterbury minister Solomon Paine requesting the right to worship apart from the churches of the standing order in accordance with the 1689 Toleration Act. The list was a roll call of New England's most passionate new converts. Nathan Cole placed his signature near the head of the first column, as did Seth Youngs, the Hartford clockmaker who traveled with James Davenport during the summer of 1741 and organized revival meetings in his home. The list included obscure former godly walkers such as Ebenezer Grover, who had joined the Lynn End (now Lynnfield), Massachusetts, church two decades earlier but now questioned whether he had been "born and brought up in a land of light." One signer from Tolland, Shubal Stearns, later migrated to the southern colonies, where he emerged as the principal architect of the southern Baptist movement. The petitioners included the son of attorney John Lee, an indefatigable revival promoter and participant in the New London bonfires. Prominent among the largest group of dissenters from Lyme was Reynold

40. Williams, diaries, March, Dec. 29, 1744; McLoughlin, ed., *Diary of Isaac Backus*, I, 193–194 (quote).

41. Williams, diaries, flyleaf, April, July 1753, Sept. 10, Nov. 12, 1755; "Manuscript Memoranda," *NEHGR*, LXV (1911), 381; McLoughlin, ed., *Diary of Isaac Backus*, I, 409. For correspondence, see Edmund Williams to Isaac Backus, July 14, 1764, June 26, 1772, Nov. 25, 1774, Jan. 25, Sept. 10, Nov. 21, 1775, Apr. 7, 1777, Jan. 14, 1785, Aug. 7, 1789, nos. 643, 921, 1096, 1101, 1138, 1149, 1217, 1719, 1990, *IBP*.

Marvin, recently censured by the New London County ministerial association for exercising his gifts of spiritual discernment on Edmund Dorr.[42]

Paine's campaign to secure legal rights for the Separates, along with a similar petition drive that Isaac Backus engineered in towns from central Massachusetts to the tip of Cape Cod, galvanized isolated dissenters into networks of committed saints. Membership in the breakaway congregations differed markedly from the inclusive, territorial parishes of the Congregational establishment. Dissenting families from Middleborough and Bridgewater formed the core of Backus's church, for example, but Edmund Williams and individuals from eight other towns in the Old Colony also sought fellowship among the Titicut Separates. Geographical diversity characterized the membership of the separatist churches gathered in Mansfield and New London as well. Recording the names of the men and women who joined Ebenezer Frothingham's dissenting congregation in Middletown, Connecticut, Nathan Cole was forced to add a special column listing the town of residence for each new member. Communicants admitted to the Middletown Separate church between 1747 and 1777 hailed from two dozen communities on both sides of the Connecticut River from Suffield to New Haven—an area comprising approximately six hundred square miles.[43]

Separate churches were religious communities of an entirely different order, as Cole explained in his "Spiritual Travels." The Connecticut artisan believed Separate brethren living in distant towns were bound together by the "Spirit of God." To prove his point, Cole described several unusual incidents in which he communicated with other dissenters through the power of prayer. On one occasion, while he was at work plowing his fields, his mind ran to the saints in Middletown, and he "broke out" in prayer as if he were "in the midst of them." After finishing his work, Cole traveled down to the Separates' meetinghouse, only to discover that another member of the congregation had just arrived on the same errand. "I believe that Saints have been fetched from town to town many a time by the strength of prayer," he concluded. Estranged

42. Solomon Paine et al. to the Connecticut General Assembly, May 2, 1748, Ecclesiastical Affairs, Ser. 1: 1658–1789, X, 29a–d, Connecticut Archives, 1629–1856, CSL; Relation of Ebenezer Grover, Dec. 24, 1721, box 5, Goodhue Family Papers, 1684–1858, PEM. On Stearns, see David T. Morgan, Jr., "The Great Awakening in North Carolina, 1740–1775: The Baptist Phase," *North Carolina Historical Review*, XLV (1968), 264–283.

43. McLoughlin, ed., *Diary of Isaac Backus*, I, 61–63; Charles D. Townsend, comp., *The History of the Third Congregational Church of Middleborough Known Today as North Congregational Church United Church of Christ North Middleboro, Massachusetts* (Sarasota, Fla., 1982), 27–29; Onuf, "New Lights in New London," *WMQ*, XXXVII (1980), 633; Barnett and Barnett, *On the Trail of a Legend*, 33–34; Nathan Cole, "A Coppy of the Church Records," 1747–1777, 1–7, Nathan Cole Papers, I, CHS.

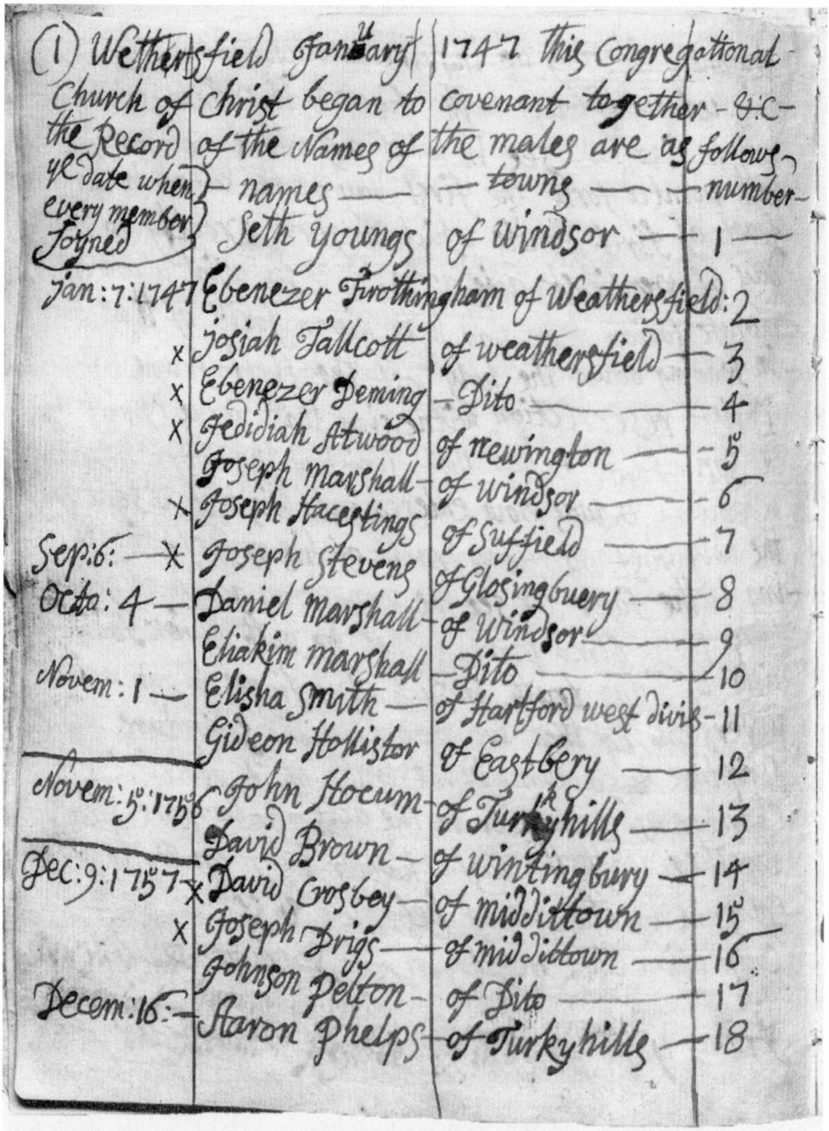
(1) Wethersfield January 11 1747 this Congregational Church of Christ began to covenant together &c the Record of the Names of the males are as follows

ye date when every member joyned		names	towns	number
		Seth Youngs	of Windsor	1
Jan:7:1747		Ebenezer Frothingham	of Weathersfield	2
	x	Josiah Tallcott	of weathersfield	3
	x	Ebenezer Deming	Dito	4
	x	Jedidiah Atwood	of newington	5
		Joseph marshall	of windsor	6
	x	Joseph Hacestings	of Suffield	7
Sep:6:	x	Joseph Stevens	of Glosingbuery	8
Octo:4		Daniel marshall	of Windsor	9
		Eliakim marshall	Dito	10
Novem:1		Elisha Smith	of Hartford west divis	11
		Gideon Hollistor	of Eastbery	12
Novem:5:1756		John Hocum	of Turkyhills	13
		David Brown	of wintingbury	14
Dec:9:1757	x	David Crosbey	of midditown	15
	x	Joseph Drigs	of middittown	16
		Johnson Pelton	of Dito	17
Decem:16		Aaron Phelps	of Turkyhills	18

FIGURE 22 Nathan Cole, "A Coppy of the Church Records." 1747–1777. "Spiritual Travels" Record Book, 1722–1780, Connecticut Historical Society, Hartford

from his cold, formalistic neighbors, Cole felt intimately—even supernaturally—drawn to Separates residing miles away.[44]

Strict Congregationalists seemed willing—even eager—to suffer material privation and even imprisonment for their dissent. Elisha Paine and at least eight other dissenting preachers were incarcerated for violating Connecticut's anti-itinerancy law. Scores of dissenters watched with mounting bitterness as town constables confiscated their oxen, cows, pewter plates, looking glasses, spinning wheels, and other valuable items of personal property after they refused to pay taxes to support the Congregational establishment. Many suffered isolation and ostracism after breaking with neighbors who remained within the churches of the standing order. Cole gave up "what the world calls a fine reputation" when he abandoned the Kensington Society church in 1747. He was "loaded with Scoffs, reproaches, and mockerys," as his "old friends grew Shy of me and forsook me." New Haven gentlewoman Sarah Pierpont took solace in that she ranked among the "little despised number" of God's elect who were "Scoffed at by the world" yet remained "dear to christ." Hannah Heaton also "lived above the world," reveling in her isolation from unconverted neighbors and resting content in the knowledge that "god had taught me to separate from their idolitrous religion." Incarcerated for refusing to pay their minister's taxes, several of Backus's parishioners and family members "found Jesus in the midst of the furnace." As Kezia Morse of Woodstock, Connecticut, summarized in a letter to her brother, "It Seemes to me that the enimies of the Lord groo Stronger against me Sence the Lord has brought me out of this Church."[45]

Separate Congregationalists imagined themselves as "Saboth Evinging [avenging] Walkers," zealous Christian soldiers struggling to restore the purity of the apostolic churches. Even as the 1748 Connecticut petitioners trumpeted the "unchainable Right" of British subjects to judge for themselves in "matters of the worship of God," they acknowledged they had withdrawn from the established churches in obedience to God's revelatory commands. In an effort to routinize Whitefieldian revivalism, they organized their new Separate churches "by order of the holy ghost."[46]

---

44. NCS, 106. For a similar argument, see Susan Juster, *Disorderly Women: Sexual Politics and Evangelicalism in Revolutionary New England* (Ithaca, N.Y., 1994), 71–72.

45. NCS, 103–104; Sarah Pierpont to Ebenezer Parkman, Aug. 9, 1745, box 3, Parkman Family Papers; Lacey, ed., *World of Hannah Heaton*, 28, 33; William Hooper to the Titicut church, Apr. 4, 1749, no. 310, *IBP*; Denison, *Notes of the Baptists, and Their Principles*, 28; Kezia Morse and Joseph Morse to John Cleaveland, Feb. 1, 1745, box 1, JCP. For additional examples, see McLoughlin, *New England Dissent*, I, 360–385.

46. Benjamin Cary to Eleazar Wheelock, Nov. 8, 1741, no. 741608, *EWP;* Paine and Smith

■ The formation of the First Church of Bennington at the close of the Seven Years' War should have been a landmark event in the history of Congregationalism. As the first Protestant institution established in the disputed frontier region known as the Hampshire Grants, the Bennington church stood at the leading edge of New England's rapidly expanding settlements. It also marked the furthest expansion of the Separate Congregational movement, for the pioneers who migrated to Bennington during the 1760s consisted almost entirely of radical religious dissenters. They came to the Grants seeking pure churches as well as cheap land and economic opportunities. The Hardwick Separates— including several descendants of Westborough deacon John Fay—formed the nucleus of the church. They were joined by separatists from Sunderland, Massachusetts, and the Newent parish of Norwich (now Lisbon), Connecticut. Bennington's first minister, an unlettered joiner named Jedidiah Dewey, had fomented a schism in Westfield, Massachusetts, and served as the pastor of a dissenting church in Amenia, New York. Leading Separate ministers from Connecticut presided over his installation in 1762.[47]

The Bennington church initially prospered. Dewey promoted more than fifty people to full communion during the first five years of his ministry. Overall, three-quarters of the settler families initially affiliated with the fledgling church. Yet, Bennington was roiled by divisions almost from its inception. Four months before Dewey's ordination, the church disciplined Samuel Montague for denying the practice of infant baptism. An outspoken group of parishioners soon grew dissatisfied with Dewey's preaching, ceased making voluntary contributions to his salary, and refused to submit to disciplinary proceedings. One of the deacons laid down his office. By 1772, many of the original members had deserted the Bennington church and were gathering in private to listen to an itinerant preacher named Ithamar Hibbard. The Bennington church admonished or excommunicated more than half of the men who joined in full communion between 1762 and 1780. Dewey's successor, an imperious Yale College graduate named David Avery, lasted only three years before he was run out of town, dogged by charges that his sermons were a *"perversion of the Gospel of Christ."* The religious disputes that led to what one Fay family member later called a "Church War" lasted for decades. By

---

to the Connecticut General Assembly, May 2, 1748, Ecclesiastical Affairs, Ser. 1, X, 29a; Samuel Drown to Solomon Paine, June 18, 1752, no. 87, JTC.

47. On the founding of the Bennington church, see Goen, *Revivalism and Separatism in New England*, 108–109. For the religious motives of Vermont's earliest settlers, see Donald A. Smith, "Green Mountain Insurgency: Transformation of New York's Forty-Year Land War," *Vermont History*, LXIV (1996), 198, 204–207.

1780, fewer than half the families in Bennington remained affiliated with the town's shattered religious institution (see Table 9).[48]

The "dust and fogg of contention and division" that enveloped Bennington church can be traced to the "Articles *of* Faith *and* Church Government," a detailed statement of separatist beliefs and practices adopted in 1745 by the founding members of the breakaway church in Mansfield, Connecticut. Published by the Windham Association in an antirevival pamphlet designed to expose the "horrible Error and Darkness" that plagued the Separate churches, the Mansfield articles circulated widely in scribal copies. According to one observer, Middletown elder Ebenezer Frothingham demanded that his parishioners assent to the principles established by Separate leaders in eastern Connecticut. Isaac Backus's church at Titicut, along with at least five other breakaway churches in southern New England, embraced the Mansfield articles with only minor alterations. The Newent Separates likely carried a copy with them on their migration to Bennington during the early 1760s.[49]

Following an opening statement in which they affirmed basic Reformed theological doctrines, the Mansfield Separates struck out in a decidedly new direction, arguing that the Holy Spirit "can and doth make a particular Ap-

48. Bennington First Church Records, I, 3, 5, 8, 10–23, 25, 28–30, 36–41 (quote, 38), 54–57, 60–61; Jonas Fay to David Avery, Sept. 27, 1792, *Papers of David Avery, 1746–1818*, microfilm, reel 9 (Princeton, N.J., 1979). On the troubled early history of the Bennington church, see Robert E. Shalhope, *Bennington and the Green Mountain Boys: The Emergence of Liberal Democracy in Vermont, 1760–1850*, Reconfiguring American Political History (Baltimore, 1996), 55–59, 179–182, 197–198, 210–218; and Michael A. Bellesiles, *Revolutionary Outlaws: Ethan Allen and the Struggle for Independence on the Early American Frontier* (Charlottesville, Va., 1993), 64–69, 234–238. For Bennington population figures, see Jay Mack Holbrook, *Vermont 1771 Census* (Oxford, Mass., 1982), xiii.

49. Bennington First Church Records, I, 30; *Result of a Council of the Consociated Churches*, 5, 20; Webster, transcr., "Letters to Joseph Bellamy," 44. Scribal copies of the Mansfield Articles include "Articles of Faith, Church Covenant etc. of the Strict Congregational Church in Stonington," Sept. 11, 1746, North Stonington, Conn., Separate Church Papers, 1746–1822, microfilm no. 584, CSL; McLoughlin, ed., *Diary of Isaac Backus*, III, 1529–1532; and George Faber Clark, *A History of the Town of Norton, Bristol County, Massachusetts, from 1669–1859* (Boston, 1859), 445–448. Southbury, Connecticut, minister John Graham, Sr., transcribed the most controversial articles of the Middletown covenant in a letter to Joseph Bellamy; and Halifax, Massuchusetts, clergyman John Cotton copied the "Articles of Faith and Church Covenant Agreed upon by a Number of *Saints* in Titticut" (box 3, Curwen Family Papers, 1637–1808, AAS). Separate churches in Canterbury and Killingly, Connecticut, and Providence, Rhode Island, adopted a less radical variant of the Mansfield articles. See *Records of the Congregational Church in Canterbury, Connecticut, 1711–1844* (Hartford, Conn., 1932), 18–22; Killingly, Conn., Separate Church, "Confession of Faith," Sept. 26, 1746, I, Diedrich Collection; and Providence, R.I., Separate Congregational Church, "The Confession of Faith of Mr. Snow's Church in Providence," n.d. [circa 1747], no. 41, Miscellaneous Volumes and Papers, *ESP*. On the diffusion of this important separatist manifesto, see Goen, *Revivalism and Separatism in New England*, 150–152.

plication" to the soul of every saint. True Christians, as Mansfield minister Thomas Marsh declared, "may know one another as certainly or clearly as a Man may know a Dog from a Sheep." Subscribers to the Mansfield articles boldly asserted that "we are of that Number who were Elected of GOD to eternal Life," and they further stated that all doubt of one's future estate was sinful and "contrary to the Command of GOD." In the minds of dissenters such as Abigail Cleaveland, a founding member of the Separate church in Canterbury, true "Christians" by definition were those who "had assurance." They believed that "CHRIST died for me," as her kinsman Elisha Paine emphatically proclaimed.[50]

The Separates' rigorous adherence to Whitefield's concept of conversion anchored a new set of restrictive church membership standards that barred covenant owners, doctrinal professors, and unconverted godly walkers. The "Doors of the Church," according to the Mansfield articles, "should be carefully kept against such as cannot give a satisfying Evidence of the Work of GOD upon their Souls whereby they are united to CHRIST." Only "true Believers (and none but such)" had the right to offer children for baptism or participate in the Lord's Supper. Consistent with the Whitefieldarians' repudiation of inclusive church admission practices, Strict Congregationalists reestablished the ideal of visible sainthood as the foundation of their purified churches. They sought what one Separate minister called an "almost invisible Church of Christ": an earthly institution that mirrored the heavenly communion of saints as closely as the Holy Spirit allowed.[51]

The ritual arm of this latest incarnation of the New England way involved the restoration of oral church admission testimonies. Anyone refusing to recite their conversion experiences before the congregation, the Mansfield articles stated, would be "Looked upon as an open Contemner of the Gospel-Commands." The Canterbury Separates even extended the practice of delivering oral relations to communicants in other congregations who sought to transfer their membership. Each time the Separates organized a new church, the founding members—both men and women—"stood confidently and zealously declared" their "Experences how the Lord brought them out of darkness into his marvelus light." These ritual acts of public speaking cemented the bonds of fellowship among the saints. Some relations functioned like awaken-

---

50. *Result of a Council of the Consociated Churches*, 7, 20; Ebenezer Cleaveland to John Cleaveland, Mar. 2, 1747, box 2, JCP; *Letter from the Associated Ministers*, 8.

51. *Result of a Council of the Consociated Churches*, 8–9; John Paine to Solomon Paine, Apr. 26, 1751, no. 70, JTC.

ing sermons. Minister Paul Parke noted that many candidates were "filled with the holy Ghost"—some to "Greate Rapture"—when they recited their conversions and were admitted into "Visable felloship" with the Separate church in Preston, Connecticut. According to Backus, Hephzibah Packard's relation "Caused many Saints to glorify God in her." When delivered with power, oral conversion narratives provided certain evidence of election, ensured the purity of Separate church membership, edified the assembled congregation, and, on rare occasions, propelled onlookers into raptures of their own.[52]

As ardent Whitefieldarians, the Mansfield Separates believed that *"GOD has yet more Light to reveal to his Church, without Contradiction to what is already revealed."* Letters that circulated among dissenting congregations opened with salutations wishing that the recipient would "Abound In the Gifts and Gracess of the Spirit of God." Church records described how parents were "Moved" to present their children for baptism by the leadings of the Holy Ghost. Separate leaders did not simply proclaim days of ritual fasting and thanksgiving. Instead, they first appointed meetings to "inquire duty of God, in order that God would make duty plain to us." Requests for assistance in settling ecclesiastical disputes called for "Gifted Bretheran" who were "full of the holy Ghost" to sit in council and "witness for god." Indeed, the Separates sought direct illumination from the "Spirit of GOD" for every action taken by their churches.[53]

Spirit-centered worship practices began with separatist ministers. Adopting the preaching techniques established by James Davenport and other charismatic itinerants during the revival years, Separate pastors rarely read from prepared sermon notes. Instead, they waited for the direct inspiration of the Holy Spirit. Backus appealed to God for suitable texts during intensive preparatory meditations. Answers in the form of biblical impulses often arrived at the last possible moment. "I was much Shut up," he noted during the winter of 1749. When the afternoon meeting came, Backus struggled to discover a text from which to preach, until the "Lord gave me one and gave me glorious Liberty in preaching from it and there was a blessed moveing among the

---

52. *Records of the Congregational Church in Canterbury,* 8; Josiah Cleaveland, Sr., to John Cleaveland, Dec. 2, 1746, box 1, JCP; Sutton, Mass., Separate Church to Canterbury, Conn., Separate Church, Sept. 28, 1752, no. 99, JTC; Anderson, comp., *Parke Scrapbook,* I, [5, 40, 51]; McLoughlin, ed., *Diary of Isaac Backus,* I, 37.

53. *Result of a Council of the Consociated Churches,* 10; John Leffingwell, Jr., to Isaac Backus, Jan. 12, 1748, no. 294.5, *IBP;* Anderson, comp., *Parke Scrapebook,* I, [34]; Clark, *History of the Town of Norton,* 448; Samuel Gustin, Jr., to Solomon Paine, Aug. 1, 1752, no. 90, JTC.

people." Similar entries dotted his diary, for an occasional period of "Barrenness and Stupidity" was a noteworthy frown of divine providence. Preaching almost daily during the early years of his career, Backus seldom lacked for inspiration.[54]

Among the most controversial features of the Mansfield articles was the provision that encouraged—and sometimes obligated—the Separates to exercise Spirit-given gifts of exhorting, prayer, or prophecy. "We believe that all the Gifts and Graces that are bestowed upon any of the Members are to be improved by them for the Good of the Whole," the Mansfield Separates explained. Backus alluded to this practice in his account of a typical meeting during the summer of 1749. "I prayed," he noted, "then one of the bretherin prayed and in his Prayer, the wind of the Spirit, began to breath upon us." On his wedding day several years later, Backus invited one parishioner to "pray before and after" the exchange of vows. And, when the Titicut church met to elect deacons, "sundry both of Brothers and Sisters Came out in declarations of great things that they Saw." A few claimed to have received revelations that God was calling certain members of the church to serve as church officers; others voiced their inspired opinions that they, themselves, had been called to preach. "These Separatists pretend to Act by Inspiration and immediate Suggestions," groused Plymouth, Massachusetts, magistrate Josiah Cotton after watching Backus's congregation later that year. During their worship exercises, he continued, "if One has anything revealed, let it be Man or Woman, The Speaker Stops and keeps Silence till the Revelation be deliver'd, and so there are Several Speakers at one and the Same Meeting." In Cotton's mind, it was no coincidence that Isaac "Bacchus" shared the same name with the Greek god of wine. He was confident that such spirit-intoxicating "Wild fire" would "run 'em into all Confusion."[55]

In contrast to the established churches that had slowly relinquished their authority over most moral and ethical trespasses to the civil courts during the previous half century, dissenting congregations zealously interrogated offending saints for seemingly minor infractions. The Separates soon found themselves "going on in a Line of disipline" with a vigilance not known in New England since the age of the puritan founders. Offences ranged from intemperance, fornication, and evil speech to stealing, dancing, and gaming. The

54. McLoughlin, ed., *Diary of Isaac Backus,* I, 52, 121. See also Goen, *Revivalism and Separatism in New England,* 175–180.

55. *Result of a Council of the Consociated Churches,* 9; McLoughlin, ed., *Diary of Isaac Backus,* I, 41, 66, III, 1536; JCH, 387.

Mansfield articles also commanded the brethren to seek resolution to "Civil Differences" within the church rather than in the provincial courts. For the first time in decades, churches resumed the practice of monitoring the business dealings of their members. Neighborly watchfulness, however, easily devolved into pettiness and backbiting. John Hayward withdrew from communion in the Titicut church after Esther Fobes refused to return some sewing items she had borrowed from his wife. The taint of unresolved conflicts even followed people when they transferred their membership between Separate churches. Letters from their former congregations ensured confession for sins committed months earlier and miles away.[56]

The decentralized ecclesiology and Spirit-filled worship practices of the Separate churches paved the way for bitter infighting and precipitated endless hearings and church councils. Records from the Separate church in Providence, Rhode Island, indicate that one in ten saints "broke covenant" and were excommunicated between 1746 and 1770. The Canterbury Separates admonished, censured, suspended, or expelled one-third of their members during Solomon Paine's ten-year pastorate. During this same period, Paine also received thirty-two requests from twenty other churches asking him to assist in resolving ecclesiastical disputes. Interchurch councils became so frequent early in the 1750s that at least one Separate congregation was forced to postpone a disciplinary hearing to accommodate delegates from other churches called to negotiate disputes elsewhere on the same day. The rising number of councils rapidly outstripped ordinations. As the formation of Separate churches slackened, dissenters turned inward and grew increasingly fractious. To one sarcastic Canterbury brother, it seemed as if the only way to avoid censure would be to sell his "soul to Devils" in exchange for a full pardon.[57]

The same ecclesiastical controversies that drew the Separates out of the standing order during the 1740s threatened to tear apart their newly formed

56. Elizabeth Backus to Isaac Backus, June 6, 1752, no. 384, *IBP; Result of a Council of the Consociated Churches*, 9; McLoughlin, ed., *Diary of Isaac Backus*, I, 436–437. Documents from a wide range of Separate church discipline cases may be found among the JTC.

57. Providence, R.I., Richmond Street Congregational Church Records, 1743–1823, III, 26–28, Plymouth Union Congregational Church Records, 1720–1974, Rhode Island Historical Society, Providence; Goen, *Revivalism and Separatism in New England*, 167; Solomon Paine, church minutes, Oct. 5, 1752–Feb. 2, 1753, no. 101, JTC. Data on council missives received by the Canterbury church is compiled from documents in the JTC and the Canterbury, Conn., Separate Church Papers, 1748–1784, microfilm no. 455, CSL. On the decline of discipline cases within established churches, see Emil Oberholzer, Jr., *Delinquent Saints: Disciplinary Action in the Early Congregational Churches of Massachusetts* (New York, 1956), 235–250. For a statistical analysis of Separate Congregational and Separate Baptist cases of church discipline, see Juster, *Disorderly Women*, 85.

churches. During the next two decades, conflicts over the proper scope of gifts of the Holy Spirit dominated disciplinary proceedings. Backus presided over a council that censured the Harwich Separate minister after he attempted to restore the apostolic practice of foot washing. Elisha Paine's younger brother, John, ran afoul of his colleagues when he audaciously proclaimed that the Bible was a useless old almanac and encouraged the saints in his congregation to allow only the indwelling Spirit to guide their actions. Churches clashed over the proper place and privileges of native and African American members. They debated the propriety of women speaking at Sabbath meetings. Separate churches even struggled to establish criteria for settling church disputes, with some members waiting for "divine testimony" to resolve matters of discipline and others emphasizing scripture-based morality. All the while, a younger and even more radical cohort of itinerants—from well-known preachers such as Joseph Croswell and Hezekiah Smith to obscure figures such as the Indian preacher Ezekiel Cole—continued to stoke the fires of religious discontent.[58]

No issue fomented greater confusion among the Separates than infant baptism. During the peak years of the Whitefieldian revivals, James Davenport and other riding ministers persuaded a handful of zealous new converts to question the efficacy of baptisms administered by purportedly unconverted ministers. Marston Cabot, the sickly minister of the north parish in Killingly (now Thompson), Connecticut, wrote nervously in his diary about "rebaptizings in the further end of the parrish" just a few weeks after the 1743 New London bonfires. Later that year, the Middleborough church censured one parishioner for denying the validity of his infant baptism. Boston's hay weigher, Nathaniel Wardell, Jr., brazenly immersed several adult members of the Old South Church at about the same time. By the end of the decade, the purifying logic of the Separate movement had incited perhaps as many as half of all Separates to reject the practice of sprinkling infants. Within only a few

---

58. Isaac Backus to Richard Chase, May 10, 1752, no. 382, *IBP;* Joseph Snow, minutes of a church council, Mar. 23, 1753, no. 115, JTC; Erik R. Seeman, "'Justise Must Take Plase': Three African Americans Speak of Religion in Eighteenth-Century New England," *WMQ,* LVI (1999), 399–402; Solomon Paine, minutes of a church council, Dec. 12, 1754, no. 3, Canterbury Separate Church Papers; Hall, diaries, June 6, 1749; Goen, *Revivalism and Separatism in New England,* 167 (quote). For Croswell, Smith, and Cole, see *Sketches of the Life, and Extracts from the Journals, and Other Writings, of the Late Joseph Croswell* ... (Boston, 1809); John David Broome, [ed.], *The Life, Ministry, and Journals of Hezekiah Smith: Pastor of the First Baptist Church of Haverhill, Massachusetts, 1765 to 1805, and Chaplain in the American Revolution, 1775 to 1780,* Warren Association (Springfield, Mo., 2004); and Douglas L. Winiarski, "New Perspectives on the Northampton Communion Controversy I: David Hall's Diary and Letter to Edward Billing," *Jonathan Edwards Studies,* III (2013), 270.

years of their founding, nearly every Separate church in New England faced a new round of disputes and schisms over the issue of adult, or believer's, baptism by full immersion.[59]

Although critics later scoffed that the Baptist dissenters "get under water to wash away their *minister's rates*," most ardent antipedobaptists cited theological, rather than financial, reasons for withdrawing from the separatist churches. Patience Adams, a founding member of the Separate church in Canterbury, offered a written explanation of her changing sentiments. "Baptism is anext to beleavours" only, Adams argued after she was "inabled by the spirit and word of God" to contemplate the meaning of Matthew 28:19. Two women overheard Zerviah Lamb of Preston proclaim that "Infant Baptism or Sprinklin was Nothing but a tradition of Men and Came from the whore of Babilon." Others felt called to withdraw from Separate churches after receiving biblical impulses, dreams, and other revelations. In the east parish of Enfield (now Somers), Connecticut, Mary Miller insisted that she had received divine teaching on the necessity of adult baptism "Right down from the burning throne" during a powerful meditation. She publicly commanded her pastor not to rebel against this new divine dispensation, for God had told her that it was a "glorious thing Leading into the New Jereusalem."[60]

The rapid spread of antipedobaptist principles grew out of the Separates' drive to purify their churches, but the transition was anything but inevitable. Most of the new churches stumbled through an extended period of uncertainty. Backus remained "Sensless and Stupid" over the issue for more than two years. Twice, he reversed his position. As their pastor sank into melancholy, the Titicut church languished. Angry members returned to the established church in Middleborough or defected to older general Baptist congregations located miles away in Rhode Island. Recriminations soon followed, as majority church factions excommunicated first the antipedobaptists and then the pedobaptists in concert with Backus's vacillating theology. Several councils met to adjudicate the dispute, but all failed to heal the gaping breach in fellowship. Finally, in 1756, the Titicut congregation disbanded and was reconstituted as the First Baptist Church of Middleborough.[61]

59. *Boston Weekly Post-Boy*, Nov. 2, 1741; Marston Cabot, "Memorabilia," 1740–1745, May 29, 1743, Mss A 1999, NEHGS; Confession of Noah Alden, Oct. 1, 1743, Middleborough, Mass., First Congregational Church Relations and Personal Records, 1702–1865, CL (available online at NEHH); *Boston Evening-Post*, Mar. 21, 1743.

60. *Boston Evening-Post*, May 17, 1773; Patience Adams to the Canterbury Separate Church, July 3, 1760, no. 157, JTC; Anderson, comp., *Parke Scrapbook*, I, [64]; Solomon Paine, minutes of a church council, Aug. 10, 1752, no. 92, JTC.

61. McLoughlin, ed., *Diary of Isaac Backus*, I, 93. For the familiar story of Backus's con-

As the Separate Baptist movement took New England by storm early in the 1750s, Strict Congregational churches teetered on the verge of collapse. "Wee are in the Militant State," declared the members of a bitterly divided native American Separate church on the Narragansett reservation in Charlestown, Rhode Island. "An Enemy is Got into the Camp and the Battle Goes hard on the Side of the faithfull." Dissenters in Enfield wrote repeatedly to the Canterbury Separates begging their brethren to "hear the Grones of this part of Zion" and pity their "Broken surcumstances." Divided into "Parties" and "going bleeding to hell," God's chosen people in a town made famous during the Whitefieldian revivals just a few years earlier now languished in the "Place of Dragons." By the mid-1750s, ecclesiastical divisions among the Sunderland Separates had grown so intractable that the members could no longer "sett down to the Table of the Lord together." The Coventry, Connecticut, Separate church had been so "Scattered, Dispers'd and Reduc'd by their Divisions and Contentions" that "there is not the form or Being of a Visible Church Remaining in Regular Standing." So many onetime saints had either withdrawn or been excommunicated from the Rehoboth, Massachusetts, Separate church over the baptism issue that elder John Paine penned his missive calling for a disciplinary council in the name of "what is left of the Church of Christ that was Commited to my Care."[62]

A few Separate Congregational churches attempted to keep their scattering flocks within the fold by practicing open or mixed communion, but this consensual ecclesiology rapidly disintegrated, as Baptist insurgents equated sprinkling with the "mark of the Beast." By 1770, half of all Strict Congregational churches had converted to antipedobaptist principles, and the number of Separate Baptist churches in southern New England had more than tripled. Separate churches continued to be wracked by further separations: the dissenters' "Insatiable Hungrings and Thirstyings after a Complete Conformity" to God's "Immage" knew no limits.[63]

---

version to antipedobaptism, see McLoughlin, *Isaac Backus and the American Pietistic Tradition*, 57–88.

62. Stephen Babcock to Solomon Paine, Apr. 26, 1752, no. 85, JTC, Ezekiel Pease to Solomon Paine, May 3, 1753, no. 119, Joseph Markham to Solomon Paine, Nov. 20, 1751, no. 80, Ebenezer Wadsworth to Solomon Paine, Aug. 27, 1753, no. 126, Alexander Miller, minutes of a church council, Mar. 24, 1756, no. 151; John Paine to the Titicut, Mass., Separate Church, Mar. 30, 1751, no. 349, *IBP*.

63. Solomon Paine to Newtown, N.H., Separate Church, Aug. 20, 1753, no. 128, JTC; John Leffingwell, Jr., to Isaac Backus, Oct. 25, 1748, no. 301, *IBP*. See also Goen, *Revivalism and Separatism in New England*, 258–267; and McLoughlin, *New England Dissent*, I, 424–425.

■ On May 17, 1781, Stephen Fay's lifeless body was laid out in the Bennington meetinghouse before being interred "decently and honourably" under an imposing tablet in the adjacent town cemetery. The town's young minister, David Avery, delivered a eulogy from Psalm 103, but his message of keeping covenant with God must have struck an equivocal note among his parishioners. Since his arrival in 1768, Fay had always been something of an oddity in Bennington. On the one hand, he was one of the town's most respected and prosperous citizens. After moving from Hardwick to the Vermont frontier during the early 1760s, Fay became the proprietor of the Green Mountain Tavern. Ethan Allen used the timber-framed inn as his headquarters when organizing the militia forces that captured Fort Ticonderoga in 1775, and a group of delegates declared Vermont an independent state in Fay's tavern two years later. Fay's sons fought with distinction at the Battle of Bennington. A dependable public servant, over the years Fay filled the posts of constable, surveyor of roads, treasurer, moderator of the town meeting, and selectman.[64]

But, even as he moved to the center of village politics during the tumultuous years of the American Revolution, Fay dropped out of New England's Congregational culture altogether. Unlike his older brother, James, he never reconciled with Ebenezer Parkman or requested a letter of dismission when he departed Westborough in 1750. Fay did not present his four youngest children for baptism in the Hardwick church, nor did he join the separatist congregation alongside his brother and extended kin. The prominent taverner's name was conspicuously absent from the earliest roster of Bennington church members. Although the wealthy proprietor of the Green Mountain Tavern socialized with Avery, Fay refused to contribute money toward his salary. None of Fay's twelve adult children and only three of their spouses ever joined the Bennington church in full communion or presented their children for baptism.[65]

What had happened to this zealous and combative Whitefieldarian? Had Fay turned away from the powerful religious experiences of his youth? Perhaps he had imbibed Allen's deistic principles. After all, Fay's prominent patriot son, Jonas, named one of his children after the controversial leader of

64. David Avery, diaries, 1771–1818, May 18, 1781, reel 1, *Papers of David Avery* (quote); Bennington, Vt., Early Town Records, typescript, Town Clerk's Office, Bennington, Vt., 35, 39, 41, 45–46, 49–50, 53–54, 57, 65, 69 (available online, *http://benningtonvt.org/departments /town-clerk/vital-records-2/early-town-records/*).

65. Walett, ed., *Diary of Ebenezer Parkman*, 159; Hardwick Congregational Church Records, 22, 25, 27, 33; Paige, *History of Hardwick*, 228; Bennington First Church Records, I, 1, 7, 10, 23, 26, 77, 81; Avery, diaries, May 11, 1780, reel 1, *Papers of David Avery*, account book, 1780–1783, reel 12.

the Green Mountain Boys; and one of his grandsons argued the negative on the question "Were the Scriptures by divine Inspiration?" during a 1788 Yale College debate. On the other hand, two of Fay's children married daughters of the notable Sturbridge Baptist leader Henry Fisk. Perhaps Fay, seeking ever purer religious congregations, elected to worship in Vermont's earliest Baptist church in the adjoining town of Shaftsbury. Or, he might have lived out the remaining years of his life worshipping in, but never establishing formal ties to, Bennington's First Church. By 1781, Fay would have fit right in with his neighbors, most of whom held all ecclesiastical institutions at arm's length.[66]

One thing is certain. Stephen Fay never returned to the land of gospel light. By the time of his death, Fay had traveled far from his roots in central Massachusetts. Born during the 1710s into one of Westborough's core parish families, Fay came of age listening to the era's most powerful riding ministers, from George Whitefield to Jonathan Edwards, James Davenport to Elisha Paine. He had witnessed family members carried to heaven in ecstatic trances, endured a powerful and physically wrenching conversion, and rebelled against his minister. Fay's religious experiences during the Whitefieldian revivals of the early 1740s propelled him out of the fold of the Congregational establishment and, perhaps, beyond all institutionalized forms of religion. He had become one of the "motley crew" of pioneers, in the words of one disenchanted Vermont settler, for whom "there was no regular place of worship, nor any likely prospect that there should, for their religions had as many shades of difference as the leaves of autumn; and every man of substance who arrived, was preacher and magistrate to his own little colony."[67]

HOLIER THAN THOU

Isaac Backus and the Separate Congregationalists faced an uncertain future during the early 1750s. Hounded by colonial authorities, scores of dissenters were fined or jailed, while hundreds more had their livestock and personal property confiscated to pay their ministerial taxes. To make matters worse, internal disputes erupted with alarming frequency and a "party spirit" seemed to prevail among the breakaway churches. Backus complained that his parish-

66. John Fay, college debate, Feb. 21, 1788, John Fay Family Papers, 1788–1819, Bailey/Howe Library, University of Vermont, Burlington. On Allen's deism, see Bellesiles, *Revolutionary Outlaws*, 217–244. The earliest Shaftsbury Baptist church records are no longer extant, but see Henry Crocker, *History of the Baptists in Vermont* (Bellows Falls, Vt., 1913), 13–20.

67. [Anne MacVicar Grant], *Memoirs of an American Lady, with Sketches of Manners and Scenery in America as They Existed Previous to the Revolution* (New York, 1909), Part 2, 162.

ioners had fallen into a "Spirit of divideing" and the Titicut separatists were roiled with an endless succession of petty disputes. Several members withdrew from communion and returned to Middleborough's established church. New admissions nearly dried up altogether. Backus attended tense conferences at Sturbridge and Exeter, Rhode Island, in which leaders of the Separate movement hotly contested adult baptism. It was a time of "many heavy plunges and distresses," he noted in his diary before pleading "Lord pity and Help my Drooping Soul!"[68]

On April 27, 1753, Backus visited the neighboring town of Bridgewater to deliver a weekday lecture. Distressed at the "dreadful Stupidity" that he perceived among his audience, he sounded a clarion call for the saints to repent and rededicate themselves to a disciplined spiritual life. The "Lord drew near," Backus later remarked with satisfaction, and the assembly was deeply moved. Following the meeting, a middle-aged woman approached the young preacher and recounted her religious experiences. Two months earlier, she had passed through a "change in her body equalent [equivalent] to Death, so that She had ben intirely free from any disorder in her Body or Corruption in her Soul ever Since." This was more than a fortuitous stretch of good health, for she also believed that her new physical and spiritual incorruptibility would last until the end of time and that she would live on earth until "Christs personal coming." Sarah Prentice declared herself to be sinless and immortal. She was also the wife of a Congregational clergyman.[69]

Contemporary critics derided Prentice's extravagant claims to immortality, and she has remained an historical oddity ever since. But Prentice was not the only person venting "Strange things" to Backus during the first decade of his ministry. Throughout the turbulent 1750s, Backus confronted numerous eruptions of what he called an "antinomian spirit" among the Strict Congregational and Separate Baptist churches. Less than a year after his ordination in 1748, he detected a "false Spirit" at work in the towns straddling the Rhode Island border in Bristol County. Conversations with colleagues brought troubling news from across New England of overzealous lay men and women who sought to make the "Spirit the rule instead of the word." Visiting his family in Norwich, Backus received reports of "Carnal antinomens" committing brazen acts of adultery in several Separate churches in eastern Connecticut. An itinerating tour of the northern frontier in 1751 brought him into contact with Richard Woodbury and the remnants of Nicholas Gilman's visionary congre-

68. McLoughlin, ed., *Diary of Isaac Backus*, I, 261, 267, 284, 290.
69. Ibid., I, 293–294.

gation in Durham, New Hampshire. Backus was troubled by the "awful wild extreams" into which they had run. Even his own sermons occasionally ignited a "wild-fire" that he could scarce contain.[70]

At the center of these "Grose and Scandolus" controversies stood Sarah Prentice and the small clique of perfectionists living on the borders of Easton, Norton, and Taunton, Massachusetts, with whom she worshipped. The purported errors promulgated by such "Sick Brain Enthusiasts" reminded some Congregational clergymen of the excesses of the Family of Love, a mystical sect persecuted in seventeenth-century England, whose members denied original sin and the resurrection of the body and averred true believers could live sinless lives of Christ-like perfection on Earth. As was the case with the Familists, the motley triumvirate of heresies that Prentice and her fellow radicals espoused—lay-administered adult baptism, spiritual marriage, and immortalism—formed no coherent denomination; yet each constituted a direct extension of the revivals of the 1740s. Perfectionist beliefs and practices flourished wherever weaknesses in the Congregational establishment allowed new converts to step out of the Calvinistical faith of their ancestors and into the Pentecostal world of the Apostles. For the most zealous Whitefieldarians, conversion was only the beginning. Belief in the indwelling presence of the Holy Spirit raised troubling theological questions regarding the relationship of corrupt bodies to regenerate souls. During the second half of the eighteenth century, Prentice and other likeminded seekers set out on a ceaseless quest for spiritual purity that led many of them to question all institutions—churches,

70. JCH, 422; McLoughlin, ed., *Diary of Isaac Backus*, I, 47, 62, 91, 149, 294, 570; Isaac Backus to Elijah Backus, Apr. 1, 1749, no. 309, *IBP*. For a pejorative assessment that marginalizes Prentice as an example of New England's "lunatic fringe," see Francis G. Walett, "Shadrack Ireland and the 'Immortals' of Colonial New England," in Frederick S. Allis, Jr., ed., *Sibley's Heir: A Volume in Memory of Clifford Kenyon Shipton*, CSM, *Publications*, LIX (Boston, 1982), 541–550 (quote, 543). My discussion of Prentice and the Winnecunnet perfectionists expands on the interpretive framework sketched by Richard Godbeer in *Sexual Revolution in Early America*, Gender Relations in the American Experience (Baltimore, 2002), 243–245, as well as the careful chronology of events reconstructed in *SHG*, VIII, 248–257; J. M. Bumsted, "Presbyterianism in 18th Century Massachusetts: The Formation of a Church at Easton, 1752," *Journal of Presbyterian History*, XLVI (1968), 243–253; William G. McLoughlin, "Free Love, Immortalism, and Perfectionism in Cumberland, Rhode Island, 1748–1768," *Rhode Island History*, XXXIII (1974), 67–85; and Ross W. Beales, Jr., "The Ecstasy of Sarah Prentice: Death, Re-Birth, and the Great Awakening in Grafton, Massachusetts," *Historical Journal of Massachusetts*, XXV (1997), 101–123. See also Erik R. Seeman, "Sarah Prentice and the Immortalists: Sexuality, Piety, and the Body in Eighteenth-Century New England," in Merril D. Smith, ed., *Sex and Sexuality in Early America* (New York, 1998), 116–131; Seeman, *Pious Persuasions: Laity and Clergy in Eighteenth-Century New England*, Early America: History, Context, Culture (Baltimore, 1999), 139–146; and Seeman, "'It is Better to Marry Than to Burn': Anglo-American Attitudes toward Celibacy, 1600–1800," *Journal of Family History*, XXIV (1999), 397–419.

communities, and families—and to generate startling new conceptions of the body and sexuality.[71]

Backus groped toward respectability as he discovered that his zeal for the gifts of the Spirit paled compared to that of other lay men and women in the region. But, where Backus recoiled from the "awful Spread" of "Antinomian principles," perfectionist seekers surged ahead. Within two generations, many of them would emerge at the forefront of the earliest networks of Methodists, Freewill Baptists, Universalists, Shakers, and other radical sectarians that ran roughshod over greater New England during the final decades of the eighteenth century.[72]

▪ There was little reason in 1740 to suspect that Norton, Massachusetts, would develop into a center of radical religious dissent. Located less than twenty miles from Isaac Backus's Separate church at Titicut, the small hamlet experienced a revival season commensurate with many of the Old Colony's rural hinterland parishes. Following visits by prominent itinerants Gilbert Tennent, Daniel Rogers, and Eleazar Wheelock, church admissions in town soared to nine times the annual average in 1741 and 1742. Within a few years, however, town minister Joseph Avery grew disenchanted with the "gross Errors in Doctrine, and many absurd Things in Practice" that threatened to "overthrow the Peace and good Order" of the established churches. In 1745,

71. McLoughlin, ed., *Diary of Isaac Backus,* I, 89; Edward Billing, diaries, 1743–1756, November 1748, Henry N. Flynt Library, Historic Deerfield, Deerfield, Mass. For a helpful review of the extensive literature on the Family of Love, see Christopher Carter, "The Family of Love and Its Enemies," *Sixteenth-Century Journal,* XXXVII (2006), 651–672.

72. Ebenezer Devotion, *The Mutual Obligation upon Ministers, and People, to Hear, and Speak the Word of GOD* (New London, Conn., 1750), 10; Eleazar Wheelock to Joseph Bellamy, Mar. 13, 1749, no. 749213, *EWP.* I borrow the useful concept of "Greater New England" from Jaffee, *People of the Wachusett,* 163. Most historians of new religious movements in early America trace the rise of the Shakers, Mormons, and other religious sectarian and utopian communities to the social ferment produced by the American Revolution and the rapid restructuring of American society during the early Republic. Prominent studies in this grain include Louis J. Kern, *An Ordered Love: Sex Roles and Sexuality in Victorian Utopias— the Shakers, the Mormons, and the Oneida Community* (Chapel Hill, N.C., 1981); Lawrence Foster, *Religion and Sexuality: The Shakers, the Mormons, and the Oneida Community* (Urbana, Ill., 1984); and Paul E. Johnson and Sean Wilentz, *The Kingdom of Matthias: A Story of Sex and Salvation in 19th-Century America,* updated ed. (New York, 2012). The argument in this section draws, instead, on the "social and cultural geography" thesis proposed by John L. Brooke, although I contend that perfectionist beliefs and practices emerged directly from the Whitefieldian revivals rather than from a transplanted mix of European "hermatic occult" traditions and radical German pietism, as he asserts in *The Refiner's Fire: The Making of Mormon Cosmology, 1644–1844* (New York, 1994), 33. I have also benefitted from Stephen C. Taysom, *Shakers, Mormons, and Religious Worlds: Conflicting Visions, Contested Boundaries,* Religion in North America (Bloomington, Ind., 2011), 100–151.

he placed his name at the head of a published list of Bristol County clergymen who closed their pulpits to George Whitefield.[73]

As Avery's opposition to the revivals increased, embittered parishioners mounted a sustained assault on his ministry. Several challenged him on ecclesiastical grounds, charging the Norton minister with refusing to call church meetings, ordain deacons and elders, visit parish families, or catechize children. To this chorus of complaints, an outspoken revival faction added their militant voices. Sarah Campbell asserted that she would "sooner burn at the stake" than listen to Avery's unedifying sermons. Her husband vehemently proclaimed that Avery and his supporters had "suckt at the breast of the church of Rome, else they could not have swallowed down and digested such Doctrine." The Norton church suspended the Campbells and a dozen other members for their vitriolic outbursts, but Avery soon met with a similar fate. Branded a "person not able nor Capebell to sustaine the office of a minester," the beleaguered clergyman was dismissed by a church vote in 1748. For the remainder of his life, he served the congregation in an ignominious capacity by sweeping the meetinghouse floor after each Sabbath.[74]

During the months leading up to Avery's removal, the Norton dissenters withdrew from communion in protest and worshipped in the home of James Briggs near Winnecunnet Pond on the outskirts of town. On September 7, 1748, they organized a Separate church, called William Carpenter to serve as their minister, and adopted the Mansfield articles of faith. Among the fifty-three original members, half were former members of Avery's church in Norton; the rest hailed from the adjacent towns of Easton and Taunton. Most of the separatists were Whitefieldian converts who had joined the church only a few years earlier. The small group of families that formed the nucleus of Carpenter's breakaway congregation grew closer during the ensuing years as young dissenters married within the tightly knit community. John Phinney, Sr., his wife, and their four children, for example, made up one-eighth of the total membership. Two of his daughters married members of the Briggs and Campbell families. None of these families were unusually poor, by prevailing standards. Phinney and Stephen Blanchard, whose names appear on a 1735 Norton tax list, fared well when compared with their neighbors.[75]

73. *The Testimony of an Association of Ministers Convened at Marlborough* ... (Boston, 1745), 5–6. See also EWD, 238–239; DDR, Oct. 28–Nov. 4, 1741; Clark, *History of the Town of Norton*, 167–168; J. M. Bumsted, "Religion, Finance, and Democracy in Massachusetts: The Town of Norton as a Case Study," *JAH*, LVII (1971), 827–831.

74. Clark, *History of the Town of Norton*, 107–108, 112, 130.

75. Ibid., 443–451; Seth Babbitt et al. to Canterbury Separate church, Aug. 15, 1748, no. 45, JTC; Howard Finney, Sr., comp., *Finney-Phinney Families in America: Descendants of John*

Absent from the earliest roster of Norton Separates was Phinney's youngest son, Solomon. A new convert who had joined Avery's church at the peak of the revivals, he had also been suspended from communion in 1748. The following year, Solomon moved to the town of Cumberland on the disputed border between Massachusetts and Rhode Island. There he set up housekeeping with his wife, a young woman named Molly Bennet. There were three problems with this arrangement. No justice of the peace or minister presided over their marriage. In addition, Molly might already have been pregnant at the time of their union. Most ominously, she was already married.[76]

The Cumberland adultery controversy might have been just another example of the youthful sexual experimentation that marked the middle decades of the eighteenth century, were it not for the religious nature of the affair. Neighbors later recalled that this was a time of "considerable discourse about marrying in the new covenant." Many young converts used marital metaphors drawn from the Song of Solomon to articulate their ecstatic experiences of conversion; some sought spouses who were "Experimentally acquainted with Vital Religion." Riding ministers, including notable Whitefieldarians such as Eleazar Wheelock, inveighed "against converted wives continuing with unconverted Husbands." Hannah Heaton recalled how James Davenport attempted to dissuade her from marrying any man who could not testify to the indwelling presence of the Holy Spirit, citing 2 Corinthians 6:14. The biblical injunction to be "not unequally yoked together with unbelievers" also provided a touchstone for many Separates as they withdrew from established churches. Unlike their puritan ancestors, Strict Congregationalists and Separate Baptists conceived of marriage as an "Instetution of God"—a divinely ordained union of souls—rather than a civil or economic arrangement. Separatists frequently elected to wait on God for further direction in the choice of a spouse. The Canterbury lawyer and separatist exhorter Elisha Paine believed that God had sent an angel to "Incline" his heart toward his future wife, asserting that they could no more doubt the "clear Demonstrations" of the divine will than question their own conversions. Even Isaac Backus stated in his wedding vows that the "all-seeing God" had revealed to him with "Blessed Clearness" that Susanna Mason was to be "my Companion and an helper meet for me." Molly Bennet pressed this emerging trend in revival discourse to its logical con-

---

Finney of Plymouth and Barnstable, Mass., and Bristol, R. I., of Samuel Finney of Philadelphia, Pa., and of Robert Finney of New London, Pa. (Richmond, Va., 1957), 8; Norton, Mass., tax records, 1735, 1840–1854, microfilm no. 903403, GSU.

76. Clark, *History of the Town of Norton,* 109, 167; McLoughlin, "Free Love, Immortalism, and Perfectionism," *Rhode Island History,* XXXIII (1974), 84.

clusion when she informed a neighbor that Solomon Phinney was "made for her." The two were "man and wife Enternally [internally] but not Externally," she maintained, for God had "made known to them that it was so." By 1750, Bennet, Phinney, and other zealous separatists had begun to distinguish these internal, "Spiritual," or "new-covenant marriages," which had been ordained by God, from the corrupt civil arrangements established by the magistrates of "Bablylon."[77]

Molly's father, Ebenezer Ward, a Separate minister who preached to small gatherings in their home during the late 1740s, defended his daughter's alleged infidelity. Shortly before her thirteenth birthday, Molly had married Joseph Bennet, one of her father's parishioners, but, in a strange turn of events three years later, the young mariner disavowed their marriage. "Ward's daughter was not his wife," Bennet declared unexpectedly, and "he had no more right to lie with her than any other woman." The members of Ward's congregation labored to disabuse Bennet of his "deluded" notions, and the lay preacher even offered to provide his son-in-law with an annual annuity to care for his troubled daughter whom contemporaries described as a "person subject to fits." Bennet rejected all offers and promptly shipped out to sea. Rumors circulated that he would never come back.[78]

Returning unexpectedly a year later, Bennet discovered his young wife in an adulterous relationship with a fellow parishioner. Molly had been living with Phinney in her father's house since his abrupt departure, and she was pregnant. Bennet immediately sued Phinney and his father-in-law. Ward's role in the strange affair remains unclear. The separatist preacher later stated that he had opposed the union until his parishioners began to debate the merits of internal, or new covenant, marriage. He tenuously indulged his daughter's wishes but continued to believe that her relationship with Phinney was not a sexual one, since the couple allegedly lay with a Bible between them. Bennet,

77. McLoughlin, "Free Love, Immortalism, and Perfectionism," *Rhode Island History*, XXXIII (1974), 82, 85; Samuel Phillips Savage to Gilbert Tennent, Feb. 2, 1742, SSP II; David Hall to Eleazar Wheelock, Sept. 23, 1741, no. 741523, *EWP;* Lacey, ed., *World of Hannah Heaton*, 13, 21–22; Jedidiah Hide to Isaac Backus, Oct. 10, 1750, no. 340, *IBP;* Elisha Paine to Obadiah Johnson, Dec. 18, 1745, no. 30, JTC; McLoughlin, ed., *Diary of Isaac Backus,* I, 65, 141, III, 1536; Isaac Backus, "Some Facts and Remarks about Baptisms at Norton and Easton," June 30, 1781, [15], no. 1480, *IBP.* On puritan attitudes toward marriage, see Edmund S. Morgan, *The Puritan Family: Religion and Domestic Relations in Seventeenth-Century New England*, rev. ed. (New York, 1966), 29–64.

78. McLoughlin, "Free Love, Immortalism, and Perfectionism," *Rhode Island History*, XXXIII (1974), 82. See also *Vital Records of Newton, Massachusetts, to the Year 1850* (Boston, 1905), 202; *Vital Records of Attleborough Massachusetts to the End of the Year 1849* (Salem, Mass., 1934), 595. On the "permissive sexual climate" of eighteenth-century New England, see Godbeer, *Sexual Revolution in Early America,* 15 (quote), 227–263.

however, maintained that Ward had "Imbibed and Cherished Certain Wicked and Strange Tenets and Principles Destructive to Government and against the Matrimonial laws and rights of the English Nation." He claimed that Ward had threatened his daughter, telling Molly that it was sinful to dwell with an unconverted husband. Turning Bennet out of his house, Ward had conspired with Phinney—a "person of like Pernicious and Evil Principles"—to seduce his own daughter. The courts agreed. Ward was jailed, Phinney received a stiff fine, and the cuckolded mariner obtained a divorce.[79]

Meanwhile, the Norton Separate church had dissolved into competing factions as the tide of Baptist schisms crested across southern New England. Minister William Carpenter initially sided with the pedobaptists, but many of his parishioners—including Solomon Phinney's extended family—did not. Around this time, Ebenezer Ward, who had served his jail sentence in Providence, appeared in Norton. The unrepentant Rhode Island separatist preacher championed adult baptism along with his unusual theological notions regarding spiritual marriage. In December 1749, he plunged John Phinney, Jr., under the icy waters of Winnecunnet Pond. Shortly thereafter, Phinney and several other separatists, including Phineas Briggs and Peter Soulard, baptized a score of other Norton dissenters. Although none of these gifted laymen had ever been ordained, they quickly gained the support of a majority of the members of Carpenter's church.[80]

By the spring of 1751, Phinney, Soulard, and the other dissenters had taken the decisive step of withdrawing from communion again, this time from the Separate church in Norton. Carpenter, who continued to sprinkle infants well into the 1750s and believed in the necessity of ordination, called for a council to discipline his former parishioners. Once in 1751, then two more times in 1753, Isaac Backus and his colleagues gathered to address the "awful erours" relating to baptism and marriage that had infected the Separate congregation in Norton. It was clear from the outset of the conflict that Molly Bennet and Solomon Phinney—who moved with Ward to Norton and persisted in their irregular marriage—espoused beliefs consistent with those of their extended family and fellow radicals at Winnecunnet Pond. John Phinney, Jr., approved of his brother's "new-covenant" marriage. He, too, had concluded that "two unconverted persons coming together in the marriage relation were not man

---

79. McLoughlin, "Free Love, Immortalism, and Perfectionism," *Rhode Island History*, XXXIII (1974), 82–83 (quotes), 85.

80. Backus, "Some Facts and Remarks About Baptisms at Norton and Easton," June 30, 1781, [1, 14], no. 1480, *IBP.* See also Isaac Backus, *A Church History of New-England, Extending from 1690 to 1784 . . .*, 2 vols. (Providence, R.I., 1784), II, 185–186, 209.

and Wife in the sight of God strictly speaking." Since marriage was a "Spiritual Union," authorities had no right to regulate matters ordained by God. Phinney's father added a millennial overtone in his defense of spiritual marriage, asserting that it was a sign of the coming "new Jerusalem." Convinced they "had not got the right women," two other Separates abandoned their lawful wives for a brief period, while a third took up "with a married man and went away with him" to New Jersey.[81]

Although a few of the Winnecunnet separatists eventually renounced their irregular marital practices, the majority refused to retract their perfectionist beliefs. In defending his right to perform the sacrament of baptism without an external ordination, John Phinney, Jr., relied on the entrenched tradition of biblical impulses. He had expressed reservations about Ward's right to re-baptize adult believers, but his fears melted away when the Holy Spirit illuminated his mind through the words of God to Peter in Acts 10:20, "I have sent him." Peter Soulard and several others also believed they had received an internal call to perform baptisms and administer the Lord's Supper without prior ordination or ecclesiastical license. John Phinney, Sr., maintained that God called his son to teach and baptize, and he "went into the water with him in obedience to Gods command." Mary, the wife of John, Sr., asserted she had obtained "divine teaching into baptism." If a "person does but obey the command of God in baptism," she argued defiantly before Backus and the assembled Separate leaders during one of the ecclesiastical councils, "it is no matter if the devil was the administrator!" In addition, several dissenters boldly proclaimed that they were "Getting into a state of Perfection in this World so as to be free from all Sinckings And trouble, and so that they Shall Never Die." Soulard even described an unusual ritual in which the separatists purged their souls by pretending to "vomit up their Sins."[82]

Following two days of heated meetings, Backus and his colleagues had heard enough. Fifteen members of the Norton Separate church sided with Carpenter. John Phinney, Jr., and the rest of the recalcitrant saints—roughly half of the church—were excommunicated for espousing perfectionist ideals

---

81. McLoughlin, ed., *Diary of Isaac Backus*, I, 141, 570–571; Backus, "Some Facts and Remarks about Baptisms at Norton and Easton," June 30, 1781, [6, 15], no. 1480, *IBP*, Samuel Peck, "At a Council of 4 Churches," Mar. 5, 1753, [2], no. 402, Backus, notes on church councils, June 27–Sept. 18, 1764, no. 638. Carpenter's baptismal records may be found in Norton, Mass., First Baptist Church Records, 1747–1835, Andover-Newton Theological Seminary, Newton, Mass.

82. Peck, "Council of 4 Churches," Mar. 5, 1753, [4], no. 402, *IBP*, Backus, "Some Facts and Remarks about Baptisms at Norton and Easton," June 30, 1781, [6–8], no. 1480; McLoughlin, ed., *Diary of Isaac Backus*, I, 141

of spiritual marriage and sanctioning the baptismal immersions performed by Ward and the other brethren. Three months later and less than ten miles away from the shores of Winnecunnet Pond, Sarah Prentice declared her immortality.[83]

■ Born in England around 1716, Sarah Prentice was the daughter of a wealthy Huguenot merchant named Nathaniel Sartell, who migrated to New England and settled in Groton, Massachusetts. Family folklore suggests that she was a precociously pious youth, although it is unlikely that she passed through a distinct conversion experience before 1740. On October 26, 1732, Sartell married a young Harvard College graduate named Solomon Prentice. An unassuming, quiet student, Prentice had recently been ordained over the newly gathered church in Grafton, Massachusetts. Sarah joined in full communion shortly before the birth of the first of their ten children later that year. The following decade brought more births and baptisms and several traumatic family deaths. Then her life took a radical turn.[84]

Like many church members thrown into consternation during the Whitefieldian revivals, Sarah experienced a wrenching conversion. The proximate cause of her religious convictions was the unexpected death of her father in Groton on January 16, 1742. Three days later, Solomon described his wife mired in deep distress. "Can I Mourn for a dead Father," she exclaimed, "when I have a dead *Soul!*" Repudiating her previous "Prof[e]ssion and Outward Shew of Godliness," Sarah consigned herself to eternal damnation. As her spiritual crisis intensified, Sarah frequently cried out to Jesus for saving grace. Then, one night, beaten down by her sense of sin, her body went taut, "Nerves and Sinews" contracted, and her tongue stiffened and "felt like an Iron bar in her Mouth." Prentice begged for the strength to speak that "She Might Shew forth the Wondras work of the Lord," and her prayers were answered. Biblical impulses from the Song of Solomon rained down on her soul, and she cried out *"its Lovely! its Lovely!"* As Jesus, the mystical bridegroom, penetrated her heart, the minister's wife counted herself among the blessed saints at last.[85]

Buoyant following the conversions of his wife and several other parish-

83. Backus, "Some Facts and Remarks about Baptisms at Norton and Easton," June 30, 1781, [3–4], no. 1480, *IBP*; McLoughlin, ed., *Diary of Isaac Backus*, I, 276, 294.

84. Grafton, Mass., First Church Record Book Hassanamisco, 1731–1774, 18, 22, 25–26, 29–30, CL (available online at NEHH); *SHG*, VIII, 248–257. For genealogical information and family lore, see C. J. F. Binney, comp., *The History and Genealogy of the Prentice, or Prentiss Family, in New England, Etc., from 1631 to 1883*, 2d ed. (Boston, 1883), 11–14.

85. Ross W. Beales, Jr., ed., "Solomon Prentice's Narrative of the Great Awakening," MHS, *Proceedings*, 3d Ser., LXXXIII (1971), 134–135.

ioners, Solomon labored to expand the burgeoning revival in Grafton by encouraging numerous riding ministers to visit his awakened parish. There was no shortage of visitors, for Grafton and the towns of southern Worcester County stood at the crossroads of New England. Jonathan Edwards, James Davenport, and a host of itinerants preached their way through the region in 1742. Observers reported that the "glorious work of the Lord" was in full swing among "all Ranks and Ages of Persons" in Grafton later that spring and throughout the summer. By the end of the year, Prentice had admitted nearly a score of new converts to the Grafton church, most of whom, like his wife, had experienced what he called a "thoro' And Saving Change."[86]

In January 1743, Solomon organized the "Grafton Exercises," outdoor revival meetings that drew large crowds and featured preaching from morning to night by regional clergymen. He repeated the event in Mendon, Massachusetts, one month later. To Prentice, the piercing outcries, visionary phenomena, and somatic conversions that attended the meetings were plentiful showers of the Holy Spirit; but, to others, including one strident newspaper critic, all the roaring and gesticulating, howling and hugging, seemed a "Wretched Delusion." A wild melee broke out at one point, after Hopkinton minister Samuel Barrett ordered the constable to remove several disruptive congregants. During the months that followed, Prentice clashed with his colleagues in the Marlborough ministerial association over theological matters, the experiences of new converts, church practices, and published revival reports in the *Christian History*. Once, he delivered an angry sermon in which he attacked the growing number of revival opposers. By the summer of 1743, he had stopped attending their meetings altogether.[87]

The Grafton minister's problems deepened the following spring, when a group of aggrieved parishioners charged him with thirty articles of misconduct. The staunch revival opposers condemned Prentice for preaching that true Christians possessed perfect assurance of their own salvation and that it was their prerogative to discern sainthood in others, for asserting that the heartfelt prayers of the unregenerate were abominable in the eyes of God, and for praying from the pulpit that those who opposed the revivals "might be struck dead in a Moment in their Sins." Other complaints stemmed from

---

86. Beales, ed., "Solomon Prentice's Narrative," MHS, *Procds.*, 3d Ser., LXXXIII (1971), 134, 136–137. See also Tracy, *Great Awakening*, 207–210; Hall, diaries, May 17, 1742; and Grafton First Church Record Book Hassanamisco, 35–37.

87. Walett, ed., *Diary of Ebenezer Parkman*, 89; *Boston Evening-Post*, Mar. 14, 1743. See also Beales, ed., "Solomon Prentice's Narrative," MHS, *Procds.*, 3d Ser., LXXXIII (1971), 138–140; and Marlborough Association of Ministers, Records, 1725–1802, 43–46, 49, CL (available online at NEHH).

Prentice's unguarded expressions, including his controversial pronouncement that fewer than one-quarter of the full church members in Grafton had passed through the new birth. Opponents rebuked Prentice for supporting James Davenport's gospel labors and allowing lay exhorters such as Elisha Paine to preach from his pulpit, while simultaneously condemning his purportedly un-converted colleagues in the Marlborough Association along with their flocks, who would "tumble over them into Hell" on the Day of Judgment. And, they were uneasy with Prentice's millennial speculations that New Englanders lived in extraordinary times during which the charismatic gifts of the Spirit would be poured out on the faithful.[88]

The ecclesiastical council that met in October 1744 to resolve the dispute confirmed twenty of the articles of grievance and enjoined Prentice to "receive them as Motives to his Humiliation and future Caution." The Grafton minister initially appeared contrite, but rumors soon circulated that he planned to ignore the published *Result* and had no intention of making a public confession for his conduct. "I find and feel Myselfe very much hurt" by the council, he wrote in the Grafton church record book. Prentice severed all ties with the Marlborough Association just three months later and demanded that his name be razed from their records. Westborough minister Ebenezer Parkman complied and scratched Prentice's signature from the association's covenant in a series of bold, crosshatched strokes. And, so, the conflict in Grafton continued to smolder. "A great storm seem'd to be rising," Parkman warned in his diary.[89]

Ministers watched with mounting concern as events in Grafton and the surrounding towns spiraled out of control. During the months following a visit from George Whitefield during his second New England preaching tour in 1745, Prentice's parish was beset by a wave of traveling separatist lay preachers from eastern Connecticut bent on sewing discord within the established churches. They included Thomas Marsh of Mansfield and the Paine brothers, Elisha and Solomon, of Canterbury. By the end of the year, a small group of disaffected parishioners had left the Grafton church. The conflict quickly en-

88. *A Result of a Council of Churches at Grafton, October 2d, 1744* [Boston, 1744], 3–4. For Prentice's early support of the Paine brothers, see Ebenezer Parkman to Robert Breck, Aug. 22, 1743, Early Springfield Manuscripts, Ser. I, Lyman and Merrie Wood Museum of Springfield History, Springfield, Mass.

89. *Result of a Council of Churches at Grafton*, 10; Grafton First Church Record Book Hassanamisco, 132, 139; Walett, ed., *Diary of Ebenezer Parkman*, 110, 154. See also James F. Cooper, Jr., and Kenneth P. Minkema, eds., *The Colonial Church Records of the First Church of Reading (Wakefield) and the First Church of Rumney Marsh (Revere)*, CSM, *Pubs.*, LXXII (Boston, 2006), 184; Marlborough Association of Ministers, Records, 3, 50, CL; and Hall, diaries, Oct. 10, 1744.

gulfed David Hall's parish in the neighboring town of Sutton, where more than two dozen church members were admonished for withdrawing from communion. Paine's militant separatism shaped much of the escalating controversy. According to Hall, dissenters in Grafton and Sutton had embraced "false perceptions of a pure Church on earth and of Infallably knowing the Brethren." Their commitment to exercising gifts of spiritual discernment had unleashed a "Horrible spirit of Judging all others as unbelievers, or spiritually dead, who will not join with them in everything." The Separates were led by Ezekiel Cole, a zealous native American revival convert from Grafton who claimed to be the typological descendant of the "Captain of the Lords Hosts" described in Joshua 5:14. Hall was appalled by the "wild delusions" that he witnessed during their tumultuous worship exercises. Women preached and exhorted in public, while other members of the dissenting faction experienced ecstatic visions and held "sensible Communion with God in sleep."[90]

Caught up in the burgeoning revival radicalism, Sarah appears to have taken the lead in fomenting "Familistical and antinomian Errors" among the Separates in Grafton and Sutton. According to her husband, she "continued drinking of the Streams of Gods Delight, almost daily for Several Months" following her dramatic conversion experience in 1742. Alternating with periods of illness and bodily weakness, her raptures intensified during the next few years. Convinced she possessed "Knowledge of the Spiritual Status of Persons," Sarah interrupted her husband's Sabbath meetings and denounced his congregation as "no Church of Christ." Gossip regarding her "Visions and Revelations" swirled about town. She laid aside her household duties and might have even embraced the practice of marrying in the new covenant. Sarah defended her immediate revelations during a heated conversation with Parkman in the spring of 1747. The Westborough minister upbraided her for "giving occasion to others to suspect criminal Freedoms with the other sex, under the splendid Guise of Spiritual Love and Friendship." That same day, Sarah "declar'd herself a Separate." She remains the only known minister's spouse to have taken the unprecedented step of withdrawing from communion in an established Congregational church during the eighteenth century.[91]

90. Hall, diaries, June 5, 1747, June 6, 1749; Sutton, Mass., Separate Church to Canterbury, Conn., Separate Church, Sept. 28, 1752, 2, no. 99, JTC; Walett, ed., *Diary of Ebenezer Parkman*, 101. For Hall's involvement in controversies of the period, see Winiarski, "New Perspectives on the Northampton Communion Controversy I," *Jonathan Edwards Studies*, III (2013), 269–273.

91. Hall, diaries, Aug. 17, 1743; Beales, ed., "Solomon Prentice's Narrative," MHS, *Procds.*, 3d Ser., LXXXIII (1971), 135; Walett, ed., *Diary of Ebenezer Parkman*, 154 (see also 117, 120–121, 127, 151).

Solomon found himself fighting a two-front war, attacked on one side by colleagues and parishioners who questioned his irregular revival tactics and on the other by his wife and an emerging Separate faction that criticized his lack of zeal. Collective rituals of fasting and prayer did little to heal the gaping breach in fellowship. Several parishioners began worshipping in Parkman's more temperate parish in Westborough. Once, during the spring of 1746, Prentice noted that sixty families refused to attend the Lord's Supper. His own behavior was equally erratic, however, as he engaged in heated disputes with ministerial colleagues and sporadically failed to appear for Sabbath exercises. With the Grafton church disintegrating, the beleaguered minister unleashed his frustrations on Sarah. Solomon beat her savagely and tore at her clothes, perhaps in response to the allegations of sexual infidelity that had arisen among the Separates in Grafton.[92]

The "Grim and formidable Evils" of both the minister and his wife proved too much for the Grafton townspeople to bear. Less than two months after Sarah withdrew from communion, the church initiated disciplinary hearings through which they removed Solomon from the Grafton pulpit. The second council that gathered to confirm the vote of dismissal refused to recommend Solomon for another pastorate. Present at the hearings, Sarah burst forth in a rage, defending her separatism and warning the assembled parishioners and ministers "not to fight against God." Later that spring, Sarah and more than a dozen other Grafton dissenters appeared before the Worcester County grand jury to answer charges of "not attending the publick Worship of God in the Ussuall place." The court dismissed the charges, citing the defendants' liberty of conscience, but not before offering a stern rebuke in which they condemned the Grafton Separates for being "Actuated by an overheated and blind Zeal."[93]

After filling the vacant pulpit in Bellingham, Massachusetts, for several weeks during the summer of 1747, Solomon secured a call to the church at Easton, a small parish located next to the troubled town of Norton. Although his ordination was observed with "Decency and Order," according to one report, Prentice quickly discovered that his new congregation was in complete disarray. During the first year of his ministry, he labored to rally his parishioners. Prentice drafted a covenant, initiated disciplinary actions against moral backsliders, and presided as moderator over the council that dismissed

92. Walett, ed., *Diary of Ebenezer Parkman*, 127, 129, 148, 154, 156–157; Grafton First Church Record Book Hassanamisco, 39, 148–152.

93. Walett, ed., *Diary of Ebenezer Parkman*, 157; Worcester County, Mass., Records of the Court of General Sessions of the Peace, 1731–1862, 20 vols., II, 193, microfilm no. 859239, GSU. See also Grafton First Church Record Book Hassanamisco, 153–159.

Joseph Avery from his Norton pastorate. Cultivating a reputation for respectability, Prentice seemed to be making the most of his second chance. "I have Enjoy'd Much health, in person, and family, and am yet Labouring I trust in the Lord," he acknowledged, "and I hope not without prospect of Success."[94]

As Solomon worked to resurrect his tarnished career, Sarah continued to follow the leadings of the Holy Spirit. "My Wife is So Strong a Separate," the newly installed Easton clergyman confided in a 1748 letter to a New Jersey colleague, that "She has not heard me Preach but a few times for 2 years past." The Separate churches were the "Lords work," Sarah declared, and they prospered "wherever there are Christians, in Spite of all Opposition from Earth and Hell." No minister could "pray with the Spirit of God" against them, for the "New English Churches are degenerated and gone away from the Rules of Gospel Dissapline." God was justified in reducing them by violent schisms. Solomon disagreed with her arguments, although he was forced to admit that religion languished everywhere in the region except among the Separates, who had "wounded and broken" nearly every church in Bristol County.[95]

Resolute in her opposition to her husband's ministry, Sarah set out in search of like-minded radicals. She found "Glorious things adoing" a few miles away among the small cluster of perfectionist families living along the shores of Winnecunnet Pond. Like her new neighbors, Prentice possessed certain assurance of her salvation, championed Spirit-driven forms of ecstatic worship, and endorsed—and might have practiced—spiritual marriage. It was a short step to embrace the principle of believer's baptism. Prentice was likely in attendance when Ebenezer Ward arrived in Norton and plunged John Phinney, Jr., and several dissenters. One year later, she followed suit. Solomon was abroad that day, but he recorded her immersion on December 5, 1750, by Winnecunnet perfectionist Peter Soulard, whom the Easton minister condemned as a "most despicable layman." On his return, Solomon reportedly flew into a fit of rage and dowsed Sarah with a pail of water screaming "Ah, it's water, it's water is it that you want? Well, you shall have water."[96]

The Prentices' fortunes soon divided. Solomon's once-promising ministry in Easton bogged down in an acrimonious dispute over the location of a new

94. *Boston Gazette,* Nov. 24, 1747; Solomon Prentice to Jacob Green, Feb. 6, 1748, box 223, SGC II. See also William L. Chaffin, *History of the Town of Easton Massachusetts* (Cambridge, Mass., 1886), 106–107, 793–797; and Clark, *History of the Town of Norton,* 116–126.

95. Prentice to Green, Feb. 6, 1748, box 223, SGC II.

96. Prentice to Green, Feb. 6, 1748, box 223, SGC II; Chaffin, *History of the Town of Easton,* 136n; Frederick Clifton Pierce, *History of Grafton, Worcester County, Massachusetts: From Its Early Settlement by the Indians in 1647 to the Present Time, 1879* (Worcester, Mass., 1879), 548.

meetinghouse. Following a series of councils, the minister, along with the majority of full church members, renounced the "brokenness of the Constitution of the Congregational Church in New England" and joined the Boston Presbytery, a network of Scots-Irish churches scattered across New England. Meanwhile, Sarah continued to worship with the Winnecunnet perfectionists, whom she invited to meet in Prentice's parsonage. Solomon's willingness to accept the renegade perfectionists into his own home was a grievous affront to his parishioners in Easton; they voted to suspend him from celebrating the Lord's Supper. "Our peace and unity," he lamented, "seems to be strangely broken."[97]

Sarah professed her immortality to Isaac Backus seven months later. News of her wondrous transformation reverberated across southeastern New England, and she furthered her own notoriety by exhorting with success among the Separates in Grafton and Sutton. She likely met Shadrach Ireland for the first time during this trip. The obscure pipe fitter had abandoned his wife and children in Charlestown, Massachusetts, and was preaching to dissenting factions throughout the uplands of central New England. He, too, embraced perfectionist beliefs and once proclaimed to be the "very Person Jesus X [Christ]." Ireland also championed the controversial practice of internal marriage. Later, rumors alleged that Prentice slept with Ireland as her "spiritual Husband." She probably encouraged the wandering evangelist to visit the Winnecunnet perfectionists in Norton and Easton. Ireland made his first and only known appearance in Bristol County in September 1754, when he preached at the home of Simeon Babbitt, a member of the small community of perfectionists living near Winnecunnet Pond.[98]

Solomon's response to his wife's powerful new relationship with Ireland must have puzzled his contemporaries. He had beaten Sarah following allegations of her sexual infidelity in 1744, but, a decade later, he inexplicably embraced her controversial beliefs. Against the wishes of his parishioners, the Easton minister continued to permit the Winnecunnet perfectionists to worship in his home. He occasionally joined with them in prayer and even referred to them as his "fellow Christians" and "Servants of the Most high God." Dis-

97. Alexander Blaikie, *A History of Presbyterianism in New England: Its Introduction, Growth, Decay, Revival, and Present Mission* (Boston, 1881), 121–122; Chaffin, *History of the Town of Easton*, 136. On the meetinghouse dispute, see Bumsted, "Presbyterianism in 18th Century Massachusetts," *Journal of Presbyterian History*, XLVI (1968), 243–253.

98. McLoughlin, ed., *Diary of Isaac Backus*, I, 293–294; Walett, ed., *Diary of Ebenezer Parkman*, 279; Hall, diaries, Feb. 29, 1756 (quote); Dexter, ed., *Extracts from the Itineraries and Other Miscellanies of Ezra Stiles*, 418 (quote); "Manuscript Memoranda," *NEHGR*, LXV (1911), 381.

gruntled members of his flock appealed to the Boston Presbytery to resolve the matter. A council convened in Easton during the fall of 1754 and suspended Prentice for four months. According to the church records, Solomon was censured for "countenancing vagrant lay teachers" and allowing the perfectionists to "pray and talk about the Scriptures" in his house. Plymouth civil magistrate Josiah Cotton claimed to know better, noting in his memoirs that Prentice had been silenced for "adhering too much to his Wifes notions of Immortality."[99]

Solomon abandoned his pastorate in Easton and moved his family back to Grafton during the spring of 1755. There, Sarah quickly emerged as a leader in the Separate church. She exhorted and preached with surprising success, Ebenezer Parkman noted in his diary. Later that summer, Sarah itinerated all the way to Charlestown—Shadrach Ireland's former home—accompanied by another woman. "I perceive they are plung'd very deep into Errors," the Westborough minister commented, although he admitted that the traveling pair "Seem exceeding Spiritual, heavenly, and Purify'd—at least Mrs. Prentice." Solomon dined at the Westborough parsonage several weeks later, whereupon Parkman "talk'd closely with him of his Wife's pretence to Immortality" and their "Conjugal Covenant." Solomon continued to support his wife's perfectionism. He believed that Sarah was in the "Millennium State" and denied any sexual improprieties by either spouse. When Isaac Backus visited Grafton, he complained of the "loosness that has prevaild in these parts of the Land whereby many have thrown aside the use of the common means of grace, and some have pretended to be perfect and immortal." By 1757, according to David Hall, most of the Sutton Separates had returned to his church, but those in Grafton had "run into worse Errors than Ever. Mr. Prentice, and his *wife Especially* Heads them." Rumors of "Grafton witchcraft" circulated throughout the towns of central Massachusetts during this period.[100]

Parkman visited the Prentices for a final time in 1773. Solomon was pleasant, and Sarah was sociable, but the eclectic couple showed no signs of softening their uncompromising zeal. Now in his late sixties, the twice-dismissed clergyman was declining and would die within a few months. Sarah referred to her ailing husband as "Brother," using the fraternal appelation common among the Strict Congregationalists and Separate Baptists. On this occa-

---

99. Chaffin, *History of the Town of Easton*, 136–138; Blaikie, *History of Presbyterianism in New England*, 123–124; JCH, 431.

100. Walett, ed., *Diary of Ebenezer Parkman*, 290, 292; McLoughlin, ed., *Diary of Isaac Backus*, I, 430; David Hall to Jacob Green, Aug. 30, 1757, case 8, box 22, SGC I; John C. Crane, ed., "The Diary of Rev. Silas Bigelow," Worcester Society of Antiquities, *Procds.*, XVII (1900), 267.

sion, she once again related the details of her miraculous change twenty years earlier. Throughout the intervening decades, Sarah maintained, she had "not so much as Shook Hands with any Man." Once a bride of Christ and a spiritual wife, she now lived in celibate perfection.[101]

■ When Isaac Backus and a council of dissenting ministers gathered in Norton in 1753 to adjudicate the ecclesiastical disputes that had paralyzed William Carpenter's Separate church, they enjoined the Winnecunnet perfectionists to confess their "Travels" in immortalism, spiritual marriage, and other antinomian heresies. Their admonition tapped a rich vein of Whitefieldian discourse. During the revivals, observers described convicted sinners "travelling in the New birth"; new converts "travelled for sinners" in their prayers and meditations. One separatist defended her decision to withdraw from communion in a written statement that opened with an evocative greeting directed to "dear felow travilers for an never ending Eternity." Backus and other dissenters often conflated the term "travils" with "experiences." Prospective church membership candidates in the Separate churches were expected to recount their "travel from time to time" on the road to salvation. Founding pillars pledged to "travel together acording to the Gospel of Christ" and kept detailed records of their "travel in dicipline." Dissenting ministers opened their correspondence with salutations "from your Brother In Travil and Companion In Tribulation." The etymological slippage between the travels of riding ministers, the travail of the new birth, and the trials of the Separate movement was not incidental. Nathan Cole spoke for many radical Whitefieldarians of his generation when he inscribed the running heads "Spiritual Travels" and "Spiritual Tryals" on the facing pages of his autobiography. His carefully chosen words capitalized on a strikingly modern religious sensibility. They marked the eclipse of the parish-based world of the early eighteenth century and the ascendance of a combative, voluntaristic, seeker-driven culture.[102]

101. Ebenezer Parkman, diaries, 1742–1782, Feb. 23, 1773, Ebenezer Parkman Papers, 1718–1789, MHS (I thank Ross W. Beales, Jr., for sharing his transcription of Parkman's diaries).

102. McLoughlin, ed., *Diary of Isaac Backus*, I, 273; Samuel Phillips Savage, "Extract from a Letter from Piscataqua," n.d. [Dec. 3, 1741], SSP I; Lacey, ed., *World of Hannah Heaton*, 12; Josiah Cleaveland, Sr., to John Cleaveland, Dec. 2, 1746, box 1, JCP; Testimony of Sarah Martin, n.d. [April 1749], Sturbridge Separatist Church Records; Isaac Backus, "Some Brief Account of My Travels and Experiences," n.d. [Dec. 15, 1750], no. 345, *IBP*; Sutton, Mass., Separate Church to Canterbury, Conn., Separate Church, Sept. 28, 1752, 1, no. 99, JTC; Montville, Conn., Baptist Church Records, 1749–1827, 1, microfilm no. 960619, GSU; Suffield, Conn., First Baptist Church Records, 1769–1872, 5, American Baptist Historical Society, Atlanta; Drown to Paine, June 18, 1752, no. 87, JTC; NCS, 91–92, 104. On the emerg-

Sarah Prentice and the Winnecunnet perfectionists gloried in their spiritual travels—and travails. For them, the antinomian controversies of the 1750s were only the beginning. Fascinated with discrete, somatic conversion experiences; predisposed to heed biblical impulses, dreams, visions, and new revelations; committed to decentralized forms of religious authority and worship; and stridently opposed to established ministers, small clusters of inspired men and women crystallized into a coherent network that extended from the central New England uplands, across the northern frontier, and into Atlantic Canada. Even leaders of the Separate movement, including the prominent itinerant preacher Joseph Croswell, recognized that sectarians professing a wide range of perfectionist beliefs were gaining ground, as what he called a "holier than thou" subculture developed among Whitefieldian new converts and their descendants.[103]

Most of the zealous lay men and women who traveled in perfectionism during the second half of the eighteenth century hailed from one of three crucibles of sectarian unrest in southern New England. In the hinterland parishes of Bristol County, the same controversies that nearly destroyed the Norton Separate church simmered for decades and sometimes rose to a boil. New reports of "wild, antinomian Schemes" involving radical dissenters who attempted to "put away their lawful Wives and Husbands" surfaced in neighboring towns. On several occasions, Backus refused to admit members of the Winnecunnet circle to his church at Titicut. Two more councils convened in Easton in 1764 to resolve the ongoing dispute. Both ended in failure. Although a few of the excommunicated Separates renounced their "former intanglement in an antinomian spirit," the majority continued to profess their perfectionist beliefs and clung tenaciously to the authenticity of their irregular baptisms into the 1780s. By then, John Phinney, Jr., had long since died, and Ebenezer Ward had moved to Greenwich, Connecticut. Backus encountered Ward by chance in 1774 and noted that he appeared to be a "steady solid man." His grandson, the child of the spiritual union of Solomon Phinney and Molly

---

ing culture of seekerism in eighteenth-century America, see David D. Hall, "'Between the Times': Popular Religion in Eighteenth-Century British North America," in Michael V. Kennedy and William G. Shade, eds., *The World Turned Upside-Down: The State of Eighteenth-Century American Studies at the Beginning of the Twenty-First Century* (Bethlehem, Pa., 2001), 146, 153–154; and Alan Taylor, "The Free Seekers: Religious Culture in Upstate New York, 1790–1835," *Journal of Mormon History*, XXVII, no. 1 (Spring 2001), 44–66. Taylor's essay expands on the argument originally advanced in his *Liberty Men and Great Proprietors*, 123–153.

103. *Sketches of the Life, and Extracts from the Journals, and Other Writings, of the Late Joseph Croswell*, 51.

Bennett, fought in the Revolutionary War and founded a pioneer settlement near Cincinnati, Ohio, that bears the family name.[104]

In the towns surrounding Grafton, a second major network of perfectionists coalesced around a charismatic layman named Nat Smith. Converted during the 1740s, he developed a reputation for disrupting Sabbath exercises in Hopkinton, Massachusetts. Disciplined by the church and jailed for his verbal outbursts, Smith later astounded his neighbors by proclaiming that he was the "Most High God." Bedecked in a cap embroidered with the word "GOD," Smith spent much of his time riding around town in a "Holy Chair" and sounding "Ramshorns" to topple the walls of Jericho—the Hopkinton meetinghouse— just as James Davenport had done during the heady days of the revivals. His small band of perhaps a dozen followers "declared themselves IMMORTALS" and practiced spiritual marriage. Sarah Prentice allegedly worshipped with them during the 1750s.[105]

Ministers were convinced that the beliefs and practices espoused by Smith and his fellow "Live-forevers" carried them beyond the pale of Calvinism, but even these "wild enthusiasts" were merely the tip of the iceberg. A third hotbed of perfectionism developed in the separatist strongholds of eastern Connecticut. The Separate church in the Newent parish of Norwich (now Lisbon), in particular, was plunged into a "strange mistery of Iniquity" and nearly rent to pieces by marital controversies. Shortly after the breakaway congregation was organized in 1748, a prominent layman named Bliss Willoughby pronounced a young woman named Mary Smith to be his spiritual wife. For several months, Willoughby allowed his legal spouse to continue living in their house while he coupled with Smith and refused to heed the admonitions of the Newent Separates. Although Willoughby eventually renounced his adulterous relationship as a delusion of the Devil, Smith moved on and partnered with another married member of the Newent congregation, John Burnam. In a surprising turn of events, Burnam's wife approved of their match and was "charged with being confederate with her husband in striving to hid his sin." Then, in 1758, church members discovered a shocking set of papers in which Keziah, the wife of Caleb Bishop, "set forth a most wicked plan" to abandon her lawful husband

---

104. McLoughlin, ed., *Diary of Isaac Backus,* I, 572, II, 921 (see also I, 455–456, 523–524, 570–573, II, 703, 853, 879); Ebenezer Frothingham, *A Letter, Treating upon the Subject and Mode of Baptism* (Hartford, Conn., [1768]), v.

105. Dexter, ed., *Extracts from the Itineraries and Other Miscellanies of Ezra Stiles,* 418. For Smith's earlier radicalism, see *Manual of the First Congregational Church in Hopkinton, Mass.* (Boston, 1881), 44; Walett, ed., *Diary of Ebenezer Parkman,* 91, 197; and Louise Parkman Thomas, transcr., "Journal of the Rev. Israel Loring," 57, no. 12193, SA.

and live with a Baptist exhorter. "How is the Gold become dim and the most fine gold changed in fermentation," Newent elder John Palmer lamented during the peak years of the controversy. He had little choice but to "purge out the old Leaven" by excommunicating his recalcitrant parishioners for their "God provoking, family destroying and soul" damning practices.[106]

One of several scandals involving spiritual unions and new covenant marriages, the Keziah Bishop affair followed a pair of even more shocking events in the neighboring town of Canterbury. The first case involved a single woman named Mary Wilkinson, who had developed a reputation during the revivals as a "Person of Evil Name and fame." In 1746, the nearby Congregational church in the Scotland parish of Windham, Connecticut, banished Wilkinson, her mother, and two siblings after they declared that minister Ebenezer Devotion presided over a "Church of Antichrist." As Backus later indicated, Wilkinson fell in with a small clique of radicals who believed that "they had passed the first resurrection, and were prefect and immortal." By 1748, she appears to have been living with the Bishops in Canterbury. During the same month that Willoughby was censured for his marital heresy a few miles away in Newent, Wilkinson stunned the Canterbury Separates with her blasphemous outbursts. "I am Jesus Christ and You are the Divel, git you behind me Satan," she shouted at a young man named Thomas Bates. "If you Will Come and lie in my Crotch I will Bless you, and you Shall be Saved, But if you Will Not I Will Curse you and you Shall be Damned." Wilkinson pulled up her skirts, exposing her "Naked Thighs, in a very Obsean manner," and she leapt about the room "offering to Expose her nakedness forther to him."[107]

The following year, John Smith, another member of the Separate church in Canterbury, ominously declared that God had revealed Mary Smith to be his spiritual wife and would soon clear the way for their union by removing Mehetabel, his legal spouse and the mother of his four children. Separatist minister Solomon Paine feared that Smith's strange pronouncement "carried *murder* in its nature." For several months, neighbors had overheard Mary Smith uttering "dredful wishes" against Mehetabel Smith and railing that she "mit be damd eternelly." The Canterbury Separates formally admonished John and Mary during the winter of 1749 for "acting and talking Carnally at

106. Pierce, *History of Grafton*, 174n; Dexter, ed., *Extracts from the Itineraries and Other Miscellanies of Ezra Stiles*, 418; "Newint Appendix," in Bennington First Church Records, 8, 10, 12–13, 16–17, 23.

107. Dominus Rex v. Mary Wilkinson, November 1748, box 86, New London County Court Files, 1691–1774, CSL; Scotland Congregational Church Records, 45; Backus, *Church History of New-England*, II, 185.

Divers times" and excommunicated them the following fall. Then, the couple took matters into their own hands. John purchased a vial of arsenic from an apothecary in Norwich that Mary mixed into a fried pancake and presented to her rival. Mehetabel fell ill and died within hours. During the autopsy that followed, a coroners' inquest discovered evidence of foul play. John and Mary were remanded to jail in Windham, where they awaited trial for murder.[108]

The legal proceedings against the three Canterbury perfectionists ended in ambiguity. Haled before the county court magistrates, Wilkinson confessed her "vile and Prophain, Discorse and actions" and paid a fine. But she also excused her strange tirade in words that echoed Davenport's published *Retractations* following the New London bonfires. "For Som Years past," Wilkinson explained, she had been "under the Government of a fals and Delusive Spirit Possesing hir mind that There was Nither good nor Evel in any Expresions or actions under whatsoever Circumstances thay ware Spoke or acted." To the "astonishment of many," the Connecticut superior court acquitted Mary Smith of murder in June 1750 and rejected the indictment against John Smith. Although they had been freed from prison, the couple was forced to bear staggering court costs exceeding five hundred pounds. One year later, they obtained a legal marriage and started a new family. At the time of his death during the Seven Years' War, John owned a small farm, kitchen implements, furniture, bedding, a spinning wheel, and a few old books, all of which was sold off to pay his creditors. Mary remained in Canterbury for the rest of her life, living miserably, according to Backus.[109]

Gaps in the surviving court records make it difficult to know how the separatist community responded to the sensational murder trials of John and Mary Smith. Three dozen people testified in court, including Solomon Paine and his Separate church members, although only a few of their depositions have survived. Some evidence suggests that at least some of them might have continued to support the Smiths' unusually heterodox theological beliefs

108. Isaac Backus, *A Fish Caught in His Own Net* (Boston, 1768), in William G. McLoughlin, ed., *Isaac Backus on Church, State, and Calvinism: Pamphlets, 1754–1789*, John Harvard Library (Cambridge, Mass., 1968), 254; Dominus Rex v. John Smith, March–June 1750, box 173, Windham County Superior Court Files, 1726–1913, CSL; Solomon Paine to John Smith, Feb. 20, 1749, no. 51, JTC; Backus, *Church History of New-England*, II, 186. See also Dominus Rex v. Mary Smith, March–June 1750, box 173, Windham County Superior Court Files; and Solomon Paine to Mary Smith, Mar. 5, 1749, no. 53, JTC.

109. Dominus Rex v. Mary Wilkinson, November 1748, box 86, New London County Court Files; Backus, *Fish Caught in His Own Net*, in McLoughlin, ed., *Isaac Backus on Church, State, and Calvinism*, 254. See also Connecticut Superior Court Records, February 1749–June 1752, XIII, 125–126, CSL; and Estate of John Smith, 1761, no. 1929, Probate Files, 1747–1854, Plainfield, Conn., Probate District, CSL.

regarding spiritual marriage. One year after the trial, Mary Backus—a distant relative of the Titicut minister—was censured by the Separate church in Canterbury after she criticized the excommunication proceedings against John Smith. A "Child of God ought not be Cast out of the Visable Church" for any reason, Backus averred. Since Smith had been perfected in his conversion, his "Elect soul" could never sin—regardless of the purported failings of his body. Backus's statement represented an early instance of a set of theological principles that would come to be known as annihilationism: the belief that only the souls of the elect would be saved, while their bodies—along with both the souls and bodies of the unregenerate—would be destroyed. Comparable ideas reverberated among Strict Congregational, Separate Baptist, and perfectionist circles for decades.[110]

Separate Leaders realized that spiritual unions and new covenant marriages were cunning heresies, for they constituted a radical extension of the basic beliefs and practices the dissenters had nurtured among their breakaway churches. In a candid letter written to Isaac Backus several months after Mary Smith's murder trial, Norwich Separate minister Jedidiah Hide positioned internal and new covenant marriages within a broader, and more dangerous, "Negetiving Spirit" that threatened his congregation. Hide traced a slippery slope from antinomianism to infidelity. It began with parishioners who refused to pray until they had experienced conversion, then renounced their infant baptisms, and, finally, asserted that "marriage is an Institution of God and I Never was married in faith." If left unchecked, Hide concluded, Whitefield's concept of the new birth would inevitably convey overzealous saints "along in this Lyne" from the Separate movement, through adult baptism, and into spiritual marriage, the great "mistery of Iniquity."[111]

Far from isolated or sensational incidents of religious extremism, eruptions of immortalism and spiritual marriage reveal the contours of a shadowy network of perfectionists that spread across the northern New England frontier and into Atlantic Canada during the second half of the eighteenth century. Many of the principal figures knew one another, sought fellowship among likeminded neighbors in distant towns, migrated to new settlements together, and passed down their perfectionist beliefs and practices to subsequent generations. Bliss Willoughby was a case in point. After confessing his adulter-

---

110. Solomon Paine, church minutes, 1751, no. 78, JTC. Stephen Marini has argued that annihilationism was "marbled through New Light popular religion from the Great Awakening forward." See Marini, "The Origins of New England Universalism: Daughter of the New Light," *Journal of Unitarian Universalist History*, XXIV (1997), 70.

111. Hide to Backus, Oct. 10, 1750, no. 340, *IBP*.

ous errors, the zealous layman assumed leadership of the Newent Separate church, converted to Baptist principles, and led an exodus of dissenters to Bennington and Shaftsbury, Vermont, where they linked up with the visionary members of the Fay clan and other religious radicals. Following the Seven Years' War, Willoughby carried a petition to England requesting permission to sponsor a new settlement on the Chignecto Isthmus of Nova Scotia. Although he never immigrated to Atlantic Canada, his brothers did, along with more than seven thousand New Englanders, some of whom, like Willoughby, carried perfectionist controversies with them.[112]

A disproportionate number of the earliest Nova Scotia Yankees hailed from towns in southeastern Connecticut and the Old Colony that had witnessed powerful revivals and repeated church schisms. Hampered by weak social institutions and evangelized by a younger cohort of itinerant preachers, including the zealous Whitefieldarian Henry Alline, the planter settlements of Nova Scotia suffered through repeated eruptions of the "foulest Antinomianism" during the New Light Stir of the 1770s and the "new dispensation" movement two decades later. Charismatic female prophets proclaimed that the "Spirit of God" had commanded them to "go beyond all order." They denounced the Bible as a dead letter, rejected all sacraments, and promoted new revelations. Many exercised gifts of discernment and claimed the ability to identify Christians by sight. Among the key tenets of their "new Sceme" were the same controversial doctrines that perfectionists in southern New England had cited in their defense of spiritual marriage a generation earlier. In 1776, the fledgling church in Yarmouth, Nova Scotia, disciplined Temperance Richardson, who had once worshipped with the Wilkinson family in Scotland, Connecticut, for stealing legal documents, menacing her stepson with a knife, and engaging in "carnal Merriment" with a man who was not her husband. Richardson defended her actions by asserting that she had received "full Assurance of God's Love" and achieved perfect holiness. During the 1790s, Lydia Randall of Cornwallis shocked her neighbors when she declared that "Marriage was from the Divel" and vowed to live apart from her unconverted "Husband, for it was as much sin for her to have children by him as by any other man." Other "new-light preachers" in Nova Scotia adopted annihilationist beliefs that echoed those of Mary Backus of Canterbury. They denied even the possibility of true saints getting drunk or committing acts of murder or adultery, for they held

---

112. "Newint Appendix," in Bennington First Church Records, 18, 23–24; Andrew Tracy to Canterbury Separate Church, Nov. 7, 1753, no. 130, JTC, Bliss Willoughby to Solomon Paine, Sept. 2, 1756, no. 155; Maurice W. Armstrong, *The Great Awakening in Nova Scotia, 1776–1809* (Hartford, Conn., 1948), 39; Crocker, *History of the Baptists in Vermont*, 16–17.

that only the bodies of the saints—not their converted and perfected souls—were capable of sin. "A believer is like a nut thrown into the mud," Alline famously explained, "which may dirty the shell, but not the kernel."[113]

The connections linking small pockets of perfectionists in disparate communities were surprisingly direct. "GOD" Smith's followers, for example, lived only a few miles away from Solomon Prentice's parsonage in Grafton. During the Whitefieldian revivals, Smith worshipped alongside Ebenezer Ward, who lived in Hopkinton before carrying his radical notions of perfectionism and spiritual marriage to Cumberland, Rhode Island, and, eventually, to Norton and Easton. The Winnecunnet perfectionists attracted the attention of Shadrach Ireland. Dogged by allegations of spousal abandonment, the Charlestown craftsman and lay preacher spent several years itinerating in Grafton and Hopkinton before settling in the small farming village of Harvard, Massachusetts. In 1769, Ireland gathered a group of followers, pronounced a widow named Abigail Lougee to be his "spiritual companion," and supervised the construction of a large building later known as the Square House—complete with secret chambers, hidden staircases, and a makeshift alarm system of ropes and bells that allowed Ireland to elude detection. For more than a decade, the Irelandites in Harvard clandestinely practiced their perfectionist piety in the first of New England's many communal utopias. They seldom referred to their leader by name, calling him instead *"the man."* Members dissolved their marriages and observed strict rules of celibacy. They held all property in common and exercised gifts of the Holy Spirit, including faith healing and, according to one report, raising the dead. During his final hours in 1781, Ireland instructed his followers not to bury him, for he would rise again on the third day. "Time is very Short," the immortalist maintained, for "God is a coming to take the church." The Square House residents deposited his body

113. Thomas Jackson, ed., *The Lives of Early Methodist Preachers* ..., 3d ed., 6 vols. (London, 1865–1878), V, 271; Gordon T. Stewart, ed., *Documents Relating to the Great Awakening in Nova Scotia, 1760–1791*, Champlain Society, *Publications*, LII (Toronto, 1982), 46, 55; Brian C. Cuthbertson, ed., *The Journal of the Reverend John Payzant (1749–1834)* (Hantsport, N.S., 1981), 44–45, 47; Joshua Marsden, *The Narrative of a Mission to Nova Scotia, New Brunswick, and the Somers Islands* ... (London, 1816), 49. For a more detailed discussion of these examples, see George A. Rawlyk, "'A Total Revolution in Religious and Civil Government': The Maritimes, New England, and the Evolving Evangelical Ethos, 1776–1812," in Mark A. Noll, David W. Bebbington, and Rawlyk, eds., *Evangelicalism: Comparative Studies of Popular Protestantism in North America, the British Isles, and Beyond, 1700–1990*, Religion in America (New York, 1994), 137–155. For Alline's career, see J. M. Bumsted, *Henry Alline, 1748–1784* (1971; Hantsport, N.S., 1984); and Gordon Stewart and George Rawlyk, *A People Highly Favoured of God: The Nova Scotia Yankees and the American Revolution* (Hamden., Conn., 1972), Part Two. On the New Light Stir, see Marini, *Radical Sects of Revolutionary New England*, 40–59.

FIGURE 23 Shaker Square House, Harvard, Massachusetts. Early twentieth century. Picture postcard, 9 × 14 cm. Shaker Collection. Courtesy, Hamilton College Library, Special Collections, Clinton, N.Y.

in a lime-filled box in the cellar, where he remained until the overpowering stench of his decomposing corpse forced his disciples to dispose of his remains in a cornfield under the cover of darkness.[114]

Meanwhile, in Cumberland, Rhode Island, the congregation that Ebenezer Ward had organized in 1748 evolved into a Separate Baptist society under the leadership of a combative minister named Daniel Miller. Among its earliest members was James Ballou, who broke with Cumberland's regular Baptist church during the 1760s. Several years later, Ballou moved his family to Richmond, New Hampshire, where he soon associated with a group of zealous Separate Baptists who had exchanged their "old flood wives" for "spiritual wives." Although Ballou eventually rejected the principle of *"spiritual wifery,"* as the controversial practice of marrying in the new covenant came to be known among the critics of nineteenth-century sectarian movements,

114. Thomas Hammond, "Sketches of Ireland, the Square House, Mother Ann, Father William, and Father James," Sept. 26, 1812, 4, VII B 27, Shaker Collection, 1723–1952, Western Reserve Historical Society, Cleveland, Ohio; Abel Jewett et al., "Circumstances Respecting the Square House," 1846, VII A 2, Shaker Collection; Isaac Holden to Isaiah Parker, May 18, 1784, no. 1669, IBP.

he was captivated by the preaching of a young itinerant named Caleb Rich. Raised by parents of divided religious loyalties in Sutton, Massachusetts, just over the border from Grafton, Rich emerged during the 1770s as a powerful rural prophet. One of the controversial messages that Rich received during his visionary experiences was the revelation that divine benevolence ensured that the "first Adam and every individual of his posterity from the beginning of this world to the end" would be saved. Ballou followed the logic of perfectionism from the Whitefieldian revivals into a period of spiritual marriage and immortalism, finally coming to rest with Rich's doctrine of universal salvation. In the decades to come, members of his extended family would emerge as leaders of the nascent Universalist denomination, which swept across the northern New England hill country.[115]

Another notable member of Miller's Separate Baptist church in Cumberland was Jemima Wilkinson, a young woman from the neighboring town of Smithfield, Rhode Island. Converted by George Whitefield during his final New England tour in 1770, Wilkinson withdrew from the Quaker meeting in which she had been raised and affiliated briefly with the Separate Baptists. Languishing with typhus during the British occupation of Providence in 1776, Wilkinson fell into a feverish trance during which she was visited by a pair of angels clad in white robes and wearing golden crowns. The figures spoke in biblical quotations, informing her that death was imminent but that God was preparing her body for the "Spirit to dwell in." Rising from her bed, Wilkinson proclaimed that she was the "person of Jesus Christ come forth and now appears in her body with all the miraculous Powers of the Messiah." The genderless *"Public Universal Friend"* soon left the Baptists in Cumberland and took to the highways as an itinerant preacher, dressing in men's clothing and speaking to vast audiences in a "grum and shrill" voice that confounded and titillated her many critics. The celibate Friend lived by dreams, visions, and other immediate revelations, exhibited spiritual gifts of prophecy and discernment, cast out demons, and performed faith healings. Refusing to respond to the name for the soul that once animated Wilkinson's body, the Friend claimed to have existed "from Eternity" and exhorted audiences

115. Adin Ballou, *An Elaborate History and Genealogy of the Ballous in America* (Providence, R.I., 1888), 80; Marini, *Radical Sects of Revolutionary New England*, 74. On the growth of universalism, see Peter Hughes, "The Origins of New England Universalism: A Religion Without a Founder," *Journal of Unitarian Universalist History*, XXIV (1997), 31–63; Marini, "Origins of New England Universalism," *Journal of Unitarian Universalist History*, XXIV (1997), 64–75; and Ann Lee Bressler, *The Universalist Movement in America, 1770–1880*, Religion in America (New York, 2001).

to live "fully in a State of Perfection," with "no Liability of Error, or Possibility of Defect in any Respect." After gathering followers in southeastern New England and Philadelphia during the 1780s, the Friend founded New Jerusalem, a communal society in western New York, which flourished into the nineteenth century.[116]

Untethered from the Congregational establishment, as well as the Strict Congregational and Separate Baptist churches spawned by the revivals of the 1740s, the radical new lights who traveled in perfection across greater New England during the second half of the eighteenth century developed starkly dualistic ideas about the relation of their immortal souls to their all-too-earthly bodies. At one end of the spectrum stood people like Jane Drinkwater, who conflated the words of the scriptures with God. For her, the notion that divinity might take material form made little sense. Even the Bible was *"at best but a Creature"* "produced in *Time,"* and infinitely removed from the incorporeal substance of the divine word. At the other end were individuals like Isaac Worden, a new convert who joined Joseph Fish's congregation in the north parish of Stonington in 1742 only to be censured for his "Strange Doctrines" two years later. In contrast to Drinkwater, Worden arrived at the belief that the "Living and True God has *bodily* Parts" and could "Mortellize himself." Like many of his contemporaries, Worden puzzled over the relationship between elect souls and sinful bodies. Dividing humanity into the "Children of Cain" and the "Seed of Abraham," Worden reasoned that the former could never be saved, since they had been created directly by Satan. Following Adam's fall, the souls and bodies of the descendants of Abraham "must die, and so quicken out of Dust into Life again before they Can Enjoy Happiness with God." Drinkwater and Worden reached opposite conclusions on the issue of whether God was a pure spirit or could take bodily form; but both denied

116. [Jemima Wilkinson], "A Memorandum of the Introduction of That Fatal Fever, Call'd in the Year 1776, the Columbus Fever," n.d. [circa 1776], microfilm, Jemima Wilkinson Papers, 1771–1849, Division of Rare and Manuscript Collections, Cornell University Library, Ithaca, N.Y.; Dexter, ed., *Literary Diary of Ezra Stiles,* II, 380, III, 334; Abner Brownell, *Enthusiastical Errors, Transpired and Detected* ([New London, Conn.], 1783), 5, 7. For Wilkinson's early life and the Friend's later career, see Paul B. Moyer, *The Public Universal Friend: Jemima Wilkinson and Religious Enthusiasm in Revolutionary America* (Ithaca, N.Y., 2015). See also Catherine A. Brekus, *Strangers and Pilgrims: Female Preaching in America, 1740-1845,* Gender and American Culture (Chapel Hill, N.C., 1998), 80–97; Susan Juster, "'Neither Male nor Female': Jemima Wilkinson and the Politics of Gender in Post-Revolutionary America," in Robert Blair St. George, ed., *Possible Pasts: Becoming Colonial in Early America* (Ithaca, N.Y., 2000), 357–379; and Scott Larson, "'Indescribable Being': Theological Performances of Genderlessness in the Society of the Publick Universal Friend, 1776–1819," *Early American Studies,* XII (2014), 576–600.

the doctrine of the Trinity and rejected all ecclesiastical authorities. And, both withdrew from communion in their respective Congregational churches during the 1740s and never returned.[117]

Working through the logic of homespun theologies such as these, lay men and women across New England developed several controversial positions on marriage and sexuality. Some, such as Molly Bennet, the Newent Separates, and Shadrach Ireland elevated marriage to an internal spiritual union, which set the stage for the spouse-swapping adultery incidents that paralyzed the Separate churches in eastern Connecticut during the 1750s. Although Sarah Prentice initially embraced this position, she and other perfectionists such as the Public Universal Friend turned in the opposite direction and attempted to transcend their bodies by denying marriage altogether and practicing a rigorous sexual asceticism. Still others, including Canterbury Separate Mary Wilkinson, the new dispensationists of Nova Scotia, and scores of lesser-known visionists, seekers, and self-proclaimed prophets resolved the issue by splitting soul from body, denying the resurrection of the latter, and affirming that the former was sinless, perfect, and immortal—whatever the carnal failings of its physical husk. Many of the Separate Baptists who followed this line of reasoning migrated into New England's earliest Universalist congregations. A few traveled even further.[118]

■ "Madam *Prentice* of Grafton has been with the *Shakers*," a physician informed Ebenezer Parkman during the fall of 1782. For Sarah Prentice, visiting with one of the most controversial sects of the eighteenth century was an understandable choice. She undoubtedly listened to the *"Elect Lady,"* Ann Lee, when the charismatic founder of the "Shaking Quakers" preached in Grafton during her first missionary tour of New England in 1781. Several weeks later, Lee moved on to the village of Harvard, where she quickly organized the dispirited residents of Shadrach Ireland's Square House into the first Shaker village in New England.[119]

---

117. Thomas Foxcroft to Nicholas Loring, Apr. 17, 1747, Thomas Foxcroft Papers, 1690–1770, Mark and Llora Bortman Collection, HGARC; North Stonington Congregational Church Records, 94. For more on Drinkwater, see Part 3, note 70, above.

118. For an additional example, see Taylor, *Liberty Men and Great Proprietors*, 146.

119. Parkman, diary, Oct. 11, 1782, Parkman Papers; Dexter, ed., *Literary Diary of Ezra Stiles*, II, 511; *Independent Ledger, and the American Advertiser* (Boston), Oct. 25, 1784, in Glendyne R. Wergland, ed., *Visiting the Shakers, 1778–1849* (Clinton, N.Y., 2007), 17. See also Seth Chandler, *History of the Town of Shirley, Massachusetts: From Its Early Settlement to A.D. 1882* (Shirley, Mass., 1883), 269; and *Testimonies of the Life, Character, Revelations, and Doctrines of Our Ever Blessed Mother Ann Lee* (Hancock, Mass., 1816), 84–85.

The beliefs and practices espoused by the earliest generation of Shakers drew together many of the disparate strands of perfectionism that Prentice had been exploring for more than forty years. "They say that Christ promised to give his Church in all ages the power of working miracles," reported one early visitor to the Harvard Shaker village. The Elect Lady taught her earliest converts that they were the "only pure and holy people" and that their church was infallible; "no person can be a member of it till he is perfectly free from all sin and impurity." Lee encouraged her followers to labor with their bodies to achieve sinless perfection and purge the "seeds of death" that remained within them. Early Shaker worship exercises featured "wild and extravagant" bodily exercises—dancing, whirling, shaking, clapping hands, and stamping on the floor. They howled and shouted, sang psalms in "whining, canting tones," and spoke in tongues. Some members of the community claimed to converse with angels. Like the Irelandites before them, the Shakers established a community of goods, segregated the sexes, practiced celibacy, and waited for the millennial moment in which the "church now militant" would emerge as the "church triumphant."[120]

During the next two decades, the Shaker village at Harvard attracted a familiar cast of characters. Disproportionately drawn from the ranks of Strict Congregationalists, Separate Baptists, and independent seekers, early converts hailed from the radical heartlands of eastern Connecticut, the perfectionist havens of Easton, Norton, and Taunton in the Old Colony, and towns in central Massachusetts that had been evangelized repeatedly by notable itinerant preachers since the 1740s. Stephen, son of the Separate Baptist diarist Edmund Williams, for example, hosted Shaker meetings at his home in Raynham. The grandchildren of Seth Youngs, the Hartford clockmaker and confederate of James Davenport, provided critical leadership for the movement during the first half of the nineteenth century, as did descendants of the Meacham and Markham families of Enfield, many of whom had witnessed Edwards's stirring performance of *Sinners in the Hands of an Angry God*. The children of several leading families within the Winnecunnet perfectionist circle—the Babbitts, Blanchards, and Phinneys—gravitated to the sect as well. Sarah Prentice's connection to the Harvard Shakers was also a direct one. Not only had she lived, preached, and, perhaps, slept with Shadrach Ireland, but she

120. F. B. Sanborn, ed., "The Original Shaker Communities in New England," *New England Magazine: An Illustrated Monthly*, n.s., XXII (1900), 305, 307–309. On the formative period in Shaker history, see Stephen J. Stein, *The Shaker Experience in America: A History of the United Society of Believers* (New Haven, Conn., 1992), 10–38.

was related by marriage to a group of Prentice family members—including two of her husband's siblings—who migrated to Harvard from Cambridge and later converted to Shakerism.[121]

Although Prentice had numerous familial and religious ties to the upstart perfectionist community, she ultimately decided not to settle at Harvard with her kin and fellow perfectionists. During the years leading up to her death in 1792, she lived with her son in Ward (now Auburn), Massachusetts. Still, Prentice's initial interest in the teachings of the Elect Lady was a reasonable outgrowth of the spiritual convictions that had guided her life since her conversion half a century earlier: an unceasing quest for spiritual purity, a fascination with the charismatic gifts of the Holy Spirit, militant opposition to the corrupt churches of the standing order, and an unshakeable faith in the immortality of her perfected, regenerate soul.

WOULD NOT CONVERT A RAT

As he entered his seventieth year in January 1750, Josiah Cotton paused in his annual memoirs to consider the volatile state of religious affairs in New England. During the previous century, the Plymouth, Massachusetts, civil magistrate, Indian missionary, and ardent revival opposer grumbled, "Arminianism was exceedingly Opposed by the best sort of Men." The colonies had been settled by "People of Calvinistical Principles" who accepted the "Imputation of Adam's first Sin to his Posterity, and the Corruption of the whole Humane Nature by the Fall, Justification by Faith alone, Perserverance of the Saints," and other staples of the Reformed tradition. But Cotton worried that Arminianism—a constellation of doctrines, often associated with the sixteenth-century Dutch theologian Jacob Arminius, that centered on free will and conditional election—had emerged "open and bare fac'd" in the preaching and published works of a younger cohort of New England clergymen and "very much Infected" their congregations. "Since the Year 1740, and the Extravagancies of

121. McLoughlin, ed., *Diary of Isaac Backus*, II, 1117; Glendyne R. Wergland, *One Shaker Life: Isaac Newton Youngs, 1793–1865* (Amherst, Mass., 2006), 18; Priscilla J. Brewer, *Shaker Communities, Shaker Lives* (Hanover, N.H., 1986), 6–7; A. Johnson, Geo. H. Booth, and L. H. Pease, *Historical Sketch of the Town of Enfield* ... (Hartford, Conn., 1876), 22; William Bradford Browne, *The Babbitt Family History, 1643–1900* (Taunton, Mass., 1912), 57. For a map of Lee's missionary tours of New England, see Stein, *Shaker Experience in America*, 20–21. Genealogical information documenting Prentice's ties to the Harvard Shakers may be found in Suzanne R. Thurman, *"O Sisters Ain't You Happy?" Gender, Family, and Community among the Harvard and Shirley Shakers, 1781–1918*, Women and Gender in North American Religions (Syracuse, N.Y., 2002), 184–192.

New Light," towns between Plymouth and Boston had hired ministers who espoused heterodox beliefs. Everywhere, Cotton complained, "Arminian Books suit the present Taste exceedingly, and are much hugged and embrac'd."[122]

To Cotton and other alarmists, the specter of Arminianism lurked everywhere in New England during the 1750s. As was the case with antinomianism—the opposing heresy with which it was often paired—allegations of Arminianism appeared regularly in ministers' writings and occasionally in the works of the laity. Nathan Cole conceded that he had been an "Arminian untill I was *near* 30 years of age." Revival narratives published in transatlantic magazines such as the *Christian History* were larded with similar assessments. Josiah Crocker believed that Arminianism had "awfully prevailed" among his congregation in Taunton before 1740. A few correspondents even turned the lamp of criticism on themselves. The zealous revival advocate Jonathan Parsons admitted that he had once been in "Love with *Arminian* Principles," although the surviving sermons from the early years of his ministry in Lyme, Connecticut, betray no significant departure from the preaching of his contemporaries. "When I got my religion in the *New Light* time," one Yale College graduate later recalled, "I became a more zealous Calvinist. I had a great aversion to the opposers of New Light religion; and those opposers in New England, where I then lived, were generally supposed to be Arminian, or tinged with Arminian principles."[123]

What passed for Arminianism at mid-century was less a coherent theological alternative to Calvinism than a general term of derision employed by the revival advocates to pillory their opponents. Only a handful of ministers were censured for holding Arminian beliefs before 1745. As late as 1738, John Cotton, Josiah's son and the minister of the small farming village of Halifax, Massachusetts, asserted in a letter to an English relative that most New England divines were "rigid Calvinists," although he admitted that the "modish"

---

122. JCH, 393–394. Previous studies that trace the rise of theological liberalism in eighteenth-century New England include Wright, *Beginnings of Unitarianism in America;* James W. Jones, *The Shattered Synthesis: New England Puritanism Before the Great Awakening* (New Haven, Conn., 1973), 131–197; Corrigan, *Hidden Balance,* 20–58; Ava Chamberlain, "The Theology of Cruelty: A New Look at the Rise of Arminianism in Eighteenth-Century New England," *Harvard Theological Review,* LXXXV (1992), 335–356; and E. Brooks Holifield, *Theology in America: Christian Thought from the Age of the Puritans to the Civil War* (New Haven, Conn., 2003), 128–135.

123. NCS, 92; Josiah Crocker, "An Account of the Late Revival of Religion at Taunton," *CH,* no. 93 (Dec. 8, 1744), 324; Jonathan Parsons, "Account of the Revival of Religion at Lyme West Parish in Connecticut, Continued" *CH,* no. 68 (June 16, 1744), 123; "Sketch of the Life of Rev. Jacob Green," *Christian Advocate (Philadelphia),* X (1832), 147. For Parsons's prerevival sermons, see Part 4, note 92, above.

heresy of Arminianism was on the rise at Harvard College. As the Whitéfield-arians repudiated the sandy foundations of the godly walk and embraced the extraordinary work of the Holy Spirit, they attacked sermons once viewed as "Catholick." Clashes between emerging clerical factions increasingly focused on sharpening definitions of what one Boston minister called the "Calvinisti-cal scheme" of their puritan ancestors. On several occasions during the 1750s, intramural sniping broke out into full-scale pamphlet wars.[124]

The well-publicized debates over Arminianism do not appear to have reached a broader popular audience. Only a handful of church discipline cases involving parishioners who questioned traditional Reformed doctrines such as original sin, Christ's atonement, or justification by faith alone sur-faced in the churches of the standing order during the three decades follow-ing the Whitefieldian revivals. Instead, as Congregational ministers were busy spilling ink over theological controversies, hundreds of families in towns across New England quietly began transferring their religious affiliation to the Church of England. The two issues were closely related. As was the case with lay men and women who traveled in perfectionism, disaffected Congre-gationalists who embraced liberal doctrines or who conformed to the Church of England expressed a deep sense of frustration with the disordered state of religion in New England. In contrast to their enthusiastic kin and neighbors who reveled in the extraordinary workings of the Holy Spirit, self-professed Arminians and Anglicans sought shelter from the growing ecclesiastical storm in rational faith and orderly worship.

■ Josiah Cotton was delighted to learn that his nephew, John Brown, Jr., son of the recently deceased clergyman of Haverhill, Massachusetts, had been called to minister to the people of Cohasset, a small parish located less than thirty miles from his farm in Plymouth. He recorded the news of his kins-man's ordination in 1747 alongside that of Solomon Prentice in Easton, and he prayed to God that they would become "burning and shining Lights in their Several Orbs." Within a few years, Cotton had lost patience with both

---

124. John Cotton (of Halifax, Mass.) to John Cotton (Isle of Wight, England), Mar. 10, 1737, HUG 300, Harvard University Archives, Harvard University, Cambridge, Mass.; "Auto-biography of the Rev. John Barnard," MHS, *Collections*, 3d Ser., V (Boston, 1836), 186. On the decline of "Catholick theology" during the 1740s, see John Corrigan, *The Prism of Piety: Catholick Congregational Clergy at the Beginning of the Enlightenment*, Religion in America (New York, 1991), 133. The argument in this section builds on Gerald J. Goodwin, "The Myth of 'Arminian-Calvinism' in Eighteenth-Century New England," *NEQ*, XLI (1968), 213–237. For ecclesiastical controversies before 1740 involving allegations of Arminianism, see Wright, *Beginnings of Unitarianism in America*, 1–27.

ministers. During the same months that Prentice and his wife worshipped with the Winnecunnet perfectionists in Norton, Cotton became embroiled in a heated theological exchange with his upstart kinsman. Brown had been studying John Taylor's *Scripture Doctrine of Original Sin*, a controversial treatise whose English author denied the imputation of Adam's sin to his posterity. "I cant but Wish," the Plymouth judge complained of his cousin's theological liberalism, "that You would adhere to what the Church of God has Esteemed Orthodox from the Beginning, for if We don't Stop there, We cant tell where We shall Stop." Cotton eventually wearied of sparring with the brash young "*Scripturalist.*" "Bishop" Brown, as he came to be known over his long pastorate at Cohasset, continued to question everything: the utility of creeds, the traditions of his puritan ancestors, and even the authority of the Bible.[125]

Brown was the latest in a series of liberal ministers who had assumed leadership in half a dozen parishes in Boston and along Massachusetts's South Shore during the previous decade. The changing of the guard began in 1746, when William Rand, one of the most vocal revival opposers in New England, exchanged his pulpit in the Connecticut Valley for one in Kingston, Massachusetts. Boston's fashionable West Church ordained Martha's Vineyard native Jonathan Mayhew one year later. Congregations in between— Braintree, Scituate, Duxbury, Pembroke, and Marshfield—all hired men with similar theological inclinations. Trained at Harvard College under John Leverett, these young clergymen had studied the works of British natural philosophers and latitudinarian divines such as John Locke and John Tillotson. The churches over which they were ordained were located in parishes that George Whitefield had bypassed during his second preaching tour of New England. And, nearly all of the members of this emerging liberal cohort of pastors found a home in the Hingham Association—a powerful ministerial organization molded by Ebenezer Gay, the resolute patriarch of Hingham's venerable Old Ship meetinghouse.[126]

Gay and his young colleagues advanced their controversial theological doctrines in a series of pamphlets, books, and published sermons. The first blast came in 1749, when Lemuel Briant, the minister of Braintree's north parish (now Quincy, Massachusetts), delivered an inflammatory sermon at

125. JCH, 378, 415; Josiah Cotton to John Cushing, Jr., July 3, 1754, William Cushing Papers, 1664–1814, MHS. On the career of John Brown, Jr., see *SHG*, XI, 12–17.

126. Wilson, *Benevolent Deity*, 121–168. Key studies of the liberalization of Harvard College during the early decades of the eighteenth century include Norman Fiering, "The First American Enlightenment: Tillotson, Leverett, and Philosophical Anglicanism," *NEQ*, LIV (1981), 307–344; and Corrigan, *Prism of Piety*, 17–27.

Mayhew's West Church. Published under the belligerant title *The Absurdity and Blasphemy of Depretiating Moral Virtue*, Briant's discourse enlisted Taylor's *Scripture Doctrine* in a sustained assault on the doctrine of original sin. The Bible, Briant claimed, had been "wretchedly abused to serve the Purposes of Error, Superstition and Vice" in all times and places but never more so than during the recent revivals in New England. The example he targeted for intensive scrutiny was Isaiah 54:6, a text in which the prophet likened the righteous acts of the Israelites to filthy rags. Seventeenth-century puritan theologians had argued that this passage referred to the good works of the unregenerate, and the trope played an important role in the sermons of George Whitefield and his followers during the revivals. Briant, however, believed that entrenched notions of human depravity dampened incentives toward ethical action and robbed yearning saints of a suitable foundation for hope in salvation. Human beings were moral agents capable of performing good works. Christianity was the "most refined System of Morality the World was ever blessed with." "It is the Righteousness of the Saints," he asserted in the sermon's most controversial passage, "that renders them amiable in God's Sight." Salvation was the inevitable consequence of a life spent in the diligent pursuit of moral virtue—a virtue that had been, according to the Braintree pastor, perverted by the Whitefieldarians. Cotton called it a "Virulent, Scurrilous, Scandalous Pamphlet."[127]

Later that same year, Jonathan Mayhew's *Seven Sermons* provided a more systematic defense of Briant's incendiary remarks on original sin. Ever since he had traveled to York, Maine, to witness the outpouring of the Holy Spirit, Mayhew had been distancing himself from the "religious phrenzy" of the revivals. By the time he ascended the pulpit of Boston's West Church for the first time in 1747, the bold young clergyman was prepared to go to considerable theological lengths to restore balance to a religious system that he believed had careened out of control. "Christianity is principally an institution of life and manners," Mayhew argued, "designed to teach us how to be good men." Rejecting all creeds as "imperious and tyrannical," he asserted that God had endowed humanity with sensory faculties and the power of reason. Intellectual liberty was the "basis of *all religion*, whether natural or revealed," he explained in a 1755 sermon series. Only a cruel deity would punish sinners for transgressions that had taken place ages before their birth. "However free the grace of God is," Mayhew concluded, "it is manifest that he has required some-

---

127. JCH, 415; Lemuel Briant, *The Absurdity and Blasphemy of Depretiating Moral Virtue* (Boston, 1749), 6–7, 9, 20. For one example of the "filthy Rags" trope in Whitefield's sermons, see his *What Think Ye of Christ?* (Philadelphia, 1739), 13.

thing of us in order to our salvation." The performance of good works and devotional duties lay within the reach of all earnest believers.[128]

Ebenezer Gay attacked the issue of free will on metaphysical grounds in his celebrated 1759 Dudleian Lecture on natural philosophy. Preaching to a packed auditory of clergymen, tutors, and scholars at Harvard College, the Hingham minister argued that religion was "practicable" depending on the strength of individual character. Gay believed that human beings were more than "merely so much lumpish Matter." They contained a "special Endowment" of "Freedom of Choice" within. The "original Design" of the Creator included an "inward Spring of Motion" that naturally pulled human beings toward God, the "Centre of their Perfection, and consummate Object of their Happiness." If this "Energy were not obstructed," all people would act righteously, for an "Inclination to Religion" was the "Gravitation" of God's noblest creatures. Following in the footsteps of noted English natural philosophers, Gay argued that all individuals could use their powers of reason to determine the existence of God. Diligent Christians made a "continual Advance in Religion" that would eventuate in a *"perfect Man,* in the reintegrated State of Nature."[129]

In time, the published works of the Boston and South Shore establishment coalesced into a coherent liberal theology that culminated in Charles Chauncy's controversial writings of the 1780s. For Chauncy, Gay, and their younger colleagues, God was a benevolent deity that sought the good of his creatures and his own glorification. Revealed religion squared with natural philosophy. Divinely endowed human reason had been tarnished, not tainted, by Adamic sin. Devotional practices contributed to self-improvement and civic virtue. Human beings striving to live in obedience to divine prerogatives could achieve ever-higher states of moral perfection. They exhibited their moral virtue through good works. Sinners were "prisoners of hope," as one South Shore clergyman summarized, who were "Invited to Come to and for Salvation." Only a virtuous minority would enter at the strait gate, but most liberal ministers assumed that salvation lay within the reach of all earnest and diligent Christians.[130]

128. Jonathan Mayhew, *Seven Sermons upon the Following Subjects* ... (Boston, 1749), 60–61, 152–153; Mayhew, *Sermons upon the Following Subjects* ... (Boston, 1755), 300; Mayhew, *Striving to Enter in at the Strait Gate Explain'd and Inculcated* ... (Boston, 1761), 23. See also Akers, *Called unto Liberty,* 66–75, 122–127; and Corrigan, *Hidden Balance,* 30–36.

129. Ebenezer Gay, *Natural Religion as Distinguished from Revealed* (Boston, 1759), in Sydney E. Ahlstrom and Jonathan Sinclair Carey, eds., *An American Reformation: A Documentary History of Unitarian Christianity* (Middletown, Conn., 1985), 49–50, 59. See also Wilson, *Benevolent Deity,* 171–184.

130. "Diaries of Rev. William Smith and Dr. Cotton Tufts, 1738–1784," MHS, *Procds.,* 3d Ser., XLII (1908–1909), 458. For Chauncy's contributions to theological liberalism, see Grif-

Controversial doctrines involving free will, original sin, and moral virtue provoked bitter debate, both in the Boston press and in local ecclesiastical affairs. Yet, there is little evidence to suggest that the "Orthodox Mayhew-metans," as Josiah Cotton derided them, and their controversial publications reached a broader audience. To be sure, their books and pamphlets as well as similar works by liberal English divines circulated widely among Congregational ministers and their most learned parishioners. But, for every prominent intellectual who pored over treatises that questioned the doctrines of original sin and predestination, there were thousands of lay men and women such as Joseph Andrews. On the day that Ebenezer Gay delivered his landmark Dudleian Lecture at Harvard College, his young Hingham parishioner "Went to Weymouth to Gitt a frame hew'd for a barn." Puzzling questions remain regarding the impact of Arminian theological ideas between 1750 and 1780. If the South Shore clergy infused their weekly sermons with controversial doctrines, did their parishioners embrace them?[131]

The diary of Thomas Josselyn, the wealthy proprietor of a large iron works and mill complex in the town of Hanover, Massachusetts, provides a rare opportunity to survey the spread of liberal theological doctrines among the laity. Descended from the noted English puritan divine Ralph Josselin, Thomas was born in 1702 and baptized as a young adult. He joined the Scituate church in full communion in 1726 and assisted in the organization of the church in Hanover two years later. Josselyn and his wife presented each of their nine children for baptism within a month of their births. Elected deacon in 1739, he represented the Hanover church at ordinations in neighboring churches and spent his leisure time reading devotional literature. Most important, Josselyn compiled a detailed "account of The Affairs of Divine providence Concerning myself and my family and the Church of God." On and off for more than three decades, the Hanover ironmonger chronicled business ventures, notable events, Sabbath attendance, and private devotional performances.[132]

---

fin, *Old Brick*, 109–125; and Colin Wells, *The Devil and Doctor Dwight: Satire and Theology in the Early American Republic* (Chapel Hill, N.C., 2002).

131. Josiah Cotton to John Cushing, Jr., July 28, 1755, William Cushing Papers; Joseph Andrews, journals, 1752–1787, May 9, 1759, MHS.

132. Thomas Josselyn, diary, 1731–1775, Jan. 1, 1743, Mss C 3489, NEHGS. See also John S. Barry, *A Historical Sketch of the Town of Hanover, Mass., with Family Genealogies* (Boston, 1853), 60, 338–339; Jedidiah Dwelley and John F. Simmons, *History of the Town of Hanover Massachusetts with Family Genealogies* (Hanover, Mass., 1910), 18, 27, 29, 31, 33, 78, 80, 205; Wilford J. Litchfield, ed., *Scituate Massachusetts Second Church Records (in Abstract), 1645–1850* (Boston, 1909), 21, 46; and L. Vernon Briggs, ed., *History and Records of the First Congregational Church, Hanover, Mass., 1727–1865 ...* (Boston, 1895), 2, 4, 55, 57,

Moving to Hingham in 1745, Josselyn struck up a friendship with Ebenezer Gay. They traveled to Boston together in a riding chair on the occasion of Gay's election-day sermon. Their families sailed on pleasure cruises and picnicked together at the World's End—a picturesque peninsula of rolling hills with striking views of Boston Harbor. During the next two years, Josselyn took notes on more than one hundred and fifty sermons delivered from the Old Ship pulpit. Gay preached the overwhelming majority, and his discourses were highly polished and erudite. To his detailed expositions of biblical texts, which he occasionally glossed in Greek and Hebrew, Gay yoked extended metaphors that rendered his learned exegetical observations accessible to audiences composed of well-educated merchants and impoverished dockworkers alike. In addition, Josselyn listened to regular sermons, fast and thanksgiving homilies, election-day addresses, funeral discourses, and sacramental lectures delivered by many prominent liberal ministers of Boston and the South Shore, including Lemuel Briant, John Brown, Jr., Charles Chauncy, Jonathan Mayhew, and William Rand. His sermon notes provide a unique weekly record of liberal preaching at a critical moment, while the prayers and meditations that he recorded in his diary reveal the extent to which his beliefs merged with those of Gay and visiting ministers. As the newest member of Hingham's gentry elite, Josselyn was as likely a convert to Arminian principles as anyone in New England.[133]

By midcentury, Hingham had evolved into a bustling commercial center, with numerous mill complexes and a sizeable fishing and coastal trading fleet. Gay's parish mirrored the town's hierarchical social structure. Deacons and other church officers hailed from wealthy families, and the layout of the pew boxes in the Old Ship meetinghouse reinforced the stratified social order. Gay enjoyed unflagging popular support throughout his six-decade career. Eschewing the test of a relation and the practice of owning the covenant, he succeeded in developing inclusive membership standards that ensured high rates of household church affiliation throughout the eighteenth century. Over the course of Gay's seven-decade pastorate, more than 85 percent of all Hingham families affiliated with the First Church or one of its satellites and an equal percentage of children born in town were baptized as infants. Diaries kept by

---

71, 119–121, 123, 126, 131–132. For Josselyn's English puritan ancestry, see Alan Macfarlane, *The Family Life of Ralph Josselin, a Seventeenth-Century Clergyman: An Essay in Historical Anthropology* (New York, 1977).

133. Josselyn, diary, May 28, July 10, Aug. 3, 1745. For examples of Gay's sermons, see Gay Family Sermons, 1718–1782, AAS.

Josselyn and other members of Gay's congregation suggest that his parishioners rarely missed a Sabbath meeting (see Tables 6 and 9).[134]

At first glance, Josselyn's sermon notes appear to be laced with many of the controversial doctrines that fomented the pamphlet wars and parish squabbles of the late 1740s. During the fall of 1745, Gay preached a sermon that cut against the grain of the revivals. In contrast to the Whitefieldarians, who emphasized the unbridgeable chasm between God and unregenerate sinners, the Hingham pastor asserted that even those in an unconverted state were "not far from The Kingdom of God." Charles Chauncy blurred the boundaries between saints and sinners when he endorsed the validity of churches composed of both regenerate and unregenerate members. It was the "will of Christ that both should Grow together untill the Harvist." One visiting ministerial candidate even skirted the boundaries of universal salvation when he remarked that Christ died for the "Elect of God or al that should believe in him." Gay also addressed the "Good will Cindness and Love" exhibited by God to humanity—an early precursor to the Arminian position on the benevolence of the deity.[135]

The liberal ministers of the South Shore suggested that human obedience to divine law was both necessary and possible—and, perhaps, by extension meritorious. God would "Respect and Reward" his faithful forever, visiting minister Ezra Carpenter suggested, if only they would offer him their best efforts at moral sincerity. "There is a Good work Begun In all Good Christians," Gay contended. Earnest men and women of "Good Chear," who labored to obey God's laws and lived "soberly Righteously and Godly" in this world, would reap a "Reward of Blessedness at the apearing of Jesus X [Christ]." At times, the Hingham minister and his South Shore colleagues seemed to reduce salvation to a volitional act.[136]

Even as Josselyn recorded what seemed to be Arminian sermons in his diary, the majority of Gay's performances focused on a traditional theme: the necessity of walking obediently in the sight of God. On the first Sabbath after he moved to Hingham, Josselyn listened as Gay outlined the variety of ways

134. John J. Waters, "Hingham, Massachusetts, 1631–1661: An East Anglian Oligarchy in the New World," *Journal of Social History*, I (1968), 351–370; Daniel Scott Smith, "Population, Family, and Society in Hingham, Massachusetts, 1635–1880" (Ph.D. diss., University of California, Berkeley, 1973), 84–204; Wilson, *Benevolent Deity*, 33–37, 192–197. Diaries kept by other Hingham residents include Andrews, journals; Anonymous farmer, diaries, 1750, 1763, Benjamin Lincoln Papers, 1635–1964, MHS; Quincy Thaxter, diary, 1774–1778, Thaxter Family Papers, 1774–1791, MHS.

135. Josselyn, diary, June 9, 16, 30, Sept. 15, 1745.

136. Ibid., Oct. 6, Dec. 8, 1745, May 25, Nov. 2, 1746, Apr. 26, May 3, 1747.

in which people should glorify God: confessing their sins and living a "Life of Religion and Vertue and of Holi obedence to the Divine will of God." During the months that followed, Gay reiterated the importance of walking "agreeable to the Gospell" and cultivating a "Good Conversation." Earthly pilgrims needed to employ "all apointed means" to reach a "Better Country" in heaven. What an "Excelent Thing it is to do Good," William Rand of Kingston reminded the Hingham assembly, "It makes us Like the Holy Angels and Like the Blessed Jesus who went abought Doing Good." Godly walking and doing good were staples of early-eighteenth-century preaching. In the charged atmosphere of the late 1740s, however, these sermons would have struck most Whitefieldarians as perilously close to Arminianism.[137]

Josselyn's sermon notes suggest that Gay never abandoned the traditional Reformed doctrines of original sin, conversion, or salvation by faith alone. The Hingham minister and his liberal colleagues understood that the pursuit of a "Holy Life" followed, rather than preceded, justification by the Holy Spirit. Godly walking always took the form of a conditional statement. A "Christian Corse," Gay believed, was the pathway to salvation, but he was careful to note that "no man Can order his Steps aright nor Direct Them as he should." Only after the "kingdom of God is set up In the Soull," Lemuel Briant concurred, would faithful Christians "shew forth the same In acts of kindnes and Benificence" to others. Gay even preached occasionally on the sandy foundations of faith. In a sermon that might just as easily have come from itinerant preachers Eleazar Wheelock or Daniel Rogers, the Hingham pastor sternly warned striving sinners who rested content in their raised affections, outward moral behavior, or performance of religious duties that they would never enter God's kingdom without grace. Gay cautioned his auditors to examine their souls and ensure that their righteous actions were "Built On a sound and Saving faith in X [Christ]." No ardent Whitefieldarian could have sounded more orthodox.[138]

Josselyn was impressed by Gay's weekly sermons, and he regretted moving his family back to Hanover during the spring of 1747. Based on the occasional prayers he inscribed in his diary, the former deacon took the Hingham minister's preaching to heart. Josselyn was a successful entrepreneur who operated a lucrative iron forge and engaged in a variety of other profitable business schemes. Yet, as with earlier generations of New England puritans, he also recognized the providential springs from which his good fortune came. In one sermon on Genesis 19:17, Gay urged sinners to "Escape from out of the state

---

137. Ibid., July 14, Aug. 18, Dec. 29, 1745, Mar. 30, 1746.
138. Ibid., Aug. 18, Oct. 18, Dec. 31, 1745.

of sin" just as Lot had fled from Sodom and Gomorrah, and he attempted to show that escape was possible through obedience to God's commands. Despite the Arminian implications of Gay's sermon, Josselyn improved the discourse in thoroughly conventional fashion, praying to God for "Grace to flee to X [Christ]," "faith to Repent of all Sin," and a "Life of Herty obedience."[139]

Josselyn never embraced any of the liberal Arminian doctrines attributed to Gay and his South Shore colleagues. When he resumed writing in his diary in 1772, following a two-decade hiatus, he penned a long birthday meditation begging God to preserve him in his old age and to pardon his sins, which were more numerous than the "Hairs of my head" or the "Sands on the Seashore." Increasingly infirm and living with family members in the town of Pembroke, Massachusetts, the aging ironmonger continued to fear the loud voice of God that sounded in thunderstorms, droughts, epidemics, mill accidents, and other frowns of divine providence. He remained convinced that "God was nigh at Hand and not afar" and that "my times are In thy Hands"; and he pleaded to be "Pardoned Justified and Sanctified in the name of the Lord Jesus and by the Holie Sperit." When his wife died in 1774, Josselyn responded just as godly walkers had done for more than a century. He elevated his devotional routines, renewed his personal covenant with God, and submitted a prayer bill for himself and his children, desiring the prayers of the Pembroke church "that the Death of my Dear wife and their mother might [be] Sanctefied to us all [by] Almigty God." In the burst of diary ruminations that followed, the grieving widower attempted to transmute affliction into spiritual gain, beseeching God to "make me a New Creature." For more than seventy years Josselyn had struggled to live a godly life, knowing that God alone enabled him to "Live well," "Die well," and "Live forevermore."[140]

▪ Surprisingly, most of the earliest ecclesiastical disputes involving direct charges of Arminianism did not erupt in Ebenezer Gay's Hingham parish or in any of the other towns along the South Shore that were led by notable liberal ministers such as John Brown, Jr. Nor did they figure prominently in the ecclesiastical politics of western New England, where an emerging cohort of New Divinity clergymen closed ranks and worked to dampen religious radicalism of all kinds. Instead, the most fertile ground for liberal religious dissent developed in the central New England uplands. The same towns in Worcester County and eastern Connecticut that had been wracked by schisms and out-

139. Ibid., May 26, 1745.
140. Ibid., Sept. 18, 21, 1772, Nov. 13, Dec. 25, 27, 1774, Jan. 1, 1775.

breaks of the wildest antinomianism following the Whitefieldian revivals also witnessed a surprising number of church discipline cases involving charges of Arminianism.

As early as April 1746, Sutton minister David Hall reported being assaulted by a group of angry parishioners in Worcester who refused to believe that the stain of Adam's original sin had been passed down through the ages. During the same months in which Westborough minister Ebenezer Parkman struggled to corral the attacks of the outspoken separatist Stephen Fay, he also squared off against a former parishioner named Robert Bradish. Like Fay, the brash layman from the neighboring town of Upton travelled from house to house proclaiming that Parkman preached "Corrupt and Damnable Doctrine"; but his "proud and obstinate" critique came from the opposite theological direction. Bradish rejected the "Doctrine of Justification by Faith alone, and that we are saved by Grace and not by works." Three years later, in October 1749, Parkman served on a council that convened to adjudicate the charges that Shrewsbury, Massachusetts, physician Joshua Smith denied the doctrine of original sin. Among the council members who advocated on Smith's behalf and walked out of the proceedings in protest was Ebenezer Gay of Hingham. Another supporter, Bradford, Massachusetts, minister William Balch, espoused similar liberal beliefs and was at the time embroiled in a pamphlet war with his antagonists in Essex County.[141]

During the 1750s, a small but outspoken group of New England ministers renounced their puritan theological heritage. One notable example from central New England was John Bass. Ordained over the Congregational church in Ashford, Connecticut, in 1743, Bass initially considered himself to be a professed member of the *"Calvinian* Class." But the "eagle-eyed" new converts in his hill country hamlet harried him with charges of Arminianism. Withdrawing from communion, a dissenting faction called for an ecclesiastical council in 1750 to vent their grievances. Bass's disaffected parishioners accused the Ashford minister of denying the imputed guilt of Adam, disdaining to preach on original sin or the new birth, and refusing to acknowledge the innate depravity of infants during the administration of baptism. In his response, Bass shocked all parties when he affirmed the articles of complaint. For some time, Bass acknowledged, he had been studying his Bible assiduously but could discover no evidence supporting the *"Calvinistic* Faith." Unlike the liberal min-

---

141. Hall, diaries, Apr. 25, 1746; Walett, ed., *Diary of Ebenezer Parkman*, 132–133, 148, 201–202, 204; Parkman, commonplace book, 114, Parkman Papers. See also Israel Loring, journal, 1748–1750, 23, no. 12195, SA. For Balch's Arminian leanings, see *SHG*, VII, 296–304.

isters of the South Shore who clung to a broader theological tradition, Bass flatly rejected basic Reformed doctrines including original sin, limited atonement, and the perseverance of the saints. He had, as he later put it, "come into a new and different Scheme." Acting with the support of the Windham County ministerial association, the members of the Ashford church demanded his immediate dismissal.[142]

Meanwhile, the Arminian controversies in Worcester County finally came to a head in Westborough, when Eliezer Rice requested permission to baptize a sickly child in a private ceremony during the spring of 1751. Rice had owned the covenant two decades earlier, and his wife was a full church member. For several years leading up to the conflict, however, Rice had openly criticized Parkman's ministry, absenting himself from Sabbath meetings and weekday lectures and declaring "himself against the Commonly recognized Doctrine of Original Sin" and the "Imputation of Adams Guilt to his Posterity." Parkman discussed the issue with Jonathan Edwards and colleagues in the Marlborough ministerial association, only to discover that "Some advis'd one way and Some another." For his part, Rice "did not appear to be very expert in the Controversy" when pressed to defend his liberal beliefs during a church meeting, and his wife flatly disagreed with his heterodox opinions. After four years of dispute, Parkman finally agreed to baptize the members of Rice's growing family, but only with the explicit understanding that the sacrament would be administered under his "Wife's Account." In the wake of the Whitefieldian revivals, the threats to Parkman's ministry came from several directions. Whereas some long-standing church members, including members of the Fay family, questioned his ministry based on their experience of the indwelling presence of the Holy Spirit, Rice's dissatisfaction stemmed from his growing concern about the validity of the fundamental doctrines of Reformed Protestantism—concerns that set him apart not only from his neighbors but from his own family.[143]

Although few would have recognized it at the time, the most notable Arminian in central Massachusetts during the 1750s was the future second president of the United States, John Adams. Born in Lemuel Briant's Braintree parish in 1735, Adams worked as a schoolmaster and studied law in Worcester for several years following his graduation from Harvard College in 1751. There, he fell in with a small group of freethinking religious radicals. Culled

---

142. John Bass, *A True Narrative of an Unhappy Contention in the Church at Ashford . . .* (Boston, 1751), 3–4, 12. See also Wright, *Beginnings of Unitarianism in America,* 72–74.

143. Walett, ed., *Diary of Ebenezer Parkman,* 238, 240, 288. See also Westborough Congregational Church Records, 90–92, 102.

from the ranks of magistrates, lawyers, merchants, and shopkeepers, the members of the clique were "great Readers of Deistical Books" and "fully satisfied that all Religion was a cheat, a cunning invention of Priests and Politicians." Adams's law instructor, Joseph Putnam, for example, was convinced that the "Apostles were a Company of Enthusiasts. He says we have only their word, to prove that they spoke with different Tongues, raised the Dead, and healed the sick." Adams began to question nearly every aspect of the Calvinist tradition in which he had been raised. He rejected the doctrines of original sin and limited atonement, preferring instead to associate religious truth with natural law, moral reasoning, and civic virtue. He sparred with Worcester minister Thaddeus Maccarty and scorned the sermons of the Whitefieldarians. Within a few years, the people of Worcester had pegged him as an *"Orminian."* It was a fair assessment of the young lawyer's early religious development.[144]

Self-professed Arminians are often difficult to identify, in part, because they tended not to affiliate with established Congregational churches. But it was also the case that many who were already full church members remained within their churches despite their changing convictions. Sometime around 1760, Joseph Bellamy, the former itinerant preacher and minister of Bethlehem, Connecticut, dispatched a cautionary letter in which he bore testimony against the "Dangerous" beliefs espoused by Silas Filer, the leader of a prayer society in the Wintonbury parish of Windsor (now Bloomfield), Connecticut. Bellamy overheard Filer denying that sinners were "Saved by the Special peculiar Distinguishing Sovereign grace of God." The "turning point" of conversion, as Filer put it, stemmed entirely from the sinner's "free will, in the Arminian Sense of the Phrase." Abandoning staple Reformed doctrines of original sin, atonement, and justification by faith, Filer arrived at the position that the new birth was strictly a matter of human volition. Curiously, Filer and his wife elected to remain within the Wintonbury Congregational church, despite his misgivings about Calvinist theology. He presented at least two more children for baptism after Bellamy had raised the alarm about his heterodox beliefs.[145]

144. L. H. Butterfield et al., eds., *Diary and Autobiography of John Adams,* The Adams Papers, Ser. I, 4 vols. (Cambridge, Mass., 1961), I, 6, 14–15, 20–21, III, 264–265; John Adams to Charles Cushing, Apr. 1, 1756, Adams Papers Digital Editions, MHS (available online at *www.masshist.org/publications*). See also C. Bradley Thompson, "Young John Adams and the New Philosophic Rationalism," *WMQ,* LV (1998), 259–280.

145. Joseph Bellamy to unknown, n.d. [circa 1759–1762], no. 81401, Joseph Bellamy Papers, Case Memorial Library, Hartford Seminary, Hartford, Conn.; Mary Kingsbury Talcott, ed., "Records of the Church in Wintonbury Parish (now Bloomfield), Conn.," *NEHGR,* LXXI (1917), 75, 154–155, 158, 161. Two names appearing at the bottom of the Bellamy manuscript provide the range of dates for the Filer case: William Manley, who was elected deacon in 1759, and Peletiah Mills, who died in 1762.

Church members who were disciplined for questioning the doctrines of original sin or justification by faith alone usually remained within the Congregational fold. Eliezer Rice, for example, made his peace with Ebenezer Parkman and resumed his place in the Westborough meetinghouse, although he never renounced his Arminian views or confessed his error. Ashford minister John Bass secured a new pulpit in Providence, Rhode Island, just one year after he abandoned Calvinism. Unlike his father, a longtime deacon, John Adams never became a full church member, but he married one: Abigail, the daughter of William Smith, the Weymouth, Massachusetts, minister and a close friend of Ebenezer Gay. In later years, Adams admitted that his religious beliefs were "not exactly conformable to that of the greatest Part of the Christian World"; by the 1810s, he and Abigail were describing themselves as Unitarians. During the 1760s and 1770s, however, they presented all five of their children for baptism a few days after their births. They owned a pew box and worshipped for the rest of their lives in the Quincy Congregational meetinghouse.[146]

These examples reveal a crucial point of difference between purported Arminians and Whitefieldarian dissenters and sectarians. Liberal critics of the Congregational establishment rarely formed factions or fomented schisms, and few of them permanently withdrew from communion. What Jonathan Edwards once called the "great noise" about Arminianism that resounded across New England during the revivals years was just that—a blustery but inconclusive theological debate among a small coterie of sniping clergymen and well-educated lay people. During the decades following the Whitefieldian revivals, the real liberal threat to the gospel land of light came from an unlikely quarter, as Edwards well knew. The "Church of England in New England," he warned in a 1750 letter to a Scottish colleague, "is, I suppose, treble of what it was seven years ago."[147]

146. John Adams to Abigail Adams, Jan. 28, 1799, *Adams Family Papers: An Electronic Archive*, MHS (available online at *http://www.masshist.org/digitaladams/*). For the Adams's church affiliations and baptismal presentations, see Charles W. Akers, *Abigail Adams: An American Woman* (Boston, 1980), 7–8; *The Manifesto Church: Records of the Church in Brattle Square, Boston, with Lists of Communicants, Baptisms, Marriages, and Funerals 1699–1872* (Boston, 1902), 185–186; Quincy, Mass., Church Records, 1762–1870, transcr. Waldo Chamberlain Sprague, MS SG SPR 17, NEHGS (available online at *www.american ancestors.org*); and Frederick A. Whitney, "A Church of the First Congregational (Unitarian) Society in Quincy, Mass., Built in 1732," *NEHGR*, XVIII (1864), 119, 122–123. See also John Fea, "John Adams and Religion," in David Waldstreicher, ed., *A Companion to John Adams and John Quincy Adams*, Wiley-Blackwell Companions to American History (New York, 2013), 184–198; and Woody Holton, *Abigail Adams* (New York, 2009), 46, 114, 271–272, 291, 307–308, 325–326, 403–404.

147. Jonathan Edwards to Benjamin Colman, May 30, 1735, in *WJE*, XVI, *Letters and Personal Writings*, ed. Claghorn, 50, Edwards to William McCulloch, July 6, 1750, 357.

■ Fueled by lingering antirevival sentiment and rising British patriotism generated by the Seven Years' War, Anglicanism exploded across New England between 1745 and 1775. Churchmen had first appeared in the region's seaports during the 1680s. A century later, they formed a small presence in many towns throughout the region, from the Connecticut hinterlands to the Maine frontier. Two decades after the infamous 1722 apostasy at Yale College, in which several tutors and ministers abandoned the Congregational establishment and sought appointments in the Society for the Propagation of the Gospel in Foreign Parts (S.P.G.), Stratford minister Samuel Johnson counted roughly two thousand "adult Church people" in Connecticut. During the next three decades, the total number of Anglicans in the New England colonies swelled to perhaps as many as twenty-five thousand worshippers organized into seventy-four congregations administered by approximately fifty missionaries.[148]

"Notitia Parochialis"—biannual statistical reports filed by S.P.G. missionaries to their superiors in the London—reveal steady growth during the 1750s in both the number of families that affiliated with the Church of England and the geographical range of towns from which they came. On the eve of the Whitefieldian revivals, Ebenezer Punderson counted seventy communicants and perhaps two hundred "Professors of the Church of England" in his Groton, Connecticut, parish. As his zealous Congregational competitor Andrew Croswell and other notable riding ministers such as James Davenport fomented a powerful religious revival in coastal Connecticut, Punderson redoubled his efforts. To combat the growing "Religious Delirium," he expanded his preaching labors to incorporate the neighboring towns of eastern Connecticut. By 1749, his itinerant ministry carried him as far west as Litchfield, more than eighty miles away. Punderson attracted new parishioners even in bastions of

---

148. E. Edwards Beardsley, ed., *Life and Correspondence of Samuel Johnson, D.D.: Missionary of the Church of England in Connecticut, and First President of King's College, New York* (New York, 1874), 114. See also George Woodward Lamb, comp., "Clergymen Licensed to the American Colonies by the Bishops of London: 1745–1781," *Historical Magazine of the Protestant Episcopal Church*, XIII (1944), 128–143; Bruce E. Steiner, "New England Anglicanism: A Genteel Faith?" *WMQ*, XXVII (1970), 122; and Steiner, "Anglican Officeholding in Pre-Revolutionary Connecticut: The Parameters of New England Community," *WMQ*, XXXI (1974), map facing 374–375. On the expansion of Anglicanism in eighteenth-century New England, see Steiner, "Samuel Seabury and the Forging of the High Church Tradition: A Study in the Evolution of New England Churchmanship, 1722–1796" (Ph.D. diss., University of Virginia, 1962), 48–75; Irving Henry King, "The S.P.G. in New England, 1701–1784" (Ph.D. diss., University of Maine, 1968), 193–242; John Frederick Woolverton, *Colonial Anglicanism in North America* (Detroit, Mich., 1984), 107–123, 126–131, 200–202; Michael Winship, "Samuel Hopkins and the Coming of the Church of England to Great Barrington," *Historical Journal of Massachusetts*, XVI (1988), 34–53; and James S. Leamon, *The Reverend Jacob Bailey, Maine Loyalist: For God, King, Country, and for Self* (Amherst, Mass., 2012), 77–100.

the Separate movement such as Mansfield and Canterbury. In less than a decade, he had doubled the number of communicants at Groton and his mission field encompassed more than fifteen hundred families scattered across eastern Connecticut. Punderson worked tirelessly to furnish his parishioners with prayer books and religious literature; he started a school that drew children from Anglican and dissenting households as well as local native Americans; and he petitioned the S.P.G. for funds to construct new churches and furnish salaries for additional missionaries.[149]

The new "conformists," as those who decamped to the Anglicans called themselves, were not recent immigrants to the colonies but rather disaffected men and women of old puritan stock who withdrew from established Congregational churches because of the religious commotions of the 1740s. During the peak months of the revivals, Johnson and his S.P.G. colleagues proclaimed that their fledgling churches were increasing daily as a result of the "Tempest of Enthusiasm" that ravaged the Congregational establishment. Bolstered by antirevival books and pamphlets donated by benefactors in London, New England's S.P.G. missionaries shielded their parishioners from "Mr. Whitefield and his Disciples." In Boston, Timothy Cutler reported a steady influx of "very tractable and teachable" new members, many of whom traveled up to thirty miles to receive communion at King's Chapel. Portsmouth, New Hampshire, minister Arthur Browne feared that his parishioners were "wavering" during the powerful awakening that commenced during the fall of 1741 in York, Maine. Within two years, however, he was writing glowing reports of an "uncommon prospect" in his parish, as many of the port town's Congregationalists recognized the "Necessity of Church Government and Order, and the unreasonableness of departing from their Mother Church." Congregational churches that had suffered through the "late spirit of enthusiasm," concluded Henry Caner, witnessed the largest surge in Anglican conformists during the 1740s and 1750s. "Many of those deluded people, having lost themselves in the midst of error, wearied in the pursuit" the Fairfield, Connecticut, minister explained, and, "as their passions subsided, sought for rest in the bosom" of the Church of England.[150]

149. Kenneth Walter Cameron, ed., *The Church of England in Pre-Revolutionary Connecticut: New Documents and Letters concerning the Loyalist Clergy and the Plight of Their Surviving Church* (Hartford, Conn., 1976), 56–57, 60, 72 (see also 58–59, 61–63, 65–66, 68–69, 71, 73–74). For a sketch of Punderson's career, see Franklin Bowditch Dexter, *Biographical Sketches of the Graduates of Yale College*, 6 vols. (New York, 1885–1912), I, 336–338.
150. Francis L. Hawks and William Stevens Perry, eds., *Documentary History of the Protestant Episcopal Church, in the United States of America*, 2 vols. (New York, 1863–1864), I, 195, 201; Perry, ed., *Historical Collections Relating to the American Colonial Church*, III, 357,

Anglican lay leaders cited disillusionment with the revivals as the principal cause of their growing parishes. "The present Distraction amongst the Dissenters Occasioned by Whitfield and his followers Inclines great numbers of the Discreetest amongst them to Declare for the Church," crowed the wardens of Saint Paul's Church in Newbury, Massachusetts. Disaffected Congregationalists had "great reasons to applaud our System," concurred the vestrymen in nearby Salem. Separation and schism during the years following the revivals had "opened the Eyes of some so as to see the Beauty of our Church." Five men from the Northbury Society in Waterbury (now Plymouth), Connecticut, provided a detailed explanation of their decision in a petition to the bishop of London. "We were all educated in this land, under the instruction of Independent teachers," they wrote, and prejudiced against the Anglicans "from our cradles." Then Whitefield passed through the land "condemning all but his adherents" followed by a host of riding ministers who aped his "insufferable enthusiastick whims and extemporaneous jargon." Northbury and the surrounding parishes were thrown into confusion, as residents watched the established Congregational churches descend into conflict and schism. Beset with ceaseless ecclesiastical turmoil, the Northbury petitioners concluded, "we fled to the Church of England for safety."[151]

Anglicans hailed from all ranks of society: merchants and magistrates, college graduates and yeoman farmers, shopkeepers, mariners, mechanics, and artisans. Conforming families, especially those living in rural parishes, tended to be poorer than their Congregational kin and neighbors; yet many Churchmen were elected to public office in the local, county, and provincial governments. S.P.G. missionaries sprinkled their correspondence with examples of courageous figures such as Jonathan Simpson of Boston, who "dared singly to step out of his father's house" and "openly embraced the Church of England." Even small country towns witnessed defections. In Westborough, Ebenezer Parkman discovered a copy of the Book of Common Prayer in one of his parishioners' homes. Other members of his congregation crossed over the border to attend Christmas services in the Anglican chapel at Hopkinton. S.P.G. missionary Roger Price claimed that several farmers from Westborough and

367, 396; "Letter from Rev. Arthur Brown," *NEHGR*, VI (1852), 264–265; Arthur Browne to Philip Bearcroft, Feb. 6, 1743, Ser. B, XI, 100, microfilm, Records of the Society for the Propagation of the Gospel in Foreign Parts, 1630–1901, Library of Congress. See also Steiner, "Anglican Officeholding in Pre-Revolutionary Connecticut," *WMQ*, XXXI (1974), 389–395; and Jeremy Gregory, "Refashioning Puritan New England: The Church of England in British North America, *c.* 1680–*c.* 1770," Royal Historical Society, *Transactions*, XX (2010), 85–112.

151. Perry, ed., *Historical Collections Relating to the American Colonial Church*, III, 379, 389; Hawks and Perry, eds., *Documentary History of the Protestant Episcopal Church*, I, 211.

the surrounding towns had moved to Hopkinton to be closer to his church. Another fascinating conformist to the Church of England during the 1740s was Joseph Prince, brother of the minister of Boston's Old South Church. A onetime dabbler in astrology, reader of pornography, aspiring lawyer, and member of the Sandwich Congregational church, Prince took to the seas as a coastal trader and settled in Stratford, Connecticut, where he purchased a pew in 1743 near the altar of the newly consecrated Christ Church.[152]

Prince's brother, Nathan, was one among a growing cohort of disaffected Congregational clergymen who traveled to London seeking orders from the bishop of London during the decades following the revivals of the 1740s. Of the fifty S.P.G. missionaries who labored in New England between 1745 and 1775, three-quarters were native sons, 70 percent had graduated from the colleges at Harvard or Yale, and two-thirds hailed from families with long-standing ties to the Congregational establishment. The roster included former ardent revival opposers such as John Fowle of Cohasset, Massachusetts, and Solomon Palmer of Cornwall, Connecticut. William Hooper, the Scottish-born minister of the West Church in Boston whose antirevival tract had been consumed in the New London bonfires, shocked his parishioners when he sailed for England in 1747 seeking ordination in the S.P.G. Three sons of respected Congregational clergymen in eastern Massachusetts—Mather Byles, Jr., William Clark, and William Walter—defected to the Church of England; so, too, did the college-educated children of deacons, schoolmasters, and core parish families from towns across New England. By 1770, a growing number of these Yankee missionaries presided over Anglican churches from Georgia to Nova Scotia.[153]

Perhaps the most intriguing clerical conformist during the second half of the eighteenth century was Samuel Fayerweather. While studying at Harvard

152. Steiner, "New England Anglicanism," *WMQ*, XXVII (1970), 122–135; Steiner, "Anglican Officeholding in Pre-Revolutionary Connecticut," *WMQ*, XXXI (1974), 372–379; Perry, ed., *Historical Collections Relating to the American Colonial Church*, III, 358 (quote), 438; Walett, ed., *Diary of Ebenezer Parkman*, 115, 193, 205, 207, 229, 282; Douglas L. Winiarski, "The Education of Joseph Prince: Reading Adolescent Culture in Eighteenth-Century New England," in Peter Benes, ed., *The Worlds of Children, 1620–1920*, Dublin Seminar for New England Folklife, Annual Proceedings 2002 (Boston, 2004), 60–61. For Prince's early life, see Part 1, note 104, above.

153. Hawks and Perry, eds., *Documentary History of the Protestant Episcopal Church*, II, 205. Statistics derived from Lamb, comp., "Clergyman Licensed to the American Colonies," *Historical Magazine of the Protestant Episcopal Church*, XIII (1944), 131–143; Dexter, *Biographical Sketches*, I, 387–388, 575, 651–652, 687–688, 729–731, II, 35–36, 39–43, 362–364, 482–487, 520–521, 557–560, 568–570, 701–706, 709–710, 788, III, 154–158, 425–427; and *SHG*, IX, 151–155, X, 110–112, XI, 97–107, 221–229, 340–359, XII, 519–535, XIII, 6–26, 202–204, 413–416, 522–545, 681–684, XIV, 111–121, 353–364, 393–402, XV, 15–19, XVI, 46–49, 76–84.

College during the 1740s, the prominent Boston merchant's son had emerged as an ardent Whitefieldian new convert. He experienced dramatic visions of Satan and embraced Andrew Croswell's assessment that the college's "President and Tutors were arminians." After presenting an unusual church admission testimony at Old South Church in 1742, however, Fayerweather began to question his youthful radicalism. Over the next two decades, he reinvented himself as a genteel Anglican divine. Fayerweather served as a chaplain during the 1745 Louisbourg expedition, preached in various towns in New England, and visited George Whitefield's orphanage in Savannah, Georgia, which he praised in a 1748 letter to Boston ministers Thomas Prince and Thomas Foxcroft. The following year, Fayerweather received a call to serve as the junior colleague of Charleston's Presbyterian minister, Josiah Smith—one of the most prominent Whitefieldarians in the southern colonies—but he declined the invitation and returned to New England. Then, in 1755, he abruptly changed direction and sailed for England, where he accepted an honorary master's degree from the University of Cambridge and was ordained by the bishop of London as an S.P.G. missionary. Returning to the colonies, Fayerweather ministered to several small Anglican parishes in South Carolina before taking a permanent position at Saint Paul's Episcopal Church in North Kingston, Rhode Island. During the last two decades of his life, Fayerweather developed a reputation for his literary wit, theological ecumenism, and refined tastes, which were on full display in the portrait that John Singleton Copley produced for him during the 1760s.[154]

Like provincials in Virginia and elsewhere in the British Empire, New Englanders were drawn to the Church of England for its promise of order. Those who "conform'd to the Episcopal Church" regarded their new religious identities as standing in direct opposition to the individual experiences of the Whitefieldians. The church's liturgical calendar, rich sensorium of music and material culture, refined architecture, and open access to the sacraments— baptism especially—engendered a sense of stability, rationality, and toleration among its adherents. Yankee missionaries in the S.P.G. emphasized these qualities in letters to their superiors in London. Solomon Palmer described his parishioners in Litchfield, Connecticut, as a "body of religious, sober, and

154. Edward T. Dunn, ed., "The Diary of Tutor Henry Flynt of Harvard College, 1675–1760," 3 vols., typescript (Buffalo, N.Y., 1978), 1458, 1484 (quote); *SHG*, XI, 221–229; Lilla Mills Hawes, ed., "A Description of Whitefield's Bethesda: Samuel Fayerweather to Thomas Prince and Thomas Foxcroft," *Georgia Historical Quarterly*, XLV (1961), 363–366. For Fayerweather's youthful radicalism, see Part 2, note 133, above; his 1742 relation may be found in Appendix C.

FIGURE 24 John Singleton Copley, *Reverend Samuel Fayerweather*. Probably 1760–1761. Oil on gold-leafed copper, 7.6 × 6.4 cm. Mabel Brady Garvan Collection, Yale University Art Gallery, New Haven, Connecticut

orderly people, steady in their principles, and constant in their attendance upon the public worship and service of the Church." Remarking on the "usual Good State" of his flock, Scituate, Massachusetts, minister Ebenezer Thompson noted that "we live very happy, in love and peace, not only with our Brethren of the Church of England, but with the Dissenters of the various Denominations." Where the Whitefieldarians and their descendants were "Rancorous and Spiteful" in their noisy, chaotic revival meetings, the Anglicans, by contrast, were calm, attentive, prudent, and, above all, "regular" in their religious observances—a keyword in eighteenth-century Anglican discourse that signaled consistency of form and a willingness to submit to ecclesiastical authority. For many godly walkers who had lived through the maelstrom of the revivals of the 1740s, the "Ocular demonstration" of ordered ritual during church services provided welcome relief to the relentless strife that plagued established Congregational churches during the 1750s and 1760s.[155]

■ During the summer of 1755, Josiah Cotton discovered to his dismay that his son-in-law, John Cushing, Jr., had become an "Admirer" of the liberal Congregational clergyman Jonathan Mayhew. The "Colonel," as Cotton called the prominent Scituate, Massachusetts, magistrate, attended Mayhew's West Church whenever his duties as a justice of the Massachusetts superior court of judicature brought him to Boston. To make matters worse, Cushing sent his father-in-law a copy of Mayhew's controversial *Seven Sermons*. Cotton was unimpressed. "I have now read Your Book above half through," he responded, "and find it writ with a great deal of argument, Life and Air." That was no compliment. Cotton quipped that it might be said of Mayhew's sermons, as it was of those by the famed Boston poet Mather Byles, that "1000 of 'em would not Convert a Rat." Although he conceded that his harsh judgment was uncivil, Cotton maintained that Mayhew's "Fleering" contempt for the theological works of "Good and Worthy Men" warranted the response. He was especially troubled by Mayhew's rejection of the doctrine of justification by faith. Where the West Church minister made moral obedience to divine law the "Matter of Our Justification before God," Cotton complained, "he Combats the Orthodox."[156]

155. Benjamin Webb, diary, 1748–1769, Oct. 27, 1748, Webb Family Papers, 1734–1769, Ser. II, box 3, Henry Herbert Edes Collection, 1648–1917, MHS; Hawks and Perry, eds., *Documentary History of the Protestant Episcopal Church*, II, 11; Perry, ed., *Historical Collections Relating to the American Colonial Church*, III, 465, 493, 503, 515. The argument in this paragraph follows Louis P. Nelson, *The Beauty of Holiness: Anglicanism and Architecture in Colonial South Carolina* (Chapel Hill, N.C., 2008), esp. 217–249.

156. JCH, 442–443; Cotton to Cushing, Jr., July 28, 1755, William Cushing Papers.

Cotton's dispute with Cushing had been brewing for a decade. Not only was his son-in-law reading liberal theological works, he had disengaged from the Congregational establishment. In 1744, Cushing and his second wife— Cotton's daughter Mary—had waited six months to baptize their eighth child; they held back for nearly two years before presenting their next child; and their last son, Roland, does not appear to have been baptized at all. By 1753, Cotton described his son-in-law as "one of the Episcopal Communion." At the same time, Cushing also demanded the right to receive the Lord's Supper in the Scituate Congregational church—an unusual privilege that was granted by a unanimous vote, perhaps on the basis of his status as one of the colony's wealthiest and most influential residents. "The Sacrament among the Ancient Romans was a Military Oath binding them to be true to their Commanders," Cotton groused in his annual memoirs, "And Oh that We who Sometimes Partake of the Christian Sacrament May be true to Our Leader and Commander Jesus Christ." To Cotton, the colonel's promiscuous religious allegiances were a dangerous sign of the times.[157]

Cotton's daughter remained a lifelong member of the Scituate church, but her husband never returned to the congregation in which he had been baptized and raised. Cushing spent his Sabbaths worshipping alone in Saint Andrew's Episcopal Church. As with Strict Congregationalists, Separate Baptists, and sectarian perfectionists—but for very different reasons—the Whitefieldian revivals had impelled John Cushing, Jr., and thousands like him to abandon the religious traditions of their puritan ancestors.

TOHU AND BOHU

Count Vavasor could scarcely contain his rage. The date was May 18, 1751, and the circumstances precipitating his furious, pseudonymous letter to the "Venerable Elders" gathered in Northampton, Massachusetts, were highly unusual. Two days earlier, a council of leading clergymen from eastern Massachusetts had convened to reconsider the church's recent decision to dismiss Jonathan Edwards from his pastorate. The delegation came at the invitation of Edwards and Timothy Dwight, the prominent merchant, magistrate, and militia colonel who had witnessed the extraordinary fits of Martha Robinson

---

157. JCH, 425. For Cushing's religious affiliations and irregular baptismal presentations, see James S. Cushing, [comp.], *The Genealogy of the Cushing Family: An Account of the Ancestors and Descendants of Matthew Cushing, Who Came to America in 1638* (Montreal, 1905), 48–49; and Litchfield, ed., *Scituate Massachusetts Second Church Records*, 20, 24, 39–40, 44, 47, 49, 53, 56, 58, 60, 70, 73, 75, 78, 80.

during the Whitefieldian revival in Boston. By the spring of 1751, Dwight and a small clique of supporters were scheming to organize a second church in Northampton with Edwards reinstalled as their pastor. In a surprising turn of events, Boston minister Thomas Prince and the other delegates approved their separatist scheme. Written by John Baker, an elderly parishioner posing as an English aristocrat, Count Vavasor's scathing epistle heaped contempt on the entire affair, condemning Dwight as the "firebrand and ringleader of A few benighted Witlings better qualified to be imployed in draging Garbage to tygers and Monsters." Acting without the sanction of the Hampshire County ministerial association, the Dwight faction had ignited a "Conflagration." That a group of interloping clergymen would foment schism in Northampton was "insuperable," Vavasor fulminated. The rogue council had "brought forth A monster."[158]

The chain of events that had led to the dismissal of one of New England's most distinguished ministers started several years earlier, when Edwards unexpectedly announced that he intended to change the procedures by which he admitted parishioners to full communion. For half a century, the Northampton church had followed what Vavasor called the "uniform and Established" doctrines of Edwards's grandfather and former senior colleague, the "Celebrated" and "Ever blessed" Solomon Stoddard. Skeptical of the possibility of distinguishing true saints from hypocrites, Stoddard eschewed relations and, instead, allowed all adult townspeople who could demonstrate a "Catechisticall knowledge of the Principalls of Religion" to participate in the sacraments. Edwards adhered to his grandfather's open communion practices for more than two decades, but revival events in Northampton and elsewhere in New England during the 1740s had convinced him of the need for more restrictive qualifications for participation in the Lord's Supper. He hinted at his change of heart briefly in his 1746 *Treatise concerning Religious Affections,* and he later produced depositions verifying that he had been considering the issue for a number of years. After searching the scriptures, reading books by leading English divines, and consulting with colleagues, Edwards made up his mind. Quietly and without the consent of his church, he began asking candidates to draw up a written "profession of saving faith" as a requirement for joining the Northampton church in full communion.[159]

---

158. Douglas L. Winiarski, "New Perspectives on the Northampton Communion Controversy III: Count Vavasor's Tirade ...," *Jonathan Edwards Studies,* IV (2014), 376–377.

159. Ibid., 376; Thomas M. Davis and Virginia L. Davis, eds., *Edward Taylor vs. Solomon Stoddard: The Nature of the Lord's Supper,* II, *Unpublished Writings of Edward Taylor,* American Literary Manuscripts (Boston, 1981), 63; Jonathan Edwards, "Narrative of Com-

When Edwards finally "declared the matter fully" to a church committee in February 1749, his parishioners rebelled. Within weeks, they were calling for his resignation. In the tangled negotiations that followed, Edwards struggled and failed to persuade his congregants to accept his restrictive qualifications for church membership and participation in the Lord's Supper. Angry congregants fought him every inch of the way, barring him from preaching on the subject, shunning his weekly lectures, and refusing to read his hastily published defense, *An Humble Inquiry*. On June 19, 1750, an ecclesiastical council voted by a narrow margin to recommend dissolving relations between the embattled clergyman and his embittered people. "Arms flew as if they went with Springs," recalled an observer, as the people of Northampton overwhelmingly confirmed the council's advice. Edwards's opponents outnumbered his supporters ten to one.[160]

Edwards remained in Northampton for more than a year after delivering a stern *Farewel-Sermon* in which he warned all of the contending parties that they would one day be summoned before God to account for their roles in "our late grand controversy." The chastened clergyman occasionally preached on supply in his vacated pulpit, while scheming with Dwight and his supporters and discussing his options with colleagues in New England and Scotland. Following the tumultuous second council of 1751 and facing the relentless abuse of "Railers" like Count Vavasor, Edwards laid aside his plans to gather a new Congregational church in Northampton. He retreated to the frontier town of Stockbridge, Massachusetts, where he spent the next six years preaching to a small community of Mahican Indians and writing the treatises for which he would later achieve enduring fame as the era's greatest theologian.[161]

munion Controversy," in *WJE*, XII, *Ecclesiastical Writings*, ed. David D. Hall (New Haven, Conn., 1994), 507. See also Jonathan Edwards, *A Treatise concerning Religious Affections* (Boston, 1746), in *WJE*, II, *Religious Affections*, ed. John E. Smith (New Haven, Conn., 1959), 415–418; Joseph Bellamy et al., "Depositions," 1750, *WJEO*, XXXVIII, *Dismissal and Post-Dismissal Documents*, and Edwards, "Sacrament Book I."

160. Dexter, ed., *Extracts from the Itineraries and Other Miscellanies of Ezra Stiles*, 503 (quote); Jonathan Edwards to John Erskine, July 5, 1750, in *WJE*, XVI, *Letters and Personal Writings*, ed. Claghorn, 353. For Edwards's account of the events leading up to his dismissal, see Edwards, "Narrative of Communion Controversy," in *WJE*, XII, *Ecclesiastical Writings*, ed. Hall, 507–619.

161. Edwards, *Farewel-Sermon*, in *WJE*, XXV, *Sermons and Discourses, 1743–1758*, ed. Kimnach, 476; Timothy Dwight, "Petition of the Northampton Minority," n.d. [circa 1751], *WJEO*, XXXVIII, *Dismissal and Post-Dismissal Documents*. On the relationship between Edwards's missionary career and his major theological works of the 1750s, see Rachel M. Wheeler, "Edwards as Missionary," in Stephen J. Stein, ed., *The Cambridge Companion to Jonathan Edwards*, Cambridge Companions to Religion (New York, 2007), 196–214; and Wheeler, *To Live upon Hope: Mohicans and Missionaries in the Eighteenth-Century Northeast* (Ithaca, N.Y., 2008), 206–222.

For several years before his dismissal, Edwards had been wrangling his congregation over his salary and church discipline cases involving the sexual indiscretions of young men from prominent Northampton families. But these minor incidents were not directly related to the communion controversy, nor were they cited in the protracted debates that ensued. Instead, Edwards challenged his parishioners at the fundamental level of religious experience by raising the qualifications for church membership. A brief survey of post-1745 relations from parishes across New England provides a more direct context for the "great Degree of unchristian Bitterness" that erupted in Northampton and reveals widening fissures in what had once been a unified religious culture. Most church admission testimonies that survive from the second half of the eighteenth century contain narrative elements that Edwards sharply criticized in *An Humble Inquiry*. Taken together, they expose the broad gulf that separated Edwards from his contemporaries, including his strongest supporters.[162]

The Northampton qualifications controversy signaled the beginning of the end for the churches of the Congregational standing order. The Whitefieldian revivals of the 1740s and the bitter theological debates and church schisms that soon followed had so polarized the region that few people—Vavasor and Edwards included—were willing to find common ground when confronted with one of the central questions of the day: what constituted an authentic religious experience? Recoiling from his earlier radicalism, Edwards came to believe that only a "public profession of religion" would insulate his parish from the centrifugal threats of Arminian formalism and antinomian enthusi-

---

162. Ebenezer Pomeroy, "Northampton Church Committee on the Petition of the Minority," n.d. [circa 1751], *WJEO*, XXXVIII, *Dismissal and Post-Dismissal Documents*. Studies that attribute Edwards's dismissal to broader sources of social discord include Patricia J. Tracy, *Jonathan Edwards, Pastor: Religion and Society in Eighteenth-Century Northampton*, American Century Series (New York, 1979), 147–194; Nobles, *Divisions Throughout the Whole*, 59–74; Kevin Michael Sweeney, "River Gods and Related Minor Deities: The Williams Family and the Connecticut River Valley, 1637–1790" (Ph.D. diss., Yale University, 1986), 429–457; Kenneth Pieter Minkema, "The Edwardses: A Ministerial Family in Eighteenth Century New England" (Ph.D. diss., University of Connecticut, 1988), 311–356; Ava Chamberlain, "Bad Books and Bad Boys: The Transformation of Gender in Eighteenth-Century Northampton, Massachusetts," *NEQ*, LXXV (2002), 179–203; George M. Marsden, *Jonathan Edwards: A Life* (New Haven, Conn., 2003), 341–374; Chamberlain, "Jonathan Edwards and the Politics of Sex in Eighteenth-Century Northampton," in Harry S. Stout, Kenneth P. Minkema, and Caleb J. D. Maskell, eds., *Jonathan Edwards at 300: Essays on the Tercentenary of His Birth* (Lanham, Md., 2005), 111–122; and Philip F. Gura, *Jonathan Edwards: America's Evangelical* (New York, 2005), 135–164. My argument in this section builds on David D. Hall, "Editor's Introduction," in *WJE*, XII, *Ecclesiastical Writings*, ed. Hall, 1–4, 51–68, 77–86; and Christopher Grasso, "Misrepresentations Corrected: Jonathan Edwards and the Regulation of Religious Discourse," in Stephen J. Stein, ed., *Jonathan Edwards's Writings: Text, Context, Interpretation* (Bloomington Ind., 1996), 19–38.

asm. But, in a religious culture that had lost its center, the "stingy principles" that Edwards attributed to New England's puritan forefathers further eroded any remaining consensus. Edwards's dismissal from Northampton laid bare the gaping fissures that had emerged in the gospel land of light, as ministers and lay people struggled to distinguish traditional relations and professions of doctrine from the inspired narratives of conversion. "All are agreed that a publick profession of religion is necessary in order to persons being admitted into the church," acknowledged one of Edwards's many critics. "But then we Shall differ as to this profession."[163]

■ Western New England was "exceeding full of noise" about the Northampton communion controversy. The dispute over Edwards's "late Sentiments engrosses Most of the Conversation," noted Joseph Hawley, one of his principal antagonists. Count Vavasor's tirade was perhaps the most extreme example of the "hot headed" rhetoric that marked the conflict, but he was hardly alone. "Let Northampton Sink or Swim," proclaimed Timothy Dwight, the leader of the dissenting faction, "Mr. Edwards should be settled over them Again." Another angry parishioner declared that "It would be well" if Edwards's head was "Seven feet under ground," although he thought "Six would do his turn." Members of the ecclesiastical council that voted against Edwards's dismissal turned on their colleagues and condemned the proceedings in a pamphlet that induced the Hampshire Association to publish a rebuttal. Hot letters alleging misconduct, misrepresentation, and public abuse swirled through epistolary networks. "I pity poor bleeding Northampton," lamented Boston minister Thomas Foxcroft. The town was "tohu" and "Bohu"—in total confusion, "without form, and void"—a neighboring minister reported, quoting a Hebrew phrase from Genesis 1. Edwards, too, was not immune from inflating the controversy. "It Seems I am born to be a Man of Strife," he declared to a young colleague at the outset of the conflict. Soon he was reveling in his role as a martyr for the cause of Christ. He felt as if he were casting himself "off from a precipice."[164]

163. Jonathan Edwards, *An Humble Inquiry into the Rules of the Word of God, concerning the Qualifications Requisite to a Compleat Standing and Full Communion in the Visible Christian Church* (Boston, 1749), in *WJE*, XII, *Ecclesiastical Writings*, ed. Hall, 203; Edwards, *An Humble Attempt to Promote Explicit Agreement and Visible Union of God's People in Extraordinary Prayer* . . . (Boston, 1747), in *WJE*, V, *Apocalyptic Writings*, ed. Stephen J. Stein (New Haven, Conn., 1977), 359; Anonymous, "Discourse on the Theology of Jonathan Edwards," n.d. [circa 1750], microfilm, reel 7, frame 1124, Eleazer Williams Papers, 1634–1964, Wisconsin Historical Society, Madison, Wisc.

164. Edwards to Thomas Foxcroft, May 24, 1749, in *WJE*, XVI, *Letters and Personal Writings*, ed. Claghorn, 284; Joseph Hawley to Elisha Hawley, Aug. 11, 1749, Joseph Hawley

The Northampton communion controversy was cloaked from the start with a certain amount of misinformation and outright ignorance on all sides. Many of the participants, Edwards included, admitted that they knew little of church admission requirements in other parts of New England. Count Vavasor and his opponents in Northampton refused to consider any alternatives to Stoddard's open communion practices. Copies of *An Humble Inquiry,* which the publisher described as undersubscribed, did not circulate widely or enjoy the extensive readership for which Edwards had hoped. Foxcroft, Thomas Prince, and several other Boston ministers signed the preface to his apologetic treatise before they even had a chance to peruse his argument.[165]

As a result, clergymen in eastern Massachusetts expressed genuine puzzlement over the "Strange Spirit of Allienation" that had gripped the Northampton church. Foxcroft, for example, wrote an exhaustive appendix for Edwards's *Humble Inquiry* in which he cataloged dozens of works by Reformed theologians in Old and New England that reinforced the Northampton minister's position on church membership. To him, Edwards's demands seemed reasonable, even axiomatic. Foxcroft's cross-town colleague, Prince, agreed. He urged all parties to settle on a common principle and reconcile their seemingly minor differences. After corresponding with Edwards, Salem Village minister Peter Clark was "at a Loss to apprehend, wherein the main ground of the Controversy, between you, and your people lies." To sympathetic outsiders, Edwards's purported "new-modeling of his church" was hardly new at all.[166]

Papers, 1653–1804, Manuscripts and Archives Division, New York Public Library (available online at *http://archives.nypl.org/mss/1360*); Dwight, "Petition of the Northampton Minority," n.d. [circa 1751], *WJEO*, XXXVIII, *Dismissal and Post-Dismissal Documents;* Thomas Foxcroft to Timothy Dwight, Aug. 4, 1752, *WJEO*, XXXII, *Correspondence by, to, and about Edwards and His Family;* Billing, diaries, May 1750; John Searle to Jonathan Edwards, June 4, 1750, *WJEO*, XXXII, *Correspondence by, to, and about Edwards and His Family*, B88. For the council result and rebuttal, see *The Result of a Council of Nine Churches Met at Northampton ...* [Boston, 1750]; and *An Account of the Conduct of the Council Which Dismissed the Rev. Mr. Edwards ...* [Boston, 1750].

165. Edwards to Foxcroft, May 24, 1749, in *WJE*, XVI, *Letters and Personal Writings,* ed. Claghorn, 283; Samuel Kneeland to Joseph Bellamy, Sept. 4 and Oct. 2, 1749, *WJEO*, XXXII, *Correspondence by, to, and about Edwards and His Family*, C83a–C83b; Peter Clark to Ebenezer Pomeroy, Apr. 4, 1750, in Edwards, "Narrative of the Communion Controversy," in *WJE*, XII, *Ecclesiastical Writings*, ed. Hall, 612; Prince to Dwight and the Northampton Minority, n.d. [circa early winter 1751], *WJEO*, XXXII, *Correspondence by, to, and about Edwards and His Family*, C91; Edwards, *Humble Inquiry*, in *WJE*, XII, *Ecclesiastical Writings*, ed. Hall, 172.

166. Hall, diaries, May 26, 1751; Peter Clark to Jonathan Edwards, May 21, 1750, *WJEO*, XXXII, *Correspondence by, to, and about Edwards and His Family*, B86. See also Thomas Foxcroft to Jonathan Edwards, June 26, 1749, in Edwards, *Humble Inquiry*, in *WJE*, XII, *Ecclesiastical Writings*, ed. Hall, 326–348; Thomas Prince to Timothy Dwight and the Northampton Minority, n.d. [circa early winter 1751], *WJEO*, XXXII, *Correspondence by, to,*

Most of Edwards's eastern colleagues accepted what Clark called the "commonly received and well-grounded distinction" between visible saints, or earnest communicants who might have been deceived in their decision to join the church, and invisible saints whom God had predestined for salvation. The church of Christ in the world, Clark further reasoned, would inevitably comprise both "good and bad, sound and unsound Christians." Until the Day of Judgment, true saints and deluded hypocrites would appear side by side at the communion table and present their children for baptism. For Clark, membership in the visible church nonetheless required a "credible profession," which he defined as a "competent measure of Christian knowledge, together with a good conversation joined to a serious and solemn consent to the covenant of the gospel." And this, of course, was precisely what godly walkers in eastern Massachusetts described in their relations for more than half a century before the revivals of the 1740s.[167]

Even as Edwards moved to impose church membership professions in Northampton, Foxcroft and Prince, two of his strongest supporters during the communion controversy, were leading their Boston congregations in the opposite direction. In 1756, Foxcroft's parishioners voted to allow candidates who "have a Scruple upon their Minds about making a Relation as usual" to exhibit a written statement of their theological knowledge instead. Members of the Old South Church eliminated the test of a relation altogether, replacing it initially with a standardized profession of doctrine and, by 1770, with a statement of candidates' beliefs written in their own words. At the height of the revivals of the 1740s, both ministers used church admission testimonies to corral the excessive zeal of new converts. During the next two decades, relations produced by candidates in Boston evolved into elaborate theological professions, rather than narratives of religious experiences.[168]

Composed in April 1749 as the communion controversy raged in Northampton, Robert Treat Paine's relation marked a transitional moment in the evolution of the genre. Like many godly walkers, he began by acknowledging his "Birth in a Land of Gospell Light" and giving thanks for the privileges of living under the means of grace. Although Paine wrote with flair about

---

and about Edwards and His Family, C91; Peter Clark to Ebenezer Pomeroy, Apr. 4, 1750, in Edwards, "Narrative of the Communion Controversy," in *WJE,* XII, *Ecclesiastical Writings,* ed. Hall, 613.

167. Clark to Pomeroy, Apr. 4, 1750, in Edwards, "Narrative of the Communion Controversy," in *WJE,* XII, *Ecclesiastical Writings,* ed. Hall, 613.

168. Richard D. Pierce, ed., *The Records of the First Church in Boston, 1630–1868,* XXXIX, CSM, *Pubs.,* XXXIX (Boston, 1961), 213; Hamilton Andrews Hill, *History of the Old South Church (Third Church) Boston, 1669–1884,* 2 vols. (Boston, 1890), II, 95–96, 112.

his sinful nature, however, he devoted little attention to experiences of any kind. Whereas candidates a generation earlier had emphasized their family upbringing and the loud calls of divine providence and new converts during the 1740s accented the formative role of powerful itinerant preachers, the young schoolmaster, aspiring lawyer, and future signer of the Declaration of Independence focused instead on the terms of salvation offered in the gospel. Professing to believe in the Bible and consenting to the tenets of Reformed theology outlined in the Westminster Confession of Faith, Paine closed his relation with a standard sacramental refrain: "I have for some time had a desire to attend upon the Lords Supper and to Come to that divine Institution of a Dying Redeemer, And I trust I'm now convinced that it is my Duty Openly to profess him least he be ashamed to own me An Other day." Paine was a pious man quite capable of writing with emotional candor in his diary and correspondence, but he seemed unwilling to render his inward piety visible to the Old South congregation in his church admission testimony.[169]

Other Boston relations shifted even further away from experiential disclosures. Hannah Blake's 1751 statement included a florid introduction, written in her flowery hand, in which she described God as a "Most Holy wise Creator, and Mercifull Father of Spirits" who had molded "So Exact an Elegant a Creature as man out of the dust of the Earth, in which that Enestamable Jewell the Soul, was to take its Lodging." Old South clergyman Joseph Sewall might have found her relation wanting, for he canceled several evocative phrases and introduced extensive marginal notations that emphasized Blake's "lost perishing Condition," her willingness to submit to Christ, and her desire to "walk agreeable" to her profession. Harvard College student John Fairfield's 1760 relation consisted entirely of doctrinal affirmations and supporting scriptural passages, which he desired to take for the "Rule of my Life." Other prospective communicants in Boston's two leading churches hoped to obtain "some Advantage" by joining the church. A comprehensive statement of the candidates' doctrinal knowledge and a "well Ordered Conversation" had emerged as the primary criteria for admission to the sacraments. For many Boston parishioners, the language of religious experience had drained out of the genre.[170]

Elsewhere in New England, the traditional relation of faith formula remained unchanged during the second half of the eighteenth century. This

---

169. Appendix B, Boston, Third (Old South) Church, 8. On Paine as a religious figure, see Mark Valeri, *Heavenly Merchandize: How Religion Shaped Commerce in Puritan America* (Princeton, N.J., 2010), 238–239.

170. Appendix B, Boston, Third (Old South) Church, 2; Appendix B, Boston, First Church, 6, 9, 11.

was the case in the hinterland parishes of central Massachusetts, including the small farming hamlet of Westborough, Massachusetts. Despite occasional scrapes with zealous new converts such as members of the Fay family and Sarah Prentice, Ebenezer Parkman remained a warm proponent of the revivals and one of Edwards's most stalwart defenders. Parkman owned a copy of An *Humble Inquiry*, the embattled clergyman's controversial "Book against his Grandfather," and he praised his Northampton colleague for being "much Study'd" on the subject of religious experience after reading his *Treatise concerning Religious Affections*. Edwards visited and corresponded with Parkman during the communion controversy, while Timothy Dwight kept the Westborough clergyman informed of the latest developments during his travels to Boston. Edwards even nominated Parkman to serve as a member of the council that met in 1750 to consider the charge of dismissal, although the Westborough church refused to allow their minister to participate.[171]

Over a period spanning more than half a century, Parkman's parishioners diligently appeared at his parsonage bearing "ample, Serious, Pathetick" relations that rarely deviated from the generic conventions that had taken root in eastern Massachusetts early in the eighteenth century. Fifty-five percent of all church membership candidates in Westborough deployed the traditional language of puritan tribalism, blessing God they had been "borne in a Land of Light," "early given up to god by baptism," and "Instructed in my duty to God" by "Christian Parents" (Table 7). Professions of belief also figured prominently in their narratives. Two years after the birth of a son who would one day revolutionize the American textile industry, Eli and Elizabeth Whitney composed a pair of theological statements in which they traced the arc of salvation history from the original disobedience of Adam and Eve to the atoning sacrifice of Christ on the cross. Long after the revivals of the 1740s had subsided, Parkman's parishioners continued to believe that it was the sacramental duty of all Christians to partake of the Lord's Supper—whatever the state of their souls. The threatening words of 1 Corinthians 11:29 remained the most frequently quoted scriptural passage in the Westborough relations, and candidates surmounted their fears of eating and drinking damnation by citing the same cluster of encouraging biblical texts that had anchored church admission testimonies for more than a century. A few cited the powerful impact of devastating temporal afflictions, including Isaac Miller, who was stirred to join

171. Walett, ed., *Diary of Ebenezer Parkman*, 146 (quote), 203 (quote), 216–217, 219, 221, 224, 236–238; Edwards, "Narrative of the Communion Controversy," in *WJE*, XII, *Ecclesiastical Writings*, ed. Hall, 618; Edwards to Ebenezer Parkman, Sept. 11, 1749, in *WJE*, XVI, *Letters and Personal Writings*, ed. Claghorn, 291–293.

TABLE 7 Content Analysis of Selected Eighteenth-Century Relations of Faith Collections by Church

Church	Total Relations (N)	Average Word Length	Profession of Beliefs (%)	Tribalism (%)	Providential Afflictions (%)	Sacramental Theology (%)	Confession of Sin (%)
Granville, Mass., First Church (circa 1756–circa 1777)	14	591	7.1	14.3	28.6	85.7	21.4
Haverhill, Mass., First Church (1719–1745)	235	241	57.4	58.3	38.7	91.5	13.2
Ipswich (now Essex), Mass., Chebacco Separate Congregational Church (1750–1785)	64	635	3.1	6.3	29.7	4.7	6.3
Medfield, Mass., First Church (1697–1766)	106	720	16.0	81.1	60.4	90.6	4.7
Middleborough, Mass., First Church (1748–1777)	40	467	7.5	67.5	40.0	60.0	15.0
Sturbridge, Mass., First Church (1737–1764)	38	509	10.5	68.4	50.0	86.8	13.2
Westborough, Mass., First Church (1736–1786)	84	436	65.5	54.8	20.2	79.8	4.8

Note: Average length excludes fragmentary relations. Dates for Granville, Chebacco, and Middleborough are delimited by the pastorates of Jediah Smith (dismissed 1776), John Cleaveland (died 1799), and Sylvanus Conant (died 1777). For methodology, see Appendix A.

Sources: Appendix B; Granville, Mass., First Congregational Church Records, circa 1760–1913, CL (available online at NEHH); Middleboro, Mass., First Congregational Church Relations and Personal Records, 1724–1865, CL (available online at NEHH).

the church after losing his hand in a mill accident. Others confessed to committing various sins during the days of their youth. When prospective communicants such as Adam Rice considered "what I must do on my Part to inharit atarnal life," the answer was one that would have been familiar to his parents and grandparents: "live as becometh an heir of the Kingdom of Grace" and "walk worthy of the vocation wherewith we are called."[172]

Across New England, in towns that had suffered through divisive revival seasons and those that had not, many lay men and women continued to submit relations that remained closely tied to the older ideal of the godly walk. Even in revival hotbeds such as Malden and Norton, Massachusetts, and Suffield, Connecticut, people still envisioned church membership in the contractual terms of sacramental obligations. Other candidates living in parishes whose ministers had opposed the revivals offered extended professions of beliefs and buttressed their decision to close with the church with familiar scriptural promises: Isaiah 55:1, Matthew 11:28, and John 7:37. Even parishioners in the small hamlet of Freetown, Massachusetts, who called former Shepherd's Tent radical Silas Brett to be their minister in 1747, continued to thank God for casting their lot in a "Land of Gospel Light."[173]

Despite their geographic diversity and occasional variations in stylistic conventions, one thing was clear: none of the relations from Boston, Westborough, or elsewhere in New England would have passed muster with Edwards. Lay men and women in these churches seldom addressed what the Northampton minister called the "great things wherein godliness consists" or the "essentials of true piety." Had colleagues in eastern Massachusetts scrutinized his *Humble Inquiry* with greater care or listened to the lectures he delivered in Northampton during the winter of 1750, they would have instantly realized that his nar-

---

172. Ross W. Beales, Jr., "Literacy and Reading in Eighteenth-Century Westborough, Massachusetts," in Peter Benes, ed., *Early American Probate Inventories*, Dublin Seminar for New England Folklife, Annual Proceedings 1987 (Boston, 1989), 48; Appendix B, Westborough, Mass., First Church, 12, 25, 53–54, 58, 60, 83 (see also 56, 81–82). For the full text of Whitney's relation, see Appendix C. For a similar argument, see Juster, *Disorderly Women*, 73n.

173. J. M. Bumsted, "Emotion in Colonial America: Some Relations of Conversion Experience in Freetown, Massachusetts, 1749–1770," *NEQ*, XLIX (1976), 106. See also Relation of Polly Emerson, n.d. [circa 1740s], private collection (I thank Phyllis Cole for sharing a copy of this manuscript); Clark, *History of the Town of Norton*, 71–72; Anonymous relation, n.d. [mid-eighteenth century], tipped in Suffield Congregational Church Records; anonymous, relations, n.d. [mid-eighteenth century], box 1, First Parish Church in Dorchester Records, 1636–1981, MHS; Relation of Mary Green, n.d. [circa 1740s], Nathan Stone Papers, 1726–1832, MHS; Erik R. Seeman, "Lay Conversion Narratives: Investigating Ministerial Intervention," *NEQ*, LXXI (1998), 631–632; and Winiarski, "New Perspectives on the Northampton Communion Controversy II: Relations, Professions, and Experiences, 1748–1760," *Jonathan Edwards Studies*, IV (2014), 132–135.

row definition of a "credible Profession of real Christianity" diverged significantly from their more inclusive concept of a church admission relation. In fact, Edwards's new sentiments reprised the stinging critique of the godly walk that he had once deployed in powerful revival sermons such as *Sinners in the Hands of an Angry God.* The diligent performance of religious duties—or what candidates in places like Westborough called walking "agreeable" to their professions—was insufficient. Prospective church members needed to square the sign of their professions with what Edwards called the "thing signified": the "essence of Christian piety," "saintship *itself,* or real grace and true holiness." Candidates who pledged merely to obey God's commands by observing their sacramental duties at the Lord's Table engaged in acts of "mere evasion." Those who were baptized as infants, owned the covenant, uttered vows, or demonstrated their catechetical knowledge of Reformed theological doctrines acted as mere spectators to salvation, rather than those "immediately concerned in the affair." Edwards reserved his harshest criticism for church membership candidates, such as those in Boston's First and Old South churches, who professed what he derided as a "historical" knowledge of Reformed doctrine. Mired in what Edwards called an "intermediate sort of state," they made a "mere sham of a solemn public profession of Christianity." Those who rested content in devotional performances or a "good conversation" missed the mark. "They will only build upon the sand," he concluded, echoing the same phrase that Whitefieldian itinerants had used with devastating power during the revivals earlier in the decade.[174]

Edwards's arguments during the communion controversy frequently devolved into attacks on the spiritual estates of candidates themselves, as he derided the "practice of promiscuous admission" as little more than sloth and hypocrisy. He asserted that the test of a relation practiced elsewhere in New England was "superficial" and "lukewarm"—even "abominable" and "hateful to Christ." To outside observers, including Edwards's former student, Samuel Hopkins, the division between the Northampton minister and his opponents seemed stark: "He look'd upon it to be the Duty of none, but only such as were visibly truly gratious Persons to enter into full Communion," while his critics presumed that "all Persons of Sober Life" and "Competante Knowl-

174. Jonathan Edwards to William Hobby, n.d. [June 1751], in *WJE,* XVI, *Letters and Personal Writings,* ed. Claghorn, 371; Winiarski, "New Perspectives on the Northampton Communion Controversy III," *Jonathan Edwards Studies,* IV (2014), 372; Appendix B, Westborough, Mass., First Church, 71; Edwards, *Humble Inquiry,* in *WJE,* XII, *Ecclesiastical Writings,* ed. Hall, 179, 185, 190, 206, 210, 221, 273, 316; Edwards, "Lectures on the Qualifications for Full Communion in the Church of Christ," in *WJE,* XXV, *Sermons and Discourses, 1743-1758,* ed. Kimnach, 359.

edge" had a "Right to enter into full Communion and that it was their Duty."
Edwards's position, to be fair, was more nuanced, but the uncompromising
rhetoric of his hastily written communion treatise put him at odds not only
with his parishioners but also with his most supportive colleagues in eastern
Massachusetts.[175]

Edwards's preoccupation with determining internal and real states of holiness left him open to criticism that he was promoting the same antinomian
errors that had scandalized the revivals during the previous decade. Critics,
he feared, would contend that he "insisted on persons being assured of their
being in a state of salvation" as a term of communion or that he was demanding a particular account of the "time and manner" of his parishioners' conversions. Some would claim that he was attempting to revive James Davenport's controversial practice of spiritual discernment by making an "exact and
certain distinction between saints and hypocrites" or that he had "arrogated
all the power of judging of the qualifications of candidates for communion
wholly" to himself. Edwards knew that his opponents would attempt to por-
tray him as one of "those wild people, who have lately appeared in New England, called 'Separatists.'" Given the fractured state of religion in the Connecticut Valley and elsewhere, he had good reason to be concerned.[176]

■ Edwards did not stand alone against Count Vavasor and his "turbulent"
and "stiff-necked" parishioners during the Northampton communion controversy. He estimated that twenty families embraced his controversial church
admission standards, as did nearly half of the council of ministers that met
to adjudicate the dispute. "We disapprove the Separation of the Reverend
Mr. *Edwards* from his People," William Hobby of Reading, Massachusetts,
asserted in a pamphlet decrying the dismissal proceedings. Edwards's sentiments on church membership were "perfectly harmonious with the Mind
of our LORD JESUS CHRIST, and strictly conformable to the Practice of the
Apostles, and that of the Reformed Churches in general through the World."
To "fling open the sanctuary" to those who professed "nothing Higher" than
a "Historical knowledge of Christianity, and a visibly Regular Life," council
member David Hall of Sutton complained to Edward Billing, would "prosti-

175. Edwards, *Humble Inquiry*, in *WJE*, XII, *Ecclesiastical Writings*, ed. Hall, 323;
Edwards, "Lectures on the Qualifications for Full Communion in the Church of Christ," in
WJE, XXV, *Sermons and Discourses, 1743–1758*, ed. Kimnach, 360; Dexter, ed., *Extracts
from the Itineraries and Other Miscellanies of Ezra Stiles*, 501–502.

176. Edwards, *Farewel-Sermon*, in *WJE*, XXV, *Sermons and Discourses, 1743–1758*, ed.
Kimnach, 488–489.

tute Sacred Mysteries" to the enemies of God. When Billing published a "very injurious Letter" in the *Boston Gazette* in which he declared his unwavering support for Edwards and vowed to institute similar procedures in his own parish in Cold Spring (now Belchertown), Massachusetts, he, too, was dismissed from his pulpit.[177]

With the removal of Edwards and Billing, the Hampshire Association appeared to have purged the upper Connecticut Valley of potential radical Whitefieldarians and pure church schismatics. But the region seethed with dissent, and churches continued to debate the merits of Edwards's restrictive admission practices. One community that reversed its course and implemented church membership procedures similar to those advocated by Edwards was the Berkshire hamlet of Granville, Massachusetts. Two years after dismissing the town's first minister—Edwards's brother-in-law Moses Tuttle—in 1754, the Granville church members drafted a new covenant in which they acknowledged that "grace is of absolute necessity in order to a right Receiving the Lord's Supper." They repudiated the "Stodarian principal" and "what is called the halfway Covenant." A second provision barred from membership anyone who believed that the sacrament was a converting ordinance. Henceforth, all candidates for church membership would be required to meet with a committee of lay leaders, draft a suitable relation in which they detailed their religious experiences, and consent to having the document read in public. To cement their restrictive admission standards, the townspeople offered their vacant pulpit to Jedidiah Smith. The recent Yale College graduate hailed from the neighboring village of Suffield—the scene of Edwards's greatest revival triumph more than a decade earlier.[178]

Within a year, the "pious young minister" had sparked a "very remarkable awakening and revival of religion" in Granville, as Edwards reported in a letter to a Scottish correspondent. Although he undoubtedly approved of Granville's bold decision to embrace his controversial position on qualifications for church membership, Edwards would have been horrified by the results. More

177. Jonathan Edwards to Thomas Gillespie, July 1, 1751, in *WJE*, XVI, *Letters and Personal Writings*, ed. Claghorn, 381, 386; *Result of a Council of Nine Churches*, 6; Winiarski, "New Perspectives on the Northampton Communion Controversy I," *Jonathan Edwards Studies*, III (2013), 278, 280; *Boston Gazette, or Weekly Journal*, June 16, 1752. On the Billing case, see Nobles, *Divisions Throughout the Whole*, 73–74.

178. "Church Constitution," June 14, 1754, Granville, Mass., First Congregational Church Papers, circa 1756–1913, CL (available online at NEHH). On Smith's career, see Dexter, *Biographical Sketches*, II, 240–241. For a more detailed discussion of the formation and trials of the Granville church, see Gregory H. Nobles, "In the Wake of the Awakening: The Politics of Purity in Granville, 1754–1776," *Historical Journal of Western Massachusetts*, VIII (1980), 48–62; and Nobles, *Divisions Throughout the Whole*, 96–103.

than a dozen relations survive from Smith's pastorate, including several that date to the 1757 revival. They were riven with many of the same errors that Edwards had spent nearly a decade condemning in his revival tracts, sermons, and personal correspondence and for which he had been roundly condemned by his opponents during the communion controversy.[179]

From the opening lines of their relations, Granville parishioners narrated their religious experiences in an assertive idiom that reflected the radical innovations of the Whitefieldian revivals. "Our Reverand paster haveing A desire that I should make a relation for the Edefication of the Church and for the conviction of sinners," began Samuel Coe, "I am willing and theirfore proseed as follows." His narrative stood in stark contrast to those penned by prospective communicants in eastern Massachusetts, where candidates labored to fit their experiences into established literary conventions. Instead, the Granville layman understood the test of a relation as an opportunity to enliven those who listened as it was read. In adopting Edwards's membership criteria, the Granville church created a situation in which prospective communicants felt they needed to prove their conversions, or give what one woman called "Better Satisffaction" on the issue of whether they possessed true grace. As a result, their testimonies veered away from the standard litany of doctrinal knowledge, family pedigree, healing vows, and upright conversation and toward dramatic narratives of conversion.[180]

What the Granville parishioners omitted from their relations was as important as the details they included. Only one woman, Jane McLeon, infused her 1762 relation with a "publick profession" of her theological beliefs. She and John Seward were also among the very few Granville candidates who cited their infant baptism or family upbringing as evidence of their fitness to participate in the Lord's Supper. None of Smith's parishioners praised God for living in the gospel land of light, nor did they close their statements with a pledge to walk answerable to their professions. References to what Seward called the "Diligent way of Duty"—a godly conversation—were noticeably absent in the Granville testimonies. Few prospective communicants expressed "fears of unworthiness" regarding their sacramental obligations or cited the terrifying words of 1 Corinthians 11:29 as a stumbling block. Instead, most boldly signified their "Great and ardent Desire to Come to the Lords table"—

179. Jonathan Edwards to John Erskine, Apr. 12, 1757, in *WJE*, XVI, *Letters and Personal Writings*, ed. Claghorn, 705.

180. Relations of Martha Benjamin, n.d. [circa 1757], Samuel Coe, n.d. [circa 1757], Granville First Congregational Church Papers. For the full text of Coe's relation, see Appendix C.

an assertive tone almost entirely absent from relations composed during New England's sacramental renaissance a generation earlier (see Table 7).[181]

If Smith's parishioners minimized the tribal and theological components of the traditional relation of faith formula and recast sacramental statements regarding lay scrupulosity, they lavished attention on their dramatic conversion experiences. Most of the Granville relations assumed a coherent narrative form in which candidates chronicled the stages of what one forthright parishioner called "my Journy heavenward." Even those who cited providential afflictions did so to pinpoint their first convictions. Surveying their private devotional routines, several parishioners turned to the "Sandy foundation" metaphor made popular by the Whitefieldarians and dismissed secret prayer, bible study, and closet meditation as crafty stratagems that led only to spiritual dullness. As with many new converts during the revivals of the 1740s, Granville parishioners confronted frightening images of Satan more often than prospective church members earlier in the century, and they described being driven "allmost to dispare" by the prospect of "hell opened wide." A few people described unusual visionary phenomena, including Charles Spelman, who was awakened out of his "Dul stupid frame" after "Dreaming twice in one night of the Day of Judgment" and the "heavens all in flames."[182]

Granville candidates scanned their experiences for evidence of the precise moment when Christ began "Courting my Backward Soul," as one woman explained. Many people described specific events in which they were "freed from my Distress" in an "Instant," or suddenly discovered by "Experience" a "new way of Living Different from what I Ever new before." Sunk low in despair and seeing nothing but hell before him, Samuel Coe felt a strange alteration one night after listening to his wife singing hymns. In words strikingly similar to those made famous by the English Methodist John Wesley in his autobiography, Coe described how his cold heart "began to grow warm." Similarly, the prominent magistrate and future Revolutionary War colonel Timothy Robinson was converted during a dramatic vision in which "all Nater Semd to vanish" and his soul entered into the "World of Spirets." After gazing on an "Ecseding [exceedingly] Lovley" Jesus for half an hour, he awoke near midnight in great bodily pain. Later during a second vision, as he stood in terror before the gates of hell gazing on the Devil and the torments of the damned,

181. Relations of Lois Baldwin, n.d. [circa 1762], Jane McLeon, n.d. [circa 1762], John Seward, n.d. [circa 1757], Granville First Congregational Church Papers.

182. Relations of Thomas Goss, n.d. [circa 1757], Charles Spelman, n.d. [circa 1765], Stephen Spelman, June 12, 1768, Granville First Congregational Church Papers.

Robinson heard a voice that dispelled all his fears, calling to him in words from Jeremiah and the Psalms.[183]

Robinson's relation underscored the central place of oracular words from scripture in the Granville relations. The Granville narratives were much longer than testimonies composed in eastern Massachusetts, and they included significantly more biblical quotations and allusions. Prospective church members in Granville also referenced a much wider range of scriptural texts. The four most frequently cited verses—Isaiah 1:18, Isaiah 55:1–7, Mathew 11:28, and 1 Corinthians 11:29—in Westborough accounted for 35 percent of all biblical citations, but that figure dropped more than fifteen points in Granville. The eclecticism of Smith's parishioners translated into important changes in the language that they used to describe their encounters with scripture. In Westborough, three-quarters of all scriptural references were simply cited or quoted. By contrast, just under half of all biblical references among the Granville relations assumed the form of "them words" that darted into the candidate's head unexpectedly. Biblical impulses, the revival phenomenon that lay men and women associated with conversion and the indwelling presence of the Holy Spirit, had become the single most distinctive marker of Granville's new requirement for admission to full church membership (Table 8).[184]

The degree to which Granville candidates referred to these intrusive biblical texts as "impressions" in their relations measured their distance from other communities and earlier generations. Joseph Swetman believed that the Holy Spirit allowed him to see the scriptures in a "Differing form" than ever before. Charles Spelman described a spiritual force that dispelled the opacity of "Misterious" biblical passages. Others spoke of being stalked by the Bible, of scriptural texts that sounded in their ears or ran in their heads, and of passages they thought God "Spak unto me" alone. Biblical impulses dominated the Granville relations to such an extent that Smith's parishioners soon began stringing them together into composite statements. The booming voice that Timothy Robinson heard after his dramatic visions of heaven and hell called to him in the words of Psalm 2:7, Jeremiah 31:3, and Micah 6:8. Similarly, the Spirit spoke to Thomas Goss in a jumble of biblical phrases cobbled from Matthew 11:28, Revelation 22:17, Isaiah 55:1, John 17:10, Psalm 16:11, and

183. Relations of Martha Benjamin, n.d. [circa 1757], Samuel Coe, n.d. [circa 1757], John Griswold, n.d. [circa 1762], Timothy Robinson, n.d. [circa 1757], Mary Seward, n.d. [circa 1757], Granville First Congregational Church Papers.

184. Relation of Martha Benjamin, n.d. [circa 1757], Granville First Congregational Church Papers. Data on the relative percentages of frequently cited biblical verses in Granville and Westborough derived from content analysis of sources in Appendix B.

TABLE 8 Scriptural References in Selected Eighteenth-Century Relations of Faith Collections by Church

Church	Total Relations (N)	Total Citations (N)	Average Number of Citations	Cited or Quoted (%)	Heard in Sermon or Discussed in Conversation (%)	Read, Studied, or Meditated On (%)	Incorporated as Figural Language (%)	Received as Impulse or Impression (%)
Granville, Mass., First Church (circa 1756–circa 1777)	14	105	7.5	32.4	3.8	1.9	13.3	48.6
Haverhill, Mass., First Church (1719–1745)	235	971	4.1	80.1	3.8	0.6	13.2	2.3
Ipswich (now Essex), Mass., Chebacco Separate Congregational Church (1750–1785)	64	174	2.7	16.7	21.3	4.6	31.6	25.9
Medfield, Mass., First Church (1697–1766)	106	601	5.7	50.2	13.0	7.2	17.1	12.5
Middleborough, Mass., First Church (1748–1780)	40	118	3.0	32.2	9.3	3.4	21.2	33.9
Sturbridge, Mass., First Church (1737–1764)	38	142	3.7	23.9	14.1	6.3	33.1	22.5
Westborough, Mass., First Church (1736–1786)	84	206	2.5	74.8	1.5	2.9	18.9	1.9

Note: Dates for Granville, Chebacco, and Middleborough delimited by the pastorates of Jedidiah Smith (dismissed 1776), John Cleaveland (died 1799), and Sylvanus Conant (died 1777). For methodology, see Appendix A.

Sources: Appendix B; Granville, Mass., First Congregational Church Records, circa 1760–1913, CL (available online at NEHH); Middleboro, Mass., First Congregational Church Relations and Personal Records, 1724–1865, CL (available online at NEHH).

Song of Solomon 8:6. The Spirit even spoke in a vernacular idiom, for many of the words that sounded in the minds of Smith's parishioners had no scriptural referent.[185]

In an especially evocative example of this trend, Stephen Spelman described his encounters with intrusive scriptures as if they were warring for his salvation. At first, he feared that the words "will you not Come to me who have Spared you So Long"—a biblical impulse drawn partly from John 5:40—had been "Spoken to me with infinite Power." Spelman languished in a miserable condition until one night God was pleased to take away his burden with an encouraging promise from Colossians 3:3, "your life is hid with Christ in God." Spelman fell into despair again less than an hour later, however, as a passage from Zephaniah proclaiming a "Day of Darkness and Gloomyness" poured into his head. Back and forth, all night long, raging biblical verses vied for control of Spelman's soul. At one point, he was almost overcome by a pair of hopeful verses, but this "Lasted not Long for harrow of mind Seased me" when words from Isaiah 66:15 and Galatians 6:7 threatened those who mocked God with vengeance in flames of fire. Finally, "god was Pleased as I hope in infinite Mercy to Speak a word in from his own Mouth." This last composite impulse, comprised of Jesus's instructions to doubting Thomas and a passage from 1 John, "Captivated the whole and Set me beyond my fears." The Granville layman emerged from his conversion ordeal like a newborn babe seeking "Spiritual milk and food" through a succession of intrusive biblical texts that he associated with the converting work of the indwelling Holy Spirit.[186]

Spelman's relation was exactly the kind of conversion narrative that Edwards had grown to despise and for which he was tarred by his opponents during the Northampton communion controversy. By the mid-1750s, Edwards had been struggling for more than a decade to convince his former parishioners and transatlantic reading audience of the dangers of biblical impulses, visions, somatic exercises, and other forms of delusive enthusiasm. Throughout the communion controversy, Edwards denied that he advocated the practice of "relating, or giving an account of experiences, or what is so commonly called, as a term of communion." But he walked a knife's edge. On the one hand, Edwards rejected the traditional relation of faith formula adopted in places such as Westborough and Boston's First and Old South churches,

185. Relations of Martha Benjamin, n.d. [circa 1757], Thomas Goss, n.d. [circa 1757], Timothy Robinson, n.d. [circa 1757], Charles Spelman, n.d. [circa 1765], Joseph Swetman, n.d. [circa 1759], Granville First Congregational Church Records.

186. Relation of Stephen Spelman, June 12, 1768, Granville First Congregational Church Papers.

where candidates testified only to their moral sincerity and historical knowledge of Reformed doctrines; yet he also condemned the boastful experiences described by the men and women of Granville, who brazenly proclaimed that they had passed through the new birth. Edwards was frustrated by what he derided in his theological notebooks as the "superabundant talk of experiences." Prideful conversion stories were like "suckers at the root of a tree" that drew nourishment away from the fruits of true grace.[187]

Looking back on the circumstances that ended his Northampton ministry, Edwards arrived at the sobering conclusion that his parishioners placed too much emphasis on the "particular steps and method of their first work." Too often they failed to "distinguish between impressions on the imagination, and truly spiritual experiences." They possessed strong faith, he admitted, but "without spiritual light." "We have had, and have to this day, multitudes of such strong believers," he confided to a Scottish colleague, whose bold confidence in their conversions had "given the greatest wound to the cause of truth and vital religion that ever it suffered in America." He might just as easily have leveled the same criticism against his overzealous supporters in Granville, many of whom had recently migrated from towns in the Connecticut Valley where he had preached with power only a decade earlier. Try as he might during the next decade, Edwards never succeeded in his efforts to "beat them out" of their "wrong notions." His dismissal was as much the result of their radical enthusiasm as it was an outcome of the alleged religious laxity of his Northampton parishioners.[188]

■ So what did Edwards expect? "I should content myself with a few words," he explained in a letter to a colleague, in which candidates professed the "great things wherein godliness consists," rather than detailed accounts of their good estate. Edwards refused to limit the length or content of his proposed professions; he even acknowledged that qualified individuals might scruple whether they had ever experienced conversion. The sample statements that he shared with prospective church members in Northampton before the controversy, moreover, were unusually terse by contemporary standards. "I hope, I do truly find a heart to give up myself wholly to God, according to the tenor of that

187. Jonathan Edwards, *Misrepresentations Corrected, and Truth Vindicated* ... (Boston, 1752), in *WJE*, XII, *Ecclesiastical Writings*, ed. Hall, 367; Edwards, Miscellany 951, in *WJE*, XX, *The "Miscellanies," (Entry Nos. 833–1152)*, ed. Amy Plantinga Pauw (New Haven, Conn., 2002), 210.

188. Jonathan Edwards to Thomas Gillespie, Apr. 2, 1750, in *WJE*, XVI, *Letters and Personal Writings*, ed. Claghorn, 328, Edwards to Gillespie, July 1, 1751, 383.

covenant of grace which was sealed in my baptism," read the shortest version, "and to walk in that way of that obedience to all the commandments of God, which the covenant of grace requires, as long as I live." When it came down to specifics, Edwards's concept of a church membership profession was "So Loose and General," countered one critic, that sectarians of all stripes would inevitably "put their own Sense upon the word."[189]

Edwards presented his most detailed exposition of his new position on church membership, not in his personal correspondence or communion controversy treatises, but in a succinct set of manuscript notes—known today as his "Directions for Judging of Persons' Experiences"—that he compiled during the 1740s. In contrast to the "superficial pangs, flashes," and "freaks" that marked the conversion narratives of new converts in towns like Granville, Edwards advocated professions that were "reasonable" and "solid." True visible saints, he believed, felt the "insufficiency and vanity of their own doings." They possessed an abiding "sense of the sufficiency" of Christ's atonement and his "divine, supreme, and spiritual excellency." They yearned for "perfect freedom from sin"; yet they were resigned to the "justice of God in their damnation." When they spoke of their own experiences, true Christians downplayed "their own discoveries and affections" and delighted instead in the beauty of God's moral perfection and divine plan of salvation. Above all, Edwards reminded himself to "See to it" that he measured the experiences of his parishioners by the operation of the heart, rather than on the mental faculties of the imagination or the intellect.[190]

A handful of relations written during the decades following the communion controversy conformed to Edwards's directions, and several might have been directly influenced by his published writings on the subject. "I think it not Sufficient to obtain Salvation to give a bare assent in the gospel that Christ is the redeemer of mankind," Charles Brigham wrote in a relation composed only a few weeks after Edwards's apologetic *Humble Inquiry* issued from the Boston press, "but it is necessary I Should have Such a Faith as will bring me into Obedience and Subjection to himself." Brigham was one of several residents in Grafton, Massachusetts, who applied to join Ebenezer Parkman's church in

189. Jonathan Edwards to Peter Clark, May 7, 1750, in *WJE*, XVI, *Letters and Personal Writings*, ed. Claghorn, 345; Edwards, *Misrepresentations Corrected*, in *WJE*, XII, *Ecclesiastical Writings*, ed. Hall, 360–361; Anonymous, "Discourse on the Theology of Jonathan Edwards," n.d. [circa 1750], microfilm, reel 7, frame 1123, Eleazer Williams Papers. See also "Drafts of Professions of Faith," *WJEO*, XXXIX, *Church and Pastoral Documents*.

190. Jonathan Edwards, "Directions for Judging of Persons' Experiences," in *WJE*, XXI, *Writings on the Trinity, Grace, and Faith*, ed. Sang Hyun Lee (New Haven, Conn., 2003), 522–524.

nearby Westborough after witnessing the revival excesses of Solomon Prentice and his inspired wife. As a result, Brigham declined to comment on his beliefs or narrate revelatory experiences. Instead, he prayed for God to "enlighten the Eyes of my understanding" and "Discover to me the Beauties and excelencies of the Lord Jesus Christ." Two decades later, Lois Rice carefully distinguished between a "historical" faith and a "true and a saving knowlidge of Christ," just as Edwards had done in An *Humble Inquiry*. Several Westborough candidates worried about hypocrisy and self-deception and distanced themselves from charges of enthusiasm by acknowledging that they were unsure "that I have had a Work of Grace wrought in me." "I don't know that I am Elected," summarized Abigail Kenney in her 1774 relation, "but I can truely Say I hope I have been so far Called of God as that my Mind is very different, and my Disposition and Inclination changd from what it once was." These relations, however, were exceptions to the rule. Overall, only a handful of Parkman's parishioners employed Edwardsean language in their testimonies.[191]

Of the major collections of church admission testimonies that survive from the second half of the eighteenth century, relations from Chebacco Parish in Ipswich, Massachusetts, best exemplify the standards outlined in Edwards's instructions for assessing his parishioners' experiences. The statements that minister John Cleaveland recorded during the 1750s and 1760s departed from prevailing conventions in neighboring churches in eastern Massachusetts in several noteworthy ways. References to family upbringing nearly vanished from the Chebacco narratives altogether. Abraham Choate applied for admission to full communion in 1767, "not merely" because he had been "born in a Land of Gospel-Light and Liberty" and dedicated to God by his parents, but because he had witnessed the "outpouring of his blessed Spirit, Wherein, I trust, I have been made a saving Partaker of it." In contrast to their peers in Boston and Westborough, Chebacco candidates minimized or dismissed altogether the diligent performance of traditional devotional practices as "Dependances," or a "sandy foundation." Fewer than one in twenty prospective church members referenced any of the doctrinal, sacramental, or tribal concerns that dominated relations composed in nearby Haverhill a generation earlier (see Table 7). Cleaveland's parishioners remained wary of "striving to make a stepping-stone of their Duties and Qualifications to step up on Christ."[192]

Instead, some Chebacco candidates filled their relations with detailed accounts of the "great revival" that enveloped numerous towns in New England

191. Appendix B, Westborough, Mass., First Church, 13, 47, 51, 64.
192. Appendix B, Ipswich (now Essex), Mass., Chebacco Separate Church, 7, 19, 36, 40, 50.

shortly after the Seven Years' War. They described powerful late-night religious gatherings, stirring sermons by visiting itinerants, and impassioned revival letters read in public. Several new converts were deeply affected by the sight of friends, neighbors, and relatives coming "out of Darkness into God's mervellous Light." The men and women of Chebacco paid close attention to the specific moment in which they were "first bro't under concern." They described the circumstances in which their "burden of guilt went off," they "received Comfort," or they were "bro't into the Light" of God's grace. Biblical impulses and other auditory forms of divine communication occasionally accompanied these transformative moments, and a few candidates even declared that they experienced a definitive "saving Discovery of Christ." "The Lord has done that for me that none else could do," proclaimed Mary Low, "I trust I find a Change in my soul." Like the people of Granville, some Chebacco parishioners seemed too concerned with reciting what Edwards criticized as the "times and circumstances" of "particular exercises of grace."[193]

Viewed from a different angle, many of the Chebacco relations incorporated Edwards's most important criterion: "fixed and strong resolutions, attended with fear and jealousy of their own hearts." On balance, the majority of Cleaveland's congregants were less confident about their spiritual estates than their contemporaries in Granville. Most Chebacco candidates tempered their relations with a recognition of the incompleteness of their conversions. Several expressed fears of deception, while others acknowledged that they lacked a "more clear and strong Faith." One woman even admitted that she had been "seized with fear" after meeting with the Chebacco elders, "lest I had said more than I had really experienced." They thirsted for "perfect holiness," abhorred the sin that remained within them, and yearned for a "heart as big as the world" with which to praise God. Downplaying their own elevated experiences during the 1764 revival, prospective church members in Chebacco more often spoke of a newfound "Love to the People of God" and a "Desire that all may be converted."[194]

In addition, Cleaveland's parishioners framed their experiences around an

193. McLoughlin, ed., *Diary of Isaac Backus*, I, 553; Appendix B, Ipswich (now Essex), Mass., Chebacco Separate Church, 5, 9, 12, 17, 24, 37, 42, 48; Edwards, *Treatise concerning Religious Affections*, in *WJE*, II, *Religious Affections*, ed. Smith, 417. On the broader context of the 1764 revivals, see Seeman, *Pious Persuasions*, 174–177; and Thomas S. Kidd, *The Great Awakening: The Roots of Evangelical Christianity in Colonial America* (New Haven, Conn., 2007), 267–287.

194. Appendix B, Ipswich (now Essex), Mass., Chebacco Separate Church, 2, 8–9, 27, 58, 69; Edwards, "Directions for Judging of Persons' Experiences," in *WJE*, XXI, *Writings on the Trinity, Grace, and Faith*, ed. Sang Hyun Lee, 524. See also Juster, *Disorderly Women*, 71.

Edwardsean epistemology of sensation. They were preoccupied with sensing—seeing, in particular, but also occasionally tasting—God's plan for salvation, rather than affirming the authority of various Reformed theological doctrines. "I was made to see the Justice of God in my condemnation," explained several candidates, echoing Edwards's directions. "My Soul did really hunger and thirst after holiness," admitted Abigail Marshall. Then, she added: "I trust I was filled with some comfort in delighting in the Beauty of holiness." Others recalled viewing, not mystical visions of Jesus enthroned in heaven, but his "fulness," "Loveliness," "alsufficiency," and, above all, "excellence." Unlike their contemporaries elsewhere in New England, Chebacco's new converts appear to have been groping toward the moderate church admission professions that Edwards had described in his communion controversy treatises. They had learned to speak about their religious experiences as an inclination or orientation of the will akin to what Edwards famously described in his *Treatise concerning Religious Affections* as a "spiritual, supernatural understanding of divine things" or, more simply, a "sense of the heart."[195]

It is ironic that the relations that most closely approximated Edwards's "Directions for Judging of Persons' Experiences" were penned by one of the foremost leaders of the Separate Congregational movement. After all, John Cleaveland had been expelled from Yale College in 1745 after attending Separate meetings with his family in Canterbury. The "New-Gathered Congregational Church in Chebacco" over which he was ordained in 1746, moreover, comprised a group of outspoken dissenters that seceded from communion in Theophilus Pickering's established church during the years following the Whitefieldian revivals. Chebacco's Strict Congregationalists simultaneously looked backward and forward in their theology and church practices. On the one hand, Cleaveland's church restored the office of elder, eliminated the practice of owning the covenant, and required church membership candidates to recite their religious experiences in private conferences. Yet, as with other Separate societies, the Chebacco church reached well beyond traditional parish boundaries. Members hailed from all three Ipswich parishes and the neighboring towns of Manchester, Gloucester, Beverly, and Wenham. Nor was Cleaveland an unlettered rabble rouser; he counted many leading Whitefield-

---

195. Appendix B, Ipswich (now Essex), Mass., Chebacco Separate Church, 3, 30, 32, 36, 52, 65, 67 (for the full text of Lucy Andrews's relation, see Appendix C); Edwards, *Treatise concerning Religious Affections,* in *WJE,* II, *Religious Affections,* ed. Smith, 270, 272. See also John E. Smith, "Religious Affections and the 'Sense of the Heart,'" in Sang Hyun Lee, ed., *The Princeton Companion to Jonathan Edwards* (Princeton, N.J., 2005), 103–114; and Terrence Erdt, *Jonathan Edwards: Art and the Sense of the Heart* (Amherst, Mass., 1980), 21–42.

arians among his close friends and correspondents. During his long pastorate, he emerged as a principled and combative leader of a new type of Congregational community—warm in piety, yet conservative in its ecclesiology. His separatist path through New England's era of great awakenings represented the road not taken by the more cautious Edwards.[196]

Although Edwards maintained that he never "promoted separations under a notion of setting up pure churches," well-founded rumors persisted—and with good reason. Following his dismissal in 1750, the embattled Northampton clergyman schemed with Timothy Dwight and a rump group of parishioners to organize a second church in Northampton. He spent the spring of 1751 discussing his options with colleagues in Boston and Essex County, Massachusetts. On one occasion, Edwards appears to have met with Jonathan Parsons, the former revival firebrand from Lyme, Connecticut, and minister of the Separate Congregational church in the waterside parish of Newbury. Two years earlier, Parsons had led his congregation into the Boston Presbytery. He had encouraged other separatists in the region to follow suit, including the breakaway churches in Chebacco and Exeter, New Hampshire, where the former itinerant preacher Daniel Rogers was installed in 1748. For a brief period during the early 1750s, Solomon Prentice's troubled church in Easton also joined the unusual alliance of independent Congregational and Scots-Irish societies.[197]

Although the evidence is circumstantial, it seems likely that Edwards met with Parsons in Newbury during the spring of 1751 to discuss the possibility of affiliating the proposed new Northampton church with a "Presbittery" that operated independent of New England's Congregational establishment. By the late 1740s, Edwards had come to value the "Presbyterian way" as "most agreeable to the Word of God." Over the years, he had developed a robust correspondence with Scottish colleagues that culminated in his 1747 efforts to orchestrate a transatlantic concert of prayer. He had experimented with hier-

---

196. The phrase "New-Gathered Congregational Church in Chebacco" appears on numerous documents in the JCP; for one example, see Seeman, "'Justice Must Take Plase,'" *WMQ*, LVI (1999), 407. On Cleaveland's expulsion from Yale College and early career, see Christopher M. Jedrey, *The World of John Cleaveland: Family and Community in Eighteenth-Century New England* (New York, 1979), 17–57. For a different perspective on the formation of the Chebacco Separate church, see Anne S. Brown, "Visions of Community in Eighteenth-Century Essex County: Chebacco Parish and the Great Awakening," *EIHC*, CXXV (1989), 239–262.

197. Edwards to Clark, May 7, 1750, in *WJE*, XVI, *Letters and Personal Writings*, ed. Claghorn, 343. For Edwards's Boston and Essex County itinerary, along with circumstantial evidence that he stopped in Newbury to consult with Jonathan Parsons, see Winiarski, "New Perspectives on the Northampton Communion Controversy III," *Jonathan Edwards Studies*, IV (2014), 362–363.

archical forms of church governance in Northampton during the years leading up to the communion controversy. Edwards maintained cordial relations with Robert Abercrombie, the Scots-Irish minister of Pelham, Massachusetts, and a founding member of the Boston Presbytery; and he even preached in James Moorehead's Presbyterian meetinghouse in Boston while consulting with Thomas Foxcroft and Thomas Prince only a few weeks before the 1751 Northampton church council. Edwards knew that he would never cross the Atlantic with his family and take up a pulpit in Scotland, as his British admirers hoped. The prospect of organizing a Presbyterian church in Northampton, however, briefly revealed a pathway through the maze of contention and schism in Northampton. The ecclesiastical and disciplinary mechanisms of the Boston Presbytery would have served as forums for debating the merits of Edwards's qualifications for church membership, and the denominational solidity of the Scots-Irish churches in New England would have insulated Edwards against the charge of separatism he suffered throughout the ordeal.[198]

By the spring of 1751, all of the parties in the conflict—the Dwight faction, the Northampton majority, the eastern ministers, and Edwards himself— seemed poised to break with their opponents rather than to seek compromise or accommodation. Packed with Edwards's close supporters and excluding his most bitter opponents closer to home, the anticouncil that met on May 16 encouraged Edwards to accept a position at the Stockbridge Indian mission. But they also vindicated his church membership principles, sternly criticized his former parishioners for heaping "Calumnies and Reproaches" on their minister, and urged Edwards's supporters to continue absenting themselves from Sabbath meetings until their numbers warranted the formation of a "distinct Society or Church." Most Congregational councils—even rump anticouncils called solely by aggrieved factions—culminated in a written statement in which the assembled ministers encouraged the contending parties to reconcile their differences. The published result of the second Northampton council, however, made no effort to resolve the simmering dispute. Edwards's

198. Daniel Giddings, church meeting minutes, Jan. 23, 1747, box 2, JCP; Edwards to Erskine, July 5, 1750, in *WJE*, XVI, *Letters and Personal Writings*, ed. Claghorn, 355. On the development of the Boston Presbytery, see Blaikie, *History of Presbyterianism in New England*, 109–112. For Edwards's interest in Presbyterian forms of church polity and the Concert of Prayer, see Kenneth P. Minkema, "Jonathan Edwards and the Heidelberg Catechism," *Nederduitse Gereformeerde Teologiese Tydskrif,* LIV, nos. 3–4 (September–December 2013), 292–302; Stephen J. Stein, "Editor's Introduction," in *WJE*, V, *Apocalyptic Writings*, ed. Stein, 29–48; and Nicholas T. Batzig, "Edwards, McLaurin, and the Transatlantic Concert," in *Jonathan Edwards and Scotland,* ed. Kelly van Andel, Adriaan C. Neele, and Kenneth P. Minkema (Edinburgh, 2011), 77–87.

principles on the qualifications for admission to the Lord's Supper had finally pushed a council of established clergymen to sanction the creation of an independent Congregational church.[199]

This was the "monster" of separatism that John Baker, the self-styled "Count Vavasor," bitterly condemned in the tirade he dashed off anonymously to the assembled ministers in Northampton shortly after the proceedings concluded. Although the anticouncil effectively ended Edwards's pastorate, the ecclesiastical turmoil that he and Dwight had fomented during the spring of 1751 continued to reverberate across New England for decades—especially within Separate circles. Leaders of the movement applauded Edwards's *Humble Inquiry*. Ebenezer Frothingham, minister of the Separate church in Middletown, Connecticut, recommended Edwards's book to the "serious Perusal of every Person of all Ranks and Denominations," and he prayed that the "allwise and merciful God would bless it, and make it Instrumental of bringing the Saints in *New-England* into the real Order of the Gospel." Baptist leader Isaac Backus also praised Edwards's "excellent rules," asserting that they provided the "capital article that the Separate churches were built upon." And, as the Chebecco relations suggest, Edwards's concept of a church membership profession found its fullest expression among those Separate Congregationalists who believed, in the words of one parishioner, that it was their "Duty to Joyn with the most pure Church."[200]

Not surprisingly and with good reason, colleagues within the Congregational establishment responded angrily to Edwards's "Stiff Adherence" to his restrictive church membership principles and the "Extraordinary Steps" he had taken to secure a second pulpit in Northampton. With so many "Giddy" lay men and women "Running into Antinomianism" or "flocking to the Arms of Arminianism," warned Solomon Williams of Lebanon, Connecticut, Edwards's unguarded actions during the qualifications controversy had undermined the foundations of New England's ecclesiastical establishment. One anonymous critic framed the broader stakes of the controversy in this way. Noting that Edwards had been "Something out of business Since the

---

199. Winiarski, "New Perspectives on the Northampton Communion Controversy III," *Jonathan Edwards Studies*, IV (2014), 373, 375. I borrow the helpful phrase "anticouncil" from James F. Cooper, Jr., *Tenacious of Their Liberties: The Congregationalists in Colonial Massachusetts*, Religion in America (New York, 1999), 187.

200. Winiarski, "New Perspectives on the Northampton Communion Controversy III," *Jonathan Edwards Studies*, IV (2014), 377; Ebenezer Frothingham, *The Articles of Faith and Practice, with the Covenant, That Is Confessed by the Separate Churches of Christ in General in This Land* ... (Newport, R.I., 1750), 34; Backus, *Church History of New-England*, II, 189; Abigail Leach to Benjamin Toppan, May 2, 1747, box 2, JCP.

late religious Commotions in the Land have So far Subsided," he sarcastically assured his Northampton colleague that "all the Separates in this Land will heartily forgive" his growing conservatism on revival errors. After all, Edwards had emboldened these "overzealous people" to "Disturb their fellow christians and make Schism in the church of God." "I cant but think Sir," the anonymous critic warned Edwards, "if you Should See our churches rent to pieces by your Book and flung into all manner of confusion by your principles you would have Some Severe Self reflections."[201]

■ Jonathan Edwards's ministry in Northampton foundered when he attempted to fix with precision an experience that had roiled families, neighborhoods, towns, and ministerial associations. In 1750, what did it mean to be a professor, a new convert, a visible saint, or an experienced Christian? What was the proper way to narrate what the Cambridge *Platform* a century earlier had called "Gods manner of working upon the soul"? Which experiences counted? Historical or catechetical knowledge of the *Assemblies Catechism?* Baptismal obligations and a religious pedigree? Afflictions and healing vows? Evidence of the indwelling presence of the Holy Spirit? Biblical impulses and extraordinary dreams and visions? Seeing the excellencies of Christ? After a decade of close observation, pastoral counseling, theological speculation, and published polemic, Edwards was confident he knew. But, in the shattered religious culture that emerged from the Whitefieldian revivals of the 1740s, he had little chance of persuading any large group of people of the truth of his position or of the righteousness of his cause.[202]

The bitter *Farewel-Sermon* that Edwards preached in Northampton on June 22, 1750, marked his defeat as a pastor and a revivalist. For more than two decades, he had labored for his congregants' eternal welfare. He had spent the prime of his life in their service; and, despite his perennial infirmities, he had not been idle or negligent in pastoral duties. "How often have we met together in the house of God," he wondered aloud. "How often have I spoke to you, instructed, counseled, warned, directed and fed you, and administered ordinances among you"? Now, Edwards concluded somberly, "my work is finished." Northampton had rejected him. Edwards nonetheless took heart that one day he would confront his antagonists "before the tribunal of the Great

201. Solomon Williams to John McLaurin, Sept. 3, 1751, JWC; Anonymous, "Discourse on the Theology of Jonathan Edwards," n.d. [circa 1750], microfilm, reel 78, frame 1120, Eleazer Williams Papers.

202. Williston Walker, comp., *The Creeds and Platforms of Congregationalism* (1893; rpt. New York, 1991), 223.

Judge." On the day of judgment, "every error and false opinion," "deceit and delusion" would vanish, and "there shall no longer be any debate, or difference of opinions." Edwards remained confident that he would receive "another decision at that great day," when his unpopular position on church admission professions was reexamined in the "searching, penetrating light of God's omniscience and glory."[203]

For a time, Edwards continued to advocate for the creation of an independent church in Northampton. He exhorted Timothy Dwight and his supportive former parishioners to step up their demands for "Christian satisfaction" and "not to patch up a mock reconciliation" with the church majority. But, as he set out for his new Indian mission post in Stockbridge, the embittered minister withdrew from ecclesiastical debates and rededicated himself to confronting in print the pressing theological issues that had galvanized a transatlantic cohort of Reformed clergymen in England, Scotland, and the American colonies: freedom of the will, original sin, the nature of true virtue, and the end for which God created the world.[204]

As Edwards refocused his intellectual labors, inspired lay men and women continued to follow the experiential paths that he had helped to blaze a decade earlier. No individual better exemplified the laity's enduring fascination with the work of the Holy Spirit than Samuel Coe. The future Granville deacon decided to apply for the privileges of full church membership in 1757, after a period in which he had been "very warm in secret prayer." During this intensified season of private meditations, a pair of unusual phrases dropped into Coe's mind: "watch and pray" and "double your diligence." The words "followed" him around as he pursued his daily routines during the next several weeks, Coe explained in his relation. In time, they fused into a single statement and reverberated through his mind over and over again. What began as a meditation soon turned into a powerful biblical impulse. When combined with additional scriptural phrases and hymns that "run in my mind for sum time," the words convinced Coe both of his divine election and of the necessity of joining the Granville church.[205]

203. Edwards, *Farewel-Sermon*, in *WJE*, XXV, *Sermons and Discourses, 1743–1758*, ed. Kimnach, 466–467, 475–476, 478.

204. Jonathan Edwards to Timothy Dwight, Feb. 27, 1752, in *WJE*, XVI, *Letters and Personal Writings*, ed. Claghorn, 448. On Edwards's rededication to formal theological issues during the 1750s, see Mark Valeri, "Jonathan Edwards, the New Divinity, and Cosmopolitan Calvinism," in Oliver D. Crisp and Douglas A. Sweeney, eds., *After Jonathan Edwards: The Courses of the New England Theology* (New York, 2012), 17–30.

205. Relation of Samuel Coe, n.d. [circa 1757], Granville First Congregational Church Papers. For the full text of Coe's relation, see Appendix C.

The genesis of Coe's composite biblical impulse was unique. The words "watch and pray" derived from Matthew 26:4, but the phrase "double your diligence" had no scriptural referent. Together, they appeared in only one place: the final pages of Edwards's published *Farewel-Sermon*. "You had need to double your diligence, and watch and pray lest you be overcome by temptation," he had warned his Northampton parishioners. In an extraordinary twist of fate, an obscure man from a small Berkshire hamlet had done the unthinkable. Coe had transformed Edwards's words into the converting voice of the indwelling Holy Spirit.[206]

NOTHINGARIANS

During the spring of 1781, Ebenezer Parkman, the aging minister of Westborough, Massachusetts, sent a brief letter to Ezra Stiles, the president of Yale College. The two men had corresponded for nearly two decades. On this occasion, Parkman wrote to request information on the Moravians—the controversial German sect whose radical theology and religious practices had incited riots and vigilante violence earlier in the century—as well as reflections on Stiles's extensive conversations with the Jewish rabbis of Newport, Rhode Island.[207]

Beneath the epistolary pleasantries and the convivial exchange of religious intelligence lay deeper and more pressing concerns regarding what Parkman viewed as an increasingly alarming state of religious affairs in central Massachusetts. Rumors of celibate perfectionists and wife-swapping immortalists continued to swirl in the adjacent towns of Grafton, Sutton, and Hopkinton; the remnants of the Irelandites remained ensconced in the Harvard Square House, despite the recent death of their inspired leader. The pace of Separate Baptist church formation had quickened during the previous decade. Elsewhere in the region, the publications of the English theologian John Murray circulated alongside controversial annihilationist ideas peddled by future Universalist founder Caleb Rich. To the west, Ann Lee, the Elect Lady of the Shak-

206. Relation of Samuel Coe, n.d. [circa 1757], Granville First Congregational Church Papers; Edwards, *Farewel-Sermon*, in *WJE*, XXV, *Sermons and Discourses, 1743-1758*, ed. Kimnach, 481.

207. Parkman, commonplace book, Parkman Papers, 37. For Stiles's friendship with Parkman, see Dexter, ed., *Literary Diary of Ezra Stiles*, II, 230–231; and Parkman, diary, Jan. 8, 1767, July 18–19, 1770, Jan. 29, 1771, June 24, 27, 1775, Sept. 8, 1776, and Nov. 20–21, 1777, Parkman Family Papers, AAS; Parkman, diary, Apr. 2, Sept. 26–27, 1781, Aug. 24, 1782, Parkman Papers, MHS (I thank Ross W. Beales, Jr., for sharing his transcription of Parkman's diaries).

ing Quakers at Niskayuna, New York, had just embarked on her first missionary tour of New England; Parkman and his colleagues in the Marlborough
ministerial association would meet to assess the "strange Conduct and Temper" of her followers later that fall. Desperate for news, he begged Stiles to send
him "anything else" he knew of "modern, present Excentricity—for we have
not a few, who are strangely wild, infesting some of our parts of the Country."
Ominous forces of radical dissent were gathering on the borders of the "holy
Enclosure" that Parkman had safely guarded for more than half a century.[208]

The "dear and worthy Friend" to whom the Westborough minister directed
his letter was ideally positioned to comment on religious developments in
New England. Scion of a vociferous revival critic, Ezra Stiles came of age during the tumultuous 1740s. After graduating from Yale College, he spent the
next decade before his 1755 ordination in Newport, studying law and touring New England. During this period, Stiles began recording a wide variety
of observations in a series of small travel journals. His "Itineraries," as he
called them, reveal an unquenchable thirst for knowledge. Stiles was fascinated by subjects as diverse as astronomy and demography, meteorology and
genealogy, silk production and rum distilling, classical languages and native
American pictographs. Above all, he excelled in gathering materials for a
projected volume on the "Ecclesiastical History of New England and British
America." Stiles created exhaustive lists of Congregational, Baptist, and Anglican clergymen, compiled statistics on Indian missions, sketched meetinghouses and measured their dimensions, and filled his notebooks with extracts
from church record books and summaries of councils; and he corresponded
with dozens of colleagues across New England on a wide variety of ecclesiastical issues.[209]

Stiles started drafting his ecclesiastical history in January 1769. Although
he returned to the manuscript occasionally during the next decade, he never

208. Marlborough Association of Ministers, Records, [147]; Parkman, commonplace
book, 37, Parkman Papers; Parkman to Paine and Fay, May 19, 1743, box 3, Parkman Family
Papers. On the rapidly changing religious landscape of central Massachusetts, see John L.
Brooke, *The Heart of the Commonwealth: Society and Political Culture in Worcester Country,
Massachusetts, 1713-1861* (Amherst, Mass., 1989), 66–96, 158–188. On the Moravian threat,
see Aaron Spencer Fogleman, *Jesus is Female: Moravians and Radical Religion in Early
America*, Early American Studies (Philadelphia, 2007). For Stiles's relationship with the Jew-
ish community in Newport, see William Pencak, *Jews and Gentiles in Early America: 1654-
1800* (Ann Arbor, Mich., 2005), 83–115; and Michael Hoberman, *New Israel / New England:
Jews and Puritans in Early America* (Amherst, Mass., 2011), 161–201.

209. Parkman, diary, Sept. 26, 1781, Parkman Papers; Dexter, ed., *Literary Diary of Ezra
Stiles*, I, 3. See also Morgan, *Gentle Puritan*, 130–157.

progressed past the Pilgrim settlement at Plymouth in 1620. By the mid-1770s, he had laid the project aside, despite the repeated urgings of friends and colleagues, including Parkman and Charles Chauncy of Boston. Stiles's failure stood in marked contrast with the publication success of his contemporary, Isaac Backus, whose multivolume *History of New-England* appeared in 1777. Backus wrote with urgency, casting the rise of the Separate Baptist movement as a heroic struggle against the forces of ecclesiastical tyranny. Stiles, who shared his unfinished draft with Backus, seemed more inclined toward collecting facts than organizing them into a finished narrative.[210]

Issues of authorial temperament aside, Stiles's inability to produce his ecclesiastical history was also the direct result of living in a religious culture that increasingly lacked a coherent center. His first pastorate in Newport brought him into contact with a dizzying array of competing denominations. Within a few blocks of Stiles's church stood two Baptist societies, a Quaker meetinghouse, a Moravian chapel, Touro Synagogue, and the imposing Anglican edifice of Trinity Church, which dominated the central street in town. The arrival of Jonathan Edwards's former student Samuel Hopkins, who was ordained over Newport's original Congregational church in 1770, forced Stiles to accommodate a stark Calvinist theology he and many of his colleagues derided as the *"new Divinity."* Down the backstreets, English, African, and native American cunning folk plied their occult trades to an eager clientele of sailors and travelers. Even after Stiles retreated to Yale College during the American Revolution, he continued to confront religious diversity at every turn. He witnessed the genderless Public Universal Friend preach in New Haven, sketched the Shaker meetinghouse in New Lebanon, New York, and recorded detailed notes on the imported divinity of upstart Scottish sectarian Robert Sandeman, whose advocacy of unusual ritual practices, including foot washing and the kiss of peace, had precipitated a handful of church schisms in Connecticut and New Hampshire.[211]

210. Dexter, ed., *Literary Diary of Ezra Stiles*, I, 3, 199, 508; McLoughlin, ed., *Diary of Isaac Backus*, II, 931. Stiles's draft, early notes, and later Yale College lectures may be found among the Quincy, Wendell, Holmes, and Upham Family Papers, 1633–1910, microfilm, reel 15, MHS.

211. Dexter, ed., *Extracts from the Itineraries and Other Miscellanies of Ezra Stiles*, 307 (quote); Dexter, ed., *Literary Diary of Ezra Stiles*, III, 243, 289; Ezra Stiles, "Memoirs of Mr. Sandeman on His First Coming to America," Dec. 4, 1764, no. 340, microfilm, reel 16, Miscellaneous Volumes and Papers, *ESP*, Stiles, "Memoir of Rev. John Murray," May 10, 1769, no. 481, microfilm, reel 17. On the religious landscape of Newport, see Benjamin L. Carp, *Rebels Rising: Cities and the American Revolution* (New York, 2007), 99–142. For Stiles's relationship with Hopkins, see Conforti, *Samuel Hopkins and the New Divinity Movement*, 95–108.

Perhaps it was his mild temperament. Perhaps it resulted from spending more than two decades working in a religiously diverse port city on the periphery of New England's Congregational establishment. Perhaps it arose out of his experiences compiling church membership statistics and mapping the religious landscape as he prepared to write his ecclesiastical history. Whatever the cause, Stiles discovered earlier than most New Englanders that the gospel land of light had splintered into a sprawling, competitive religious marketplace. The Whitefieldian revivals of the 1740s emboldened lay men and women to affiliate where they pleased, switch communions whenever they chose, or profess no religious allegiances at all. The cosmopolitan president of Yale College eventually resigned himself to changing times, but, for many of Stiles's contemporaries, accepting the new religious order of things came slowly—if at all.

■ Although Ezra Stiles once described himself as one of the "good old Puritans," he was a more cosmopolitan Protestant, a "citizen of the intellectual world" who remained tolerant of religious diversity throughout his life. Stiles seldom criticized those with whom he disagreed, and he rarely hurled the epithets "enthusiasm" or "Arminianism" against his opponents. He filled his itineraries with information on church schisms dating back to "Whitefieldian Times," yet he hardly ever offered his own commentary on these controversies. An exception to this pattern was the brief essay he inscribed in one of his notebooks several months before he began writing his ecclesiastical history. Stiles's "Eye Salve" was an attempt to come to terms with the effects produced by the revivals of the 1740s on New England's religious establishment. "When a Church and Congregation became generally New Lighted," Stiles maintained, a "new minor Old Light Church has been gathered." This had been the situation in Massachusetts parishes with large revival factions, such as Concord, Ipswich, and Plymouth. Churches that remained "Old Light" frequently generated "minor New Light Churches." In still other cases, when ministers preached against purported revival excesses, Separate churches broke away from the "New Lighted Churches." These dissenting institutions inaugurated

---

On the flourishing occult subculture of southeastern New England, see Douglas L. Winiarski, "Native American Popular Religion in New England's Old Colony, 1670–1770," in Joel W. Martin and Mark A. Nicholas, eds., *Native Americans, Christianity, and the Reshaping of the American Religious Landscape* (Chapel Hill, N.C., 2010), 110–115. For Sandemanians and Murrayites, see John Howard Smith, *The Perfect Rule of the Christian Religion: A History of Sandemanianism in the Eighteenth Century* (Albany, N.Y., 2008); and Kathryn Gin Lum, *Damned Nation: Hell in America from the Revolution to Reconstruction* (New York, 2014), 13–42.

a "new species of Ordinations" by "illiterate Pastors," including notable figures such as Isaac Backus and Elisha Paine.[212]

Stiles's brief but convoluted "Eye Salve" essay reflected his struggle to impose linguistic order on the unruly field notes he had been compiling for more than a decade. He was searching for patterns within a fractured religious culture. Then, his ruminations took a remarkable turn. At the close of one of the earliest descriptions of the Old Light–New Light taxonomy that would rise to canonical status among modern historians, Stiles conceded that all New England churches were in "Essence true Churches." Established or Separate, peaceable or fractious, led by college-educated ministers or unlettered elders, Congregational or Presbyterian in polity, moralistic or tinctured with enthusiasm — all of them were on some level, or at least for some faction of earnest Christians, legitimate. To accent his point, Stiles closed his excursus by recording an encounter with a junior colleague who claimed not to know the meaning of the phrase "Old Lights," although he had been raised in the household of a man whom Stiles called a "mighty New Light" clergyman. Wearied by years of ecclesiastical wrangling, the young man's father had his "Eyes anointed" sometime around the year 1745 and had stopped criticizing his opponents. The unnamed minister's son grew up wishing to have the "Differences between the Whitefieldians and his Opposers cease and be buried in Oblivion." To Stiles, an ecumenical spirit of toleration seemed to be the only salve capable of healing the wounds inflicted by New England's era of great awakenings.[213]

Whether he was chronicling the legal harassment of Baptist dissenters, calculating the proportion of Anglican and Quaker families in various towns, or compiling lists of Separate ordinations, Stiles could not escape the conclusion that the Congregational standing order no longer commanded undivided allegiance. Even his fascination with measuring the dimensions of dissenting meetinghouses lent conceptual solidity to the Separate Congregational and Baptist movements. Visual representations of those structures appearing in his notebooks amplified the situation. Eighteenth-century maps of the New England colonies, such as Moses Park's 1766 *Plan of the Colony of Connecticut*, used symbols of Congregational meetinghouses to identify population centers. Designed for a broader, imperial audience, they worked to efface dissent from a seemingly homogenous Protestant landscape. Although Stiles traced

212. Ezra Stiles to Abigail Dwight, Nov. 30, 1770, reel 3, *ESP*; Abiel Holmes, *The Life of Ezra Stiles, D.D. LL.D. . . .* (Boston, 1798), 18; Dexter, ed., *Extracts from the Itineraries and Other Miscellanies of Ezra Stiles*, 233, 251–252.

213. Dexter, ed., *Extracts from the Itineraries and Other Miscellanies of Ezra Stiles*, 251–252.

Park's map for his projected volume on ecclesiastical history, he populated it with "nearly all the Congregational, Baptist and Separate Meeting-houses" in New England, "besides the Episcopal Churches." He filled his itineraries with detailed maps of towns that had witnessed bitter schisms, such as Lyme and Canterbury, Connecticut, and Providence, Rhode Island. In each case, Stiles accented Congregational authority by placing a cross atop the established meetinghouses, but he also marked Anglican, Separate, and Baptist societies with buildings labeled "E," "S," and "B."[214]

Stiles devoted sustained attention to quantifying the religious affiliations of families living in New Haven, a town that had suffered through bitter religious conflicts during the years following the Whitefieldian revivals. Yale College and the adjacent "Nine Squares" district had attracted many of the most notable riding ministers, beginning with George Whitefield and Gilbert Tennent. But the problems in New Haven started in August 1741, when James Davenport arrived in town and declared minister Joseph Noyes to be unconverted and the members of his congregation "Sheep without a Shepherd." Jonathan Edwards attempted to cool overheated tempers a few days later with his commencement address on *The Distinguishing Marks of a Work of the Holy Spirit*, but the revival that Davenport had unleashed could not be quelled. Within weeks of his visit, a cabal of zealous parishioners began agitating against Noyes. A few experienced dramatic visions in which they claimed to have seen the New Haven clergyman and his fellow revival opposers roasting in the flames of hell. The scholars at Yale College grew so restless that rector Thomas Clap temporarily closed the school and eventually expelled David Brainerd and John Cleaveland. By the end of the year, more than one hundred church members had withdrawn from communion and petitioned the crown seeking legal status as dissenters. One year later, they covenanted to form the renegade "White Haven" Society.[215]

A comparison of two manuscript maps shows the lasting divisions created by the schism within the New Haven church (Maps 4–5). Stiles's copy of an early-eighteenth-century map indicates that more than two-thirds of the households in the Nine Squares had affiliated with the First Church be-

214. Dexter, ed., *Extracts from the Itineraries and Other Miscellanies of Ezra Stiles*, 220, 226; Dexter, ed., *Literary Diary of Ezra Stiles*, I, 4 (quotes); Stiles, map of Connecticut, Feb. 25, 1769, no. 475, reel 17, Miscellaneous Volumes and Papers, *ESP*. See also Stiles, Itineraries, 1760–1794, I, 22, 551, II, 570, reel 6, *ESP*. On the Park map, see Thompson R. Harlow, "The Moses Park Map, 1766," *CHS Bulletin*, XXVIII (1963), 33–37.

215. *Boston Weekly Post-Boy*, Oct. 5, 1741. For a more detailed analysis of the New Haven schism, see Stowe, "Opposers Are Very Much Enraged," *CHS Bulletin*, LVI (1991), 211–235.

fore 1724. When Yale College student James Wadsworth produced his "Plan of the Town of New Haven with All the Buildings" a quarter century later, many households stood on opposite sides of the bitter divide fomented by Davenport and his followers. The First Church and White Haven Society meetinghouses faced off against each other on Church Street, scarcely twenty rods apart. Noyes would have trudged past the dissenters' sky-blue building each week on the way to his own pulpit. Across the common stood the stately home of one of his former parishioners, James Pierpont, the wealthy leader of the Separate faction. Members of the White Haven congregation lived on every block in town. The percentage of unaffiliated households appears to have risen by 10 percent between 1724 and 1748. Some of these families had converted to Anglicanism, which was steadily expanding throughout southern Connecticut during the years before the construction of Trinity Church in 1752.[216]

The divisions in New Haven intensified during the next two decades, as the White Haven Society blossomed into a thriving congregation. In 1762, Stiles spent several days compiling an exact list of the "Number of Inhabitants in compact part of the Town of New Haven" and noting the religious meetings attended by the members of each household. Each of the twelve most common surnames on Stiles's census were divided between First Church and White Haven Society, and a few of these kin groups included Anglican defectors as well. A handful of families split down the middle, with spouses worshipping in separate meetinghouses. Together, New Haven's dueling Congregational churches still accounted for 82 percent of the town's population, while the Anglicans and a small group of displaced Catholic "French Neutrals" from Acadia rounded out the list. Despite their numerical superiority, however, Stiles elected to subsume all four groups under the heading "Sects etc.," legitimating the emergence of a burgeoning pluralistic religious culture in the land of steady habits.[217]

Traveling throughout New England during the 1760s, Stiles occasionally visited resilient bastions of Congregational authority and conversed with ministers who had resisted the incursion of Strict Congregationalists, Separate Baptists, Anglicans, Quakers, and other radical dissenters. Some parishes, including Israel Loring's congregation in Sudbury, Massachusetts, and Jonathan Edwards's former pastorate in Northampton, maintained high rates of household affiliation well into the second half of the century. In the west parish of

216. On the Wadsworth map, see Peter Benes, *New England Prospect: A Loan Exhibition of Maps at the Currier Gallery of Art* (Boston, 1981), 64–65.

217. Dexter, ed., *Extracts from the Itineraries and Other Miscellanies of Ezra Stiles*, 42, 50.

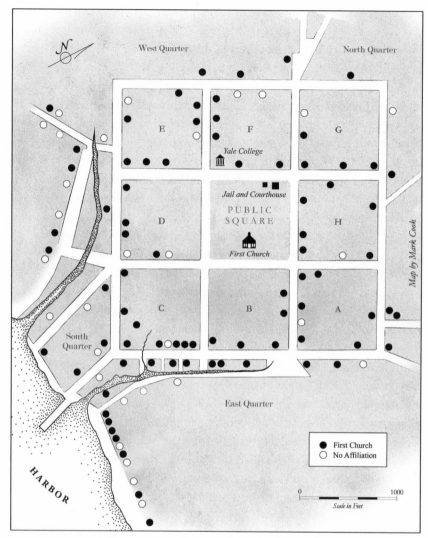

MAP 4 Religious Affiliation by Household in the "Nine Squares" District of New Haven, Connecticut, 1724. Drawn by Mark Cook

Hartford, the small hamlet of Walpole, Massachusetts, and a few other recently gathered churches, the number of yearly baptisms kept pace with the annual birth rate. Stiles was especially impressed with Ebenezer Gay's parish in Hingham. "The people," he noted, were "sober, industrious, don't go to Taverns, generally pray in families and a great number hopefully pious and truly religious"; there was scarcely a family in town whose children had not been baptized. Likewise, Stiles's friend and correspondent, Ebenezer Parkman, ap-

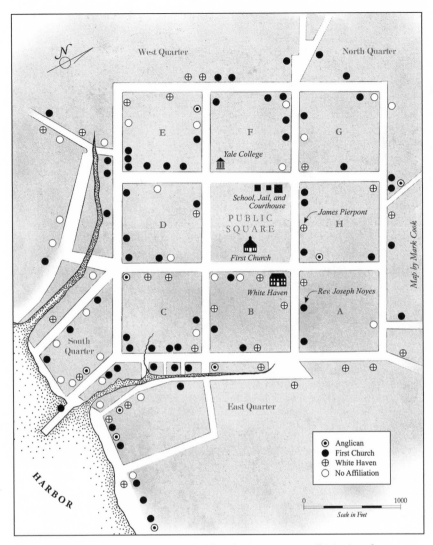

MAP 5 Religious Affiliation by Household in the "Nine Squares" District of
New Haven, Connecticut, 1748. Drawn by Mark Cook

peared to have weathered the storms of the 1740s. The percentage of families
affiliated with his Westborough church declined, but only from 89 percent
in 1724 to 78 in 1762. Haverhill's venerable First Church—praised by John
Brown's parishioners half a century earlier as the very seat of gospel light—
also maintained a relatively high percentage of affiliated families, despite the
rapid growth of Hezekiah Smith's upstart Separate Baptist church (Tables 6
and 9). One factor united these disparate and infrequent Congregational suc-

TABLE 9 Religious Affiliation by Household in Selected New England Towns and Parishes, 1740–1800

Town or Parish	Total Households	Congregational (%)	Other/Mixed/ No Affiliation[a] (%)
Bennington, Vt. (List of Freemen, 1778–1779)	65	40.0	60.0
Haverhill, Mass., First Parish (Tax List, 1774)	99	67.7	32.3
Hingham, Mass., First Parish (Tax List, 1784)	123	87.8	12.2
New Haven, Conn., "Nine Squares" (Ezra Stiles's Census, 1762)[b]	270	43.0	57.0
Norwich, Conn., First Parish (Tax List, 1754)	122	63.2	36.8
Stratham, N.H. (Map, 1793)	113	32.7	67.3
Suffield, Conn., First Parish (Tax List, 1769)	81	50.6	49.4
Westborough, Mass. (Tax List, 1762)	108	77.8	22.2

Notes:

[a]Limitations in extant church records make it difficult to identify the precise household affiliation strategies of families that did not belong to the Congregational church. This comprehensive category, therefore, includes families in which one or both spouses can be identified as Anglicans, Strict Congregationalists, Separate Baptists, Quakers, or Catholics and those whom Ezra Stiles called "Nothingarians": households with no formal ties to any religious society.

[b]Congregational households in New Haven included 115 First Church families (42.3%) and 2 families that worshipped in the chapel at Yale College (0.7%). Other/Mixed/No Affiliation households included 109 White Haven Church families (40.1%), 34 Trinity Episcopal Church families (12.5%), 5 French Acadian Catholic families (1.8%), and 7 mixed families (2.6%) in which spouses attended different religious meetings.

Sources: Appendix A.

cess stories: all were parishes in which ministers and lay people rejected the purported excesses of the Whitefieldian revivals and retained or implemented inclusive church admission standards.[218]

Towns that had witnessed powerful revival seasons during the 1740s, suffered through decades of conflict and decline. The proportion of affiliated households in Benjamin Lord's Norwich parish, for example, which had hovered around 80 percent during the 1730s, slipped to 63 by 1754, as Isaac

218. Ibid., 200–201, 207–208, 246, 259–260 (quote), 328–329.

Backus's family and other disgruntled parishioners departed for the Separate Baptists and Anglicans. In nearby Stonington, a dispirited Nathaniel Eells informed Stiles that one-quarter of the children in his parish remained unbaptized and the only woman admitted to full communion during the previous fifteen years had demanded to be immersed. A rough accounting of the annual number of baptisms in Stiles's uncle's parish in Woodstock, Connecticut, revealed a disturbing decline, from a high of 46 in 1742 to only 14 in 1763. By the mid-1760s, Stiles estimated that the Congregational church in Wallingford commanded the allegiance of only half the town's families. Dissenters in the tiny hamlet of Freetown, Massachusetts, outnumbered Congregationalists two to one. One-third of the Ripton parish in Stratford (now Huntington), Connecticut, had gone over to the Anglicans. Gloucester, Massachusetts, was "mostly Baptists." The Providence, Rhode Island, pulpit stood vacant, its minister hounded out of town by zealous Whitefieldarians. In Plainfield, Connecticut, the "Separates became such a Plurality" that they forced establishment Congregationalists to accept the ordination of an "unlearned Minister" by Solomon and Elisha Paine. "Swallowed up with Exhorters," the Hull, Massachusetts, church had almost disbanded, Stiles lamented, owing to the labors of the "Reverend and crazy Solomon Prentice," who preached in town briefly after losing his second pulpit in Easton.[219]

The most notable example of the "Broken State" of the Congregational establishment during the second half of the eighteenth century was the famously awakened town of Suffield. The prosperous Connecticut Valley farming village had been the scene of the largest revival in early American history. One year after Jonathan Edwards electrified Suffield with a pair of stirring sermon performances on the eve of his more famous visit to neighboring Enfield in July 1741, however, the church slid into bitter strife that lasted for years. The protracted controversy began when the young minister Ebenezer Gay— nephew and namesake of the prominent Hingham clergyman—attempted to implement the traditional test of a relation and fortnight propounding period in his new parish. Although familiar to residents in eastern Massachusetts, these orderly but restrictive practices fomented "Schism and ruine" in Suffield. Angry parishioners railed against Gay's sermons and challenged his pastoral authority. By 1750, many of the town's most ardent new converts had withdrawn from communion and formed a strict Congregational church. Before George Whitefield's visit to Suffield during the fall of 1740, more than

219. Ibid., 80, 250, 295 (see also 71, 77, 99, 119, 137, 159, 195–196, 214, 219, 237).

80 percent of all households in town had affiliated with the Suffield church. Thirty years after Edwards preached *Sinners in the Hand of an Angry God*, that figure had been reduced by more than a third (see Tables 6 and 9). The "Glorious Work" of the revivals, as Gay's uncle predicted in 1742, had "Chang'd into a ruinous War."[220]

The situation seemed even bleaker in Suffield's west parish, an outlying village renowned both for "extraordinary warmth" in revival zeal and for "engagedness of spirit" in ecclesiastical controversies. Despite his earnest support for revival innovations, minister John Graham wrangled with his fractious parishioners over issues ranging from homiletics to church discipline. During the 1760s, the conflict grew so desperate that Graham suspended the Lord's Supper for several years. Taking stock in 1781, Graham decried the declining fortunes of his pastorate. At the time of his ordination in 1746, nine out of every ten households were represented in the west parish church by both spouses; Graham could count the number of unbaptized children on one hand. A little more than a generation later, the total number of communicants had declined by nearly one half. Of the 136 families in Graham's parish, fewer than one in three were affiliated with his church through either spouse. Membership in Suffield's new Baptist church had tripled during the previous decade, and unbaptized children numbered in the hundreds. Early in his career, Graham noted in his diary, the "public worship of God" had been "daily, zealously and universally attended" and his people were "hungry for the word." "But, alas how different is it Now? And what a different temper appears now?" By 1781, "prayless" families—the exact number Graham could not determine—formed the majority in his parish. They neglected their morning and evening prayers, he complained, and "go to their meals like Swine to their troughs and live like the Brutes."[221]

As he surveyed the fractured situation in towns across New England, Stiles noted with mounting concern the growing number of people who seemed in-

220. Dexter, ed., *Extracts from the Itineraries and Other Miscellanies*, 232, 325, 352 (quote); Stephen Williams, diaries, 1715–1782, 10 vols., IV, 24, typescript, Storrs Library, Longmeadow, Mass. (available online at *http://longmeadowlibrary.wordpress.com/*); Ebenezer Gay to Ebenezer Gay (of Suffield), Dec. 6, 1742, case 8, box 22, SGC I. On Gay's troubled ministry, see Douglas L. Winiarski, "Jonathan Edwards, Enthusiast? Radical Revivalism and the Great Awakening in the Connecticut Valley," *Church History*, LXXIV (2005), 715–727.

221. Jonathan Edwards to Stephen Williams, Jan. 1, 1745, in *WJE*, XVI, *Letters and Personal Writings*, ed. Claghorn, 153; John Graham, Jr., journal, [1739], 1776–1785, Jan. 26, 1781, box 1, Graham Family Papers, 1731–1849, WCL. See also West Suffield, Conn., Second Congregational Church Papers, 1766–1768, Kent Memorial Library, Suffield, Mass.; and McLoughlin, ed., *Diary of Isaac Backus*, II, 1093.

different to the Congregational establishment altogether and "very seldom" came to Sabbath meetings. He struggled to develop a vocabulary to describe these "Non Communicants," "Neutrals," people of "no Denomination," and "stay at home Christians." Eventually, Stiles settled on a single word to describe their anomalous status. He called them "Nothingarians." In places like New Haven and Suffield, "Nothingarians" were on the rise.[222]

■ Several years before Ezra Stiles began working on his ecclesiastical history of New England, colleagues in the Rhode Island ministerial association invited him to preach at their annual convention. The published version of Stiles's "ingenious performance," *A Discourse on the Christian Union*, became an instant best seller admired throughout the colonies for the author's "candor and good Judgment." But Stiles's *Discourse* was more important for what it occluded than for what it revealed about the present state of the *"congregational* denomination." Like the council of ministers overmantel painting that graced the study of Newbury minister John Lowell, Stiles's address contributed to a broader post-revival movement among established clergymen toward reconciliation, toleration, and ecumenism.[223]

Stiles devoted the first half of his *Discourse on the Christian Union* to the "fundamental principles of christianity and ecclesiastical polity" on which, he believed, ministers of all persuasions were agreed. Most clergymen, Stiles asserted with confidence, shared basic Reformed beliefs in the existence and nature of God, divine creation, the necessity of Christ's atonement, justification by faith, the inspired origins of the scriptures, and the inevitability of future judgment. Purported divisions between *"calvinism* and *arminianism"* were overstated, Stiles continued, now that the churches of New England had in "some measure cooled and recovered themselves" from the revivals of the 1740s. "I am persuaded from a very thorough disquisition and search," he concluded triumphantly, "that there is no body of churches in the protestant

222. Dexter, ed., *Extracts from the Itineraries and Other Miscellanies of Ezra Stiles*, 54, 105–106, 298–299; Dexter, ed., *Literary Diary of Ezra Stiles*, I, 208, 278. Stiles's use of this provocative term predates nearly all of the examples cited in the *Oxford English Dictionary* and may well have been the source for Jedidiah Morse's more famous observation in *The American Geography* (Elizabethtown, N.J., 1789), 206, that many people in Rhode Island "can be reduced to no particular denomination, and are, as to religion, strictly *Nothingarians.*"

223. Francis Alison to Ezra Stiles, Mar. 24, 1762, reel 1, *ESP*; Stiles, *A Discourse on the Christian Union* (Boston, 1761), 8. On Stiles's ecumenism, see Carl Bridenbaugh, *Mitre and Sceptre: Transatlantic Faiths, Ideas, Personalities, and Politics, 1689–1775* (New York, 1962), 3–22; and Beneke, *Beyond Toleration*, 81–87.

world more nearly recovered to the simplicity and purity of the apostolic age" than the Congregational churches of Massachusetts, Connecticut, and New Hampshire.[224]

Toward the end of his *Discourse*, Stiles marshaled his considerable knowledge of demography and church history in a provocative hypothesis regarding the future "proportion of the sects" in New England. If Congregational clergymen stayed true to their principles, exercised the "utmost charity and benevolence to others," and remained united in "faith and fellowship," more than five thousand meetinghouses would dot the American landscape by 1860. The "ancestorial religion" of the New England puritans would expand into yet unsettled western provinces and claim the allegiance of more than seven million people. Stiles recognized that his calculations were based on a series of questionable assumptions. New patterns of immigration, "proseliting and shifting communions," and a rising tide of "public enthusiasm" might draw some New Englanders into competing denominations and sects. Stiles nonetheless pressed forward to assert his confident conclusion. Congregationalists would enjoy "remarkable increase" during the next century, he predicted, "which some of the present generation may live to see."[225]

Stiles had spent nearly a decade mapping and measuring the vitality of New England's Congregational establishment in his "Itineraries"; but the self-congratulatory demographic experiment must have struck even his staunchest allies as implausible, even naïve. Stiles presumed that a commitment to basic theological principles and ecclesiastical practices would ensure a "diffusive harmony," yet his *Discourse on the Christian Union* sidestepped the "late enthusiasm" that had driven multitudes of New Englanders "seriously, soberly and solemnly out of their wits": sudden conversions, bodily exercises, biblical impulses, visions, and extraordinary gifts of preaching and spiritual discernment. These more fundamental experiential issues lay at the root of the controversies over baptism, ordination, and church councils that he assumed would wither away with time and in the light of "free inquiry" and reasoned debate. Stiles's demographic projections reflected his deep-seated desire for ecclesiastical unity rather than the troubling demographic facts that he had been compiling in his notebooks.[226]

Church admission relations reveal the plural languages of religious experience that emerged within the established Congregational churches during the

224. Stiles, *Discourse on the Christian Union*, 8, 50–51, 95.

225. Ibid., 112, 114–115. For Stiles's preliminary calculations, see Dexter, ed., *Extracts from the Itineraries and Other Miscellanies of Ezra Stiles*, 105–106.

226. Stiles, *Discourse on the Christian Union*, 50, 94, 115.

second half of the eighteenth century. Across New England, churchgoers increasingly recited their religious experiences in a variety of competing and, at times, mutually unintelligible experiential dialects. Unlike the relentlessly uniform testimonies produced by candidates a generation earlier, the Middleborough and Sturbridge relations, in particular, exhibited a wide range of literary tropes (see Table 7). Many prospective communicants continued to cling to their "goodly Heritage" or acknowledged that they were seeking access to the sacrament of baptism for their children. Although many continued to believe that they had "Profited by the means of grace" and were joining the church in response to sacramental imperatives, others repudiated what one Middleborough man called the "relegion in my head" and lamented that they derived little comfort from their devotional practices. Several years before he was harried into exile for his Loyalist sympathies, Middleborough's most prominent resident, Peter Oliver, Jr., drafted a perfunctory, 125-word relation in which he tersely noted his "Duty to offer myself a Member of this Church," after stating his belief in the "Supreme Governor of the Universe." Two years later, an enslaved man named Cuffee Wright composed a relation four times as long in which he struggled to described how God had carried him "out of [the] Land of Dearkness unto the Land of gloryous gosple Light." In both towns, professors and new converts worshipped side by side, often presenting competing evidence in their testimonies.[227]

The Middleborough and Sturbridge relations also reflect a wide range of perspectives on the Whitefieldian new birth. Besides the providential afflictions which continued to provide incentives to close with the church, candidates in both parishes added detailed descriptions of revival meetings and powerful preaching—some of their memories stretching back decades to the "time of the general awakining" during the 1740s. One Sturbridge woman conflated her "Safe Deliverance in Child bareing" with her liberation from "my State of Sin and misery." Although some prospective church members acknowledged that they could not give a "perticular account of a Change wrot on my ♥," others described a "very sensible alteration" in which "all doutes and Sorows vanieshed away." Intrusive scriptural passages played a key role in many of these narratives (see Table 8). Ichabod Billington summarized the tangled situation in his 1762 relation. Citing the religious privileges of

---

227. Appendix B, Sturbridge, Mass., First Church, 2, 10; Relations of Nathan Eddy, Jan. 23, 1765, and Peter Oliver, Jr., Jan. [13], 1771, Middleborough First Congregational Church Relations and Personal Records, CL; James F. Cooper, Jr., "Cuffee's 'Relation': A Faithful Slave Speaks through the Project for the Preservation of Congregational Church Records," *NEQ*, LXXXVI (2013), 309. For the full text of Oliver's relation, see Appendix C.

his youth, the loud calls of divine providence in a thunderstorm, biblical impulses, and a mystical vision, the Middleborough yeoman recalled how God had used "Soo Many Wase [ways] and mens [means] to Bring me to the Sight of my Salf."[228]

Devotional writings composed during the second half of the eighteenth century by lay men and women who remained within what Stiles termed "our denomination" can be mapped along a similar spectrum. At one end, stood stolid godly walkers like John and Ruth Stanwood, members of the south parish church in Ipswich, whose infrequent meditations followed a pattern that had changed little across the generations. The Stanwoods marked the births of their children on the pages of a small leather-bound volume and struggled to sanctify God's "holy hand of provedence" in the sicknesses and deaths of extended family members. They were "Earnest in Seeking"—but never fully achieved—an "Aquaintance with God." Mehetabel Williams occupied the opposite pole. Growing up in the north parish of Norton (now Mansfield), Massachusetts, only a few miles away from the perfectionist community at Winnecunnet Pond, the lifelong single woman experienced a "true regenerateing saveing change" during the 1740s. As with many new converts, however, Williams oscillated between protracted periods of "darkness and distress" and fleeting moments of inner illumination, as she examined herself for certain evidence of a "work of grace in my heart." Even as she meditated on events ranging from the raising of a new meetinghouse to the repeal of the Stamp Act, Williams filled her journal with reports of dreams, voices, visions, and dramatic encounters with Jesus and Satan. Hers was a religious life sustained by "discoveries of divine things" through a never-ending string of "those words" that "kept runing in my mind."[229]

Other writers occupied the broad middle space between the traditional ideal of the godly walk and visionary enthusiasm. During the same decade in which he sat for a handsome pastel portrait by John Singleton Copley, Ebenezer Storer, the cosmopolitan merchant and deacon of Boston's Brattle Street church, began keeping a devotional diary that he filled with occasional medi-

228. Relations of Ichabod Billington, Mar. 9, 1762, Abijah Cobb, Sept. 14, 1765, Thomas Cole, 1747 [adm. Feb. 14, 1748], Fear Redding, 1763, Middleborough First Congregational Church Relations and Personal Records; Appendix B, Sturbridge, Mass., First Church, 10, 15, 26.

229. Stiles, *Discourse on the Christian Union*, 101; Record of the John Stanwood and Moses Smith Families, 1750–1789, [7–8], Mss A 2045, NEHGS; Abijah Leonard, transcr., diary of Mehitable Williams, 1765–1770, [5, 12, 17, 34, 43, 51], Mss A 2059, NEHGS. For an extended analysis of Williams's diary, see Douglas Leo Winiarski, "All Manner of Error and Delusion: Josiah Cotton and the Religious Transformation of Southeastern New England, 1700–1770" (Ph.D. diss., Indiana University, 2000), 335–340.

tations written in an elegant hand. Like the Stanwoods, Storer turned to his diary two or three times per year and usually in response to affliction, sacramental observances, or important life-course events. At the same time, Storer borrowed heavily from the emerging poetics of sentiment that appeared in the hymns of Isaac Watts and British literary magazines. In contrast to the Boston merchant's effusive coffeehouse piety, Elizabeth Robbins, the wife of a prominent New Divinity clergyman, seldom used her devotional diary to ruminate on temporal affairs. Instead, she channeled her infrequent writing activities toward recording the "various dealings of God to my soul"—most of which were negative. Robbins joined the church in Norfolk, Connecticut, in 1766 and presented thirteen children for baptism in regular order during the next two decades, but she rarely experienced "Spirituall communion" with God. Even during the powerful revivals that punctuated her husband's prosperous ministry, Robbins felt "exceeding dull and stupid and senceless." She worried incessantly that she had "no Interest in Christ nor never Saveingly closd with him."[230]

Throughout the second half of the eighteenth century, competing ways of experiencing religion empowered the New England laity and set them at odds with their neighbors and ministers. For more than five decades following her conversion in 1743, Sarah Osborn of Newport, Rhode Island, ruminated on the state of her soul in the largest series of devotional diaries to survive from the colonial era. Osborn's relentless quest for spiritual certainty allowed her to push, but never to exceed, the gender boundaries prescribed for her. During the 1740s, she organized a female religious society and later emerged as the leader of a powerful religious community among enslaved African Americans. Her experiences differed dramatically from those of Framingham, Massachusetts, deacon Edward Goddard. Although he also recorded meditations during the 1740s and 1750s in which he attempted to determine whether he had "experienced that great change which imparts a New Nature," Goddard sparred with his clerical contemporaries, championed liberty of conscience, and fomented a bitter schism that nearly destroyed the church to which he had belonged for decades.[231]

230. Ebenezer Storer, diary, 1749–1764, Mss C 2004, NEHGS; Elizabeth Robbins, diary, 1766–1783, [1, 10–11, 18], Robbins Family Papers, 1719–1850, MS 1169, YUA. Robbins's church activities may be found in *Baptisms, Marriages, Burials, and List of Members Taken from the Church Records of the Reverend Ammi Ruhamah Robbins, First Minister of Norfolk, Connecticut, 1761–1813* (n.p., 1910), 5, 8, 24–27, 29, 31, 34, 36, 38, 40, 44.

231. Harry S. Stout and James F. Cooper, Jr., "The Self-Examination of Edward Goddard," AAS, *Procds.*, XCVII (1987), 97. Osborn has been the subject of a number of important studies, including Mary Beth Norton, "'My Resting Reaping Times': Sarah Osborn's

FIGURE 25 John Singleton Copley, *Ebenezer Storer II*. Circa 1767. Pastel on paper mounted on canvas, 58.7 × 43.5 cm. Purchase, Morris K. Jessup Fund and Lila Acheson Wallace Gift, 2008. Courtesy, Metropolitan Museum of Art, New York

The struggles of Eunice Andrews provide a final example of the powerful ways in which diverging religious experiences fundamentally transformed the Congregational churches as institutions. Baptized as an infant in Ipswich Hamlet (now Hamilton), Massachusetts, Eunice married George Andrews in 1747 and started attending Sabbath meetings with the Separates in the neighboring Chebacco parish. In a church admission testimony written several years later, Andrews dated her earliest religious convictions to the Whitefieldian revivals, when "God had first begun to pour out his Spirit in this our Day and I came to hear the Enlivened Ministers preach." Brought to the "very brink of Eternity" following the birth of her first child, Andrews received comfort from a vision in which she saw Christ "Interceeding with God for me." During the years that followed, Andrews struggled to overcome "worldy cares" and pondered whether her newfound faith was only the result of a "Sick-bed Repentance." Still full of "Staggerings," Andrews eventually summoned the courage to relate her experiences to John Cleaveland and placed her mark in the Chebacco church record book on September 16, 1750.[232]

The following decade, at the height of the powerful revival that gripped Chebacco, Andrews and her husband moved to Ebenezer Parkman's parish in Westborough. Cleaveland sent a letter to Parkman endorsing Andrews's upright Christian conversation and dismissed her to his pastoral care. After soliciting reports from colleagues in Essex County about the formation of the Separate church in Chebacco, however, Parkman refused to accept her letter of

Defense of Her 'Unfeminine' Activities, 1767," *Signs: Journal of Women in Culture and Society*, II (1976), 515–529; Barbara E. Lacey, "The Bonds of Friendship: Sarah Osborn of Newport and the Reverend Joseph Fish of North Stonington, 1743–1779," *Rhode Island History*, XLV (1986), 127–136; Charles E. Hambrick-Stowe, "The Spiritual Pilgrimage of Sarah Osborn (1714–1796)," *Church History*, LXI (1992), 408–421; Sheryl A. Kujawa, "The Great Awakening of Sarah Osborn and the Female Society of the First Congregational Church in Newport," *Newport History*, LXV (1994), 133–153; and Catherine A. Brekus, *Sarah Osborn's World: The Rise of Evangelical Christianity in Early America* (New Haven, Conn., 2013). Examples of Goddard's correspondence and private devotional writings may be found in the Nathan Stone Papers; box 3, Curwen Family Papers; Goddard, *Brief Account of the Formation and Settlement of the 2nd Church and Congregation in Framingham;* and Goddard, diary, 1752–1753, RG 1343, box 1, Charles Morton Papers, 1752–1867, American Baptist Historical Society.

232. Parkman, diary, Jan. 8, 1767, Parkman Family Papers (I thank Ross Beales, Jr., for sharing his transcription of Parkman's diary); Appendix B, Ipswich (now Essex), Mass., Chebacco Separate Church, 3. For genealogical information, see "Descendants of John Andrews of Ipswich," *Essex Antiquarian*, III (1899), 100. On the Andrews controversy, see also Keith W. F. Stavely, *Puritan Legacies: Paradise Lost and the New England Tradition, 1630–1890* (Ithaca, N.Y., 1987), 167–197; and Ross W. Beales, Jr., "The Smiles and Frowns of Providence," in Peter Benes, ed., *Wonders of the Invisible World: 1600–1900*, Dublin Seminar for New England Folklife, Annual Proceedings 1992 (Boston, 1995), 95–96.

dismission. The following year, Andrews petitioned to present her new infant for baptism and to receive the Lord's Supper in the Westborough meetinghouse as a "Transient Communicant." The details of her request were significant. Andrews had no intention of transferring her membership from Chebacco because she disagreed with Parkman's inclusive admission procedures. "I don't believe that Mr. P. has a spark of Grace in him," neighbors overheard Andrews declare, "for I never could see any." Her husband refused to pay his ministerial rate. In the protracted dispute that followed, Andrews maintained that she belonged to a "Reguler Church" at Chebacco. As one of Christ's "true followers," she was entitled to participate in the sacrament in Westborough, regardless of her concerns about the state of Parkman's soul or her reservations regarding the church over which he presided.[233]

Parkman's parishioners remained divided over the *"Andrews* Controversie." Since the Westborough minister and his colleagues in the Marlborough Association refused to hold communion with the Chebacco Separates, he denied Andrews's request to sit at the Lord's Table in Westborough when "She was not in Charity with the Pastor." The members of his church opposed schism, Parkman explained in a letter to Cleaveland, and they would admit Andrews only after she had confessed her error in electing to worship in Chebacco's Separate church during the "Times of Darkness and Temptation" that had prevailed during the decades following the Whitefieldian revivals.[234]

Meanwhile, a vocal clique defended Andrews in a series of "very rough" altercations. "Full of wrath and hard speeches," they branded Parkman a *"Wicked Man"* and waggishly suggested that he and his colleagues condemned Cleaveland simply because the Chebacco preacher "so much out-shined them, and People esteemed him so much higher." To make matters worse, Cleaveland visited the Andrewses during the dispute, preached in town without Parkman's consent, and baptized several Westborough children. And he attempted to expose Parkman's grievous abridgment of Christian charity by publishing a selection of letters from the controversy in a spirited defense of the Chebacco

233. Parkman, church minutes, Oct. 17, 1766, box 2, Parkman Family Papers; Parkman, diaries, Sept. 26, 1766, Parkman Family Papers; Eunice Andrews to Ebenezer Parkman, Jan. 1, 1768, box 3, Parkman Family Papers. See also Westborough Congregational Church Records, 128–129, 134–138; and John Cleaveland to Samuel Chandler and John Rogers, Nov. 20, 1765, box 2, JCP.

234. Parkman, diary, Aug. 1, Nov. 6, 1766, Parkman Family Papers; John Cleaveland, *A Short and Plain Narrative of the Late Work of God's Spirit at Chebacco in Ipswich in the Years 1763 and 1764 ...* (Boston, 1767), 51. See also Marlborough Association of Ministers, Records, [115], CL.

revivals. "O how my Heart grieves for this bitter Contention," the Westborough minister lamented. It was a shocking "Frown" of divine providence.[235]

After four years of wrangling, tempers cooled and positions softened. Parkman persuaded his congregation to put a stop to the "fruitless controversies and Contests" that had wracked his parish. The Westborough church voted to make Andrews a "professor in General and not as a Member of one particular Church or another." She presented the last of her nine children for baptism in the Westborough meetinghouse and participated in the Lord's Supper alongside Parkman for nearly a decade until her death in 1776. The Westborough minister even noted several occasions in his diary in which he sat down to tea with Andrews and her husband, who treated him "with great Civility." She remained an outsider to the Congregational establishment, however, and never renounced her membership in Chebacco's Separate church.[236]

Parkman's acquiescence to Andrews's demands signaled the ascendancy of individual experience over corporate discipline. Church membership no longer related to parish boundaries, ecclesiastical order, or community expectations. Instead, as Cleaveland's parishioners in Chebacco explained in a landmark series of votes, all individuals had the right to judge for themselves where to worship, regardless of "Lines drawn by the civil Majestrate," and any church member could move from one congregation to another based solely on the "Principle of Edification." Churches that refused to grant an orderly dismissal to such dissenters, the Chebacco parishioners maintained, made "themselves a Prison, contrary to the rules of Gospel."[237]

Separatist Eunice Andrews and the godly walking Stanwoods, dogged Calvinist Sarah Osborn and visionary Mehetabel Williams, dour Elizabeth Robbins and cosmopolitan Ebenezer Storer—all were Congregationalists by Ezra Stiles's reckoning. And yet they also embodied more than what he called "different species of congregationalism," for they shared little beyond a general commitment to basic Reformed theological tenets. By the end of the eighteenth century, New England's established churches had developed into arenas for testing and contesting religious experience. They were riven with

235. Parkman, diary, Sept. 26, Oct. 17, Nov. 5–6, 1766, May 19, July 23, 1767, Parkman Family Papers.

236. Parkman, church minutes, Jan. 11, 1768, box 2, Parkman Family Papers; Parkman, diary, Mar. 14, 1768, Mar. 22, 1770, Parkman Family Papers. See also Westborough Congregational Church Records, 140–143.

237. Cleaveland, *Short and Plain Narrative*, 36–37, 42. For a similar argument, see Timothy D. Hall, *Contested Boundaries: Itinerancy and the Reshaping of the Colonial American Religious World* (Durham, N.C., 1994), 112–116.

petty feuds and ripe for controversy and schism. Many ministers continued to refer to their parishioners' church admission testimonies as relations, but some began to call them "Experimental" relations or simply "Experiences." Not only did lay men and women have a story to narrate, they had something to prove.[238]

In 1768, as the Andrews conflagration in Westborough cooled to embers, Stiles sent a letter to one of Parkman's colleagues in the Marlborough Association. Reprising the argument he had first advanced in his *Discourse on the Christian Union,* Stiles proclaimed that the New England churches were "happy beyond any Churches throughout the World." The most learned clergyman in British North America still believed that the next century would belong to the Congregationalists. But, in most towns, the numerical superiority of the once-puritan churches failed to outlast the span of Stiles's own life. A revolutionary era of religious voluntarism, liberty of conscience, and freedom of choice had dawned in the gospel land of light.[239]

238. Stiles, *Discourse on the Christian Union,* 88; Appendix B, Sturbridge, Mass., First Church, 18. See also Douglas L. Winiarski, "Religious Experiences in New England," in Amanda Porterfield, ed., *Modern Christianity to 1900,* A People's History of Christianity, VI (Minneapolis, Minn., 2007), 210, 230–232.

239. Ezra Stiles to Nathan Stone, Jr., Apr. 25, 1768, Nathan Stone Papers.

Epilogue

Each year, for more than half a century, Samuel Lane painstakingly trimmed, folded, and stitched together sheets of paper to form what he called his "new Fashoned almanack," a personal journal in which he "pen'd down" the "Remarkable Providences" of his life. Daily entries chronicled a wide range of affairs, from meteorological events and mundane business transactions to family crises and imperial conflicts. The most valuable components of Lane's almanacs were the yearly commentaries he inscribed on the first and last pages. The prosperous Stratham, New Hampshire, farmer, tanner, and surveyor reserved the latter for general observations on the productivity of his fields and livestock, the value of various economic commodities, the health of his community, and noteworthy political events. Commencing in 1741 and continuing intermittently into the 1790s, the first page of each almanac contained brief reflections on ecclesiastical affairs in New England. Collectively, these short memoranda constituted one of the longest running religious histories of the eighteenth century.[1]

Lane's annual reports on the state of religion in New England were relentlessly negative: "Lamentable Lamentable Lamentable," he wrote emphatically on one occasion during the 1740s. In the wake of the Whitefieldian revivals, Lane resorted to tidal metaphors to describe the malaise that gripped the established Congregational churches. "Religon in the Country is now at a verry low ebb," he complained at the close of 1746, "and those amongst us that us'd to be verry forward in Religious Matters, are now verry Dull and backward." Young people had grown increasingly "Loose Rude and Vain." "Worldly

---

1. Samuel Lane, almanacs, 1737–1801, cover for 1738, Ser. II, box 2, LFP; Extracts published in Charles Lane Hanson, ed., *A Journal for the Years 1739–1803 by Samuel Lane of Stratham, New Hampshire* (Concord, N.H., 1937). For an excellent biography, see Jerald E. Brown, *The Years of the Life of Samuel Lane, 1718–1806: A New Hampshire Man and His World*, ed. Donna-Belle Garvin (Hanover, N.H., 2000).

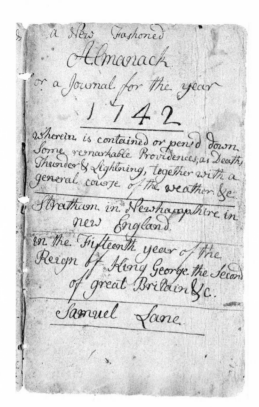

FIGURE 26 Samuel Lane, "A New Fashoned Almanack or a Journal for the Year 1742." Box 2, Lane Family Papers, 1727–1924. Courtesy, New Hampshire Historical Society, Concord

Mindedness" seemed to prevail everywhere, as people hungered after land speculation schemes in the newly opened interior settlements. Repeated epidemics of smallpox and diphtheria, protracted droughts, a powerful earthquake in 1755, and the staggering early military defeats of the Seven Years' War were "threatning tokens of the Displeasure of heaven" against a sinful New England, yet Lane saw no evidence of moral reformation among his Stratham neighbors. "It is a verry Dead and Maloncholy time with respect to Religon," he concluded, "and 'tis Said that Religon is at as low an Ebb as ever was known."[2]

At first glance, Lane's lamentations appeared to echo the pronouncements of leading Congregational clergymen, as the torrent of religious excitement and the flood of church admissions that attended the revivals of 1741 and 1742 quickly receded and nearly dried up altogether. But Lane was no ardent Whitefieldarian. It was not the abrupt cessation of the revivals that troubled

2. Samuel Lane, almanacs, religious memoranda for 1746, 1748, 1752, 1753, and 1758, Ser. II, box 2, LFP.

him most. Quite to the contrary, Lane believed that his neighbors had become far too enamored with the wrong kind of religion. In 1756, he attributed
the region's "Universal Lethergie" to a growing rash of divisions in "Church
and State affairs." These ecclesiastical schisms had been perpetrated, in Lane's
view, by a younger cadre of unlettered itinerants who descended on the northern frontier, preaching house to house, sowing discord wherever they went,
and seducing earnest lay people into heterodoxy and sectarianism. Lane repeatedly yoked his disparaging commentaries on the "Low Ebb" of religious
affairs to the "Commotions" associated with the revivals and the "Scheemers"
who promoted them. For him, the emergence of competing denominations in
New England during the second half of the eighteenth century was a troubling
sign of religious decline.[3]

Lane grew to maturity in a world in which religion and the family were in-
separable and the established, tax-supported Congregational churches dominated most New England towns uncontested. In Hampton, New Hampshire,
where he was born and baptized, 95 percent of all households affiliated with
the Congregational church during the first half of the eighteenth century (see
Table 6). The Lanes were no exception. Each of Samuel's fifteen younger siblings covenanted shortly after marriage and presented their children for baptism in an orderly progression. Knowledgeable in Reformed theology yet less
preoccupied with issues of conversion than earlier generations of New England puritans, families like the Lanes understood church membership as
both a duty incumbent on all people and a privilege that ensured temporal
and spiritual benefits for anxious parents who pledged to walk answerable to
their professions.

Samuel and his father, Joshua Lane, a deacon in the Hampton church, lived
to see the unmaking of that broadly shared religious culture. Both men lamented the sudden proliferation of the distinctly Whitefieldian theology of the
new birth that supplanted the steady ideal of the godly walk during the turbulent decade of the 1740s. They were wary of narratives that described conversion as a discrete and often datable event attended by wrenching, somatic,
and visionary experiences. Powerful preaching on the sandy foundations of
faith set individuals in motion, seeking new forms of religious community
that carried them outside the boundaries, both physically and experientially,
of New England's parish-based Congregational system. Lane's youngest son,
Jabez, eventually reconciled himself to the new world of denominational diversity that emerged during the decades following the American Revolution.

3. Ibid., religious memoranda for 1756, 1770, Ser. II, box 2, LFP.

Through personal religious writings that spanned four generations and nearly a century, the Lanes bore witness to the travail of New England Congregationalism and the rise of American evangelicalism.

▓ Born in 1696, Joshua Lane was a prosperous tanner and shoemaker who hailed from a respectable clan of New Hampshire joiners, tailors, and gravestone carvers. At the time he joined the Hampton church in 1719, Lane had been married for a little more than a year to Bathsheba Robie. Although they were younger than typical church membership candidates, the Lanes had a good reason to affiliate. With the birth of their first child, Samuel, the previous fall, they were seeking access to the sacrament of baptism. During the next two decades, Joshua and Bathsheba presented each of their sixteen infants in the Hampton meetinghouse within the first week of life and seldom more than two months after birth.[4]

In the aftermath of the Great Earthquake of 1727, Joshua elevated his devotional routines by starting a religious journal. Unlike the almanacs that his son began compiling a decade later, the elder Lane wrote sporadically. Life-course transitions, natural disasters, and family afflictions triggered each of the introspective entries he recorded during the next two decades. Although Lane hoped to be fitted for another world, he more often appealed to God for sparing mercies. Lane also used the journal to record two kinds of community events: town deaths and admissions to full communion in the Hampton church. Monitoring his own reactions to affliction and accounting for the public display of religion, the young father and rising townsman hoped that he and his neighbors might be made fruitful in this world and prepared for the next. A "life of Constant devotedness," Lane believed, was the only way to ensure the health, safety, and prosperity of his family and his community.[5]

Shortly after Lane was struck dead by lightning in 1766, his son, Jeremiah, published an essay extolling the Hampton deacon's "exemplary walk and conduct." The younger Lane recalled the many ways in which his father's "heavenly conversation" was "interwoven with all his secular affairs, and worldly pursuits." Joshua had provided his children with a religious education; he was

4. Hampton, N.H., Records of the First Congregational Church, 1667–1902, 91, microfilm, reel 1 (Watertown, Mass., 1986), NEHGS; George Freeman Sanborn, Jr., and Melinde Lutz Sanborn, [comps.], *Vital Records of Hampton, New Hampshire, to the End of the Year 1900,* 2 vols. (Boston, 1992–1998), II, 23–24, 26, 28–30, 32, 34, 36, 50, 52, 55, 57, 59, 63. For genealogical information, see Jacob Chapman and James H. Fitts, comps., *Lane Genealogies,* I, *William Lane of Boston, Mass., 1648 ...* (Exeter, N.H., 1891), 11, 17–30.

5. Joshua Lane, journal, 1727–1755, [40], Ser. I, box 1, LFP. For Lane's death records, see Sanborn and Sanborn, [comps.], *Vital Records of Hampton, New Hampshire,* II, 457–472.

attentive to the providential calls of God; he was earnest in his "constant use of the appointed means of grace." Renowned for his temperance, meekness, gravity, and sobriety, the Hampton deacon was a tender parent and a compassionate neighbor who "served God and his generation." Jeremiah praised his father as a man who imitated Christ through his humble "walk with God." The elder Lane had been rewarded during his earthly pilgrimage with longevity, material goods, and an unusually large family. Jeremiah never presumed that his father had experienced conversion, but he had little reason to doubt that Joshua was one of the "true citizens of Zion."[6]

Samuel, Joshua's eldest son, joined the Hampton church in May 1736, during one of New England's most devastating epidemics. The previous year, diphtheria had broken out in the neighboring town of Kingston, New Hampshire, and, within months, the epidemic was raging across the northern frontier. In his devotional journal, Lane's father recorded more than sixty deaths in town from the mortal distemper. Most were children under the age of eight. Samuel was among the two dozen men and women who closed with the Hampton church during the spring of 1736. More than half of this cohort was unmarried. "Our young people," minister Ward Cotton noted approvingly, "seem to be very much awaknd."[7]

Written in his own hand, Lane's church admission relation suggests that he applied for the privileges of participating in the Lord's Supper partly out of a sense of self-preservation. Apprenticed to his father and five years away from his marriage to Mary James, Samuel feared that his iniquities would provoke God to cast him into the grave with the other victims of the epidemic. "I desire to Bless God that I am alive and that I am yet numbred amongst the Living," he explained. Lane also relied on many of the standard rhetorical tropes that had defined the ideal of the godly walk for half a century. He cited classic encouraging biblical passages—Isaiah 1:18 and Matthew 11:28—that reinforced his decision to join the church. He professed his knowledge of basic Reformed theology. Most important, Lane acknowledged that he had been baptized as an infant, as he pledged to "renew my Baptismal covenant and to come up to that holy ordinance of the Lords Supper." The recent providences of God

6. Jeremiah Lane, *A Memorial, and Tear of Lamentation, with Improvement of the Death of Pious Friends* (Portsmouth, N.H., 1766), 6–8, 10, 15.

7. Hampton Records of the First Congregational Church, microfilm, reel 1, 26; Sanborn and Sanborn, [comps.], *Vital Records of Hampton, New Hampshire*, II, 462–465; Ward Cotton to John Cotton (of Halifax, Mass.), May 10, 1736, box 2, Curwen Family Papers, 1637–1808, AAS. See also Jabez Fitch, *An Account of the Numbers That Have Died of the Distemper in the Throat, Within the Province of New-Hampshire, with Some Reflections Thereon* (Boston, 1736), 3.

might have accelerated the pace of Lane's religious life, but he continued to think of church membership in terms that mirrored those of most godly walkers of his generation.[8]

Samuel's religious development was punctuated by gaps and lapses, as he slowly grew to manhood. Lane made the connection between religion and the life-course explicit in an extended meditation that he recorded on a loose sheet of paper on his twenty-first birthday, October 6, 1739. During the years following the diphtheria epidemic, Samuel occasionally slipped into adolescent vanities including disobeying his parents and "indulging myselfe in the lusts of the flesh." He berated himself for serving God "only by the by when the world would best allow of it." The assumption of adult responsibilities provided an opportunity to renew and elevate his pious disciplines. He drafted a religious covenant in which he pledged to "do my duty in every particular instance" by watching over both the "inward motions of my heart" and the "outward actions of my life." Samuel's birthday covenant coincided with the expiration of his tanning apprenticeship to his father. As if to signal his newfound independence in both spiritual and temporal realms, he started compiling his financial accounts on the same day. For the rest of his life, Lane's quest to "make religion my business" would go hand-in-hand with recording "my proceedings and Business in the World."[9]

■ George Whitefield stopped briefly in Hampton on his excursion to York, Maine, during the fall of 1740. Samuel Lane recorded only short references to the touring Anglican evangelist's two sermon performances. As powerful revivals erupted in nearby Portsmouth and surged across the northern frontier the following year, Lane began to note the "uncommon concern on the minds of People about their souls." Now married and living in Stratham, Lane initially welcomed the awakening. The townspeople appeared "verry desirous of hearing the word," he recalled, "and ministers forward to preach it, and for some time there was Lectures almost every Day or night in many places." Sparked by leading Whitefieldarians Gilbert Tennent, Daniel Rogers, Samuel Buell, and an engaged cohort of local ministers, the burgeoning revival spread throughout the surrounding towns. Late in the fall of 1741, Lane listened as Boston minister David McGregore delivered a powerful sermon in Stratham

8. Relation of Samuel Lane, Mar. 26, 1736, in Samuel Lane, "A Record of Those Persons Which Have Been Taken into the Church of Christ in Hampton and Stratham," in Hampton Records of the First Congregational Church, microfilm, reel 2, [10, 12].

9. Samuel Lane, confession of sins, Oct. 6, 1739, Ser. II, box 3, LFP; Hanson, ed., *Journal for the Years 1739–1803*, 23.

excoriating professors who contented themselves with the *"false Foundations"* of "CHURCH PRIVILEDGES," "OUTWARD DUTIES," "SOUNDNESS *in the Principles of Religion,"* and "their CIVILITY and OUTWARD SOBRIETY." Men and women of "all ages and Sexes Black and White, but chiefly on young People" were struck down by the sermons of visiting itinerants, Lane explained in his almanac memoranda. He and his father kept careful accounts of church admissions during the Whitefieldian revivals. Three dozen new converts closed with the Stratham church in less than a year, while more than 120 joined in Hampton, including 41 on a single sacrament day in March 1742.[10]

By then, the revivals had taken a radical turn, especially in nearby Durham, New Hampshire, where Nicholas Gilman was actively cultivating his young parishioners' visionary experiences. Once prized as divinely appointed agents of the Holy Spirit, riding ministers soon emerged as a flashpoint of controversy, as they turned to "Judging and censering" the souls of others. Rogers was particularly active in Stratham and neighboring Exeter following his ordination as an itinerant in 1742. Preaching with "Freedom and Enlargement" against formal professors, he reported dramatic physical exercises and piercing outcries among the young converts. Although many in Stratham greeted Rogers warmly, town minister Henry Rust voiced grave reservations. During the months that followed, several outspoken laymen proclaimed that they had received special commissions to preach and exhort in public. Lane vented his frustration with the ominous turn of events in his 1742 memoranda. There is a "great deal of talk in the country about Religion," he grumbled, but also "great oppositions and difference in opinions." Revival innovations had set "Ministers aginst Ministers and People aginst People; and Ministers against People and People against their Ministers." Nightly religious meetings continued in several neighboring towns, but Lane increasingly viewed these gatherings as sites of "great Releigeous Commotions," not revival.[11]

The conflict in Stratham worsened during the next several years. Many people that a "year or two ago, Seem'd greatly concern'd for their Souls, and to have hopeful beginings," Lane lamented in 1743, "now seem to run into great extreems on many accounts." Church members in Stratham and the surround-

10. *GWJ*, 466–467; Samuel Lane, almanacs, religious memorandum for 1741, Ser. II, box 2, LFP; David McGregore, *Professors Warn'd of Their Danger* (Boston, 1742), 8–12; Lane, "Record of Those Persons Which Have Been Taken into the Church," in Hampton Records of the First Congregational Church, microfilm, reel 2, [9, 18]; Hampton Records of the First Congregational Church, reel 1, 34–44.

11. Samuel Lane, almanacs, religious memoranda for 1742 and 1743, Ser. II, box 2, LFP; DDR, June 12–13, 1742; NGD, 284.

ing towns began withdrawing from communion in the established Congregational churches. Rogers fanned the flames of schism by preaching regularly to dissenting factions. "Ministers are meer Instruments," he told a Stratham audience, "God Works by 'em, or without 'em, just as He pleases." An eclectic cast of unlearned riding ministers passed through town, including Joseph Prince, the ubiquitous blind itinerant, Salem, Massachusetts, baker Richard Elvins, the English Baptist Benjamin Dutton, and the notorious perfectionist Richard Woodbury. Local Congregational clergymen responded by closing their pulpits to the interlopers, and some went even further. The minister in the neighboring town of Kensington, New Hampshire, sent Rogers a letter forbidding him to preach within the limits of his parish, and he dispatched several parishioners armed with clubs to string a chain across the main road into town. When Whitefield visited the region during his second New England tour in 1745, an irate militia officer brandished his musket and threatened to dispatch him "either to heaven or hell." "These Separate People are cal'd by Many New-Lights and Scheemers," Lane observed, and their unusual "practices cause many people to Stumble at, and be much Set against what they some time ago, cal'd a good work."[12]

In Exeter, the separatists remonstrated against their recalcitrant minister, John Odlin, in a series of contentious church councils. It was a familiar story of ecclesiastical breakdown in which the aggrieved parties condemned Odlin for opposing the "Remarkable work of God's Holy Spirit" and infringing on their "Christian Liberties." But, in Stratham, the situation was quite different. Although Rust upbraided the new converts in his parish who "pretend to be favoured with the divine inspiration of heaven," he was among the minority. On September 30, 1744, the majority faction that had withdrawn from communion in the Stratham church created an "unaccountable uproar" in the meetinghouse when they brazenly demanded that Rust share his pulpit with a former parishioner, fiery Harvard College graduate Dudley Leavitt. "Dont Sir Think that we are in Jest," warned the members of a town committee charged with apportioning the use of the meetinghouse between the two rival preachers. "We Trust that we are persuing the welfare of our precious and Immortal Souls which requires Zeal and Earnestness." Leavitt excoriated his new colleague one week later, declaring that he "Could as well Joyn with the devil" or "Joyn with the pope in saying Mass" as with Rust in prayer. The local sheriff forcibly removed Leavitt from the meetinghouse, but not before

12. Samuel Lane, almanacs, religious memorandum for 1743, Ser. II, box 2, LFP; DDR, May 12 (quote), June 6–7, Aug. 4–5, 1743, Mar. 8, 11, 28–29, Sept. 20, 1744; *GWJ*, 553.

one parishioner Dorothy Jewett branded the beleaguered Stratham minister a "Son of the Divel." These slanderous outbursts occasioned two weeks of "Law Business" in Portsmouth, according to Lane, as county magistrates dragged Leavitt into court for disturbing the peace.[13]

Leavitt moved on to Salem, but Stratham's dissenting faction quickly stepped up their efforts to gather a Separate church. By the end of 1744, they had outfitted the home of one of the separatists with pews and were holding Sabbath exercises. Several months later, fifty-eight men, representing roughly one-third of the families in town, signed a letter offering their makeshift pulpit to Joseph Adams, a "young zealous Itinerant" who previously had preached among the separatists in Newbury, Massachusetts. In response, Stratham townspeople loyal to Rust sent their own petition to the New Hampshire Assembly in which they argued that dividing the town between two churches would impoverish their estates and "Destroy that Love Peace and Unity that ought to be kept and maintained amongst us as the Professors of Christ." Undaunted, the separatists ignored their demands and installed Adams as their pastor. A Boston newspaper correspondent called it the "most unaccountable Ordination" in the history of the colonies.[14]

Rust's unexpected death in March 1749 left the Separates firmly in control. Adams's parishioners took possession of the Stratham meetinghouse and even refused to allow one of Rust's pallbearers to deliver an elegy from the former minister's pulpit. Frustrated by the escalating ecclesiastical strife in town, Lane quietly withdrew from church affairs. During the next six years, he appears to have established a business schedule that frequently carried him to Hampton or Exeter on the Sabbath. In other weeks, Lane likely kept at home, engaged in reading and praying with his family. Although they continued to present each of the three children born between 1750 and 1755 for baptism,

13. "Aggrieved Brethren" to John Odlin, n.d. [circa 1743], Blandina Diedrich Collection, I, WCL; Samuel Lane, sermon notebook, 1745–1747, Ser. II, box 3, LFP, Samuel Lane, almanacs, Sept. 30 (quote), Oct. 7–8, Dec. 4, 1744, religious memoranda for 1744–1745, [3], Ser. II, box 2; John Sinkler, George Veazey, Jr., and Thomas Wiggin v. Dudley Leavitt, 1744, no. 25518, Provincial Court Cases, circa 1670–circa 1771, New Hampshire Division of Archives and Records Management, Concord; Hanson, ed., *Journal for the Years 1739–1803*, 31. On the Exeter schism, see Douglas K. Fidler, "John Odlin of Exeter and the Threat to Congregational Peace and Order in Northern New England," *Historical New Hampshire*, LV (2000), 7–24.

14. Samuel Lane, almanacs, religious memoranda for 1744–1745, Ser. II, box 2, LFP; John Blunt to Benjamin Colman, Sept. 9, 1746, Letters to Benjamin Colman, 1693–1747, MHS; Stratham, N.H., Congregational Church Records, 1746–1913, 2 vols., I, 1–9, NHHS; Nathaniel Bouton, comp. and ed., *Provincial Papers: Documents and Records Relating to the Province of New Hampshire from 1738 to 1749*, 7 vols. (Nashua, N.H., 1867–1873), V, 848; *Boston Evening-Post*, Apr. 6, 1747.

Lane and his wife elected to carry them ten miles to the Hampton meeting-house for the ceremony.[15]

Ecclesiastical affairs in Stratham eventually simmered down. During the mid-1750s, Adams began working to heal the "Strife and Contention" in town. Lane's father, Joshua, assisted in drafting a confession in which Adams's supporters lamented the "uncharible Speaches" that had been so "Distructive to the Peace and good Order" of the Stratham church and "hurt Religion in the Town Famalies." Adams followed suit by offering a pair of public confessions first to his parishioners and then to the New Hampshire ministerial association in which he, too, expressed hearty grief for having "encouraged separations in Churches." The contending parties agreed to "lay Aside all former Grudgings and Annamosities" and resolve their differences. The process of reconciliation took several years, but, by June 1757, peace appears to have been restored in one of northern New England's most bitterly divided parishes. Adams's reunited congregation liberalized church admission practices and extended the privilege of baptism to the children of all adults who were willing to own the covenant. Dissatisfied members began trickling back into the pews, including Lane, who was elected deacon in 1765.[16]

The Stratham Separates interpreted Adams's attempt to broker ecclesiastical accommodation as an act of betrayal. Within a few months of his installation, a group of disaffected parishioners withdrew from the recently reunited church. They gathered to worship by themselves, Lane noted, and resolutely refused to pay taxes to support Adams's ministry, despite threats of property confiscation and incarceration. The rancor intensified until the "Great Religious Commotions" of the 1764 revivals impelled the Stratham dissenters to organize yet another Separate church across the river in Newmarket. Joseph, brother of the outspoken Boston revivalist Andrew Croswell, reported that he had never seen the work of God spread so quickly. "Scores have been awakend in Stratham," he wrote with excitement to Isaac Backus, "and the wilderness Blossoms, like a Rose." Now in full retreat from the radicalism he had

15. Samuel Lane, almanacs, Feb. 5, Mar. 20, 24, 1749, Sept. 8, 1751, Apr. 22, 1753, Apr. 20, 1755, Ser. II, box 2, LFP; Sanborn and Sanborn, [comps.], *Vital Records of Hampton, New Hampshire*, II, 73–74, 98.

16. Warrant for a church council, Aug. 21, 1755, "Confession of Mr. Adams and His People," Jan. 1, 1756, "Paper of Union and Ministers Advice to the People of Stratham," Jan. 28, 1756, box 3: Miscellaneous Papers, 1742–1876, Stratham Town Records, New Hampshire Division of Archives and Records Management; Joshua Lane, "To Those Brethren of Streatham Who Adheard to the Revd. Mr Rust," n.d. [Jan. 1, 1756], Ser. I, box 1, LFP; "A Record of the Transactions of the Annual Convention of Ministers in the Province of N: Hampshire ...," NHHS, *Collections*, IX (1889), 29; Stratham Congregational Church Records, I, 12–32. See also Samuel Lane, almanacs, Aug. 21, 1755, Jan. 22, 28, June 22, 24, 1756, Ser. II, box 2, LFP.

espoused two decades earlier, Adams worried that "many that are call'd New-Lights" were in danger of falling into "wild false Notions and Extravagant Opinions." Following his election as deacon, Lane counted a slim majority of households in which one or both spouses had affiliated with the established church. Soon, he was crossing off additional names of members that had withdrawn to worship with the Newmarket separatists.[17]

The new insurgency reached a boiling point in 1770, when Backus and two Separate Baptist ministers Hezekiah Smith and Samuel Shepherd appeared in Stratham and immersed a dozen of Adams's former congregants in the Winnicut River before a crowd numbering between seven and eight hundred. Where Smith and Backus greeted the mass baptisms as "precious tokens" of a "glorious day" that had "not been before known in New-England," Lane saw only betrayal. "Many of those People Called Separates," he complained, naming each of the twelve renegades in his religious memoranda, had turned Baptist merely to "Save their Ministers Rate" and evade paying taxes to the established church by claiming dissenter status. Their subversive activities stood in stark contrast to the mature George Whitefield. By 1770, the portly, temperate evangelist had moderated the uncompromising message that he had unleashed on his New England audiences three decades earlier. Lane watched him preach one of his final sermons before his death in Newburyport later that year.[18]

During the next two decades, Lane turned inward and grew increasingly conservative in his religious outlook. A meditation penned on Thanksgiving Day in 1793 emphasized the benefits dispensed by God. Personal and family health; his Bible and other "Useful Books"; the ordinances of public worship; his land, clothing, animals, and crops; his watch and surveying tools—Lane blessed God for them all. In his personal covenant, which he adapted from a popular devotional guidebook and renewed each week, the Stratham dea-

17. Samuel Lane, almanacs, religious memoranda for 1756, 1758, 1764 (quote), Ser. II, box 2, LFP; *Sketches of the Life, and Extracts from the Journals, and Other Writings, of the Late Joseph Croswell* ... (Boston, 1809), 54–55; Joseph Croswell to Isaac Backus, June 24, 1764, no. 637, *IBP;* Joseph Adams to [Benjamin Adams], 1766, Portsmouth Athenaeum, Portsmouth, N.H.; Samuel Lane, "Church Book," 1765–1804, [6], box 3: Miscellaneous Papers, 1742–1876, Stratham Town Records.

18. William G. McLoughlin, ed., *The Diary of Isaac Backus*, 3 vols. (Providence, R.I., 1979), II, 765, 767–768; John David Broome, ed., *The Life, Ministry, and Journals of Hezekiah Smith: Pastor of the First Baptist Church of Haverhill, Massachusetts, 1765 to 1805, and Chaplain in the American Revolution, 1775 to 1780,* Warren Association (Springfield, Mo., 2004), 366; Samuel Lane, almanacs, June 20, Sept. 28, 1770, religious memorandum for 1770 (quote), Ser. II, box 2, LFP. For Whitefield's final years, see Thomas S. Kidd, *George Whitefield: America's Spiritual Founding Father* (New Haven, Conn., 2014), 225–247.

con dedicated his material possessions, bodily members, mental faculties, and social influence to God's service as long as "thou Continuest me in Life." Lane took a special interest in debates held by the New Hampshire ministerial association in 1786 on the question of whether the *"Presbyterian form of Church Government"* with its greater centralization of clerical authority would "Strengthen the Bond of Union" among Congregationalists throughout the state. Although Lane continued to purchase books of practical piety— primarily as gifts for his children—he also collected ordination sermons, works on church government by notable Scottish Presbyterians, and theological treatises by Joseph Bellamy and other former Whitefieldarians. As the Separate Baptist movement expanded into northern New England, Lane purchased every antirevival pamphlet from the 1740s he could find, including Jonathan Edwards's *Distinguishing Marks of a Work of the Holy Spirit* and his *Farewel-Sermon.*[19]

Even as Lane worked to shore up the foundations of his own religious identity, he found himself caught in a rising tide of sectarian dissent. Five decades of relentless ecclesiastical schism and rancor had taken its toll on Stratham's established Congregational church. At the time Lane was elected deacon in 1765, the church consisted of eighty-five communicants, along with a handful of individuals who had owned the covenant. Although the population of Stratham declined slightly during the next half century, the total number of church members dwindled to thirty-six by the time Adams's successor, James Miltimore, was ordained in 1786. Seven years later, an enterprising schoolteacher and surveyor named Phinehas Merrill produced a detailed map in which he meticulously plotted and labeled every building in Stratham. Religious affiliation had plummeted among the 113 households on his plan. Congregationalists and Separate Baptists were spread evenly throughout the town, yet they accounted for only half of all Stratham families. The largest group—41 percent of all households appearing on Merrill's map—had no official ties to any religious institution. In 1799, nearly one in five Stratham families claimed dissenting status and no longer paid taxes to support Miltimore's ministry; by 1806, the year of Lane's death, the figure had doubled (Map 6; see also Table 9).[20]

19. Samuel Lane, "Thoughts on a Thanksgiving Day," Nov. 21, 1793, Ser. II, box 3, LFP, Samuel Lane, "An Example of Self Dedication," n.d., Ser. II, box 3, Samuel Lane, "Copy from a Paper I Had from Mr. Miltimore," Oct. 11, 1786, Ser. II, box 3, Samuel Lane, "An Account of the Books I Own," Mar. 6, 1762, Ser. II, box 3. Lane adapted his personal covenant from P[hilip] Doddridge, *The Rise and Progress of Religion in the Soul* ... (London, 1745), 161–166.

20. Samuel Lane, "Church Book," [1–6], box 3: Miscellaneous Papers, 1742–1876, Stratham Town Records; Samuel Lane, "An Account of the Church Money Receiv'd," 1774–1803, [1],

In 1791, Lane once again lamented the "Considerable Religious Commotions" that abounded in northern New England. Where many of his contemporaries welcomed this latest season of grace, Lane could only see threats to established social hierarchies. Itinerant preachers flocked to Stratham, "and almost anybody thinks themselves capable, and do undertake to preach, and Speak in publick, women and girls not Excepted." "The Baptists Seem to increase in Many places," Lane grumbled the following year. Although he continued to compile his almanacs for another decade, this terse entry was the last of the religious memoranda he had been composing for half a century.[21]

■ Samuel Lane's youngest son, Jabez, came of age in a religious culture transformed by the Whitefieldian upheavals of the mid-eighteenth century. When he joined the Stratham Congregational church in full communion during the summer of 1801, he drafted a conversion narrative recounting a long awaited discovery of the "opperations of Gods Spirit" on his soul. As with many of his generation who were born during the decades following New England's era of great awakenings, the younger Lane had grown accustomed to thinking of conversion as a singular, transformative event. "I Should have known the time to a minute when so great a change passed upon me," Jabez wrote, yet he long struggled to determine the "Time of my Conversion."[22]

The years 1799 and 1800 brought renewed "Attention to Religion" and a "Great and Solemn Seriousness" to northern New England. In despair, Jabez watched scores of townspeople pass from darkness into the light of the new birth, while his own heart remained "adamant and nothing would move it." Slowly, after months of introspective searching, the younger Lane arrived at the conclusion that he, too, had been converted. His experiences were never as "Clear and Sensible" as those reported by his neighbors, but Lane eventually had his "Doubts in a great measure resolved" and obtained a "Satisfactory Evidence that I was in reality a new born Soul."[23]

---

box 3: Miscellaneous Papers, 1742–1876, Stratham Town Records; Jabez Lane, "Miscellanies," 1791–1805, Ser. I, box 1, [9], LFP; "Stratham Records of Invoice and Assessment: Book 1," VI, 43–50, box 2, Stratham Town Records. On Merrill's career, see Peter Benes, *New England Prospect: A Loan Exhibition of Maps at the Currier Gallery of Art* (Boston, 1981), 44–47. For the population of Stratham, see Evarts B. Greene and Virginia D. Harrington, *American Population Before the Federal Census of 1790* (1932; rpt. Gloucester, Mass., 1966), 79, 84; and *Heads of Families at the First Census of the United States Taken in the Year 1790: New Hampshire* (Washington, D.C., 1907), 10.

21. Samuel Lane, almanacs, religious memoranda for 1791–1792, Ser. II, box 2, LFP.

22. Relation of Jabez Lane, n.d. [circa August 1801], box 3: Miscellaneous Papers, 1742–1876, Stratham Town Records. For the full text of Lane's relation, see Appendix C.

23. Jabez Lane, journals, 1789–1810, Oct. 23, 1799, religious memoranda for 1799, Ser. II,

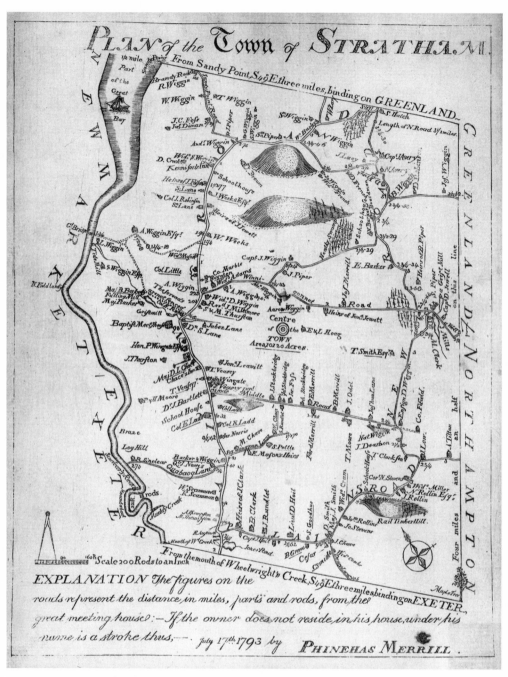

FIGURE 27 Phinehas Merrill, "Plan of the Town of Stratham." 1793.
Courtesy, New Hampshire Historical Society, Concord

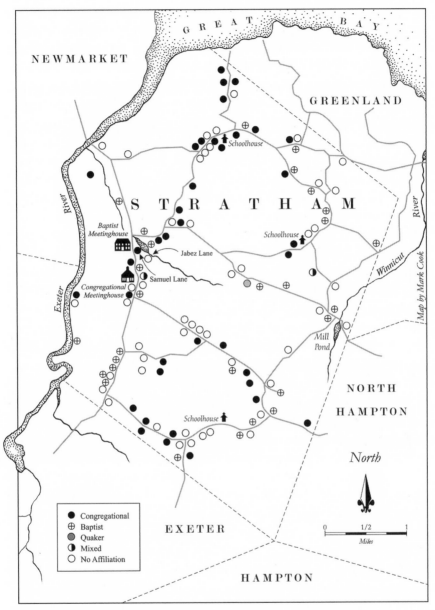

MAP 6 Religious Affiliation by Household in Stratham, New Hampshire, 1793.
Drawn by Mark Cook

Married for nearly two decades and the father of five children, the forty-one-year-old convert was unlike the young converts who swelled the ranks of the Stratham church during the Whitefieldian revivals; and his decision to affiliate was not related to the protective family strategies that had structured Congregational lay piety a century earlier. Unlike his grandfather, Lane disavowed the connection between church membership and family formation. In an unprecedented act of repudiation, Jabez stated his "Settled opinion" regarding the legitimacy of his own baptism in the closing lines of his relation. "I have no doubt but my parents did what they tho't was their duty," he admitted, refusing to rest on his religious pedigree, "but I have tho't and still think that it is not my duty to offer my Children for Baptism." Without an "Experimental Acquaintance with religion," Jabez continued, baptism "cannot in my Opinion be of any Saving benefit to them."[24]

Seen from one angle, the Lanes' world had changed little over the course of the eighteenth century. Jabez followed in the footsteps of his father and grandfather, plying his trade as a tanner and shoemaker. His work routines, reading interests, and even his journal-writing habits mirrored those of his father. In matters of the spirit, however, the evangelical convert of what came to be called the Second Great Awakening bore little resemblance to his progenitors. The differences separating the generations of Lane men appear in subtle ways across the pages of Jabez's yearly "Journal of Remarkables." He planted crops and fenced the fields surrounding Stratham's Baptist meetinghouse; he assisted the Baptists in auctioning their pew boxes; and he worked with neighbors of both denominations to haul the Baptist meetinghouse to a new location—all without negative commentary. Jabez regularly interacted with townspeople of different religious persuasions: tanning hides, exchanging commodities, hauling timber, plowing and harvesting, slaughtering livestock, traveling, conducting town business, and managing legal affairs. His charity "towards those who differed from him in circumstantials of religion," as his obituary writer put it, might well have prompted him to attend a wider variety of religious meetings, including Sabbath exercises with the Newmarket separatists, Freewill Baptist gatherings with relatives in the nearby town of Lee, and even an Anglican Christmas service in Portsmouth. Jabez occasionally invited Baptist itinerants to lead prayer meetings in his home; and

---

box 3, LFP; Relation of Jabez Lane, n.d. [circa August 1801], box 3: Miscellaneous Papers, 1742–1876, Stratham Town Records. See also Stratham Congregational Church Records, I, 39–40.

24. Relation of Jabez Lane, n.d. [circa August 1801], box 3: Miscellaneous Papers, 1742–1876, Stratham Town Records.

he attended the 1792 ordination of Elias Smith, the charismatic leader of the emerging Christian Connection, a loose network of religious radicals who rejected all religious creeds and ecclesiastical institutions.[25]

The tolerance, respect, and support Jabez extended to his Baptist neighbors in Stratham must have rankled his father, for Samuel struggled throughout his life to accept religious diversity. At the height of the 1799 revival, Stratham's Congregational minister, Miltimore, agreed to baptize several new communicants by immersion in Lane's mill pond. Miltimore omitted the details of this dramatic concession to his upstart Baptist rivals in his church record book, but Samuel bitterly condemned the irregular baptisms in his alamanac. Jabez, in contrast to both, warmly embraced the immersions, noting their locations and the number of participants. Samuel grudgingly reported a surge in Congregational church admissions in 1799, but his son carefully counted new converts among both Stratham's established and dissenting societies. The boisterous religious meetings that his father derided as "Considerable Religious Commotions" Jabez praised as a remarkable revival of "real religion" that transcended denominational and parish boundaries. To Jabez, the chaotic and competitive religious marketplace that had developed in New Hampshire by 1800 seemed little cause for concern. He was more likely to complain of partisan politics among Federalists and Jeffersonians than religious rancor, although the latter abounded across northern New England during the early decades of the nineteenth century.[26]

According to his obituarist, Jabez "continued to the last to retain that system of Christian doctrine and that mode of worship denominated Congregational." Many of his neighbors, however, cast aside the inherited traditions of their puritan ancestors. Following Miltimore's dismissal in 1807, the Stratham Congregational church languished without a pastor for almost two decades. Unable to hire a suitable replacement, the townspeople watched their parish collapse into a mission field for the Society for Propagating the Gospel among

25. Jabez Lane, journals, Aug. 15, 1792, Dec. 25, 1798, Nov. 19, 1800, May 25, June 15, Sept. 1, 1802, Nov. 8, 1807, Oct. 9, 1809, Jan. 2–3, 1810, Ser. II, box 3, LFP; Chapman and Fitts, comps., *Lane Genealogies*, I, 215. For similar examples, see "Josiah Brown His Book," 1790–1816, typescript (Stratham, N.H., 1987), NEHGS. See also Karen V. Hansen, *A Very Social Time: Crafting Community in Antebellum New England* (Berkeley, Calif., 1994), 149–152. On Smith and the Christian Connection, see Nathan O. Hatch, *The Democratization of American Christianity* (New Haven, Conn., 1989), 68–81.

26. Stratham Congregational Church Records, I, 39; Samuel Lane, almanacs, cover page for 1799, Ser. II, box 2, LFP, Jabez Lane, journals, June 30, Aug. 13, Oct. 23, Nov. 1, 24–25, 1799, memoranda for 1799 (quote), 1800, Ser. II, box 3. See also Samuel Lane, "A List of the Names of Those Persons Who Have Been Admitted to the Fellowship of the Church," 1786–1800, Ser. II, box 3, LFP.

the Indians and Others in North America—one of several Congregational organizations founded during the final decades of the eighteenth century to counter sectarian dissent on the northern frontier. Upstart denominations rushed to fill the void. Stratham families produced a dozen clergymen during Jabez's lifetime, but most of them eventually were ordained over Freewill Baptist, Methodist, and Universalist congregations in towns from Maine to the Ohio Valley. Other Strathamites joined Smith's Christian Connection, found their way to the Shaker village at Canterbury, New Hampshire, or even linked up with the renegade Jacob Cochran and his notorious sect of free love perfectionists. Religious seekers—"flaming professors," as one Congregational missionary put it, "jealous of their civil and religious liberties" and "irrecoverably lost"—dominated New Hampshire and northern New England by 1815. Their spiritual travels grew directly out of the Whitefieldian revivals of the 1740s, which had irreparably shattered the orderly, parish-based religious world of eighteenth-century Congregationalism.[27]

Lane's refusal to baptize his children after joining the Stratham church in 1801 reflected his sympathies for sectarian dissent, but it also signaled something perhaps more important: his belief that the rising generation should claim their own religious destinies. And that is precisely what they did. A cryptic entry in his journal for 1808 stating that "Patty came to Meeting" hints at the probability that Jabez's daughter had been worshipping elsewhere. The following year, a Baptist minister immersed her sister Mary in the Exeter River. Shortly before Jabez's untimely death in 1810, the Methodists raised a meetinghouse in the neighboring town of Greenland. Within weeks of his passing, his eldest son, George—who had taken over writing in his journal—began entertaining a newly appointed Methodist circuit rider and traveling to Greenland for Sabbath exercises. Three of Jabez's nine children remained in Stratham and eventually covenanted with the Congregational church, but

---

27. Chapman and Fitts, comps., *Lane Genealogies*, I, 215; Charles B. Nelson, comp., *History of Stratham, New Hampshire, 1631–1900* (Somersworth, N.H., 1965), 119–120, 153–155; N. F. Carter, *The Native Ministry of New Hampshire* ... (Concord, N.H., 1906), 732–737; James Otis Lyford, *History of the Town of Canterbury, New Hampshire, 1727–1912*, 2 vols. (Concord, N.H., 1912), I, 353–354; Jonathan Homer to James Freeman, Aug. 5, 1816, CL. On the Cochranites, see Joyce Butler, "Cochranism Delineated: A Twentieth-Century Study," in Charles E. Clark, James S. Leamon, and Karen Bowden, eds., *Maine in the Early Republic: From Revolution to Statehood* (Hanover, N.H., 1988), 146–164. My argument in this paragraph draws on Alan Taylor's description of the "Yankee diaspora" in "The Free Seekers: Religious Culture in Upstate New York, 1790–1835," *Journal of Mormon History*, XXVII, no. 1 (Spring 2001), 44–66; and Shelby M. Balik's analysis of the Congregationalists' emerging "itinerant system" in *Rally the Scattered Believers: Northern New England's Religious Geography*, Religion in North America (Bloomington, Ind., 2014), 5, 148–178.

three others affiliated with the Methodists and at least one joined Smith's Christian Connection.[28]

The last entry that George Lane inscribed in his father's journal stands as a fitting epitaph for New England's gospel land of light. "Love feast here," he wrote on November 28, 1810, referencing the distinctive Methodist communal meal he hosted in a house built by a third-generation Congregational deacon across the road from a Separate Baptist meetinghouse.[29]

28. Jabez Lane, journals, Nov. 6, 1808 (quote), Sept. 22, 1809, July 29, Aug. 7, 29, Sept. 2, 9, 30, Oct. 15, 28, Nov. 7–8, 1810, Ser. II, box 3, LFP; Chapman and Fitts, comps., *Lane Genealogies*, I, 68–72; "Josiah Brown His Book," [56]. On the rise of Methodism in New England, see Richard D. Shiels, "The Methodist Invasion of Congregational New England," in Nathan O. Hatch and John H. Wigger, eds., *Methodism and the Shaping of American Culture* (Nashville, Tenn., 2001), 257–280; and Eric Baldwin, "'The Devil Begins to Roar': Opposition to Early Methodists in New England," *Church History*, LXXV (2006), 94–119.

29. Jabez Lane, journals, Nov. 28, 1810, Ser. II, box 3, LFP. On love feasts, see John H. Wigger, *Taking Heaven by Storm: Methodism and the Rise of Popular Christianity in America*, Religion in America (New York, 1998), 87–89.

A Note on Church Affiliation Statistics

More than half a century ago, Edmund Morgan challenged early American historians to recover the "diversity of New England Puritanism" by investigating local church records. Practitioners of what soon came to be called the "new social history" rallied to the cause, producing a battery of community studies that provided a wealth of statistical data on eighteenth-century church members. Through painstaking demographic research, J. M. Bumsted, Philip Greven, Kenneth Lockridge, Gerald Moran, William Willingham, James Walsh, and others have demonstrated that church membership in provincial New England served as a marker of social maturation before the Whitefieldian revivals of the 1740s. Men and women who had grown up in core parish families with deep roots in the community were typically admitted to full communion in their mid- to late-twenties. New England's era of great awakenings temporarily reversed this general trend, as unmarried youths and small groups of native and African Americans joined churches in a brief burst of activity between 1741 and 1744.[1]

1. Edmund S. Morgan, "New England Puritanism: Another Approach," *WMQ*, XVIII (1961), 237; Darrett B. Rutman, "The 'New Social History' in America," in Rutman with Anita H. Rutman, *Small Worlds, Large Questions: Explorations in Early American Social History, 1600–1850* (Charlottesville, Va., 1994), 17. Early efforts to quantify church membership data in New England include Darrett B. Rutman, "God's Bridge Falling Down: 'Another Approach' to New England Puritanism Assayed," *WMQ*, XIX (1962), 408–421; Cedric B. Cowing, "Sex and Preaching in the Great Awakening," *American Quarterly*, XX (1968), 624–644; Ross W. Beales, Jr., "The Half-Way Covenant and Religious Scrupulosity: The First Church of Dorchester, Massachusetts, as a Test Case," *WMQ*, XXXI (1974), 465–480; J. M. Bumsted, "Religion, Finance, and Democracy in Massachusetts: The Town of Norton as a Case Study," *JAH*, LVII (1971), 817–831; Gerald F. Moran, "Conditions of Religious Conversion in the First Society of Norwich, Connecticut, 1718–1744," *Journal of Social History*, V (1972), 331–343; James Walsh, "The Great Awakening in the First Congregational Church of Woodbury, Connecticut," *WMQ*, XXVIII (1971), 543–562; Philip J. Greven, Jr., "Youth, Maturity, and Religious Conversion: A Note on the Ages of Converts in Andover, Massachusetts, 1711–1749," *EIHC*, CVIII (1972), 119–134; William F. Willingham, "Religious Conversion in the Second Society of Windham, Connecticut, 1723–43: A Case Study," *Societas*, VI (1976), 109–119; Moran, "Religious Renewal, Puritan Tribalism, and the Family in Seventeenth-Century Milford, Connecticut," *WMQ*, XXXVI (1979), 236–254; and Willingham, "The Conversion Experience during the Great Awakening in Windham, Connecticut,"

Darkness Falls on the Land of Light builds on these pioneering studies by providing church affiliation data for eight eighteenth-century parishes—Haverhill, Hingham, Medfield, Sandwich, and Westborough, Massachusetts, Norwich and Suffield, Connecticut, and Hampton, New Hampshire—as well as household affiliation data for several additional communities. I have selected these towns based on several criteria. Relatively complete sets of church records survive for each congregation during the eighteenth century. In most cases, the ministers' record books are supplemented by unusually detailed collections of town records, personal papers, or church admission testimonies. In addition, the selected churches represent a broad geographical range of towns and a variety of ecclesiastical practices. Hampton, Haverhill, Hingham, Norwich, and Sandwich were founded during or shortly after the puritan Great Migration; Medfield and Suffield were second-generation congregations organized in outlying farming districts; and Westborough represented the many interior villages organized in the central New England uplands during the early decades of the eighteenth century. The data I have collected on more than five thousand full church members and covenant owners from these eight churches generally confirm the findings of earlier studies (see Tables 1 and 4).

At the same time, this study breaks new ground by combining traditional methods of family reconstitution with innovative tools and interpretive frameworks, including content and spatial analysis, to quantify the religious experiences of Darrett Rutman's "man in the village lane." One of the primary goals of this project is to revise our understanding of the meaning of church membership over the long eighteenth century. Lacking sources "usually under the jurisdiction of the historian of ideas," as Gerald Moran acknowledged in a seminal 1979 *William and Mary Quarterly* essay, social historians yoked their quantitative assessments of eighteenth-century church membership trends to Edmund Morgan's well-known definition of visible sainthood and the puritan "morphology of conversion." Data on the sex, age, and marital status of new church members purportedly revealed the "conditions and circumstances" accompanying conversion, the "crowning point in a Puritan's journey towards salvation." Meanwhile, scholarship on the "puritan conversion narrative" by literary historians and religious studies scholars often moved briskly from Thomas Shepard's Cambridge, Massachusetts, confessions of the 1640s to Jonathan Edwards's conversion narratives of the 1730s. Quantitative and qualitative studies thus combined to flatten the meaning of church mem-

---

Connecticut History, XXI (1980), 34–61. See also Brooks B. Hull and Moran, "A Preliminary Time Series Analysis of Church Activity in Colonial Woodbury, Connecticut," *Journal for the Scientific Study of Religion*, XXVIII (1989), 478–492; Stephen R. Grossbart, "Seeking the Divine Favor: Conversion and Church Admission in Eastern Connecticut, 1711–1832," *WMQ*, XLVI (1989), 696–740; Harry S. Stout and Catherine Brekus, "A New England Congregation: Center Church, New Haven, 1638–1989," in James P. Wind and James W. Lewis, eds., *American Congregations*, I, *Portraits of Twelve Religious Communities* (Chicago, 1994), 14–102; Hull and Moran, "The Churching of Colonial Connecticut: A Case Study," *Review of Religious Research*, XLI (1999), 165–183; and Kenneth P. Minkema, "Old Age and Religion in the Writings and Life of Jonathan Edwards," *Church History*, LXX (2001), 674–704.

bership, leaving scholars struggling to account for the unexpected conflicts and schisms that developed in the wake of the Whitefieldian revivals.[2]

My approach to studying eighteenth-century church membership trends starts with Susan Juster's revisionist insight that provincial relations differed significantly from seventeenth-century oral church admission narratives. The formulaic content of the testimonies that New England ministers began composing on behalf of prospective communicants beginning in the 1690s makes them well-suited to quantitative analysis. As religious studies theorist Thomas Tweed has argued, literary tropes "function as one source of change in the history of religions." Measuring the evolution of generic elements in eighteenth-century church admission testimonies, I hope to provide a baseline for assessing shifts in religious experience across a broad spectrum of the population.[3]

Tables 7 and 8 present preliminary data from a long-term content analysis study that, when completed, will include roughly twelve hundred relations from more than forty Congregational churches over a period spanning two centuries. For this study, I selected 581 relations from seven of the largest collections of eighteenth-century church admission testimonies—Granville, Haverhill, Medfield, Middleborough, Sturbridge, Westborough, and the Chebacco Separate Church in Ipswich (now Essex)—and coded them in two ways. First, I identified whether each relation contained one or more statements in five thematic areas: profession of beliefs, tribalism, providential afflictions, sacramental theology, and confession of sin. Second, I recorded the number and range of biblical texts cited in each relation. One of the key findings of this study, which I discuss in detail in Part 3, is that lay men and women during the Whitefieldian revivals of the 1740s learned to associate conversion with darting biblical texts they attributed to the indwelling presence of the Holy Spirit. For this reason, I have also tracked what might be described as the candidate's relationship with or experience of the Bible: whether a

2. Darret B. Rutman, "The Mirror of Puritan Authority," in Rutman with Rutman, *Small Worlds, Large Questions,* 71; Moran, "Religious Renewal, Puritan Tribalism, and the Family," *WMQ,* XXXVI (1979), 254; Edmund S. Morgan, *Visible Saints: The History of a Puritan Idea* (New York, 1963), 66; Moran, "Conditions of Religious Conversion," *Journal of Social History,* V (1972), 331; Patricia Caldwell, *The Puritan Conversion Narrative: The Beginnings of American Expression,* Cambridge Studies in American Literature and Culture (New York, 1983), 6. Studies of the morphology of conversion that sidestep the period between 1680 and 1740 and draw a straight line from the puritans to Jonathan Edwards and the Great Awakening include Daniel B. Shea, Jr., *Spiritual Autobiography in Early America* (Princeton, N.J., 1968); Rodger M. Payne, *The Self and the Sacred: Conversion and Autobiography in Early American Protestantism* (Knoxville, Tenn., 1998); and D. Bruce Hindmarsh, *The Evangelical Conversion Narrative: Spiritual Autobiography in Early Modern England* (New York, 2005). For important correctives to this trend, see Susan Juster, *Disorderly Women: Sexual Politics and Evangelicalism in Revolutionary New England* (Ithaca, N.Y., 1994); and Sarah Rivett, *The Science of the Soul in Colonial New England* (Chapel Hill, N.C., 2011).

3. Juster, *Disorderly Women,* 53–54; Thomas A. Tweed, *Crossing and Dwelling: A Theory of Religion* (Cambridge, Mass., 2006), 68. See also Charles Lloyd Cohen, *God's Caress: The Psychology of Puritan Religious Experience* (New York, 1986), 22n, 273–274; and Erik R. Seeman, "Lay Conversion Narratives: Investigating Ministerial Intervention," *NEQ,* LXXI (1998), 630n.

particular scriptural passage was cited or quoted; heard in a sermon or discussed in a conversation; read, studied, or meditated on; incorporated into the relation as a figure of speech; or, most important, received as an impulse or impression.[4]

The results of this basic content analysis challenge static definitions of church membership employed in previous studies by social and literary historians. During the last quarter of the seventeenth century and the first four decades of the eighteenth, the meaning of church membership associated with the test of a relation shifted away from the standards of visible sainthood outlined in the 1648 Cambridge *Platform*. Most testimonies composed between 1690 and 1740 were not conversion narratives; nor was conversion a "typical requirement for church membership." Surviving relations from Haverhill, Medfield, and Westborough differed in content, tone, and physical appearance from the earliest puritan confessions. Men and women typically joined provincial churches to establish their identities as adult members of the community, perform their sacramental duties at the Lord's Supper, demonstrate their knowledge of Reformed theology, and, most important, secure the privilege of baptizing their children. With the rise of Whitefieldian revivalism, however, church membership candidates in places such as Middleborough, Sturbridge, Chebacco, and, especially, Granville began filling their church admission testimonies with dramatic accounts of revival preaching, intrusive biblical texts, and, occasionally, visionary phenomena. Relations composed during the second half of the eighteenth century reveal important narrative innovations in the genre, as the expectations for judging the fitness of prospective members in some—but not all—Congregational churches turned toward accounts of individual conversion experiences that many scholars associate with early evangelicalism.[5]

A second and related methodological problem involves determining what Morgan called the "penetration" of puritan beliefs and practices within society, or what sociologists Roger Finke and Rodney Stark have defined as the "market share" of New England's established Congregational churches. Drawing on the work of colonial clergyman Ezra Stiles and nineteenth-century antiquarians, scholars during the 1970s attempted to gauge the overall religious vitality of various New England towns by cross-referencing the total number of church members with the names of male householders appearing on tax lists. Their findings confirmed Perry Miller's declension thesis and helped to fuel the development of the "communal breakdown model" of New England social history.[6]

4. For a helpful introduction to content analysis methods, see Kimberly A. Neuendorf, *The Content Analysis Guidebook* (Thousand Oaks, Calif., 2002).

5. Grossbart, "Seeking the Divine Favor," *WMQ*, XLVI (1989), 697 (quote).

6. Morgan, "New England Puritanism," *WMQ*, XVIII (1961), 237; Roger Finke and Rodney Stark, *The Churching of America, 1776–2005: Winners and Losers in Our Religious Economy*, 2d ed. (New Brunswick, N.J., 2005), 55; Christine Leigh Heyrman, *Commerce and Culture: The Maritime Communities of Colonial Massachusetts, 1690–1750* (New York, 1984), 16. The genealogy of proportional measurements of religious vitality in early New England runs from the new social historians through Edmund Morgan and William Warren Sweet to John Gorham Palfrey and Ezra Stiles. See Morgan, "New England Puritanism," *WMQ*, XVIII (1961), 240; Morgan, *The Puritan Family: Religion and Domestic Relations in Seventeenth-*

By this logic, the gap between church and town widened in Boston during the first three decades of settlement; and barely half of all householders were communicants in the Dedham, Massachusetts, and Milford, Connecticut, churches by mid-century. Fewer than one in five Salem taxpayers near the end of the seventeenth century, only one-third in towns along the Connecticut River by 1700, and fewer than one in ten in Concord a generation later had joined their respective Congregational churches. Other studies offer an even bleaker assessment of those "unchurched" men and women who hung back from the communion table and their "nonelect" households. Although scholars studying puritan theology, popular religion, and religious practice have revised Miller's thesis during the past four decades, many historians continue to assume that overall rates of church affiliation declined in New England between 1660 and 1740 among what Jon Butler has called an "increasingly secular population."[7]

Proportional measurements of Congregational vitality during the provincial period entail significant problems. Most calculations omit women, as several scholars have noted, although they accounted for as many as three-quarters of all new church members after 1660. More important, the unit of measurement used in many of these studies—individual church members—does not comport with shifts in the meaning of church affiliation that developed during the latter decades of the seventeenth century. Even Morgan recognized that New Englanders "thought of their church as an organization made up of families rather than individuals." Anne Brown, David Hall, Gerald Moran, Mark Peterson, and Mary Ramsbottom have described church membership as a "family strategy"—a joint decision made by husbands and wives seeking access to baptism for their children. The social time of the family life-course structured the religious lives of lay men and women, rather than the evangelical time of individual salvation often associated with the Whitefieldian conversion paradigm. Once derided by Morgan as

Century New England, rev. ed. (New York, 1966), 171; W. W. Sweet, "The American Colonial Environment and Religious Liberty," *Church History,* IV (1935), 52–53; and John Gorham Palfrey, *History of New England,* 5 vols. (Boston, 1858–1890), III, 41n. I address the potential value and the significant limitations of Stiles's early research on the ecclesiastical history of New England in Part 5.

7. Darrett B. Rutman, *Winthrop's Boston: A Portrait of a Puritan Town, 1630–1649* (Chapel Hill, N.C., 1965), 146–148; Kenneth A. Lockridge, "The History of a Puritan Church, 1637–1736," *NEQ,* XL (1967), 411–412; Moran, "Religious Renewal, Puritan Tribalism, and the Family," *WMQ,* XXXVI (1979), 245–246; Richard P. Gildrie, *Salem, Massachusetts, 1626–1683: A Covenant Community* (Charlottesville, Va., 1975), 159; Paul R. Lucas, *Valley of Discord: Church and Society along the Connecticut River, 1636–1725* (Hanover, N.H., 1976), 141–142, 244n; Robert A. Gross, *The Minutemen and Their World* (New York, 1976), 19; Benjamin C. Ray, "Satan's War against the Covenant in Salem Village, 1692," *NEQ,* LXXX (2007), 78–79 ("nonelect," 78), 92; Minkema, "Old Age and Religion in the Writings and Life of Jonathan Edwards," *Church History,* LXX (2001), 699n ("unchurched"); Jon Butler, *Awash in a Sea of Faith: Christianizing the American People,* Studies in Cultural History (Cambridge, Mass., 1990), 61. See also Barbara E. Lacey, "Gender, Piety, and Secularization in Connecticut Religion, 1720–1775," *Journal of Social History,* XXIV (1991), 799–800; and Hull and Moran, "Churching of Colonial Connecticut," *Review of Religious Research,* XLI (1999), 177–178.

symptomatic of a "tottering" ecclesiastical system, "Puritan tribalism" emerges in the most current scholarship as the bulwark of the New England way during the decades leading up to the revivals of the 1740s.[8]

In this study, the more neutral and inclusive term "affiliation" denotes the strategies through which men and women in provincial New England established formal ties to local churches by owning the covenant, presenting children for baptism, or joining in full communion. The maps and tables in this book displaying rates of household affiliation (see Tables 6 and 9 and Maps 2, 4, 5, and 6) are based on information collected in MS-Access databases that mirror the traditional family reconstitution forms developed by English historical demographers more than half a century ago. After identifying the members of each household appearing on various types of census records using vital statistics, town histories, and published and online genealogies, I cross-referenced each family group with lists of baptisms, covenant owners, and full church members. Adopting Mark Peterson's concept of "primary affiliation," I define an "affiliated household" as one in which either husband or wife had owned the covenant, joined the church, or presented at least one child for baptism in or before the year in which the map, census, land division, or tax list was created.[9]

This approach to studying religious affiliation through family units places greater emphasis on baptismal records than earlier studies. I have calculated age data for nearly seven thousand children baptized in the eight selected churches

8. Morgan, *Puritan Family*, 136, 161, 185; Anne S. Brown and David D. Hall, "Family Strategies and Religious Practice: Baptism and the Lord's Supper in Early New England," in Hall, ed., *Lived Religion in America: Toward a History of Practice* (Princeton, 1997), 43; Gerald F. Moran and Maris A. Vinovskis, "The Puritan Family and Religion: A Critical Reappraisal," in Moran and Vinovskis, ed., *Religion, Family, and the Life Course: Explorations in the Social History of Early America* (Ann Arbor, Mich., 1992), 13. See also Mary Macmanus Ramsbottom, "Religious Society and the Family in Charlestown, Massachusetts, 1630 to 1740" (Ph.D. diss., Yale University, 1987), 88; Anne Speerschneider Brown, "'Bound Up in a Bundle of Life': The Social Meaning of Religious Practice in Northeastern Massachusetts, 1700–1765" (Ph.D. diss., Boston University, 1995), 61–64; Mark A. Peterson, *The Price of Redemption: The Spiritual Economy of Puritan New England* (Stanford, Calif., 1997), 70–71; Hall, "From 'Religion and Society' to Practices: The New Religious History," in Robert Blair St. George, ed., *Possible Pasts: Becoming Colonial in Early America* (Ithaca, N.Y., 2000), 159. Several of these works draw on the conceptual frameworks outlined in Natalie Zemon Davis, "Ghosts, Kin, and Progeny: Some Features of Family Life in Early Modern France," *Daedalus*, CVI, no. 2 (Spring 1977), 87–114; and Tamara K. Hareven, "Family Time and Historical Time," *Daedalus*, CVI, no. 2 (Spring 1977), 57–70. I borrow the categories of "social" time and "evangelical" time from Hall, "'Between the Times': Popular Religion in Eighteenth-Century British North America," in Michael V. Kennedy and William G. Shade, eds., *The World Turned Upside-Down: The State of Eighteenth-Century American Studies at the Beginning of the Twenty-First Century* (Bethlehem, Pa., 2001), 149–150. For an important corrective to gender bias in earlier studies of church affiliation, see Harry S. Stout and Catherine A. Brekus, "Declension, Gender, and the 'New Religious History,'" in Philip R. Vandermeer and Robert P. Swierenga, eds., *Belief and Behavior: Essays in the New Religious History* (New Brunswick, N.J., 1991), 15–37.

9. Peterson, *Price of Redemption*, 70. For a similar assessment of key terms, see Patricia U. Bonomi and Peter R. Eisenstadt, "Church Adherence in the Eighteenth-Century British American Colonies," *WMQ*, XXXIX (1982), 249–253.

before 1790 (see Table 2). In addition, I assigned an identification number to each occasion on which a family brought one or more children to be baptized. These baptismal presentation events were then ordered sequentially for each family. A couple's first baptismal presentation following marriage plays an important role in this study, for it serves as a rough index of parents' preparedness to assume their adult religious responsibilities. Most parents who joined the church or who owned the covenant as young adults planned to present their children for baptism one by one in a regular order—usually within the month following each birth. As the data in Table 3 shows, the phenomenon that David Hall has evocatively described as children "brought to baptism in bunches, like grapes" rarely persisted into the second quarter of the eighteenth century, and then only in towns with unusually restrictive church admission practices, such as Sandwich, Massachusetts.[10]

As with all works of early American social history, my attempts to code, quantify, and map church affiliation practices involves conjecture, creative choices, and occasional guesswork. Matching reconstituted families with church records can be difficult—especially for married women whose family surnames remain unknown. Birth records often went unrecorded. A few town residents—ministers, most notably—do not appear on early tax lists, maps, or related census documents. The fragmentary nature of many Congregational church record books before 1720, moreover, makes it difficult to establish the primary affiliation data of some households with precision. As a result, the maps and statistical tables presented in this book exclude cases for which there is insufficient data. Rates of household affiliation omit nonresident taxpayers who worshipped in neighboring congregations, single men, and individuals for whom no genealogical data survives. The baptismal presentation data in Tables 3 and 5 excludes several types of unusual cases: adult baptisms; children brought by single mothers, grandparents, guardians, and masters; and situations in which the family's first baptismal presentation took place in a different parish or before extant church records begin.[11]

Despite the limitations of the data, family reconstitution based on church records, maps, tax lists, land division records, and other census documents remains the single best method for assessing the changing religious composition of eighteenth-century New England. Readers, however, should recognize the statistical elements of this study for what they are: suggestive interpretations of popular religious practice in provincial New England using old and new analytical techniques and the best available data from a broad range of well-documented communities. The quantitative methods developed for this book reveal a religious world strikingly at odds with prevailing social history models. By 1740, most towns in New England were composed overwhelmingly of affiliated Congregational fami-

10. David D. Hall, "The New England Background," in Stephen J. Stein, ed., *The Cambridge Companion to Jonathan Edwards*, Cambridge Companions to Religion (New York, 2007), 66.

11. On the limitations of colonial vital records and tax lists, see Philip J. Greven, Jr., *Four Generations: Population, Land, and Family in Colonial Andover, Massachusetts* (Ithaca, N.Y., 1970), 6–8; and Jackson Turner Main, *Society and Economy in Colonial Connecticut* (Princeton, 1985), 8, 37–39.

lies; upward of three-quarters of all children were born, baptized, and raised in the gospel land of light. Provincial New Englanders were dutiful and committed Protestants; and it was precisely their diligence that incited the attacks of zealous Whitefieldarians during New England's era of great awakenings.

■ The following bibliography lists the principal church records, tax lists, census records, maps, and other documents employed in the compilation of the visual and statistical data that appear throughout the preceding pages. Sources employed in family reconstitution include a wide range of published vital records, town histories, family bible records, cemetery records, and published and online genealogies too numerous to be included here.

Andover, Mass.: Andover, Mass., North Parish Church Records, 1686–1810, microfilm, Stevens Memorial Library, North Andover, Mass.; Andover, Mass., North Parish Church Records: Tax Lists, 1712–circa 1780, microfilm, Stevens Memorial Library.

Bennington, Vt.: Bennington, Vt., First Church Records, 1762–1820, typescript, 2 vols., I, 1–81, Bennington Museum, Bennington, Vt.; E. B. O'Callaghan, ed., *The Documentary History of the State of New-York,* 4 vols. (Albany, N.Y., 1850–1851), IV, 584–585; Lewis Cass Aldrich, ed., *History of Bennington County, Vt., with Illustrations and Biographical Sketches of Some of Its Prominent Men and Pioneers* (Syracuse, N.Y., 1889), 248–250; David Avery, account book, 1780–1783, microfilm, reel 12, David Avery Papers, 1765–1818, CHS.

Beverly, Mass.: William P. Upham, ed., *Records of the First Church in Beverly, Massachusetts, 1667–1772* (Salem, Mass., 1905); Sidney Perley, "Beverly in 1700," *EIHC,* LV (1919), 81–102, 209–229, 273–303, LVI (1920), 33–49, 98–110, 209–222.

Hampton, N.H.: Hampton, N.H., Records of the First Congregational Church, 1667–1902, microfilm, reel 1 (Watertown, Mass., 1986), NEHGS; Seaborn Cotton, commonplace book, 1650–1752, Mss A 1454, NEHGS; George Freeman Sanborn, Jr., and Melinde Lutz Sanborn, comp., *Vital Records of Hampton, New Hampshire, to the End of the Year 1900,* 2 vols. (Boston, 1998), II, 1–121; Hampton, N.H., tax list, 1732, New Hampshire Division of Archives and Records Management, Concord, N.H.; Pauline Johnson Oesterlin, comp., *New Hampshire 1742 Estate List,* New Hampshire Society of Genealogists, Special Publication, no. 1 (Bowie, Md., 1994), 56–89.

Haverhill, Mass.: Mary F. M. Raymond, comp., "Records of First Parish, Haverhill," 2 vols., unpublished MS, 1895, Haverhill Public Library, Haverhill, Mass.; Haverhill, Mass., Records of the North Parish Congregational Church, 1730–1905, typescript, Haverhill Public Library; Haverhill, Mass., West Parish Congregational Church Records, 1735–1761, CL (available online at NEHH); Haverhill, Mass., East Parish Congregational Church Records, 1743–1785, typescript, 1936, Haverhill Public Library; Haverhill, Mass., First Baptist Church Records, 1765–1816, Haverhill Public Library; George Wingate Chase, *The History of Haverhill, Massachusetts, from Its First Settlement, in 1640, to the Year 1860* (1861; rpt. Somersworth, N.H., 1983), 235, 310–315; Oesterlin, comp., *New Hampshire 1742 Estate List,* 120–142; Haverhill, Mass., East Parish tax list, 1744, Essex County Manuscripts Collection, 1639–1959, PEM; Haverhill, Mass., West Parish tax list, 1745, Haverhill Public Library; Haverhill, Mass., Tax Records of the First Parish, 1751–1807, Haverhill Public Library.

Hingham, Mass.: C. Edward Egan, Jr., [ed.], "The Hobart Journal," *NEHGR,* CXXI (1967), 3–25, 102–127, 191–216, 269–294; Hingham, Mass., First Congregational Church Records, 1718–1786, box 8, First Parish (Hingham, Mass.) Records, 1635–1961, MHS; James Hawke, account book, 1679–1684, box 8, First Parish (Hingham, Mass.) Records; Frank D. Andrews, ed., *Names of Tax Payers of Hingham, Massachusetts, 1711* (Vineland, N.J., 1913); Hingham, Mass., tax lists, 1748, 1755, 1770–1771, Cushing Family Papers, 1633–1884, MHS; Hingham, Mass., tax list, 1749, Office of the Town Clerk, Hingham, Mass. (available online at *www .ancestry.com*); Hingham, Mass., tax list, Sept. 1, 1784, box 17, First Parish (Hingham, Mass.) Records.

Lebanon, Conn.: Lebanon, Conn., First Congregational Church Records Index, 1700–1883, typescript, 1942, Connecticut Church Records Abstracts, 1630–1920, CSL (available online at *www.ancestry.com*); "List of the Polls and Rateable Estate of the Inhabitants of the First Society in Lebanon," 1730–1733, Lebanon, Conn., First Congregational Church Records and Papers, CHS.

Medfield, Mass.: Medfield, Mass., First Congregational Church Records, 1697–1866, Medfield Historical Society, Medfield, Mass.; Medfield, Mass., tax lists, 1693, 1718, Medfield (Mass.) Papers II, 1693–1818, MHS; Medfield, Mass., tax list, n.d. [1717], box 11, MSS 624, Dorchester Antiquarian and Historical Society Collection, 1635–1874, NEHGS; E. O. Jameson, *The History of Medway, Mass., 1713 to 1885* (Providence, R.I., 1886), 40–41, 45; Medfield, Mass., tax lists, 1723, Medfield Historical Society.

Newbury (now West Newbury), Mass.: West Newbury, Mass., Congregational Church Records, 1698–1797, Essex County Manuscripts Collection; Newburyport, Mass., Saint Paul's Episcopal Church Records, 1715–1854, microfilm no. 1290171, GSU; William Stevens Perry, ed., *Historical Collections Relating to the American Colonial Church,* 5 vols. (Hartford, Conn., 1870–1878), III, 94, 104; West Newbury, Mass., tax list, 1696, "Early Records of the Parishes and Churches at the West End of the Newbury Settlement," 1696–1930, Belleville Congregational Church, Newburyport, Mass.; John J. Currier, *"Ould Newbury": Historical and Biographical Sketches* (Boston, 1896), 392–393.

New Haven, Conn.: Franklin Bowditch Dexter, comp., *Historical Catalogue of the Members of the First Church of Christ in New Haven, Connecticut (Center Church), A.D. 1639–1914* (New Haven, Conn., 1914); New Haven, Conn., First Congregational Church Records Index, 1639–1937, 2 vols., typescript, 1947, Connecticut Church Records Abstracts (available online at *www.ancestry.com*); New Haven, Conn., United [White Haven] Church Records, 1742–1933, microfilm no. 577, CSL; Samuel W. S. Dutton, *The History of the North Church in New Haven: From Its Formation in May, 1742, during the Great Awakening, to the Completion of the Century in May, 1842* (New Haven, Conn., 1842), 7; *Catalogue of the Members of the Church in the United Society in New Haven, Formed by the Union of the White-Haven and Fair-Haven Churches . . .* (New Haven, 1855), 12–19; Lists of those entered as Mr. Noyes's Party and Mr. Bird's Party, Jan. 10, 1757, Ecclesiastical Affairs, Ser. 1: 1658–1789, XI, 99–100, Connecticut Archives, 1629–1856, CSL; Donald Lines Jacobus, "Records of St. James's Church, Derby, Conn., 1740–1796," *NEHGR*, LXXVI (1922), 130–153; Dean B. Lyman, Jr., comp., *An Atlas of Old New Haven or "The Nine Squares" as Shown on Various Early Maps* (New Haven, Conn., 1929); James Wadsworth, *A Plan of the Town of New Haven: With all the Buildings in 1748* ([New Haven, Conn.], 1806); Franklin Bowditch Dexter, ed. *Extracts from the Itineraries and Other Miscellanies of Ezra Stiles, D.D., LL.D., 1755–1794* (New Haven, Conn., 1916), 42–50, 317–318.

Norwich, Conn.: Norwich, Conn., First Congregational Church Records, 1699–1917, microfilm no. 85, CSL; Kenneth Walter Cameron, ed., *The Church of England in Pre-Revolutionary Connecticut: New Documents and Letters concerning the Loyalist Clergy and the Plight of Their Surviving Church* (Hartford, Conn., 1976), 49; Norwich, Conn., Christ Church Records, 1747–1901, microfilm no. 3, CSL; Norwich, Conn., tax lists, 1729–1731, 1734–1737, 1739, 1742–1743, Town of Norwich Records, 1729–1900, CSL; Norwich, Conn., tax lists, 1744–1757, First Congregational Church Records, 1699–1928, microfilm no. 585, CSL.

Salem Village (now Danvers), Mass.: Paul Boyer and Stephen Nissenbaum, eds., *Salem-Village Witchcraft: A Documentary Record of Local Conflict in Colonial New England*, 2d ed. (Boston, 1993), 260–263, 268–312, 383–414; Henry Wheatland, ed., "Baptisms at Church in Salem Village, Now North Parish, Danvers," *EIHC*, XVI (1879), 235–238; Richard D. Pierce, ed., *The Records of the First Church in Salem, Massachusetts, 1629–1736* (Salem, Mass., 1974).

Sandwich, Mass.: Sandwich, Mass., First Church Records, 1692–1853, Mss 638, NEHGS; Caroline Lewis Kardell and Russell A. Lovell, Jr., comp., *Vital Records of Sandwich, Massachusetts to 1885*, 3 vols. (Boston, 1996), II, 1371–1436; Sandwich, Mass., tax lists, 1696, 1698, Miscellaneous Bound Manuscripts, MHS; John G. Locke, ed., "Extracts from Rev. Benjamin Fessenden's Manuscript," *NEHGR*, XIII (1859), 30–31.

Stratham, N.H.: Stratham, N.H., Congregational Church Records, 1746–1913, 2 vols., NHHS; Samuel Lane, "Church Book," 1765–1804, box 3: Miscellaneous Papers, 1742–1876, Stratham Town Records, New Hampshire Division of Archives and Records Management; Lane, "An Account of the Church Money Receiv'd and Paid Away for the Support of the Communion Table," 1774–1803, box 3: Miscellaneous Papers, 1742–1876, Stratham Town Records; Lane, "A List of the Names of Those Persons Who Have Been Admitted to the Fellowship of the Church," 1786–1800, Ser. II, box 3, LFP; Charles B. Nelson, *History of Stratham, New Hampshire, 1631–1900* (Somersworth, N.H., 1965), 146–147; Stratham, N.H., Baptist Church Records, 1808–1863, NHHS; Lane, "Ministers Rate," 1764, box 3: Miscellaneous Papers, 1742–1876, Stratham Town Records; "Stratham Records of Invoice and Assessment: Book 1," 1805–1815, VI, box 2, Stratham Town Records; Phinehas Merrill, "Plan of the Town of Stratham," July 17, 1793, NHHS; Merrill, "Plan of the Town of Stratham," May 17, 1806, New Hampshire Division of Archives and Records Management.

Suffield, Mass. (now Conn.): Records of the Congregational Church in Suffield,

Conn. (Except Church Votes), 1710–1836 (Hartford, Conn., 1941); Suffield, Conn., First Baptist Church Records, 1769–1872, American Baptist Historical Society, Atlanta; Suffield, Conn., First Baptist Church, articles of incorporation, n.d. [circa 1769], Kent Memorial Library, Suffield, Conn.; summary of Suffield church records, 1679–1710, n.d. [nineteenth century], Suffield Genealogical Materials, CHS; Separatist church petitions, Apr. 22, May 25, 1765, May 10, 1770, Ecclesiastical Affairs, Ser. 1, XV, 236, 238, 240, Connecticut Archives; Hezekiah Spencer Sheldon, ed., *Documentary History of Suffield, in the Colony and Province of the Massachusetts Bay, in New England, 1660–1749* (Springfield, Mass., 1879), 178–181, 192–193; Suffield, Conn., tax lists, 1763, 1769, Kent Memorial Library; John Graham, Jr., diary, [1739], 1776–1785, box 1, Graham Family Papers, 1731–1849, WCL.

Westborough, Mass.: Westborough, Mass., Congregational Church Records, 1724–1808, microfilm, Westborough Town Library, Westborough, Mass.; Westborough, Mass., tax lists, 1756, 1762, 1771, 1776, Tax Lists, 1756–1852, Office of the Town Clerk, Westborough, Mass.

Westford, Mass.: Chelmsford, Mass., First Congregational Church Records, 1741–1901, microfilm no. 868444, GSU; Westford, Mass., Congregational Church Records, 1727–1889, typescript, microfilm no. 902078, GSU; William B. Prescott, ed., *Westford, Massachusetts: Eight Tax Lists 18 October 1730 to 15 November 1731* (Round Brook, N.J., 1998); Edwin R. Hodgman, *History of the Town of Westford, in the County of Middlesex, Massachusetts, 1659–1883* (Lowell, Mass., 1883), 25–33.

Major Relations of Faith Collections

Darkness Falls on the Land of Light builds on a unique database of more than twelve hundred eighteenth-century church admission relations from dozens of towns scattered across New England. The list below facilitates locating individual relations from the largest collections cited throughout this study. A handful of these texts have been published, for which see the accompanying notes. Dates associated with relations may reflect one of several events, including the day on which the narratives were composed, the day on which candidates were propounded (prop.), or the day on which they were admitted (adm.) to full communion. I have supplied the date of admission in square brackets for undated (n.d.) relations. In a few cases involving testimonies for people with the same name, I have supplied a brief parenthetical reference identifying the candidate's role as a husband (h.), daughter (d.), son (s.), or wife (w.). The codes after each entry correspond to the following manuscript collections: MS Am 524, BPL [B1]; Parker-Legal Opinion, etc. 1809, no. 4, MS G.361.10, BPL [B2]; Thomas Foxcroft Papers, 1690–1770, Mark and Llora Bortman Collection, HGARC [B3]; Autograph File, F, 1447–1994, HL [B4]; John Davis Papers, 1627–1846, MHS [B5]; Letters to Benjamin Colman, 1693–1747, MHS [B6]; Miscellaneous Bound Manuscripts Collection, MHS [B7]; Robert Treat Paine Papers, 1659–1916, Ser. III, MHS [B8]; box 10, Park Family Papers, 1701–1929, YUA [B9]; Essex, Mass., First Congregational Church Papers, MSS 256, Essex County Manuscripts Collection, 1639–1959, PEM [C1]; box 1, JCP [C2]; box 2, JCP [C3]; Personal Records, 1719–1745, Haverhill, Mass., First Congregational Church Records, 1719–2012, CL (available online at NEHH) [H1]; Buttonwoods Museum, Haverhill, Mass. [H2]; box 1, Pomeroy Family Papers, 1735–1817, CHS [H3]; Joseph Baxter Papers, 1710–1742, Dedham Historical Society, Dedham, Mass. [M1]; Amos Adams Sermon, 1704–1768, MHS [M2]; Baxter-Adams Family Papers, 1699–1889, box 1, MHS [M3]; Medfield, Mass., Congregational Church Records, 1697–1866, Medfield Historical Society, Medfield, Mass. [M4]; Miscellaneous Church Papers, 1693–1857, Medfield Historical Society, Medfield, Mass. [M5]; Sermon Collection, box 3, Mss. A S87, NEHGS [M6] (available online at NEHH); Sturbridge, Mass., Congregational Church Records, 1736–1871, CL (available online at NEHH) [S1]; box 2, Parkman Family Papers, 1707–1879,

AAS [W1]; box 3, Parkman Family Papers [W2]; "'Relations of Belief and Confessions prior to 1800,'" Office of the Town Clerk, Westborough, Mass. [W3].

BOSTON, FIRST CHURCH (1702–1767)

1. Brooks, Mary, n.d. [adm. Dec. 31, 1727] [B3]
2. Coburn, Rebecca, n.d. [adm. Nov. 25, 1739] [B3][1]
3. Cravath, John, n.d. [adm. Mar. 31, 1728] [B1]
4. Currier, Ann, prop. Nov. 10, 1731 [adm. Jan. 9, 1732] [B3]
5. Dix, Hannah, n.d. [adm. July 31, 1726] [B3]
6. Fairfield, John, Sept. 6, 1760 [adm. Sept. 7, 1760] [B3][2]
7. Fisher, Sarah, n.d. [adm. May 31, 1741, or May 17, 1742] [B3]
8. Marsh, Daniel, n.d. [adm. Sept. 26, 1742] [B3]
9. Marsh, Sarah, Apr. 25, 1767 [B3]
10. Osborn, Ruth, n.d. [adm. Nov. 29, 1724] [B3]
11. Stephenson, Elizabeth, n.d. [adm. May 27, 1759] [B3][3]
12. Thorn, Samuel, Mar. 24, 1740, [adm. Mar. 30, 1740] [B3]
13. Walter, Abigail, n.d. [adm. Oct. 25, 1702] [B3]
14. Unknown (fragment), n.d. [B3]

BOSTON, THIRD (OLD SOUTH) CHURCH (1721–1751)

1. Allen, Sarah, adm. May 24, 1741 [B2]
2. Blake, Hannah, adm. Oct. 27, 1751 [B7][4]
3. Brewer, Abigail, adm. July 19, 1741 [B5]
4. Fayerweather, Samuel, adm. May 24, 1741 [B4][5]
5. Gale, Mary, n.d. [adm. Feb. 11, 1733] [B9]
6. Holland, Mary, adm. May 24, 1741 [B2]
7. Lowden, Mary, adm. Aug. 13, 1721 [B6]
8. Paine, Robert Treat, adm. Apr. 16, 1749 [B8][6]
9. Simpson, John, adm. July 11, 1725 [B5]
10. Walley, Bethiah, n.d. [adm. Mar. 25, 1744][7]

HAVERHILL, MASS., FIRST CHURCH (1719–1745)

1. Ames, Joseph, prop. October 1736, adm. Oct. 31, 1736 [H1]
2. Ayer, Abigail, prop. Dec. 25, 1720, adm. Jan. 15, 1721 [H1]

1. Appendix C.
2. Douglas L. Winiarski, "New Perspectives on the Northampton Communion Controversy II: Relations, Professions, and Experiences, 1748–1760," *Jonathan Edwards Studies*, IV (2014), 138–139.
3. Ibid., 137–138.
4. Ibid., 136–137.
5. Appendix C.
6. Stephen T. Riley and Edward W. Hanson, eds., *The Papers of Robert Treat Paine*, MHS, *Collections*, LXXXVII (Boston, 1992), 48–49.
7. Hamilton Andrews Hill, *History of the Old South Church (Third Church) Boston, 1669–1884*, 2 vols. (Boston, 1890), I, 309n.

3. Ayer, Hannah, prop. July 14, 1728, adm. Aug. 4, 1728 [H1]

4. Ayer, John, Jr., prop. May 16, 1736, adm. May 30, 1736 [H1]

5. Ayer, Nathaniel, prop. June 23, 1728, adm. July 7, 1728 [H1]

6. Ayer, Rachel, prop. Nov. 19, 1727, adm. Dec. 1, 1727 [H1]

7. Ayer, Ruth, prop. July 12, 1719, adm. July 26, 1719 [H1]

8. Ayer, Susannah, prop. Nov. 19, 1727, adm. Dec. 1, 1727 [H1]

9. Badger, Hannah, adm. Feb. 28, 1742 [H1]

10. Badger, Joseph, prop. Mar. 17, 1728, adm. Mar. 31, 1728 [H1]

11. Bayley, John, prop. Jan. 24, 1725, adm. Feb. 7, 1725 [H1]

12. Bayley, Sarah, prop. Nov. 6, 1737, adm. Dec. 18, 1737 [H1]

13. Belknap, Abiah, prop. June 9, 1728, adm. June 30, 1728 [H1]

14. Bond, Mercy, prop. May 6, 1720, adm. June 5, 1720 [H1]

15. Boynton, John, prop. May 9, 1736, adm. May 30, 1736 [H1]

16. Boynton, Joshua, prop. Dec. 3, 1727, adm. June 9, 1728 [H1]

17. Bradley, Abigail, adm. Feb. 8, 1736 [H1]

18. Bradley, Daniel, prop. Apr. 21, 1728, adm. May 5, 1728 [H1]

19. Bradley, Elizabeth (alias Calef), prop. Oct. 8, 1738, adm. Oct. 29, 1738 [H1]

20. Bradley, Isaac, prop. Mar. 5, 1727, adm. July 30, 1727 [H1]

21. Bradley, Joseph, prop. Sept. 1728, adm. Nov. 24, 1728 [H1]

22. Buck, Ebenezer, prop. Dec. 3, 1727, adm. Dec. 31, 1727 [H1]

23. Carleton, Edward, prop. Jan. 7, 1728, adm. Jan. 21, 1728 [H1]

24. Clark, Abigail, prop. Aug. 12, 1722, adm. Aug. 26, 1722 [H1]

25. Clark, Edward, prop. June 1726, adm. July 17, 1726 [H1]

26. Clark, Gift, prop. Nov. 26, 1727, adm. Dec. 3, 1727 [H1]

27. Clark, Samuel, prop. Aug. 12, 1722, adm. Aug. 26, 1722 [H1]

28. Clement, Abigail, adm. Nov. 29, 1730 [H1]

29. Clement, Hannah, prop. Feb. 11, 1728, adm. Mar. 10, 1728 [H1]

30. Clement, John, prop. July 14, 1723, adm. July 28, 1723 [H1]

31. Clement, Jonathan, prop. Sept. 8, 1728, adm. Oct. 6, 1728 [H1]

32. Clement, Joseph, adm. June 27, 1742 [H1][8]

33. Clement, Lydia, prop. July 12, 1719, adm. July 26, 1719 [H1]

34. Clement, Obadiah, prop. July 28, 1728, adm. Aug. 11, 1728 [H1]

35. Corlis, Elizabeth, prop. Mar. 24, 1728, adm. Apr. 5, 1728 [H1]

36. Corlis, Rebecca, adm. Oct. 26, 1729 [H1]

37. Corlis, Ruth, Nov. 19, 1727, adm. Dec. 1, 1727 [H1]

38. Currier, Abigail, prop. May 8, 1720, adm. June 19, 1720 [H1]

39. Currier, Elizabeth, prop. Jan. 13, 1723, adm. Jan. 27, 1723 [H1]

40. Currier, Grace, prop. June 19, 1720, adm. July 3, 1720 [H1]

41. Currier, Reuben, prop. Nov. 19, 1727, adm. Dec. 1, 1727 [H1]

42. Davis, Anna, prop. Feb. 10, 1734, adm. Mar. 3, 1734 [H1]

8. Douglas L. Winiarski, "Gendered 'Relations' in Haverhill, Massachusetts, 1719–1742," in Peter Benes, ed., *In Our Own Words: New England Diaries, 1600 to the Present*, I, *Diary Diversity, Coming of Age*, Dublin Seminar for New England Folklife, Annual Proceedings 2006/2007 (Boston, 2009), 67.

43. Davis, Deborah, prop. Dec. 10, 1727, adm. Feb. 11, 1728 [H1]
44. Davis, Hannah, prop. June 21, 1719, adm. July 19, 1719 [H1]
45. Davis, Katherine, prop. Dec. 3, 1727, adm. Jan. 7, 1728 [H1]
46. Davis, Rebecca, prop. Jan. 26, 1729, adm. Feb. 9, 1729 [H1]
47. Davis, Samuel, Nov. 26, 1727, adm. Dec. 3, 1727 [H1]
48. Dow, Judith, prop. Nov. 12, 1727, adm. Nov. 26, 1727 [H1]
49. Dow, Samuel, prop. Mar. 10, 1728, adm. Mar. 31, 1728 [H1]
50. Dow, Stephen, adm. May 4, 1729 [H1]
51. Duston, Hannah, prop. May 17, 1724, adm. May 31, 1724 [H2][9]
52. Duston, Lydia, prop. Aug. 14, 1726, adm. Aug. 28, 1726 [H1]
53. Duston, Mary (w. Thomas, Jr.), prop. Nov. 5, 1727, adm. Nov. 19, 1727 [H1]
54. Duston, Mary, prop. Feb. 28, 1731, adm. Apr. 4, 1731 [H1]
55. Duston, Sarah, prop. Nov. 19, 1727, adm. Dec. 1, 1727 [H1]
56. Duston, Thomas, n.d. [adm. Mar. 1, 1724] [H2]
57. Eastman, Mehetabel, prop. Jan. 7, 1728, adm. Feb. 4, 1728 [H1]
58. Eastman, Sarah (w. Ebenezer), prop. Feb. 16, 1724, adm. Mar. 8, 1724 [H1]
59. Eastman, Sarah, prop. June 9, 1728, adm. June 23, 1728 [H1]
60. Eaton, Hannah, prop. Sept. 14, 1729, adm. Oct. 5, 1729 [H1]
61. Eaton, Mary (w. Job), prop. Aug. 30, 1719, adm. Sept. 13, 1719 [H1]
62. Eaton, Mary, prop. Nov. 26, 1727, adm. Dec. 10, 1727 [H1]
63. Eaton, Mehetabel, prop. Aug. 28, 1726, adm. Sept. 18, 1726 [H1]
64. Ela, John, prop. July 21, 1734, adm. Aug. 4, 1734 [H1]
65. Ela, Mary, prop. Nov. 19, 1727, adm. Dec. 1, 1727 [H1]
66. Ela, Sarah, adm. May 23, 1742 [H1]
67. Ely, Abigail, prop. July 24, 1720, adm. Aug. 7, 1720 [H1]
68. Emerson, Elizabeth, adm. Aug. 1, 1725 [H1]
69. Emerson, Hannah, prop. Sept. 5, 1725, adm. Sept. 19, 1725 [H1]
70. Emerson, Jonathan, prop. May 17, 1724, adm. May 31, 1724 [H1][10]
71. Emerson, Michael, adm. July 26, 1730 [H1]
72. Ewing, William, adm. Dec. 31, 1727 [H1]
73. Ford, Hannah, prop. Nov. 12, 1727, adm. Dec. 1, 1727 [H1][11]
74. Ford, Lydia, prop. Mar. 24, 1728, adm. Apr. 5, 1728 [H1]
75. Foster, David, prop. Jan. 7, 1728, adm. Jan. 21, 1728 [H1]
76. Gale, Benjamin, prop. Dec. 17, 1727, adm. Dec. 31, 1727 [H1]
77. Gile, Daniel, prop. Jan. 21, 1728, adm. Feb. 2, 1728 [H1]
78. Gile, Ebenezer, prop. Aug. 30, 1719, adm. Sept. 13, 1719 [H1]
79. Gile, Ebenezer (h. Lydia), prop. June 17, 1733, adm. July 22, 1733 [H1]
80. Gile, Elizabeth, prop. June 24, 1722, adm. July 22, 1722 [H1]
81. Gile, Ephraim, prop. Dec. 10, 1727, adm. Dec. 31, 1727 [H1]
82. Gile, Joanna, prop. Nov. 26, 1727, adm. Dec. 31, 1727 [H1]
83. Gile, Samuel, prop. Nov. 26, 1727, adm. Dec. 10, 1727 [H1]

9. Ibid., 78.
10. Ibid., 78.
11. Appendix C.

84. Gile, Sarah, prop. Jan. 28, 1728, adm. Feb. 4, 1728 [H1]

85. Gordon, Elizabeth, prop. Nov. 19, 1727, adm. Dec. 1, 1727 [H1]

86. Gordon, Mary, prop. Dec. 17, 1727, adm. Dec. 31, 1727 [H1]

87. Greely, Mary, prop. Nov. 12, 1727, adm. Nov. 26, 1727 [H1]

88. Greely, Rachel, prop. July 14, 1723, adm. July 28, 1723 [H1]

89. Greely, Samuel, prop. Dec. 10, 1727, adm. Dec. 31, 1727 [H1]

90. Green, Elizabeth, prop. May 5, 1728, adm. May 19, 1728 [H1]

91. Green, Martha, prop. July 19, 1719, adm. Aug. 2, 1719 [H1]

92. Green, Peter, prop. May 19, 1728, adm. June 9, 1728 [H1]

93. Griffing, Elizabeth, prop. Jan. 21, 1728, adm. Feb. 11, 1728 [H1]

94. Gutterson, William, prop. July 18, 1725, adm. Aug. 1, 1725 [H1]

95. Hassaltine, Hannah, prop. June 4, 1738, adm. June 18, 1738 [H1]

96. Hassaltine, Judith, prop. Nov. 22, 1733, adm. Feb. 3, 1734 [H1]

97. Hassaltine, Mary, prop. Feb. 4, 1728, adm. Feb. 18, 1728 [H1]

98. Hassaltine, Nathaniel, prop. Nov. 5, 1727, adm. Jan. 28, 1728 [H1]

99. Hastings, Elizabeth (w. Robert), prop. May 21, 1721, adm. June 11, 1721 [H1]

100. Hastings, Elizabeth (w. Robert, Jr.), prop. July 21, 1723, adm. Aug. 4, 1723 [H1]

101. Hastings, Robert, Jr., prop. Nov. 26, 1727, adm. Dec. 3, 1727 [H1]

102. Haynes, Sarah, prop. Dec. 31, 1727, adm. Jan. 21, 1728 [H1]

103. Hazzen, Richard, Jr., prop. July 15, 1722, adm. Aug. 5, 1722 [H1]

104. Hazzen, Sarah (w. Richard, Jr.), prop. Nov. 5, 1727, adm. Nov. 19, 1727 [H1]

105. Hazzen, Sarah, prop. Jan. 10, 1731, adm. Jan. 24, 1731 [H1]

106. Heath, Elizabeth, prop. Dec. 3, 1727, adm. Dec. 31, 1727 [H1]

107. Heath, Frances, prop. Aug. 30, 1719, adm. Sept. 13, 1719 [H1]

108. Heath, Joseph, prop. 1721, adm. Apr. 1, 1722 [H1]

109. Heath, Lydia, prop. Nov. 15, 1730, adm. Dec. 6, 1730 [H1]

110. Heath, Phebe, prop. Jan. 7, 1728, adm. Jan. 21, 1728 [H1]

111. Herriman, Mary, prop. June 30, 1728, adm. July 21, 1728 [H1]

112. Herriman, Sarah, adm. Jan. 31, 1729 [H1]

113. Hinckley, Sarah, prop. Nov. 1, 1724, adm. Nov. 15, 1724 [H1]

114. Howe, Martha, prop. July 27, 1729, adm. Aug. 17, 1729 [H1]

115. Hutchins, Hannah, prop. Aug. 28, 1726, adm. Sept. 18, 1726 [H1]

116. Hutchins, James, prop. Nov. 26, 1727, adm. Dec. 3, 1727 [H1]

117. Hutchins, Zerviah, prop. Aug. 12, 1733, adm. Sept. 2, 1733 [H1]

118. Ingals, Hannah, prop. Mar. 3, 1723, adm. Mar. 31, 1723 [H1]

119. Johnson, Abigail, adm. Mar. 16, 1729 [H1]

120. Johnson, John, prop. Jan. 28, 1728, adm. Feb. 4, 1728 [H1]

121. Johnson, Lydia, prop. Jan. 21, 1728, adm. Feb. 4, 1728 [H1]

122. Johnson, Mary (w. James), prop. Sept. 3, 1721, adm. Sept. 24, 1721 [H1]

123. Johnson, Mary (w. Jonathan), prop. Jan. 7, 1728, adm. Jan. 28, 1728 [H1]

124. Johnson, Mehetabel, prop. May 21, 1727, adm. June 4, 1727 [H1]

125. Johnson, Rachel, prop. Dec. 31, 1727, adm. Jan. 21, 1728 [H1]

126. Johnson, Ruth (d. Thomas), prop. Jan. 14, 1728, adm. Jan. 28, 1728 [H1]

127. Johnson, Ruth (d. Thomas, Jr.), prop. Jan. 14, 1728, adm. Jan. 28, 1728 [H1]

128. Johnson, Susannah, prop. May 5, 1728, adm. May 19, 1728 [H1]
129. Johnson, Susannah (w. Daniel), prop. Nov. 24, 1734, adm. Dec. 1, 1734 [H1]
130. Johnson, Thomas, Jr., prop. Mar. 24, 1728, adm. Apr. 5, 1728 [H1]
131. Johnson, Thomas, prop. Mar. 31, 1728, adm. Apr. 7, 1728 [H1]
132. Kelly, Richard, prop. Jan. 7. 1728, adm. Jan. 21, 1728 [H1]
133. Kelly, Samuel, prop. Aug. 30, 1727, adm. Sept. 13, 1719 [H1]
134. Kimball, Jemima, prop. Nov. 17, 1728, adm. Dec. 1, 1728 [H1]
135. Kimball, Mary, prop. June 21, 1719, adm. July 19, 1719 [H1]
136. Kimball, Richard, adm. Nov. 17, 1734 [H1]
137. Lad, Mary, prop. Nov. 12, 1727, adm. Nov. 26, 1727 [H1]
138. Little, Thomas, prop. Feb. 24, 1734, adm. Mar. 31, 1734 [H1]
139. Lovejoy, Hannah, prop. Mar. 14, 1725, adm. Mar. 28, 1725 [H1]
140. Main, Amos, prop. Sept. 17, 1729 [H1]
141. Marsh, David, prop. Mar. 5, 1727, adm. Mar. 19, 1727 [H1]
142. Marsh, Ephraim, prop. Nov. 30, 1729, adm. Dec. 21, 1729 [H1]
143. Marsh, John, prop. Dec. 10, 1727, adm. Dec. 31, 1727 [H1]
144. Marsh, Sarah, prop. Dec. 10, 1727, adm. Dec. 31, 1727 [H1]
145. McHard, Margaret, adm. Mar. 28, 1736 [H1]
146. Merrill, Lucy, prop. Sept. 13, 1719, adm. Oct. 11, 1719 [H1]
147. Merrill, Lydia, prop. July 9, adm. July 30, 1727 [H1]
148. Merrill, Mary (w. Peter), prop. Aug. 2, 1724, adm. Aug. 22, 1724 [H1]
149. Merrill, Mary (w. Jonathan), prop. June 16, adm. June 30, 1728 [H1]
150. Merrill, Nathan, prop. Nov. 12, 1727, adm. Nov. 26, 1727 [H1]
151. Merrill, Stephen, Jr., prop. Jan. 28, 1728, adm. Feb. 4, 1728 [H1]
152. Messer, John, prop. Nov. 19, 1727, adm. Jan. 7, 1728 [H1]
153. Messer, Mehetabel, prop. Nov. 12, 1727, adm. Nov. 26, 1727 [H1]
154. Messer, Sarah, prop. Nov. 19, 1727, adm. Jan. 7, 1728 [H1]
155. Middleton, Dorothy, prop. Mar. 19, 1721, adm. Apr. 23, 1721 [H1]
156. Mingo, Thomas, prop. July 1736, adm. Sept. 5, 1736 [H1]
157. Mitchell, Andrew, Jr., prop. Nov. 26, 1727, adm. Dec. 3, 1727 [H1]
158. Mitchell, Susannah, prop. Mar. 31, 1728, adm. May 5, 1728 [H1]
159. Osgood, Lydia, prop. Feb. 10, 1734, adm. Mar. 3, 1734 [H1]
160. Page, Abiah, prop. Nov. 10, 1734, adm. Dec. 1, 1734 [H1]
161. Page, Cornelius, prop. Nov. 19, 1728, adm. Jan. 7, 1728 [H1]
162. Page, Edmund, prop. May 5, 1728, adm. May 19, 1728 [H1]
163. Page, Elizabeth (w. Lewis), prop. Mar. 14, 1725, adm. Mar. 28, 1725 [H1]
164. Page, Elizabeth, prop. May 16, 1725, adm. May 30, 1725 [H1]
165. Page, Elizabeth (w. Caleb), adm. Mar. 2, 1729 [H1]
166. Page, Hannah, prop. Nov. 19, 1727, adm. Dec. 1, 1727 [H1]
167. Page, John, prop. Nov. 19, 1727, adm. Dec. 1, 1727 [H1]
168. Page, Joseph, prop. July 21, 1719, adm. Aug. 2, 1719 [H1]
169. Page, Judith, prop. May 15, 1720, adm. June 5, 1720 [H1]
170. Page, Lewis, prop. Dec. 12, 1736, adm. Jan. 2, 1737 [H1]
171. Page, Lydia, prop. Dec. 12, 1736, adm. Jan. 2, 1737 [H1]
172. Page, Mary (w. Joseph), prop. July 19, 1719, adm. Aug. 2, 1719 [H1]

173. Page, Mary (w. Cornelius), prop. Aug. 17, 1735, adm. Aug. 31, 1735 [H1]

174. Page, Nathaniel, prop. Jan. 8, 1721, adm. Jan. 22, 1721 [H1]

175. Page, Susannah, prop. Nov. 19, 1727, adm. Dec. 1, 1727 [H1]

176. Page, Timothy, prop. Aug. 25, 1728, adm. Sept. 29, 1728 [H1]

177. Parker, Bethia, n.d. [adm. Dec. 1, 1728] [H1]

178. Pattee, Elizabeth, prop. Nov. 12, 1727, adm. Nov. 26, 1727 [H1]

179. Pattee, Sarah, prop. June 21, 1719, adm. July 19, 1719 [H1]

180. Peaslee, Abigail, prop. Dec. 3, 1727, adm. Dec. 31, 1727 [H1]

181. Peaslee, Elizabeth, prop. May 12, 1728, adm. May 26, 1728 [H1]

182. Peaslee, Judith, prop. Sept. 10, 1721, adm. Sept. 24, 1721 [H1]

183. Peaslee, Lydia, prop. Dec. 10, 1727, adm. Dec. 31, 1727 [H1]

184. Peaslee, Nathaniel, prop. Dec. 10, 1727, adm. Dec. 31, 1727 [H1]

185. Peaslee, Rebecca, prop. Nov. 5, 1727, adm. Nov. 19, 1727 [H1]

186. Peaslee, Susannah, prop. Aug. 25, 1728, adm. Sept. 29, 1728 [H1]

187. Pike, Hannah, prop. May 19, 1723, adm. June 2, 1723 [H1]

188. Richards, Abigail, prop. Feb. 25, 1728, adm. Mar. 10, 1728 [H1]

189. Roberds, Ephraim, prop. Dec. 10, 1727, adm. Dec. 31, 1727 [H1]

190. Roberds, Hannah, prop. June 18, 1721, adm. July 23, 1721 [H1]

191. Roberds, Martha, prop. July 28, 1728, adm. Aug. 11, 1728 [H1]

192. Rue [Rony], Abigail, prop. Nov. 1719, adm. Dec. 6, 1719 [H1]

193. Sanders, Abigail, prop. July 19, 1719, adm. Aug. 2, 1719 [H1]

194. Sanders, Judith, prop. July 12, 1719, adm. July 26, 1719 [H1]

195. Sanders, Mary, prop. Jan. 7, 1728, adm. Feb. 4, 1728 [H1]

196. Sawyer, John, n.d. [adm. Nov. 24, 1745] [H1]

197. Scribner, Elizabeth, prop. Feb. 4, 1728, adm. Feb. 18, 1728 [H1]

198. Shepard, Hannah, prop. Oct. 1731, adm. Nov. 3, 1731 [H1]

199. Shepard, Samuel, prop. Dec. 7, 1735, adm. Dec. 21, 1735 [H1]

200. Silver, Sarah, prop. July 12, 1719, adm. July 26, 1719 [H1]

201. Silver, Susanna, prop. June 13, 1736, adm. Aug. 1, 1736 [H1]

202. Simonds, Prudence, prop. June 9, 1728, adm. June 23, 1728 [H1]

203. Simonds, Sarah, prop. June 30, 1728, adm. July 21, 1728 [H1]

204. Singletary, Sarah, prop. Jan. 13, 1723, adm. Jan. 27, 1723 [H1]

205. Smith, Abigail, prop. Apr. 4, 1725, adm. May 16, 1725 [H1]

206. Smith, Samuel, prop. Nov. 26, 1727, adm. Dec. 3, 1727 [H1]

207. Smith, Sarah, prop. Nov. 26, 1727, adm. Dec. 3, 1727 [H1]

208. Smith, Susannah, prop. May 3, 1730, adm. May 31, 1730 [H1]

209. Stanly, Ruth, prop. Apr. 28, 1728, adm. May 19, 1728 [H1]

210. Staples, Abigail, prop. Mar. 31, 1728, adm. Apr. 7, 1728 [H1]

211. Staples, Elizabeth (w. Thomas), prop. May 12, 1728, adm. May 26, 1728 [H1]

212. Staples, Elizabeth, prop. June 13, 1736, adm. June 27, 1736 [H1]

213. Staples, Thomas, prop. Jan. 21, 1728, adm. Feb. 2, 1728 [H1]

214. Watts, Dorothy, adm. Apr. 4, 1729 [H1]

215. Webster, Abigail, prop. Oct. 1, 1727, adm. Oct. 22, 1727 [H1]

216. Webster, John, prop. Jan. 28, 1728, adm. Feb. 4, 1728 [H1]

217. Webster, Stephen, prop. Jan. 16, 1732, adm. Jan. 30, 1732 [H1]

218. Webster, Tryphena (w. John), prop. Jan. 28, 1728, adm. Feb. 4, 1728 [H1]

219. Webster, Tryphena, prop. Feb. 28, 1731, adm. Apr. 4, 1731 [H1]

220. Weed, Mary, prop. Mar. 10, 1728, adm. Mar. 31, 1728 [H1]

221. White, Abigail, prop. Dec. 10, 1727, adm. Dec. 31, 1727 [H1]

222. White, James, prop. Mar. 3, 1728, adm. Mar. 31, 1728 [H1]

223. White, Nicholas, prop. Aug. 2, 1719, adm. Aug. 16, 1719 [H1]

224. White, Timothy, prop. July 31, 1720, adm. Aug. 21, 1720 [H1]

225. Whittaker, Jacob, prop. Jan. 7, 1728, adm. Jan. 28, 1728 [H1]

226. Whittaker, Mary (w. Jacob), prop. Nov. 26, 1727, adm. Dec. 3, 1727 [H1]

227. Whittaker, Mary (w. William), prop. Mar. 31, 1728, adm. Apr. 7, 1728 [H1]

228. Whittaker, Sarah, prop. Mar. 24, 1728, adm. Apr. 5, 1728 [H1]

229. Whittaker, William, prop. Jan. 21, 1728, adm. Feb. 2, 1728 [H1]

230. Whittier, Nathaniel, adm. June 1, 1729 [H1]

231. Whittier, William, prop. Feb. 25, 1728, adm. Apr. 7, 1728 [H1]

232. Wilson, Rebecca, prop. Mar. 3, 1728, adm. Apr. 5, 1728 [H1]

233. Wincott, Olive, prop. May 12, 1728, adm. May 26, 1728 [H1]

234. Wise, Abigail, adm. Mar. 7, 1742 [H1]

235. Worthen, Hannah, prop. Mar. 10, 1728, adm. Mar. 31, 1728 [H1]

HEBRON, CONN., FIRST CHURCH (1736–1739)

1. Derby, John, June 21, 1736 [H3]

2. Filer, Samuel, July 12, 1736 [H3]

3. Hutchinson, Aaron, n.d. [circa 1730s] [H3]

4. Hutchinson, Mary, Jan. 15, 1736 [H3]

5. Man, Mercy, n.d. [circa 1730s] [H3]

6. Porter, Abigail, n.d. [circa February 1739] [H3]

7. Porter, David, Jr., n.d. [circa 1730s] [H3]

8. Porter, Joseph, n.d. [circa February 1739] [H3]

9. Post, Thomas, n.d. [circa 1730s] [H3]

10. Root, Rachel, Feb. 23, 1736 [H3][12]

11. Root, Rebecca, n.d. [circa February 1739] [H3]

12. Wright, Aaron, n.d. [circa February 1739] [H3]

13. Wright, Elizabeth, Feb. 9, 1739 [H3]

IPSWICH (NOW ESSEX), MASS., CHEBACCO SEPARATE CHURCH (1750–1816)

1. Allen, Sarah, prop. June 17, 1764, adm. June 29, 1764 [C2]

2. Andrews, Eunice, prop. Aug. 26, 1750, adm. Sept. 16, 1750 [C2][13]

3. Andrews, Lucy, prop. Nov. 11, 1764 [adm. Nov. 21, 1764] [C3][14]

4. Andrews, Martha, n.d. [adm. Mar. 3, 1764] [C2]

5. Bear, Hannah, prop. Aug. 26, 1764 [adm. Oct. 3, 1764] [C2]

6. Bennett, Anna, prop. June 17, 1764, adm. June 29, 1764 [C2]

---

12. Appendix C.

13. Thomas Henry Billings, "The Great Awakening," *EIHC*, LXV (1929), 94–96.

14. Appendix C.

7. Brown, Ebenezer, prop. June 17, 1764, adm. June 29, 1764 [C2]

8. Brown, Sarah, n.d. [adm. Mar. 26, 1764] [C2]

9. Burnham, Abigail, prop. Apr. 22, 1764 [adm. May 4, 1764] [C2]

10. [Burnham, Lucia], adm. Feb. [2], 1765[15]

11. Burnham, Martha, n.d. [adm. Mar. 3, 1764] [C2]

12. Burnham, Nathan, prop. Aug. 26, 1764 [adm. Oct. 3, 1764] [C2]

13. Burnham, Peggy, adm. Aug. 23, 1807 [C1]

14. Burnham, Sukey, adm. Aug. 23, 1807 [C1]

15. Butler, Sarah, prop. Apr. 22, 1764 [adm. May 4, 1764] [C2]

16. Butler, Sarah, Jr., adm. Mar. 30, 1764 [C2]

17. Cheever, Ezekiel, prop. Oct. 13, 1765, [adm. Oct. 30, 1765] [C1]

18. Cheever, John, prop. Aug. 26, 1764 [adm. Oct. 3, 1764] [C2]

19. Choate, Abraham, prop. July 12, 1767 [adm. July 31, 1767] [C2]

20. Choate, Jacob, n.d. [adm. Mar. 3, 1764] [C2]

21. Choate, Sarah, adm. Oct. 31, 1801 [C1]

22. Choate, Thomas, adm. Mar. 30, 1764 [C2]

23. Cleaveland, Abigail, prop. Jan. 23, 1785, adm. Feb. 9, 1785 [C2]

24. Cleaveland, Mary, n.d. [adm. Mar. 3, 1764] [C2]

25. Cogswell, Elizabeth, adm. Sept. 15, 1807 [C1]

26. Cogswell, Phyllis, prop. Apr. 22, 1764 [adm. May 4, 1764] [C2][16]

27. Dodge, Jemima, prop. June 17, 1764, adm. June 29, 1764 [C2]

28. Edwards, Hannah, prop. Nov. 11, 1764 [adm. Nov. 21, 1764] [C2]

29. Eveleth, Sarah, prop. Sept. 16, 1764 [adm. Oct. 3, 1764] [C2]

30. Foster, Bethiah, prop. Feb. 2, 1766 [adm. Feb. 28, 1766] [C2]

31. Galloway, Abigail, prop. June 17, 1764, adm. June 29, 1764 [C2]

32. Giddings, Abigail, prop. Aug. 26, 1764 [adm. Oct. 3, 1764] [C2]

33. Giddings, Daniel, Jr., adm. Mar. 30, 1764 [C2]

34. Haskell, Judith, prop. Aug. 26, 1764 [adm. Oct. 3, 1764] [C2][17]

35. Hassock, Ruth, prop. Aug. 26, 1764 [adm. Oct. 3, 1764] [C2]

36. Holmes, Mercy, adm. Mar. 30, 1764 [C2]

37. Ingersoll, Elizabeth, prop. June 17, 1764, adm. June 29, 1764 [C2]

38. Kinsman, Jeremiah, prop. Apr. 22, 1764 [adm. May 4, 1764] [C2]

39. Kinsman, Sarah, prop. June 17, 1764, adm. June 29, 1764 [C2]

40. Kinsman, Sarah, Jr., prop. Apr. 22, 1764 [adm. May 4, 1764] [C2]

41. Lee, Edward, adm. Mar. 30, 1764 [C2]

15. John Cleaveland, *A Short and Plain Narrative of the Late Work of God's Spirit at Chebacco in Ipswich, in the Years 1763 and 1764* ... (Boston, 1767), 25–31. The "young Woman's" relation that Cleaveland inserted into his published revival narrative corresponds to Lucia Burnham, the only person admitted to full communion in the Chebacco Separate church in February 1765. See Essex, Mass., Second (Separate) Congregational Church Records, 1746–1774, 17, PEM.

16. Erik R. Seeman, "'Justise Must Take Plase': Three African Americans Speak of Religion in Eighteenth-Century New England," *WMQ*, LVI (1999), 413–414.

17. Erik R. Seeman, ed., "Appendix to 'Justise Must Take Plase': Three African Americans Speak of Religion in Eighteenth-Century New England" (available online at *http://oieahc .wm.edu/wmq/Apr99/seeman.html*).

42. Lee, Hannah, prop. June 17, 1764, adm. June 29, 1764 [C2]

43. Lee, Mary, n.d. [adm. Mar. 30, 1764] [C2]

44. Lendal, John, adm. Mar. 30, 1764 [C2]

45. Low, Aaron, prop. Apr. 22, 1764 [adm. May 4, 1764] [C2]

46. Low, Daniel, n.d. [adm. Jan. 2, 1765] [C2]

47. Low, Hannah, n.d. [adm. Mar. 3, 1764] [C2]

48. Low, Mary, n.d. [adm. Mar. 3, 1764] [C2]

49. Low, Rachel, adm. Mar. 30, 1764 [C2][18]

50. Low, Susanna, n.d. [adm. Mar. 3, 1764] [C2][19]

51. Manning, Mary, prop. June 17, 1764, adm. June 29, 1764 [C2]

52. Marshall, Abigail, prop. June 17, 1764, adm. June 29, 1764 [C2]

53. Marshall, Elizabeth, adm. Mar. 30, 1764 [C2]

54. Perkins, Elizabeth, n.d. [adm. Mar. 3, 1764] [C2]

55. Procter, Isaac, n.d. [adm. Mar. 3, 1764] [C2]

56. Procter, Isaac, Jr., adm. Mar. 30, 1764 [C2]

57. Proctor, Lucy, prop. June 17, 1764, adm. June 29, 1764 [C2]

58. Rogers, Mary, prop. Aug. 26, 1764 [adm. Oct. 3, 1764] [C2]

59. Rust, Joseph, prop. Aug. 15, 1771, adm. Sept. 1, 1771 [C2]

60. Rust, Mary, prop. Aug. 26, 1764 [adm. Oct. 3, 1764] [C2][20]

61. Sargeant, Hannah, adm. Mar. 30, 1764 [C2]

62. Sewall, Mary, adm. December 1816 [C1]

63. Story, Lucy, adm. Aug. 25, 1807 [C1]

64. Story, Mary, prop. June 17, 1764, adm. June 29, 1764 [C2][21]

65. Story, Thomas, prop. June 17, 1764, adm. June 29, 1764 [C2]

66. Tarring, Abigail, prop. Aug. 26, 1764 [adm. Oct. 3, 1764] [C2]

67. Tarring, Mary, prop. Oct. 21, 1764 [adm. Nov. 21, 1764] [C2]

68. Williams, Esther, adm. Mar. 30, 1764 [C2]

69. Woodbury, Mary, prop. Feb. 2, 1766 [adm. Feb. 28, 1766] [C2]

70. Unknown, January 1765[22]

MEDFIELD, MASS., FIRST CHURCH (1697–1766)

1. Adams, Elizabeth, adm. June 26, 1720 [M5]

2. Allen, Aaron, adm. Nov. 4, 1739 [M3]

3. Allen, Hannah, adm. July 29, 1739 [M5]

4. Allen, Mary, adm. Apr. 3, 1726 [M5]

5. Allen, Mehetabel, adm. Feb. 27, 1743 [M3]

6. Allen, Sarah, adm. July 11, 1731 [M5]

7. Baker, Hannah, adm. Aug. 21, 1720 [M2]

8. Ballard, William, adm. Mar. 15, 1728 [M3]

9. Barber, Abial (w. Zachariah), adm. June 4, 1699 [M3]

18. Ibid.
19. Ibid.
20. Ibid.
21. Ibid.
22. Cleaveland, *Short and Plain Narrative*, 20–25.

10. Barber, Abial, adm. Sept. 30, 1711 [M3]
11. Barber, George, adm. Aug. 6, 1710 [M1]
12. Barden [Barns], Mehetabel, adm. Mar. 19, 1719 [M6]
13. Battle, Abigail, adm. Jan. 21, 1728 [M6]
14. Bowers, Hannah, adm. Dec. 24, 1727 [M2]
15. Boyden, Keziah, adm. May 11, 1740 [M3]
16. Boyden, Mary, adm. Sept. 25, 1697[23]
17. Bullard, Ebenezer, Jr., adm. Aug. 20, 1738 [M5]
18. Bullard, Eleazar, n.d. [adm. Feb. 10, 1734] [M5]
19. Bullard, Susanna, adm. July 18, 1742 [M5]
20. Bullard, Unknown (w. Josiah), adm. July 29, 1739 [M5]
21. Bullen, Keziah, adm. Dec. 6, 1741 [M5]
22. Bullen, Sarah, adm. Mar. 25, 1739 [M3]
23. Chamberlain, Moses, adm. Mar. 28, 1729 [M3]
24. Chenery, Hannah, adm. May 23, 1742 [M6]
25. Chenery, Rachel, adm. Feb. 27, 1743 [M3]
26. Cheney, Mehetabel, adm. Sept. 26, 1697 [M6]
27. Clap, Hannah, adm. June 8, 1729 [M5]
28. Clap, Joshua, adm. May 16, 1708 [M2]
29. Clap, Mary, adm. June 18, 1704 [M2]
30. Clap, Thomas, adm. Oct. 20, 1728 [M6]
31. Clark, David, adm. Apr. 20, 1735 [M3]
32. Clark, Deborah, adm. June 27, 1731 [M3]
33. Clark, Edward, adm. June 15, 1712 [M3]
34. Clark, Hannah, adm. June 15, 1712 [M3]
35. Clark, Mary, adm. July 6, 1735 [M6]
36. Clark, Mehetabel, adm. July 18, 1742 [M5]
37. Clark, Phebe, adm. Jan. 31, 1742 [M5]
38. Clark, Rowland, adm. Mar. 28, 1742 [M5][24]
39. Clark, Ruth, adm. Feb. 26, 1721 [M5]
40. Clark, Susannah, adm. May 14, 1704 [M6]
41. Clark, Sarah, adm. Feb. 18, 1728 [M5]
42. Cook, Nathan, adm. July 18, 1742 [M5]
43. Daniel, Joseph, Jr., adm. Feb. 21, 1703 [M6]
44. Daniel, Mary, adm. Aug. 30, 1713 [M3]
45. Dwight, Elizabeth, adm. Jan. 16, 1715 [M5]
46. Ellis, Patience, adm. July 16, 1727 [M3]
47. Ellis, Rachel, adm. May 14, 1727 [M6]
48. Evans, Sarah, adm. Mar. 15, 1713 [M3]
49. Evans, Susanna, adm. Nov. 21, 1697 [M6]

23. Ross. W. Beales, Jr., unpublished typescript (circa 1970s) of a missing manuscript previously in the collections of the Medfield Historical Society.

24. Douglas Leo Winiarski, "All Manner of Error and Delusion: Josiah Cotton and the Religious Transformation of Southeastern New England, 1700–1770" (Ph.D. diss., Indiana University, 2000), 396–397.

50. Fales, Peter, Sr., adm. Apr. 1, 1705 [M5]
51. Fales, Peter, Jr., adm. Dec. 26, 1725 [M5]
52. Fisher, Dorcas, adm. July 2, 1738 [M5]
53. Fisher, Hannah, adm. Jan. 2, 1743 [M5]
54. Force, Benjamin, adm. Nov. 28, 1728 [M6]
55. Force, Jemima, adm. Mar. 19, 1727 [M6]
56. Harding, Abraham, n.d. [adm. Apr. 23, 1699] [M5]
57. Harding, Mary, adm. Mar. 26, 1727 [M3]
58. Hinsdale, Susanna, adm. May 3, 1741 [M3]
59. Holbrook, Daniel, adm. Mar. 3, 1728 [M6]
60. Kingsbury, Joanna, adm. Oct. 24, 1724 [M5][25]
61. Lovel, Abigail, adm. Apr. 8, 1711 [M5]
62. Lovel, Alexander, adm. Mar. 14, 1731 [M5]
63. Lovel, Hannah, adm. May 14, 1727 [M5]
64. Lovel, Hopestill, adm. Jan. 31, 1742[26]
65. Lovel, Lydia, adm. Apr. 21, 1728 [M5]
66. Lovel, Nathaniel, adm. Feb. 25, 1705 [M3]
67. Lovel, Rachel, adm. Oct. 19, 1735 [M3]
68. Mason, Abigail, adm. Feb. 1, 1736 [M5]
69. Mason, Elizabeth, adm. Mar. 15, 1713 [M3]
70. Mason, Sarah, adm. Sept. 26, 1742 [M5]
71. Morse, Joshua, adm. July 16, 1727 [M3]
72. Morse, Mary, adm. June 26, 1720 [M6]
73. Morse, Nathaniel, adm. June 17, 1733 [M5]
74. New, James, adm. June 18, 1721 [M6]
75. New, Mary, adm. June 18, 1731 [M6]
76. Noyes, Lydia, adm. Dec. 24, 1727 [M3]
77. Partridge, Eleazar, adm. June 8, 1712 [M2]
78. Partridge, Hannah (w. William), adm. June 18, 1704 [M6]
79. Partridge, Hannah (w. Samuel), adm. May 5, 1706 [M5]
80. Partridge, William, Sr., adm. Feb. 4, 1728 [M5]
81. Partridge, William, Jr., adm. Mar. 31, 1728 [M5]
82. Peters, Hannah, adm. Mar. 3, 1734 [M6]
83. Plimpton, Benjamin, n.d. [adm. Sept. 7, 1729] [M5] (revised draft by Joseph Baxter [M6]).
84. Plimpton, Keziah, adm. May 17, 1730 [M5]
85. Richardson, Hannah, adm. Mar. 15, 1713 [M3]
86. Richardson, Joseph, adm. Mar. 19, 1727 [M6]
87. Robbins, Ebenezer, adm. July 6, 1729 [M6]
88. Rockwood [Rocket], Hannah, adm. Nov. 21, 1697 [M6]
89. Rockwood [Rocket], Josiah, adm. Sept. 12, 1697 [M5]

25. Ibid., 395–396.

26. Beales, unpublished typescript of a missing manuscript previously in the collections of the Medfield Historical Society.

90. Rockwood [Rocket], Mary, adm. Aug. 1, 1697 [M5][27]

91. Sanders, Daniel, n.d. [adm. Jan. 31, 1742] [M5]

92. [Smith, Ezra], adm. Feb. 9, 1766 [M5]

93. Smith, Mary, n.d. [adm. Aug. 30, 1713] [M6]

94. Smith, Nathaniel, Sr., adm. Feb. 11, 1728 [M6]

95. Smith, Nathaniel, Jr., adm. Dec. 6, 1741 [M3]

96. Smith, Ruth, adm. May 6, 1733 [M3]

97. Smith, Samuel, adm. Apr. 28, 1700 [M4][28]

98. Sparhawk, Timothy, adm. Mar. 28, 1742 [M5]

99. Thurston, Joseph, adm. Mar. 2, 1728 [M5]

100. Wight, Joseph, Jr., adm. Mar. 31, 1728 [M6]

101. Wight, Margaret, Aug. 5, 1733 [M6]

102. Wight, Mercy, adm. Feb. 19, 1744 [M5]

103. Wight, Sarah, adm. June 6, 1736 [M6]

104. Unknown (fragment), n.d. [M3]

105. Unknown (fragment), n.d. [M3]

106. Unknown, n.d. [M6]

STURBRIDGE, MASS., FIRST CHURCH (1737–1764)

1. Allen, Lucy, n.d. [adm. May 16, 1762] [S1]

2. Babbitt, Mary, n.d. [adm. July 19, 1761] [S1]

3. Beal, Sarah, n.d [adm. May 16, 1762] [S1]

4. Bond, Martha, adm. Sept. 11, 1757 [S1]

5. Bond, Thaddeus, n.d. [adm. Jan. 20, 1751] [S1]

6. Ellis, Reuben, n.d. [adm. Oct. 28, 1750] [S1]

7. Fay, Abigail, n.d. [adm. May 16, 1762] [S1]

8. Fosket, Jonathan, Jr., n.d. [adm. May 16, 1762] [S1]

9. Foster, Edward, and Rachel, n.d. [adm. May 22, 1737] [S1]

10. Harding, Jemima, prop. Mar. 1, 1764, [adm. Mar. 18, 1764] [S1][29]

11. Hatfield, William and Elizabeth, adm. July 10, 1757 [S1]

12. Holbrook, Moses, n.d. [adm. Nov. 20, 1748] [S1][30]

13. Holbrook, Ruth, n.d. [adm. Nov. 20, 1748] [S1][31]

14. Holbrook, Sarah, adm. Sept. 11, 1757 [S1][32]

15. Howard, Benjamin, n.d. [adm. Mar. 11, 1762] [S1][33]

16. Howard, Thomas, Jr., and Mary, n.d. [adm. Aug. 21, 1757] [S1]

17. Livermore, Rebecca, n.d. [adm. July 22, 1750] [S1]

27. Appendix C.

28. William S. Tilden, *History of the Town of Medfield, Massachusetts, 1650–1886* ... (Boston, 1887), 481–483.

29. Winiarski, "All Manner of Error and Delusion," 402–403.

30. George H. Haynes, *Historical Sketch of the First Congregational Church, Sturbridge, Massachusetts* (Worcester, Mass., 1910), 38–39.

31. Appendix C.

32. Haynes, *Historical Sketch*, 39–40.

33. Ibid., 39.

18. Lyon, Aaron, prop. Dec. 6, 1761, [adm. Jan. 10, 1762] [S1][34]

19. Lyon, Mary, n.d. [adm. Sept. 13, 1761] [S1]

20. Marcy, Elijah, n.d. [adm. Jan. 17, 1763] [S1]

21. Marcy, Miriam, n.d. [adm. Mar. 11, 1762] [S1]

22. Marcy, Sarah, n.d. [adm. Mar. 11, 1762] [S1]

23. Mason, Eunice, adm. May 16, 1762 [S1]

24. Partridge, Sarah, prop. Jan. 3, 1762, [adm. Jan. 10, 1762] [S1]

25. Plimpton, Prudence, prop. July 26, 1761 [adm. Aug. 9, 1761] [S1]

26. Rood, Sarah, Jan. 28, 1762, prop. Jan. 31, 1762 [adm. Feb. 21, 1762] [S1]

27. Rood, Solomon, Jan. 28, 1762, prop. Jan. 31, 1762 [adm. Feb. 21, 1762] [S1]

28. Shumway, Mary, n.d. [adm. Mar. 11, 1762] [S1]

29. Stacy, Isaac, and Elizabeth, prop. Jan. 17, 1763, [adm. Apr. 10, 1763] [S1]

30. Tarbel, John, and Esther, adm. Nov. 12, 1758 [S1]

31. Towne, Benjamin, and Hannah, n.d. [adm. Sept. 8, 1751] [S1]

32. Turner, Silence, n.d. [adm. July 4, 1756] [S1]

33. Upham, Asa, n.d. [adm. Sept. 14, 1762] [S1]

34. Upham, Lydia, n.d. [adm. Sept. 14, 1762] [S1]

35. Upham, Rebecca, n.d. [adm. Sept. 17, 1756] [S1]

36. Ward, Sarah, n.d. [adm. Jan. 20, 1751] [S1]

37. Weld, Joshua and Mary, n.d. [adm. Apr. 3, 1758] [S1]

38. Weld, Moses, and Elizabeth, n.d. [adm. Sept. 18, 1757] [S1]

WESTBOROUGH, MASS., FIRST CHURCH (1736–1786)

1. Ball, Benjamin, adm. [July 4,] 1784 [W3]

2. Ball, Lucy, adm. [July 4,] 1784 [W3]

3. Batherick, Abigail, n.d. [adm. Mar. 17, 1771] [W1]

4. Batherick, Jonathan, n.d. [adm. Mar. 17, 1771] [W1]

5. Batherick, Lydia, n.d. [adm. Aug. 27, 1749] [W1][35]

6. Beals, Elizabeth, prop. Mar. 9, 1764, adm. Mar. 11, 1764 [W1]

7. Beeman, Eleazar, n.d. [adm. Oct. 18, 1741] [W1]

8. Bond, Lydia, n.d. [adm. May 21, 1769] [W1]

9. Bond, Thomas, n.d. [adm. May 21, 1769] [W1]

10. Bowman, Joseph, n.d. [adm. Aug. 28, 1757] [W1]

11. Bradish, Ruth, n.d. [adm. Sept. 2, 1739] [W1]

12. Brigham, Antipas, adm. Oct. 16, 1785 [W3][36]

13. Brigham, Charles, n.d. [adm. Aug. 6, 1749] [W1][37]

14. Brigham, Edmund, n.d. [adm. Apr. 16, 1786] [W3]

15. Brigham, Elizabeth, n.d. [adm. Apr. 16, 1786] [W3]

---

34. Ibid., 38.

35. Winiarski, "New Perspectives on the Northampton Communion Controversy II," *Jonathan Edwards Studies*, IV (2014), 131–132.

36. Heman Packard DeForest and Edward Craig Bates, *The History of Westborough, Massachusetts* (Westborough, Mass., 1891), 205–206.

37. Winiarski, "New Perspectives on the Northampton Communion Controversy II," *Jonathan Edwards Studies*, IV (2014), 137–130.

16. Brigham, Esther, adm. Apr. 19, 1785 [W3]
17. Brigham, Gershom, Jr., adm. Apr. 19, 1785 [W3]
18. Brigham, Gershom III, adm. 1785 [W3]
19. Brigham, Hephzibah, adm. Oct. 16, 1785 [W3]
20. Brigham, Levi, n.d. [adm. Apr. 12, 1747] [W1]
21. Brigham, Mehetabel, n.d. [adm. Nov. 19, 1749] [W1]
22. Brigham, Sarah, adm. 1785 [W3]
23. Brigham, Susanna, n.d. [adm. Apr. 12, 1747] [W1]
24. Broaders, Catherine, n.d. [July 23, 1786] [W3]
25. Buck, Ruth, n.d. [adm. Aug. 16, 1778] [W3]
26. Chamberlain, Edmund, adm. May 1, 1768 [W1]
27. Chamberlain, Ruth, adm. May 1, 1768 [W1]
28. Chase, Mary, adm. June [15], 1760 [W1]
29. Crosby, Hepzibah, n.d. [adm. Apr. 9, 1749] [W1][38]
30. Entwhistle, Mindwell, [adm. May 25,] 1784 [W3]
31. Fay, Benjamin, n.d. [adm. July 26, 1741] [W1]
32. Fay, Deliverance, n.d. [May 29, 1763] [W1]
33. Forbush, Eli, n.d. [adm. Oct. 21, 1744] [W2]
34. Forbush, Hannah, Jr., n.d. [adm. Mar. 3, 1751] [W1]
35. Forbush, Lucy, n.d. [adm. Oct. 5, 1755] [W1]
36. Frost, Ruhamah, adm. Oct. 16, 1785 [W3]
37. Gale, Abigail, n.d. [adm. Apr. 28, 1751] [W1]
38. Gale, Abijah, n.d. [circa early 1750s] [W1]
39. Grout, Hannah, n.d. [adm. Feb. 5, 1764] [W1]
40. Grout, Jonathan, n.d. [adm. Feb. 5, 1764] [W1]
41. Hardy, Constantine, Nov. 27, 1763 [W1]
42. Hardy, Jemima, n.d. [adm. Feb. 12, 1764] [W1]
43. Harrington, Elizabeth, n.d. [adm. Oct. 5, 1740] [W1]
44. Harrington, Joseph, n.d. [adm. Nov. 1, 1767] [W1]
45. Harrington, Ruth, n.d. [adm. Nov. 1, 1767] [W1]
46. How, Martha, n.d. [adm. Feb. 12, 1764] [W1]
47. Kenny, Abigail, adm. Feb. 20, 1774 [W1]
48. Leland, Mehetabel, n.d. [adm. May 25, 1784] [W3]
49. Maynard, Hannah, n.d. [adm. Nov. 8, 1741] [W1]
50. McAllister, Mary, adm. Apr. 29, 1770 [W1]
51. Metcalf, Pelatiah, n.d. [adm. July 27, 1763] [W1]
52. Miller, Elizabeth, n.d. [adm. Nov. 19, 1749] [W1]
53. Miller, Elizabeth, 1784 [adm. Dec. 14, 1783] [W3]
54. Miller, Fortunatus, n.d. [adm. Dec. 14, 1783] [W3]
55. Miller, Huldah, Apr. 18, 1785 [W3]
56. Miller, Isaac, n.d. [adm. May 27, 1764] [W1]
57. Miller, Mary, n.d. [adm. Sept. 28, 1766] [W1]
58. Nurse, Sarah, n.d. [adm. Aug. 21, 1785] [W3]

38. Ibid., 124–126.

59. Parkman, William, n.d. [adm. Feb. 23, 1766] [W3]
60. Rice, Adam, n.d. [adm. May 1, 1763] [W1]
61. Rice, Anna, adm. Aug. [29], 1736 [W1]
62. Rice, Eunice, n.d. [adm. Oct. 5, 1755] [W1]
63. Rice, Hannah, n.d. [adm. Aug. 12, 1764] [W1]
64. Rice, Lois, n.d. [adm. May 1, 1763] [W1]
65. Rice, Priscilla, n.d. [adm. June 19, 1763] [W1]
66. Rice, Prudence, n.d. [adm. July 29, 1770] [W1]
67. Rice, Zebulon, prop. May 21, 1743, [adm. June 5, 1743] [W1]
68. Robbins, Eleanor, n.d. [adm. July 23, 1786] [W3]
69. Robbins, Joseph, n.d. [adm. July 23, 1786] [W3]
70. Sever, Lucy, n.d. [adm. Mar. 16, 1766] [W1]
71. Smith, Ezekiel, n.d. [adm. Oct. 19, 1766] [W1]
72. Smith, Ruth, n.d. [adm. Oct. 19, 1766] [W1]
73. Snow, Hannah, adm. July 16, 1769 [W1]
74. Snow, Jabez, Jr., adm. July 16, 1769 [W1]
75. Tainter, Benjamin, adm. Nov. [6], 1748 [W1][39]
76. Warrin, Mary, n.d. [adm. Aug. 27, 1738] [W1]
77. Warrin, Moses, n.d. [adm. Nov. 30, 1752] [W1]
78. Warrin, Persis, n.d. [adm. Nov. 30, 1752] [W1]
79. Wheelock, Abigail, adm. Aug. 21, 1785 [W3]
80. Whipple, Francis, Jr., n.d. [adm. Oct. 16, 1766] [W1]
81. Whitney, Eli, adm. Dec. 6, 1767 [W1][40]
82. Whitney, Elizabeth, adm. Dec. 6, 1767 [W1]
83. Wood, John, adm. Feb. 3, 1765 [W1]
84. Wood, Martha, adm. Feb. 3, 1765 [W1]

39. Ibid., 122–123.
40. Appendix C.

Selected Relations of Faith, 1697–1801

The thirteen church admission relations that follow chronicle the evolution of this distinctive genre of early American religious literature from the 1690s, when written testimonies replaced oral narratives, to the early 1800s, by which time the practice had fallen out of favor in most Congregational churches. The decade-by-decade sample includes classic examples of the godly walk paradigm described in Part 1 of this study as well as relations that incorporate the controversial aspects of the Whitefieldian revivals of the 1740s, including reports of itinerant preaching and references to biblical impulses.[1]

Eighteenth-century relations were composed by ministers and lay people with a wide range of literacy skills. I have attempted to reproduce the texts as they were originally written, with a few notable exceptions. Transcriptions follow the expanded method described in Mary-Jo Kline, *A Guide to Documentary Editing*, 2d ed. (Baltimore, 1998), 157–158, 161–164, and Samuel Eliot Morison, "Care and Editing of Manuscripts," in Frank Freidel, ed., *The Harvard Guide to American History*, rev. ed., 2 vols. (Cambridge, Mass., 1974), I, 28–31. Conjectural readings, grossly misspelled or missing words, and scriptural references appear in square brackets. I have supplied the date on which the candidate was admitted (adm.) to

1. For additional published collections of eighteenth-century church admission testimonies, see Appendix B as well as George Faber Clark, *A History of the Town of Norton, Bristol County, Massachusetts, from 1669–1859* (Boston, 1859), 71–72; J. M. Bumsted, ed., "Emotion in Colonial America: Some Relations of Conversion Experience in Freetown, Massachusetts, 1749–1770," *NEQ*, XLIX (1976), 97–108; Kenneth P. Minkema, ed., "The East Windsor Conversion Relations, 1700–1725," *CHS Bulletin*, LI (1986), 7–63; Minkema, ed., "A Great Awakening Conversion: The Relation of Samuel Belcher," *WMQ*, XLIV (1987), 121–126; Minkema, ed., "The Lynn End 'Earthquake' Relations of 1727," *NEQ*, LXIX (1996), 473–499; Erik R. Seeman, "Lay Conversion Narratives: Investigating Ministerial Intervention," *NEQ*, LXXI (1998), 629–634; Douglas Leo Winiarski, "All Manner of Error and Delusion: Josiah Cotton and the Religious Transformation of Southeastern New England, 1700–1770" (Ph.D. diss., Indiana University, 2000), 394–405; James F. Cooper, Jr., "Cuffee's 'Relation': A Faithful Slave Speaks through the Project for the Preservation of Congregational Church Records," *NEQ*, LXXXVI (2013), 293–310; and Winiarski, "New Perspectives on the Northampton Communion Controversy II: Relations, Professions, and Experiences, 1748–1760," *Jonathan Edwards Studies*, IV (2014), 110–145. Several of the largest collections of eighteenth-century relations are available online at NEHH.

full communion when this information is missing from the manuscript. The accompanying notes provide biographical sketches and information on the physical characteristics of the manuscripts.

MARY ROCKWOOD [ROCKET], MEDFIELD, MASS., AUGUST 1, 1697[2]

In my youthful days my Parents were often instructing of me, and exhorting me to love, feare, and serve God. But I was apt to set light by their counsels, and Exhortations, thinking that I was young, and it would be time enough hereafter to mind the concerns of my soule, and thus I was putting off my repentance time after time, and neglecting of my worke. Afterwards I entred into a married estate wherein I met with many sorrowes, troubles, and afflictions, which did something awaken me. But I still ramained cold unto my duty, and did not bring forth that early fruite unto God, which I ought to beare unto him: but was still delaying, and putting off my worke. After this it pleased God to take away my Father suddenly by death,[3] without giving me leave to heare anything from him which Sorely troubled me because the words of dying Persons, and especially of dying relations doe usually take impression on those that doe survive. Hereupon I was sorely troubled thinking that God was angry with me. That place of Scripture coming to my mind in Matthew 3:10, The Axe is now laid to the root of the tree, every tree which brings not forth good fruite is cutt downe, and cast into the fire. This startled me I fearing that the axe was now laid to the root of the tree, and that I was in danger of being cutt downe for my unfruitfulnesse, and so I remained a long time in greate trouble of minde thinking that if any of Gods People knew my condition they would pray hard for me. But yet I was prevailed with by Satan to keep his counsel, and not make knowne my case, and condition to any, until it pleased God that my mother came to me, and seeing me in a Dejected Posture desired to knowe what was the reason of it. When I told her she encouraged me to pray hard to God, and endeavoured to comfort me with many promises as that in Isaiah 55:7, let the wicked forsake his way, and the unrighteous man his thoughts, and let him returne unto the lord and I will have mercy upon him, and unto our God, and he will abundantly pardon and other promises [she] mentioned. Still I thought that these did not belong unto me. My mother counselled me still to pray to God. But I thought I could not pray so well as others could, and that God would not heare me. Then Those words came to my mind in Isaiah 38:14, like a crane, or a Swallowe so did I chatter, which words were a greate comfort to me. I thought that if I prayed so well as

2. Mary, the daughter of Benjamin and Mary (Riggs) Twitchell, was born in Dorchester, Massachusetts, on September 1, 1658. She married Josiah Rockwood, or Rocket, a soldier in King Phillip's War, in 1677 and died in 1699. The Rockwoods had eight children born in Medfield between 1677 and 1696. Ralph Emerson Twitchell, comp. and ed., *Genealogy of the Twitchell Family: Record of the Descendants of the Puritan—Benjamin Twitchell—Dorchester, Lancaster, Medfield, and Sherborn, Massachusetts, 1632-1927* (New York, 1929), 12–13; William S. Tilden, ed., *History of the Town of Medfield, Massachusetts, 1650-1886 . . .* (Boston, 1887), 472–473.

3. Puritan immigrant Benjamin Twitchell was killed during a native American raid on Medfield at the outset of King Phillip's War in 1676. See Twitchell, comp. and ed., *Genealogy of the Twitchell Family*, 2–3.

I could God would heare my prayers. But then againe I fell into doubts, and fears, and discouragements, thinking that I was such a Poor Sinful Creature that none of the promises did belong to me, till I heard Mr. Wilson[4] in a sermon wherein he shewed that Poor doubting Souls who were afraid that none of the promises belonged to them might know that such promises belong to them if they came to them at such times when they are under doubts, and discouragements, whose Discourse at that time did suite my condition as well as if he had been acquainted therewithal. After this I was encouraged to be earnest with God in prayer and to lay hold on the promises which are made by God in his worde. And although I have been many times labouring under doubts, and discouragements, yet God hath helped me to be committing my case unto him, and to be going unto him by prayer, whereby I have often found greate comfort, and encouragement, and have been desiring to cast myselfe upon the lord Jesus Christ, and to waite upon him in the enjoyment of all his holy Ordinances. I have formerly had longing desires to come unto the lords supper, but to my greate sorrowe did neglect it untill I was deprived of an opportunity, and now lately hearing Mr. Green[5] who shewed that if a Person had a sparke of true Grace he had better come to the lords table then stay away, I was hereby greatly encouraged to come. And then soon after It was shewed that it is the Indispensable duty of all to get themselves prepared for, and come unto the table of the lord from those words in 1 Corinthians 11:24, This doe in remembrance of me. It was convincingly laid before me that it was my unquestionable duty to get myself prepared with a wedding garment [Matt. 22:11–12], and come unto the supper of the lord. Since which time I thought I could have no quiet (it being such an unquestionable duty) without coming unto this ordinance. And now finding in myselfe hungring, and thirsting desires after the same, I doe humbly offer myselfe to this church that I may enjoye all the ordinances of Christ, earnestly begging the prayers of all Gods People that I may be enabled to walke as becomes all those that doe enter into solemne engagements to be the lords.[6]

4. John Wilson (1621–1691) graduated from Harvard College in 1642 and settled in Medfield, where he served for nearly four decades as the town's first schoolmaster, physician, and minister. *SHG,* I, 65–66.

5. This is probably a reference to Joseph Green (1675–1715), a 1695 graduate of Harvard College who served as schoolmaster in Roxbury and might have been one of the thirty-six candidates who preached on probation in Medfield before 1696, when the church called Joseph Baxter. Green eventually secured a pastorate in the troubled parish of Salem Village in 1697. The tone of the sacramental sermon described in Rockwood's relation is consistent with the stern letters on the subject that Green circulated among his relatives during the 1690s, for which see Part 1, note 39, above. For Green's life and career, see *SHG,* IV, 228–233. Rockwood's preceding allusion to being "deprived of an opportunity" to participate in the Lord's Supper likely refers to the death of Medfield minister John Wilson during the summer of 1691.

6. Relation of Mary Rockwood [Rocket], August 1, 1697, Miscellaneous Church Records, 1693–1857, Medfield Historical Society, Medfield, Mass. Medfield minister Joseph Baxter composed Rockwood's relation on the inner sides of a large folded sheet of paper. His notation on the front side reads "The Relation of Mary Rocket the wife of Josiah Rocket., who was received to full communion August 1st 1697."

ANONYMOUS, PERHAPS PLYMOUTH, MASS., FIRST CHURCH, N.D.
[EARLY EIGHTEENTH CENTURY]

I desire to be [thankful] to God that i was brought up in a Land of Light [where] Gods word has bin sow ofen sounding in my ears. [God's] marsys [mercies] to mee have been very Grat and distinguishing in spareing my Life hearuntoo. I was entered into Covenant with God by Baptism and was then brought under strong ingagements to be the Lords. But I Ecknledge [acknowledge] I have been going too much astray from God in the ways of sin. I blieve that the souels of believers are at their death made Perfect in holiness. I have had a Grate desire for sum time to Gine [join] to the Church but i have been under feeirs [fears] Least i shold Cum unwothly [unworthily] and so eat and drink my one [own] damnation [1 Cor. 11: 29] but the Considdarration of the Cummand of Crist and of my Grate need of a inttrest in him has brought mee to a reslution not to stay away anni Longer. Thear are many Places in Gods word wich made mee feere Lest I shold Cum unworthely and so eat and drink my one [own] damnation but Cum unto mee all ye that Labore and are heavey Laden and i will Give you Rest [Matt. 11:28] Witch much incurridged mee hoping to find Rest for my souel. I doo belive that God has bin striveing with mee in his word and by his Providencs But they have been worn of [off] too much allreddy. I have been awakened of Lat by a flash of Lightning which was very neer wich Put in mind that dath may Come suddenly. I feere Lest Cuming sudingly it shold finding mee unprepared. I belive in the Holy Gost the Lord and giver of Life who Proceedeth from the father and the son.[7]

BENJAMIN PHINNEY, BARNSTABLE, MASS., WEST PARISH CHURCH, N.D.
[ADM. JUNE 30, 1717][8]

I desire to bless God that I was born in a land of light and have set under the dispensation of the gosple and that I was born of Godly parents who have instructed me in [the] ways of God and instilled into me the principles of religion and often told me the danger I was in while I remained in a natural and unconverted state,

---

7. Anonymous relation, n.d. [early eighteenth century], Individual Manuscripts Collection, PHM. This unsigned and undated relation was composed on the front side of a single sheet of paper. Based on the provenance of the manuscript, the candidate likely lived in Plymouth or a neighboring town in southeastern Massachusetts. The content of the testimony is consistent with relations composed elsewhere in New England during the first half of the eighteenth century. A later notation in a different hand, written sideways along the edge of the back side, reads: "No. 3 / Relation etc."

8. Born in Barnstable on June 18, 1682, Benjamin, the son of John and Mary (Rogers) Phinney, married Martha Crocker in 1709 and Elizabeth Ames in 1747. Several months after his admission to the west parish church, Phinney presented three children for baptism; he and his first wife, who joined the church in 1719, brought three additional children to the sacrament between 1718 and 1723. Phinney was a middling yeoman farmer and an active participant in town affairs. He died in Barnstable in 1758. See Robert J. Dunkle, trans., *Records of Barnstable, Massachusetts*, CD-ROM (Boston, 2002); Howard Finney, Sr., comp., *Finney-Phinney Families in America: Descendants of John Finney of Plymouth and Barnstable, Mass., and of Bristol, R. I., of Samuel Finney of Philadelphia, Pa., and of Robert Finney of New London, Pa.* (Richmond, Va., 1957), 2, 5–6.

biding of me to remember my creator in the days of my youth [Ecc. 12:1]. I have been many times under convictions but they have worn off and I have returned again to my Sinful course. I thought it was time enough for me to repent and mind the Affair of my immortal Soul til god awakened me by an awfull providence in taking away one [of] my intimate frinds by death. This put me upon Seeking earnestly to God that he would fit me for Such a great change. But these good beginings Soon wore of [off] and I returned again to my former course of Sin So that I have Cause to Say with the Psalmist *O Lord remember not against me the Sins of my youth* [Ps. 25:7]. I hope I was brought to See my own wretchedness by nature and how vile and miserable I had made myself by my actual transgressions. I hope I was brought to See the need I stood in of Christ. But I was afraid to come to Christ my Sins were So many and So great. But that place of Scripture came to my mind Revelation 20:8 but the fearfull and unbelieving Shall have their part in that Lake *wich burns with* fire and brimstone. I thought I would earnestly look after the enternel welfare of my immortal soul, and did desire to lay hold on the promises and *that place of Scripture* was an incouragement to me Matthew *11:28* and *55* of Isaiah 1. So also 1 of Isaiah 18. I hope I can truly Say that I desire to come to Christ and depend on him alone for life and Salvation. God was pleased after Some time to bring me into a married State where I met with new duties and new difficulties. I often set about the great duty of Secret prayer and family prayer but with much deadness, dullness and lukewareness. Those words came often into my mind cursed be he that doth the work of the Lord deceitfully [Jer. 48:10] which put me on praying to God that he would enable me to Serve him better and more Sincerely. When God was pleased to lay his hand on any of mine I was ready to make promises that if God would be pleased to restore them I would not neglect to bring them under the wing of the covenant, but Still being under temptation to neglect it. That place came into my mind 5 of Ecclesiastes 4, when thou vowest a vow uttered to God defer not to pay it for he hath no pleasure in fools. I desire to be humbled before God for all my Sins. I desire to take Christ for my prince and Saviour. I desire to take him in all his offices, and I hope I am longing to injoy him in all his ordinances and of late by the preaching of the word I have been Stired up to consider my duty and consult my interest. I desire to joyn in communion with this church if Gods people Shall think me fit beging your prayers for me that God would enable me to work out my own salvation with fear and trembling [Phil. 2:12] and that he would keep me by his almighty power through faith unto salvation.

Benjamin Phinney[9]

9. Relation of Benjamin Phinney, n.d. [adm. June 30, 1717], Lemuel Shaw Papers, 1648–1923, microfilm, reel 1, MHS. Phinney's relation was composed on the front side of a large sheet of paper. The undated manuscript has been mislabeled "1748?" on the back.

HANNAH FORD, HAVERHILL, MASS., FIRST CHURCH, DECEMBER 1, 1727[10]

Im Sensible I'm a very great Sinner and without a Christ to pardon me I'm miserable and undone. When I was young I was exercised with weakness and God was striving with me by many Convictions. I had then thots of offering myself to the Church, but when I came to gain strength again, I grew more wild and wicked than ever. Now since I renewed my Covenant[11] I have had tho'ts of it again but thot I woud tarry till I was more fit for it. But now under the Great Earthquake I tho't the day of Judgment was come and I was in great Horror. The first and greatest Sin that came to my mind, was that I had under all [of] God's Mercies been crucifying † [Christ] all my days. I thot I was then as one of the Foolish Virgins [Matt. 25]. But I found there was nowhere to go but to God to put confidence in him and if I perished to perish at his feet, and gave myself to God as well as I could. In the midst of my distress the 46 psalm was a great Encouragment to me. I promised if God woud spare me I would lead a new Life. I desire accordingly now to come to the Lords Table. I desire to come renouncing my own Righteousness. I desire to return Thanks to God in giving me so long space of time to consider my Evil ways. [I] desire never to forget his Goodness and Mercy to me. [I] desire to give myself to God and the Church. [I] desire their prayers for me that I may be a Welcome Guest, that I maynt come unworthily so as to eat and drink Judgment to myself [1 Cor. 11:29].

Hannah Ford[12]

10. Born in Haverhill on February 19, 1705, and baptized later that year, Hannah, the daughter of James and Lydia (Ross) Ford, married Timothy Clement in 1728. During the next three years, they presented the first two of their ten children for baptism before moving to the new settlement of Pennacook (now Concord), N.H. The Clements returned to Haverhill during the Seven Years' War. Hannah died sometime after 1749. See Kathleen Canney Barber, Janet Ireland Delorey, and Alan Bruce Sherman, "The Ross Families of Ipswich, Massachusetts," *NEHGR*, CLVII (2003), 234–236; *Vital Records of Haverhill, Massachusetts, to the End of the Year 1849*, 2 vols. (Topsfield, Mass., 1910–1911), I, 66–69, 127, II, 121; Mary F. M. Raymond, comp., "Records of First Parish, Haverhill," 2 vols., II, 88, 103, unpublished mss, 1895, Haverhill Public Library, Haverhill, Mass.

11. Hannah Ford owned the covenant in Haverhill on June 18, 1727. See Raymond, comp., "Records of First Parish, Haverhill," II, 76.

12. Relation of Hannah Ford, December 1, 1727, Haverhill, Mass., First Congregational Church Records, 1719–2012, CL (available online at NEHH). As with most of the relations he composed for his parishioners, Haverhill minister John Brown wrote Ford's testimony on a small, trimmed sheet of paper. He docketed the relation by folding it in half, inscribing Ford's name at the top of the back side, assigning an identification number (208), and noting the date on which she was propounded (Nov. 12, 1727) and admitted to full communion.

RACHEL ROOT, HEBRON, CONN., FIRST CHURCH, FEBRUARY 23, 1736[13]

Sometime Last summer I began to be more Concernd for my soul than ever I had been before; and began to seek God more earnestly and to shun and avoid sin; but Continuing under concern, for some time at Length began as I tho't to perform duty better than I had done, whereupon was ready to conclude there was some good in me. I tho't I Loved God and his ways better than the ⊙ [world] and Sin and vanity, and was encouraged to hope that I was in a right way and shou'd obtain my [salvation] but was soon convinc'd that I trusted to my own righteousness, and brot into great distress again, and now my own duties seemed to fail me, and my way seem'd to be hedged up, that I Coudn't turn to the right hand or the Left nor go forward, and Close behind me seem'd Like hell as if one step back wo'd place me in hell. In this time I had fearful apprehensions of Hell, and seem'd as it were to see the flames, Smell the Scent of that horrible pit. In this distress those words of † [Christ] come unto me all ye that Labour and are heavy Laden etc. [Matt. 11: 28] were Comforting to me but yet my way seemed to be block'd up, that I codn't [couldn't] take a step forwards, and was also pressed down and almost overborn with the burden of my sins. Whereupon I had these thots cast thy burden upon the Lord and he will deliver thy Soul [Ps. 55:22]. I seemed now to dispair of help in myself, and if I had any hope it was in god, and Soon after this I seem'd as it were to break thro the opposition that was in the way, and having got thro, I seemd to see + [Christ] stand with open arms to receive me. Whereupon I was filld with Joy, and my heart went forth in praises to god and + [Christ] for the great deliverance and enlargement granted me. I thot I wanted to have everybody Join with me in praising god. I seemd to have a Love for god and + [Christ], and have since found my soul much ravishd with his Love, So that I Coud willingly part with all for him, and have even Longed to depart and be with him, tho I am sometimes in darkness, and find my heart too far from God and too much set upon the ⊙ [world], but yet I have a hope that God has begun his work in my soul which shall be Carried on to perfection [Phil. 1:6]. I desire to wait upon god in all his ordinances and to Sit down at his table and desire the prayers of the Church for me that I maynt be [an] unworthy partaker etc.

Rachel Root[14]

13. Rachel, the daughter of Daniel Root of Northampton, Mass., was born in Hebron, Conn., on December 28, 1721. She married Zerubbabel Rollo in 1738. They had six children born in Hebron between 1739 and 1755. See James Pierce Root, *Root Genealogical Records, 1600-1870, Comprising the General History of the Root and Roots Families in America* (New York, 1870), 111; and John Hollenbeck Rollo, [comp.], *A Genealogical Records of the Descendants of Alexander Rollo, of East Haddam, Conn., 1685-1895* (Wilmington, Del., 1896), 8-9.

14. Relation of Rachel Root, February 23, 1736, box 1, Pomeroy Family Papers, 1735-1817, CHS. Hebron minister Benjamin Pomeroy composed Root's relation on both sides of a small sheet of paper. His notation at the top of the front side reads "The Relation of Rachel Root, Written February 23, 1735/6." Pomeroy inscribed Root's name twice on the back side of the manuscript.

REBECCA COBURN, BOSTON, FIRST CHURCH, NOVEMBER 25, 1739[15]

I was in my Infancy Given up to god in Baptism and in my Childhood often put in mind of the Engagements I Ly under to keep all Gods holy Commandments. And I have had Great Experience of the Goodness of god to me through the whole course of my life, which Should have Led me to repentance. And I hope I am made heartily Sorry for all my Sins and brought to Abhor sin as the Worst of Evills. The Spiritt of God hath been often Striving with me, and I hope and trust not altogether in Vain, but has made some Saving Impressions on my Soul. I have been verry thoughtfull of renewing my Baptismall Covenant and Coming to the table Christs, but fears and Doubts have kept me back, Least Coming Unworthily, I Should Eat and Drink Judgment to myself [1 Cor. 11:29]. But I have been Encouraged by Such texts of Scripture as these: in Isaiah the 55th and 1st, Ho Every One that thirsteth come ye to the Waters and he that hath no money come ye buy and Eat yea come buy wine and milk without money and without Price. John the 6th and 37th, him that Cometh unto me I will in no wise Cast out. The blood of Jesus Christ his Son Cleanseth us from all Sin [1 John 1:7]. I Desire to Come Unto Christ weary and heavy Laden that I may find rest unto my Soul [Matt. 11:28]. I hope God has made me in some measure Sensible of my Sin and Error, in neglecting that Command of my Saviour Jesus Christ, who hath Said do this in remembrance of me [Luke 22:19; 1 Cor. 11:24]. And I am Come to a Resolution that I Will by the help of Gods Grace have respect to this as well as all other Gods Commands, hoping that in the Use of this Ordinance I Shall be growing in Grace and in the knowledge of my Lord and Saviour Jesus Christ. I Ask your Acceptance of me into your Communion, and prayers for me, that I may walk worthy of the Lord Jesus Christ, to all pleasing.

Rebecca Coburn[16]

---

15. Rebecca, daughter of Samuel and Susanna (Heaton) Hill of Charlestown, Massachusetts, was baptized on May 18, 1718, and married Ebenezer Coburn in Boston in 1736. Her husband, also a full member of Boston's First Church, expressed his distaste for the irregularities of the Whitefieldian revivals by subscribing to Charles Chauncy's *Seasonable Thoughts on the State of Religion in New-England.* The Coburns had seven children between 1737 and 1746, all of whom were baptized in a timely fashion. Rebecca likely died from childbirth complications. Her gravestone, bearing the date February 10, 1746 [1747], still stands in Boston's historic Granary Burying Ground. See Thomas Bellows Wyman, *The Genealogies and Estates of Charlestown, in the County of Middlesex and Commonwealth of Massachusetts, 1629–1818,* 2 vols. (Boston, 1879), I, 500; George A. Gordon and Silas R. Coburn, comp., *Genealogy of the Descendants of Edward Colburn/Coburn* ... (Lowell, Mass., 1913), 31; Richard D. Pierce, ed., *The Records of the First Church in Boston, 1630–1868,* CSM, *Publications,* XXXIX–XL (Boston, 1961), 114–115, 406, 408, 411–412, 414; Charles Chauncy, *Seasonable Thoughts on the State of Religion in New-England* ... (Boston, 1743), 5; *A Report of the Record Commissioners of the City of Boston, containing Boston Births from A.D. 1700 to A.D. 1800,* XXIV (Boston, 1894), 228, 232, 239, 242, 248, 252, 259; and *Gravestone Inscriptions and Records of Tomb Burials in the Granary Burying Ground, Boston, Mass.* (Salem, Mass., 1918), 64.

16. Relation of Rebecca Coburn, n.d. [adm. Nov. 25, 1739], Thomas Foxcroft Papers, 1690–1770, Mark and Llora Bortman Collection, HGARC. Boston minister Thomas Foxcroft

SAMUEL FAYERWEATHER, BOSTON, OLD SOUTH CHURCH, N.D.

[ADM. MAY 24, 1741][17]

I Desire to[18] Praise Almighty God for his Infinite goodness to me, in casting my lot in a land of Gospel Light, and in favouring me with the unspeakable Priviledge of Baptism[19] in my infant days, and also in enabling my Parents to bring me up in the nurture and Admonition of the Lord [Eph. 6:4], and for their putting me in mind of remembring my Creator in the days of my youth [Ecc. 12:1]; but alas I cannot but[20] be ashamed to think, how little I regarded them, and how ill I have treated my Dear Redeemer, who has been striving with me so long by his holy Spirit, and calling me to accept of him, but instead of accepting him, I have been crucifying him, and doing everything that is Displeasing in his Sight. For I thought it was time enough to serve God, when I come to be old, and so I put it of [off] with the Evil Day [Amos 6:3]; yet I always was Conscientious in keeping up a Form of Religion,[21] and thought that was enough tho' I did not abstain from Sin, which I apprehend, proceeded from the force of my Ignorance and Blindness. But O astonishing goodness of God in exercising so much Patience and Forbearance towards me, and in Discovering to me my Error and Danger which he has of late done by his Faithful ministers. He has shown me that I was a lost and undone Creature without Christ, and that the Foundation I had been building my hopes of Salvation upon was false, and behold when I came to myself, I thought what a

---

composed Coburn's relation on both sides of a small folded sheet of paper. Coburn appears to have signed the document. For reasons that remain unclear, Foxcroft or another person later placed a pair of darkly etched parentheses around the biblical texts in Coburn's relation from "in Isaiah the 55th and 1st" to "John the 6th and 37th."

17. Samuel, the son of Thomas, a prominent merchant, and Hannah (Waldo), Fayerweather, was born in Boston on February 3, 1725. Graduating from Harvard College in 1743, he served as a chaplain during the New England expedition against the French fortress at Louisbourg and preached on probation in Boston and the surrounding towns. Unable to secure a regular pastorate in New England, Fayerweather lived for a time in Georgia and South Carolina, where he turned down an offer to serve as the junior colleague to Charleston's prominent Presbyterian minister, Josiah Smith. After several additional false starts in Wells, Maine, New Haven, Connecticut, and Newport, Rhode Island, Fayerweather eventually traveled to England in 1755, where he was awarded an honorary degree from Cambridge University and was ordained as a missionary in the Society for the Propagation of the Gospel in Foreign Parts. He returned to the colonies in 1757 and served several small Anglican parishes in South Carolina before finally securing a permanent position at Saint Paul's Episcopal Church in North Kingston, Rhode Island. Fayerweather married Abigail Hazard in 1763. He resigned his pastorate in 1774 after refusing to read prayers on behalf of George III and died in 1781. See *SHG*, XI, 221–229.

18. Deleted, perhaps by Boston's Old South Church minister Thomas Prince, Sr.: "~~Bless and~~."

19. Deleted: "~~which I enjoyed~~." Fayerweather was baptized in Boston's First Church, where his mother was a member in full communion, on February 7, 1725. See Pierce, ed., *Records of the First Church in Boston*, CSM, *Pubs.*, XXXIX–XL (Boston, 1961), XXXIX, 109, XL, 393.

20. Deleted: "~~Blush and~~."

21. Prince corrected Fayerweather's original phrasing, which read: "but I always kept up a Form of Religion."

Prodigal I had been, and how miserable I should be If I died in that State, and so I resolved to return to my Heavenly Father, Confessing and forsaking all of my Sins, and in Expectation of finding Mercy and Favour with God, since that Jesus Christ came into the world to save Sinners [1 Tim. 1:15]. I was incouraged to seek him, and I resolved by the assistance of God to seek till I died; but I found many oppositions in the way, and was toss'd to' and Fro' with the temptations of the Devil,[22] but I trust God has appeared for me, and delivered me out of them all, and that I have found him whom my Soul Loveth. O how Sweet is Christ *he is altogether Lovely and the Chief among Ten thousands* [Song. 5:10, 5:16]. There is nothing to be compared with his Love, for it passes all understanding [Phil. 4:7]. O What reason have I to Lie down in the Dust, and admire the free and Soveraign Grace of God, that he should pluck me as a Firebrand out of the Burning [Amos 4:11], and make me a Partaker of his Love, when most part of the world are Destitute of it. *Bless the Lord O my Soul and forget not all his Benefits* [Ps. 103:2]. And seeing God has thus manifested himself unto such a poor wretch as I am, it should be an Incouragement to all young People to seek Christ in their early Days. For the Lord has said *I Love them that Love me, and those that seek me early shall find me* [Prov. 8:17]. And when he was upon Earth, he invited Children to come to him, *and he took them up in his Arms and laid his hands upon them and Blessed them* [Mk. 10: 16], and so he will do by you. O dont my Dear young Brethren refuse this Blessed Jesus who invites you to come to him, and stands with open Arms ready to receive you. And those of you that are under Convictions, as I trust there is some here, be incouraged to seek the Lord now while he is near to you [Is. 55:6], and dont Grieve his Blessed Spirit to withdraw from You, for if you do, God knows whether you will ever have another Opportunity, and remember now you have put your hands to the Plough, and if you look back, you will not be fitt for the Kingdom of God [Luke 9:62]. O be incouraged then to keep on Seeking, and dont rest short of Christ and I hope you will in his due time find him. Think of the Glorious Physician which God has provided for you sin sick Souls, and think of the willingness of Christ to accept of you that so you may be animated and enlivened in your Christian Course.

And now I would account it a faithful Saying and worthy of all acceptation, that Jesus Christ came into the world to save Sinners of whom I am the Chief [1 Tim. 1:15]. And as I believe the Holy Scriptures to be Given by Inspiration of God, as a Perfect Rule of Faith and Life, and the Assemblies Shorter Catechism to be [for] the substance agreable to them,[23] I do resolve by the assistance of God, to shun

22. In January 1741, Henry Flynt noted in his diary that several Harvard College students had experienced visions, including Fayerweather, who "pretended to see the divil in [the] Shape of a bear coming to his bedside." See Edward T. Dunn, ed., "The Diary of Tutor Henry Flynt of Harvard College, 1675–1760," 3 vols., typescript (Buffalo, N.Y., 1978), 1458.

23. Prince replaced the deleted word "now" with this long passage in which he attempted to corral Fayerweather's exhortation to young people and bring the text into line with the standard conventions of the relation of faith genre. Originally published in 1647, *The Shorter Catechism Agreed upon by the Reverend Assembly of Divines at Westminster* (Cambridge, Mass., 1682) circulated widely in New England during the first half of the eighteenth century and was cited regularly in church admission testimonies. See Part 1, note 26, above.

and flee every youthful Lust and Vanity [2 Tim. 2:22], and go out of myself, and rely on the Lord Jesus alone for Salvation, as he is offered to Sinners in the Gospel, And also do promise to come up to all God's Ordinances. And now being Convinced that it is my duty to give up myself to God in a perpetual Covenant never to be broken I would now out of Love and Obedience to my Glorious Saviour's dying Command *do this in remembrance of me* [Luke 22:19] come up to his holy Table to Commemorate his dying Love, and I would now take this Opportunity to ask your Prayers to God for me that I may be sincere and hearty in the solem dedication of myself, unto the Great God Father Son and holy Ghost, and that I may walk worthy of the near Relation that I may be taken into with himself and with you his Church and People.

Per me Samuel Fayrweather[24]

RUTH HOLBROOK, STURBRIDGE, MASS., N.D. [NOVEMBER 20, 1748][25]

I desier to bless god that I was born in the land of lite and livead under the preaching of the gospel all my days and that I decended of Such parence [parents] that gave me up to god in baptism in my infancy but I have rebeld against god and my parence in living in allmost all manner of Sin in Sabath braking and Company keeping and in disabaying my parnce [parents'] good Counsl and instructions that thay gave me in telling of me it was my duty to Seak to god in prayer and keep his commands. Thay told me that I must renew my baptismal covenant. I being young thought it time Enough but it has pleased allmytey god to awaking me by thunder many a time which is terrifying to me and puts me in mind of my duty. But I have been afraid if I Should offer myself to come to the table of the Lord that I should

24. Relation of Samuel Fayerweather, May 24, 1741, Autograph File, F, 1447–1994, HL. Fayerweather composed his relation on both sides of a large sheet of paper. Prince wrote the following biographical information on the back side: "He is the 2d now living son of Mr. Thomas Fayrweather deceesed and Hannah his wife; a sophimore at College and aet 17." Below this inscription, Prince appended a list of twelve people "⊙ ([admitted] per May 24, 1741" to the Old South Church. Prince's list, which begins with Fayerweather's name and is numbered from 167 to 178, corresponds to the roster of new communicants appearing in Hamilton Andrews Hill and George Frederick Bigelow, *An Historical Catalogue of the Old South Church (Third Church) Boston, 1669–1882* (Boston, 1883), 41.

25. Ruth Holbrook led a peripatetic life following her admission to full communion in the Sturbridge church in 1748. Daughter of Richard and Anna (Hawes) Puffer, she was born in Wrentham, Massachusetts, on June 25, 1722. She married Moses Holbrook in Bellingham in 1744 and moved to Sturbridge, where the first five of their eight children were born and baptized between 1747 and 1758. In later years, the Holbrooks lived in Wrentham and Upton, Massachusetts, before moving to the northern frontier settlement of Townshend, Vermont, in 1768 with a group of settlers that included members of their extended family. See Thomas W. Baldwin, comp., *Vital Records of Wrentham, Massachusetts, to the Year 1850*, 2 vols. (Boston, 1910), I, 126, 173; *Vital Records of Bellingham, Massachusetts, to the Year 1850* (Boston, 1904), 119; *Vital Records of Sturbridge, Massachusetts, to the Year 1850* (Boston, 1906), 67–69; *Vital Records of Upton, Massachusetts, to the End of the Year 1849* (Worcester, Mass., 1904), 31–32, 168; Sturbridge, Mass., Congregational Church Records, 1736–1896, 40, 42, 44, 61, MS copy, microfilm no. 863530, GSU; James H. Phelps, *Collections Relating to the History and Inhabitants of the Town of Townshend, Vermont* (Brattleboro, Vt., 1877), 71.

come unworthily.[26] For he that eateth and drinketh unworthily eateth and drinketh damnation to himself not discerning the lords body [1 Cor. 11:29] is vry [very] discouraging to me. And then another Place Came into my mind which is incouraging to me Isaiah 55 and 1 and I hop [hope I] dont alow myself in the omission of any none [known] duty nor in the commission of any none [known] Sin and I desire your prayers for me and your axceptance of me that I may walk acording to the profession that I have maid.[27]

SAMUEL COE, GRANVILLE, MASS., FIRST CHURCH, N.D. [CIRCA 1757][28]

Our Reverand paster[29] haveing A desire that I Should make a relation for the Edefication of the Church and for the conviction of sinners I am willing and theirfore proseed as follows. Haveing had sumthing of the spirit of god from time to time at work upon my sole from my youth but allways grieved and quenched it untill this last fall of the year I being under sum concern I resolved to lay Aside the world as to the profits and pleasurs theirof and to seek god for which resolution I bless god. As I was walking in the field meditating upon the sins of my past life a sight theirof was [Encreased] being but a glims which made me to cry out being from about that time very warm in secret prayer and so continuing for sum time. At length those words came to me watch by which I was taught to watch as well as pray. Then those words came to me double Your deligence. And so they fallowed me watch and pray double your diligence[30] untill I was constrained to be very carefull in speaking

26. Sentence interlineated by Sturbridge minister Caleb Rice.

27. Relation of Ruth Holbrook, n.d. [Nov. 20, 1748], Sturbridge, Mass., Congregational Church Records, 1736–1871, CL (available online at NEHH). Ruth Holbrook's relation appears to have been written on her behalf by her husband, Moses, who joined the church on the same day. He composed her relation on the front side of a single sheet of paper. Sturbridge minister Caleb Rice docketed the manuscript, identified "the wife of Moses Holbrook" at the bottom of the testimony, and inscribed the words "Moses Holbrook wife" on the back side.

28. Born on August 5, 1726, Samuel was the son of Ephraim and Hannah (Miller) Coe of Middletown, Connecticut. He was baptized the following year in the neighboring town of Durham. During the late 1740s, Coe joined a group of Durham families that migrated to the new settlement of Granville. He married Dorcas Allen of Middletown in 1746 and Hope Hubbard in Granville sometime around 1750. Coe presented each of the twelve children from his second marriage for baptism shortly after their births. Two years after his admission to full communion, Coe was elected deacon of the Granville church, a position that he held until his death in 1790. A respected citizen, Coe received an innkeeper's license for several years during the 1760s, and he served as selectman in 1777. See J. Gardner Bartlett, comp., *Robert Coe, Puritan: His Ancestors and Descendants, 1340–1910, with Notices of Other Coe Families* (Boston, 1911), 100, 134–135; William Chauncey Fowler, *History of Durham, Connecticut, from the First Grant of Land in 1662 to 1866* (Hartford, Conn., 1866), 261; Albion B. Wilson, *History of Granville, Massachusetts* (Hartford, Conn., 1954), 28, 35, 37, 47, 310, 338.

29. Jedidiah Smith (1727–1776) graduated from Yale College in 1750 and was ordained in Granville in 1756. Dismissed for his Loyalist sympathies, Smith died during an expedition to Natchez, Mississippi, in 1776. See Franklin Bowditch Dexter, *Biographical Sketches of the Graduates of Yale College, with Annals of the College History*, 6 vols. (New York, 1885–1912), II, 240–241.

30. The first part of this composite biblical impulse, "watch and pray," derives either from Mark 13:33 or Matthew 26:41. The second phrase, "double your diligence," does not appear

and so remaining sum time. Two sabbiths I keept fast one of which was the last sacrament to the intent that I might be the more capable of receiving the word. At the time of that ordanance I was very desierous to see the members pertake. After meting was done I went out at the dore and as I stood upon the steep the door was shut. I sought in my mind for some house where I might find sum sutable discorse but I found none. At length I was resovled to open the dore and go in and so I did. Oh what longings had I to pertake. Before the ordanance was over I trembled every limb. Not long after I began to grow cold and formel which terified me very much. One sabbath after I Cam home I felt all alive. I thought wheather or no I was not Converted but I could not enteertain these thoughts. I think the next sabbath day morning as I opened my eyes these words were in my mind when I awake I am still with the [thee] [Ps. 139:18] which run in my mind for sum time. After this I grew so cold that I was afraid that I had grieved the holy spirit which causeed me to labour hard in prayer. My eyes grew dry in secret. I began to be very much discorraged thinking that I had done all that I could. I beleived that christ would save me if I could but come aright for two sabbaths. In the last of my discouragements I could not receive the word but being sunck very lo the last sabbath which was the first sabbath in febuary I Come home in almost dispare haveing a secret in me that I had never bin born or that I had bin sumthing [dead] hell being before me and no way to escape it. Sumtime before this I had a desire to know what form god was of wheather In the form of a man or in sum other shape. Then those words would come to me ye worship ye know not what [John 4:22] and wearying myself I gave that up. This evening I had been out abroad and as I came into my house my wife was singing a hime [hymn]. One verce being as falloweth dispare Is such a sin of sins it cannot be forgiven while other sins hels ways do pave that bars the gates of heaven[31] which caused A strange alteration in me. After I had thought theiron my cold heart began to grow warm. I being calm and easey slept easey. When I awoke in the morning I felt chearfull and so continouing in cherfull meditation until towards noon my eyes were opened. I cannot write the joys that I felt. I beheld god and christ and that adams sin lay against me. If it was nothing else that must cost christ his blood for Justice was wronged but christ had sattisfied it and that god could not hurt me for god could not lay [lie]. And those words came to me him that cometh unto me I will in no wise cast of [off] [John 6:37] and my heart made answer o lord I come I will fallow the [thee]. Tho thou slay me tho thou kill me I will not let the [thee] go [Job 13:15, Gen. 32:26]. I also found a yoke and that was to keep my thoughts from wandering and ranging and so I continued to the end of that Joyfull day keeping the yoke upon me that not one thought might

---

to have a biblical referent. The two phrases appear together in Jonathan Edwards's famous *Farewel-Sermon,* which he delivered shortly after his dismissal from his Northampton pastorate in 1750. Edwards's sermon reads: "You had need to double your diligence, and watch and pray lest you be overcome by temptation." See Jonathan Edwards, *A Farewel-Sermon Preached at the First Precinct in Northampton* ... (Boston, 1751), *WJE,* XXV, *Sermons and Discourses, 1743–1758,* ed. Wilson H. Kimnach (New Haven, Conn., 2006), 481.

31. [John Mason and Thomas Shepard], *Penitential Cries in Thirty Two Hymns,* 2d ed. (London, 1693), 11.

wander if possiable. And I beg the prayers of this Church to allmighty god that he would keep me from the assaults of satan and that I may grow in grace and in knowledge. Now to god the father god the son and god the holy ghost be given everlasting praise. Amen.

Samuel Coe[32]

LUCY ANDREWS, IPSWICH (NOW ESSEX), MASS., CHEBACCO SEPARATE CHURCH, NOVEMBER 11, 1764[33]

What bro't me first under concern, was my Brother Edward Lees[34] being bro't out into Light and comfort last Winter. I was awakened to a Sight of my lost condition, that I had been a Sinner all my Days and had done nothing but sin. And [I] Saw that I deserved to be damn'd for my actual sins but could not see it was just that I should be damn'd for my original sin. But after awhile, I Saw that I deserv'd to be damned for that sin too. I Saw that every sin deserved Damnation, and that I was cut off. And then I had a view of Christ's Loveliness and of his wonderful conscending Love in coming down to dye for sinners. And My Burden was carried off. And I had Some comfort, tho' I did not then think I had received any Comfort. And I Saw Sin to be so vile, I desired I might never sin any more. But after awhile I tho't I had lost all my concern and had found no Christ, but hearing of one and another of my acquaintance having found Christ, I was bro't under concern fearing I should now be wholly lost and was greatly cast down. And those words came to me, why art thou cast down o my soul? And why art thou disquieted within me? Hope thou in God for I Shall yet praise him [Psalm 42:11]. And I found Comfort

32. Relation of Samuel Coe, n.d. [circa 1757], Granville, Mass., First Congregational Church Papers, circa 1756–1913, CL (available online at NEHH). Coe composed his relation on both sides of a large sheet of paper. Granville minister Jedidiah Smith folded and docketed the manuscript, writing the phrase "Samuel Coes Relation" along the edge of the back side. In an intriguing shift in language, nineteenth-century minister Timothy Mather Cooley wrote the words "Samuel Coe's *Experience*" beneath his predecessor's original notation.

33. Lucy, the daughter of Edward and Hannah (Allen) Lee, was born in Manchester, Massachusetts, on February 12, 1733. She married a mariner named Benjamin Andrews in 1753. The first of their five children, Ezekiel, was born in Manchester on July 25, 1754, well beyond the seven-month period that typically resulted in the church disciplinary action to which she confessed in her relation. Lucy and her husband worshipped in the established Congregational church in Manchester until at least 1763, when their youngest daughter was baptized. Two months before Lucy joined the Chebacco Separate church, her husband was lost at sea during a return voyage from the West Indies. She does not appear to have remarried, nor is the date or location of her death known. See Thomas Amory Lee, "The Lee Family of Marblehead," *EIHC*, LII (1916), 147–148; "Descendants of John Andrews of Ipswich," *Essex Antiquarian*, III (1899), 99–100; *Vital Records of Manchester, Massachusetts, to the End of the Year 1849* (Salem, Mass., 1903), 19–20, 136, 236.

34. Admitted to full communion in the Chebacco Separate church on Mar. 30, 1764, Edward Lee was born in Manchester on November 29, 1729, and died on December 23, 1793. In his later years, he became a Methodist exhorter and was the subject of a nineteenth-century American Tract Society pamphlet entitled *The Apostolic Fisherman: A Tale of the Last Century* (Philadelphia, 1850). See Lee, "Lee Family of Marblehead," *EIHC*, LII (1916), 225–227. For Lee's relation, see Appendix B., Ipswich (now Essex), Mass., Chebacco Separate Church, 41.

in my Soul and had such a sense of Christ's Love and loveliness, that I could part with all for him, and tho't I could dye for him. I now found the Same Comfort as when my Burden the first time was carried off. I find my mind is changed, that my heart is towards God and in *Religion*, whereas it was before wholly in and after the world. I desire more Grace, and the Prayers of God's people for me that I may be made to press forward in the Christian Life.

And altho' I have publickly acknowledged my having broke the 7 Commandment in having my first Child too Soon, yet I am willing before this congregation to take Shame for it again, and as I hope God of his Grace has forgiven me, So I desire forgiveness of all men and of this Church in particular.[35]

ELI WHITNEY, WESTBOROUGH, MASS., DECEMBER 6, 1767[36]

I beleave there is one God who is Infinite in being and perfection. In the unity of the Godhead there be three persons of one Substance power and Eternity God the Father God the Son God the Holy gost. I beleave that our first parents being Seduced by the Subtlety and Temptation of Saton Sinned in Eating the forbidden fruit. This their Sin God was pleased According to his wise and Holy Counsel to permit having purposed to Order it to his Own Glory, and that by this Sin fell from their Original Righteousness and Communion with God and So became Dead in Sin and wholly Defilled In all the faculties and parts of Soul and body. And that theay being the Root of all mankind the Guilt of this was Imputted to all their posterity Desending from them by Ordinary Generation. But God was pleasd to Enter

35. Relation of Lucy Andrews, Nov. 11, 1764, box 1, JCP. Chebacco minister John Cleaveland composed Andrews's relation on a large sheet of paper. He drew a line across the page near the bottom and proceeded to record the relation of Hannah Edwards, who was propounded to full communion on the same day. On the back side, at the conclusion of Edwards's relation, Cleaveland drew a second line and wrote the following notation: "Chebacco November 11th 1764. Lucy Andrews and Hannah Edwards were propounded for Communion with the 4th Church in Ipswich, And said Lucy's Acknowledgement was accepted by the said Church. Attests John Cleaveland, Pastor."

36. Eli, the youngest son of Nathaniel and Mary (Child) Whitney, was baptized in Westborough on May 3, 1741. He married twice: Elizabeth Fay in 1765 and Judith Hazeltine of Sutton, Massachusetts, in 1779. On November 10, 1767, Westborough minister Ebenezer Parkman noted in his diary that "Mr. Eli Whitney had been here in the Day about his own and his Wife's joining with the Church"; he propounded the couple to full communion on November 22. The Whitneys presented four children for baptism between 1768 and 1770, including Eli, Jr., the future inventor of the cotton gin. Active in religious affairs, the elder Whitney was elected one of Westborough's first choristers; he served on a variety of church committees, hosted prayer meetings at his home, and regularly supported Parkman's ministry by donating labor, goods, and, on several occasions, his horticultural knowledge. He died in 1807. See *Vital Records of Westborough, Massachusetts, to the End of the Year 1849* (Worcester, Mass., 1903), 106–107, 220, 257; Westborough, Mass., Congregational Church Records, 1724–1808, 58, 143–144, 148, microfilm, Westborough Town Library, Westborough, Mass.; Ebenezer Parkman, diaries, 1723–1778, July 21, 1756, Jan. 12, 1761, Nov. 10, 22, 1767, Dec. 24, 1770, Parkman Family Papers, 1707–1879, AAS; Parkman, diaries, 1771–1782, June 27, 1771, Apr. 8, 17, 1773, May 8, 1775, Mar. 17, 1779, microfilm, Ebenezer Parkman Papers, 1718–1789, MHS (I thank Ross W. Beales, Jr., for sharing his transcription of Parkman's diaries).

into A new and better Covenant A covenant of Grace and Christ being the media-tor pardon and Life and Salvation are through him.

I wold thank God that I have ben brot up in A religous famuly and in a Land whear the Gosple is preached and Have Leved under the ministration of the word of God and have ben geven up to him in Baptism. And I would humbly hope I have bin Awakned by the Spiret of God to See what an Amazeing thing it is to go Into Eternity unprepard and that I could do Nothing of myself and wold Hope that I have ben brot to Rsign [resign] myself unto Christ for pardoning mercy and have been brot to Accept of him as he is offered to poor Sinners in the Gosple. I would ask the forgiveness of all that I Have Offended, and your Accepttence of me and your prayers for me that I may be a Sincere and worthy Communicent at the Lords Table.

Eli Whitney[37]

PETER OLIVER, JR., MIDDLEBOROUGH, MASS., JANUARY [13], 1771[38]

It being a Duty incumbent upon all, to live in such a Manner, as may honour the Religion they profess, I look upon it as my Duty to offer myself a Member of this Church to enter into full Communion with them. I think it hath pleas'd God to convince me of my Sinfulness and my Need of an Almighty Saviour beleiving in one God, the Supreme Governor of the Universe and in Jesus Christ the true Saviour of Mankind, that in and thro' him alone my Sins can be forgiven by a Sin-cere Repentance, that the holy Scriptures are revealed from God as a Rule of Life and Faith, resolving by the Assistance of the divine Spirit to regulate my Life ac-cording to them.

Peter Oliver, Jr.[39]

37. Relation of Eli Whitney, Dec. 6, 1767, box 2, Parkman Family Papers. Whitney com-posed and signed his own relation on the front side of a large sheet of paper. Parkman's en-dorsement on the back side reads "The Relation of Eli Whitney. Admitted December 6, 1767."

38. Peter, Jr., the son of Peter and Mary (Clarke) Oliver, was born in Boston on June 17, 1741, and raised on his father's estate in Middleborough, Massachusetts. The elder Oliver, a prominent merchant, iron manufacturer and chief justice of the Massachusetts Superior Court of Judicature, sent his son to live with Presbyterian clergyman Aaron Burr in Newark, New Jersey. Peter, Jr., studied briefly at Princeton College before returning to New England. Oliver served an apprenticeship to a prominent Scituate, Massachusetts, physician follow-ing his graduation from Harvard College in 1761. He settled in Middleborough and married Sally Hutchinson in 1770. Threatened with mob violence during the American Revolution, Oliver abandoned his comfortable Georgian home, which still stands in Middleborough, and moved to Boston, Falmouth (now Portland), Maine, and, eventually, London. While in England, he continued his medical studies and eventually received a degree from Marischal College, Aberdeen, in 1790. Oliver and his wife had four children. He died in Shrewsbury, England, in 1822. See *SHG*, XV, 82–87.

39. Relation of Peter Oliver, Jr., January [13], 1771, Middleboro, Mass., First Congrega-tional Church Relations and Personal Records, 1724–1865, CL (available online at NEHH). Oliver composed his brief relation on the front side of a trimmed sheet of paper. Middle-borough minister Sylvanus Conant's endorsement on the back reads "Peter Oliver Jr. / Janu-ary 1771."

JABEZ LANE, STRATHAM, N.H., N.D. [ADM. AUGUST 1801][40]

Soon after the commencement of the late revival of Religion in this Town, I was convinced that it was the work of the Spirit of God. I rejoiced thereat and wished earnestly that I might be a Shearer therein. It went on for a considerable time and many Were brot in, but I felt no Extraordinary awakening tho I greatly desired and earnestly prayed that I might be made a Subject of Gods renewing Grace. At last I began to thenk that the work would soon be over and I should be left un-renewed, and that if I was not awakened at such a time of remarkable outpouring of the Spiret of God, the probability was, that I never should be effectually Called. It seemed as if I was not under any serious impressions and my heart was hard as adamant and nothing would move it. My only consolation was, that conversion was Gods work and hard as my heart was, he was able to do the work. With this frame of mind I went to Meeting and heard a Sermon from Isaiah 40:29 He giveth power to the faint and to him that hath no might he increaseth strength. In the first part of the sermon I thot there was food for others, but not a crumb for me. Oh tho't I what a hard heart have I that nothing will Soften, but in the close of the Discourse I thot there was something for me. Those words in particular are you willing to forego all interest in the Saving Mercy of the Lord! To give up all claim to the favour of God! To renounce Christ and his Salvation forever! Are you indifferent whether you can ever come to the possession of an heartfelt interest in the Salvation of the Gospel etc. Seemed to go to the heart and the answer of my very Soul was O no no.[41] In Answering to myself the Questions that were there asked I thot I discovered that I was really a Subject of the operations of Gods Spirit. I rejoiced at the discovery and tears of Joy flowed plentifully down my Cheeks which I endeavoured to conceal. What rejoiced me was this, I thot that God had begun a good work on my heart and I knew that when God begun a good work, he always finished it [Phil. 1:6]. In this frame I passed Some considerable time expecting every day to have convictions on my mind. At length I heard a sermon from these words Except a Man be born again he cannot see the kingdom of God [John 3:3]. In describing the new Birth and the exercises of a renewed and doubting Soul it seemd as if ever word was designed for me and Suited my Case. The Discourse affected and rejoiced me which drew tears in abundance, tho' I hardly knew for what reason. For thot I, it can hardly be possible that I have been born again for I should certainly have knew the time to a minute when so great a change passed upon me, and beside I have never had such convictions as I always supposed preceded Conversion. Thus I passed a number of days not knowing what to think of myself, but

40. Jabez, son of the tanner, surveyor, and diarist Samuel Lane and his first wife, Mary James, was born on May 16, 1760. He married his stepsister, Eunice Colcord, in 1783. They had nine children between 1784 and 1805. Jabez died in 1810 and was buried across the street from the house that he inherited from his father. For more on the Lane family, see the Epilogue. See also Jacob Chapman and James H. Fitts, comps., *Lane Genealogies, I, William Lane of Boston, Mass., 1648* ... (Exeter, N.H., 1891), 32, 68–72.

41. The passage that begins "Those words in particular" was written sideways in the margin.

without Saying a word on the subject to any person, providentially came to my hand a Book intitled a Guide to the Doubting and a Cordial to the fainting Christian. I run over the Contents and found one doubt answered which was, I fear I am not a Christian because I know not the Time of my Conversion. I read the chapter and found that some who were thot to be real Christians knew not the time of their conversion and an Eminent Minister of the Gospel who declared he neither new the day nor the year when he began to be Sincere, and with respect to great convictions I found it was the opinion of Some Christians and countenanced by some passages of Scripture that great convictions were not Supposed always to preceede conversion.[42] I felt some encouraged by these things Compared with the state of my mind formerly to entertain a hope that I was born again.

I had serious impressions on my mind from time to time when I was a Child. I was much affected with reading Dr. Watts's World to come and frequently said to myself, if ever I am converted I believe it will be by reading this Book.[43] When I was about 14 or 15 years old I was greatly Stirred up to attend secret prayer and had at that time such a realizing sense of the greatness and importance of Spiritual things that it appeared to me matter of surprise that real Christians spak a word about anything else. If I ever experienced a change of heart I suppose it was about this time, tho' not in that clear and sensible way that I had prefigured to myself. For I really thot, that I should be as sensible of the change, as Naaman would have been of the cure of his Leprosy if the cure had wrought in the way he Expected [1 Kings 5]. I afterwards returned to the vanities of the world, but I think if my heart does not deceave me I have always had at times, a relish for and Delight in Christian Exercises and Christian discourse and Company and frequently I have been ready to entertain hopes of myself which would again be dash'd by Considering that I had not an evidence of a new birth.[44]

In the fore part of the month of May last in attending on the preaching of the word at several times I got my Doubts in a great measure resolved and obtained what appeared to me a Satisfactory Evidence that I was in reality a new born Soul and not many days after God was pleased to manifest himself to me in So Clear and Sensible a manner that my whole Soul Appeared to be filled with the Love of God so that I felt no Desire to Ask for anything more it appearing to me I had as much as I could contain. My Doubts were now all at an End, and I had no Idea that ever I should have any more. I thot I should always walk in the light of Gods countenance [Ps. 89:15], and that I Could go on my way rejoicing to my Journeys end that temptations were over and all the tryals of this Life appeared as nothing. I tho't I could go thro' anything without any Difficulty. The Society of Christians appeared to me now more Desirable than ever. I longed to be with them, that I might with David Say, come all ye that fear God and I will declare what he hath done for my soul [Ps. 66:16]. But alas! I soon found myself under such a cloud that I began

---

42. Benj[amin] Wadsworth, *A Guide for the Doubting, and Cordial for the Fainting, Saint* ... (Boston, 1711), 94–99.

43. I[saac] Watts, *The World to Come; or, Discourses on the Joys or Sorrows of Departed Souls at Death, and the Glory or Terror of the Resurrection* ... (London, 1739).

44. Lane's narrative breaks off here and continues further down the page in a lighter ink.

to call in Question all I had Experienced. I feared I had been deceived, but I found on Examination that I could not give up my hope, that feble as it was nothing in this world would induce me to part with it.

I have since at times enjoyed very comfortable seasons and when I enjoy the Divine presence I feel Satisfyed and tho' I do not always feel satisfied as to my Interest in Christ yet my Satisfaction is Such at Times that I think it is my Duty to Join myself to those who have Joined themselves to the Lord If they can extend the arms of their Charity to receive me, and renew my Covenant with the Lord at his holy Table. Altho' the thoughts that perhaps I may be an unworthy receiver and thereby Eat and Drink Judgment to myself not Discerning the Lords body [1 Cor. 11:29] at times strike a great dread upon me, yet I think I Shall not be wilfully Guilty, and I desire to trust in the mercy of God thro' Jesus Christ for Acceptance.

With respect to Baptism I would observe that it has been my settled opinion for a number of years that if I Should see my way clear to ask admittance to Church priviledges and Should Join in full Communion as I was Baptised in infancy[45] I should have no desire to have it repeated. I have no doubt but my parents did what they tho't was their duty, but I have tho't and still think that it is not my duty to offer my Children for Baptism it being a Matter in Dispute as to their right to the ordinance and it cannot in my Opinion be of any Saving benefit to them, and often makes difficulty and perplexity in their minds who make too much of Baptism as to the validity of it when by the Grace of God any of them are brot to an Experimental Acquaintance with religion, that in my Opinion it would be as well, at least I think it would for me to omit it. This is my present Idea of the Subject. So far as the Lord makes my Duty known to me I am Willing to obey.

I Sometimes wished for an oportunity to divulge the State of my mind to Some Christian friend, but when I had oportunity could not prevail on myself to do it. I have been daily imploring the giver of every good and perfect Gift that he would discover my situation to me, and make me willing to see it as it is that if I am yet in the gall of bitterness and in the bonds of iniquity [Acts 8:23] I may be delivered therefrom, and that if I am in reality a new born soul I may be enabled to give God the Glory and take the comfort to myself and that my whole Soul may be filled with the Love of God, and that I may not be deceived in a Matter of such infinite importance. I have of late been led to think that I have been wrong in keeping the exercises of my mind so intirely to myself and that, that may be the reason why I am so much in the dark as to my Spiritual State and this consideration has induced me to this step.[46]

45. Jabez was baptized on May 18, 1760. See Stratham, N.H., Congregational Church Records, 1746–1913, 2 vols. I, 16, NHHS.

46. Relation of Jabez Lane, n.d. [circa August 1801], box 3: Miscellaneous Papers, 1742–1876, Stratham Town Records, New Hampshire Division of Archives and Records Management. Lane composed his relation on three sides of a large, folded sheet of paper. An earlier draft is also in the collection.